NOVELL'S®

Guide to Creating
IntranetWare Intranets

D1519101

N O V E L L ' S

Guide to Creating
IntranetWare Intranets

KARANJIT SIYAN, Ph.D.

NOVELL

PRESS®

Novell Press, San Jose

Novell's Guide to Creating IntranetWare Intranets

Published by
Novell Press
2180 Fortune Drive
San Jose, CA 95131

Library of Congress Catalog Card No.: 97-072190

ISBN: 0-7645-4531-0

Printed in the United States of America

10 9 8 7 6 5 4 3 2 1

1A/RX/QX/ZX/FC

Distributed in the United States by IDG Books Worldwide, Inc.

Distributed by Macmillan Canada for Canada; by Contemporanea de Ediciones for Venezuela; by Distribuidora Cuspide for Argentina; by CITEC for Brazil; by Ediciones ZETA S.C.R. Ltda. for Peru; by Editorial Limusa SA for Mexico; by Transworld Publishers Limited in the United Kingdom and Europe; by Academic Bookshop for Egypt; by Levant Distributors S.A.R.L. for Lebanon; by Al Jassim for Saudi Arabia; by Simron Pty. Ltd. for South Africa; by Pustak Mahal for India; by The Computer Bookshop for India; by Toppan Company Ltd. for Japan; by Addison Wesley Publishing Company for Korea; by Longman Singapore Publishers Ltd. for Singapore, Malaysia, Thailand, and Indonesia; by Unalis Corporation for Taiwan; by WS Computer Publishing Company, Inc. for the Philippines; by WoodsLane Pty. Ltd. for Australia; by WoodsLane Enterprises Ltd. for New Zealand. Authorized Sales Agent: Anthony Rudkin Associates for the Middle East and North Africa.

For general information on IDG Books Worldwide's books in the U.S., contact our Consumer Customer Service department at 800-762-2974. For reseller information, including discounts and premium sales, contact our Reseller Customer Service department at 800-434-3422. For information on where to purchase IDG Books Worldwide's books outside the U.S., contact our International Sales department at 415-655-3078 or fax 415-655-3281. For information on foreign language translations, contact our Foreign & Subsidiary Rights department at 415-655-3018 or fax 415-655-3281. For sales inquiries and special prices for bulk quantities, contact our Sales department at 415-655-3200 or write to the address above. For information on using IDG Books Worldwide's books in the classroom or for ordering examination copies, contact our Educational Sales department at 800-434-2086 or fax 817-251-8174. For authorization to photocopy items for corporate, personal, or educational use, contact the Copyright Clearance Center, 222 Rosewood Drive, Danvers, MA 01923, or fax 508-750-4470. For general information on Novell Press books in the U.S., including information on discounts and premiums, contact IDG Books at 800-434-3422 or 415-655-3200. For information on where to purchase Novell Press books outside the U.S., contact IDG Books International at 415-655-3021 or fax 415-655-3295.

John Kilcullen, *CEO, IDG Books Worldwide, Inc.*
Brenda McLaughlin, *Senior Vice President & Group Publisher, IDG Books Worldwide, Inc.*
The IDG Books Worldwide logo is a trademark under exclusive license to IDG Books Worldwide, Inc., from International Data Group, Inc.

Lois Dudley, *Novell Press, Inc.*
Novell Press and the Novell Press logo are trademarks of Novell, Inc.

Welcome to Novell Press

Novell Press, the world's leading provider of networking books, is the premier source for the most timely and useful information in the networking industry. Novell Press books cover fundamental networking issues as they emerge — from today's Novell and third-party products, to the concepts and strategies that will guide the industry's future. The result is a broad spectrum of titles for the benefit of those involved in networking at any level: end-user, department administrator, developer, systems manager, or network architect.

Novell Press books are written by experts with the full participation of Novell's technical, managerial, and marketing staff. The books are exhaustively reviewed by Novell's own technicians and are published only on the basis of final released software, never on prereleased versions.

Novell Press at IDG Books Worldwide is an exciting partnership between two companies at the forefront of the information and communications revolution. The Press is implementing an ambitious publishing program to develop new networking titles centered on the current version of IntranetWare, GroupWise and on Novell's ManageWise products. Select Novell Press books are translated into 14 languages and are available at bookstores around the world.

Lois Dudley, Novell Press, Inc.

Novell Press

Publisher
Lois Dudley

Acquisitions Editor
Jim Sumser

Development Editor
Kevin Shafer

Copy Editors
Kevin Shafer
Anne Friedman

Technical Editors
Peter Rybaczyk
Vincent Tran

Project Coordinator
Tom Debolski

Quality Control Specialist
Mick Arellano

Production Staff
Mario Amador
Vincent F. Burns
Laura Carpenter
Jude Levinson
Christopher Pimentel
Dina F Quan

Proofreader
Annie Sheldon

Indexer
Nancy Anderman Guenther

Illustrator
David Puckett

Cover Design
Archer Design

Cover Photo
Rieder & Walsh / Photonica

About the Author

Karanjit Siyan is president of Kinetics Corporation. He has authored international seminars on Solaris & SunOS, TCP/IP networks, PC Network Integration, Windows NT, Novell networks, and Expert Systems using Fuzzy Logic. He teaches advanced technology seminars in the United States, Canada, Europe, and the Far East. Dr. Siyan has published articles in *Dr. Dobbs Journal*, *The C Users Journal*, *Database Advisor*, and research journals, and is actively involved in Internet research. Karanjit holds a Ph.D. in Computer Science, a Masters degree in Electrical Engineering and Computer Science, and a Bachelor's degree in Electronics and Electrical Communication Engineering. He is a member of IEEE and ACM, and his career achievements are recorded in *Marquis' Who's Who in the World*, *Who's Who in America*, *Who's Who in Finance and Industry*, and *Who's Who in Science and Engineering*.

To Mother and my beloved Bapu, the Ascended Master El Morya.
With all my love and gratitude!

Preface

IntranetWare is a powerful platform from Novell that includes many important services (such as File, Print, Directory, and Application services). One of the very important application services that is bundled with IntranetWare is the Novell Web Server. This book examines how the Novell Web Server can be used as the centerpiece of an intranetwork (or *intranet*) strategy within an organization. The book is important for anyone who wants to evaluate or deploy the Novell Web Server in an intranet.

This book is organized as follows:

- ▶ *Chapter 1.* This chapter explains the role of intranetworks and examines the business needs of intranets. Intranets can be built with a variety of protocols and components, which are discussed in this chapter.

- ▶ *Chapter 2.* This chapter explains in depth the features of the Novell Web Server that are most useful in the context of an intranet.

- ▶ *Chapter 3.* The Novell Web Server runs on top of NetWare 4. Before you can install the Novell Web Server, you must have an existing NetWare 4 server to install the Novell Web Server. If you don't have an existing NetWare 4 server platform that you can use, you must install a new NetWare 4 server. This chapter shows you not only how to install a Novell Web Server, but also how to install a NetWare 4 server from scratch. The installation procedures are described step-by-step with detailed information on how to make the decisions for installing the software. The procedures for installing Web browser clients and Internet Protocol Exchange (IPX) gateways are also explained.

- ▶ *Chapter 4.* Once the Novell Web Server is installed, you must configure it. The Novell Web Server comes with configuration tools such as the Web Manager. This chapter discusses procedures for configuring the Novell Web Server. The Web Manager keeps configuration information for the Novell Web Server in some critical files. The syntax of these critical files is described.

▶ *Chapter 5*. After the Novell Web Server has been configured, you must create the content for the Web site. This chapter discusses the fundamentals of Hypertext Markup Language (HTML), which is the language for specifying Web content. All the basic HTML features are explained with several examples so that you can create Web content, or understand how various authoring tools create Web content.

▶ *Chapter 6*. The Common Gateway Interface (CGI) is used to link external applications to the Web server, and to create dynamic content. This chapter discusses the Remote Common Gateway Interface (RCGI) and Local Common Gateway Interface (LCGI) mechanisms of the CGI for the Novell Web Server, including numerous examples of RCGI and LCGI scripts. The Multipurpose Internet Mail Extensions (MIME) types that are used for identifying Web content and the MIME encoding method are explained. CGI code to process form data and handle search queries is discussed. CGI program security issues and CGI interfaces to UNIX systems are also discussed.

▶ *Chapter 7*. CGI scripts can be written in Perl, BASIC, and NetBasic. This chapter begins a discussion on each of the languages by providing a tutorial on Perl, which is presented in sufficient depth for you to begin writing sophisticated CGI scripts.

▶ *Chapter 8*. This chapter presents an in-depth tutorial on the BASIC and NetBasic languages.

▶ *Chapter 9*. This chapter discusses the elements of the Java language for use in the Novell Web Server environment, and presents examples of how to use Java to provide dynamic content.

▶ *Chapter 10*. This chapter discusses the use of Server Side Includes (SSIs) to provide dynamic content.

▶ *Chapter 11*. This chapter discusses details of integrating the Novell Web Server with Novell Directory Services (NDS).

▶ *Chapter 12.* This chapter discusses the details of installing and configuring NetWare/IP and the Domain Name System (DNS) services.

▶ *Chapter 13.* This chapter discusses the details of installing and configuring Dynamic Host Configuration Protocol (DHCP) services.

▶ *Chapter 14.* This chapter discusses the details of installing and configuring file-transfer protocol (FTP) services.

All the examples in the book are included in the CD-ROM that accompanies this book. This CD-ROM also contains a Win32 version of Perl for practice in writing Perl CGI scripts.

Acknowledgments

One of the more pleasurable tasks of being an author is to thank the people responsible for the success of a book. My heartfelt thanks to my wife Dei for her love and support. I wish to thank my father, Ahal Singh, and my mother Tejinder; my brothers Harjeet, Jagjit; my sisters Kookie and Dolly. Special thanks to Mother, Saint Germain, El Morya Khan, Kuan-Yin, Bhagwan Krishna, and Babaji. Without their spiritual support, this book would not have been possible.

I want to thank Bob Sanregret and Anders Amundson, who initially got me interested in writing teaching materials about computers. I also wish to thank the many people at Learning Tree for their help and support on various projects. In particular I would like to thank Professor John Moriarty, Rick Adamson, Dr. David Collins, Eric Garen, Marti Sanregret, Richard Beaumont, Mark Drew, David O'Neil, Robin Johnston, and Tom Spurling.

I wish to thank Kevin Shafer, the development editor, for his experience and professionalism, and IDG Books Worldwide for their help in developing this book. Special thanks to the staff at IDG Books Worldwide and Novell Press: Jim Sumser, Ann Hamilton and David Kolodney for some wonderful dinners and conversations, especially David Kolodney for sharing some of his poetry; Colleen Bluhm and Lois Dudley for their help with copies of Novell's products. I want to thank Novell for creating IntranetWare. In these changing times, it has not been easy for Novell. But I must go on record as saying that many of the developers and engineers at Novell are some of the finest people I have met — they have a sense of honor, honesty, and integrity that is rare in an industry that is often plagued by marketing rhetoric and mind manipulation that, among other things, is misleading. It is my sincere hope that Novell, as a company, does not let these people down.

Thanks also to Peter and Maria Elizabeth Rybaczyk for watching the Ramayana video tapes with us while I was writing this book. I also wish to thank Drew and Blythe Heywood for their friendship, support, and encouragement throughout the many years it has been my pleasure to know them; and thanks to Drew Heywood for suggesting that I write for Novell Press.

Contents at a Glance

Contents

## CHAPTER 1

Defining Intranets and Internets

At the beginning of the 1990s, the Internet was popularized with the introduction of World Wide Web (WWW) application services. Most people who had never heard of this "Internet" were surprised that the Internet had existed for more than a decade. As businesses and individual users began using the Internet applications (such as WWW services, e-mail, file transfer, and remote login), they became very familiar with the user interface of these applications. Many network designers began to appreciate the potential benefits of using traditional Internet services in a corporate-wide network, and this led to the creation of the *intranetworks*, or *intranets*. What is an intranet? Corporate networks that use Internet applications are called "intranets." The choice of the term "intranets" to describe these corporate networks is appropriate because it emphasizes one of the key distinctions between an internal network, as opposed to the external worldwide Internet. This chapter discusses the essential differences between the Internet and intranets.

Before examining the differences between Internet and intranets, you should first understand the characteristics of each of these networks. The Internet has had an interesting evolution, and, in order to better understand what it represents now, you should understand how it has evolved.

Understanding the Internet

In many ways, the circumstances that resulted in the creation of the Internet resulted from the launch of the Sputnik spacecraft. In 1957, the former U.S.S.R. launched Sputnik, which had far-reaching consequences. In response to this, the U.S. government created the Advanced Research Projects Agency (ARPA) to fund research projects that would enable the U.S. to remain competitive in space research and the potentially defense-related applications of this research.

In the late 1960s, the Defense Advanced Research Projects Agency (DARPA) began connecting different military installations and research sites together to facilitate collaboration between research and development efforts. The agency soon had an old, but familiar, problem on its hands.

The problem was that, by this time, a rapid proliferation of computers had occurred in military communications. Computers, because they could be easily programmed, provided a flexibility in achieving network functions that was not available with other types of communications equipment. The computers that were used in military communications were manufactured by different vendors and were designed to interoperate with computers from that vendor only.

Vendors used proprietary protocols in their communications equipment. The military had a multivendor network, but no common protocol to support the heterogeneous equipment from different vendors.

This problem is particularly instructive, because the computer industry faces a similar challenge today with applications. How can you write programs that can run on any computer with little or no change? One solution is to buy applications/equipment from only a single vendor. This has been done in the past with companies such as IBM and others, and, if the past is any guide, such approaches are not only costly to the users, but also to the industry at large.

A Case for Networking Standards

To solve the network interoperability problems, the U.S. Department of Defense (DoD) mandated a common set of protocols. Some of the reasons for having a common set of protocols were as follows:

▶ *Procurement simplification.* By mandating a common set of protocols it was possible for the military to have a Request for Proposal (RFP) specifying that communications products use the common protocol.

▶ *Fostering competition among vendors.* Vendors could compete with each other based on the merits of their implementation of a standard protocol. If a common set of protocols was not required, vendors would implement their proprietary protocols against which other vendors could not compete.

▶ *Interoperability.* By having vendors use a common set of protocols, interoperability between equipment from different vendors became a reality. If equipment from different vendors (implementing a common protocol) did not interoperate, you could suspect the problem to be one of difference in implementation. The vendors could then refer to the standard specification of the protocol to isolate the problem.

▸ *Vendor productivity and efficiency*. Vendors could focus attention on a single protocol, rather than spread their efforts trying to implement several protocols. This made the efforts of vendors more productive.

In 1969, an interesting experiment was conducted in order to use a computer network to connect the following four sites:

▸ University of California, Los Angeles (UCLA)

▸ University of California, Santa Barbara (UCSB)

▸ University of Utah

▸ SRI International

This was the beginning of the famous Advanced Research Project Agency Network (ARPAnet). The experiment was a success. Additional sites were added to the network.

In 1972, an ARPAnet demonstration was performed with 50 Packet Switched Nodes (PSNs) and 20 hosts. Like the previous four-node experiment, this, too, was a success, and it set the stage for large-scale deployment of PSNs and hosts on the ARPAnet.

From ARPAnet to the Internet

The ARPAnet continued to grow and went through a series of transformations. Prior to 1989, the ARPAnet consisted of specialized military networks connected with the ARPAnet. After 1989, the specialized military networks formed their own network that was not connected to any other network. The Defense Data Network (DDN) was created with links to the ARPAnet.

By 1986, the ARPAnet had expanded to encompass all major universities, the military network called MILNET, research laboratories such as Cadre and Tartan at Carnegie-Mellon University (CMU), and satellite links to several international sites.

Gradually the ARPAnet itself was replaced by the Internet. The Internet is experiencing a rapid commercialization, and is no longer the exclusive domain of universities and research organizations. Currently, more network traffic comes from commercial organizations than any other source on the Internet.

The earlier Internet community consisted of universities (such as Stanford University, UCLA, MIT, the University of California at Santa Barbara, the University of Utah, University of Hawaii, and University of California at Berkeley) and research organizations such as SRI International, Rand Corporation, the Institute of Advanced Computation, and Bolt, Beranek and Newman (BBN).

Currently, the Internet community has expanded to include commercial organizations and individual users. The Internet community includes all major universities, research organizations, corporations, individual users, and Internet providers.

Internet providers are commercial organizations that sell access to the Internet. Table 1.1 shows a list of some of the Internet providers.

TABLE 1.1 Internet Providers	INTERNET ACCESS PROVIDER	CONTACT
	AlterNet	UUNET Technologies, Inc. 800-488-6383 703-204-8000 alternet-info@uunet.uu.net
	AT&T WorldNet Service	AT&T 1-800-831-5259 worldnet@attmail.com
	Community News Service (CNS)	719-520-1700 ID "new", password "newuser" Local access area codes: 303, 719 klaus@cscns.com
	DELPHI	800-365-4636 Local access areas: Boston, Kansas City walthowe@delphi.com
	Dial-in-cerf	Provided by CERFNET 800-876-2373 or 619-455-3900 Local access area codes: 213, 310, 415, 510, 619, 714, 818 help@cerf.net
	NEARnet	617-873-8730 Local access codes: 508, 603, 617 nearnet-join@nic.near.net
	NETCOM	408-554-UNIX info@netcom.com

(continued)

T A B L E 1.1	INTERNET ACCESS PROVIDER	CONTACT
Internet Providers (continued)	NorthWestNet	206-562-3000 nic@nwnet.net
	NYSERnet	315-453-2912 info@nysernet.org
	PSInet	703-620-6651 all-info@psi.com
	Well	The Whole Earth 'Lectronic Link 415-332-6106 ID "newuser" info@well.sf.ca.us
	World	Software Tool & Die 617-739-9753 ID "new" 617-739-0202 office@world.std.com

The TCP/IP Standard

The primary transport protocol used on the Internet is *Transmission Control Protocol/Internet Protocol* (TCP/IP). This protocol is published as an open protocol that is not controlled by any vendor. While TCP/IP was originally designed for *wide area networks* (WANs) with slow links, the protocol can also be used on *local area networks* (LANs) that have faster data transfer rates.

In fact, one of the first uses of TCP/IP in LANs was at the University of California, Berkeley. It was here that TCP/IP was implemented in the kernel of the Berkeley Software Distribution (BSD) 4.2 UNIX operating system. BSD 4.2 UNIX was a very seminal version of UNIX, and is one of the reasons for TCP/IP's widespread popularity. Most universities and many research organizations use BSD UNIX. Today, most host machines on the Internet run a direct descendant of BSD UNIX. In addition, many commercial versions of UNIX (such as SUN's SunOS and Digital's Ultrix) were derived from BSD 4.2 UNIX. Also heavily influenced by BSD UNIX is UNIX System V TCP/IP implementation.

Application Protocols on the Internet

The earlier applications on the Internet were the Simple Mail Transfer Protocol (SMTP), terminal emulation protocol (TELNET) for remote logon, file-transfer protocol (FTP). Figures 1.1 to 1.3 show examples of using some of these earlier protocols.

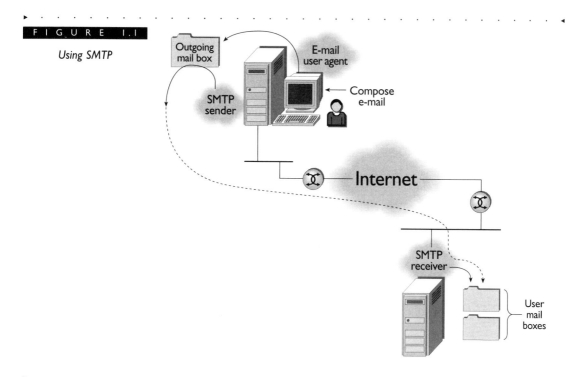

FIGURE 1.1

Using SMTP

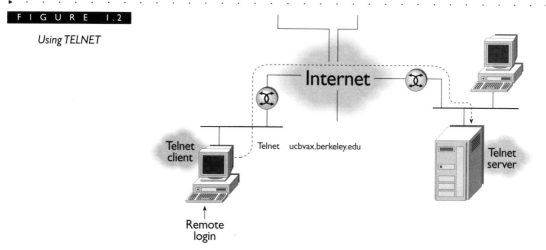

FIGURE 1.2

Using TELNET

FIGURE 1.3

Using FTP

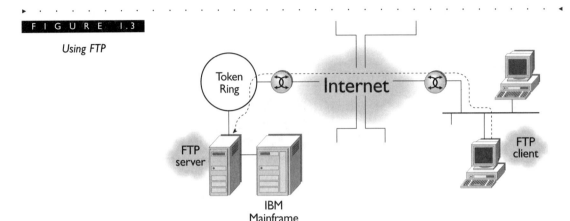

The application protocols that are used on the Internet all run on top of TCP/IP. Since TCP/IP can run equally well on LANs, these older applications can also be used on corporate networks that typically use LANs.

The late 1980s saw the emergence of new types of application protocols. The earlier application protocols dealt primarily with mail data or traditional computer data files. In fact, earlier implementations of mail protocols treated mail as file data for the purposes of transferring mail to other computers on the network. These new application protocols defined newer types of structures within data. Examples of these types of files are multimedia files that contain not only pictures or sound, but also *hyperlinks*. Hyperlinks enable users of multimedia files to move at designated points inside the same file, other files, and even files on other computers (see Figure 1.4).

The modern Web application protocol was created in 1989 at the European Particle Physics Laboratory, CERN. The Web protocol was developed by Tim Berners-Lee as part of a project that led to an effort to create standards for passing hyperlink-enabled text and multimedia information on the Internet.

The Web protocol consisted of the following two components:

▶ A standard for creating the multimedia hypertext files

▶ A standard for serving these standardized files when they were requested.

F I G U R E   1.4

Hyperlinks and the Web protocol

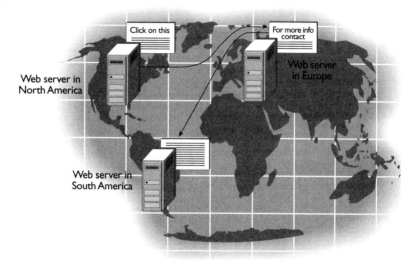

The standard for creating the multimedia hypertext files is called Hypertext Markup Language (HTML), which is a simplified subset of another standard called the Standard General Markup Language (SGML).

The standard for serving the HTML files is called Hypertext Transfer Protocol (HTTP). The Web server consists of a program that implements the HTTP server. On UNIX systems the HTTP server program is called the HTTP daemon (see Figure 1.5). Many non-UNIX systems (such as NetWare) also have adopted this vocabulary. In fact, the Novell Web Server is called HTTP.NLM.

F I G U R E   1.5

HTTP daemon on a UNIX system

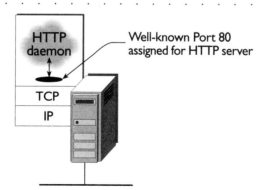

Because multimedia files can be created in a standard way, client software (called Web *browsers*) can be defined and built to retrieve the files from an HTTP server, as well as render the multimedia document (HTML file) for display (see Figure 1.6). As part of the rendering of the multimedia document, hyperlinks are displayed in such a way that users can use a pointing device to select these links. The original Web browsers were text-based interfaces. The development of NCSA's Mosaic technology, which provided a graphical user interface (GUI) soon changed this. Today, you have the choice of many Web browsers with easy-to-use graphical interfaces.

HTTP and HTML

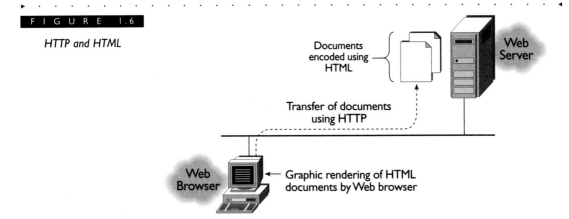

Selection of these links enables the users to navigate through hyperlinked documents. The power of this method of navigating documents has led to the popularity of the Web as an application and an increased use of the Internet. It provides an easy way of accessing a complex maze of documents. Documents are broken into pages that fit the size of standard display units in computer systems. Users can examine documents as a sequence of pages, or use hyperlinks to branch off and navigate other documents. Another reason to break these documents into pages is to give the user the option of deciding what to view. It also improves network bandwidth by reducing the amount of data that is transferred to the client. The Web server has become a major component of corporate intranetworks and can be used as a distributed document store that can be navigated by using a Web browser.

Many of today's Web browsers can keep track of the history of pages that were navigated. This enables the user to "backtrack" to a previously viewed page, or continue browsing from the place at which the user jumped off by using a hyperlink. This navigation process is popularly called *Web surfing*. (This is similar to channel surfing for TV, but it is, hopefully, more productive.)

Browsers typically also have the option of being configured to automatically retrieve a specific HTML page when they are started. This initial page is also called the *home page* for the Web browser. Web servers are also configured with a default page, which is also called the home page. It is stored in index.htm or index.html file. If an HTML document is not specified by the Web browser, this default home page is sent to the Web browser for display. The home page typically contains an index. The global collection of pages and hyperlinks on the Internet is known as the World Wide Web (WWW or W3). For users who only use a Web browser to interact with the Internet, the World Wide Web provides a virtual view or virtual world of the Internet, a virtual world that is sometimes called *cyberspace*.

The WWW method of publishing documents is unlike the paper medium used for publishing. When composed with such languages as Java, HTML documents can provide dynamic content, as opposed to the static content of the paper medium. Additionally, anyone who has access to the Internet can become an "instant" publisher. The HTML page can be set up to keep track of who is reading the page, and even how many people have accessed the page (called *hits*). Because anyone can set up a link to your HTML page, you cannot keep track of who is referencing your page. This is the reversal of the paper medium, where a periodical index is available that lists all the articles referencing a specific article, but there is no way to tell when someone reads that article.

Understanding Intranets

The protocols and applications that are used on the Internet (and the Web, in particular) can also be deployed on the internal network of an organization (see Figure 1.7). The term "intranet" was derived from the explosion of Web technology into enterprise networking. These applications and protocols actually have faster performance on the internal network, since most internal networks have faster bandwidths than the Internet. Contrast a user in Figure 1.7 who has access to the Web server on a 10 Mbps Ethernet with a user on the Internet (see Figure 1.8) who has access to the Web server at 28.8 Kbps to 64 Kbps.

FIGURE 1.7

Deploying Internet
applications on an internal
network

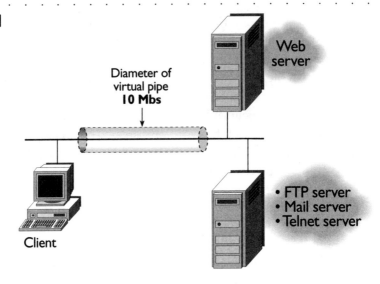

FIGURE 1.8

Limited bandwidth of
Internet connections

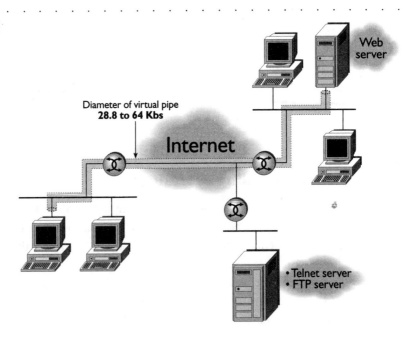

The Web browser client that is used to retrieve and display the HTML documents can also be used to view documents on an internal Web server. The Web browsers have a GUI with which many users find the interface intuitive and simple to use. This same Web browser software can be used on the internal network to access information on internal Web servers. The types of information you can publish on the Web server are endless. Here are just a few examples:

- Company stock data

- Company policies

- Personnel forms

- Job applications within the company

- Vacation applications

- Time sheets

- Access to corporate databases

- Company wide telephone directories

- Bulletin boards

- Search capabilities to documents

- Mail system

If network access to the outside world is restricted, the internal network must not be strapped as much with security issues. If one has access to an external network (such as the Internet), a firewall and/or data encryption must be considered (see Figure 1.9) to restrict the traffic and access from the outside world to data.

▶ · ◀

FIGURE 1.9

Security considerations for connection to an external network

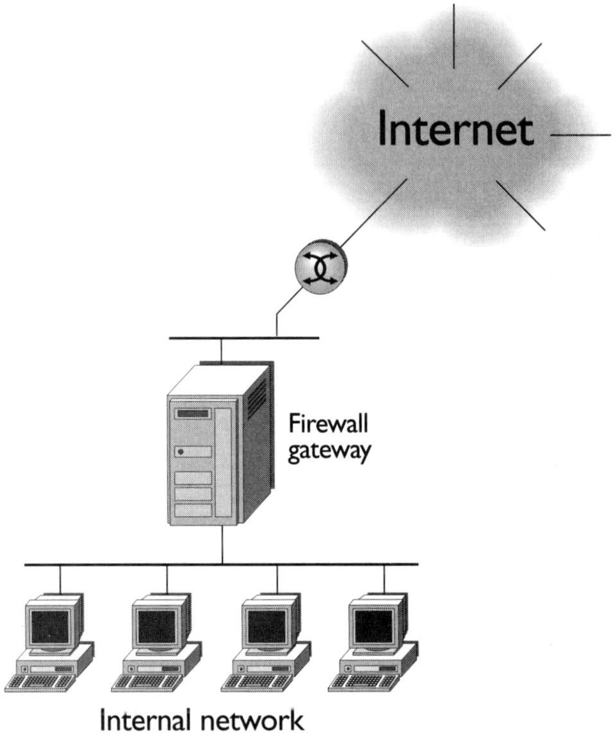

Using a Universal Client

Because browsers exist for many client platforms (such as UNIX, MS-Windows, OS/2, Macintosh, and so on), an organization can use the Web browser as a universal client to access data (see Figure 1.10). Browsers that can display the text portions of the accessed documents are also available for non-GUI systems.

The Web browser can act as a universal client that can retrieve data not only HTML files, but also data on other systems. The Web Server can be linked to other computer systems and more conventional corporate databases. The Web browser can submit the query, and the Web server can redirect this query to another system, obtain the results, and send the results back as an HTML-formatted document to the Web client. The Web client then displays the results as it would any other HTML document.

F I G U R E   1.10

Universal client access

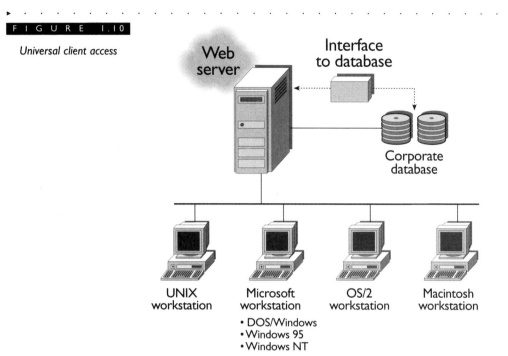

Figure 1.11 shows how a Web client can act as a universal client to provide access to legacy applications on mainframe computers. This figure shows a command being issued from the Web browser as an HTTP Get command. The Web server translates this command to a query sent to the mainframe. The mainframe could be on the same network as the Web client, or on a separate network. What matters is that the Web server has network access to the mainframe. The mainframe processes the query and sends it back to the Web server. The Web server translates the mainframe results to an HTML document, which is then sent to the Web client. Figure 1.12 shows a similar interaction being performed against a specialized database server machine. In this example, the database server is on the same network as the Web client.

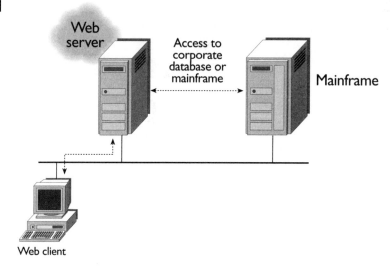

FIGURE 1.11

Universal client access to legacy applications on mainframes

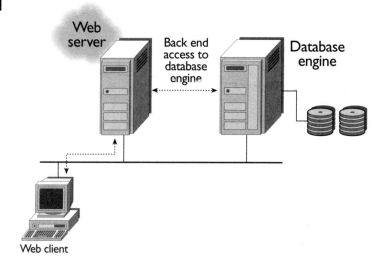

FIGURE 1.12

Universal client access to database servers

What is important to realize after examining Figures 1.11 and 1.12 is that the protocols used to interact between the Web client and the Web server, and the protocols that the Web server uses to interact with the database servers, are quite different. For example, the Web client and the Web server use HTTP running on top of TCP/IP. The Web server and the computer that houses the database may or may not use TCP/IP, but the application level protocol is, for legacy applications, entirely different than HTTP. The Web server provides a translation between the TCP/IP and HTTP protocols to the protocols required for communicating with the database computer. In essence, the Web server acts as a gateway between the Web client and the database computer.

As an example of the scenario illustrated in Figure 1.11, IBM is using the HTML and the Web Universal client interface to provide its IBM 3270 and 5250 terminal users access to intranets. This is being done in attempt to shift the terminal traffic from the protocol-dependent systems network architecture (SNA) software to a protocol-indifferent approach. By IBM's estimate, as of 1996, $20 trillion was invested in SNA applications and more than 40,000 SNA networks worldwide. Because of this large investment and installed base, it is not practical to rewrite the applications and software to accommodate emerging intranet technologies. However, what does make good sense, in this case, is to provide gateway capabilities to access Web services. For dumb terminals, Figure 1.13 shows an HTML gateway running a Web browser that translates IBM 3270 and 5250 terminal traffic to IP-encapsulated data streams, which are sent to the intranet or Internet. The IP-encapsulated data stream carries the application-level HTTP protocol between the Web server and the HTML gateway. The HTML gateway, therefore, provides translation between terminal and HTTP data streams.

For IBM PCs that use IBM 3270/5250 terminal emulation to access mainframes, a more direct approach is used (see Figure 1.14). The IBM Personal Communications line of 3270 and 5250 terminal emulation software have Web browsing capability incorporated in the software itself. Contrasting this approach to that of Figure 1.13, you can see that the HTML gateway functions are performed within the terminal emulation software itself. For PCs that use terminal emulation software to access Web resources only, there will be no SNA traffic sent from the PC. The terminal traffic will be converted to HTTP traffic within the PC itself.

Using the Universal Web client means that the client portion of the client/server application must not be written, and only the Web gateway to the server must be written. The universal client is readily available as one of the many off-the-shelf Web browsers (such as Mosaic, NetScape Navigator, Internet Explorer, Web Explorer, Web Surfer, and so on). With traditional clients, a programmer must design how information will flow to the client and how it must be displayed. The use of hyperlinks in an HTML document provides a flexible way for the user of the application to determine how the information will flow to the client. This also provides the user with the ability to piece together the data to best accomplish the task at hand.

HTML gateway for
IBM terminals

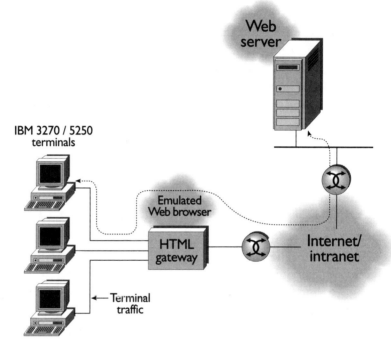

The Web universal client was designed with accessing Web resources in mind, but it is flexible enough so that it can be used as a client for other traditional applications, such as FTP, TELNET, SMTP, and Network News Transfer Protocol (NNTP). Most Web browsers can directly access FTP or TELNET sites as long as the Uniform Resource Locator (URL) is properly constructed. The URL has the following syntax:

```
protocol://hostname/pathname
```

The *protocol* can be a protocol such as HTTP (Web access), FTP (FTP client access), TELNET (TELNET client access). Most Web client users are used to seeing the HTTP protocol. The following are some examples of URLs using HTTP:

▸   `http://www.ibm.com`

▸   `http://cnn.com`

▸   `http://www.tsl.org`

▸   `http://www.usa.net`

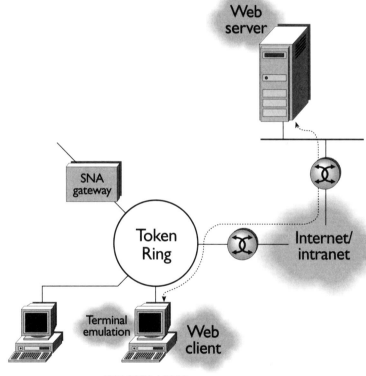

*Web browser capability for
3270/5250 terminal
emulation software*

To access an FTP server, the user would replace *protocol* with *FTP* and then specify the hostname. Similarly, you can replace *protocol* with *telnet* to remotely log in to a TELNET server from a Web browser. Using the Novell Web Server, you can use the Web browser to dynamically index the directory you are browsing so that you can see the directory.

Some Web browsers can be configured with helper applications for SMTP mail and Network News that can be launched from within the Web client. Other Web clients (such as Netscape) have their own mail and Network News clients built into them.

From these examples, you can see the versatility of the Web client, and the fact that it indeed can be used as a universal client.

Effectiveness of Using Intranets

The ease-of-use of the universal Web client opens up the use of network computing for the masses. As masses of people rush into using the Web, they are developing skills that they can use within an organization that has deployed intranets.

On the Internet, the Web is being positioned as a means for marketers to gather information to get exposure for an organization, and to sell products directly to customers. While, to a certain extent, some of this potential is being realized, venturing into the Internet has not been successful for many.

The intranet, on the other hand, can be used by organizations to save costs of internal operations. When the intranet Web server is also exposed to the Internet, it can serve as an effective means of communication between an organization and its customers and clients. For example, many software vendors now provide software patches, updates, demonstration products, and support information on the Web server.

The internal users see the Web server as an intranet server, and to users outside the organization, the Web server is seen as an Internet server (see Figure 1.15). Some organizations are even using the Web server to distribute and sell new software by using a *commerce-enabled Web server* (see Figure 1.16). A commerce-enabled Web server uses encryption and digital authentication techniques to protect the exchange of a customer transaction that can contain private information (such as credit card numbers, phone numbers, and address information). Examples of commerce-enabled servers are the Netscape Suite Spot servers and the Novell Web Server, which implement Secure Socket Layers (SSLs) to provide an encrypted channel between the Web browser and the Web server.

F I G U R E   1.15

Intranet/Internet Web server
for software distribution

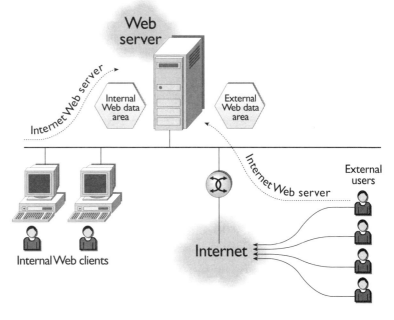

Other important uses of an intranet/Internet Web server would be to answer common queries about the business, or to distribute white papers, press releases, and so on. These informational queries would otherwise normally be handled by a customer service representative. For example, Novell uses its Web server to distribute information on its products, provide technical support, and so on. Wells Fargo Bank has a Web server that customers can use for inquiring about personal bank account balances and recent transactions via an encrypted transaction. Federal Express uses a Web server to check the location and status of specific overnight packages, even to the point of finding out the name of the person who signed for the package. State governments in the U.S. are using Web servers to help citizens find jobs. Theaters and movie houses publish times and location of entertainment events. Even politicians are using Web servers to distribute public service announcements and various other information.

All of these are examples of queries that would typically be handled by a customer service representative. Automated answer machines could be used, but these do not have the range of dynamic content provides by a Web server.

. . . . ◄

FIGURE 1.16

A commerce enabled intranet server

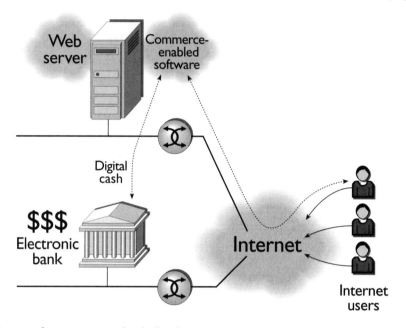

Another boon of intranets is the help they can provide to the overburdened worker. This technology-based society has spawned the concept of a *knowledge worker*, or a worker whose effectiveness and ability to function in a technology-based competitive market is dependent on having access to the right information at the right time. As part of the daily work routine, the modern knowledge worker is bombarded with vast amounts of information, only some of which is useful. This has led to a new type of stress called the *information overload*, truly a malady of our times.

In an attempt not to miss out on information that might be useful some day, people try to maintain some semblance of organizing this information. Even after discounting the inevitable pile of "junk" mail, much of the information is sent to an employee, just in case it might be useful. With the advent of photocopy machines, and e-mail, it is easy to duplicate the information and send it to lists of people "just-in-case" they may need it. The problem, therefore, intensifies with people getting copies of memos and reports that are marginally useful, if that at all. So the knowledge worker is constantly faced with a high-volume, low-value information system, and even with information that may be stored in multiple formats.

A solution to duplicating the "just-in-case" information is to have available a single copy of information that can be accessed "just-in-time" on demand. This is the area in which an intranet server can be very useful. First of all, documents and text information are maintained in the common HTML format, reducing the problem of incompatible formats.

The "just-in-time" approach is not a new approach. It has been associated with access to database files and database servers. However, *ad hoc* access to this information is not easy for the average user. Structured Query Language (SQL) access methods have been created to access databases, but this requires that the user learn a complex set of commands and access procedures. Even after the application is accessed, there is the question of how this information should be displayed. Usually custom applications are written by in-house database support staff to navigate through the accessed information. For standard types of queries and applications, the user must learn how to navigate this use interface, and this is part of the user's training.

However, for *ad hoc* queries for information, this approach is not flexible enough. To solve this problem, some enterprises have attempted to create a master information system with a single access and single interface. Such systems have not been able to keep pace with changing requirements, primarily because of the inflexibility of their architectures. The tools to manage these master information systems were designed to support the discrete data of transaction-based processes. Modern information needs have shifted toward support for complex data and information-based processes and the master information systems have not been able to keep pace.

The Web technology provides "just-in-time" information, but is flexible enough to support changes to the distributed information easily. The authoring, publishing, and management of documents is straightforward and does not require the complexity of the older centralized systems. You need not rely on programmers to add the information. The Web browser acts as a universal client that a user can use to retrieve, view, and print information without having to know about complex commands and access procedures. The intranet Web-based technology actually shifts control of information flow from the database support staff to the information users. As long as the user has the ability to easily retrieve and view the information when needed, there is no need to copy the information just-in-case someone needs it. Publishing a document is separated from automatic distribution—a problem that exists with e-mail.

Intranets for Managing Information Flows

Another important application of intranets is in the area of information flow and distribution within the organization. Many large organizations have their information resources stored in a variety of different *information stores*. These information stores are databases or a collection of files on a host computer's file system, and, in some cases, they may not even interoperate with each other. In some cases, the employees may see different, and often inconsistent, views on a particular subject because the information is stored on different centralized systems, and because there is no automated means of maintaining consistency and synchronization of this information.

In an attempt to solve some of these problems, *groupware technologies* have been used to provide a distributed, synchronized database. However, some users do not find these groupware technologies intuitive to use. If the user wants a different view of the data, or wants to use an application not already integrated with their proprietary groupware package, custom applications must be written, often in the proprietary scripting or development language of the groupware package. Such custom development is usually a fairly significant effort, requires a high level of skill, and may also be expensive to implement. Market leaders in groupware technologies such as IBM's Lotus Notes, provide Web support so that Lotus documents can be viewed as HTML documents.

Web-based technologies are usually less expensive to implement, deploy and maintain than the proprietary groupware counterparts. If the organization is already using TCP/IP based technologies such as UNIX workstations, or NetWare and Windows NT networks that use TCP/IP, then the organization already has the skill set to implement and maintain the protocol infrastructure of intranets. It is easy for users to create, publish, and access information in HTML format. In many cases, simple word processors can be used. Some word processors (such as WordPerfect and MS Word) even have interfaces that permit the saving of the document in HTML formats.

Because the Web servers provide unprecedented ease-of-use for any employee in an organization to publish documents that can be viewed by a large number of people, the organization must try to prevent workers from becoming too involved in low-level maintenance of Web pages at the expense of the tasks that would most benefit the enterprise. The challenge is to meet the needs and overall goals of the organization without destroying the independence of decision making and action that usually results in a strong and flexible organization.

Groupware Versus Intranet Web Servers

Groupware products have become a dominant and established solution for creating a collaborative working environment that enables users to communicate and share information. The primary players in this market are IBM, Novell, and Microsoft. IBM's Lotus Notes is the front-runner and, by some estimates, has captured approximately a third of a market that is valued at close to $1 billion per year. The groupware market is expected to grow exponentially.

With the arrival of open Web-based technologies, many organizations are now questioning the need for groupware products, and wondering if intranet solutions can offer a less-expensive, more open, and equally effective solution. So, it is worthwhile to consider what the groupware products and Web-based technologies have to offer.

Groupware provides users simultaneous access to corporate information and the ability to communicate electronically with other users. In an enterprise, this communication enables customers, employees, and business partners to collaborate and be more effective as an organization. Most groupware products are built using a client/server architecture, where the clients (users) access over a corporate network with document databases (object stores) that are located on a single site or distributed across multiple sites. Groupware documents are multimedia documents and can consist of text, images, audio, and video information. However, their internal formatting and representation are usually proprietary, unlike the case of Web-based technologies such as HTML (which is based on a standard). Groupware software enables users to enter data using a form interface, and the data can be stored in remote databases.

Data stores in groupware products can be distributed on several groupware servers. A key issue in maintaining consistency of distributed data is synchronization of replicated information. Information is replicated for increasing the reliability in case one of the groupware servers is down. Groupware servers additionally provide the following capabilities:

- GUI

- E-mail capability

- Server security

- Customized templates for common business applications

- Support for multiple platforms

Many of these capabilities are also provided by groupware intranet technologies. The intranet Web server can be configured to provide collaborative computing at a much lower cost than the groupware products. Because of their longer history in the groupware market, groupware products are currently more mature than their intranet counterparts. However, even this is rapidly changing with many intranet Web servers providing capabilities that rival and sometimes exceed groupware product offerings.

The multimedia documents published on intranet Web servers are relatively easier to produce and publish when compared with groupware products. They are all based on HTML. In addition to word processors that can produce HTML text, there are a number of authoring tools such as HotMetal, HotDog, and many others that are available either free or at a very low cost. The document creation for intranets can be done by the same people who create the ideas and the document content. This means that information gets published quickly, and the originator of the document can more closely monitor how the actual document compares with the original idea. This results in greater accuracy of the documents, and quicker dissemination of information.

The intranet solutions are based on open technology, one of the important benefits of its evolution on the Internet. These technologies are primarily derived from the World Wide Web which has seen an explosion since 1992. As a side effect of this explosion, there has been the rapid increase in the number of tools that are freely available for Web Client and Web Server development. It is, therefore, much easier for the intranet Web servers to incorporate emerging technologies that are designed to be compatible with Web usage. Examples of these technologies include Virtual Reality Markup Language (VRML), Multimedia, and Java.

Current intranet products deliver all the capability to allow people to easily and quickly share information, but the majority of them do not provide the full-blown functionality of a collaborative groupware. As they evolve, they will begin to match the collaborative computing capabilities of groupware products.

Intranet Web servers can speed access to information by providing a cached copy of the information using proxy server technologies. If the data and the Web server reside on the same server, the Common Gateway Interface (CGI) can be used to deliver data in real-time. With the use of Java clients, even the CGI interface can be eliminated, thus providing rapid access to data on servers.

Deploying Intranet Technologies

Interestingly enough, internal Web usage-the start of the intranet-has often begun as an "underground," "unofficial," or "skunk works" project kept alive by the keen technical interest of an organizations local Internet experts. Now that the term "intranet" has become fashionable and glamorous, these projects have been coming out of the woodwork. Some of these projects enjoy a high visibility, and have become official full-scale efforts. In some cases, where management is not sure of how intranet technologies fit into the corporate networks, these projects are still managed as skunk projects, but with official blessing and limited or modest management support.

The following are three basic approaches being used to deploy intranets today:

▶ *Use the intranet server as a bulletin board.* This enables the intranet server to act as a bulletin board. Users can post commonly used information such as telephone directories.

▶ *Use the intranet server as a foundation for moving information.* In this example, the intranet server is used much like the way e-mail and groupware systems operate.

▶ *Use the intranet server for the core decision-support systems.* In this example, the corporate databases are linked to the intranet server and used for daily business functions and tracking of sales information.

You can use any of these approaches in building intranets. The remainder of this book focuses on how you can build intranets using the products from Novell.

Summary

In this chapter you have been introduced to the concepts of intranets and Internets. Corporate networks that use Internet applications are called *intranets*. One of the key distinctions between these networks is that intranets are internal networks over which an organization has greater control, as opposed to the Internet where an organization may have little control.

## CHAPTER 2

Novell Web Server as an Intranet/Internet Server

The Novell Web Server provides a powerful platform for intranet services. These intranet services include Web services, and several support services (such as DNS and dynamic IP address assignment) that are needed to build an enterprise-wide intranet. This chapter provides an overview of the services offered by the Novell Web Server. Later chapters describe the critical components of the intranet services in detail.

Identifying Services Offered by the Novell Web Server

The Novell Web Server runs on top of the NetWare 4 Server platform (see Figure 2.1). The NetWare 4 Server platform provides a number of features that make NetWare 4 a very fast and efficient server for providing the following basic services:

▶ Global directory services called Novell Directory Services (NDS)

▶ Fault-tolerant distributed file system services

▶ Print services that can be controlled by NDS

▶ Multiple protocol support (IPX, TCP/IP, AppleTalk, OSI, and so on)

▶ File-transfer protocol (FTP) and Trivial File-Transfer Protocol (TFTP) services

▶ XCONSOLE services to permit management of a server from UNIX workstations on the Internet/intranet.

▶ Network File System (NFS) services

▶ AppleTalk file and print services

▶ UNIX/NetWare bidirectional print services

▶ Systems Network Architecture (SNA) gateway services

▸ Storage management (compression, real-time data migration, backup agents, and redundant array of inexpensive disks, or RAID)

▸ Network management support (SNMP over IP and IPX)

▸ MultiProtocol Router (MPR) services

▸ Support for Simple Network Management Protocol (SNMP)

▸ Internet access server

▸ Remote access services

▸ Mobile IPX services

▸ NetWare/IP

▸ IPX/IP gateway services

▸ Novell GroupWise with SMTP mail gateway

▸ Protocol analysis tools (Lanalyzer)

▸ Client support (UNIX, DOS/Windows, Windows 95, Windows NT, OS/2, and Macintosh)

▸ Embedded Java support

▸ Web publishing capabilities via the Web server.

▸ Language interpreters (Perl, BASIC, and NetBasic)

▸ Dynamic Host Configuration Protocol (DHCP) and Boot Protocol (BOOTP) services

▸ Domain Name System (DNS) services

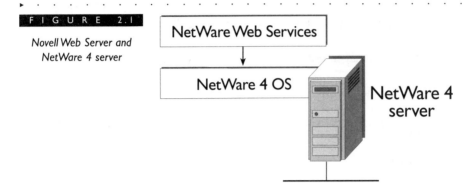

FIGURE   2.1

*Novell Web Server and
NetWare 4 server*

Web services such as those provided by the Novell Web Server and the Novell
Netscape Navigator run on top of the basic NetWare 4 services. Depending on the
needs of the intranet, you can add any of the service elements in the previous list
to build your intranet.

Overview of the Required Networking Technology

To build an intranet, you need the following basic technologies and services:

▸ *TCP/IP protocol support for the Web client and the Web server.* TCP/IP
   support is essential at the Web server. At the Web client, TCP/IP
   support is optional. You can use IPX clients to access intranet
   services, provided you have configured an IPX/IP gateway.

▸ *DNS server.* DNS services provide naming services for the TCP/IP
   protocol. Using DNS services enables Web clients to refer to servers
   and other workstations by their symbolic name, rather than by their
   IP addresses.

▸ *Web server.* The Web server provides access to documents that are
   published using the HTML standard. The Web server must include
   support for the CGI (Common Gateway Interface) to access services
   available on the Web server. The Web server must provide for a
   method to develop CGI programs.

▸ *Web client.* The Web client is the front end used to access the services on the Web server. The Web client can access services from a cluster of Web servers by using a naming scheme called the Uniform Resource Locator (URL). Because URL addresses typically use DNS names, DNS name resolution is needed.

▸ *Routers.* Protocol devices such as Internet Protocol (IP) routers extend the range of the network beyond a single network segment. If IPX is used by the Web clients, then IPX routers are also essential.

▸ *IP address allocation scheme.* You can assign IP address, subnet masks and other IP configuration parameters manually per Web client. However, as the number of clients increases, and the network changes, manual maintenance of IP parameters is a time-consuming task that is also prone to human error. A better method is to assign IP parameters automatically. This can be done using a BOOTP server or a DHCP server. A DHCP server is preferable because IP parameters can be leased on a first-come, first-served basis. If IPX is used as the communication protocol there is no need for an IP or IPX address assignment scheme, because IPX is dynamically configurable.

Figure 2.2 shows the intranet built around the TCP/IP protocol and Figure 2.3 shows the intranet built around the IPX protocol. In Figure 2.2 the Web, DNS, and DHCP services are shown running on different servers, but it is not essential that they run on separate servers. You can run some or all of these services on the same physical server. Figure 2.3 shows an example of how a single server supports multiple services.

The Web server, DNS server, and DHCP server can all run on the same NetWare 4 server platform, or you can spread these services on multiple servers. Figure 2.4 shows an example of an intranet built around the NetWare 4 server platform.

▶ · ◀

FIGURE 2.2

Example intranet using TCP/IP

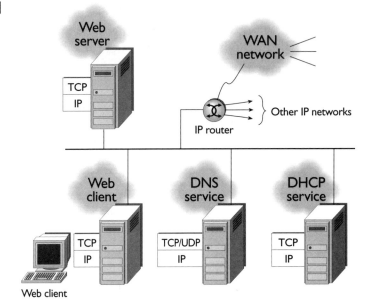

▶ · ◀

FIGURE 2.3

Example intranet using IPX

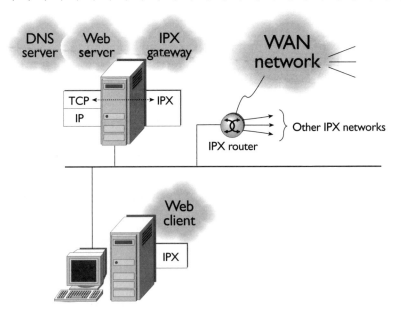

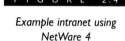

FIGURE 2.4

Example intranet using NetWare 4

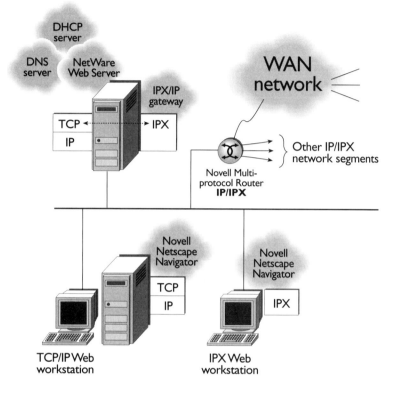

Services Provided by the Novell Web Server

The Novell Web Server provides the basic Web services. In addition the Novell Web Server provides a CGI interface to run programs on the server. This allows you to develop CGI programs that can deliver to Web clients services other than simple document access. Documents can be generated dynamically and can contain information on a variety of network and application services. The Novell Web Server provides the following services:

▸ HTTP Web services

▸ CGI interface

- CGI scripting languages (Perl, BASIC, NetBasic)

- CGI NLM programs written in C/C++

- Server Side Includes (SSIs)

- Image maps

- Restricted access via NDS authentication

- User publishing of Web documents

- NDS browsing

- Virtual directories

- Secure Socket Layer (SSL) protocol

- Multihoming

- Novell Quickfinder

- Navie Oracle support via NetBASIC

Server Side Includes (SSIs) are the ability of the server to process the documents and replace special tags called *SSI tags* with information from the Web server. This enables you to generate dynamic documents without resorting to writing special CGI programs. You can set the Novell Web Server as a simple firewall for Web clients so that only the specified Web clients can access the Web server. You can restrict Web clients on the basis of

- User access to the Web server

- IP address of Web client

- Domain name of Web client

Figure 2.5 illustrates how Web clients and users can be restricted.

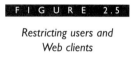

FIGURE 2.5

*Restricting users and
Web clients*

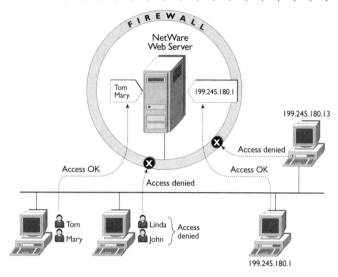

The Web server allows users to publish HTML pages from their home directories. By default, users are allowed to publish documents by placing them in the PUBLIC.WWW directory relative to their home directory. You can control whether user publishing of HTML pages is enabled or disabled. Additionally, the Web server permits NDS tree browsing from a Web client. You can disable or enable NDS browsing as part of the Novell Web Server configuration.

Novell Web Server Configuration Scenarios

You can configure the Novell Web Server on a single LAN, as shown in Figure 2.6. If you do not have the expertise to configure and maintain a DNS server or a DHCP server on the network, you can use manually allocated IP addresses. This configuration is adequate for small workgroup LANs consisting of about 30 stations or less.

If you want to extend the range of your intranet to have an additional one or two network segments, you can do this by using the Novell Web Server as an MPR itself (see Figure 2.7). You must use a different IP address class for the different networks, or use IP address classes with subnetting. In Figure 2.7, a class B address of 150.33.0.0 is being used with subnetting. The Novell Web Server acts as a central server resource machine in Figure 2.7 in the sense that all the Web, file system, and other shared resources are kept on the server. Depending on the size of the network, it is advisable to have the Web server act as a DNS and a DHCP server. The DNS server will enable you to use symbolic names instead of IP addresses and the DHCP server will enable you to dynamically allocate IP addresses.

F I G U R E   2.6

Novell Web Server on a single LAN

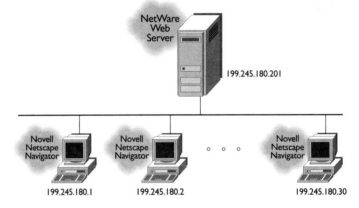

F I G U R E   2.7

Novell Web Server on an interconnected LAN

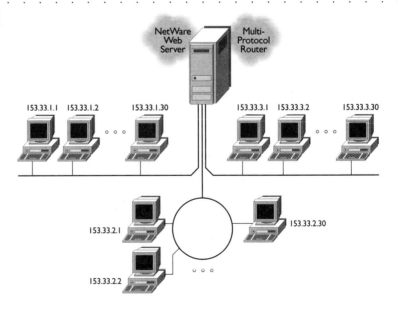

If you want to extend the range of your intranet over several geographical locations, you can use a wide area network (WAN). A WAN can consist of an X.25 network, Frame Relay, Asynchronous Transfer Mode (ATM), Switched Multimegabit Data Service (SMDS), dedicated leased lines, T1/E1 lines, and so on. Figure 2.8 shows such an intranet/internetwork where the WAN technology is shown as a cloud and may use any of the technologies previously mentioned. Each site separated by the WAN should have its own DNS service to avoid the overhead of transmitting DNS traffic over the relatively slower WAN links. In addition, such an enterprise network may have a DHCP server at each site to ease the problem of maintaining consistent values for the IP parameters for that site. MPR devices will also be needed to connect the sites to the WAN network. Unless the decision is made to go with an entirely IPX or IP network, the routers must be configured for both IPX and IP. It is possible for each site to maintain its own Web server (as shown in Figure 2.8), or use a common Web server.

FIGURE 2.8

Novell Web Servers on a WAN

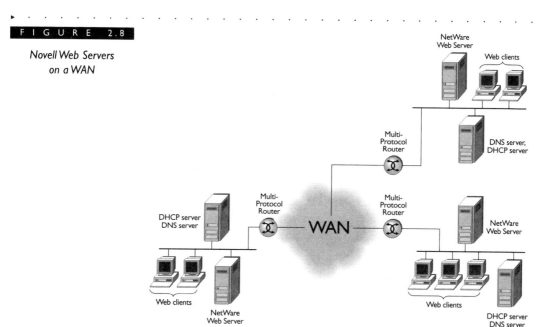

Summary

The NetWare server is a powerful platform for providing intranet services. These intranet services include in addition to other services Web services, DNS, DHCP services, and MPR services. These services can be used to build an enterprise-wide intranet. This chapter has discussed the basic services provided by the Novell Web Server, different configuration scenarios that demonstrate how intranets can be built using the Novell Web Server, as well as other support services.

## CHAPTER 3

Installing the Novell Web Server

This chapter discusses the Novell Web Server installation process. Normally, software installation can be performed as a first step without considering serious design issues. However, the Novell Web Server runs on top of the NetWare 4 operating system. The NetWare 4 operating system is a powerful network operating system with support for Novell Directory Services (NDS). Before installing the Novell Web Server, you should have already installed the NetWare 4 operating system.

This chapter has a twofold purpose. The first purpose is to teach you how to install the NetWare 4 server, which provides the infrastructure for running the Novell Web Server. The second purpose is to show you how to install the Novell Web Server on top of the installed NetWare 4 server. If you have already installed the NetWare 4 server, you can skip the first part of the chapter and go directly to the section, "Guided Tour for Installing the Novell Web Server."

Installing the NetWare 4 Server

A very important aspect in the design of the IntranetWare-based network is the NDS structure. During NetWare 4 installation, you are asked to make decisions about the NDS structure for your network. It is, therefore, essential that you have a solid understanding of the NDS tree for your organization. Remember, once you have chosen the basic NDS tree structure, extra effort is required to make changes. You can save yourself time and effort by doing things right the first time. The installation process assumes that you are familiar with NDS.

The installation requirements for the NetWare server fall into two categories: hardware and software.

Hardware Requirements

In terms of hardware, the server must be an Intel 80386 or higher processor with at least 20 MB of RAM, and an internal or external hard disk of at least 105 MB partitioned for NetWare. The server disk must have a minimum of 15 MB DOS partition, plus a minimum of 90 MB for the NetWare partition. You will need an additional 60 MB on the NetWare partition if you plan to install the DynaText viewer and the accompanying Novell documentation. It is not necessary to install the DynaText viewer or Novell documentation on the server. Instead, you can install this at a workstation.

The server must also have at least one Network Interface Card (NIC) with the correct NetWare Loadable Module (NLM) driver. One of the areas of improvement in NetWare 4 is that the distribution software comes with a list of a larger number of network drivers and automatic detection of most well-known NICs.

If NetWare does not automatically detect and support the NIC of your choice, consult the NIC vendor. You can download drivers from bulletin board systems (BBSs) and Web sites. These drivers contain instructions on how to use them in the NetWare 4 installation process. You will also need a CD-ROM for installing the server software. Other optional pieces of hardware are a tape backup and an optical jukebox for data migration.

To summarize: the minimum hardware requirements for NetWare 4.x are as follows:

- ▶ Intel 80386 processor (or better)

- ▶ 20 MB of RAM

- ▶ Server disk size of at least 105 MB for the NetWare server (140 MB for installing other products such as the Novell Web Server)

- ▶ Additional 60 MB for optional installation of DynaText viewer and Novell documentation

- ▶ 15 MB DOS partition for storing server startup files

- ▶ Supported NIC

- ▶ CD-ROM drive

To find out the actual server memory requirements, you can use the following equation:

$$M = 20 + D*0.008 + 4$$

where M is the server RAM in megabytes and D is the disk space in megabytes. The 20 MB in the formula is the minimum server RAM, and the 4 MB is additional RAM for cache buffers. Simplifying the formula, you have the following equation:

```
M = 24 + D*0.008
```

Therefore, for a server that has 4 GB of disk space, the server RAM is computed as follows:

```
M = 24 + 4000*0.008 = 24 + 32 = 66 MB
```

For a more accurate estimation of server RAM, see Appendix A of the Novell document called "Installing NetWare 4."

An important (but often overlooked) hardware attribute is that the server should have an accurate time clock, especially if will act as a Single Reference time server, Primary time server, or Reference time server. These time servers are needed for NDS operations to be properly synchronized. NDS implements a distributed database that acts as a repository for network resources. Because the database is distributed on servers on the network, the operations on the database must be performed in reference to a common network time. The different time server types help to provide this common network time. A Reference time server should, by definition, have an accurate time clock. However, the Single Reference time server and the Reference time server are usually ordinary computers, and should have a reasonably accurate clock.

The first NetWare 4 server that you install defines the initial NDS partition, which also contains the [Root] object of the NDS tree. For this reason, the first NetWare 4 server that is installed is called the *root* server. The root server should be a 100 MHz Intel 80486 computer or better. A faster machine is preferred as a root server, because the root server contains the master replica of the NDS root partition and may be accessed for some global NDS operations.

Software Requirements

One of the software requirements for NetWare 4 is DOS for the initial loading of the server software. The versions of DOS that are supported are DOS 3.1 and higher for a standard Intel platform with an Industry Standard Architecture (ISA), Enhanced Industry Standard Architecture (EISA) bus, or Peripheral Control Interconnect (PCI) bus. Micro Channel Adapter (MCA) computers must use a

DOS 3.3 or higher. Another requirement is the NetWare 4 software and license disk. You can also build a registration disk (different from the license disk) that is used to copy registration information on the installed NetWare 4 software. Registration can be accomplished by sending the completed registration disk to Novell. Though recommended, registration is not a requirement for completing NetWare 4.*x* installation.

NetWare 4 requires DOS for the initial load of the server. You can install the NetWare server from a CD-ROM or over the network. If this is your first NetWare 4 server on the network, you must select the CD-ROM method (see Figure 3-1). The network installation method is faster than the CD-ROM installation method, but requires an existing NetWare server with sufficient space to store the NetWare files, or a NetWare 4 CD-ROM that is mounted as a NetWare volume (see Figure 3-2).

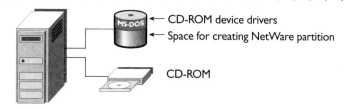

FIGURE 3.1

NetWare 4 CD-ROM installation method

← CD-ROM device drivers
← Space for creating NetWare partition

CD-ROM

NetWare 4 server

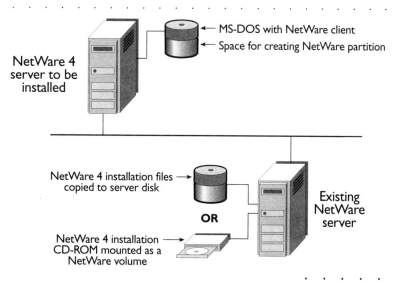

FIGURE 3.2

NetWare 4 remote network installation method

NetWare 4 server to be installed

← MS-DOS with NetWare client
← Space for creating NetWare partition

NetWare 4 installation files → copied to server disk

OR

NetWare 4 installation → CD-ROM mounted as a NetWare volume

Existing NetWare server

Installation Procedure

This section reviews the installation procedure and discusses the details of performing the installation. The installation procedure is presented as a guided tour that consists of the following 20 steps:

▶ *Step 1:* Selecting the installation method

▶ *Step 2:* Selecting the server language and type of installation

▶ *Step 3:* Assigning the server name

▶ *Step 4:* Assigning the server IPX internal network number

▶ *Step 5:* Copying the server boot files to the DOS partition

▶ *Step 6:* Assigning the locale configuration

▶ *Step 7:* Specifying special SET commands

▶ *Step 8:* Starting the server

▶ *Step 9:* Loading and configuring disk drivers

▶ *Step 10:* Loading and configuring network drivers

▶ *Step 11:* Creating the NetWare 4.*x* disk partition

▶ *Step 12:* Creating the NetWare 4.*x* volume

▶ *Step 13:* Selecting NetWare file groups

▶ *Step 14:* Installing NDS (time configuration and context)

▶ *Step 15:* Licensing the NetWare operating system

▶ *Step 16:* Creating or modifying the startup files

▶ *Step 17:* Copying files

▸ *Step 18:* Performing other installation options

▸ *Step 19:* Completing the installation

▸ *Step 20:* Booting the server from the startup files

Step 1: Selecting the installation method

Decide on the installation method: CD-ROM or network installation.

For *CD-ROM installation*, you must have a CD-ROM attached locally to the server machine on which you will be installing NetWare 4. This means that the CD-ROM must be recognizable by DOS. You must boot with DOS and have appropriate CD-ROM drivers in the CONFIG.SYS file on the DOS partition. Typically, you will boot the machine with a DOS-formatted floppy disk that has appropriate drivers for the CD-ROM. You should also have at least 12 file handles and 15 buffers specified in the CONFIG.SYS file, as follows:

```
FILES=12
BUFFERS=15
```

Since each CD-ROM manufacturer has a different set of installation procedures and CD-ROM drivers, you should follow the manufacturer's instructions. After the CD-ROM drivers are installed and activated by booting the server machine, you should change your directory to the CD-ROM drive.

For *network installation*, mount the CD-ROM as a NetWare volume on an existing server, or copy the CD-ROM distribution software on an existing NetWare server volume. Next, use the client software to log on to the network and then map to the directory on the server that contains the NetWare 4 server installation files.

After changing your current drive to the CD-ROM or the network drive containing the distribution files, issue the INSTALL command:

```
INSTALL
```

Step 2: Selecting the server language and type of installation

The NetWare Install menu appears. Select the choice corresponding to the language option you will use for this server. For English the choice is "Select this line to install in English." The Novell license terms and conditions then appear. Page through the license terms and conditions by pressing any key.

A menu called "Select the type of installation desired" then appears. Your choices are the following:

- ▸ NetWare Server Installation

- ▸ Client Installation

- ▸ Diskette Creation

- ▸ Readme files

Select "NetWare Server Installation." You are then given the choice for which server product to install or to view README files:

- ▸ NetWare 4.*x*

- ▸ NetWare 4.*x* SFT III

- ▸ Display Information (README) File

Note that the *x* is the version number for the NetWare OS. At some time, browse through the README files by selecting the "Display Information (README) File" option to find tips on resolving installation problems.

Select the "NetWare 4.*x*" option to install a new NetWare 4.*x* server. Select the type of NetWare server installation you are performing. Your choices are the following:

- ▸ Simple Installation of NetWare 4.*x*

- ▸ Custom Installation of NetWare 4.*x*

- ▸ Upgrade NetWare 3.1*x* or 4.*x*

The "Simple Installation" allows the installation program to make most choices. It assumes the following:

- ▸ An existing DOS partition on the server of at least 15 MB with DOS already installed on the partition.

▸ Remaining disk space that is not used for the DOS partition will be used for a NetWare partition.

▸ Each disk can have only one NetWare volume.

▸ The Server will boot from the hard disk and not from the floppy.

▸ IPX numbers will be randomly generated.

▸ No changes will be made to the STARTUP.NCF or AUTOEXEC.NCF files.

▸ The NDS tree will have a single container for all objects.

If these assumptions are not true, select the "Custom Installation." If you are selecting the "Upgrade NetWare 3.1x or 4.x" option, back up your data before performing the upgrade, even though no existing data files will be deleted.

The Simple Installation is a subset of the Custom Installation. Therefore, the remainder of this discussion describes the most general Custom Installation procedure.

Step 3: Assigning the server name

Select the Custom Installation and you are prompted for the server name. Enter a server name, which can be from 2 to 47 characters and include alphanumeric characters (A-Z, 0-9), hyphens, and underscores. You cannot use a period as the first character. The server name must be different from any other server or directory name on the network.

After installation, the server name is saved in the AUTOEXEC.NCF file. When the SERVER.EXE program loads during normal startup of the NetWare server, the server name is read from this file. You can change your server name by editing the AUTOEXEC.NCF file and changing the server name parameter.

Step 4: Assigning the server IPX internal network number

You now see a prompt for an internal network number. The installation program generates a number at random. You can select this internal network number (since it is not likely to conflict with an existing internal network number) or select your own unique internal network number.

It is best to select your own internal network number according to your own scheme, or to register the IPX network number with Xerox (who now maintains a registry of IPX network numbers).

Internal network numbers can be eight hexadecimal digits long. These numbers must be different from other internal network numbers and from the network numbers used to identify the cable segments. The internal network number describes a logical network that uniquely identifies the NetWare Core Protocol (NCP) processing engine at the heart of the NetWare server. Internal network numbers were introduced in NetWare 3.0 to solve routing anomalies common in NetWare 2.*x* networks, where the NCP processing engine had a network number that was the same as that of the network installed on LAN A (the first network adapter on the server).

Step 5: Copying the server boot files to the DOS partition

The installation will then copy the server boot files to the DOS partition. If this partition has not been created, the installation program guides you through creating the DOS partition. You are asked to verify the source and destination paths for copying the server boot files.

The *default source path* is the drive from which you booted. Normally, you should not have to change the source path if you are installing by using the floppy disk or local CD-ROM method. If you were installing from across the network, you can press the F2 key, and then specify the network drive and path from which to read the software distribution.

The *default destination path* is C:\NWSERVER. Accept this default, unless you have your own standard as to where the server files are copied. To change the destination path, press F4 and then specify the network drive and path from which to read the software distribution.

Press Enter to verify the source and destination paths and to continue with the installation. A status display screen shows the files that are copied to the DOS partition.

Step 6: Assigning the locale configuration

You are now asked to select a locale configuration for the server. The configuration that is displayed is that for the server. However, the displayed default values are taken from the DOS configuration you are using to run the INSTALL program. Previous versions of NetWare did not support country-specific conventions (such as differences in keyboard layout). NetWare 4.*x* supports internationalization and allows other keyboard layouts.

The *country code* is a three-digit country code. Consult the COUNTRY.SYS entry in your DOS manual for the applicable country code. The U.S. country code is 001.

The *code page* is a country-dependent three-digit page code. For U.S. English, the code page value is 437. This defines the character sets that are used for screen display.

Keyboard mapping supports keyboard layout differences that are specific to a language. The keyboard mapping values that are supported are France, Germany, Italy, Spain, and the United States.

To edit a field, highlight it and press Enter. When you are finished making changes, select the option "Press <Enter> here to continue."

Step 7: Specifying special SET commands

You are then asked if you want to specify any special startup SET commands. There are several SET commands that can be placed in the STARTUP.NCF file only. The STARTUP.NCF file resides on the DOS partition and in the directory where the SERVER.EXE program was copied. It contains commands to load disk drivers and name spaces, and special commands such as SET AUTO REGISTER MEMORY ABOVE 16 MEGABYTES=OFF. (Set to ON to automatically add memory above 16 MB for EISA bus server machines.) With NetWare 4.02 and higher, set "Reserved Buffers below 16 MB" to 200 if the server has device drivers that use memory below 16 MB.

Select Yes only if your server configuration demands that you need to set special parameters in the STARTUP.NCF file. Otherwise, select No. You can always edit the STARTUP.NCF file at a later stage.

Step 8: Starting the server

You are then asked if you want AUTOEXEC.BAT to load SERVER.EXE. If you answer Yes, your AUTOEXEC.BAT is modified to contain the following commands to start the server automatically, every time the machine is booted:

```
REM The following lines were created by the server
installation program.
REM They will cause the server to come up whenever this
computer is booted.
:BEGIN_SERVER
C:
cd C:\NWSERVER
```

```
SERVER
:END_SERVER
```

If you select No, you must manually start the SERVER.EXE program. Select Yes, unless you have special circumstances, such as situations where you expect to troubleshoot the server. You can always edit the AUTOEXEC.BAT file (at a later time) to add other commands (such as the DOS command PAUSE to give you a chance to break out of the AUTOEXEC.BAT file).

If you select Yes to have the INSTALL program add SERVER.EXE to the AUTOEXEC.BAT file, you are then asked to verify the location of the AUTOEXEC.BAT file.

The SERVER.EXE program loads at this point.

Step 9: Loading and configuring disk drivers

A screen display now informs you that NetWare is scanning for available drivers, after which you see a list of disk drivers. Select the disk driver that matches your server disk controller. If the driver you want is not listed, press the Insert key to load the disk driver from a distribution medium from the disk manufacturer.

You are presented with a screen for selecting the parameter settings for your disk controller. These include Port value, Interrupt number, DMA value, ABOVE16 (Y for Yes, N for No), and so on.

Make any corrections and verify that the parameter settings match disk controller settings. Select "Save parameters and continue" to save changes and continue with installation. Follow the instructions to load additional disk drivers and continue with installation.

Step 10: Loading and configuring the network drivers

The message "Scanning for available drivers" should appear, and you are presented with a list of network drivers. Note that, at this point, the NetWare 4.*x* server cannot transmit or receive messages on the network. Only after you load and bind the driver to the protocol stack does the NetWare 4 server become an active participant on the network.

Scroll through the list of network drivers and select the correct network driver for your NIC. If your driver is not listed, press the Insert key to load a driver from a floppy disk. If the driver is in a different source than floppy drive A:, use F3 to specify an alternate source.

You are presented with a default set of parameter values for your driver, such as the following:

- ► Port value

- ► Memory address

- ► Interrupt number

- ► Direct Memory Address (DMA) value (if your NIC uses DMA)

- ► Frame types

The port value, memory address, interrupt number, and DMA values should match the hardware settings on the NIC. If they do not, you must change the default settings on the screen to that of the network card by selecting "Select/Modify driver parameters and protocols." Note that the supported frame type values are shown in Table 3.1

For Ethernet, the default frame types that are loaded are ETHERNET_802.3 and ETHERNET_802.2. Though ETHERNET_802.2 is the default frame type for NetWare 4.*x*, the ETHERNET_802.3 frame type is also loaded for compatibility with existing NetWare 3.*x* clients.

For Token Ring frames, you can specify a local address that overrides the Media Access Control (MAC) address of the Token Ring on the board. (Each IEEE-specification LAN board has a unique 6-octet MAC address.) You should normally not have to override this address, unless interacting with other networks (such as SNA networks).

The default order of Token Ring frame transmission is that the Most Significant Bit (MSB) is transmitted first. Normally, you should not have to change this, unless the board vendor recommends it. To change this value to an LSB (Least Significant Bit) order, use the toggle key F4 on the highlighted frame in the Frame Type List. You can get to the Frame Type List by selecting the Frame Types field.

If you decide to change the bit order of address transmission, you must also specify that the order of node (MAC) address transmission is MSB or LSB. The default is MSB. The node address transmission order is changed by selecting the value in the Node Address field.

TABLE 3.1

*Server Frame Types
Supported*

FRAME	FRAME PARAMETER NAME	DEFAULT LOGICAL NAME	DESCRIPTION
IEEE 802.3	ETHERNET_802.3	*boardname_*IE_802.3	Novell's raw Ethernet frame type. Does not include an LLC (IEEE 802.2).
IEEE 802.2	ETHERNET_802.2	*boardname_*IE_802.2	Default frame type for NetWare 4.*x*. Essentially IEEE 802.3 frame with an LLC (IEEE 802.2) sublayer.
IEEE 802.3 with SNAP extension	ETHERNET_SNAP	*boardname_*IE_SNAP	Used for Appletalk networks. Essentially an IEEE 802.2 frame with an additional 3-octet Organization Unit Identifier (OUI) and a 2-byte Ether Type field.
Ethernet II	ETHERNET_II	*boardname_*IE_II	Ethernet II frame, which differs from IEEE 802.3. Main distinction is the presence of a 2-octet Ether Type field instead of a 2-octet length field (IEEE 802.3).
IEEE 802.5	TOKEN-RING	*boardname_*IT_RING	Standard IEEE 802.5 frame.
IEEE 802.5 with SNAP extension	TOKEN-RING_SNAP	*boardname_*IT_SNAP	Used for Appletalk networks. Essentially an IEEE 802.5 frame with an additional 3-octet OUI and a 2-byte Ether Type field.
ARCnet	RX-NET	*boardname_*RX-NET	Only one frame type is used with ARCnet.

You can change a frame's default logical name by highlighting it in the Frame Type List and using F3. Alternatively, you can edit the LOAD BoardDriver statement in the AUTOEXEC.NCF file, after the installation.

For Token Ring, the default frame type is TOKEN-RING.

If the network board parameters match the ones on the screen, select "Save parameters and continue." Repeat this step to add any additional network drivers.

After you select the network drivers with the correct parameters, and added any additional network drivers, you are presented with a summary of your choices for disk and network drivers. Select "Continue installation" to accept your choices and continue with the installation.

You should see a status of files as they are copied and loaded. If the network driver cannot recognize the board, the loading of the network driver fails. You must have a network board installed on your server that matches the LAN driver settings.

If you specified more than one frame type for the driver, the network driver is loaded *reentrantly.* (In other words, the program code for the driver is shared and differences in the frame type information are kept in a separate data area for each frame type.)

The Installation program will scan the network for existing network numbers used for the IPX network and for the frame types for the network driver. A random address is generated if this is the first server on a new network, but you should select a network number according to your own standards.

If you are installing on an existing IPX network, NetWare 4 installation searches the network for the network number on the network segment.

Step 11: Creating the NetWare 4.x disk partitions

You are given a choice of creating disk partitions "Manually" or "Automatically." "Manually" allows you to specify partition sizes, Hot Fix, and mirroring. "Automatically" allows you to create an unmirrored NetWare partition in the disk space available. Note that "Automatically" will destroy any existing data on a NetWare partition.

Follow the instructions on the screen to create your NetWare partition.

Step 12: Creating the NetWare 4.x volume

After you create the NetWare partition, you are presented with the Manage NetWare Volumes screen. This screen shows a summary of all the proposed volume changes. Press Enter to continue to the next screen.

The SYS: volume is always the first volume that is created. It is created automatically on device 0, and must have a minimum size of 50 MB.

You can modify the volume parameters and you can change all volume names, except the volume name SYS:. Other parameters you can change on a volume are as follows:

> ▶ *Volume Block Size.* The volume block size can be set to multiples of 4 KB, up to 64 KB (4 KB, 8 KB, 16 KB, 32 KB, 64 KB). The volume block size has a default value that is set according to the size of the volume. Table 3.2 shows the default volume size that is selected.

TABLE 3.2	DEFAULT BLOCK SIZE (KB)	VOLUME SIZE (RANGE IS IN MB)
Default Block Size versus Volume Size	4	0 to 31
	8	32 to 149
	16	150 to 499
	32	500 to 1,999
	64	2,000 and above

Because of disk suballocation, a larger block size is not wasted for small files. Once selected, the disk block size cannot be changed. Select a block size of 64 KB because most disk controllers perform best at this block size. Also, disk block suballocation ensures that space is used efficiently, even for larger block sizes.

▶ *File Compression.* This ensures that files that have not been accessed for a specified period of time are compressed to save on disk space. Once file compression for a volume is enabled, it cannot be disabled. After installation, individual files and directories can be marked with or without compression by using the FLAG command (or the FILER utility).

▶ *Block Suballocation.* This feature optimizes disk space by ensuring that unused fragments of disk blocks are not wasted. Actual disk space is used in 512-byte sizes. Leftover space in a block is shared by other files. The default value for Blocks Suballocation is On.

▶ *Data Migration.* This allows movement of files to a near-line storage device such as an optical jukebox. The default value for Data Migration is Off. Unless you have a High-Capacity Storage System (HCSS) installed, leave this value set to Off. Note that you can only have one NetWare partition per disk, but you can have up to eight volume segments on the NetWare partition.

After making volume changes, save them by pressing the F10 key, and continue with installation. The volumes you have created will be mounted.

Step 13: Selecting NetWare file groups

You will see a screen informing you of the path from which NetWare files will be installed. If the path is incorrect, use the F3 key to change it. Press the Enter key to continue.

You will see the File Copy Status as files are copied. This is a preliminary copy of the files. The main file copy is done later.

When the preliminary file copy is completed, you see a message on the screen informing you to press Enter to continue. Press Enter.

Step 14: Installing NDS (time configuration and context)

The NetWare server then searches the network for the existence of a directory tree. If it finds one, it displays the name of the directory tree. You can select this tree, or create a new tree by pressing the Insert key.

If this is the first server on the network, you must select a name for the directory tree. If you are installing on an existing network, make sure that your server is connected to the network. If a new [Root] and directory tree is created, and this is not what you want, you must integrate this with an existing network by using the DSMERGE tool. If you attempt to create a new tree when one already exists, a warning message informs you of some of the consequences of your actions.

Starting with NetWare 4.02, you can select a simple NDS installation or custom NDS installation. The simple NDS installation creates a single-level NDS tree with a single organization container. If you select the simple NDS installation, follow the screen instructions. The remainder of this section describes the custom NDS installation.

You are prompted to select a time zone. Selecting the correct time zone is important if you will be connecting to networks in other time zones. You are presented with a form that contains the following time configuration information for the installed server:

> ▶ *Time server type.* Enter either a Single Reference time server, Reference time server, Primary time server, or Secondary time server. If you select the Single Reference time server, you cannot have a Primary time server or another Reference time server. With Single Reference time server, only the Secondary time servers can exist.

▸ *Standard time zone abbreviation.* Enter the abbreviation code for your time zone. This string is for display purposes only. You can enter any value, but it is best to enter a value that is standard for your time zone. The important parameter to set for time zone offset is *Standard time offset from UTC.* The standard time zone abbreviation can also be changed in the AUTOEXEC.NCF file.

▸ *Standard time offset from UTC.* Verify that the time-offset for your zone is correct. You can set the time offset in the format *hh:mm:ss* (hours:minutes:seconds) behind or after UTC.

▸ *DST.* Many areas of the world have daylight savings time (DST), and several others do not. NetWare 4.*x* provides the flexibility of changing the daylight savings time criteria, or disabling it altogether. To enable daylight savings time, answer Yes to "Does your area have daylight savings time (DST)?" To disable daylight savings time, answer No to this parameter.

▸ *DST time zone abbreviation.* This specifies a string for daylight savings time that is used for display purposes only. The daylight savings rules are set by the *DST offset from standard time, DST Start,* and *DST End* parameters. The *DST time zone abbreviation* can also be changed in the AUTOEXEC.NCF file.

The *DST offset from standard time* is a parameter that represents the time difference between daylight savings time and standard time. This can have the value *hh:mm:ss* and can be set to be ahead or behind the standard time.

The *DST Start* and the *DST End* times indicate the start and end of daylight savings time. The values for these parameters can be programmed to be on a weekday of a specified month at a specific time, or on a specific day of the month at a specific time. For example, in areas of the U.S. that use daylight savings time, the daylight savings time commences at 2:00 a.m. on the first Sunday of the month of April, and ends at 2:00 a.m. on the last Sunday of the month of October. Should the laws change to a different daylight savings start and end, NetWare 4.*x* provides the flexibility to provide for these changes from the server console.

The time settings are recorded in the AUTOEXEC.NCF file. The listing that follows shows a sample AUTOEXEC.NCF file that has the time settings. The commands dealing with time settings have been highlighted.

```
set Time Zone = MST7MDT
set Daylight Savings Time Offset = 1:00:00
set Start Of Daylight Savings Time = (APRIL SUNDAY FIRST
2:00:00 AM)
set End Of Daylight Savings Time = (OCTOBER SUNDAY LAST
2:00:00 AM)
set Default Time Server Type = SINGLE
set Bindery Context = O=ESL
file server name FS1
ipx internal net 2C74169E
   load SMC8000 mem=D0000 int=3 PORT=280 FRAME=Ethernet_802.3
NAME=SMC8000_1E_802.3
bind IPX to SMC8000_1E_802.3 net=255
   load SMC8000 mem=D0000 int=3 PORT=280 FRAME=Ethernet_802.2
NAME=SMC8000_1E_802.2
bind IPX to SMC8000_1E_802.2 net=E8022
```

Press F10 to save changes in the time configuration information for the server. Verify that you want to save the time configuration.

A screen appears and prompts you to specify a context in which this server should be placed. In the Company or Organization field, enter the name for your primary organization. This should be a name that is readily recognizable by the users of the network. For example, the company International Business Machines could simply use the abbreviation IBM for the organization name.

You are given the option to specify three suborganization units:

▸ Level 1 Sub-Organizational Unit (optional)

▸ Level 2 Sub-Organizational Unit (optional)

    ▸ Level 3 Sub-Organizational Unit (optional)

The organizational unit levels are optional, because a minimal NDS tree can consist of only the organization container. To create the context in which the newly installed server should be placed, consult your NDS tree design.

You are building only a partial tree here. The full directory tree can be built using the NETADMIN or the NetWare Administrator tool. If you have created a new directory tree, the root partition is installed on the NetWare server that you have just installed. Once the server is installed it cannot be moved using the INSTALL.NLM. If you want to change its location, you must use the Partition Manager or DS Manager tools.

The server object is created at installation only. The INSTALL.NLM can create the server object, but cannot be used to perform general NDS management. NETADMIN and NetWare Administrator can be used for managing the NDS tree. The first server installed in a container gets a Master replica of that partition if the container does not exist. Other servers installed in the same context receive a Read/Write replica of that partition. If the container that holds the server already exists, all servers installed in that container get a Read/Write replica of the partition holding the container. These partitions can be further modified by using the PARTMGR utility or the Partition Manager tool.

As you enter the values for the organization unit levels, you see the Server Context value change to reflect the names of the organization unit levels that you have entered.

If you want to place the server in a tree branch containing the country object, you can modify the server context fields by adding .c=xx at the end of the server context, where xx is the two-letter country code.

The Administrator Name field describes the Common Name (CN) for the administrator of the network. It is set to Admin by default, and is placed in the organization container. The Admin user object can be renamed, moved, and even deleted. Before deleting the Admin user object, you must make sure that there are other user objects that have Supervisor rights, so that the NDS tree can be maintained.

You must know the context of the Admin user, and decide on the initial Admin password, when designing the directory tree. The Password field is for the Admin user object password. Setting a password is a requirement for completing the installation. The password for the Admin object can be changed using the NETADMIN utility or NetWare Administrator tool.

After making the changes, press F10 and answer Yes to the query for saving your changes. You see a message informing you that NDS services are being installed and the NDS schema is being adjusted.

The INSTALL program reports the number of volume objects installed in the directory. The volume objects are installed with a CN that consists of the file server name and the following physical volume name:

`servername_volumename`

If the server name is *FS1*, its first volume name (*SYS*) has the following CN:

`CN=FS1_SYS`

Press Enter to continue. You are asked to note the following information:

- ▸ Directory tree name

- ▸ Directory context (or the NDS context in which the server was placed)

- ▸ Administrator name

Press Enter to continue.

Step 15: Licensing the NetWare operating system

You will now be asked to enter the license disk. Enter the license disk in drive A:. If this is an upgrade, you must fax your serial number to Novell and obtain a key that you will use to unlock the license disk (using the program called NUNLOCK on the license disk). See the documentation that accompanies the license disk for additional information.

Step 16: Creating or modifying the startup files

If the STARTUP.NCF file is displayed, edit this file as necessary and press F10 to save changes and continue. If the AUTOEXEC.NCF file is displayed, edit this file as necessary and press F10 to save changes and continue.

Step 17: Copying files

You will see the File Copy status screen displayed as the main copy is performed.

Step 18: Performing other installation options

You are presented with the Other Installation Options screen. The following options are available:

- ▶ Create a registration disk

- ▶ Make diskettes

- ▶ Install NetWare IP

- ▶ Install NetWare DHCP

- ▶ Configure Network Protocols

- ▶ Install Legacy NWADMIN Utility

- ▶ Install Novell Web Server

- ▶ Install 3.1x Print Services

- ▶ Install an Additional Server Language

- ▶ Change server language

- ▶ Install NetWare for Macintosh

- ▶ Install NetWare Client for Mac OS

- ▶ Configure NetWare Licensing Services (NLS)

Step 19: Completing the installation

Press F10 to go to the final installation screen that contains advice on the manuals to which you can refer for managing the network. Press the indicated key to exit to system console screen.

Step 20: Booting the server from the startup files

Enter the following to shut down the server and restart it to verify your installation:

```
down
exit
Reboot server
```

This completes the detailed installation of the NetWare 4 server which serves as a base platform for the Novell Web Server, which is an important component of the IntranetWare server. It is the primary component that gives the IntranetWare server its intranet capabilities.

To install the Novell Web Server, you should have additional sufficient free disk space on your server disk to copy the distribution files on the server. Starting with Novell Web Server 3.0, you can place Web files on other file servers, so the free space requirement can be reduced. Directories residing on other file servers are called *virtual directories*. To run the Novell Web Server on an installed NetWare 4 server, you need an additional 4 MB of RAM on the server. The Novell Web Server uses the TCP/IP protocol and, therefore, you should have installed and configured your NetWare 4 server to use TCP/IP. If you have not configured your NetWare 4 server to use TCP/IP, you must do so before you can use the Novell Web Server.

Configuring TCP/IP for the IntranetWare Server

There are two methods for configuring TCP/IP. The first method uses LOAD and BIND statements that you manually enter into the AUTOEXEC.NCF file. The second method uses the INETCFG.NLM to create a configuration database of network protocol and bindings. The second method is the preferred method according to Novell. However, both methods are discussed here because the first method (though less automated) provides a better understanding of how TCP/IP is configured on your NetWare server.

Configuring TCP/IP Using AUTOEXEC.NCF

When the NetWare server is installed, you will see statements in the SYS:SYSTEM\AUTOEXEC.NCF file that has commands to configure the IPX protocol stack. These commands load the network card driver with specific frame types and bind the protocol to the network card driver. One way of configuring your NetWare 4 server to use TCP/IP is to add statements in the AUTOEXEC.NCF file to load the TCP/IP protocol stack and bind the IP protocol to the appropriate network driver.

Figure 3.3 summarizes the loading and configuration steps for TCP/IP NLMs using the AUTOEXEC.NCF file.

The NetWare 4 server must be properly installed using the steps outlined earlier in this chapter. You can use the same network board for TCP/IP that is used for IPX communications. You can do so because the network board drivers are based on the Open Data-link Interface (ODI) that allows multiple protocol stacks to use the same board. If the NetWare 4 server is to connect to both an IPX and a TCP/IP network, you may want to have an additional network board at the NetWare server that connects the NetWare server to the TCP/IP network (see Figure 3.4)

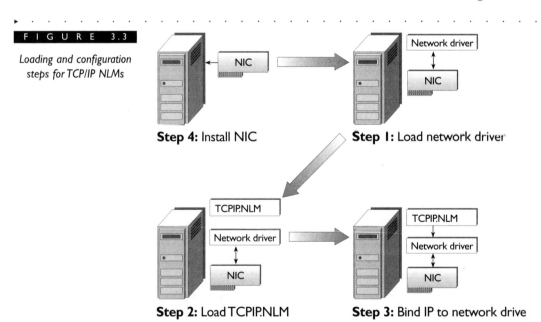

FIGURE 3.3

Loading and configuration steps for TCP/IP NLMs

Step 4: Install NIC

Step 1: Load network driver

Step 2: Load TCP/IP.NLM

Step 3: Bind IP to network drive

Step 1: Loading the network driver

In Step 1 of Figure 3.3, the network board driver must be loaded using the LOAD command. The LOAD command is issued at the server console to load and run the network board driver NLM. The network board drivers for the NetWare servers are written as NLMs. The LOAD command has the following general syntax:

```
LOAD NETDRIVER [parameters]
```

The *NETDRIVER* is replaced by the name of the ODI driver. By convention, ODI drivers on a NetWare server have a .LAN extension. Examples of these drivers are SMC8000.LAN, NE2000.LAN, TOKEN.LAN, and so on.

The *parameters* that follow the name of the driver specify the interrupt request number, I/O port address, memory base address, DMA channel, and so on, used by the network board. Network board drivers are written with a range of allowable parameter values. You must select a parameter value that matches the network board settings. When the network board driver loads, it initializes the network board. If the parameters specified on the LOAD command for the network board driver do not match the network board settings, you see an error message on the console. Most network board drivers are written so that they will not load in server memory, unless they can communicate with the network adapter.

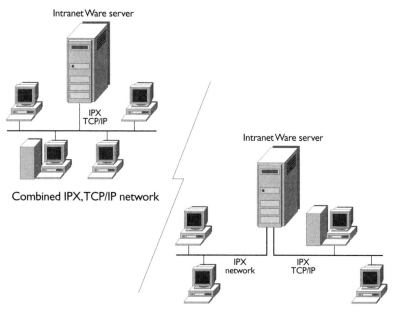

FIGURE 3.4

Connecting IntranetWare server to an IPX and TCP/IP network

Table 3.3 shows typical parameters used for a large number of network board drivers. Token Ring boards require special parameters, which are listed in Table 3.4.

TABLE 3.3	PARAMETER	MEANING
Card Parameters in LOAD NETWORK_DRIVER Command	DMA	Specifies the DMA channel number of NIC.
	INT	Specifies the IRQ level NIC is set to.
	MEM	Refers to the base memory address of RAM on driver.
	PORT	Specifies the I/O port address setting of NIC.
	NODE	Overrides node address on NICs that permit it (such as NICs that use IEEE MAC-addressing schemes).
	RETRIES	Denotes the number of times NIC driver retries failed packet transmissions. Default for most adapters is 5. Can be set to as high as 255.
	SLOT	Used for MCA and EISA bus computers. Tells the network operating system (NOS) to which NIC to link driver. Hardware parameters (such as I/O port and IRQ) are set by using the reference disk.
	NAME	Specifies a unique name (up to 17 characters) for an NIC. Useful for many NICs of the same type. NAME can be used in the BIND command.
	FRAME	Specifies the type of MAC layer encapsulation to be used. Used for Ethernet and Token Ring.

TABLE 3.4	PARAMETER	MEANING
Token Ring Specific Parameters for LOAD TOKEN Command	LS	Specifies the number of IEEE 802.5 link stations.
	SAPS	Denotes the number of Service Access Points (SAPs) for Token Ring driver.
	TBC	Refers to the Transmit Buffer Count for Token Ring driver. The default is set to 2.
	TBZ	Refers to the Transmit Buffer Size for Token Ring driver. Values range from 96 to 65,535, although not all values are supported. The default value is 0, and it implies the maximum that works for the NOS or the NIC.

The one parameter that may require some explanation is the FRAME parameter in Table 3.3. The FRAME parameter can be used for Ethernet and Token Ring

NICs and tells the network driver the type of header to be used for packets. In other words, the FRAME parameter controls the MAC layer encapsulation.

The TCP/IP protocol stack on NetWare servers, when configured for Ethernet network board, requires an Ethernet II encapsulation. The Ethernet II has a 2-byte type field immediately following the 6-byte destination and source address fields. The IEEE 802.3 frame also uses the 6-byte destination and source address fields, but these are followed by a 2-byte length field that specifies the length of the packet. The Ethernet type field of Ethernet II frame has a value of more than 1500 (decimal). This enables the Ethernet II frame to be easily distinguished from the IEEE 802.3 frame that uses the length field whose value is less than or equal to 1500. Remember that 1500 is the maximum legal size of the data portion of an Ethernet or IEEE 802.3 packet.

To communicate with TCP/IP based networks that typically use an Ethernet II frame encapsulation, NetWare provides the flexibility of changing the MAC layer encapsulation to Ethernet II (see Figure 3.7). This is done by setting the FRAME parameter in the LOAD NETWORK_DRIVER command to ETHERNET_II.

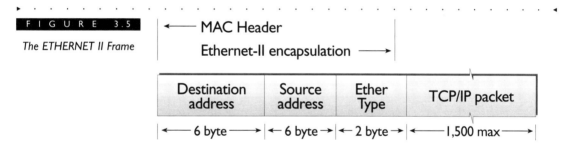

FIGURE 3.5

The ETHERNET II Frame

If the network driver has already been loaded with a frame type of ETHERNET_802.3 or ETHERNET_802.2, you must reload this driver with the ETHERNET_II frame type if you are configuring the network board for TCP/IP. When you load a network board driver that has already been loaded, only one copy of the network board driver is kept in memory. The additional load of the network driver is called a *reentrant load*, because it uses a single copy of the program code for the driver.

Consider the following LOAD commands in a AUTOEXEC.NCF file that is set up for IPX communications on an Ethernet SMC8000 board:

```
LOAD SMC8000 port=300 INT=10 MEM=CC000
```

Because no frame parameter was specified in the LOAD command, a default frame type is assumed. If the LOAD command was issued on a NetWare 3.11 server, the frame type of ETHERNET_802.3 would be used. On a NetWare 3.12 or NetWare 4.x server, the frame type of ETHERNET_802.2 would be used. If the same SMC8000 board is to be used for TCP/IP communications, you must use a frame type of ETHERNET_II. This can be done by another LOAD command that loads the driver a second time. The following statements illustrate this concept:

```
LOAD SMC8000 port=300 INT=10 MEM=CC000 name=IPX_NET
LOAD SMC8000 port=300 INT=10 MEM=CC000 frame=ETHERNET_II
NAME=IP_NET
```

The second LOAD command uses the same copy of the network driver loaded by the first LOAD command, but it has a different frame type, ETHERNET_II, that can be used by the TCP/IP protocols. The NAME parameter is used as a means of distinguishing between the different LOAD statements in the BIND command discussed in the section "Step 3: Binding the IP protocol to the network driver."

Another value for the FRAME parameter for is ETHERNET_SNAP. The ETHERNET_SNAP frame encapsulation is used on Macintosh-based networks. If you are using a Macintosh client to communicate with a NetWare TCP/IP server, you should additionally configure the Ethernet interface on the NetWare server with ETHERNET_SNAP.

The "SNAP" in ETHERNET_SNAP stands for Sub-Network Access Protocol. SNAP, described in RFC 1042, was developed as a means to send IP datagrams and Address Resolution Protocols (ARPs) used in the Internet, over IEEE 802.3, IEEE 802.4 (Token Bus), IEEE 802.5 (Token Ring), and FDDI networks. IP datagrams historically have been tied to Ethernet II frames. SNAP offers a way of transporting the IP datagrams across non-Ethernet II networks while preserving the Ethernet_II frame syntax. The SNAP mechanism is not confined to IP networks; it is general enough to be used by other protocols (such as AppleTalk Phase 2 used for Macintosh networks). NetWare 4 supports AppleTalk and TCP/IP-based networks and defines a FRAME value of ETHERNET_SNAP for Ethernet and TOKEN-RING_SNAP for Token Ring networks.

For Token Ring, the possible FRAME values are TOKEN-RING and TOKEN-RING_SNAP. The TOKEN-RING frame value is used for sending IPX data, and the TOKEN-RING_SNAP is a requirement for TCP/IP packets. TOKEN-RING uses the IEEE 802.2 header in its data portion, and TOKEN-RING_SNAP uses the SNAP header in the data portion of the Token Ring frame .

Consider the following LOAD commands in an AUTOEXEC.NCF file that is set up for IPX communications on an IBM Token Ring board.

```
LOAD TOKEN
```

Because no frame parameter was specified in the LOAD command, a default frame type is assumed. On NetWare 4 servers, the default frame type of TOKEN-RING would be used. If the same Token Ring board is to be used for TCP/IP communications, you must use a frame type of TOKEN-RING_SNAP. This can be done by another LOAD command that loads the driver a second time. The following statements illustrate this concept:

```
LOAD TOKEN
LOAD TOKEN frame=TOKEN-RING_SNAP
```

The second LOAD command uses the same copy of the network driver loaded by the first LOAD command, but it has a different frame type, TOKEN-RING_SNAP, that can be used by the TCP/IP protocols.

Step 2: Loading the TCP/IP NLM
After the network drivers have been loaded, Step 2 (see Figure 3.3) of the TCP/IP configuration requires the TCPIP.NLM to be loaded.

The TCPIP.NLM is loaded using the following LOAD command:

```
LOAD TCPIP
```

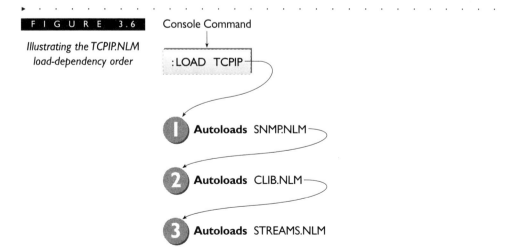

FIGURE 3.6

Illustrating the TCPIP.NLM load-dependency order

Console Command

:LOAD TCPIP

1 Autoloads SNMP.NLM

2 Autoloads CLIB.NLM

3 Autoloads STREAMS.NLM

The TCPIP.NLM depends on a number of other NLMs. If these are not in memory at the time of loading TCPIP.NLM, they are automatically loaded (autoloaded). Figure 3.6 shows the TCIP.NLM load-dependency order.

The TCPIP.NLM depends on SNMP.NLM. The SNMP.NLM is the Simple Network Management Protocol (SNMP) agent that runs on NetWare servers, and can be used by SNMP management workstations to query parameters about the NetWare server. If SNMP.NLM is not loaded in the server memory at the time of loading TCPIP.NLM, the SNMP.NLM is autoloaded.

The SNMP.NLM in turn depends on CLIB.NLM. If CLIB.NLM is not loaded in the server memory at the time of loading TCPIP.NLM, the CLIB.NLM is autoloaded. The CLIB.NLM in turn depends on STREAMS.NLM. If STREAMS.NLM is not loaded in the server memory at the time of loading TCPIP.NLM, the STREAMS.NLM is autoloaded. The CLIB.NLM and STREAMS.NLM are used by other application NLMs, and may already be loaded at the server. If these NLMs are not already loaded, you will see console messages on the screen as they are autoloaded.

The following is the full syntax for loading the TCPIP.NLM:

```
LOAD TCPIP [FORWARD={Yes|No}] [RIP={Yes|No}]  [TRAP=IP Address]
```

The parameters used to configure TCPIP are for IP routing, Routing Information Protocols RIPs), and SNMP traps. Table 3.5 shows a brief description of the TCPIP.NLM parameters.

T A B L E 3.5

TCPIP.NLM Parameters

PARAMETER	DESCRIPTION
FORWARD	Enables or Disables IP forwarding. If set to Yes (Enabled), server acts as an IP router. If set to No (Disabled), disables forwarding of IP packets. Default is No.
RIP	Enables or Disables RIP. If set to Yes (enabled) and forwarding is enabled (FORWARD=Yes), the NetWare server will actively participate in the RIP algorithm. It will use RIP to broadcast information on routes it knows. If set to No (disabled), server will not use RIP messages or send RIP messages. The default value is Yes, which means that RIP operation is enabled at the server.
TRAP	Specifies the destination IP address to which SNMP agent (SNMP.NLM) running at the server sends trap messages. The default value is the software loop back IP address of 127.0.0.1. If the TRAP messages are sent to another NetWare server, it must be configured for TCP/IP and have the SNMP logger running at the server, if messages are to be logged in a file.

The following are a few examples of loading TCPIP.

Example 1: To enable RIP and IP forwarding, but not send SNMP messages, you can use the following:

```
LOAD TCPIP FORWARD=Yes RIP=Yes
```

or

```
LOAD TCPIP FORWARD=Yes
```

The RIP parameter was left out in the second LOAD statement because its default value is Yes.

Example 2: To disable RIP and disable IP forwarding, you can use the following:

```
LOAD TCPIP FORWARD=No RIP=No
```

or

```
LOAD TCPIP  RIP=No
```

The FORWARD parameter was left out in the second LOAD statement because its default value is No.

Example 3: To forward trap messages to SNMP Manager at 199.245.180.33 and enable IP forwarding and RIP, you can use the following:

```
LOAD    TCPIP TRAP=199.245.180.33 RIP=Yes FORWARD=YES
```

or

```
LOAD    TCPIP FORWARD=YES  TRAP=199.245.180.33
```

The RIP parameter was left out in the second LOAD statement because its default value is Yes. The second statement also illustrates that the parameters can be placed after the LOAD TCPIP in any order.

TCPIP may fail to load, if the protocol numbers assigned to IP and ARP have been assigned to other protocols. Normally, this should not happen, because ARP and IP have been assigned the protocol numbers of 806 (hex) and 800 (hex) respectively by the Internet standards. If you are running experimental protocol modules on the server that are using the protocol numbers assigned to ARP and IP, TCPIP.NLM will not load and will produce either of the following messages:

```
Could not register ARP
Could not register IP (LSL error code=xx)
```

The solution to this problem is to remove the protocol software that is claiming the protocol numbers assigned to IP and ARP.

Step 3: Binding the IP protocol to the network driver

After the TCPIP.NLM has been loaded, Step 3 (see Figure 3.3) of the TCP/IP configuration requires the binding of the IP protocol to the network driver. Binding of IP to the network board driver sets the communications between the TCP/IP stack and the LAN driver.

When the TCPIP.NLM is loaded, it is only resident in server memory, and it does not know about the network board that it will be using. The TCPIP.NLM must be informed about the network interface in a separate step called *binding the protocol to the network driver*. This binding process is similar to that used for IPX, but because the protocol is IP, it requires a different set of parameters.

The general syntax for binding IP to the network board driver is the following:

```
BIND IP NETDRIVER  [parameters]
```

The *parameters* specify IP Address, subnet mask, and routing information. Table 3.6 summarizes the BIND parameters that are used for IP, and Table 3.7 shows the default values of these parameters and which parameters are required and optional.

TABLE 3.6

BIND Parameters for IP

PARAMETER	DESCRIPTION
ADDR	This is the IP Address of the network interface that IP will be using. This must be specified and there is no default value. If not specified, TCPIP prompts you for value. IP requires a different IP address for each interface to which it is bound. If you assign a duplicate IP address to an interface, you will see an error message that says "The interface, IP Address1, is connected to the same network as the interface using IP Address2." If you are using the server router with two network boards, each network board must be assigned a different and unique IP address that is compatible with the IP address of the network they connect to. The TCP/IP software checks for illegal addresses (such as addresses that are not class A, B, or C, or an attempt to use a loop back address for a network interface). On detecting illegal parameter values, an appropriate message is sent to the server console. In addition, the host field cannot be all zeros or all ones. An attempt to make the host field in the IP address, all zeros or ones will produce the error message "IP Address is illegal. Host field zeros or all ones.".

BIND Parameters for IP
(continued)

PARAMETER	DESCRIPTION
MASK	This is the subnet mask and it is used to implement subnetting. All nodes on the same physical network must have the same subnet mask. A physical network is defined as one that does not cross a router boundary. If a subnet mask is not specified, IP assumes that the network is not subdivided into subnetworks, and a default is used. For class A, B, and C addresses, the default masks are respectively 255.0.0.0, 255.255.0.0, and 255.255.255.0. The subnet number field cannot be all zeros or all ones as per RFC 950. An attempt to make the subnet number field in the IP address, all zeros or ones will produce the error message "IP Address is illegal. Subnet field is zeros or all ones." If you use different subnet masks within the same network and create duplicate IP addresses, the TCP/IP software can detect these error conditions, and will generate error messages of the form "Cannot support IP Address1 with subnet mask Mask1 because it conflicts with IP Address2 with subnet mask Mask2, an address IP is already supporting on another interface."
BCAST	This is the broadcast address used for the network interface. The default value is all ones (255.255.255.255) which means a local broadcast. This is normally not changed. TCP/IP software derived from BSD 4.2 may not understand the local broadcast. In this case, you can change the BCAST parameter to use a broadcast address that is compatible with other nodes on the network. Software derived from 4.2 BSD UNIX, typically use an all zeros broadcast. This means for a class B network address of 135.23, the all zeros broadcast address would be 135.23.0.0. If you are using a mix of 4.2 BSD UNIX nodes and NetWare servers, it is best to use an all ones broadcast address. In the example of network address 135.23, an all ones broadcast address would be 135.23.255.255. BSD UNIX nodes can be configured to use an all ones broadcast address by using the ifconfig UNIX utility. Limited broadcasts do not cross router boundaries. If you must broadcast to a network or subnetwork, you should use directed broadcast. For example the broadcast address for the subnetwork 144.19.74.0 is 144.19.74.255.
ARP	Specifies if you are using ARP. Must be set to Yes for broadcast networks such as LANs. When set to No, the host portion of the address is mapped directly to the local hardware address. Mapping the host portion of the address to the local hardware address is possible with Ethernet, and is used in DECnet.
GATE	Specifies IP address of default router for this network. IP uses this gateway value to reach other networks that are not directly connected to the NetWare server. If this parameter is not used, NetWare TCP/IP gathers default route information from RIP. If RIP is set to Yes, Novell does not recommend using the GATE parameter. There is no default value for this parameter. When the GATE parameter is specified a status message of "Using IP Address as a default gateway" is returned.
DEFROUTE	If set to Yes, the server advertises itself as a default router for other nodes on the network. The default value is No. When DEFROUTE=YES is specified, a status message of "Configured as default router for this network" should be returned.

(continued)

TABLE 3.6

BIND Parameters for IP
(continued)

PARAMETER	DESCRIPTION
COST	Specifies metric cost to be used with RIP in a decimal value that can range from 1 to 16. The value of 16 means that the interface is unreachable and corresponds to a cost of 16. So, you should use values from 1 to 15. The default value for the COST parameter is 1. The lower cost value interfaces are selected over higher cost interfaces for routing of packets. When the COST parameter is specified, a status message informing you that the "Interface cost is set to *xx*" is returned.
POISON	Controls use of "Poison Reverse" in RIP. *Poison reverse* is a mechanism that determines how routing updates on failed links are sent on the network. When POISION=YES is specified, you will see a status message "Using 'poison reverse' in RIP's split horizon".

TABLE 3.7	PARAMETER	ARGUMENT VALUE	DEFAULT VALUE	REQUIRED/ OPTIONAL
Summary of Default and Required/optional Status of Bind Parameters	ADDR	IP address	None	Required
	MASK	Network mask	Standard	Optional
	BCAST	IP address	255.255.255.255	Optional
	ARP	Yes/no	Yes	Optional
	GATE	IP address	None	Optional
	DEFROUTE	Yes/no	No	Optional
	COST	Integer	1	Optional
	POISON	Yes/no	No	Optional

If the server has insufficient memory, the BIND IP command can fail with any of the following error messages:

```
Could not add interface to routing database
Interface allocation failed
IP could not get enough memory to remember interface
```

If you get the message that "ARP could not allocate resource tag," it indicates that server is short on memory. You must unload other NLMs or add more RAM to the server computer.

The following are examples of using the BIND IP parameters.

Example 1: To specify an IP address of 132.13.46.1 for the interface and a subnet mask of 255.255.0.0, use the following:

```
BIND IP  TO  IPNET ADDR=132.13.46.1 MASK=255.255.0.0
```

or

```
BIND IP  TO  IPNET ADDR=132.13.46.1
```

Note that the IPNET used in this and the following examples refers to the name of the network board driver that is loaded with the appropriate frame type. For example, if a NE2000 Ethernet board is being used for TCP/IP, and you wanted to identify it by the name IPNET, you would use the following:

```
LOAD SMC8000 port=280 int=3 frame=ETHERNET_II name=IPNET
BIND IP TO IPNET ADDR=199.245.180.10
```

Example 2: To specify an IP address of 144.19.74.22 for the interface and a subnet mask of 255.255.255.0, if the following statement was used. Will it work?

```
BIND IP TO IPNET ADDR=144.19.74.22
```

Answer: No. The previous statement assumes a default mask of 255.255.0.0, because 144.19.74.22 is a class B address and no MASK parameter is specified. The default mask of 255.255.0.0 is different from the mask of 255.255.255.0 that was required in the example.

The following is the correct BIND statement for Example 2:

```
BIND IP TO IPNET ADDR=144.19.74.22 MASK=255.255.255.0
```

Example 3: To specify an IP address of 200.225.100.5 for the interface and a subnet mask of 255.255.255.192 and a broadcast mask of 200.225.100.5, you can use the following:

```
BIND IP TO IPNET ADDR=200.225.100.5 MASK=255.255.255.192
BCAST=199.245.180.63
```

Example 4: To specify poison reverse be used for the IP address of 200.225.100.11 for the interface and a subnet mask of 255.255.255.240, and that the interface be used as a default router on the network, you can use the following:

```
BIND IP TO IPNET ADDR=200.225.100.11 MASK=255.255.255.240
POSION=YES DEFROUTE=YES
```

Complete TCP/IP Configuration Examples

The previous sections have discussed the different steps of configuring TCP/IP. To make this discussion practical, several examples in this section show the commands needed to provide complete TCP/IP configuration.

Example 1: The NetWare server is on an Ethernet network and has the following statements in its AUTOEXEC.NCF file:

```
LOAD NE2000 INT=3 PORT=300  NAME=IPXNET
BIND IPX TO IPXNET  NET=6000
```

Write down the configuration statements to configure a TCP/IP interface on the same network so that the interface has an IP address of 130.125.15.2 a subnet mask of 255.255.255.0 with no forwarding of IP packets and with RIP enabled.

Answer: The configuration statements that should be placed in the AUTOEXEC.NCF file can be the following:

```
LOAD NE2000 INT=3 PORT=300  NAME=IPXNET
BIND IPX TO NOVNET  NET=6000
LOAD NE2000 INT=3 PORT=300 FRAME=ETHERNET_II NAME=IPNET
LOAD TCPIP FORWARD=NO RIP=YES
BIND IP TO IP_A ADDR=130.125.15.2 MASK=255.255.255.0
```

Example 2: The NetWare server is on a Token Ring network and has the following statements in its AUTOEXEC.NCF file:

```
LOAD TOKEN  NAME=TRNET
BIND IPX TO TRNET  NET=7F31
```

Write down the configuration statements to configure a TCP/IP interface on the same network so that the interface has an IP address of 201.245.180.193 a subnet mask of 255.255.255.224 with no forwarding of IP packets, with RIP enabled and a broadcast address of 201.245.180.255

Answer: The configuration statements that should be placed in the AUTOEXEC.NCF file can be the following:

```
LOAD TOKEN  NAME=TRNET
BIND IPX TO TRNET  NET=7F31
LOAD TOKEN NAME=TR_IPNET FRAME=TOKEN-RING_SNAP
LOAD TCPIP FORWARD=NO RIP=YES
BIND IP TO TR_IPNET ADDR=201.245.180.193
MASK=255.255.255.224 BCAST=201.245.180.255
```

Unloading TCP/IP

If you want to reconfigure the TCP/IP parameters (such as IP address, subnet mask, broadcast address, and other parameters) on the NetWare server, you can do so without shutting down the server. Changing TCP/IP parameters that are specified in the BIND or LOAD TCPIP statements means that you must execute these commands after you unbind or unload the TCPIP.NLM. The procedure for unloading TCPIP.NLM is described in Figure 3.12.

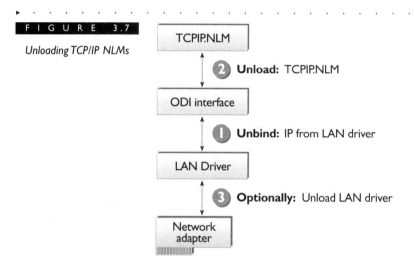

To unload the TCP/IP NLM, the following steps must be performed in the reverse order of the load sequence:

1. • Unbind IP from LAN driver. This is done using the UNBIND IP FROM *NETDRIVER* command

2. • Unload TCPIP NLM. This is done using the UNLOAD TCPIP command

3. • Optionally unload *NETDRIVER* if not in use

Configuring TCP/IP Using INETCFG (Preferred Method)

Using INETCFG.NLM to configure TCP/IP is the second method for TCP/IP configuration. The INETCGF utility presents a menu system with parameter choices for configuring the TCP/IP NLMs. The INETCFG menu controls the setting of the following:

- Network Boards

- Protocols

- Bindings

If you use INETCFG.NLM, the LOAD and BIND statements in the AUTOEXEC.NCF are commented by placing the # character preceding each such statement. Additionally, the following statements are added to the AUTOEXEC.NCF file:

```
LOAD CONLOG
LOAD SNMP
INITIALIZE SYSTEM
    .
    .
    .
UNLOAD CONLOG
```

The CONLOG.NLM utility captures console messages generated during server startup and logs them to the SYS:ETC\CONSOLE.LOG file. This is a text file and can be examined for troubleshooting server startup problems.

The INITIALIZE SYSTEM statement initializes the processing of information entered through the INETCFG.NLM.

The UNLOAD CONLOG statement is placed at the end of the AUTOEXEC.NCF file and stops the logging of console messages in order to conserve disk space. If obtaining a log of console messages is more important than conserving disk space, you can remove the UNLOAD CONLOG statement from the AUTOEXEC.NCF file.

Although INETCFG.NLM can be used for configuring other network protocols (such as IPX and AppleTalk), this section focuses on TCP/IP configuration only.

Using INETCFG

To run INETCFG, type the following command at the console server:

LOAD INETCFG

When INETCFG is loaded for the very first time from a server console, you see a menu asking you if you want to transfer LAN driver, protocol and remote commands to the configuration files maintained by INETCFG.NLM (see Figure 3.13). Select Yes. The two configuration files used by INETCFG.NLM are SYS:ETC\INITSYS.NCF and SYS:ETC\NETINFO.CFG.

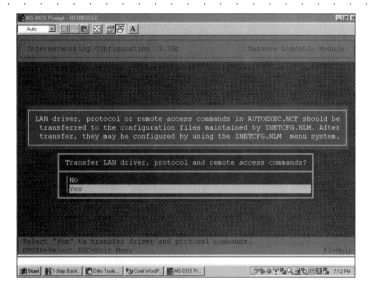

FIGURE 3.8

INETCFG screen on first load

The statements that are transferred out of the AUTOEXEC.NCF are commented in the file and left there for reference. You are also given an option for performing a fast setup if you are configuring permanent WAN connections (see Figure 3.9). If you are configuring TCP/IP, you should not select the Fast Setup option.

You should see the Internetworking Configuration menu (see Figure 3.10). The Boards option enables the configuration of network cards that are installed in the file server. If you are configuring TCP/IP on an existing board, you do not need to select this option. If you are configuring TCP/IP on a new board for which network drivers have not been loaded, you should select the Boards option to load the network driver. Figure 3.11 shows a view of the drivers selected for an IntranetWare server. To add additional boards press the Insert key and select the network drivers (see Figure 3.12), and then follow the instructions on the screen to select board parameters such as the interrupt (IRQ), I/O port, and shared memory address.

FIGURE   3.9

Fast Setup option in
INETCFG.NLM

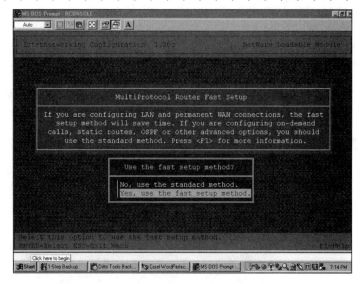

If you must change any of the board parameters, highlight the configured board and press Enter. You must also change the board settings on the physical board itself (such as through jumper settings or with software tools supplied by the manufacturer of the board). To delete a misconfigured board, highlight the problem board and press the Delete key.

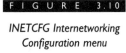

FIGURE   3.10

INETCFG Internetworking
Configuration menu

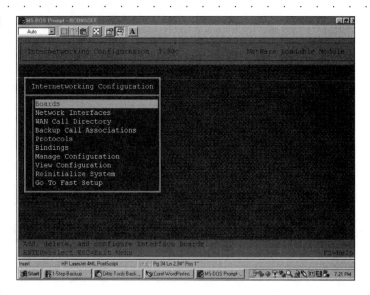

FIGURE 3.11

Example Boards option

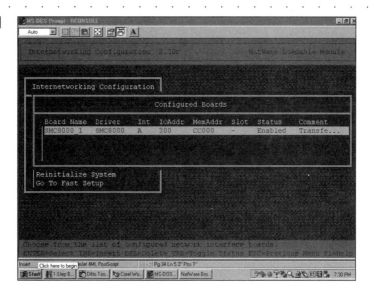

FIGURE 3.12

Adding a network board

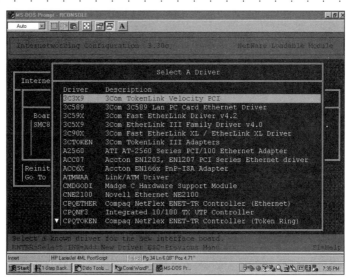

The Network Interfaces option (see Figure 3.13) enables you to review your board definitions. You can use this to temporarily disable or enable a network board. This option displays an entry for every defined network board.

FIGURE 3.13

Network Interfaces option

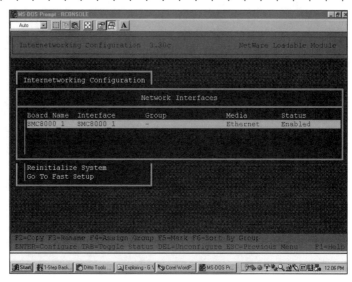

If you had WAN boards, you would configure them by using the WAN Call Directory and Backup Call Associations. Configuring the WAN Call Directory requires the NetWare MPR, which is bundled with IntranetWare.

FIGURE 3.14

Protocols option for INETCFG

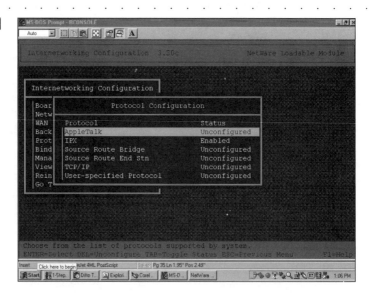

After the network board drivers have been configured, select the Protocols option to configure the TCP/IP protocol. Figure 3.14 shows a typical Protocols option screen showing that only IPX has been configured. Note that the TCP/IP protocol has not been configured. To configure the TCP/IP protocol, highlight the TCP/IP protocol entry and press Enter. You should see the TCP/IP Protocol Configuration screen (see Figure 3.15). To make any changes, select the appropriate option and press Enter. You can use the help key (F1) to get additional information on the field. After making changes, press Esc, and update your changes.

After configuring the protocol, you must bind it to the network driver. You can do this by selecting the Bindings option from the INETCFG main menu. To add a binding for TCP/IP press the Insert key. You should see a list of protocols available for binding. Select TCP/IP, and then from the "Bind To?" menu, select "A Network Interface."

When you are presented with a menu to select a configured network interface, select the network interface over which TCP/IP will be run. If you have more than one network interface over which TCP/IP will be run, you must select each interface in turn and perform the bindings that are described next. Figure 3.16 shows the parameters for binding TCP/IP to a network interface.

FIGURE 3.15

*TCP/IP Protocol
Configuration for INETCFG*

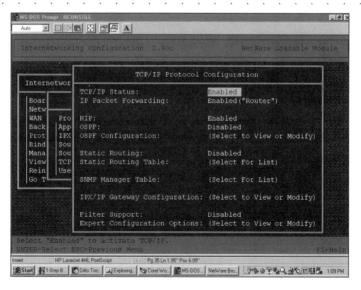

Binding TCP/IP to a LAN interface

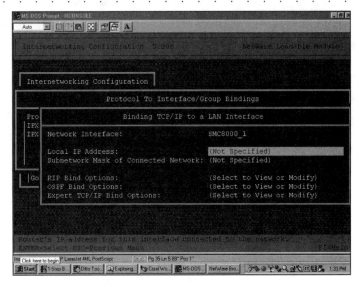

Use the "Local IP Address" field to specify the IP address of the network interface. The subnet mask will be set to a default value for the IP address. If the IP address is a class A, the subnet mask will default to 255.0.0.0; for a class B, it will default to 255.255.0.0; and for a class C, it will default to 255.255.255.0. If you are using subnetting, edit the field "Subnetwork Mask of Connected Network" appropriately. If the IntranetWare server is to act as an IP router, you should configure either the "RIP Bind Options" or "OSPF Bind Options" (see Figure 3.16).

Figure 3.17 shows the RIP Bind Options and Figure 3.18 shows the OSPF Bind Options. Use the help screens to configure these options appropriately.

The RIP is a simple distance-vector protocol used to create and maintain routing tables. RIP table entries can be either dynamic or static. *Dynamic RIP table entries* are created through periodic broadcast exchanges between routers. *Static RIP table entries* are configured manually when static routing is enabled. A RIP table entry consists of the distance required to reach the final destination, IP addresses of the destination networks, and the direction or vector required to reach the destination. The direction is represented by the IP address of the next router.

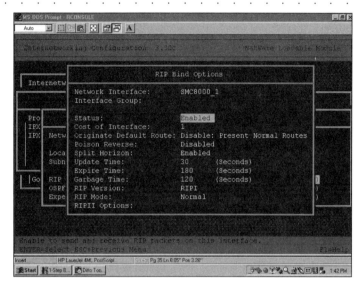

FIGURE 3.17

RIP Bind options

RIP *distance* is defined as the number of routers an IP packet must traverse before reaching its destination, and is referred to as the number of *hops*. An IP RIP has a limitation of a maximum of 15 hops. A destination with a hop count of 16 is considered to be unreachable. A packet that has a hop count of 16 will be discarded.

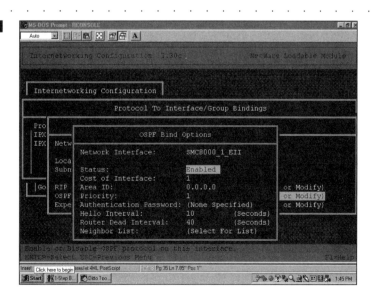

FIGURE 3.18

OSPF Bind options

RIP routers send out updates at a default interval of 30 seconds. You can modify the update interval by editing the Update Time field (see Figure 3.17). If an update for a route is not received in the Expire Time interval (see Figure 3.17), that route is invalidated. When a router is down, the route will not be discarded until the Garbage Time interval.

RIP typically refers to the original RIP, version I. A new version of RIP, RIP II, has been developed to deal with some of the limitations of the original RIP. RIP II is described in detail in RFC 1732, and provides better security through authentication and support for variable subnet masks.

The Open Shortest Path First (OSPF) protocol was developed to overcome the limitations of RIP. OSPF is considered to be a link-state protocol, and the algorithm it uses to compute routes is entirely different from that of RIP. Instead of maintaining distances to all possible destinations in an internetwork, OSPF routers maintain a "topological map" of the network. This map consists of the descriptions or the state of the links in an internetwork. A *link* is considered to be a segment connecting any two routers. It is identified by the interface identifiers of the connected routers, a link number, and a metric.

OSPF was designed to be a scalable routing protocol that would facilitate routing in large internetworks. OSPF supports *hierarchical routing* through the concept of *areas*. Each area acts as an independent network and is uniquely identified by an area ID. Routers belonging to a given area must be assigned the same area ID. An *area ID* is a 32-bit number that's expressed in a dotted decimal notation like an IP address. However, area ID addresses should not be confused with IP addresses. Multiple areas in an internetwork are joined together through a *backbone area*, which by default has an ID of 0.0.0.0. Routers that connect OSPF areas to the backbone area are known as *area border routers* (ABRs). The backbone area must be physically contiguous to act as a backbone. In the event that a backbone area becomes partitioned for geographical reasons, different OSPF areas can still be reconnected through the use of "virtual links."

The advantage of OSPF areas is that most of the routers in a given area must be aware of the topology of only that area. This translates into a smaller database of the "topology map" from which the routes are calculated, and improves the router performance. Only the ABRs that connect OSPF areas to the backbone must maintain multiple sets of the link-state or topology map databases. ABRs maintain one link-state database for the area to which they belong, and a summary of link-state databases for other areas connected to the backbone. OSPF must be configured through the OSPF Configuration option explained in the next section.

In OSPF, large internetworks can be broken into routing domains known as *autonomous systems*. Different autonomous systems may run different routing protocols. Communication between autonomous systems takes place through the autonomous system boundary routers or ASBRs. ASBRs typically run a protocol such as Exterior Gateway Protocol (EGP), and Border Gateway Protocol (BGP, in addition to OSPF. ASBRs further facilitate hierarchical routing. When an OSPF router is configured as an ASBR, OSPF allows this router to learn about routes supplied by EGP coming from other autonomous systems. ASBRs should not be confused with ABRs, which connect different OSPF areas to the backbone. ASBRs can also be configured to exclude specific routes. This requires the enabling of the filter support parameter and configuring of the exclusion routes through the FILTCFG menu-driven NLM.

After making the changes for TCP/IP parameters, press the Esc key and save the changes. Figure 3.19 shows the Bindings screen where TCP/IP has been enabled and configured. To save your changes, exit INETD.CFG by pressing the Esc key. When asked if you want to save changes, answer Yes. Next you should shut down the IntranetWare server and start it up again.

Special configuration for the STARTUP.NCF file

In addition to configuring the TCP/IP protocol you should make the following changes to the STARTUP.NCF file. This file resides on the DOS boot partition on the IntranetWare server.

```
SET MINIMUM PACKET RECEIVE BUFFERS=400
SET MAXIMUM PACKET RECEIVE BUFFERS=1000
```

These settings provide optimum performance for the Novell Web Server. If you have other NLMs that require a different setting of these parameters, use the highest value required by any of the NLMs.

FIGURE   3.19

Configured TCP/IP in the Protocol Bindings screen

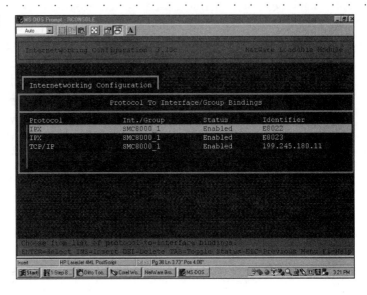

Installing the Novell Web Server

Now that you have installed and configured your IntranetWare server with TCP/IP, you are ready for the last phase of the installation-installing the Novell Web Server. Before installing the Novell Web Server, you should ensure that you have an additional 10 MB of free disk space, and an additional 4 MB of RAM on the server. The following is a guided tour for installing the Novell Web Server. If you do not have the Novell Web Server, version 3, you can download it from www.novell.com. It is a self-extracting file and, for ease of installation, you may want to extract it on the server volume.

I   •   Mount the CD-ROM containing the NetWare 4.*x* Operating System distribution software as NetWare volume on the server. You can do this by executing the following commands from the server console:

```
LOAD CDROM
CD DEVICE LIST
CD MOUNT NW411  (or the volume name of the CD containing the
Novell Web Server distribution files)
```

2 • Load the INSTALL NLM from the server console.

LOAD INSTALL

3 • You should see the INSTALL screen shown in Figure 3.20.

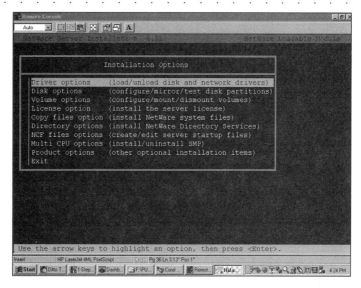

4 • Select "Product Install." You should see the screen in Figure 3.21.

5 • Select "Install a product not listed." You should see a screen shown in Figure 3.22 that asks you to specify the source of the product.

6 • Press F3 and enter the source installation path, which contains the Novell Web Server distribution files. Next, type in the location of the Web Server files. You should see a status of files as they are copied to the NetWare server. You will also see several license screens. Press Enter after accepting the license agreement.

7 • When the files are copied, you will see a message about the README.TXT file that you should view at your earliest convenience to see important facts about the Novell Web Server product. Press Esc to continue.

FIGURE 3.21

Product Install screen

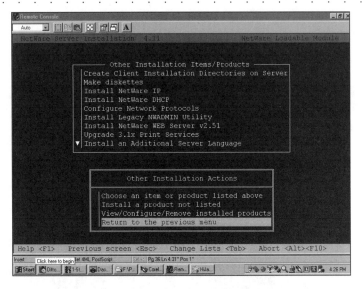

FIGURE 3.22

Specifying product source message

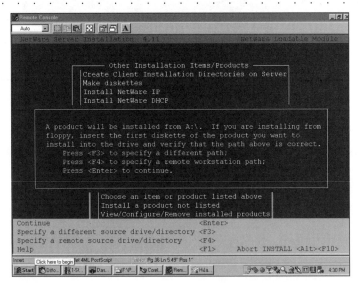

8 • The installation will create two new directories: SYS:INW-WEB and SYS:WEB. Online documentation is kept in the INDEX.HTM file in SYS:WEB/DOCS. If you are upgrading your Novell Web Server, the Novell documentation will be copied to NOVELL.HTM instead, leaving your original INDEX.HTM page intact. The INDEX.HTM is the default HTML page for the Novell Web Server.

9 • The installation will continue and you will see the installation status messages.

10 • You will be asked to enter the Web server password (see Figure 3.23). Select a secure password and enter it. You will be asked to enter it again for verification.

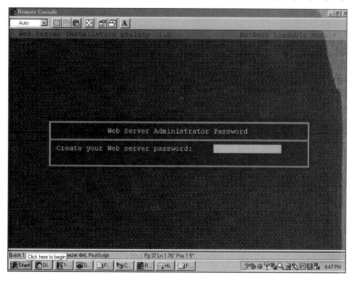

FIGURE 3.23

Web server password screen

11 • You will see a status message announcing the completion of the Novell Web Server installation. Press Esc to continue.

12 • You will see some additional status messages, and you will be returned to the screen shown in Figure 3.21.

13 • From the "Other Installation Actions" menu select "View/Configure/Remove installed products" to review the components that are installed.

14 • Exit the INSTALL NLM by pressing Esc a few times and answering Yes when asked to verify your actions.

15 • Restart the server and verify the installation as follows.

```
DOWN
RESTART SERVER
```

NOTE

Note that you can restart or stop the Web server from the server console by using the commands WEBSTART and WEBSTOP.

Installing the Novell Netscape Navigator

If you do not have a Web client installed at a workstation on the network, you can install the Novell Netscape Navigator to see if you can browse the default Web documents on the recently installed Novell Web Server.

To install the Novell Netscape Navigator, ensure that the workstation is configured with TCP/IP and then install the Novell Netscape Navigator. You can use a Windows 3.x, Windows 95, Windows NT, or a UNIX workstation as a Web client. The procedures for configuring TCP/IP depend on the operating system you are running at the workstation. This section describes configuring a Windows 95 workstation with TCP/IP.

Note that if you plan to use the Novell IPX/IP gateway, you do not need to install TCP/IP at the workstation. However, you must install and configure the Novell IPX/IP gateway on your Novell Web Server from the Novell Internet Access Server CD, and then configure the NetWare Client32 to use this gateway. Newer versions of Netscape Navigator are available for download from www.novell.com.

Configuring TCP/IP on a Windows 95 Workstation

Your Windows 95 workstation should have already been installed with NetWare Client32 software. If you have not installed the NetWare Client32 software, map a drive to the SYS: volume of the Novell Web Server, and run the following setup file from the Windows 95 workstation:

```
\public\client\win95\setup.exe
```

Follow the instructions on the screen for completing the installation of the NetWare Client32.

As part of the NetWare Client32 software installation, the network drivers will already be installed on the workstation. So, the next step is to install the TCP/IP protocol. Before installing TCP/IP on the Windows 95 workstation, ensure that you have the Windows 95 distribution CD because the setup may need to copy some files from this CD. The following steps outline the instructions for installing the Microsoft TCP/IP stack:

1 • From the Start menu select Settings.

2 • Select Control Panel.

3 • Select the Network icon.

4 • From the Network panel, select the Add button.

5 • From the Select Network Component Type dialog box, highlight Protocol and the select the Add button.

6 • From the manufacturer's list in the Select Network Protocol dialog box, select Microsoft.

7 • From the Network Protocol list, select TCP/IP, and then select OK.

8 • When returned to the Network panel, select OK and follow instructions on the screen to complete the installation.

9 • By default the TCP/IP installation selects the protocol for configuring the workstation's IP address, subnet mask, default gateway, DNS server, and so on.

10 • If you do not have a DHCP server setup, you should manually configure the workstation's IP parameters.

11 • To manually configure the TCP/IP parameters, repeat Steps 1 to 3 to get to the Network panel.

a) Highlight the "TCP/IP —> Network Adapter" binding from the list of network components and select the Properties button.

b) Select the IP Address tab, and select the "Specify an IP address" option. Enter the IP address and subnet mask of the workstation.

c) Select the other tabs to set the default gateway, DNS server, and so on.

12 • When prompted to reboot the workstation during setup, do so.

Installation of Novell Netscape Navigator

The following is an outline for installing the Novell Netscape Navigator.

1 • Go to the following directory on the Novell Internet Access Server CD as follows:

```
\NETSCAPE\32       (for 32-bit Windows)
\NETSCAPE\16       (for 16 bit Windows)
```

2 • Run the SETUP program from within Windows.

3 • You will see the Novell Netscape Navigator installation screen (see Figure 3.24)

4 • Select the Next button. You will be shown the default location where the Netscape browser will be installed (see Figure 3.25). You can change this location by selecting the Browse button.

5 • Select the Next button. You will see a status of files as they are copied (see Figure 3.26). A program folder for Netscape browser will be created.

6 • The setup will complete and you will be prompted to read the README file. Read the README file and quit the installation.

FIGURE   3.24

Novell Netscape Navigator installation screen

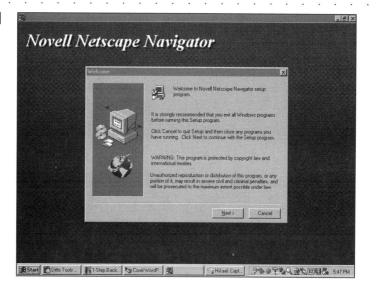

FIGURE   3.25

Selecting destination directory

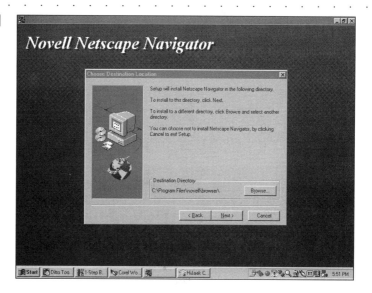

7 • On Windows 95, a desktop shortcut to the Netscape browser will be created. Start the Netscape browser, and verify that you see the default home page for Novell (see Figure 3.27).

F I G U R E   3.26

Netscape files copy status

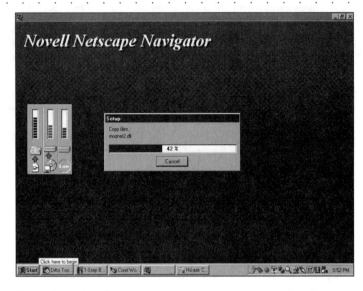

After installing the Novell Netscape Navigator, point the browser to the following URL for your Web server:

    http://webserver/

F I G U R E   3.27

Novell Netscape Browser's default home page

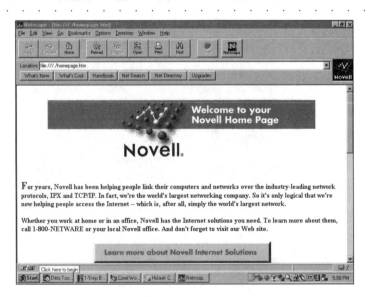

Replace *webserver* with the IP address (or hostname, if you have DNS setup) of the Novell Web Server that you just installed. If your installation has been successful, you will see the default home page on the Novell Web Server (see Figure 3.28). This default home page is in the file SYS:WEB/DOCS/INDEX.HTM.

F I G U R E   3.28

Default home page on the Novell Web Server

Summary

This chapter discussed the Novell Web Server installation process. There are three major steps to installing the Novell Web Server. First, you must install the NetWare 4 server. This chapter discussed the details of installing the NetWare 4 server. Second, you must configure the NetWare server with TCP/IP because the Novell Web Server communicates using TCP/IP. Lastly, you must install the Novell Web Server.

This chapter also discussed how to install the NetWare Client32 and TCP/IP protocol on a Windows 95 computer. You learned how to install the Novell Netscape Navigator and use this to verify the Novell Web Server installation.

CHAPTER 4

Configuring and Administering the Novell Web Server

Chapter 3 discussed the Novell Web Server installation procedure. Once the server is installed you must configure the Web server and learn how to administer it. This chapter discusses the configuration directories and files needed for the Novell Web Server configuration. The Novell Web Server comes with a Web Manager tool that you can use to perform many of the administration tasks. You will learn to use the Web Manager tool to change the default configuration for the directories, set up access control configuration, and access log files.

Novell Web Server Configuration Files

The default location for installing the Novell Web Server is the SYS:WEB directory. Underneath this directory are a number of directories and configuration files created by the Novell Web Server installation process. Figure 4.1 shows the Novell Web Server directory structure and Table 4.1 describes the functions of the Web server directories.

Novell Web Server directory configuration

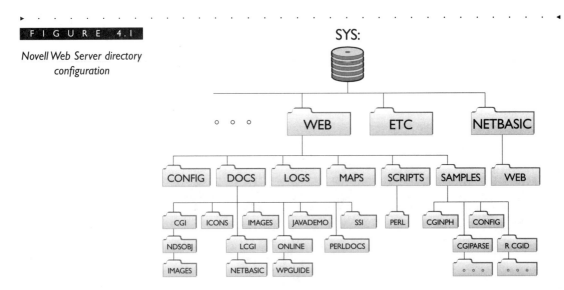

T A B L E 4.1

Novell Web Server
Configuration Directories

DIRECTORY	DESCRIPTION
SYS:WEB	Root directory structure.
SYS:WEB\CONFIG	Web server configuration directory.
SYS:WEB\DOCS	Root directory for HTML documents.
SYS:WEB\DOCS\CGI\ NDSOBJ	Configuration files for the NDS access demo.
SYS:WEB\DOCS\CGI\ NDSOBJ\IMAGES	GIF images for NDS objects.
SYS:WEB\DOCS\ICONS	Icon images in the XBM format.
SYS:WEB\DOCS\IMAGES	Images referenced in Web documents generally placed here.
SYS:WEB\DOCS\JAVADEMO	Java Demos placed here.
SYS:WEB\DOCS\LCGI\ NETBASIC	NetBasic documentation placed here (HTML docs).
SYS:WEB\DOCS\ONLINE\ WPGUIDE	Dynamic Web Programming guide (HTML docs).
SYS:WEB\DOCS\PERLDOCS	Sample Perl scripts (HTML docs).
SYS:WEB\DOCS\SSI	Server Side Includes support documentation.
SYS:WEB\LCGI\NETBASIC	CGI interface to NetBasic files.
SYS:WEB\LOGS	Web server log files are kept here.
SYS:WEB\MAPS	Image map files are kept here.
SYS:WEB\SAMPLES\CGIAPP	Sample CGI applications written in the C language are kept here. The RCGI.H and RCGI.C files can be found in this directory.
SYS:WEB\SAMPLES\CGINPH	Sample CGI applications written in the C language that shows how non-parsed header CGI programs can be written are kept here. Contains separate subdirectories for source, object, include, and directory files.
SYS:WEB\SAMPLES\CGIPARSE	Sample CGI applications written in the C language that shows how parsed header CGI programs can be written are kept here. Contains separate subdirectories for source, object, include, and etc. directory files.

(Continued)

	DIRECTORY	DESCRIPTION
TABLE 4.1 *Novell Web Server Configuration Directories (Continued)*	SYS:WEB\SAMPLES\CONFIG	Sample configuration files for the Novell Web Server kept here.
	SYS:WEB\SAMPLES\RCGID	Files for building the RCGI daemon to run on remote UNIX servers are kept here. The daemon is written in the C language and must be compiled on the target UNIX platform. Complete source files including make files are available. The compiled binaries for BSD UNIX, Solaris, Unixware are kept in separate subdirectories. Sample Perl and shell scripts for UNIX are also kept here.
	SYS:WEB\SCRIPTS	BASIC language CGI program scripts (.BAS extension) are kept here.
	SYS:WEB\SCRIPTS\PERL	Perl language CGI program scripts (.pl extension) are kept here.
	SYS:NETBASIC\WEB	NetBasic scripts used by the Novell Web Server are located here.

In addition to the standard Novell Web Server directory structure, the SYS:ETC directory structure is also important for configuring the Novell Web Server. The SYS:ETC directory contains the configuration files that are needed for configuring the TCP/IP protocol stack on the Web server.

The Novell Web Server is started by the UNISTART.NCF file, which contains the commands to start the Novell Web Server and other support services dealing with UNIX or IP connectivity. The following is a sample UNISTART.NCF file:

```
load netdb.nlm
load http.nlm -d sys:web
load basic.nlm -d sys:web
load perl.nlm
```

The -d sys:web parameter specifies that Web server root directory is SYS:WEB. You can change this parameter but before doing so, you should use the Web Manager tool discussed in the next section to ensure the consistency of the Web server document tree is maintained.

The NLMs that are loaded to start the Novell Web Server have the following roles:

▶ *NETDB.NLM*. This NLM is used for the network database access configurations and IP address information.

▶ *HTTP.NLM*. This is the Novell Web Server NLM. The Novell Web Server is a Hypertext Transfer Protocol (HTTP) server.

▶ *BASIC.NLM*. This BASIC language interpreter is implemented as an RCGI interface module that listens on TCP port 8001. You will learn about the RCGI interface in Chapter 6.

▶ *NETBASIC.NLM*. This is the NetBasic language interpreter implemented as an LCGI interface module that listens on port 8003. You will learn about the LCGI interface in Chapter 6.

▶ *PERL.NLM*. This Perl language interpreter is implemented as an RCGI interface module that listens on TCP port 8002.

An additional module, CGIAPP.NLM, is available as a test application for CGI NLM applications.

Configuring the Novell Web Server

You can configure the Novell Web Server by using the Web Manager program (WEBMGR.EXE), or you can alter the configuration files directly. The Novell Web Server configuration files are text files and the Web Manager provides a graphical interface to most configuration functions. If you understand the syntax of the Web server configuration files, you can use any text editor to modify these files. However, you must restart the Web server if you edit any of the configuration files.

The SYS:WEB\SAMPLES directory contains some sample configuration files for modifying the configuration files. You can use this as a basis for modifying your actual configuration files in the SYS:WEB\CONFIG directory.

The Novell Web Server is set up with a default configuration when it is installed. The following are a few of the reasons why you might want to change the default configuration:

- ▸ Changing the default port number on which the Web server listens for Web client requests

- ▸ Using host names instead of IP addresses for redirected client requests

- ▸ Changing the document root directory

- ▸ Changing the directory in which log files are saved

- ▸ Specifying the e-mail addresses of the Web server administrator

- ▸ Controlling the ability of users to publish Web documents from their home directories

- ▸ Enabling NDS browsing

The server root directory SYS:WEB (by default) contains a number of directories needed for the proper operation of the Web server. Other than the users' Web page directory in their home directories, Web clients cannot access information outside the document root. The document root, therefore, provides a built-in security mechanism.

Starting with Novell Web Server version 3.0, you can set up *virtual Web servers*. A virtual Web server is a logical copy of a Novell Web Server with its own document, log, and configuration directories. These directories can reside anywhere on the Novell intranetwork. The virtual Web server can also have its own unique Domain Name System (DNS) and IP address. A newer TCPIP.NLM has been released (starting with Novell Web Server version 3.0) that permits secondary IP addresses to be assigned to the same network interface board. Novell calls this feature *multihoming*, which is a term generally referring to any TCP/IP host that has more than one IP address associated with the host. Typically, a single IP address is assigned per network interface.

Changing the Configuration Using the Web Manager

At the time of the Novell Web Server installation, the Web Manager (WEBMGR.EXE) is installed in the SYS:PUBLIC directory. You can run the Web Manager from the command line by typing its name, or use the Windows interface to create a program item for it or a shortcut to the program.

The following is a guided tour of using the Web Manager.

1 • Log in to the network and start the Web Manager from the SYS:PUBLIC directory.

2 • The opening screen for the Web Manager appears (see Figure 4.2).

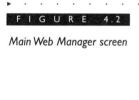

FIGURE 4.2

Main Web Manager screen

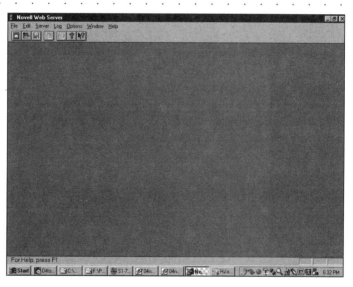

3 • To load the current server configuration, select File from the main menu and select Server. The "Select a virtual server to configure" dialog box shown in Figure 4.3 appears. You can use the Network button to map a network drive to access the server root files.

4 • Select a different drive and directory combination only if you want to configure another Web server on a different file server. Select OK.

5 • The Novell Web Server configuration dialog box shown in Figure 4.4 appears.

FIGURE 4.3

"Select a virtual server to configure" dialog box

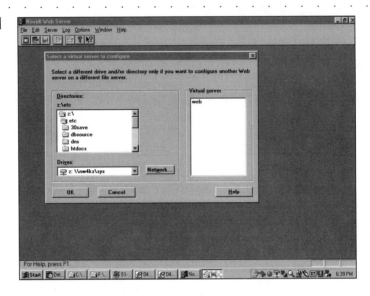

FIGURE 4.4

Web server configuration dialog box

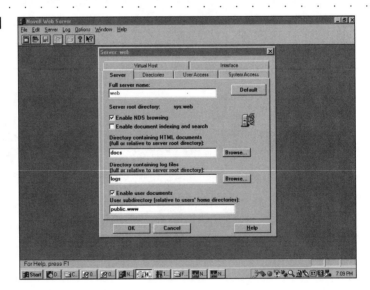

The following fields appear in the Web Server dialog box:

> ▸ *Full server name*. Edit the Full server name field to change the host name of the server or its IP address. If you enter a name, it must be

the full DNS name of the server, such as nw4ks.kinetics.com. If you do not have DNS set up on the network, you must enter the IP address of the Novell Web Server.

▶ *Enable NDS browsing.* Turning this option enables you to use the NDS browsing feature of the Novell Web Server to browse the NDS tree. For NDS browsing, the trustee [Public] must have NDS Browse rights to the containers of the NDS tree to be browsed.

▶ *Enable document indexing and search.* This enables you to use the Novell QuickFinder to perform document indexing and searching. The Novell QuickFinder is a search engine that automatically indexes more than 20 different file types, including HTML, WordPerfect, Word, Quattro Pro, Excel and PDF. The indexes are less than 10 percent of the original document size. Web authors can add customizable search forms to their sites. Searching can also be added by using the QuickFinder APIs and the NetBasic interface.

▶ *Directory containing HTML documents.* Edit the Directory containing HTML documents field, to change the document root directory. The document root can be a full path or the path relative to the server root. You need to modify this field only if you move the document root from the default SYS:WEB\DOCS directory.

▶ *Directory containing log files.* Edit the Directory containing log files field to change the directory in which the Web server creates the Access, Error, and Debug logs. This directory can be a full path or a path relative to the server root. You need to modify this field only if you want the log files written to a different location.

▶ *Enable user documents.* Edit the Enable user documents check box to change whether users can publish Web documents from their home directories on the server. Uncheck this check box if you do not want users to publish documents from their home directories.

▶ *User subdirectory.* Edit the User subdirectory field, to change the name of the subdirectory within the users' home directories where users should store documents to be published on the Web. You need to modify this field only if user documents are enabled (see previous field) and you want users to store their Web documents in a subdirectory other than the default directory of PUBLIC_WWW. The user's home page is specified using the following URL address: `http://servername/~username`. Alternatively, you can specify the NDS distinguished name of the user such as `http://servername/~username.corp.esl`.

The other configuration tabs in Figure 4.4 can be used to configure

▶ Directories

▶ User Access

▶ System Access

▶ Interface

▶ Virtual Host

These are discussed in the sections that follow.

Changing the Server Directories Using the Web Manager

Use the Directories tab page to set up a new directory in the Web server document tree. One way of adding a new directory to the document tree is to create a new directory under the document root using the DOS MD command or by using the Windows GUI. The HTML document and image files that you store in the new directory can be accessed by Web clients immediately. However, the new directory that you create will inherit directory options and access control settings from the parent directory. If you want to change the inherited directory options and access control settings, you must first add the new directory by using the Directories tab page. Figure 4.5 shows the options under the Directories tab.

FIGURE 4.5

Configuring server directories

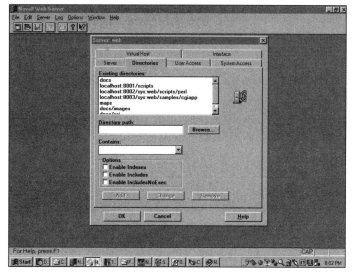

The fields in the Directories tab are as follows:

▸ *Existing directories list*. This contains a list of the directories in the document tree.

▸ *Directory path*. This specifies the path to the selected directory, or to the directory you are adding to or deleting from the document tree.

▸ *Contains*. This describes the contents of the selected directory. This field is a drop-down list that contains choices such as "Documents," "Scripts," and "Image maps" from which you choose. You must specify the Contains field when adding a new directory to the document tree. Image maps are "hot spots" within a graphic image. These hot spots represent URL addresses. Clicking a hot spot causes the corresponding URL to be accessed by the Web client.

▸ *Options*. This section contains check boxes that signify options for enabling automatic directory indexing and Server Side Includes (SSIs) for the selected directory. Server Side Includes are discussed in detail in Chapter 10. To enable automatic directory indexing check the box labeled "Enable indexing." To enable Server Side Includes, check the box labeled "Enable includes."

In addition to setting up a new directory as explained previously in this section, you can remove a directory, set up automatic indexing, and enable Server Side Includes. These procedures are described in the sections that follow.

After selecting the options you want for the new directory, select OK.

Removing a directory from the Web server document tree

To remove a directory from the document tree, follow these steps:

1 • Select File from the menu.

2 • Click Select Server.

3 • Select the virtual Web server on the drive that is mapped to the server and select OK.

4 • Select the Directories tab.

5 • Select the directory you want to remove from the "Existing directories" list.

6 • Select the Remove button.

7 • Select OK.

8 • Select Save and Restart.

9 • Type the Web server password and select OK. (You specified the Web password during the Novell Web Server installation.)

10 • Delete the directory and its contents from the server's file system.

Setting up automatic indexing of a directory

A directory index is an HTML document that describes the contents of a directory on the Web server. The following are two ways to provide directory indexes:

▶ You can create an HTML document called INDEX.HTM (or
INDEX.HTML) that describes the contents of the directory. Normally,
the home page is created in the INDEX.HTM file. In fact, the home
page is an example of a directory index to the remainder of your
HTML files. When a user types in the URL of a directory rather than
a file, the Web server automatically looks for an INDEX.HTM file to
return.

▶ You can set up the Web server to generate an index automatically
whenever a user types in the URL of the directory. This is useful when
the contents of a directory change often, or when a directory contains
many files. If the directory does not contain an INDEX.HTM file and
automatic directory indexing is not enabled, the Web server returns
an error code.

To set up automatic directory indexing, follow these steps:

1 • Select File from the menu.

2 • Click Select Server.

3 • Select the virtual Web server on the drive that is mapped to the server
and select OK.

4 • Select the Directories tab.

5 • Select the directory in which you want to enable automatic directory
indexing from the "Existing directories" list.

6 • Select the "Enable indexing" check box.

7 • Set the Index options. If you want the index entries to include icons,
file size information, and descriptions in addition to filenames, select
"Fancy indexing." If you want users to be able to click icons to
retrieve an associated file, select "Icons are links." If you want the
Web server to generate a description for each file by scanning the
HTML documents for titles, select "Scan titles."

8 • Select OK.

9 • Select Save and Restart.

10 • Enter the Web server password and select OK.

Enabling Server Side Includes

The Server Side Include (SSI) mechanism enables the Web server to insert data in HTML documents before sending them to a requesting client. SSI directives enable you to create dynamic Web documents. HTML files containing SSI directives must be saved with a .SSI extension. Chapter 10 discusses the details of the SSI directives that you can insert in an HTML document.

To set up Server Side Includes, you must enable Server Side Includes by following these steps:

1 • Select File from the menu.

2 • Click Select Server.

3 • Select the virtual Web server and directory on the drive that is mapped to the server and select OK.

4 • Select the Directories tab.

5 • Select the directory in which you want to enable SSIs from the "Existing directories" list.

6 • Enable the Enable Includes or Enable IncludesNoExec check box.

7 • Select Change.

8 • Select OK.

9 • Select Save and Restart.

Restricting System Access

After you finish adding the new directory to the Web directory tree, you can restrict access to the directory by authorized system or user. To restrict System access, select the System tab shown in Figure 4.4. The System tab form is shown in Figure 4.6.

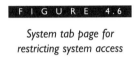

F I G U R E 4.6

*System tab page for
restricting system access*

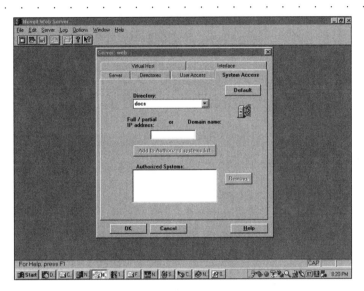

The following are the different fields shown in Figure 4.6:

▶ *Directory*. This field contains a drop-down list of all directories for which you can set up access control. The directory list is that specified in the Server tab form.

▶ *Full/partial IP address or Domain name*. Use this field to identify the systems to which you want to allow directory access. You must specify either the full or partial IP address of the systems that are allowed access, or the fully qualified DNS domain name or hostname of the systems that are allowed access to the selected directory. For example, if you want all hosts that have the class C IP address of 199.245.180 to access the selected directory, enter the partial IP address of **199.245.180** and then select the "Add to Authorized system lists" button.

> ▸ *Authorized Systems.* This field lists all IP addresses or domains that currently have access to the selected directory. To add entries to this list see the description of the previous field. You can remove entries from this list by highlighting the entry and selecting Remove.

When you restrict directory access to a list of authorized systems, the Web server checks the Web client's IP address or DNS domain name against this list before processing a document request. If the Web client is not in the authorized system list, its request is denied. As explained previously, you can restrict directory access to authorized systems by using the following:

> ▸ *Full IP address.* An example of a full IP address is 134.33.23.201. It is a full IP address because all the four bytes (32-bits) of the IP address are specified. If this is the only entry in the authorized system list, only the Web client that has this IP address can access the system.

> ▸ *Partial IP address.* An example of a partial IP address is 135.23. This address specifies the first two bytes that are the network portion of a class B address. By specifying only the partial address of 135.23, all hosts in the class B address of 135.23 will be given access to the Web server. For example, hosts with IP addresses of 135.23.1.1, 135.23.1.2, 135.23.200.32 will all have access to the Web server.

> ▸ *DNS domain name.* You can restrict access by domain names. For example, if you specify a domain name of `siyan.com`, `kinetics.com`, or `tsl.org`, only hosts that are within these domain names will have access to the Web server. Examples of hosts that will have access are `madhav.kinetics.com`, `think.siyan.com` and `emk.tsl.org`.

Follow these steps to restrict directory access to authorized systems:

1 • Select File from the main menu.

2 • Click Select Server.

3 • Select the virtual Web server and directory on the drive that is mapped to the server and select OK.

4 • Select the System Access tab.

5 • Select the directory you want to control from the Directory drop-down list.

6 • Enter the full or partial IP address, or the fully qualified DNS domain name or hostname, in the appropriate field.

7 • Select "Add to Authorized systems list."

8 • Repeat Steps 6 and 7 for each authorized system or group of systems.

9 • Select OK.

10 • Select Save and Restart.

11 • Enter the Web server password and select OK.

Restricting User Access

Use the User Access tab page to restrict directory access to authorized users. Figure 4.7 shows the User Access tab page.

The following fields are shown in Figure 4.7:

▶ *Directory.* This field contains a drop-down list of all the directories for which you can set up access control.

▶ *Authentication method.* This field describes the type of authentication used to restrict users. You can choose the user authentication method from the drop-down list.

▶ *Default NDS context.* This field defines the default NDS context for users. If no NDS context is specified, a default context is used. If an NDS context is specified, the "Network users list" will contain the list of users in the specified context.

▶ · ◀

User Access tab page

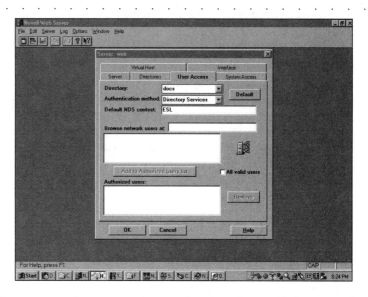

▶ *Browse network users at.* This is a list that shows all the network users and groups who are allowed access the selected directory by using the selected authentication method. This is not the same as the "Authorized users list." Note that as you change the value of the Default NDS Context field, the users that are listed also change.

▶ *Authorized users.* This field lists all users and groups who currently have access to the selected directory. You can add users to this list by selecting a user entry from the "Network users list" and clicking "Add to Authorized users list." You can remove users from this list by selecting the entry you want to remove and clicking Remove.

▶ *All valid users.* This check box enables all users who can be authenticated to have access to the selected directory. When this box is selected, the "Network users list" is disabled and you cannot select individual users from the "Network users list." Uncheck this box to allow individual users.

Follow these steps to restrict directory access to authorized users only:

1 • Select File from the main menu.

2 • Click Select Server.

3 • Select the virtual Web server directory on the drive that is mapped to the server and select OK.

4 • Select the User Access tab.

5 • Select the directory you want to control from the Directory drop-down list.

6 • Select Directory Services from the "Authentication method" drop-down list.

7 • Enter the name of the NDS context that contains the user objects you want to allow to access the directory in the "NDS context" field.

8 • Select an authorized user from the "Network users" list.

9 • Select the "Add to Authorized users list" button to add the selected user to the authorized list.

10 • Repeat Steps 8 and 9 for each authorized user.

11 • Select OK.

12 • Click Save and Restart.

13 • Enter the Web server password and click OK.

Setting Virtual Host Options

Use the Virtual Hosts option to create and manage virtual hosts on a virtual server. This tab page (see Figure 4.8) contains the "Defined virtual hosts" list, which contains a list of defined virtual hosts for a virtual server and whether they are active (On or Off). You can enable an inactive virtual host by selecting it in the "Define virtual hosts" list and clicking Disable. You can see the current configuration of a virtual host by selecting it in the "Define virtual hosts" list and clicking See Details.

FIGURE 4.8

Virtual Host option

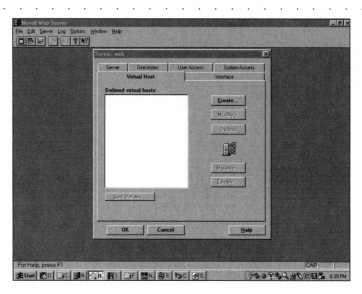

Interface Tab Option

Use the Inteface tab (see Figure 4.9) option to specify an interface for a virtual server or to enable SSL on a virtual server.

The following fields are shown in Figure 4.9:

- ▸ *Port.* This field contains the default TCP port address of the Novell Web Server. The default is set to TCP port 80. The TCP port number of 80 has been reserved for the Web server. You may want to change the TCP port number of Web servers from third-party vendors already using the TCP port number 80. The default of the Port field is 80.

- ▸ *IP addresses.* This field lists all IP addresses assigned to the virtual server. You can add an IP address to this list by clicking Add and entering the address in the Add Address dialog box. You can remove an IP address from this list by selecting the entry you want to remove and clicking Remove.

FIGURE 4.9

Interface tab option

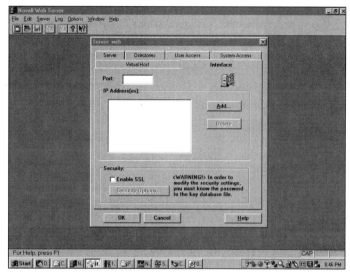

> ▶ *Security.* This box contains the Enable SSL check box to activate
> Security Sockets Layer (SSL) protocol for the virtual server. If this box
> is checked, you can select SSL options by clicking Security Options.
> When this box is not checked, SSL is disabled for the virtual server.
> Before enabling the SSL option, you must have the key database file.
> You can use the Set Key Database File option in the Options menu of
> WEBMGR to set the key dababase file.

Specifying Web Access for Non-NetWare Users

The Novell Web Server enables you to specify access for non-NetWare users.
This can be accomplished by editing the Novell Web Server configuration files.
The Novell Web Server configuration files are kept in the SYS:WEB/CONFIG
directory. This directory contains the following files:

> ▶ ACCESS.CFG—This file contains resource information (such as
> directories for user and system access).

▸ HTTPD.CFG—This is the configuration file for the HTTPD.NLM that contains basic server setup commands. You can use this file to change the location of the other configuration files.

▸ MIME.TYP—This file contains the Multipurpose Internet Mail Extension (MIME) content types that are recognized by the Web server. Chapter 6 discusses MIME types.

▸ SRM.CFG—This is the Server Resource Map file. This file contains information on where document, scripts, and icon information is stored. This file is used to map the virtual path names specified in URL addresses to the actual directory location on the Web server.

To allow non-NetWare users access to the Novell Web Server, you must modify the ACCESS.CFG file in the SYS:WEB/CONFIG directory. The ACCESS.CFG file describes the users who can have access to specific server directories. Since non-NetWare users are not authenticated by NDS, you must build a special username/password file for these users. There are two steps to completing this process:

1 • Generate the username/password file.

2 • Edit the ACCESS.CFG file.

To generate the username/password file, follow these steps:

1 • Create a text file (for example, plain.www) that contains a list of usernames and passwords in the following format:

username:password

The *password* should be the unencrypted form of the password. Here is an example:

```
linda:inner4
janice:speaker+phone
mary:vajra+
```

2 • Convert the password file to an encrypted password file by using the PWGEN.EXE utility in the SYS:PUBLIC directory:

```
pwgen plain.www encrypt.www
```

The `plain.www` is the username/password file that contained the non-encrypted passwords. A new file `encrypt.www` is produced that contains the encrypted form of these passwords. For example, the previous password file will be encoded as follows:

```
linda:OpquRduXAH+1SRJ3fwYmmw==
janice:9lnqL5FH3o/SS+S1uREXNg==
mary:z8SOlWzlbVdTWVwTxQMoCg==
```

3 • Copy the `encrypt.www` file to SYS:WEB.

You must now edit the ACCESS.CFG file as follows:

1 • Edit the ACCESS.CFG file and add the following lines if you want to provide access to the DOCS/NONW directory:

```
<Directory docs/nonw>
AuthType Basic
AuthName Access-to-my-stuff
AuthUserMethod encrypt.www
Options Indexes FollowSymLinks
```

2 • Use one of the following options to provide access to the users:

a) To allow just specific users to do a GET or a PUT, add the following lines:

```
<Limit GET PUT>
require user linda
require user janice
require user mary
</Limit>
```

Note that GET allows users to download documents, and a PUT allows users to submit data via an HTML form or some other query method.

b) To allows all users in the `encrypt.www` file access via GET or PUT, add the following:

```
<Limit GET PUT>
require valid-user
</Limit>
```

3 • Finally, add the following to complete the <Directory tag> specified earlier:

```
</Directory>
```

4 • Reload the Novell Web Server for changes to take effect.

Every time you change the configuration in the SYS:WEB/CONFIG/ ACCESS.CFG directory, you must reload the server. However, you can specify access to a specific directory by adding an ACCESS.WWW file to that directory. Adding an ACCESS.WWW file to a directory does not require that you restart the Novell Web Server. Additionally, this enables each user to set up access to his or her Web data. The syntax of the ACCESS.WWW file is similar to that discussed earlier. For example, if users wanted to control access to their Web area in their PUBLIC.WWW subdirectory of their home directory, they could do the following:

1 • Create the ACCESS.CFG file in the PUBLIC.WWW directory underneath the users' home directory and add the following lines:

```
AuthType Basic
AuthName Access-to-my-stuff
AuthUserMethod encrypt.www
Options Indexes FollowSymLinks
```

2 • Use one of the following options to provide access to the users:

a) To allow just specific users to do a GET or a PUT, add the following lines:

```
<Limit GET PUT>
require user linda
```

```
require user janice
require user mary
</Limit>
```

Note that GET allows users to download documents, and a PUT allows users to submit data via an HTML form or some other query method.

b) To allow all users in the encrypt.www file access via GET or PUT, add the following:

```
<Limit GET PUT>
require valid-user
</Limit>
```

Configuring the IPX/IP Gateway for the Intranet

If your network is primarily IPX-based, you may want to use the IPX protocol for communicating with the Novell Web Server. IPX-based workstations do not require configuration of IPX parameters, which is a good reason to use the IPX protocol as your primary protocol for NetWare-based networks. Web browsers typically understand only the TCP/IP protocol. The IPX/IP Gateway provides the conversion between the IPX clients and the IP protocol expected by the Novell Web Server.

To configure your intranet for IPX, perform the following steps:

1 • Install and configure the IPX/IP gateway at a NetWare Server.

2 • Configure NetWare IPX/IP gateway at the client workstations.

3 • Configure NDS rights for the Gateway NDS object.

Installing and Configuring the IPX/IP Gateway at a NetWare Server

The IPX/IP gateway is distributed on the Internet Access Server CD-ROM. This CD-ROM is distributed as part of the IntranetWare distribution. You must first install the IPX/IP gateway and then configure it.

Follow these steps to install the IPX/IP gateway:

1 • Mount the CD-ROM containing the Internet Access Server as NetWare volume on the server. You can do this by executing the following commands from the server console:

```
LOAD CDROM
CD DEVICE LIST
CD MOUNT NIAS4
```

2 • Unload the license API NLM if loaded, and load the INSTALL NLM from the server console:

```
UNLOAD LIC_API
LOAD INSTALL
```

3 • The INSTALL screen shown in Figure 4.10 appears.

FIGURE 4.10

Main INSTALL screen

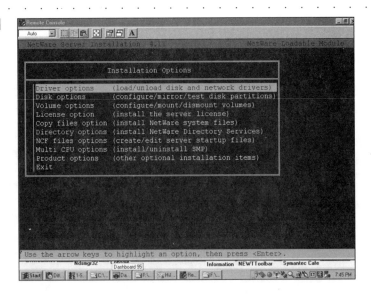

4 • Select "Product Install" and the screen shown in Figure 4.11 appears.

5 • Select "Install a product not listed" and the screen shown in Figure 4.12 appears. You are prompted to specify the source of the product.

FIGURE 4.11

Product Install screen

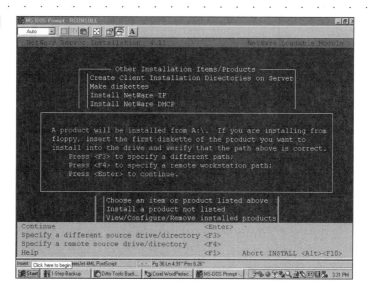

FIGURE 4.12

Specifying product source message

6 • Press F3 and enter the source installation path as follows:
`NIAS4:NIAS\INSTALL`

7 • The Install Options screen appears. Select "Install Product."

8 • A list of servers to install the product appears. Select a server and answer Yes to start the installation. If an expected server is not displayed, ensure that the latest version of the RSPAWN.NLM is loaded on that server. A copy of RSPAWN.NLM (and dependent module RSPX.NLM) can be found in \SUPPS\ALL on the Novell Internet Access Server CD-ROM. If you are performing a remote installation (that is, the Novell Web Server is being installed on a server that is different from the one on which you are performing the installation), you must press the Insert key to add servers to the list. You can then simultaneously perform the installation on multiple servers.

If you are installing to a remote server, you will be prompted to log in as an administrator. You must enter the distinguished name (complete name) of the administrator user and the password. For example, the complete name of the user Admin in the NDS context O=ESL.C=US is

`.Admin.ESL.US`

9 • A screen shown in Figure 4.13 appears and prompts you to install configuration files. If this is the first installation of the Web server, you should probably select No, unless someone has prepared for you a set of configuration files to use with the Web server.

10 • You will be asked to enter the license disk. Enter the IntranetWare server license disk in the floppy drive and follow instructions on the screen.

11 • After the license file is successfully read, you will see a status of files as they are copied to the IntranetWare server. When the files are copied, the following message indicates the successful completion of the install:

`Press <Enter> to continue and when prompted, remove the license disk from the server.`

F I G U R E   4.13

Option to install
configuration files

12 • You will see the Installation Options menu again. To see a log of the files that were copied (such as the list shown in Figure 4.14), select "Display Log File."

F I G U R E   4.14

Display Log File option

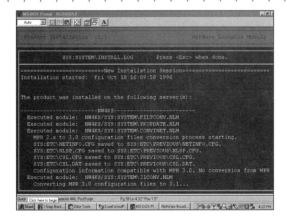

13 • Select "Exit" from the Installation Options menu, and answer Yes to exit Product Installation.

14 • From the "Other Installation Actions" menu select "View/Configure/ Remove installed products" to review the components that are installed. Figure 4.15 shows that the IPX/IP Gateway, MultiProtocolRouter, Internet Access Server, NetWare UNIX Client, and WAN Extensions are all installed as a result of this installation procedure.

In addition to updating and adding server NLMs in SYS:\SYSTEM, the Novell Internet Access Server installation process installs the client files in the SYS:\PUBLIC\CLIENT\WIN95 and SYS:\PUBLIC\CLIENT\WIN31 directories. The Netscape Navigator browser files are installed in the SYS:\NETSCAPE\32 (for Win32) and SYS:\NETSCAPE\16 (for Windows 3.*x*) directories.

F I G U R E   4.15

Viewing installed products

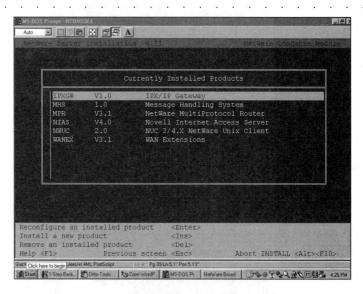

15 • Restart the server and verify the installation.

```
DOWN
RESTART SERVER
```

After the IPX/IP gateway is installed, the next step is to configure the IPX/IP gateway at the NetWare server. Follow these steps to configure the IPX/IP gateway:

1 • Load the INETCFG NLM. at the server console.

`LOAD INETCFG`

The INETCFG NLM checks for configuration information stored in AUTOEXEC.NCF that can be transferred to the INETCFG configuration files.

2 • If you are prompted to transfer commands from AUTOEXEC.NCF or to insert initialization commands into AUTOEXEC.NCF, select Yes.

3 • From the main Internetworking Configuration menu, select the Protocols option.

On a list of protocols that is displayed, you should see TCP/IP enabled (if you followed the instructions in Chapter 3 to install TCP/IP on the server).

4 • From the Protocol Configuration menu, select the TCP/IP protocol. The TCP/IP Protocol Configuration screen appears.

5 • From the TCP/IP Protocol Configuration screen, select IPX/IP Gateway Configuration (see Figure 4.16).

6 • Highlight the IPX/IP Gateway field, press Enter, then select Enabled to activate the IPX/IP Gateway.

The default is to enable the logging of clients to the Novell Web Server. If you want to disable this, select the Client Logging field and disable it. The file SYS:GW_AUDIT.LOG logs the client, the service, and the duration of accessing the service.

▶ . . . . ◀

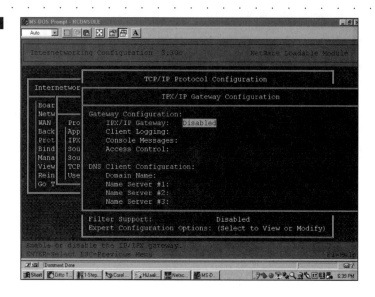

7 • You can control the level of messages that are reported on the server console by selecting the Console Messages field. The following level of messages can be set:

Errors Only

Warnings and errors

Informational, warnings and errors

8 • The default setting is "Informational, warnings and errors" and this is adequate for most purposes. The messages are also logged to the log file if logging is enabled.

9 • If you enable the field "Access Control," you can control access through the IPX/IP gateway on a per-user basis. The actual configuration of the user access restrictions is done through the client utility Network Administrator at the client workstation. If you want unrestricted access for all users to access the gateway, you should disable Access Control.

10 • In the DNS Client Configuration section of the IPX/IP Gateway Configuration screen, set a valid domain name for the NetWare server on which the gateway resides. Additionally, specify IP addresses of the DNS servers for your network.

11 • Press Esc a few times to back out of the menus. When asked if you want to update your TCP/IP configuration, answer Yes.

12 • You will be informed that the next action requires a user with Supervisor object rights to the [Root] object of the NDS tree, that the NDS schema will be extended, and that an IPX/IP gateway object will be automatically created (see Figure 4.17).

Message about creation of IPX/IP Gateway object

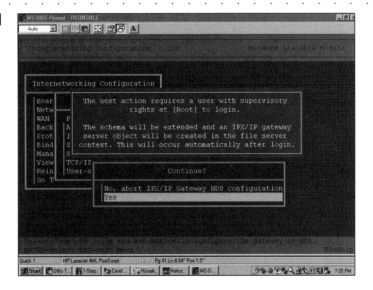

After you log in, the IPX/IP gateway object is created automatically in the file server NDS context. The gateway configuration process updates the NDS schema when the gateway object is created. The schema is extended for the User, Group, Organization, and Organization Unit classes. This causes a temporary increase in NDS traffic until all NDS servers have been updated.

13 • Select Yes to continue. Enter an administrator name and password. Press Enter at the Select To Login prompt. After the successful creation of the gateway server NDS object, you see a message informing you that the IPX/IP Gateway server NDS configuration is completed. The name of the gateway server is the name of the file server with "-GW" appended to it.

The gateway is active on all network interfaces. You must not configure the gateway on a per-interface basis.

14 • Exit INETCFG and restart the server.

15 • Ensure that the SYS:ETC\HOSTS file contains a correct entry for the server's IP address and hostname.. For example, if the server NW4EM has an IP address of 202.31.212.32, you should have the following entry in the SYS:\ETC\HOSTS file:

```
202.31.212.32   NW4EM localhost
```

You can use the EDIT NLM to check for this:

```
LOAD EDIT SYS:ETC\HOSTS
```

16 • The IPX/IP Gateway server log files (GW_INFO.LOG and GW_AUDIT.LOG) are placed in the root of the SYS: volume. The GW_AUDIT.LOG provides information about IP access for every client using the IPX/IP Gateway.

Configuring the IPX/IP Gateway at the Client Workstations

After installing and configuring the IPX/IP gateway at the NetWare server, you must configure the NetWare IPX/IP gateway at the client. The client configuration is described for a Windows 95 workstation using the Client32 software. There are two steps involved in the Client32 configuration:

1 • You must install the Client32 software.

2 • Use the Windows 95 Network Panel to add and configure the IPX/IP gateway at the client.

Installing the Windows 95 Client32 software

If you have not installed the Client32 software, follow these steps:

1 • The Client32 software enabled for IPX/IP gateway functions uses a special version of the Windows Sockets interface that can work with the IPX protocol. Novell recommends that you perform the following to avoid conflicts between Windows Sockets library files:

a) Search for WINSOCK.DLL on your workstation. Rename any WINSOCK.DLL file that is *not* in the \NOVELL\CLIENT32 or the \WINDOWS directory.

b) Search for WSOCK32.DLL on your workstation. Rename any WSOCK32.DLL file that is *not* in the \NOVELL\CLIENT32 or the \WINDOWS\SYSTEM directory.

c) Search for WLIBSOCK.DLL on your workstation. Rename any WLIBSOCK.DLL file that is *not* in the \NOVELL\CLIENT32 directory.

2 • Run the SETUP.EXE program from the Client32 distribution. If you have installed the Client32 installation files on the server, you will find the SETUP.EXE program in the directory *D*:\PUBLIC\CLIENT\WIN95 directory, where *D* is the network drive. You can also install from the Internet Access Server CD-ROM, where you will find the SETUP.EXE program in the *D*:\NIAS\GWCLIENT\WIN95 directory, where *D* is the CD-ROM drive.

3 • When the Client32 SETUP program is run, you will see the license agreement screen. After agreeing with the license, select Yes.

4 • If you are using NDIS drivers and want to upgrade to ODI drivers, enable the check box labeled "Upgrade NDIS drivers to ODI automatically, if available?".

5 • Select Start to begin the Client32 installation.

6 • If prompted to select a preferred server or other client properties select Yes, and then enter the preferred tree/server and name context information. Select Yes to continue. The "Preferred tree" is the name of the NDS tree for your network. The "NDS tree" represents a hierarchical distributed database of network information, and each NDS tree has a name. The "name context" is the location within this tree where your user account can be found.

7 • When installation completes, you will see a Customize button. Select this button.

8 • You will see the Windows 95 Network panel. Use the next section to add and configure IPX/IP gateway. After configuring the IPX/IP gateway at the client, reboot the workstation.

Using the Windows 95 Network Panel to add and configure the IPX/IP gateway

If you have already installed Client32 on the workstation, double-click the network icon from the Control Panel program group. To get to the Control Panel, select Start, then Settings, and then Control Panel. The Network Panel for Windows 95 is shown in Figure 4.18.

▶ · ◀

FIGURE 4.18

Windows 95 Network Panel

1 • Select the Add button (see Figure 4.18).

2 • Highlight the Protocol option and select Add.

3 • From the list of manufacturers, select Novell.

4 • From the list of Network Protocols that displays on the right, select "Novell NetWare IPX/IP Gateway." Select OK.

5 • Select OK again from the Network Panel screen.

6 • When asked if you want to select a preferred gateway server, select Yes.

7 • The Preferred gateway server box shown in Figure 4.19 appears. Enter the preferred gateway server. This is the NetWare server on which you have installed and configured the IPX/IP gateway. Select OK.

FIGURE 4.19

Preferred gateway server option

8 • If prompted for location for additional files, specify the location. The location could be the directory from which you ran the Setup program and/or the Windows 95 distribution files.

9 • When prompted to restart the system, select Yes.

10 • After logging on to the network using the Client32, you will see a dialog box from which you should select "Enable IPX/IP Gateway" option. This will enable the IPX/IP gateway at the workstation.

11 • Verify that the \Novell\Client32 is added to the PATH statement in the AUTOEXEC.BAT file. The \Novell\Client32 should be on the path before directories containing other WINSOCK.DLL files. Also, other WINSOCK.DLL files should not be present in the directories of applications that you invoke. If you followed the renaming of the Windows socket files described in the previous section, you should not have any problems.

Configuring NDS Rights for the Gateway NDS Object

The last step in the IPX/IP configuration is to set NDS rights for the IPX/IP Gateway object. You can set NDS rights using the NetWare Administrator tool (located in SYS:PUBLIC\WIN95\NWADMN95.EXE). Before you can use the NetWare Administrator tool you must add snap-in DLLs so that the NetWare Administrator can recognize the IPX/IP gateway objects.

If you are using the Windows 3.*x* NetWare Administrator, add the following under the [Snapin Object DLLs WIN3X] heading:

```
IPXGW3X.DLL=IPXGW3X.DLL
```

If you are using the Windows 95 NetWare Administrator, add the following under the [Snapin Object DLLs] heading:

```
IPXGW.DLL=IPXGW.DLL
```

Follow these steps to configure NDS rights for the gateway NDS object:

1 • Start the NetWare Administrator. On a Windows 95 workstation, if you have not created a shortcut for the NWADMN95.EXE on your desktop, it is recommended that you do so.

2 • Make [Public] NDS object a trustee of the Gateway object with object rights of Browse, and All Property rights of Read and Compare.

a) Right-click the Gateway object.

b) Select "Trustees of this Object…"

c) If [Public] is not in Trustees List, select Add Trustee. Change Browse Context to [Root]. Select [Public] from Available Objects and then select OK.

d) Highlight [Public] in Trustees List.

e) Check the Browse box under Object Rights.

f) Ensure that the All Properties radio button is selected, and then check the Read and Compare check boxes.

g) After making these rights changes, select OK.

3 • Make the [Public] NDS object a trustee of the file server object that is running the Novell IPX/IP gateway. Assign [Public] object rights of Browse, and Read and Compare property rights to the Network Address property to the server object.

a) Locate the server object, and right-click the server object.

b) Select "Trustees of this Object…"

c) If [Public] is not in Trustees List, select Add Trustee. Change Browse Context to [Root]. Select [Public] from Available Objects and then select OK.

d) Highlight [Public] in Trustees List.

e) Check the Browse box under Object Rights.

f) Select "Selected properties" radio button. Select Network Address from the list of properties. Select the Read and Compare check boxes.

g) After making these rights changes, select OK.

4 • Make the Gateway object a trustee of the [Root] object with object rights of Browse, and Read and Compare All Property rights.

a) Right-click the [Root] object.

b) Select "Trustees of this Object…"

c) If the Gateway object is not in Trustees List, select Add Trustee. Change Browse Context to the container in which the Gateway object is defined. Select the Gateway object from Available Objects and then select OK.

d) Highlight the Gateway object in the Trustees List.

e) Check the Browse box under Object Rights.

f) Ensure that the All Properties radio button is selected. Select the Read and Compare check boxes.

g) After making these rights changes, select OK.

You are now ready to access the Novell Web Server using the IPX protocol.

Summary

This chapter discussed the layout of the configuration directories and files needed for the Novell Web Server configuration. The primary tool for configuring the Novell Web Server is the Web Manager tool that comes with the Novell Web Server. You can use the Web Manager to perform many of the administration tasks associated with setting up the Novell Web Server. You learned to use the Web Manager tool to change the default configuration for the directories, server configuration, set up access control configuration for systems and users, and control how log files are handled. Finally, you learned how to install and configure the Novell IPX/IP gateway at the server and at the workstation.

## CHAPTER 5

Using HTML to Provide Dynamic Novell Web Server Content

Previous chapters discuss how to install and configure the Novell Web Server. The next step in making the Web server operational is to use the Web server to provide *content*. The word "content" when used with a Web server refers to the document/graphic/audio/video media that will be seen by users accessing Web browser client software. You can use any Web browser to view the documents provided by the Web server, although the preferred Web browser is Netscape Navigator (which is bundled with IntranetWare).

The language used to describe document content is called Hypertext Markup Language (HTML). The documents that are encoded in this language are called HTML documents. One of the functions of the Web browser is to take the HTML description of a document and render it as a series of graphic images. Consequently, understanding how to encode a document with HTML is important if you want to publish documents and data using the Web media.

Using HTML: The Content Enabler

HTML is an implementation of the Standard Generalized Markup Language (SGML). The SGML standard, also designated as ISO-8879 by the International Standards Organization (ISO), provides a generalized method of specifying how to represent documents that have hyperlinks. A *hyperlink* is a phrase or sentence in a document that is highlighted in a special way so that, when it is selected, another document is displayed or a specified action is performed. Examples of actions to be performed when a hyperlink is selected are displaying an image, sending mail, soliciting information from the user by using a form, initiating a remote logon or file-transfer session, querying a database, executing a program, and so on. The documents containing hyperlinks are also called *hyperdocuments*.

The current HTML standard is HTML 3.2. Many browsers have begun to support this standard. The Novell Netscape Navigator is licensed from Netscape Communications and is the top browser on the market. It supports HTML 3.2 and a few other extensions. The discussion of HTML in this chapter is based on HTML 3.2.

Reading an HTML Document

A number of HTML editors and software (including Novell's InnerWeb Publisher) enable you to create HTML documents without understanding the details of HTML syntax. The latest versions of WordPerfect and MS Word allow you to convert word processor documents to HTML format. You can even convert scanned images to HTML format with software that is bundled with many scanners. Figure 5.1 shows how a WordPerfect document can be saved in an HTML format.

F I G U R E 5.1

Publishing to HTML using WordPerfect

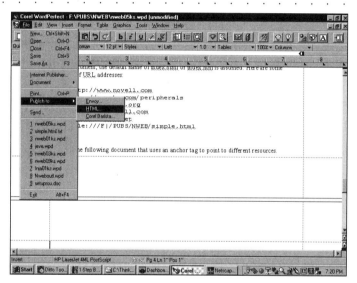

With all these different methods to help you create HTML documents, you might ask why you should bother learning the details and intricacies of HTML format. There are some very good reasons. Chief among them is that, if you want to create dynamic content, you must be able to write programs that alter the HTML document to be delivered to the Web browser. To write these programs, you must understand the basic structure and component elements of HTML documents. Another situation where knowledge of HTML comes in handy is when you are troubleshooting HTML documents that do not quite display the desired information, or when you are creating HTML documents that interact with the user.

You can learn to read HTML documents quickly by understanding some basic guidelines about how an HTML document is structured. All HTML documents contain tags that have the following structure:

```
<tag>
</tag>
```

The *tag* is a reference to special keywords that are used to describe the components of an HTML document. The end tag specifier *</tag>* ends the scope of the corresponding *<tag>*. Almost every HTML tag has a corresponding end tag specifier. For example, HTML documents begin and end with the following specifiers:

```
<HTML>

   The different elements of the HTML document go between
   these tags.

</HTML>
```

Between the <HTML> and </HTML> tags, you specify the head and body of the HTML document. The head is specified using the <HEAD> and </HEAD> tags. The body of the HTML is specified by the <BODY> and </BODY> tags.

```
<HTML>
<HEAD> The Head goes over here </HEAD>
<BODY> The Body goes here </BODY>
</HTML>
```

Blank lines and newlines placed between tags are not significant. For example, the previous HTML syntax can be written as follows:

```
<HTML><HEAD> The Head goes over here </HEAD><BODY> The Body
goes here </BODY></HTML>
```

Blank lines and newlines are generally added to improve readability of the HTML document. Also, tags are case-insensitive. This means that <HTML> is the same as <html> or <Html>. If you want to break a paragraph of text, or add a blank line that will appear in the rendering of the HTML document by the Web browser, you must add special HTML tags. Later in this chapter you learn how to do this.

Within the head section, you define the title of the HTML document. The title is defined by the tags <TITLE> and </TITLE>. The text in the title tags is displayed at the title area of the browser:

```
<HTML>
<HEAD>
  <TITLE>
        My first simple HTML page!
  </TITLE>
</HEAD>
<BODY> The Body goes here </BODY>
</HTML>
```

Figure 5.2 shows how this simple HTML document (file `simple.html`) is rendered in a Web browser. Notice that the title "My first simple HTML page!" is displayed at the top of the browser and the main display area just contains the text within the body tags. HTML documents can be any valid filename on the system, and are created using an extension of .HTML or .HTM.

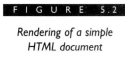

F I G U R E   5.2

*Rendering of a simple
HTML document*

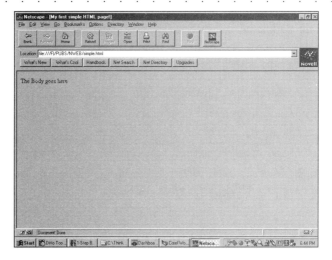

Creating URL Addresses and Hyperlinks

To create a hyperlink, use the following anchor tag:

```
<A HREF= URLaddress otherparameters> hyperlink text </A>
```

The anchor tag can have a number of parameters indicated by *otherparameters* that modify the behavior of the anchor tag. Typically, you have the HREF parameter that is set to a URL address. Remember, a URL address is a standard way of specifying a resource or location on the Internet and has the following general syntax:

```
protocol://hostname/pathname
```

The *protocol* can be any of the protocols used on the Internet (such as `http`, `ftp`, `telnet`, `gopher`, `file`, and so on) that is used to access the resource. If you were specifying an HTML document on another host computer, you would specify `http` (Hypetext Transfer Protocol) that is used to fetch an HTML document. If you were accessing a document using file transfer, you would specify the `ftp` protocol. If you were accessing a local file on the same computer on which you are running the Web browser, you would specify the `file` protocol.

The *hostname* is the IP address or DNS of the host on which the resource is located. DNS names are symbolic names for computers on the Internet or intranet. For example the name of the Web host for Novell is `www.novell.com`.

The *pathname* is the directory plus filename of the document/file that is being accessed. The *pathname* may be case sensitive if the Web server runs on a UNIX host. The *pathname* is optional. If not specified, for an HTML document, the default name of `index.html` or `index.htm` is assumed. The following are some examples of URL addresses:

```
http://www.novell.com
http://www.hp.com/peripherals
http://www.tsl.org
ftp://ftp.novell.com
telnet://usa.net
file:///F|/PUBS/NWEB/simple.html
```

Using Anchor Tags and Item Lists

Consider the following HTML document that uses an anchor tag to point to different resources. Note that comments can be embedded in an HTML document by using *<!- comment>*.

```
<HTML>
<HEAD><TITLE>Anchor tags</TITLE></HEAD>
<BODY>
<!- This is a comment for HTML documents. Notice its
```

```
syntax.>
<!
<H1>Demonstration of the use of anchor tags</H1>
<p>Anchor tags can be used to create hyperlinks. Notice how
we began this paragraph with a paragraph tag. Paragraph tags
automatically format a paragraph of text for display. When
you end with a hard new line, a line break is generated to
separate the paragraph from any text that might follow.
<br> <!- The tag to the left creates a line break. You go
to a new line>
Actually Anchor tags have many different parameters, but we
will consider only the simple ones here.
<hr><!- This creates a horizontal line>
<p> Here are the anchor tags:
<p><A HREF=http://www.novell.com>Novell's Web server</A>
<p><A HREF=ftp://www.novell.com>Novell's FTP server</A>
<p><A HREF=telnet://usa.net>Logon to USA.NET</A>
<p><A HREF=mailto:tslinfo@tsl.org>Mail us</A>
</BODY>
</HTML>
```

Figure 5.3 shows how the previous HTML code (file anchor.html) is rendered
by a Web browser. By studying the HTML code and its actual appearance in a Web
browser, you can better understand the different elements of HTML.

In the previous HTML document, the paragraph tag <p> was used to put the
different anchors on separate lines. HTML provides an ordered or unordered list
to represent items on separate lines. The *ordered list* numbers each list item and the
unordered list places a bullet before each list item. The syntax of using these lists is
as follows:

```
<!- Ordered list>
<OL>
  <LI> List item1
  <LI> List item2
       :
  <LI> List itemN
```

```
</OL>
<!- Unordered list>
<UL>
  <LI> List item1
  <LI> List item2
        :
  <LI> List itemN
</UL>
```

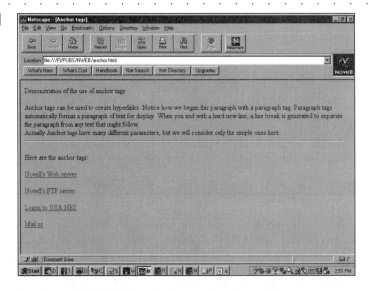

FIGURE 5.3

Use of anchors in HTML documents

The following shows the HTML code for putting the anchor tags as a numbered list. Notice that two additional anchor tags are defined. The HREF parameter contains the string preceded with the "#" character. This location refers to a position defined by an anchor tag in the same document. The location to jump to has an anchor tag that has the NAME parameter whose value is the same as the HREF value without the "#" character:

```
<HTML>
<HEAD><TITLE>Anchor tags</TITLE></HEAD>
<BODY>
<!- This is a comment for HTML documents. Notice its
```

```
syntax.>
<!
<H1>Demonstration of the use of anchor tags</H1>
<p>Anchor tags can be used to create hyperlinks. Notice how
we began this paragraph with a
paragraph tag. Paragraph tags automatically format a
paragraph of text for display. When you end
with a hard new line, a line break is generated to separate
the paragraph from any text that might
follow.
<br> <!- The tag to the left creates a line break. You go
to a new line>
Actually Anchor tags have many different parameters, but we
will consider only the simple ones
here.
<hr><!- This creates a horizontal line>
<p> Here are the anchor tags:
<B><!- Make things bold until /B>
<OL><!- Begin Ordered List>
<LI><A HREF=http://www.novell.com>Novell's Web server</A>
<LI><A HREF=ftp://www.novell.com>Novell's FTP server</A>
<LI><A HREF=telnet://usa.net>Logon to USA.NET</A>
<!- Next two Anchors cause jump to named location in current
document>
<LI><A HREF="#Heading1">Heading 1</A>
<LI><A HREF="#Heading2">Heading 2</A>
</OL><!- End Ordered List>
</B><!- End bold>
<hr>
<!- Heading levels can be from H1 to H6>
<A NAME="Heading1"><H2>Heading1 topic</H2></A>
<A NAME="Heading2"><H2>Heading2 topic</H2></A>
</BODY>
</HTML>
```

Figure 5.4 shows the rendering of the previous HTML code (file `anchor2.html`) in a Web browser. You may also notice the use of the <B> and </B> tags to display text in bold. Similarly, the <I> and </I> tags are used to display text as italics. You can also use up to six levels of headings (<H1> to <H6>) to display headings in different sizes.

F I G U R E 5.4

Ordered List anchor tags

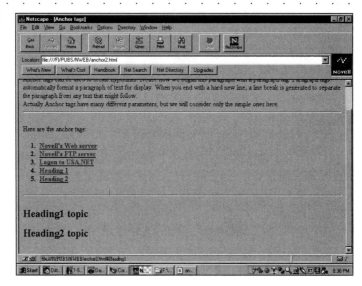

Figure 5.5 shows the same document with the ordered list replaced by the unordered list tags (file `anchor3.html`). The code for the unordered list tags is as follows:

```
<HTML>
<HEAD><TITLE>Anchor tags</TITLE></HEAD>
<BODY>
<!- This is a comment for HTML documents. Notice its
syntax.>
<!
<H1>Demonstration of the use of anchor tags</H1>
<p>Anchor tags can be used to create hyperlinks. Notice how
```

```
we began this paragraph with a
paragraph tag. Paragraph tags automatically format a
paragraph of text for display. When you end
with a hard new line, a line break is generated to separate
the paragraph from any text that might
follow.
<br> <!- The tag to the left creates a line break. You go
to a new line>
Actually Anchor tags have many different parameters, but we
will consider only the simple ones
here.
<hr><!- This creates a horizontal line>
<p> Here are the anchor tags:
<B><!- Make things bold until /B>
<UL><!- Begin Unordered List>
<LI><A HREF=http://www.novell.com>Novell's Web server</A>
<LI><A HREF=ftp://www.novell.com>Novell's FTP server</A>
<LI><A HREF=telnet://usa.net>Logon to USA.NET</A>
<!- Next two Anchors cause jump to named location in current
document>
<LI><A HREF="#Heading1">Heading 1</A>
<LI><A HREF="#Heading2">Heading 2</A>
</UL><!- End Unordered List>
</B><!- End bold>
<hr>
<!- Heading levels can be from H1 to H6>
<A NAME="Heading1"><H2>Heading1 topic</H2></A>
<A NAME="Heading2"><H2>Heading2 topic</H2></A>
</BODY>
</HTML>
```

FIGURE   5.5

Unordered List anchor tags

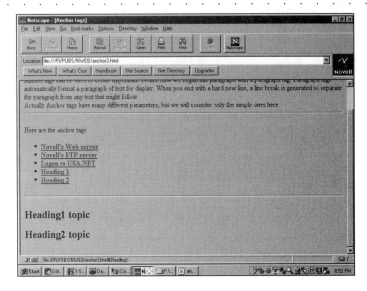

Using Style Tags

Sometimes you may want to use a special style for the text rather than have the Web browser render the HTML document using its own default styles. For example, you may want to emphasize a certain text region so that it stands out from the background text, or quote references, or use a monospaced font. The common HTML style tags are listed in Table 5.1. The bold, italics underline, Times Roman, and Helvetica tags are used for more precise control over the style of the text.

TABLE 5.1	TAG	DESCRIPTION
Common Style Tags	<STRONG></STRONG>	Strong style. This is commonly rendered as bold.
	<EM></EM>	Emphasis style. The text stands out from the background. Commonly rendered as underlined or italics text.
	<CITE></CITE>	Citation style. Used to cite titles and references within text.

TABLE 5.1	TAG	DESCRIPTION
Common Style Tags (continued)	<TT></TT>	Typewriter style. Monospaced font (every character has the same width). Commonly rendered as Courier.
	<ADDRESS></ADDRESS>	Used for address information, signatures of authors of the document, or for contact persons.
	<BLOCKQUOTE></BLOCKQUOTE>	Quoting segments of text.
	<PRE></PRE>	Treat text as preformatted text. Do not attempt to preformat. Accepts an optional WIDTH parameter that tells the Web browser the maximum line length, so that the browser can adjust margins and font to accommodate text.
	<CODE></CODE>	Used for coding samples of a computer language text. Typically rendered as monospaced font. Similar to <TT></TT>.
	<DFN></DFN>	Definition style. Typically used to define first instance of a new term or concept.
	<SAMP></SAMP>	Sample style. A sequence of literal characters.
	<STRIKE></STRIKE>	Strikethrough text. Typically used in legal documents to indicate strikethrough text.
		Subscript style. Lowers the text slightly.
		Superscript style. Raises the text slightly.
	<KBD></KBD>	Keyboard style. Typically the response of a user to be typed in exactly. This is used in instructional text.

(Continued)

TABLE 5.1	TAG	DESCRIPTION
Common Style Tags (continued)	<VAR></VAR>	Variable style. Typically the name of variable/value to be supplied by the user in instructional text.
	<TR></TR>	Times Roman style.
	<HV></HV>	Helvetica style.
	<B></B>	Makes text bold.
	<I></I>	Makes text italics.
	<U></U>	Makes text underlined.

Figures 5.6 to 5.10 show the rendering of the styles using the Novell Netscape Navigator. The HTML code shown in Listing 5.1 (file `styles.html`) was used to produce these figures:

LISTING 5.1

styles.html Code

```
<HTML>
<HEAD><TITLE>Styles demonstration</TITLE><HEAD>
<BODY>
<h1>HTML Style Examples</h1>
<h4>&ltSTRONG&gt&lt/STRONG&gt</h4>
<p><STRONG>Strong style. This is commonly rendered as
bold.</STRONG>
<h4>&ltEM&gt&lt/EM&gt</h4>
<p><EM>Emphasis style. The text stands out from the
background. Commonly rendered as underlined or italics
text.</EM>
<h4>&ltCITE&gt&lt/CITE&gt</h4>
<p><CITE>Citation style. Used to cite titles and references
within text.</CITE>
<h4>&ltTT&gt&lt/TT&gt</h4>
<p><TT>Typewriter style. Monospaced font -- every character
has the same width. Commonly rendered as courier.</TT>
<h4>&ltADDRESS&gt&lt/ADDRESS&gt</h4>
```

<p><ADDRESS>Used for address information, signatures of authors of the document or for contact persons.</ADDRESS>
<h4>&ltBLOCKQUOTE&gt&lt/BLOCKQUOTE&gt</h4>
<p><BLOCKQUOTE>When Rama noticed his arrows falling down ineffectively while the trident sailed towards him, for a moment he lost heart. When it came quite near, he uttered a certain mantra from the depth of his being and while he was breathing out that incantation, an esoteric syllable in perfect timing, the trident collapsed. Ravana, who had been so intent on vanquishing Rama with his trident, was astonished to see it fall down within an inch of him, and for a minute wondered if his adversary might not after all be a divine being although he looked like a mortal. Ravana thought to himself, "This is, perhaps, the highest God. Who can it be? Not Shiva, for Shiva is my supporter; he could not be Brahma, who is four faced; could not be Vishnu, because of my immunity from the weapons of the whole trinity. Perhaps this man is the primordial being, the cause behind the whole universe. But whoever he may be, I will not stop my fight until I defeat and crush him or at least take him as a prisoner.
<PRE>

Ramayana
</PRE>
 </BLOCKQUOTE>
<h4>&ltPRE&gt&lt/PRE&gt</h4>
<p><PRE>Treat text as preformatted text. Do not attempt to preformat.
Accepts an optional WIDTH parameter that tells the web browser the maximum line length so that the browser can adjust margins and font to accomodate text.
  @ @
   |
    \===/

```
</PRE>
<h4>&ltCODE&gt&lt/CODE&gt</h4>
<p><CODE>Used for coding samples of a computer language
text. Typically rendered as monospaced font. Similiar to
&ltTT&gt&lt/TT&gt.</CODE>
<h4>&ltDFN&gt&lt/DFN&gt</h4>
<p><DFN>Definition style. Typically used to define first
instance of a new term or concept.</DFN>
<h4>&ltSAMP&gt&lt/SAMP&gt</h4>
<p><SAMP>Sample style. A sequence of literal
characters.</SAMP>
<h4>&ltSTRIKE&gt&lt/STRIKE&gt</h4>
<p><STRIKE>Strike-out text. Typically used in legal
documents to indicate strike-out text.</STRIKE>
<h4>&ltSUB&gt&lt/SUB&gt</h4>
<p>Regular Text<SUB>Subscript style. Lowers the text
slightly</SUB>
<h4>&ltSUP&gt&lt/SUP&gt</h4>
<p>Regular Text<SUP>Superscript style. Raises the text
slightly.</SUP>
<h4>&ltKBD&gt&lt/KBD&gt</h4>
<p><KBD>Keyboard style. Typically the response of a user to
be typed in exactly. This is used  in instructional
text.</KBD>
<h4>&ltVAR&gt&lt/VAR&gt</h4>
<p><VAR>Variable style. Typically the name of variable/value
to be supplied by the user in instructional text.</VAR>
<h4>&ltTR&gt&lt/TR&gt</h4>
<p><TR>Times roman style.</TR>
<h4>&ltHV&gt&lt/HV&gt</h4>
<p><HV>Helvetica style.</HV>
<h4>&ltB&gt&lt/B&gt</h4>
<p><B>Makes text bold</B>
<h4>&ltI&gt&lt/I&gt</h4>
```

```
<p><I>Makes text italics.</I>
</BODY></HTML>
```

F I G U R E   5.6

Rendering HTML style codes with Novell Netscape Navigator — Screen 1

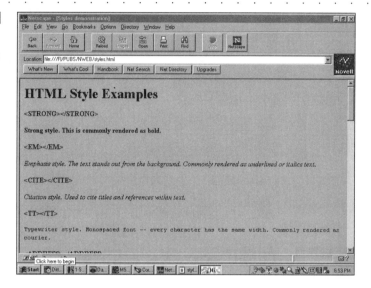

F I G U R E   5.7

Rendering HTML style codes with Novell Netscape Navigator — Screen 2

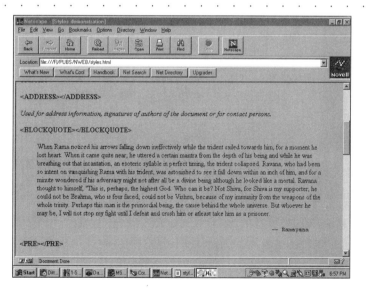

*Rendering HTML style
codes with Novell Netscape
Navigator — Screen 3*

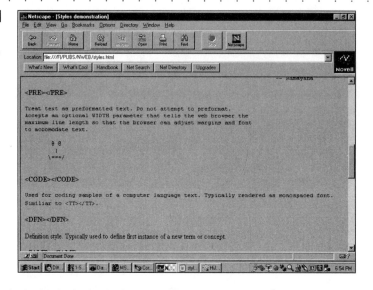

*Rendering HTML style
codes with Novell Netscape
Navigator — Screen 4*

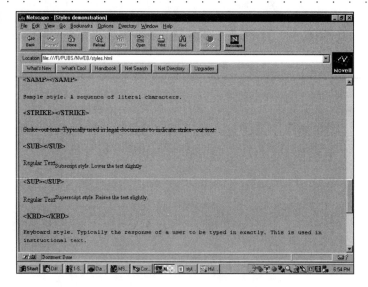

Rendering HTML style codes with Novell Netscape Navigator — Screen 5

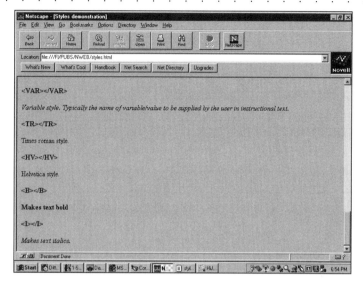

As you examine Listing 5.1, notice the use of the special character sequences &lt and &gt, which represent the characters "<" and ">," respectively. HTML provides character entities for groups of characters that have special meaning in HTML. Some of the other character entities are &amp for "&," &quot for "," and   for a nonbreaking space. There are special character entities for the ISO Latin-1 alphabet (which includes characters with accent marks).

Embedding Images in HTML

Today, a Web page without a picture is considered very unusual. Most Web pages have at least a few icon images that make the page attractive visually. The image tag <IMG> is used to specify an in-line image. The <IMG> tag does not have a corresponding end tag. This is an example of an *empty tag* (which does not have a corresponding end tag). The information about the image is specified by parameters/attributes for the image tag. The syntax of the image tag is as follows:

```
<IMG SRC=source [ALIGN=alignvalue] [ALT=altvalue]
[ISMAP=ismapvalue]>
```

The SRC attribute must be specified—it is mandatory. The value of the SRC attribute, *source*, is the URL address of the file containing the image to be embedded in the HTML page. The attributes ALIGN, ALT, ISMAP are optional.

The ALIGN attribute specifies how the image should be aligned with respect to the surrounding text. It can have a value of TOP, MIDDLE or BOTTOM.

The ALT attribute specifies a text string that should be displayed in case the Web browser is not able to draw the graphic image. The text string is displayed as an alternative to displaying the image.

The ISMAP attribute is an interactive graphic image map. When the graphic image map is selected in a browser, the current cursor coordinates are sent to the Web server. The image tag that has the ISMAP attribute is enclosed in an anchor tag whose HREF attribute points to the script or to program on the server that is to be run. This script or program reads the cursor coordinates sent to the server and maps it to the appropriate URL resource.

Figure 5.11 shows a simple image map Web page and the following is the HTML code (file `image1.html`) that was used to generate this Web page:

```
<html>
<head>
<title>Images Demo</title>
</head>
<body>
<img src="file:///F|/PUBS/NWEB/sky1.gif" align=bottom>Montana
is the state of big blue skys. As far as the eye can see
you see beautiful blue skys that strech from horizon to
horizon. It is as if eternity is in your grasp and in the
blue skys you see a glimpse of the divine...
<hr>
<A HREF="http://www.tsl.org/index.html"><img
src=file:///F|/PUBS/NWEB/water.gif align=middle>
Need more information on clean fresh water lakes?</A>
</body>
</html>
```

FIGURE 5.11

Simple image map

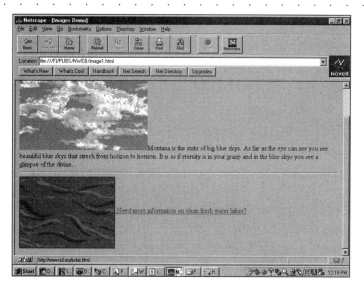

Note that the first image map simply displays the image. However, the second image map is embedded inside an anchor tag. When you click this image, the URL code in the HREF parameter of the enclosing anchor tag is executed. You may also notice that the image references are to local files where the Web browser is running.

In general, the location is the URL address of any resource on the Internet. It may be helpful to understand the peculiar syntax of the local filename such as the file:///F|/PUBS/NWEB/sky1.gif. The file:// is the standard URL protocol prefix. The filename is /F|/NWEB/sky1.gif. The vertical bar represents the colon (:) character for the drive letter F:.

In addition to graphic images in the GIF format, you can also use JPEG images, IBM image format (XIBM), or Macintosh image format (PICT). GIF and JPEG images are the most popular image format for Web documents because they are supported by a number of Web browsers.

Creating Directories and Glossaries

In some of the earlier examples of HTML documents, you saw the use of the unnumbered list and the numbered list. Another type of list that is useful is a *directory*. A directory is a list of short items that are to be displayed. The <DIR> and </DIR> tags are used to create the directory list.

Often you need to define a list of terms such as in a glossary at the end of a book or chapter. HTML provides special tags for creating a *glossary list*. A glossary is often called a *definition list*. Each item in the definition list consists of a *term* and a corresponding *definition*. The term is short text and the definition usually runs into several lines of text. If the definition consists of more than one line, the text is wrapped to the next line and aligned underneath the beginning of the previous line of text. The term occurs on its own separate line, and the definition is indented to the right of the term. Blank lines may be inserted between term and definition pairs, depending on your Web browser.

The definition list is created by using the definition list tag <DL> and </DL> as follows:

```
<DL>
   List of definitions
</DL>
```

Each definition term is defined by the empty tag <DT>. Recall that empty tags do not have a corresponding end tag:

```
<DT> term
```

Immediately following the definition tag <DT> is the actual definition. The definition is defined by the empty tag <DD>. Following the <DD> tag, you can have several lines of text. These text lines are properly formatted by the Web browser, so you do not have to enter the lines in a specific format:

```
<DD> line1
line2
line3
   :
lineN
```

Figure 5.12 shows a portion of a glossary and the following shows the HTML code (file `glossary.html`) that was used to produce this glossary:

```
<html>
<head>
<title>Glossary example</title>
</head>
<body>
<DL>
<DT>Angel
<DD>Divine spirit, herald, forerunner; messenger sent by God
to deliver his Word to his children. Ministering spirits
sent forth to comfort, protect, guide and strengthen, teach,
counsel, and warn.
<DT>Anthkarana
<DD> Sanskrit for internal sense organ. The web of life. The
network of light spanning the spirit matter cosmos that
connects and sensitizes the whole of creation within itself
and the heart of God.
<DT>Archangel
<DD>Hierarch of the angelic hosts; the highest rank in the
order of the angels. Each of the seven rays of God has a
presiding Archangel who, with his divine complement, an
Archeia, embodies the God consciousness of the ray and
directs the band of angels serving in their command on
that ray.
</DL>
</body>
</html>
```

▶ . . . . ◀

FIGURE 5.12

Glossary using HTML

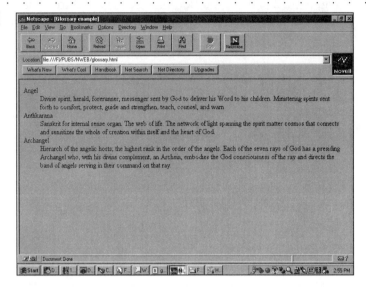

Creating Tables

One of the nicer features of HTML 3.0 is the ability to format and display information in the form of tables. A *table* is defined by the table tags <TABLE> and </TABLE> and can be used to display columnar data as follows:

```
<TABLE attributes>
  table definition
</TABLE>
```

An example of the attributes can be BORDER. This attribute determines if the entire table is enclosed in a border. If absent, the table is drawn without a border.

Tables have *columns* of headings and each heading has *rows* of data. HTML defines the row tag <TR> and </TR> that can be used to define a row. You can use the row tags to describe the column headings as well as the rows:

```
<TR>
  row definition
</TR>
```

Using the table and row tags you can define a table:

```
<TABLE>
<TR>
```

```
    column headings
</TR>
<TR>
    row definition 1
</TR>
<TR>
    row definition 2
</TR>
        :
<TR>
    row definition N
</TR>
</TABLE>
```

A table row consists of a series of cells. Each cell is defined using the table data tags <TD> and </TD>. Thus, each row definition in the previous table syntax is defined as follows:

```
<TR>
    <TD>data</TD><TD>data</TD> ... <TD>data</TD>
</TR>
```

Figure 5.13 shows an example of a simple table. The HTML code (file table_1.html) used to produce this Web page is as follows:

```
<html>
<head>
<title>
Simple tables
</title
</head>
<body>
<p>Table with border
<table border>
<tr> <!- Row 1>
    <td>Column 1</td><td>Column 2</td><td>Column 3</td>
```

```
</tr>
<tr> <!- Row 2>
  <td>data11</td><td>data12</td><td>data13</td>
</tr>
<tr> <!- Row 3>
  <td>data21</td><td>data22</td><td>data23</td>
</tr>
<tr> <!- Row 4>
  <td>data31</td><td>data32</td><td>data33</td>
</tr>
</table>
<hr>
<p>Table without border
<table>
<tr> <!- Row 1>
  <td>Column 1</td><td>Column 2</td><td>Column 3</td>
</tr>
<tr> <!- Row 2>
  <td>data11</td><td>data12</td><td>data13</td>
</tr>
<tr> <!- Row 3>
  <td>data21</td><td>data22</td><td>data23</td>
</tr>
<tr> <!- Row 4>
  <td>data31</td><td>data32</td><td>data33</td>
</tr>
</table>
</body>
</html>
```

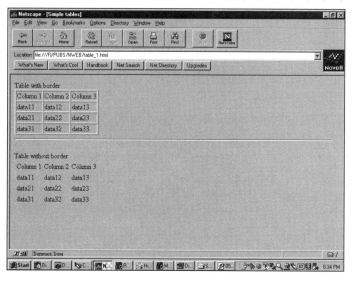

FIGURE 5.13

Simple HTML table

As you examine Figure 5.13 and the previous HTML code, notice that without the BORDER attribute in the table tag, the second table appears rather plain. Many HTML browsers permit you to treat the <TR> and <TD> tags as empty tags (that is, you can leave out the corresponding end tags). Leaving out the end tags can help simplify the writing of HTML code. Therefore, the Web page in Figure 5.13 can be produced by the following simplified HTML code (file `table_2.html`):

```
<html>
<head>
<title>
Simple tables 2
</title>
</head>
<body>
<p>Table with border
<table border>
<tr> <td>Column 1<td>Column 2<td>Column 3
<tr> <td>data11<td>data12<td>data13
```

```
<tr> <td>data21<td>data22<td>data23
<tr> <td>data31<td>data32<td>data33
</table>
<hr>
<p>Table without border
<table>
<tr> <td>Column 1<td>Column 2<td>Column 3
<tr> <td>data11<td>data12<td>data13
<tr> <td>data21<td>data22<td>data23
<tr> <td>data31<td>data32<td>data33
</table>
</body>
</html>
```

Notice that in the previous HTML listing, the end tags </tr> and </td> are eliminated and this results in less data input.

What if the rows in a table do not have the same number of cells? In this case, the rows that have fewer cells are padded to the right, as shown by the following HTML listing (file `table_3.html`) and the Web page shown in Figure 5.14:

```
<html>
<head>
<title>
Simple tables 2
</title
</head>
<body>
<p>Table with border
<table border>
<tr> <td>Column 1<td>Column 2<td>Column 3
<tr> <td>data11<td>data12<td>data13<td>data14
<tr> <td>data21<td>data22<td>data23
<tr> <td>data31<td>data32
</table>
<hr>
```

```
<p>Table without border
<table>
<tr> <td>Column 1<td>Column 2<td>Column 3
<tr> <td>data11<td>data12<td>data13<td>data14
<tr> <td>data21<td>data22<td>data23
<tr> <td>data31<td>data32
</table>
</body>
</html>
```

FIGURE 5.14

Unequal cells in rows

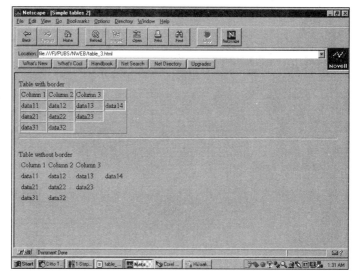

In certain situations, you may want the cell in a table to span multiple rows or column boundaries. Consider the example in Figure 5.15 and the corresponding HTML code (file `table_4.html`) shown here:

```
<html>
<head>
<title>
ROWSPAN attribute
</title
```

```
</head>
<body>
<h2>Table with different row size cells - Example 1</h2>
<table border>
<tr> <td>Column 1<td>Column 2<td>Column 3<td>Column4
<tr> <td rowspan=2>data11<td>data12<td>data13<td>data14
<tr> <td>data21<td rowspan=3>data22<td>data23
<tr> <td>data31<td>data32<td>data33
</table>
<hr>
<h2>Table with different row size cells - Example 2</h2>
<table border>
<tr> <td><b><i>Column 1</b></i><td><b><i>Column
2</b></i><td><b><i>Column 3</b></i>
      <td><b><i>Column 4</b></i><td><b><i>Column 5</b></i>
<tr> <td>data11<td>data12<td>data13<td
rowspan=3>data14<td>data15
<tr> <td rowspan=2>data21<td
rowspan=3>data22<td>data23<td>data33
<tr> <td>data31<td>data32
<tr> <td>data41<td>data42<td>data43<td>data44
</table>
</body>
</html>
```

Example 1 in Figure 5.15 shows the table cells spanning two rows in Column 1 and Column 3. Because the cell spans an additional row, the data that would normally be in a cell position is moved to the next cell position to the right. Therefore, in Example 1, you can see that data cells *data13* and *data33* are both moved to the next column to the right. Example 2 of Figure 5.15 is similar to the first example, except that some of the table cells span up to three rows. There is no limit to the number of rows spanned by a cell.

▸ • ◂

FIGURE 5.15

Cells with different row spans

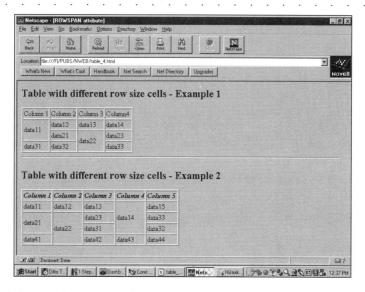

The COLSPAN attribute is similar to the ROWSPAN attribute except that you span columns instead of rows. You can also combine the COLSPAN attribute with the ROWSPAN attribute in defining a data cell. Figure 5.16 shows an example of a Web page that uses the COLSPAN attribute. The HTML code (file `table_5.html`) that produced the Web page in Figure 5.16 is as follows:

```
<html>
<head>
<title>
COLSPAN & ROWSPAN attribute
</title>
</head>
<body>
<h2>Table with different column size cells - Example 1</h2>
<table border>
<tr> <td>Column 1<td>Column 2<td>Column 3<td>Column4
<tr> <td colspan=2>data11<td>data12<td>data13<td>data14
<tr> <td>data21<td colspan=3>data22<td>data23
```

```
<tr> <td>data31<td>data32<td>data33
</table>
<hr>
<h2>Table with different row and column size cells - Example
2</h2>
<table border>
<tr> <td><b><i>Column 1</b></i><td><b><i>Column
2</b></i><td><b><i>Column 3</b></i>
      <td><b><i>Column 4</b></i><td><b><i>Column 5</b></i>
<tr> <td>data11<td>data12<td>data13<td
colspan=3>data14<td>data15
<tr> <td colspan=2 rowspan=2>data21<td colspan=3
rowspan=2>data22<td>data23<td>data33
<tr> <td>data31<td>data32
<tr> <td>data41<td>data42<td>data43<td>data44
</table>
</body>
</html>
```

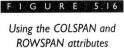

F I G U R E   5.16

*Using the COLSPAN and
ROWSPAN attributes*

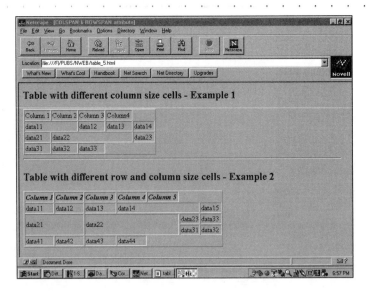

Example 1 in Figure 5.16 shows the table cells spanning multiple columns. Because the cell spans additional columns, the data that would normally be in a cell position is moved to the next cell position to the right. Therefore, in Example 1, you can see that data cells *data11* and *data22* span two and three columns, respectively. All the data cells that occur after *data11* in the same row are moved two positions to the right. Similarly, all the data cells that occur after *data22* in the same row are moved three positions to the right. Example 2 of Figure 5.15 is similar to the first example except that some of the table cells have both the COLSPAN and ROWSPAN attributes, and span several columns and rows.

In the examples that have been given so far, the *table caption* was provided by the header (<h4>) or *paragraph* (<p>) tags. HTML defines a separate tag called <CAPTION> ... </CAPTION> that is designed to create a *table title*. The syntax of the caption tag with its attributes is as follows:

```
<CAPTION ALIGN=alignvalue>
   caption text
</CAPTION>
```

The caption tag must occur inside a table tag because it pertains to tables only. The *alignvalue* can be TOP or BOTTOM. If the *alignvalue* is TOP, the caption is placed at the top of the table. If it is BOTTOM, the caption is placed at the bottom of the table. The default *alignvalue* is TOP. The caption text is centered relative to the table width.

Figure 5.17 shows examples that use captions with the TOP and BOTTOM attributes. The corresponding HTML code (file `table_6.html`) is listed next. Notice the manner of defining the caption for each table. In example 1, a default alignment of TOP is assumed, and, in Example 2, the caption is explicitly specified to be at the bottom.

```
<html>
<head>
<title>
COLSPAN & ROWSPAN attribute
</title
</head>
<body>
```

```
<table border>
<caption>Table with caption at the top - Example 1</caption>
<tr> <td>Column 1<td>Column 2<td>Column 3<td>Column4
<tr> <td colspan=2>data11<td>data12<td>data13<td>data14
<tr> <td>data21<td>data22<td>data23
<tr> <td>data31<td>data32<td colspan=2>data33
</table>
<hr><hr>
<table border>
<caption align=bottom><b><i>Table with caption at bottom -
Example 2</h2>
<tr> <td><b><i>Column 1</b></i><td><b><i>Column
2</b></i><td><b><i>Column 3</b></i>
       <td><b><i>Column 4</b></i><td><b><i>Column
5</b></i><td><b><i>Column 6</b></i>
<tr> <td
rowspan=4>data11<td>data12<td>data13<td>data14<td>data15<td>d
ata16
<tr> <td colspan=2
rowspan=3>data21<td>data22<td>data23<td>data33
<tr> <td colspan=2 rowspan=2>data31<td>data32
<tr> <td>data41
</table>
</body>
</html>
```

If you want to specify the data in a cell in boldface, you can use the <B> ... </B> tag for the text in each cell. What if, in addition to boldfacing the text, you wanted to center it also? HTML provides a special tag called the *table header* tag <TH> ... </TH> for this purpose. The text within the table header tag is in boldface and centered. The table header tag can be used in place of the table data tag <TD>. The table header tag is particularly useful for specifying column headings in bold.

Figure 5.18 shows a Web page that was created using the following HTML code (file `table_7.html`) that makes use of the <TH> tag:

```
<HTML>
<HEAD><TITLE>Table Header Demo</TITLE></HEAD>
<BODY>
<TABLE BORDER>
    <CAPTION>Table of Network Data</CAPTION>
    <TR><TH ROWSPAN=2>Network Segment<TH COLSPAN=2>Packets
Transmitted
        <TH ROWSPAN=2> <TH ROWSPAN=2>Efficiency
    <TR><TH>Input<TH>Output
    <TR><TH ALIGN=LEFT>Ethernet<TD>123<TD>455<TD><TD>54
    <TR><TH ALIGN=LEFT>Token Ring<TD>133<TD>755<TD><TD>97
    <TR><TH ALIGN=LEFT>FDDI<TD>423<TD>754<TD><TD>43
    <TR><TH ALIGN=LEFT>ATM<TD>443<TD>842<TD><TD>84
</TABLE>
</BODY>
</HTML>
```

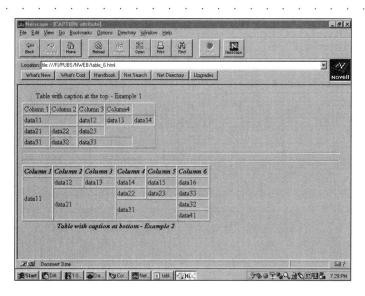

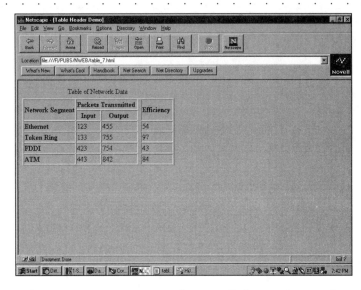

FIGURE 5.18

*Use of the Table Header
tag <TH>*

In the example in Figure 5.18, notice the use of the ALIGN attribute for the table header tag <TH>. The ALIGN attribute can be applied to a table row tag <TR>, table header tag <TH>, or a table data tag <TD>. The values of the ALIGN attribute can be LEFT, CENTER, and RIGHT. These indicate whether the data in a cell is to be left-justified, placed in the center, or right-justified. Another attribute that you can specify for the table row tag <TR>, table header tag <TH>, or a table data tag <TD> is the VALIGN attribute. This attribute performs the vertical alignment of the data in the cells, just as the ALIGN attribute performs the horizontal alignment. The values for the VALIGN attribute are TOP, MIDDLE, BOTTOM, and BASELINE. When the ALIGN and VALIGN attribute is applied to a table row <TR>, it applies to every cell in that row. Individual settings of the attribute in the data cells of a row override the settings in the corresponding table row tag. Figure 5.19 shows a Web page that was created using the following HTML code (file `table_8.html`) that makes use of the ALIGN and VALIGN attributes:

```
<HTML>
<HEAD><TITLE>Table Alignment Demo</TITLE></HEAD>
<BODY>
<TABLE BORDER>
```

```
<CAPTION>Table of Alignments</CAPTION>
<TR><TH><TH align=left>Heading Left<TH align=center>Heading
Center
    <TH align=right>Heading Right<TH align=right>Heading
Right
<TR><TH align=left>First Row
        <TD rowspan=3 valign=top>Top of data cell with
valign
      <TD rowspan=3 valign=middle>Middle of data cell with
valign
      <TD rowspan=3 valign=bottom>Bottom of data cell with
valign
      <TD rowspan=3 valign=baseline>Baseline of data cell
with valign
<TR><TH align=left>Second Row
<TR><TH align=left>Third Row
</TABLE>
</BODY>
</HTML>
```

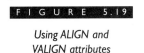

F I G U R E   5 . 1 9

*Using ALIGN and
VALIGN attributes*

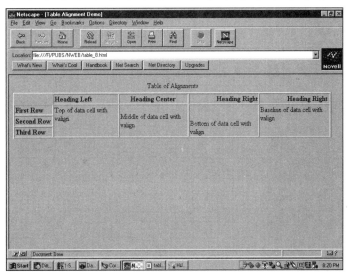

Notice in Figure 5.19 that the browser tries to fit all the columns on a single Web page and wraps any text data that is longer than the column width it uses for display. The default behavior is to perform wrapping of text in a data cell. If you do not want the browser to perform this default wrapping, you can specify the NOWRAP attribute for the table tags <TH> and <TD>. If you have specified NOWRAP, the table may not fit in the browser screen, and you may have to scroll to the right to see the entire table. Figure 5.19 shows the same Web page as in Figure 5.20 but with the NOWRAP attribute specified for the <TH> and <TD> parameters. The modified HTML code (file table_9.html) with NOWRAP attribute follows. Notice that the table does not fit on the browser screen and you must scroll to the right to see the entire table.

```
<HTML>
<HEAD><TITLE>Table Alignment with NOWRAP</TITLE></HEAD>
<BODY>
<TABLE BORDER>
<CAPTION>Table of Alignments</CAPTION>
<TR><TH><TH  NOWRAP align=left>Heading Left<TH
align=center>Heading Center
     <TH align=right>Heading Right<TH align=right>Heading
Right
<TR><TH align=left>First Row<TD NOWRAP rowspan=3
valign=top>Top of data cell with valign
        <TD NOWRAP rowspan=3 valign=middle>Middle of data
cell with valign
        <TD NOWRAP rowspan=3 valign=bottom>Bottom of data
cell with valign
        <TD NOWRAP rowspan=3 valign=baseline>Baseline of data
cell with valign
<TR><TH NOWRAP align=left>Second Row
<TR><TH NOWRAP align=left>Third Row
</TABLE>
</BODY>
</HTML>
```

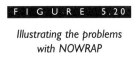

FIGURE 5.20

Illustrating the problems with NOWRAP

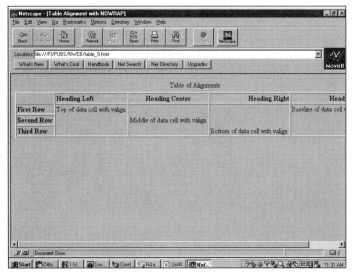

You may want to use NOWRAP if you want to take complete control over how the text is wrapped. With NOWRAP specified, you can do a "hard wrap" by using the line break tag (<BR>).

If you want your Web page to have a "newspaper look" that is multicolumnar you can do so by using the table tags with the default NOBORDER attribute. You must use the VALIGN attribute with the value set to TOP for the row of the cell. Define a data cell <TD> for each column of the newspaper article. Figure 5.21 illustrates a news article formatted using the table tags. The HTML code (file table_10.html) that produced the news article in Figure 5.21 is as follows:

```
<HTML>
<HEAD><TITLE>Newspaper article</TITLE></HEAD>
<BODY>
<h1>Flash News!</h1>
<TABLE> <!- Default is NOBORDER attribute>
<TR VALIGN="top">
<TD><CITE>July 7, 1999 - </CITE><FONT SIZE="+3">S</FONT>o on
this important
date it is time to take
perspective of how we have done since the Encyclical of
```

World Good Will was released.

The Encyclical was released by El Morya Khan and was based on long range studies on the state of the governments of the nation and the consciousness of

the people. The purpose of the Encyclical was to give a widespread knowledge and understanding of life and its purposes. It was

the hope that through the world wide application of the program some of the

major world problems could be solved.
</TD>
<TD>Here are those nine points: (1) International citizenship and responsibility.

(2) Individual expression through Essays of Integrity. (3) Universal Conscience

through Universal Participation in Current World Affairs. (4) United Faith through

United Action. (5) World Citizenship through Cultural Exchange Programs.

(6) Social Evils Attacked through Examination of Monetary Systems. (7) Speedy

adjustment of Civil Inequities through the Ombudsman. (8) Universal Equality

before the Law through the Ombudsman. (9) By word of Universal Good Will:

"I AM my Brother's Keeper".
</TD>
</TR>
</TABLE>
</BODY>
</HTML>

FIGURE 5.21

*News article formatted
using the table tags*

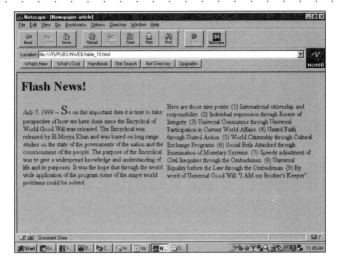

Understanding Static Versus Dynamic Content

In the HTML examples that have been discussed so far, the Web browser asks the Novell Web Server for an HTML document. The Web browser receives the HTML document and renders it on the graphic display for the Web browser (see Figure 5.22). The HTML document was prewritten on the Web server and does not change by the time it is delivered to the Web browser. These HTMLs are called *static* HTMLs and their content is called *static content.*

FIGURE 5.22

*Typical delivery of HTML
documents to a
Web browser*

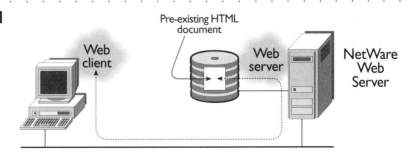

Another approach is to deliver a different HTML document depending on parameters such as the identification of the user requesting the HTML document, the time at which the Web browser accessed the HTML document, the domain name from which the Web browser requested the HTML document, the information supplied by the user, and so on. HTML documents that are transformed or generated dynamically as they are delivered to the Web browser are said to provide *dynamic content*. Typically, the dynamic HTML is created at the time the Web browser makes the request for the document. The Web server may request from the Web user information by using a special type of HTML form that enables the user to supply the requested information. Figure 5.23 shows a sample HTML form (file `form_1.html`). Notice the Send Form button in Figure 5.23 that is used to send the information entered in the form to the Web server.

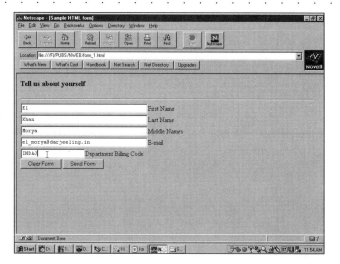

F I G U R E   5.23

Sample HTML form

Upon receiving the information supplied by the user, the Web server processes the information by running special programs. This special program may generate an HTML document to be sent to the user informing the user about whether the information supplied was accepted or not.

One way of providing dynamic content is to run special programs on the Web server that generate the dynamic HTML documents and data that is delivered to the Web browser. These special programs are run by using the Common Gateway Interface (CGI) and the programs themselves are called *CGI programs*. If the CGI programs are written in a scripting language such as Perl, NetBasic, Tcl/Tk,

Python, and so on, they are called *CGI scripts*. Later chapters discuss how to write CGI scripts in Perl, BASIC, and NetBasic.

Understanding the CGI Architecture

CGI is the interface between the Web server, the sources of data on the Web server (such as text files and SQL data) and the Web browser (see Figure 5.24). The typical action of the CGI is as follows:

1 • The user makes the request for an HTML document. The user may enter information interactively through an HTML form and send this back to the Web server.

2 • The Web server receives the information supplied by the user and passes this to a CGI program.

3 • The CGI program processes the information and sends the reply back to the server as an HTML document.

4 • The Web server passes the HTML document received from the CGI program to the Web browser.

▶ · ◀

F I G U R E   5.24

CGI Interface

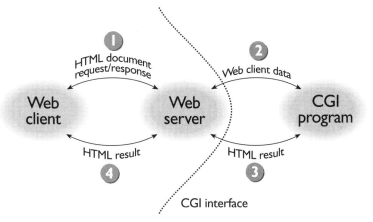

1 HTML document request/response

2 Web client data

Web client   **Web server**   **CGI program**

HTML result **4**   HTML result **3**

CGI interface

Creating Interactive Forms

A common way to obtain input from the user is the use of an HTML form. The HTML form is specified using the form tag <FORM> ... </FORM>, as follows:

```
<FORM attributes>
  form definition
</FORM>
```

The following are some common FORM attributes:

- ▸ ACTION—URL of CGI program

- ▸ METHOD—{GET | POST}

- ▸ ENCTYPE—application/x-www-form-urlencoded

The ACTION attribute specifies the URL address of a CGI program that is executed when the form data is sent to the Web server.

The METHOD attribute specifies the method of submitting the form data to the Web server. The two methods that are in use are the GET and POST methods.

If the GET method is used, the form data is sent to the CGI program as arguments and also in a special environment variable QUERY_STRING. The CGI program must obtain the user data either from the arguments passed to it, or from the QUERY_STRING variable. The GET method is the default method, which means that if the METHOD attribute is not specified, the GET method is assumed. However, the GET method is limited in terms of the amount of data it can safely pass to the Web server. Using the GET method, you are limited to an effective maximum of 255 characters, including any special characters that are used for the URL encoding of the data.

The POST method does not have the data limitation of the GET method, and can be used to transmit arbitrary amounts of data to the Web server. The POST method is the recommended method for transmitting form data to the Web server. The POST method receives its data from the standard input stream. The CGI program reads the form data as if it were reading data from the standard input device (usually the keyboard).

The ENCTYPE is the method used to encode the data. This encoding refers to MIME (Multipurpose Internet Mail Extension) encoding, which says that the data that follows should be treated as a stream of octets (bytes). Chapter 6 discusses MIME encoding.

The INPUT tag

A form consists of input fields that are described by the empty input tag <INPUT>.

```
<INPUT attributes>
```

Each input field in the form must have an input tag in the form definition. The attributes define the type of data to be input, default value of the input field, the size of the input field, the maximum amount of data that can be entered, the internal name of the input field, and so on.

The following are some common input *attributes*:

- ▶ TYPE—Type of data

- ▶ NAME—Internal variable name of field that is sent to the Web browser as `name=value` pairs

- ▶ VALUE—Default assigned value for the input field

- ▶ SRC—URL source for input field data

- ▶ SIZE—Size of input field to be displayed

- ▶ MAXLENGTH—Maximum length of input data

- ▶ ALIGN—Where to align accompanying text

The attributes that are used depend on the value of the TYPE attribute. Many different data types are defined for the input tag. The following are some of the commonly used data types:

- ▶ `text`

- ▶ `radio`

- ▶ `checkbox`

▶ textarea

▶ reset

▶ submit

The default input type is text. The input data is assumed to be text if the TYPE attribute is not specified.

A simple form definition

To make the ensuing discussion more concrete, consider a simple form definition where you want to ask the user to supply their mailing address. You would like the user to supply the following information:

```
Name: _____
Street1: _____
Street2: _____
City: _____
State/Province: _____
Postal Code: _____
Country: _____
E-mail: _____
```

The following a first attempt to define this form:

```
<html>
<head>
<title>Simple form 1</title>
</head>
<body>
<form>
<h3>Please supply this information to get on our mailing
list</h3>
<hr>
Name <input type="text" size=45 name="pname"><br>
Street1 <input type="text" size=45 name="street1"><br>
```

```
Street2 <input type="text" size=45 name="street2"><br>
City <input type="text" size=45 name="city"><br>
State/Province <input type="text" size=45
name="statepr"><br>
Postal Code <input type="text" size=30
name="postalcode"><br>
E-mail <input size=30 name="email"><br>
<br>
<input type="reset" value="Clear Form">
<input type="submit" value="Send Form">
</form>
</body>
</html>
```

Notice that the input types of the fields are text. For the "E-mail" field, no input type was specified, but it still defaults to text. type. The <br> tag is used between many of the fields to cause a line break. Without the line break, the input fields would be placed on the same line.

The last two input tags are of reset and submit, type respectively. The purpose of the reset type is to display a button that has the label of the value attribute "Clear Form." When the Clear Form button is selected, any user data entered is cleared and the user must enter the field values again. The purpose of the submit type is to display a button that has the label of the value attribute "Submit Form." When the Submit Form button is selected, any user data entered is sent to the Web browser.

This input form uses the default method GET to submit data to the Web browser. If the full display size of the fields are used, the total data sent to the Web browser will exceed 255 characters and, therefore, the GET method is not appropriate. It would be better to use the POST method, which does not have limits on form data sent to the browser.

You may also notice that the ACTION attribute for specifying the CGI program to handle the form data is not specified. The data sent to the Web browser will, therefore, not be processed. In a practical HTML form, you must specify the URL address of the CGI program that will be executed to process the form data. The following is an example of how you may specify such a form tag:

```
<FORM METHOD="POST" ACTION="http://www.kinetics.com/
cgi-bin/form1.pl">
```

The name of the CGI program that will be run is `http://www.kinetics.com/cgi-bin/form1.pl`.

Figure 5.25 shows how the form (file `form_2.html`) appears using the Novell Netscape Web browser. Notice that, though many of the input fields have the same length, they are actually not aligned, and so the appearance of the form is not so pleasing. The reason for this was that the names of the fields that are displayed are not of uniform length. You can add padding of blanks to the names of the fields so that the fields are aligned vertically, but a simpler method is to place the field labels *after* the input field.

F I G U R E   5.25

Simple form 1

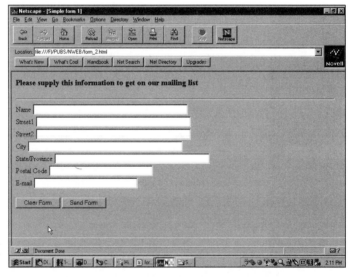

Figure 5.26 shows the appearance of this modified form. The HTML code (file `form_3.html`) used to produce this form is as follows:

```
<html>
<head>
```

```
<title>Simple form 2</title>
</head>
<body>
<form method="POST" action="http://www.tsl.org/mailst.pl">
<h3>Please supply this information to get on our mailing
list</h3>
<hr>
<input type="text" size=45 maxlength=80
name="pname">Name<br>
<input type="text" size=45 maxlength=80
name="street1">Street1<br>
<input type="text" size=45 maxlength=80
name="street2">Street2<br>
<input type="text" size=45 maxlength=80 name="city">City<br>
<input type="text" size=45 maxlength=80
name="statepr">State/Province<br>
<input type="text" size=30 maxlength=50
name="postalcode">Postal Code<br>
<input size=30 maxlength=50 name="email">E-mail<br>
<br>
<input type="reset" value="Clear Form">
<input type="submit" value="Send Form">
</form>
</body>
</html>
```

Notice that the POST method is used to send the data and a real URL address is specified for the CGI script that is to be run. Also, the maximum length of input data is specified for the fields.

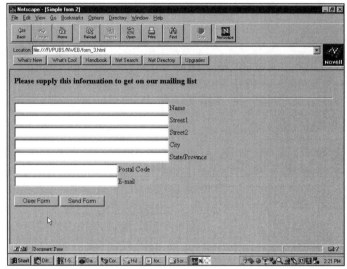

FIGURE 5.26

Simple form 2

Using other input data types

In the form examples so far, the main input data type that was used was the text type. The HTML form shown in Listing 5.2 (file form_4.html) illustrates the use of the other input data types such as checkbox, radio, optional selection, and textarea.

LISTING 5.2

form_4.html *code*

```
<html>
<html>
<head>
<title>A more complex form</title>
</head>
<body>
<h2>Please enter your travel profile information</h2>
<hr>
<form method="POST" action="http://www.tsl.org/tprofile.pl">
<input type="reset" value="Clear Form">
```

```
<hr>
<h3>Client Name</h3>
<input type="text" size=40 name="firstname">First Name<br>
<input type="text" size=40 name="lastname">Last Name<br>
<input type="text" size=40 name="phone">Phone<br>
<input type="text" size=40 name="fax">Fax<br>
<input type="text" size=40 name="email">E-mail<br>
<hr>
<h3>Frequent Flier Accounts</h3>
<input type="text" size=20 name="airline1" value="Delta">Air
Line
<input type="text" size=20 name="acct1">Account<br>
<input type="text" size=20 name="airline2"
value="United">Air Line
<input type="text" size=20 name="acct2">Account<br>
<input type="text" size=20 name="airline3"
value="American">Air Line
<input type="text" size=20 name="acct3">Account<br>
<input type="text" size=20 name="airline4" value="TWA">Air
Line
<input type="text" size=20 name="acct4">Account<br>
<input type="text" size=20 name="airline5" value="North
West">Air Line
<input type="text" size=20 name="acct5">Account<br>
<input type="text" size=20 name="airline6">Air Line
<input type="text" size=20 name="acct6">Account<br>
<hr>
<h3>Meal Preference</h3>
<input type="radio" name="meal"
value="Kosher">Kosher  
<input type="radio" name="meal" value="LVeg">Lacto-
Vegetarian  
<input type="radio" name="meal" value="Lowcal">Low
calories  
```

```
<input type="radio" name="meal" value="Lowsugar">Low
Sugar  
<input type="radio" name="meal" value="PVeg">Pure
Vegetarian  
<input type="radio" name="meal" value="Hindu">Hindu
<hr>
<h3>Seating Preference</h3>
<input type="radio" name="seat" value="aisle">Aisle
<input type="radio" name="seat" value="center">Center
<input type="radio" name="seat" value="window">Window
<hr>
<h3>Preferred times of departure</h3>
<input type="radio" name="departime" value="dc">dont care
<input type="radio" name="departime" value="5am-8am">5am-8am
<input type="radio" name="departime" value="8am-11am">8am-
11am
<input type="radio" name="departime" value="11am-1pm">11am-
1pm
<input type="radio" name="departime" value="1pm-4pm">1pm-4pm
<input type="radio" name="departime" value="4pm-7pm">4pm-7pm
<input type="radio" name="departime" value="7pm-12am">7pm-
12am
<hr>
<h3>Preferred times of arrival</h3>
<input type="radio" name="arrtime" value="dc">dont care
<input type="radio" name="arrtime" value="5am-8am">5am-8am
<input type="radio" name="arrtime" value="8am-11am">8am-11am
<input type="radio" name="arrtime" value="11am-1pm">11am-1pm
<input type="radio" name="arrtime" value="1pm-4pm">1pm-4pm
<input type="radio" name="arrtime" value="4pm-7pm">4pm-7pm
<input type="radio" name="arrtime" value="7pm-12am">7pm-12am
<hr>
<h3>Acceptable Airlines</h3>
<input type="checkbox" name="AnyAirline" value="dc">dont
```

```
care<br>
<input type="checkbox" name="prefDelta"
value="Delta">Delta<br>
<input type="checkbox" name="prefUnited"
value="United">United<br>
<input type="checkbox" name="prefAmerican"
value="American">American<br>
<input type="checkbox" name="prefNW" value="NW">North
West<br>
<hr>
<h3>Vacation Profile</h3>
<select name="vacation">
  <option> Hawaii
  <option> San Fancisco
  <option> Los Angeles
  <option> New Orleans
  <option> New York
  <option> Europe
  <option> Africa
  <option> India
  <option> Far East
  <option> Australia
</select> Vacation spot
<hr>
<h4>Other preferences</h4>
<textarea name="other" rows=5 cols=50></textarea><br>
<hr>
<input type="submit" value="Send Form">
</form>
<hr>
<address> Last updated March 15, 1997 by webmaster@xyz.org
</address>
</body>
</html>
```

The radio type input can have only one of several values. Therefore, for each of the radio button values you define the same value for the NAME attribute. You see this in all the examples of the use of radio button in the previous HTML code. The form data is URL-encoded and sent using *name=value* pairs. As an example, for the radio buttons dealing with meal preferences, only one of the following values is sent:

```
meal=Lowcal
meal=Lowsugar
meal=Pveg
meal=Hindu
```

Because of the absence of the <br> tag between the input tags for the radio button, the radio buttons are formatted on the same line. If you want the radio buttons to be on separate lines, you must use the line break <br> between them. There is normally only a single space between the radio buttons that are formatted on the single line. You can add an extra space by using the special character code   which stands for non-break space. You see the use of this in the example of the radio buttons for the meal preference.

Figures 5.27 to 5.31 show how the previous HTML form appears in the Novell Netscape Navigator. Several screens are shown because the form is too long to fit on a single screen. Figure 5.32 shows the options for the SELECT tag appear when selected. The SELECT tag uses the OPTION tag to define the list of options from which you can select. You can specify a SIZE attribute for the SELECT tag to specify the number of options that will be initially displayed (the default is a size of one).

The textarea input data type is used to get several lines of input from the user. You see the use of this in the section of the form titled "Other preferences." The ROWS and COLS attributes for the <INPUT TYPE="TEXTAREA ...> tag specify the size of the text area in rows and columns.

FIGURE 5.27

More complex HTML form — Screen 1

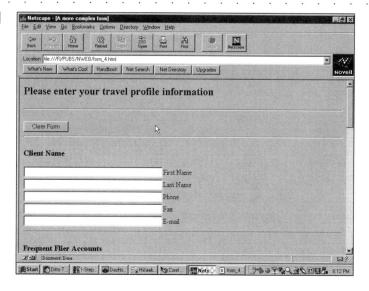

FIGURE 5.28

More complex HTML form — Screen 2

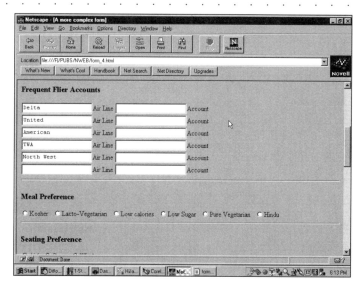

FIGURE 5.29

*More complex HTML
form — Screen 3*

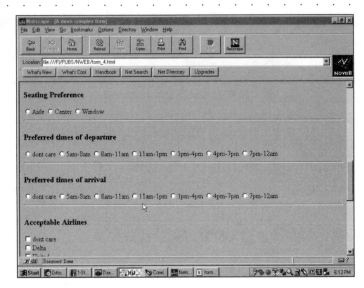

FIGURE 5.30

*More complex HTML
form — Screen 4*

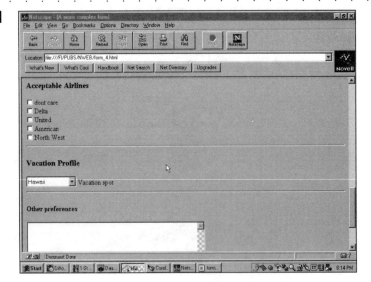

FIGURE 5.31

*More complex HTML
form — Screen 5*

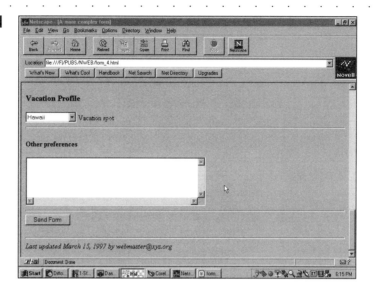

FIGURE 5.32

The SELECT tag options

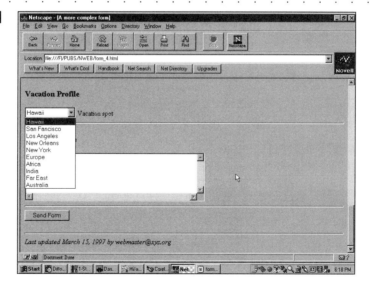

Setting Background Screen and Colors

You can set the background color and pattern of your HTML documents using additional attributes specified in the BODY tag.

The background color is set by specifying the BGCOLOR attribute in the BODY tag:

```
<BODY BGCOLOR="#RRGGBB" otherattributes>
```

The *RR*, *GG*, and *BB* are hexadecimal codes for the amount of red, green, and blue colors used to make up the color. These color values are commonly referred to as the *RGB values*. The two-digit hexadecimal codes have a value ranging from 00 to FF (decimal 255). The RGB combination can describe up to 16,777,216 colors (24-bit color value). A value of #000000 corresponds to an RGB value of (0, 0, 0)-the color white. And a value of "#FFFFFF" corresponds to an RGB value of (255, 255, 255)-the color black. Between these two extremes, you can have approximately 16 million colors. If you have the patience, you can try experimenting with all these values, or instead you can use Table 5.2 as a guide for some common color values for the background.

TABLE 5.2	#RRGGBB VALUE	MEANING
Common Values for the BGCOLOR Attribute	#000000	Black
	#0000FF	Blue
	#00FF00	Green
	#00FFFF	Cyan
	#FF0000	Red
	#FF00FF	Purple
	#FFFF00	Yellow
	#FFFFFF	White
	#000080	Dark blue
	#008000	Dark green
	#008080	Dark cyan
	#800000	Dark red
	#800080	Dark purple
	#808000	Brown (dark yellow)

TABLE 5.2	#RRGGBB VALUE	MEANING
Common Values for the BGCOLOR Attribute (continued)	#808080	Dark gray
	#A0A0A4	Medium gray
	#C0C0C0	Light gray

So, if you want a blue background, you could use the following:

```
<BODY BGCOLOR=#0000FF>
```

If you want a purple background, you would use the following:

```
<BODY BGCOLOR=#FF00FF>
```

Your monitor and display driver software may not be capable of displaying all 24-bit color values (16,777,216 colors) simultaneously. Instead, you may be limited to 256 colors. These 256 colors are your *palette* of colors. You will have to approximate the actual color that you want to one of the 256 colors. You can do this by picking a color from your palette that is closest to the desired color, leave out one of the RGB values, or use *dithering*. Dithering is used by most display software. In dithering, if you want a pixel color that is between two color values X and Y in your color palette, the display will pick two adjacent pixels, and set one to color X and the other to color Y. Because of the aggregating effect of the colors on your eyes, you will see a color that is approximately the target color. You may not always be pleased with the result, because the color will have a "grainy" appearance. For this reason, you should not try to set your color to a complex value, because displays with lower resolution will not be able to render the color exactly. Instead, try to stick to one of the standard colors.

Changing the background color may cause the text to disappear or to be shown in an unattractive color. You can change the text color (also called foreground color) by using the TEXT attribute in the BODY tag:

```
<BODY TEXT="#RRGGBB" otherattributes>
```

Again, the *RR*, *GG*, and *BB* are the hexadecimal codes for the amount of red, green, and blue colors used to make up the text color.

For example, you can use the following to have white text on a purple background:

```
<BODY TEXT="#FFFFFF" BGCOLOR="FF00FF">
```

As you change the text and background colors, you should pay attention to the hyperlink colors. The LINK attribute can be used to change the color of unvisited hyperlinks; the VLINK attribute can be used to change the color of visited hyperlinks; and the ALINK attribute can be used to change the color of an active link. An *active link* is one which the browser is trying to process. If you get impatient and try to select a link that you have already selected, but which the browser has not completed processing, the link will turn to the active link color (red on many browsers). The following is the syntax of the different link attributes:

```
<BODY LINK="#RRGGBB" VLINK="#RRGGBB" ALINK="#RRGGBB"
otherattributes>
```

The *RRGGBB* has the usual meaning of hexadecimal codes for red, green, and blue colors.

If you are not happy with the color attributes and would like to display a background pattern, you can use the BACKGROUND attribute to specify the URL of an image file:

```
<BODY BACKGROUND=urlOfImage  otherattributes>
```

If a background image is specified, the background color is not used. It is a good idea to specify the background color anyway, because many browsers will try to display the background color in case they are not able to display the background image. If the background color is not specified, changes to the text colors are ignored.

You can obtain background images at the following sites, or create your own:

```
http://home.netscape.com/assist/net_sites/bg/backgrounds.html
http://www.yahoo.com/Computers/World_Wide_Web/Browsers/
http://www.europa.com/~yyz/textures/textures.html
```

Summary

This chapter exposed you to the principles of creating Web content by using HTML. You can use the HTML language to create linked hypertext documents containing a variety of media types (such as text, graphics, audio, and video data). This chapter focused on using text and graphics data. Web browsers can support audio and video data if they can support it directly, or have been configured to use helper applications that take audio and video encoded data files and transform this to sound and images. This chapter has exposed you to the basics of practical HTML elements that you can start using to code your own HTML documents on the Novell Web Server. Chapter 9 discusses HTML extensions that enable you to launch Java applets from HTML pages. There are a variety of HTML authoring tools that are available (such as Soft Quad's HotMetal Pro, Net Object's Fusion, HotDog, and others). You can use the search engines on the Internet for the latest information on these and other tools.

## CHAPTER 6

CGI to the Novell Web Server

Chapter 5 discussed how HTML documents are created and how you can use HTML forms to solicit input from the user. This chapter builds on those concepts by providing information on how the form data is encoded and how CGI programs parse this data. It is important for you to know how form data is formatted to be sent, because you must write CGI programs to parse this data.

This chapter discusses the architecture of CGI programs and discusses the environment in which CGI programs are run. The details of writing CGI programs are covered in later chapters (when the scripting languages such as Perl and NetBasic are discussed in more detail).

Understanding HTTP as the Delivery Mechanism for HTML

The discussion in Chapter 5 showed the Web page content is encoded in HTML. However, the HTML documents are themselves transmitted using a special protocol called the Hypertext Transfer Protocol (HTTP). HTTP is actually an application-level protocol that runs on top of one of the standard communications protocols (such as TCP/IP or IPX). Figures 6.1 and 6.2 show that the HTTP protocol can run on top of TCP/IP or IPX. TCP/IP is the dominant protocol used to transmit HTML documents. However, in situations where you do not want to install a TCP/IP protocol stack at the workstation, you can use IPX as the communications transport. To accept HTTP requests encapsulated by the IPX protocol, the Novell Web Server must be configured with the IPX/IP gateway.

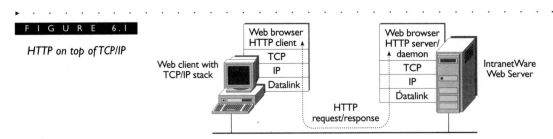

F I G U R E   6.1

HTTP on top of TCP/IP

When a Web browser requests an HTML document, a connection is established between the Web browser and the Web server. The underlying communications transport such as TCP/IP or IPX is used to establish the connection. If the TCP/IP protocol is being used as the transport, the connection is established on TCP port number 80 on the server (see Figure 6.3). You can specify other ports (such as TCP port number 8080), but the default port of 80 is reserved for HTTP.

▶ · ◀

F I G U R E 6.2

HTTP on top of IPX

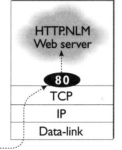

Web client without TCP/IP stack — Web browser / IPX / Data-link — IPX gateway — IPX / Data-link — Web Server HTTP server/daemon — Intranet Web server with gateway IPX/IP

▶ · ◀

F I G U R E 6.3

Establishing connection on TCP port 80 on the Web server

• Well-known TCP port number for TCP is 80

HTTP.NLM Web server

80
TCP
IP
Data-link

HTTP requests

If a nonstandard value is being used by the Web browser, the TCP port number must be specified as part of the URL address. The following is an example of a URL address requesting service from port 8080 of the Web server:

```
http://www.someorg.com:8080
```

After the connection is established, the Web browser sends a request for the document by using the HTTP protocol. The request includes the method to be used to fetch the document, the object's name and the HTTP protocol version in use at the Web browser. The HTTP protocol uses text strings so that users can more readily understand the protocol. For example, the following HTTP request might be sent by the Web browser to the Web server requesting a document:

```
GET /web/docs/index.html HTTP/1.0
```

In this request, the GET HTTP request is used to obtain the document `/web/docs/index.html`. The version number of HTTP to be used for transferring the document is 1.0.

The server responds to the request for the HTML document by sending an HTTP response. The HTTP response from the server is composed of the following three parts:

▶ Response status

▶ Response header

▶ Response data

The *response status* is a line of text that contains the version number of HTTP used by the server, a status code that describes the server result, and a text description that sheds a little more light onto what the status code means. The following is an example of a response status returned by a Web server:

```
HTTP/1.0 200 OK
```

Table 6.1 shows some of the more commonly used status codes. For a more complete description of the status codes refer to the following on the Internet:

```
http:/www.w3.org/hypertext/WWW/Protocols/HTTP/HTRESP.html
```

TABLE 6.1	CODE	DESCRIPTION
HTTP Response Codes	200	OK. Request successful.
	204	No response. On receiving this, the browser will not attempt to load the page it is trying to fetch.
	301	The document that was requested has moved.
	400	Bad HTTP request.
	401	The request is unauthorized.
	403	The request is forbidden.
	404	The resource was not found.
	500	There was an internal server error.
	501	Access request is not implemented.

After the response code comes the response header. The response header contains information on the server type, the MIME version number used to describe the content type, the content type that describes the contents to follow in the response data, and a blank line. The blank line is mandatory because it separates the response header from the response data. Here is an example of a response header:

```
Date: Tuesday, 05-Nov-96 23:42:34 GMT
Server: Novell-HTTP-Server/2.5
MIME-version: 1.0
Content-type:text/plain
Body follows after the mandatory blank line
```

MIME is a method of encoding data that was originally used in Internet mail for transmitting documents containing a mix of text, image, audio, and video data. HTTP uses MIME to describe the different data types that it must deal with. The "Content-type" is a MIME description of the data. The text/html says that the major category of the data that is to be sent is text and the subcategory is HTML. Upon seeing the text type, the browser interprets the response data that follows as HTML code. Another content type that is understood by all Web browsers is text/plain which means that the response data is to be treated as plain text.

If the document that was requested was an HTML document, the response data will contain the text in the HTML document. The following is an example of the response data:

```
<HTML>
<HEAD><TITLE>Simple HTML doc</TITLE></HEAD>
<BODY>
<P> This is a simple HTML document...
</BODY>
</HTML>
```

Putting together all of the different pieces of the Web server's response, the following is seen by the Web browser:

```
HTTP/1.0 200 OK
Date: Tuesday, 05-Nov-96 23:42:34 GMT
Server: Novell-HTTP-Server/2.5
MIME-version: 1.0
```

```
Content-type:text/plain
<HTML>
<HEAD><TITLE>Simple HTML doc</TITLE></HEAD>
<BODY>
<P> This is a simple HTML document...
</BODY>
</HTML>
```

After the HTTP request/response is complete, the underlying TCP/IP connection is terminated. A TCP/IP connection is made for each HTTP request/response.

To understand how the HTTP protocol works, you can try an experiment to connect to the Web server at port number 80. If you have access to a `telnet` client application, you can do this by using the following command:

```
telnet    webhost        80
```

You must replace *webhost* with the IP address or hostname of the Novell Web Server. The number 80 tells the `telnet` client to connet at TCP port 80 on the Web server. Without an explicit port number, `telnet` will try to connect to its default port number of 23. You can use telnet from any UNIX host or a MS Windows-based application. If you are using a GUI-enabled application, you must set the port number to 80 in the appropriate dialog box.

After you make the connection, you will see messages similar to the following from the Novell Web Server:

```
Trying 199.245.180.11...
Connected to 199.245.180.11
Escape character is '^['.
```

The previous response assumes that the IP address of the Novell Web Server is 199.245.180.11. Your Web server's IP address will undoubtedly be different.

Now you are going to simulate a Web browser client making an HTTP GET request. Enter the following command to fetch the file `index.htm`.

```
GET /index.htm HTTP/1.0
```

After you press the Enter key, you will notice that nothing happens. This is because the HTTP request must be followed by two <CR><LF> characters. So, press the Enter key one more time. You will see the HTTP response from the Web server shown in Listing 6.1 scroll by quickly:

LISTING 6.1

HTTP Response

```
HTTP/1.0 200 OK
Date: Sun, 09 Apr 1995 04:17:19 GMT
Server: Novell-HTTP-Server/2.5
Content-type: text/html
Last-modified: Thu, 29 Feb 1996 14:26:58 GMT
Content-length: 2761
<HTML><TITLE>Novell Web Server CGI SDK Home Page</TITLE>
<BODY TEXT="#000000" LINK="#FF0000">
<BODY BACKGROUND=images/blue_pap.gif>
<IMG SRC="/images/novlogo.gif" align="right" hspace=10> <P>
<H2>Novell Novell Web Server</H2>
This Novell Web Server product contains the CGI SDK that
allows programmers to extend the functionality of the Novell
Web Server.
<P>
This is the sample home page installed on your Early Access
Web Server.  You can edit this file or replace it with any
other HTML document.  This file can be found in your
document root
as <I>index.htm</I>.
<HR>
<H2>About this Web server...</H2>
This web page is served from a NetWare File server running
HTTP.NLM. The CGI implementation is beta software, and is
provided to allow
for developers to begin development of extensions to the
Novell Web Server.
<p>
<B>Please send email to the address at the bottom of this
page to let us know that you're developing applications to
the Novell Web Server,
and for any technical support issues you might have.</B>
<hr>
```

Try out these three examples of applications that are written to the NetWare CGI. The SDK provides the source code for the <I>cgiparse</I> and <I>cginph</I> applications that you can use as development templates.
<P>
1. LoadableModule   /nds/   sys:web/nds-bin/
<DD>http://localhost<A HREF="/nds/ndsobj">/nds/ndsobj</A>
<P>
2. LoadableModule /cgi/ sys:web/cgi-bin
<DD>http://localhost<A HREF="/cgi/cgiparse">/cgi/cgiparse</A>
<DD><I>Use as a template for parsed-header extensions.</I><P>
3. LoadableModule /cgi/ sys:web/cgi-bin
<DD>http://localhost<A HREF="/cgi/cginph">/cgi/cginph</A>
<DD><I>Use as a template for non-parsed header extensions.</I><P>
<hr>
The following is an implementation of an image map processor written to the NetWare CGI. The Novell Web Server implements image maps natively, but this demonstrates that you can implement your own processing if you wish.
<p>
Try clicking on the pillar, a fish's eye, the plant, etc.
<p>

<A href="/cgi-bin/imagemap.nlm/ncsafish.imp"><IMG src="/images/ncsafish.gif" ISMAP></A>
<HR>
<H2>Known problems</H2>
Sometimes there may be some problems when you UNLOAD the HTTP.NLM. The System Console may hang for a bit before unloading. Also, sometimes unloading HTTP.NLM does not successfully unload your CGI extensions. If this happens, manually unload the extensions

```
before
trying to unload HTTP.NLM again.
<P>
More examples and code will be provided with later updates.
Be sure to send us email to the address below to get on our
update list!
<HR>
<ADDRESS>Novell, Inc., San Jose, CA<br>
<A
HREF="mailto:nwwebdev@novell.com"><i>nwwebdev@novell.com</i><
/A>
</ADDRESS>
</BODY>
</HTML>
```

Notice that the HTTP response contains some header information, a blank line, and then the contents of the actual document that was requested. The HTML document that is requested may be different on your Novell Web Server because the contents of the file index.htm may be different. At the end of the HTML document transfer, the telnet connection is closed automatically. If you need to get another document with HTTP/1.0, you must open another connection. The process of opening and closing a connection each time an HTML document is transferred is somewhat inefficient, especially when several files must be downloaded to the Web browser. Newer improvements to the HTTP protocol are expected to have options to overcome these limitations.

In the previous experiment, you were fetching a document that already existed. What if you tried to fetch a document that did not exist? Try the following experiment using HTTP where you attempt to fetch a document you know does not exist. As before, make a telnet connection to the HTTP server, and type the following command:

```
GET /xyzzy.htm HTTP/1.0
```

Press the Enter key twice. You should see an output similar to the following:

```
HTTP/1.0 404 Not Found
Date: Sun, 09 Apr 1995 04:58:05 GMT
Server: Novell-HTTP-Server/2.5
```

```
Content-type: text/html
<HEAD><TITLE>404 Not Found</TITLE></HEAD>
<BODY><H1>404 Not Found</H1>
The requested URL /xyzzy.htm was not found on this
server.<P>
</BODY>
```

Notice that the HTTP response contains an HTML document announcing that the requested resource was not found. The error code that was returned was 404. Consulting Table 6.1, you can see that this error code indicates that the resource was not found. The HTML document that was returned by the Web server is a *virtual document*. It does not exist in the HTML documents directory on the server, but was created dynamically by the Web server to indicate the nature of the error.

You may want to try some other experiments such as sending an invalid request to see what kind of response is returned by the server:

```
GETX this is an invalid request
```

The Web server response will indicate an error code of 400, which means that this was a bad HTTP request:

```
HTTP/1.0 400 Bad Request
Date: Sun, 09 Apr 1995 04:58:56 GMT
Server: Novell-HTTP-Server/2.5
Content-type: text/html
<HEAD><TITLE>400 Bad Request</TITLE></HEAD>
<BODY><H1>400 Bad Request</H1>
Your client sent a query that this server could not
understand.<P>
Reason: Invalid or unsupported method.<P>
</BODY>
```

For a more complete description of the formats of the HTTP request/response, you can see the following resource on the Internet:

```
http:/www.w3.org/hypertext/WWW/Protocols/HTTP/HTTP2.html
http:/www.w3.org/hypertext/WWW/Protocols/HTTP/HTTP1.0-
ID_1.html
```

Using MIME Types for Identifying Web Content

The HTTP protocol uses MIME to specify the data type sent to the Web browser. MIME was originally created to overcome the limitations of sending non-text mail messages. The SMTP (Simple Mail Transfer Protocol) that is used on the Internet was designed to send text messages only. In order to send binary data, Internet users had to convert binary data to text by using utilities such as Uuencode (encoding binary to text) and Uudecode (decoding from text to binary). With the introduction of MIME for mail messages, this encoding of non-text data is performed automatically. MIME-complaint mail reader programs encode any non-text data such as binary files, image, audio, and video to text using an encoding method called *base64* encoding. Before the data is sent, it is prefaced by "Content-Type" information. The "Content-Type" informs the receiver of the message how to interpret the data that follows. The following is an example of a MIME-encoded message:

```
Date: Wed,  6 Nov 96 17:15:15
From: karanjit@siyan.com
Subject: Some subject
To: karanjit
X-PRIORITY: 3 (Normal)
X-Mailer: Chameleon 5.0, TCP/IP for Windows, NetManage Inc.
Message-ID: <Chameleon.847325803.karanjit@>
MIME-Version: 1.0
Content-Type: MULTIPART/MIXED;
BOUNDARY="gethostname.err:847325803:890:-1963343:41"
--gethostname.err:847325803:890:-1963343:41
Content-Type: TEXT/PLAIN; charset=US-ASCII
Here is the document we talked about
-------------------
Name: Karanjit Siyan, Ph.D.
E-mail: karanjit@siyan.com
Date: 11/6/96
Time: 5:15:16 PM
-------------------
```

```
--gethostname.err:847325803:890:-1963343:41
Content-Type: IMAGE/gif; SizeOnDisk=746; name="4homebtt.gif"
Content-Transfer-Encoding: BASE64
Content-Description: 4homebtt.gif
R01G0DdhJQA1APYPAAAAAIAAAACAAICAAAAAgIAAgACAgMDAwICAgP8AAAD/
AP//AAAA//8A/wD//////wAAAIAAAACAAICAAAAAgIAAgACAgMDAwICAgP8A
AAD/AP//AAAA//8A/wD//////wAAAIAAAACAAICAAAAAgIAAgACAgMDAwICA
gP8AAAD/AP//AAAA//8A/wD//////wAAAIAAAACAAICAAAAAgIAAgACAgMDA
wICAgP8AAAD/AP//AAAA//8A/wD//////wAAAIAAAACAAICAAAAAgIAAgACA
gMDAwICAgP8AAAD/AP//AAAA//8A/wD//////wAAAIAAAACAAICAAAAAgIAA
gACAgMDAwICAgP8AAAD/AP//AAAA//8A/wD//////wAAAIAAAACAAICAAAAA
gIAAgACAgMDAwICAgP8AAAD/AP//AAAA//8A/wD//////wAAAIAAAACAAICA
AAAAgIAAgACAgMDAwICAgP8AAAD/AP//AAAA//8A/wD//////ywAAAAAJQA1
AAYH/4AAgoOEhYaHiIIID4yNjo+QkY8HiouS15iNB5QACAiboKGio6SjlQeZ
kAgMrJKgp6mOq6wMrpuwtLm1u426D74Pr52fv7qtx4y+uovCnqiOntHFtQfA
ntDBt8PPDJa93d0sm4+szNr0xd7ps7nMtcngzcTlssbY1b/p2Zzo9A/q1YxN
g2e037xuz/KFM7Z0V7xzBxuK+yfQH8F9uMAVg9eOkTp98rhZsoctmSN6IfUt
FPgL1beCGS0diGYvYKuLKS16bAfNEzmY21RqyqWS3Tug/TSe9Cez3CyXOZV+
k1oM1aabUT9SpCp1FdKIqmi5TAbwoUGRkcTWG1vtK9qwNO811XM7MC0tVx0j
kqzFblJAYnr3bkW4aRYxjEH/RVu8ePAythDHxnLs01HKyZZBQQpZqrNnUZUQ
dBotujTp06ZTd4KIurXq16g5JZpN21AgADs=
--gethostname.err:847325803:890:-1963343:41--
```

As you look at this example of a MIME-encoded message, notice that the MIME version is 1.0, and the "Content-Type" of the overall message is MULTIPART/MIXED. The MULTIPART refers to the major content type and informs the receiver that the message has multiple parts. The MIXED is a subtype of the major content type and informs the receiver that the multiple parts are to be processed sequentially.

Other valid subtypes for MULTIPART are PARALLEL, which says that the multiple parts are to be processed in parallel (simultaneously); ALTERNATIVE, which means that the multiple parts define the same content; and DIGEST, which means this is an e-mail digest (composite of several e-mail messages). The PARALLEL subtype can be used if accompanying audio or video must be played simultaneously. The ALTERATIVE subtype can be used to describe the same information in text and image form, and is designed for message readers that cannot display images.

Table 6.2 shows some common content types for MIME messages. Each type/subtype has many parameters. In the previous message, the BOUNDARY parameter contains a text string that is used to separate the multiple parts of the message.

T A B L E 6.2	CONTENT TYPE/SUBTYPE	MEANING
Examples of MIME 1.0 Content Types	TEXT/PLAIN	Plain text.
	TEXT/RICHTEXT	Rich text containing some simple formatting.
	TEXT/ENRICHED	Enriched text containing additional formatting information.
	TEXT/HTML	Text containing HTML codes.
	MULTIPART/MIXED	The document has multiple parts. Each part must be processed sequentially.
	MULTIPART/PARALLEL	The document has multiple parts. Each part must be processed in parallel.
	MULTIPART/DIGEST	The document has multiple parts where the parts are the messages of an E-mail digest.
	MULTIPART/ALTERNATIVE	The document has multiple parts. The parts represent the same information in different format.
	MESSAGE/RFC822	This is a message type that follows the RFC822 specification. Standard e-mail message.
	MESSAGE/PARTIAL	This is a partial message (a message fragment).
	MESSAGE/EXTERNAL-BODY	This is a pointer to a message that is external to this message (for example, a pointer to a document on an FTP host).
	APPLICATION/POSTSCRIPT	The application is meant for a Postcript interpreter.

(Continued)

T A B L E 6.2	CONTENT TYPE/SUBTYPE	MEANING
Examples of MIME 1.0 Content Types (Continued)	APPLICATION/OCTET-STREAM	The application is a stream of uninterpreted octets (binary programs or data).
	IMAGE/GIF	Image file using the Graphics Interchange Format (GIF).
	IMAGE/JPEG	Image file using the JPEG format.
	AUDIO/BASIC	Audio file (8-bit ISDN mu-law encoded).
	VIDEO/MPEG	Video file using the MPEG format.

The other content types are TEXT/PLAIN for the text part of the message and IMAGE/GIF for the image part. The TEXT/PLAIN has the `charset` parameter, whose value of US-ASCII determines which character set is used to encode the text part. The IMAGE/GIF content type has a number of parameters that indicate the size and name of the file and the method of encoding.

MIME supports other forms of encoding such as *NVT ASCII*, *eight-bit set*, *binary*, *quoted-printable,* and *base64*. The most common forms are NVT ASCII (which means the ASCII character set for text messages) and the base64 (for non-text messages). Only the base64 encoding method is described here. Base64 uses the following 64 printable character set:

▸ A to Z

▸ a to z

▸ 0 to 9

▸ + /

Each of these symbols is assigned a 6-bit code. Letter "A" is assigned 000000, letter "B" is assigned 000001, ..., letter "Z" is assigned 011001 (decimal value 25). Next, letter "a" is assigned 011010 (decimal 26), and so on. The "+"character is assigned 111110 (decimal value 62) and the "/" character is assigned 111111 (decimal value 63).

Every three octets of data (24-bits) are interpreted as grouped in four groups of six bits. Each group of six-bits is then translated to its corresponding character from the 64 printable character set. As an example, consider the following three octets of data:

```
00000100  00000000  01111111
```

When these octets are grouped in as 6-bit groups, they become:

```
000001  000000  000001  111111
```

These six bit groups correspond to the following base64 encoding:

```
B     A           B   /
```

The HTTP protocol used by Web servers to send response data back to the Web browser uses the MIME content types to describe the type of data that is being sent back. The examples in the previous section show the MIME information embedded in the Web server response. The "Content-Type" line is set to `text/html`, indicating that the Web response is an HTML document.

Input/Output to the Common Gateway Interface

The data supplied by a user through a form or a keyword Web search is sent to the CGI program (see Figure 6.4). The data can be sent either using the GET or POST method. The CGI program processes the data and returns the data to the Web client using a partial header approach or a complete header. In the partial header approach, only part of the response header is returned by the CGI program to the Web server. The Web server fills out the remainder of the information in the response header and sends the completed response header to the Web client. The partial header approach requires parsing of the response header by the Web server and this approach is, therefore, also called using *parsed headers*. In the complete header approach, the CGI program is responsible for sending the complete response header to the Web client. The Web server does not have to parse the header, and this approach is also called using *non-parsed headers*.

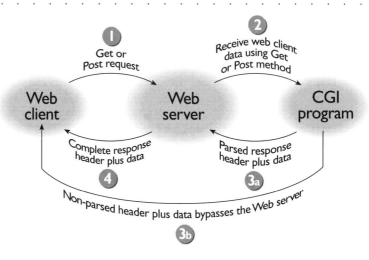

CGI interaction with parsed and non-parsed headers

Most CGI programs use the parsed header approach because this requires less processing by the CGI program and the burden of providing a complete response header is left to the Web server. The *non-parsed header* approach requires more processing by the CGI program, but no additional processing by the Web server because the complete response header is already provided by the CGI program. The *non-parsed header* approach can be advantageous in situations where you want to minimize the burden on the Web server and provide a quicker response to the Web client.

The following sections examine the issues of how CGI programs read Web client data and how they send results back to the Web client.

Reading Web Client Data Through the CGI Interface

The information that is sent by the Web client to the server is placed in CGI environment variables, passed as parameters to the CGI program, or read from the standard input channel of the CGI program. The Web server is responsible for setting up the values of environment variables. The actual data that is sent is encoded in a special way so that it does not contain any blanks.

CGI environment variables

A great deal of information is available to CGI programs through environment variables. These CGI environment variables are special variables that are set up by the Web server before passing control to the CGI program. Table 6.3 shows the CGI environment variables that are defined for CGI programs.

TABLE 6.3	CGI ENVIRONMENT VARIABLE	DESCRIPTION
CGI Environment Variables	ARGC	The number of arguments supplied on the command line. In Perl, @ARGV contains the command line arguments.
	AUTH_TYPE	Set to the authentication used to validate the user. Usually set to "Basic". For additional information see `http://www.w3.org/hypertext/WWW/Protocols/HTTP1.0-ID_40.html`.
	CONTENT_TYPE	Set to the MIME value of the query data.
	CONTENT_LENGTH	Set to the number of bytes to be read by the CGI program through the standard input.
	DOCUMENT_ROOT	Set to the root document directory of the Web server.
	GATEWAY_INTERFACE	Set to the revision level of the CGI interface.
	HTTP_ACCEPT	Set to the list of MIME types that the Web client can accept.
	HTTP_CONNECTION	Type of HTTP connection.
	HTTP_FROM	Set to the e-mail address of the user making the request. Not supported by all Web browsers.
	HTTP_REFERER	Set to the URL of the document that the Web client was pointing to prior to the execution of this CGI program.
	HTTP_USER_AGENT	Set to the Web browser name that the client uses to issue the request.
	PATH_INFO	Set to any extra path information passed to the CGI program. This represents the resource to be returned by the CGI application.
	PATH_TRANSLATED	Set to the actual or translated version of the path given in PATH_INFO.

(Continued)

TABLE 6.3

*CGI Environment Variables
(Continued)*

CGI ENVIRONMENT VARIABLE	DESCRIPTION
QUERY_STRING	Set to the query information passed to the CGI program. The string is appended with a "?" to the URL.
REMOTE_IDENT	Set to the identity of the remote user making the request. This is set if the RFC 931 (Authentication Server) is supported by the Web server.
REMOTE_ADDRESS	Set to the IP address of the computer through which the user is making the request.
REMOTE_HOST	Set to the hostname of the computer through which the user is making the request. Set to null if this information is not available.
REMOTE_USER	Set to the authenticated name of the user. The Web server must support user authentication and the CGI program must be protected from unauthorized access.
REQUEST_METHOD	Set to the method used for sending the information. In HTTP 1.0, this is set to GET, POST, PUT, HEAD, DELETE, LINK, or UNLINK. The method name is case-sensitive.
SERVER_NAME	Set to the Web server's hostname or IP address.
SERVER_PORT	Set to the TCP port number of the Web server on which the HTTP daemon is running.
SERVER_PROTOCOL	Set to the name and revision of the application level protocol on which the request was received. Usually set to HTTP 1.0.
SERVER_SOFTWARE	Set to the name and version number of the Web software that received the client request.

(Continued)

T A B L E 6.3	CGI ENVIRONMENT VARIABLE	DESCRIPTION
CGI Environment Variables (Continued)	SCRIPT_NAME	Set to the virtual path of the CGI program that is being executed. Note that the virtual path may not be the actual physical path of the CGI program on the server. The virtual path is the CGI program path that is sent in the Web client request.

Suppose that you wanted to find out the actual settings of the CGI environment variables for executing a CGI program on a Novell Web Server. One way of accomplishing this is to write a CGI program that displays the environment variable values as an HTML document. Because the CGI environment variables depend on the actual request, there is no way of creating such an HTML document value beforehand. The CGI program must determine the actual settings of the CGI environment variables for the request, and dynamically generate a virtual HTML page that displays the values of the environment variables. The following CGI program performs this task. It is written in Perl. For a detailed understanding of how to write Perl programs, refer to Chapter 7. The actual program is simple enough so that you do not have to have much knowledge of Perl to understand how it works.

```
#!/usr/local/bin/perl
# The previous line does not have any meaning for non-Unix
# hosts such as the Novell Web Server. It is a good idea
# to include it, in case you want to port this script to a
# Unix based web server.
#
print "Content-Type: text/html\n\n";
# Note that the \n\n at end of the previous string
# ensures an extra blank line between the HTTP response
# header and the HTTP response body that follows.
# What follows next is the dynamically generated virtual
HTML
# document that has the computed environment variable
values.
print "<HTML>\n";
print "<HEAD><TITLE>Display environment
```

```
        variables</TITLE></HEAD>\n";
        print "<BODY>\n";
        print "<p>AUTH_TYPE = $ENV{AUTH_TYPE}\n";
        print "<p>CONTENT_TYPE = $ENV{CONTENT_TYPE}\n";
        print "<p>CONTENT_LENGTH = $ENV{CONTENT_LENGTH}\n";
        print "<p>DOCUMENT_ROOT = $ENV{DOCUMENT_ROOT}\n";
        print "<p>GATEWAY_INTERFACE = $ENV{GATEWAY_INTERFACE}\n";
        print "<p>HTTP_ACCEPT = $ENV{HTTP_ACCEPT}\n";
        print "<p>HTTP_CONNECTION = $ENV{HTTP_CONNECTION}\n";
        print "<p>HTTP_FROM = $ENV{HTTP_FROM}\n";
        print "<p>HTTP_REFERER = $ENV{HTTP_REFERER}\n";
        print "<p>HTTP_USER_AGENT = $ENV{HTTP_USER_AGENT}\n";
        print "<p>PATH_INFO = $ENV{PATH_INFO}\n";
        print "<p>PATH_TRANSLATED = $ENV{PATH_TRANSLATED}\n";
        print "<p>QUERY_STRING = $ENV{QUERY_STRING}\n";
        print "<p>REMOTE_IDENT = $ENV{REMOTE_IDENT}\n";
        print "<p>REMOTE_ADDRESS = $ENV{REMOTE_ADDRESS}\n";
        print "<p>REMOTE_HOST = $ENV{REMOTE_HOST}\n";
        print "<p>REMOTE_USER = $ENV{REMOTE_USER}\n";
        print "<p>REQUEST_METHOD = $ENV{REQUEST_METHOD}\n";
        print "<p>SERVER_NAME = $ENV{SERVER_NAME}\n";
        print "<p>SERVER_PORT = $ENV{SERVER_PORT}\n";
        print "<p>SERVER_PROTOCOL = $ENV{SERVER_PROTOCOL}\n";
        print "<p>SERVER_SOFTWARE = $ENV{SERVER_SOFTWARE}\n";
        print "<p>SCRIPT_NAME = $ENV{SCRIPT_NAME}\n";

        print "</BODY></HTML>";    # Generate the end tags
        exit (0);                  # Exit the script
```

The first line in this Perl script contains the following line:

```
#!/usr/local/bin/perl
```

This line does not have any meaning for non-UNIX hosts such as the Novell Web Server. It is meant for UNIX hosts and tells UNIX the path name of the program interpreter to execute this script. On a Novell Web Server, this line is ignored as a comment (characters from # to the end of line are treated as comments in Perl). It is a good idea to include it, however, in case you want to port this script to a UNIX-based Web server.

The remainder of the program mainly consists of print statements. A print statement sends the text string (and any other data that is specified on the print statement) to the standard output channel. The data that is written to the standard output channel is received by the Web server, processed, and then forwarded to the Web client for display. The first print statement sends the HTTP response header:

```
print "Content-Type: text/html\n\n";
```

The "Content-Type" value is the MIME description of the data type that follows. The value of text/html indicates that the response data is an HTML document. The "Content-Type" text string that is printed ends with \n\n. The code \n generates a newline code. The first \n terminates the current line and the second \n creates an extra blank line. The extra blank line is required for separating an HTTP header with the HTTP data that follows. When you dynamically generate virtual documents, you must be careful to output a blank line after the HTTP response header.

The next three print statements generate the tags for the start of the HTML document. The Web client will see the following text for the start of the HTML document:

```
<HTML>
<HEAD><TITLE>Display environment variables</TITLE></HEAD>
<BODY>
```

The next several print statements generate HTML lines similar to the following:

```
<p>variable = $ENV{variable}
```

The *variable* stands for the environment variable. The $ENV{*variable*} is a reference to an element of the associative array %ENV. An associative array in Perl can be indexed by any variable name or data, and is not restricted to integer indexes as is often true in many programming languages. The values of the associate array %ENV is set up by the Web server and is available to CGI Perl scripts.

The last print statement generates the end tags for the HTML document:

```
</BODY></HTML>
```

The last statement, exit (0);, terminates execution of the CGI Perl script and control is returned to the Web server.

After creating this Perl script, you should copy it in the CGI directory on the Novell Web Server. By default the Perl scripts are stored in the SYS:WEB/SCRIPTS/ PERL directory. You access Perl scripts by using the following path name:

```
http://webserverhostname/perl/showenv.pl
```

If you want to change the default convention, edit the file SYS:WEB/CONFIG/ SRM.CFG and change the following default line:

```
RemoteScriptAlias /perl/ localhost:8002/sys:web/scripts/perl
```

The previous line shows that the relative path name of /perl maps to the SYS:WEB/SCRIPTS/PERL directory on the local host. If you wanted Perl scripts to be referenced by the path name /cgi-bin (common on many UNIX systems), you could add the following line to the SYS:WEB/CONFIG/SRM.CFG file:

```
RemoteScriptAlias /cgi-bin/
localhost:8002/sys:web/scripts/perl
```

Note that the changes you make to the configuration file will only be registered when you reload the Web services. You can do this by executing the WEBSTOP.NCF file, and then the WEBSTART.NCF file from the server console:

```
WEBSTOP
WEBSTART
```

In Novell Web Server version 3.0, the corresponding files were UNISTOP.NCF and UNISTART.NCF. To run Perl CGI scripts, you must have the PERL.NLM loaded on the Novell Web Server. When UNISTART is run, it loads the Perl NLM on the Novell Web Server. The Perl NLM waits for input on TCP port number 8002. The Novell Web Server takes care of sending the Perl script to this port, and returning the output of the Perl script.

The following is an example of a sample output generated by executing the showenv.pl script on the Novell Web Server by using the URL address. The showenv.pl Perl script described earlier was first copied to the SYS:WEB/ SCRIPTS/ PERL directory.

```
http://webserverhostname/perl/showenv.pl
```

Output displayed by executing the previous URL address is as follows:

```
AUTH_TYPE =
CONTENT_TYPE =
CONTENT_LENGTH =
DOCUMENT_ROOT =
GATEWAY_INTERFACE = RCGI/1.0
HTTP_ACCEPT = image/gif, image/x-xbitmap, image/jpeg,
image/pjpeg, */*
HTTP_CONNECTION = Keep-Alive
HTTP_FROM =
HTTP_REFERER =
HTTP_USER_AGENT = Mozilla/2.01E-NOV-NOV (Win95; I)
PATH_INFO = /
PATH_TRANSLATED = SYS:WEB/docs/
QUERY_STRING =
REMOTE_IDENT =
REMOTE_ADDRESS =
REMOTE_HOST = 199.245.180.16
REMOTE_USER =
REQUEST_METHOD = GET
SERVER_NAME = 199.245.180.10
SERVER_PORT = 80
SERVER_PROTOCOL = HTTP/1.0
SERVER_SOFTWARE = Novell-HTTP-Server/2.51R1
SCRIPT_NAME = /perl/showenv.pl
```

From this output, you can see that the GET method was used from the Web client at IP address 199.245.180.1 to the Web server at IP address 199.245.180.10. Also notice that not all of the CGI environment variables are set in this example.

GET versus POST method

You can use two common methods for transmitting data from a Web client to a Web server. These were discussed briefly in Chapter 5. These methods are the GET and PUT methods. For small amounts of data, the GET method can be used but it has a limitation of about 255 characters for reliable data transfer. The POST method is a much more general-purpose method that does not have limitations on the amount of data that can be transferred.

To better understand the differences between GET and POST methods, consider the following HTML document used to transmit form data to the Web server:

```
<html>
<head>
<title>Another simple form</title>
</head>
<body>
<form method="GET" action="http://www.tsl.org/cgi-
bin/simpform.pl">
<h3>Please supply this information about yourself</h3>
<hr>
<input type="text" size=45 name="pname">Name<br>
<input type="text" size=45 name="street1">Street1<br>
<input type="text" size=45 name="street2">Street2<br>
<input type="text" size=45 name="city">City<br>
<input type="text" size=45 name="statepr">State/Province<br>
<input type="text" size=30 name="postalcode">Postal Code<br>
<input size=30 name="email">E-mail<br>
<br>
<input type="reset" value="Clear Form">
<input type="submit" value="Send Form">
</form>
</body>
</html>
```

Notice that the method used in this form is GET. When the Send Form button is selected (see Figure 6.5), the information supplied in the form is appended to the URL address of the ACTION program and sent.

FIGURE 6.5

Sample form

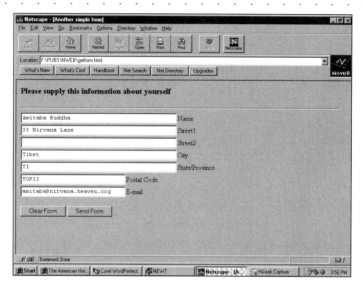

Assume that you entered the following information in the form:

```
Name:    Amitaba Buddha
Street1: 33 Nirvana Lane
Street2:
City:    Tibet
State/Province:        TI
Postal Code:   TOP33
E-mail: amitaba@nirvana.heaven.org
```

The HTTP GET request that is issued will contain this previous data encoded as the following long string:

```
GET /cgi-
bin/simpform.pl?pname=Amitaba%20Buddha&street1=33%20Nirvana%2
0Lane&street2=&city=Tibet&statepr=TI&postalcode=TOP33&email=a
mitaba@nirvana.heaven.org HTTP/1.0
```

There are several things that are noteworthy in how the GET request is formed. First, the form data is appended to the URL of the CGI program with a "?" character. The string data after the "?" is called the *query string*. The Web server sets the CGI environment variable QUERY_STRING with the query string.

The form data is encoded as `name=value` pairs separated by the "&" character. The name is the value of name attribute for the input form field and the value is the actual data entered by the user. There are no blanks permitted in the actual data. Blanks and any special characters such as "&" or "=" that are part of the data are converted into their equivalent hexadecimal form:

%HH

The *HH* refers to the hexadecimal digits. Therefore, a single blank is replaced by its hexadecimal equivalent of %20.

The data is encoded in the manner just described because both the name of the field and its value can be arbitrary text. The encoding is done so that you can always identify the `name=value` pair uniquely.

If a check box field is selected, the value specified in the value attribute is used to encode the data. Consider the following input field from the complex form example in Chapter 5:

```
<input type="checkbox" name="prefDelta" value="delta">Delta
```

If the Delta check box is selected, the following value will be sent by the Web browser:

```
prefDelta=delta
```

If the VALUE attribute is not specified in the check box input tag, and the check box is selected, a default value of "on" is sent. Therefore, if the following input check box field is selected,

```
<input type="checkbox" name="prefDelta">Delta
```

then the following value is sent by the Web browser:

```
prefDelta=on
```

For radio button fields, only a single name field is used for the group of radio buttons to be selected. Only one radio button value can be selected from the radio button group. The radio button name will be set to the value specified in the VALUE attribute. For radio buttons, it is important to specify a unique value for the VALUE attribute, because, if it is not specified, a default value of "on" will be used for the radio button name, and there will be no way of determining which radio button was selected.

One advantage of using the GET method is that you can supply the arguments for the GET query in the URL address itself, rather than obtaining the query information from a form. Therefore, the previous GET query could be generated using the following URL address in an anchor tag:

```
<A HREF=http://www.tsl.org/cgi-
bin/simpform.pl?pname=Amitaba%20Buddha&street1=33%20Nirvana%2
0Lane&street2=&city=Tibet&statepr=TI&postalcode=TOP33&email=a
mitaba@nirvana.heaven.org>Click to execute CGI program</A>
```

You can also pass the query string as extra path information to the URL address. For example, the following anchor tag passes the query string as an extension to the path information:

```
<A HREF=http://www.tsl.org/cgi-
bin/simpform.pl/pname=Amitaba%20Buddha/street1=33%20Nirvana%2
0Lane/street2=/city=Tibet/statepr=TI/postalcode=TOP33/email=a
mitaba@nirvana.heaven.org>Click to execute CGI program</A>
```

The string after the CGI program name is placed in the CGI environment variable PATH_INFO (see Table 6.1) by the Web server prior to executing the CGI program. This method is more suitable for file path information rather than form data.

When the CGI program `simpform.pl` is run, it must break the query string to its individual field elements. This means decoding the special hexadecimal encodings of the data values.

The POST method does not have the data limits of the GET method. The reason for this is that the form data is sent as a MIME object. Consider the following form example that uses the POST method:

```
<html>
<head>
<title>Another simple form</title>
</head>
<body>
<form method="POST" action="http://www.tsl.org/cgi-
bin/simpform.pl">
<h3>Please supply this information about yourself</h3>
<hr>
<input type="text" size=45 name="pname">Name<br>
```

```
<input type="text" size=45 name="street1">Street1<br>
<input type="text" size=45 name="street2">Street2<br>
<input type="text" size=45 name="city">City<br>
<input type="text" size=45 name="statepr">State/Province<br>
<input type="text" size=30 name="postalcode">Postal Code<br>
<input size=30 name="email">E-mail<br>
<br>
<input type="reset" value="Clear Form">
<input type="submit" value="Send Form">
</form>
</body>
</html>
```

This example is similar to the earlier form that used the GET method. The difference is that the POST method is used instead of the GET method. Again, assume that you enter the following information in the form:

```
Name:    Amitaba Buddha
Street1: 33 Nirvana Lane
Street2:
City:    Tibet
State/Province:        TI
Postal Code:   TOP33
E-mail: amitaba@nirvana.heaven.org
```

When you select the Send Form button, an HTTP message similar to the following is sent to the Web server:

```
POST /cgi-zbin/simpform.pl HTTP/1.0
Accept: www/source
Accept: text/plain
Accept: text/html
Accept: Content-Types of other forms of data accepted by
browser
User-Agent: name of browser
Content-Type: application/x-www-form-urlencoded
Content-Length: Number set to bytes in body of message
```

```
pname=Amitaba%20Buddha&street1=33%20Nirvana%20Lane&street2=&c
ity=Tibet&statepr=TI&postalcode=TOP33&email=amitaba@nirvana.h
eaven.org
```

After the POST HTTP command, the list of MIME content types that the browser can accept is sent. Next, the browser identifies itself in the "User-Agent" line. The "Content-Type" and "Content-Length" are the MIME specification for describing the object that follows in the body. The blank line terminates the HTTP request from the object that follows. The object that follows is the encoded value of the form data. There is no limit to the number of bytes of form data that can be sent. The "Content-Length" informs the Web server how many bytes are in the "form-urlencoded" data. The CGI program obtains the "form-urlencoded data" by reading its standard input channel. Because the data is in the special "urlencoded" format, it must be decoded to the original format by the CGI program.

Using GET in an INDEX query

From the discussion of GET versus POST methods in the previous section, you may have gathered that the POST method can be used for submitting all Web client data to a Web server. While this is true in the case of form data, there is another type of query mechanism called the ISINDEX query method that is appropriate for the GET method. In fact, the ISINDEX query method only uses the GET method. The ISINDEX query method is used for specifying a list of keywords that can be used to search a database or a collection of documents. To use the ISINDEX method, you use the ISINDEX tag inside the HEAD tag:

```
<HEAD>
  <ISINDEX HREF=URLofCGIprogram>
</HEAD>
```

The HREF attribute of the ISINDEX tag should specify the URL address of the CGI program that will be used to receive the search keywords. Consider the following simple HTML document that shows the use of the ISINDEX query:

```
<html>
<head>
<isindex href="http://morya/cgi-bin/isindex.pl">
</head>
</html>
```

Figure 6.6 shows how this HTML document appears in the Novell Netscape Navigator. If you enter the following keywords separated by a single blank character, and press the Enter key, you will see a screen similar to Figure 6.7.

```
keywd1 keywd2 keywd3
```

FIGURE 6.6

ISINDEX query

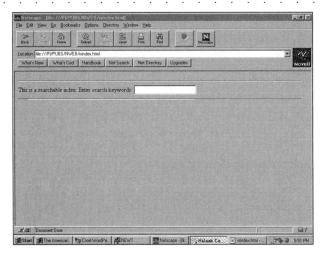

FIGURE 6.7

*ISINDEX query with
keyword searches*

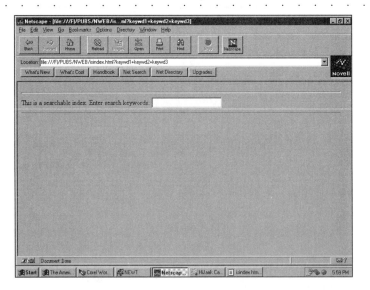

Notice that the URL address of the CGI program is appended with the following string:

```
?keywd1+keywd2+keywd3
```

The query string is formed by appending the keywords with the "?" character. Blanks that separate the keywords are replaced with the "+" character. If the keyword to search for contains special characters such as the "+" character, they are encoded using their equivalent hexadecimal codes.

Figure 6.8 shows an example of passing the following string through the ISINDEX query:

```
"k=e/y\w+/o\+|r_d  y"
```

Note that the special characters are replaced by their corresponding hexadecimal equivalents, and the two blanks preceding the "y" character are replaced by the "+" characters.

In the previous example of the ISINDEX, the BODY and the HEAD tag were missing. These tags can be used with INDEX as seen in the following HTML code and its corresponding rendering (see Figure 6.9) in the Novell Netscape Navigator:

▶ · ◀

ISINDEX encoding example

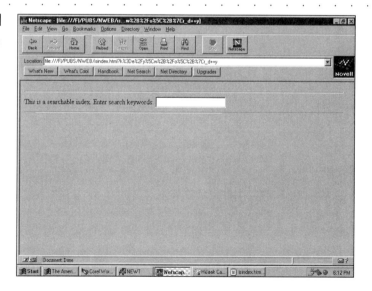

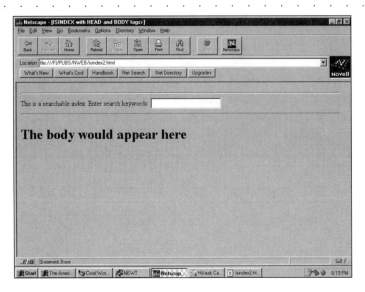

FIGURE 6.9

ISINDEX with HEAD and BODY tags

Once the CGI program receives the query, it must decode the string by converting the "+" characters to spaces and the hexadecimal codes to their equivalent characters.

Decoding form data

When a CGI program receives Web client data, it must first examine where to read the data from. If the request method was GET, the Web client data is in the command line arguments to the program and in the environment variable QUERY_STRING or PATH_INFO. If the request method is POST, the CGI program must read the standard input. The number of bytes to read from the standard input is determined by the value of the CGI environment variable CONTENT_LENGTH. After reading the data, the CGI program must decode the data into *name=value* pairs and decode any hexadecimal and special string patterns. The following is a summary of the steps that must be performed:

1 • Determine if the GET or POST method was used.

2 • For the GET method, obtain a query string from QUERY_STRING and/or PATH_INFO.

3 • For the POST method, obtain data from standard input. The size of data is in CONTENT_LENGTH.

4 • Separate the `name=value` pairs by splitting the string based on the "&" character.

5 • Decode "+" to blank, and hexadecimal codes to equivalent characters.

Step 1 is optional if you know that the data will be submitted using either a GET or POST. However, if you want to create a general-purpose program that will work with either a GET or POST, you must determine the method of data input.

There are a number of standard libraries that are available to convert a URL-encoded string to the equivalent `name=value` pairs. In the popular CGI scripting language, Perl, the `name=value` pairs are typically stored as an associative array.

Perl code to decode URL-encoded data

If you are familiar with the basics of Perl, you can study this section on how Perl can be used to decode URL-encoded query strings and form data. If you are not familiar with Perl, skip this section for now. After you understand the basics of Perl in Chapter 7, you can come back and study this section.

Listing 6.2 is Perl code (file `decode.pl`) that can be used in CGI scripts to decode the URL-encoded data. This Perl code also represents an example (although somewhat incomplete) of a CGI Perl script.

LISTING 6.2

decode.pl Perl Script

```
#!/usr/local/perl
#Above is in case you want to port to Unix
# Obtain the request method
$reqmethod = $ENV{'REQUEST_METHOD'};
if ($reqmethod eq 'GET')
{
    #  Request method is GET
    $input = $ENV{'QUERY_STRING'};
}
```

```
elsif ($reqmethod eq 'POST')
{
    # Request method is POST
    read (STDIN, $input, $ENV{'CONTENT_LENGTH'});
}
else
{
    #Unknown requesr method: generate an error HTML
document
    &senderror(400, "Bad HTTP request",
  "Unknown method $reqmethod", "karanjit@darjeeling.in");
}
#
# This is where the fun begins and we decode the URL
# encoded string.
#
@valuepairs = split(/&/, $input);
foreach $vp (@valuepairs)
{
    ($name, $value) = split(/=/, $vp);
    $value =~ tr/+/ /;
    $value =~ s/%([\da-fA-F][\da-fA-F])/pack("C",
hex($1))/eg;
    $data{$name} = $value;
}
exit(0);
# senderror subroutine: This takes the following arguments:
# $statcode    = Integer code for error status
# $statdesc    = Text description of previous code
# $msg         = The message text to be printed
# $webmaster   = The webmster's address
sub senderror
{
    local ($statcode, $statdesc, $msg, $webmaster) = @_;
    print "Content-Type: text/html\n";
    print "Status: $statcode, $statdesc\n\n";
```

```
      print <<EndSendMsg;
<html>
<head>
<title>CGI Program Error Report</title>
</head>
<body>
<h2>$statcode: $msg</h2>
<p>$msg
<hr>
<p>
Contact web master at $webmaster
<hr>
</body>
</html>
EndSendMsg
      exit(1);
}
```

The first line contains the following comment:

```
#!/usr/local/perl
```

This line is not needed for Novell Web Server scripts, but is useful if you want to reuse this Perl code on a UNIX-based Web server. It contains the path of the Perl interpreter program that is to be invoked to run the script that follows.

The next line is used to get the request method:

```
$reqmethod = $ENV{'REQUEST_METHOD'};
```

Recall that the CGI environment variables can be accessed using the Perl associative array %ENV. The use of the "%" character indicates that the array is associative. The braces {} notation is used to index the associative array, and the string 'REQUEST_METHOD' is the index to the array. The "$"character precedes the array reference to inform the Perl interpreter that the result is a scalar value. In Perl, a *scalar* is a single value (such as a number or a string) and an *array* has multiple values or numbers or strings. The request type is stored in the scalar variable $reqmethod.

The next Perl statement is a nested if statement, whose first part is the following:

```
if ($reqmethod eq 'GET')
{
    #  Request method is GET
    $input = $ENV{'QUERY_STRING'};
}
```

This says that if the request method is the string 'GET', then the statement in the { } is executed. Notice that for string comparisons the Perl keyword eq is used. Other comparison operators are ne (for not equal), gt (greater than), ge (greater than or equal), lt (less than),and le (less than or equal). The assignment statement extracts the value of the CGI-environment variable QUERY_STRING from the associative array %ENV, and stores it in the scalar variable $input. The $input contains the input data that was sent using the GET method.

The second part of the same if-statement checks to see if the request method is POST:

```
elsif ($reqmethod eq 'POST')
{
    # Request method is POST
    read (STDIN, $input, $ENV{'CONTENT_LENGTH'});
}
```

If the request method is POST, the read statement is executed. Those who are familiar with the C language will recognize this read statement to be similar to the read function call in that language. The first argument to the read statement is an input channel, which, in this case, is STDIN. The Perl script is reading from standard input, because the request method is POST. The input data that is read is stored in the scalar variable $input (the second argument). The number of bytes to read is obtained from the CGI environment variable CONTENT_LENGTH, and is passed as the third argument.

The last part of the if statement generates an error code message if the request method is not found to be GET or POST:

```
else
{
    #Unknown requesr method: generate an error HTML
document
```

```
    &senderror(400, "Bad HTTP request",
  "Unknown method $reqmethod", "karanjit@darjeeling.in");
}
```

The use of "&" before `senderror()` indicates that `senderror` is a Perl subroutine. Within the "( )" are the arguments to the subroutine. The subroutine arguments are a numeric error code, a description of the error code, an error message, and the address of the Web master to contact for further explanation. The code for the `senderror` subroutine is listed at the end of the previous Perl code.

After the input is read in `$input`, it must be decoded from its URL-encoded form. This is where you begin to see the power of Perl for pattern matching and text processing. The following statement creates an array `@valuepairs` consisting of the `name=value` strings that are separated in the input by the "&" character:

```
@valuepairs = split(/&/, $input);
```

The split function in Perl, splits the string specified in the second argument based on the string pattern in the first argument. The `/&/` represents a regular expression. Regular expressions are descriptions of a text string to be matched, and are enclosed by the "/ /" characters. Each element in the array `@valuepairs` contains the *name=value* form fields data.

The next statement is the `foreach` statement that sequences through each of the *name=value* pairs in the array `@valuepairs`:

```
foreach $vp (@valuepairs)
{
    ($name, $value) = split(/=/, $vp);
    $value =~ tr/+/ /;
    $value =~ s/%([\da-fA-F][\da-fA-F])/pack("C",
hex($1))/eg;
    $data{$name} = $value;
}
```

The `foreach` loop sets the index variable `$vp` to each element of the `@valuepairs` array in succession. For each value of `$vp`, the following processing takes place.

The statement

```
($name, $value) = split(/=/, $vp);
```

is used to split the *name=value* string along the "=" delimiter. The result is an array of two elements: the name and its value. The name is assigned to $name and its value is assigned to $value.

The statement

```
$value =~ tr/+/ /;
```

translates any occurrences of the "+" character to the blank character in the scalar variable $value.

The statement

```
$value =~ s/%([\da-fA-F][\da-fA-F])/pack("C",
hex($1))/eg;
```

substitutes any occurrences of the hexadecimal code *%HH* in $value to the equivalent character code. There are two regular expressions in the substitute (s) operator. The string $value is searched for occurrences of the regular expression /%([\da-fA-F][\da-fA-F])/. This regular expression matches the string pattern consisting of % followed by two hexadecimal digits. The [\da-fA-F] represents a character class consisting of digits 0 to 9 (indicated by \d), and letters "a" to "f" and "A" to "F." The letters represent the hexadecimal codes for 10, 11, 12, 13, 14 and 15. The first character class [\da-fA-F] matches a hexadecimal digit following the "%" character, and the second character class [\da-fA-F] matches the second hexadecimal digit. The use of the parenthesis () in a regular expression enables the matching contents within it to be stored in scalar variables $1, $2, and so on. A match with the first parenthesis is stored in $1, a match with the second parenthesis is stored in $2, and so on.

When such a match occurs, the *%HH* is replaced by the value of the second regular expression /pack("C", hex($1))/. The second regular expression consists of the pack operator. The pack function takes an array of values specified by the second argument and packs it using a template specified in the first argument. The template in the first argument is "C," which means that the values are to be packed as an unsigned character. The second argument is hex($1). The $1 refers to the contents that were matched in the parenthesis of the substitute operator's first regular expression. The matching contents are, therefore, two hexadecimal digits. The hex function takes a hexadecimal value and returns the equivalent decimal value.

This equivalent decimal value is "packed" to a character value using the pack function. The letters "e" and "g" at the end of the second regular expression in the substitute operator are options that modify the behavior of the substitute operator. The option "e" says that the second regular expression (the replacement string) must be evaluated as an expression and not treated as a replacement string. The result of the evaluation will be treated as the replacement string. The "g" option is a global option that says that all occurrences of the first regular expression are to be replaced with the second regular expression. Without the "g" option, only the first occurrence of the regular expression will be replaced.

The statement

```
$data{$name} = $value;
```

is used to build an associative array %data. An array can be built by assigning values to it. This array is an associative array because the { } is used for indexing an element of the array. The indexes to this array are the name of the field, and the value stored at the index is the value associated with the name. If the form data that was submitted by the Web client had a field name of 'pname' for the name of a person, you could access its value using $data{'pname'}.

The last statement that is executed in the Perl code is

```
exit(0);
```

This code terminates execution of the Perl code and returns an exist status code of 0. The Perl code will terminate without the exit statement, but an explicit status code is useful as it can be used for debugging programs that execute this Perl code.

The subroutine code is placed at the very end. It can be placed anywhere in the program, although it is traditional to place the subroutines at the very end in a Perl code file. The subroutine senderror is defined as the following:

```
sub senderror
{
    local ($statcode, $statdesc, $msg, $webmaster) = @_;
  # Other statements...
}
```

The sub keyword marks the beginning of the subroutine. It is followed by the name of the subroutine and its contents in { }. The arguments to the subroutine are passed in the special array @_. The use of local() around the four scalar variables define these variables to be local, which means that they cannot be accessed by the main program. The main program is the Perl code that was just described. The parameters that are passed to the subroutine are assigned to the local variables by the following statement:

```
local ($statcode, $statdesc, $msg, $webmaster) = @_;
```

The remaining statements generate a dynamic HTML document containing an error code and an error message to be sent to the Web client.

The first two print statements in subroutine `senderror` print out a MIME header to the standard output.

```
print "Content-Type: text/html\n";
print "Status: $statcode, $statdesc\n\n";
```

Note that the MIME header must end with an extra blank line. The extra blank line is printed by the extra "\n" at the end of the string in the statement:

```
print "Status: $statcode, $statdesc\n\n";
```

The next print statement is interesting because it says that the program text delimited by the print statement and the text `EndSendMsg` are to be sent to the standard output:

```
       print <<EndSendMsg;
<html>
<head>
<title>CGI Program Error Report</title>
</head>
<body>
<h2>$statcode: $msg</h2>
<p>$msg
<hr>
<p>
Contact web master at $webmaster
<hr>
</body>
</html>
EndSendMsg
```

If you examine this print statement, you will notice that it is a convenient way of generating an HTML document by just writing out the HTML code to be sent to the Web client in the Perl code itself. As a word of caution, you must not have any spaces between the ">>" and the delimiting text string that follows. Therefore, the following will cause the Perl interpreter to generate errors:

```
print << EndSendMsg;
```

The following is the correct form of the previous statement:

```
print <<EndSendMsg;
```

You can use another text delimiter besides EndSendMsg.
The last statement in the senderror subroutine is

```
exit(1);
```

This causes the CGI script to exit with an exit status of 1. The convention is to exit with a zero status for a successful execution of a program, and a non zero exit status for error conditions in a program.

You could actually write the senderror subroutine using a single print statement that contains the complete template of the HTML document that announces the error status, as shown in the following example:

```
sub senderror
{
    local ($statcode, $statdesc, $msg, $webmaster) = @_;
    print <<EndSendMsg;
Content-Type: text/html
Status: $statcode, $statdesc
<html>
<head>
<title>CGI Program Error Report</title>
</head>
<body>
<h2>$statcode: $msg</h2>
<p>$msg
<hr>
<p>
Contact web master at $webmaster
```

```
<hr>
</body>
</html>
EndSendMsg
        exit(1);
}
```

Notice that the blank line separating the MIME response header with the response data is encoded as part of the enclosed text itself.

Experimenting with GET and POST methods

The Perl script showenv.pl discussed earlier can be used to understand how the CGI environment variables are set for forms submitted using GET and PUT methods. Consider the following form HTML (file form_get.html):

```
<html>
<head>
<title>GET form</title>
</head>
<body>
<form method="GET"
action="http://199.245.180.10/perl/showenv.pl">
<h3>Please supply this information about yourself</h3>
<hr>
<input type="text" size=45 name="pname">Name<br>
<input type="text" size=45 name="street1">Street1<br>
<input type="text" size=45 name="street2">Street2<br>
<input type="text" size=45 name="city">City<br>
<input type="text" size=45 name="statepr">State/Province<br>
<input type="text" size=30 name="postalcode">Postal Code<br>
<input size=30 name="email">E-mail<br>
<br>
<input type="reset" value="Clear Form">
<input type="submit" value="Send Form">
</form>
</body>
</html>
```

You should copy this form HTML in the SYS:WEB/DOCS directory and the showenv.pl should be in the Perl scripts directory, which, by default, is SYS:WEB/SCRIPTS/PERL. Replace the Web server IP address with the hostname or IP address of your Web server. Enter some sample data and select the button Send Form. Examine how the CGI environment variables are set as shown by the showenv.pl script. You should see an output similar to the following:

```
AUTH_TYPE =
CONTENT_TYPE =
CONTENT_LENGTH =
DOCUMENT_ROOT =
GATEWAY_INTERFACE = RCGI/1.0
HTTP_ACCEPT = image/gif, image/x-xbitmap, image/jpeg,
image/pjpeg, */*
HTTP_CONNECTION = Keep-Alive
HTTP_FROM =
HTTP_REFERER = http://199.245.180.10/form_get.html
HTTP_USER_AGENT = Mozilla/2.01E-NOV-NOV (Win95; I)
PATH_INFO = /
PATH_TRANSLATED = SYS:WEB/docs/
QUERY_STRING =
pname=El+Morya&street1=33+kashi&street2=&city=Darjeeling&stat
epr=DJ&postalcode=DAJ%26%5E%25KS&email=elmorya@darjeeling.in
REMOTE_IDENT =
REMOTE_ADDRESS =
REMOTE_HOST = 199.245.180.16
REMOTE_USER =
REQUEST_METHOD = GET
SERVER_NAME = 199.245.180.10
SERVER_PORT = 80
SERVER_PROTOCOL = HTTP/1.0
SERVER_SOFTWARE = Novell-HTTP-Server/2.51R1
SCRIPT_NAME = /perl/showenv.pl
```

Notice that the QUERY_STRING contains the URL-encoded form data. Blanks in the form data are replaced with "+" and special characters are escaped using their hexadecimal values preceded with the "%" character. Also note that the CONTENT_LENGTH is not defined.

Now change the form method to use POST instead of GET and submit the same form. Replace the Web server IP address with the hostname or IP address of your Web server. The new form HTML (file form_pst.html) is as follows:

```html
<html>
<head>
<title>POST form</title>
</head>
<body>
<form method="POST"
action="http://199.245.180.10/perl/showenv.pl">
<h3>Please supply this information about yourself</h3>
<hr>
<input type="text" size=45 name="pname">Name<br>
<input type="text" size=45 name="street1">Street1<br>
<input type="text" size=45 name="street2">Street2<br>
<input type="text" size=45 name="city">City<br>
<input type="text" size=45 name="statepr">State/Province<br>
<input type="text" size=30 name="postalcode">Postal Code<br>
<input size=30 name="email">E-mail<br>
<br>
<input type="reset" value="Clear Form">
<input type="submit" value="Send Form">
</form>
</body>
</html>
```

Enter the same sample data and select the button Send Form. Examine how the CGI environment variables are set as shown by the showenv.pl script and compare it with the CGI environment variable settings for the form that used the GET method. You should see an output similar to the following:

```
AUTH_TYPE =
CONTENT_TYPE = application/x-www-form-urlencoded
CONTENT_LENGTH = 128
DOCUMENT_ROOT =
GATEWAY_INTERFACE = RCGI/1.0
```

```
HTTP_ACCEPT = image/gif, image/x-xbitmap, image/jpeg,
image/pjpeg, */*
HTTP_CONNECTION = Keep-Alive
HTTP_FROM =
HTTP_REFERER = http://199.245.180.10/form_pst.html
HTTP_USER_AGENT = Mozilla/2.01E-NOV-NOV (Win95; I)
PATH_INFO = /
PATH_TRANSLATED = SYS:WEB/docs/
QUERY_STRING =
REMOTE_IDENT =
REMOTE_ADDRESS =
REMOTE_HOST = 199.245.180.16
REMOTE_USER =
REQUEST_METHOD = POST
SERVER_NAME = 199.245.180.10
SERVER_PORT = 80
SERVER_PROTOCOL = HTTP/1.0
SERVER_SOFTWARE = Novell-HTTP-Server/2.51R1
SCRIPT_NAME = /perl/showenv.pl
```

Notice that the QUERY_STRING is not defined because the URL-encoded form data is read from the standard input. The CONTENT_LENGTH contains the number of bytes to be read from the standard input and the CONTENT_TYPE is set to `application/x-www-form-urlencoded`.

Writing Data Through the CGI Interface

The Perl scripts `showenv.pl` and `decode.pl` write data to the standard output channel. CGI script data written to the standard output channel is received by the server and transmitted to the Web client. The HTTP headers that were used in the `showenv.pl` and `decode.pl` scripts output only the "Content-Type" headers. Table 6.4 shows some of the common HTTP headers. The HTTP headers can occur in any order, but the header section must end with a blank line. The blank line acts as a delimiter between the HTTP response and HTTP data. The Refresh and Cookie headers are used only with Netscape-compatible browsers such as the

Novell Netscape Navigator or the MS Internet Explorer. Use the following to see a complete listing of HTTP headers:

```
http://www.w3.org/hypertext/WWW/Protocols/HTTP/Object_Headers
.html
```

TABLE 6.4	HTTP HEADER	DESCRIPTION
Common HTTP Headers	Content-Type	MIME content type. The MIME content types that a Web client can accept are sent by the Web client to the Web server and are initialized in the CGI environment variable HTTP_ACCEPT.
	Content-Length	Number of bytes to be sent. Used for non-text data.
	Expires	The date and time when the document has "expired." The Web client should reload the document.
	Location	Used to redirect server to send another document whose location is specified. Cannot be sent as part of complete header.
	Pragma	Used to turn on/off document caching.
	Status	Status of request. Cannot be sent as part of complete header.
	Refresh	Directs the Web client to "refresh" (or reload) the specified document. Used only with Netscape-compatible browsers such as the Novell Netscape Navigator or the MS Internet Explorer.
	Cookie	Directs the Web client to store the specified data. Used only with Netscape-compatible browsers such as the Novell Netscape Navigator or the MS Internet Explorer.

Using the "Content-Length" HTTP header

The "Content-Length" header is sent by the Web server to the Web client to guard against unexpected end of data errors. The Web client knows exactly the amount of data that is to be sent by reading the number specified in the "Content-Length" header. This is particularly important for binary data such as image files.

If you are writing the CGI program, you must determine the size of the binary file and specify it in the "Content-Length" HTTP header. If you are writing the CGI program as a Perl script, you can use the Perl stat function. The stat function for a file returns a 13-element array containing statistics for the specified file. The eighth element of the array result contains the size of the file. In Perl, arrays are indexed starting from 0, so the eighth element will be indexed by 7. For example, if you wanted to get the length of a file MYSPECIA.EXE, you could use the following Perl code fragment:

```
$file = 'MYSPECIA.EXE';
$length = (stat ($file))[7]; # $length contains
                              # size of file.
```

The stat($file) returns a 13-element array. The use of [7] returns the eighth element, which is the size of the file in bytes.

Server redirection using the "Location" HTTP Header

In the CGI program examples you have seen so far, the CGI program generated the HTML document by writing HTML header and code to the standard output. If the response will be a standard response, you can redirect the server to send a standard HTML document. For example, if you are soliciting user information, you can have the server return a standard thank-you response that you have encoded in an HTML file. You can do this by using the "Location" HTTP header:

```
Location: URLaddressOfHTMLdocument
```

Here is an example of a CGI Perl script that performs server redirection:

```
#!/usr/local/bin/perl
# The previous line does not have any meaning for non-Unix
# hosts such as the Novell Web Server. It is a good idea
# to include it, in case you want to port this script to a
# Unix based web server.
#
print "Location: /standard.html\n\n";
exit(0);
```

When this CGI script is executed, the Web server returns the standard.html document. The Web server takes care of providing the appropriate HTTP response headers so you do not have to worry about it. An example of such a standard HTML response for form data may be similar to this:

```
<html>
<head>
```

```
<title>Thanks for your information</title>
</head>
<body>
<hr>
<b><p> Thank you for supplying the information to get on our
mailing list. Your request will be processed in 7 days. If
you need additional information see our web site at
<i>http://www.tsl.org</i> or contact us at
<i>tslinfo@tsl.org</i></b>
<hr>
</body>
</html>
```

Forcing reload of document using "Pragma" and "Expires" HTTP headers

The Novell Netscape Navigator browser and many other browsers cache a document that is accessed from the server in a special directory on the Web client. If the document is accessed again, the cached copy of the document is displayed rather than another retrieve request for the same document. Caching of documents locally has the advantage of speeding up access to the same document and avoiding an extra retrieve request across the network. The Web browsers will even cache the virtual documents generated by CGI programs. This is undesirable if the virtual document generated by the CGI program is expected to be different for each access of the URL address.

To prevent the Web client from caching documents locally you can use the "Pragma" or the "Expires" HTTP headers:

```
Pragma: No-Cache
Expires: Friday, 15-Nov-96 12:00:00 AM GMT
```

The Pragma: No-Cache statement prevents the Web browser from caching the document. The "Expires" HTTP header specifies the time at which the cached HTML document will no longer considered to be current. After this time, the document must be reloaded by the Web browser.

The following shows an example of a skeleton Perl script that uses the "Pragma" header:

```
#!/usr/local/bin/perl
# The previous line does not have any meaning for non-Unix
# hosts such as the Novell Web Server. It is a good idea
# to include it, in case you want to port this script to a
# Unix based web server.
#
# Skeleton script showing the use of Pragma: no-cache
print   "Content-Type: text/html\n";
print "Pragama: no-cache\n\n";
#   Other statements to generate the virtual HTML doc.
exit(0);
```

The following shows an example of a skeleton Perl script that uses the "Expires" header.

```
#!/usr/local/bin/perl
# The previous line does not have any meaning for non-Unix
# hosts such as the Novell Web Server. It is a good idea
# to include it, in case you want to port this script to a
# Unix based web server.
#
# Skeleton script showing the use of Pragma: no-cache
print   "Content-Type: text/html\n";
print   "Expires: Friday, 15-Nov-96 12:00:00 AM GMT\n\n";
#   Other statements to generate the virtual HTML doc.
exit(0);
```

The NetWare CGI Execution Environment

The Novell Web Server is a special-purpose operating system that is optimized for fast file, printer, and application services. You can write CGI programs as Perl, BASIC, or NetBasic scripts, or as NLMs to run on the server. The Novell Web Server runs CGI scripts and programs using the following methods:

▸ Using LCGI extension

▸ Using RCGI extension

Because CGI programs extend the functionality of Web servers, they are also called *Web server extensions.*

Understanding LCGI Extensions

The Local Common Gateway Interface (LCGI) extension is used to write CGI programs called *LCGI applications.* The LCGI application must be written as NetWare Loadable Modules (NLMs) and are not portable to non-NetWare platforms.

Even though LCGI applications are not as portable as Perl scripts, they execute very quickly. LCGI applications run directly on the Novell Web Server on which they are invoked. LCGI programs do not need to establish network communications with other Web servers because, by definition, they run local to the Web server. Because LCGI programs are written as NLMs, you can take advantage of the unique architecture of the NetWare environment and access the full range of services available on that NetWare server. In short, use LCGI when you want your dynamic Web page to run most efficiently on the NetWare operating system.

Perl and BASIC CGI scripts are loaded and interpreted each time they are executed. Loading modules in the NetWare environment requires substantial overhead. LCGI application NLMs, on the other hand, are loaded only once, and can handle multiple requests. Multiple requests can be handled reentrantly. *Reentrant CGI programs* are those that can be re-entered or executed simultaneously for each Web client request. LCGI programs are ideally suited to handle high volumes of Web client requests. LCGI programs are unloaded only when the Web Server unloads. Because LCGI programs use NetWare threads, they work more efficiently than other CGI scripts. NetWare threads are "lightweight" processes and have less overhead than processes on UNIX systems. UNIX processes are called "heavyweight" processes.

Figure 6.10 illustrates how LCGI programs interact with the Novell Web Server.

▶ . . . . ◀

FIGURE 6.10

LCGI interaction

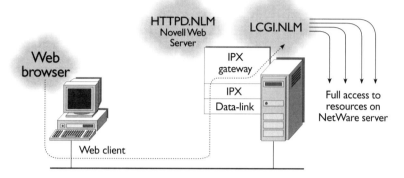

In the NetWare environment, LCGI NLMs are installed as Web Server parser/processor libraries.

The Novell Web Server has at its disposal a group of threads. When the Novell Web Server receives a request for an LCGI NLM, it uses one of its threads to perform the required processing. If the LCGI.NLM has never received a request, it is not loaded in server memory. When a request for the LCGI NLM is received, it is loaded and remains in memory. Thus, the installable NLMs behave as libraries to the Novell Web Server.

Another difference between LCGI NLMs and CGI programs running on UNIX Web servers is how the data is transmitted between the Web server process and the CGI program. In UNIX, the network file descriptors are available to CGI programs by using redirection of the standard I/O facility after creating the CGI process as a child process of the Web server process. In the NetWare environment, there are no parent/child relationships between NLMs. The Web server's network file descriptors are available to the LCGI NLM because the code is executing in the NLM context of the Novell Web Server. When the LCGI NLM needs memory to perform its tasks, it requests the memory from the memory owned by the Web server. This means that the Web server can clean up resources and close client connections, rather than rely on the LCGI NLM to perform these critical tasks.

You can use the NetBasic NLM to write CGI scripts. The NetBasic NLM is an example of an LCGI NLM. The NetBasic NLM runs only on the local NetWare server, and is not portable to UNIX platforms. NetBasic NLM has been licensed by Novell from Hitec Soft, and supports most of the standard BASIC functions, in addition to many functions that support the creation of dynamic Web pages.

Another example of an LCGI extension is the NDS Object Browser. The NDS Object Browser comes with the Novell Web Server distribution.

Once the Web server determines that the request is for an LCGI NLM, it checks to see if the NLM is already registered. If the LCGI NLM is not registered, the Web server obtains a thread and loads the NLM. The NLM begins executing its main routine. The main routine performs the following actions:

1 • Initializes global variables

2 • Registers its message table with the NetWare OS message-handling NLM

3 • Initializes any extension specific variables or structures

4 • Registers itself with the Web server

Once the main routine performs these functions, it suspends itself and waits for Web client requests.

Understanding RCGI Extensions

The Remote Common Gateway Interface (RCGI) is used to run CGI programs on the Novell Web Server or on other platforms besides NetWare (such as on UNIX servers). The RCGI interface provides communications between the Novell Web Server NLM and the CGI programs using TCP port numbers. The TCP/IP sockets programming interface is used to implement the actual communications. Figures 6.11 and 6.12 show the interaction between the Novell Web Server and the RCGI programs.

The RCGI programs can be NLMs or BASIC and Perl scripts. If BASIC or Perl scripts are used, the BASIC and PERL NLMs are loaded on the Novell server and they listen for requests on dedicated port numbers. The BASIC.NLM listens for requests on TCP port number 8001 and the PERL NLM listens for requests on TCP port number 8002 (see Figure 6.13). The BASIC and PERL NLM interpreters are examples of RCGI NLMs (that is, they are written using the RCGI interface).

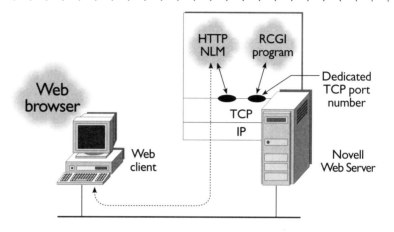

FIGURE 6.11

RCGI interface on a single Novell Web Server

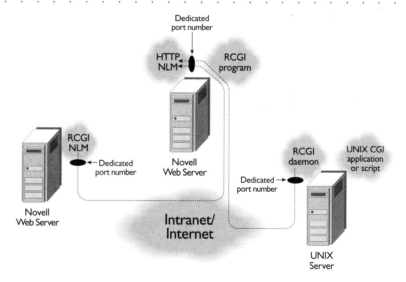

FIGURE 6.12

RCGI interface on multiple platforms

The PERL and BASIC NLMs support most of the functions available in the standard Perl and BASIC scripting languages. As seen in Figure 6.12 , the RCGI scripts can execute on any platform that supports CGI using the RCGI daemon. On UNIX systems, the scripting language of choice is Perl. So, if you want your CGI scripts to be portable across platforms, you should write your scripts in Perl.

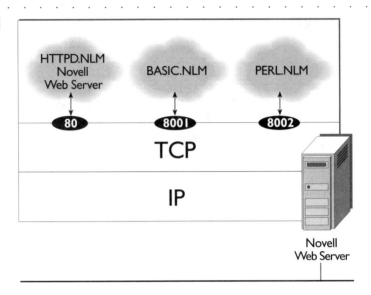

*BASIC and PERL NLMs
implemented using RCGI*

Creating URL Addresses for LCGI Extensions

The examples of running Perl scripts shown earlier in this chapter are all examples of creating URL addresses for RCGI extensions. The RCGI extension in this case is the PERL NLM. In this section you will learn how the URL addresses of LCGI extensions are formed.

To run an LCGI NLM, you must know how to refer to it using its URL address. The URL syntax is determined by placing the `LoadableModule` directive in the SYS:WEB/CONFIG/SRM.CFG file. The syntax of the `LoadableModule` directive is as follows:

```
LoadableModule          template        physical_path
```

The *template* is the logical path of the file or alias of the file that, when used in the URL address, is translated to the *physical_path* of the NLM file. Here are some examples of `LoadableModule` directive entries:

Example 1

```
LoadableModule          /lcgi/          sys:web/lcgi/nlm
```

Any URL containing a matching /lcgi/ becomes a request for NLMs in the sys:web/lcgi directory. For example, the following URL will cause the SYS:WEB/LCGI/NLM/SHOWENV.NLM to be loaded and run:

```
http://webserver/lcgi/showenv.nlm
```

Example 2

```
LoadableModule          /show/       sys:web/lcgi/nlm/showenv
```

In this example, showenv is the filename of an LCGI NLM with or without the .NLM extension. In this case, because the filename is specified in the physical path, it is not specified in the URL address. Here is an example of running the SYS:WEB/LCGI/NLM/SHOWENV.NLM:

```
http://webserver/show
```

Example 3

```
LoadableModule /netbasic/ sys:web/lcgi/netbasic/cgi2nmx.nlm
```

In this example, cgi2nmx.nlm is the filename with a .NLM extension. It is actually the name of the NetBasic NLM interpreter. This filename is not specified in creating its URL address:

```
http://webserver/netbasic
```

Example 4

```
LoadableModule          /cgi-nlm/             sys:web/nlm
```

In this example, the filename is not specified in the LoadableModule directive. Therefore, the URL must specify the filename with or without the .NLM extension. The NLM is located in the SYS:/WEB/NLM directory. The corresponding URL can have the following forms:

```
http://webserver/cgi-nlm/bday.nlm
http://webserver/cgi-nlm/bday
http://webserver/cgi-nlm/bday.nlm/path_info
http://webserver/cgi-nlm/bday.nlm?rama+krishna
```

LCGI Versus RCGI Request Process

Another difference between LCGI and RCGI is the difference in which they process requests. When the Novell Web Server receives an HTTP request for an LCGI server extension, it processes the request as follows:

1 • Convert the URL address in the request to the actual physical path by looking for the `LoadableModule` directive in the server resource configuration file, SRM.CFG.

2 • The Web server determines if it can process the request or an external LCGI NLM must be loaded. If the requested resource is an external NLM, the server scans its list of registered external LCGI NLMs by using the mapped file path from SRM.CFG.

3 • If the external LCGI NLM is not already registered, the Web server loads the NLM and waits for it to register. For registered LCGI NLMs, the Web server passes it the request.

4 • The registered LCGI NLM services the request and returns control to the Web server. Communication between the Web server and the LCGI NLM is handled through the LCGI APIs.

5 • The LCGI NLM is unloaded when the Web server unloads.

When the Novell Web Server receives an HTTP request for an RCGI server extension (such as the BASIC or PERL NLM), it processes the request as follows:

1 • Convert the URL address of the CGI program in the request to the actual physical path by looking for the `RemoteScriptAlias` directive in the server resource configuration file, SRM.CFG.

2 • The RCGI extension runs on the host and TCP port number specified in the RemoteScriptAlias directive. This directive also specifies the physical path to the script. The RCGI NLM waits for requests on the dedicated TCP port.

3 • Upon receiving the request, the RCGI executes the indicated BASIC or Perl script. A typical action by the RCGI script is to generate a dynamic HTML page.

4 • The Novell Web Server receives the dynamic HTML page on the dedicated TCP port number, and after completing the HTTP response header, sends it to the Web client.

5 • The RCGI NLM is not unloaded when you unload the HTTP NLM (Novell Web Server). For example, the BASIC and PERL NLMs will continue to run when you unload the HTTP.NLM, and must be unloaded separately. A convenient way to unload all the Novell Web Server NLMs is to use the WEBSTOP.NCF command file, as long as the WEBSTOP.NCF file does not unload other services that you may still need.

CGI Program Security

Because CGI programs allow users to run processes on your server, it is important that you control access to the script directories and implement proper security measures for all scripts on your server. At a minimum, you should implement the following security measures:

▸ Access to all directories containing scripts should be controlled using NetWare trustee rights. Only the people responsible for writing, managing, and editing scripts should have Read and Write rights to the script directories such as SYS:WEB\SCRIPTS, SYS:WEB\SCRIPTS\PERL, SYS:NETBASIC\WEB, and any other script directories you create.

▸ You should take measures to ensure that only authorized scripts should be placed in the script directories. Authorized scripts are those that are thoroughly tested and debugged before being released on a working Novell Web Server.

> ▸ Design and write your scripts with security in mind. CGI programs implemented as NLMs provide the maximum security because they are difficult to modify. Perl and BASIC scripts are essentially text files and are easier to modify if Write access is inadvertently granted to them.

Because LCGI NLMs can make use of the full range of services on a Novell Web Server, there is a special method that can be used to restrict access to LCGI programs. To restrict access to LCGI programs, create the ACCESS.WWW file (shown in Listing 6.3) in the directory where the LCGI program resides. You can use the sample ACCESS.WWW file in the SYS:WEB/SAMPLES/CONFIG directory as a template for creating your own custom ACCESS.WWW file or use the WEBMGR tool:

LISTING 6.3

ACCESS.WWW File

```
# access.www
#
# Please DO NOT use TAB charaters when editing this file.
#
# This file provides local configuration of the web
# server's access control system.  You can implement
# the access restriction of a document directory
# by simply having this local access control file in that
# directory. The default name for these local control
# files is 'access.www' and it can be set by the
# 'AccessFileName' in the resource configuration
# file: 'srm.cfg'.
#
# Please refer to the User Acess Control section of the
# readme.txt file for additional relevent information.
#
# This example demonstrates the use of an NDS group and a
# list of NDS users for the authentication list.
```

```
#
# In the global access control files, access.cfg,
# one should not specify NDS groups and NDS users
# at the same time, but you can do that in this file.
# Although the access.www can support both NDS groups
# and NDS users at the same time, this combination must
# be handled with care.  The context specified in both
# AuthUserMethod and AuthGroupMethod lines should be
# identical to minimize confusion.
#
# Syntax:
#
#   AuthType Basic <== Keyword, don't change
#
#   AuthName name
#     name can be any descriptive name that the Browser
#     will display. One can take advantage of this line
#     to show the context specified in
#     AuthUserMethod/AuthGroupMethod so those user who
#     belongs to the specified context would know that
#     they don't have to type the fully-qualified user name.
#
#   AuthUserMethod NDS .ou1.ou2...o
#     This signifies that NDS users will be specified in
#     the access list. The NDS fully-qualified parameter
#     must be a container object.
#     NOTE THE LEADING PERIOD.  IT IS REQUIRED.
#     For users in the access list (Require User list)
#     that belongs to this specified container context
#     they do not have to key in the fully-qualified name
#     when prompted for user name and password.
#
#   AuthGroupMethod NDS .ou1.ou2...o
#     This signifies that NDS groups will be specified in
#     the access list. The NDS fully-qualified parameter
#     must be a container object.
```

```
#     NOTE THE LEADING PERIOD.  IT IS REQUIRED.
#     For users in the specified group (Require Group)
#     that belongs to this specified container context,
#     they do not have to key in the fully-qualified name
#     when prompted for user name and password.
#
#  require user user1 user2 ...
#     Specifies that one or more NDS users in the access
#     list.
#     user* is the name of the user.  If the user NDS
#     context is already defined in the AuthUserMethod line,
#     then only the relative name needs
#     to be specified.  It the user belongs to another NDS
#     context, then the fully-qualified NDS name mut be
#     specified (with the leading dot).
#
#  require group gname1 gname2 ...
#     Specifies that one or more NDS groups in the access
#     list.
#     gname* is the name of the group.  The group name
#     should
#     be a fully-qualified NDS name (with the leading dot).
#
AuthType Basic
AuthName DOCS\ENGR(default context: .eng.icd.novell)
AuthUserMethod NDS .eng.icd.novell
AuthGroupMethod NDS .eng.icd.novell
<Limit GET>
require user mel .sally.mgnt.icd.novell
require group .group1.icd.novell
require group .techies.eng.icd.novell
</Limit>
```

The ACCESS.WWW file restricts access to the user `mel` in the NDS context `.eng.icd.novell`. Additionally, user `.sally.mgnt.icd.novell` and users in groups `.group1.icd.novell` and `.techies.eng.icd.novell` have restricted access.

When a Web client requests an LCGI server extension in the directory containing the ACCESS.WWW file, the client will be prompted for a user ID and password. Once a user is authenticated to use an LCGI extension, full access is granted to the Web client through the capabilities of the LCGI NLM. In the case of the NetBasic LCGI NLM, full access is granted to the NetBasic script. Similarly, once a user is authenticated to the NDS Object Browser LCGI extension, NDS browsing is available to all NDS trees via the public NDS group [Public].

There is currently no mechanism to selectively place access control on different NetBasic scripts. Also, when NDS browsing is enabled from the WEBMGR, access is not restricted.

Running RCGI Daemons on UNIX Platforms

The RCGI daemon is a process that runs on a UNIX host (see Figure 6.12) and communicates with the Novell Web Server using the RCGI APIs. The RCGI daemon enables you to run CGI scripts and programs on a UNIX host, or run existing CGI scripts and applications on the Novell Web Server from a remote UNIX host. The RCGI daemon communicates with the Novell Web Server and can be used to accept Web page requests from the Novell Web Server.

The RCGI daemon is available as an executable module called `rcgid`. Versions of `rcgid` are available for these operating systems:

▸ SunOS 4.*x*

▸ Solaris 2.*x*

▸ UnixWare 2

▸ BSD UNIX

You can also port the `rcgid` source code to other versions of UNIX. To install an RCGI daemon on a remote UNIX machine and then access it from a Novell Web Server, follow these steps.

I • Add a RemoteScriptAlias directive to the SYS:WEB\CONFIG\SRM.CFG file to configure the server to include the alias `rcgid`.

As an example, if you want to configure a UNIX host to run `rcgid` on port 8004, the SRM.CFG file should contain the following directive:

```
RemoteScriptAlias /rcgid/ unixhost:8004
```

This means that when the Novell Web Server receives a URL with a virtual path of /RCGID/, the request is forwarded to the UNIX machine (`unixhost`). You should replace `unixhost` with the hostname of your UNIX host.

2 • Restart the Web server. You can use the following commands from the NetWare console:

```
unload http
load http
```

3 • Copy the `rcgid` file to the UNIX machine using a method such as FTP, rcp or NFS. You can find the `rcgid` file in SYS:WEB/SAMPLES/RCGID/*UnixOS*. The SYS:WEB/SAMPLES/RCGID/RCGISAMP directory contains some sample CGI scripts that you can also copy these to the UNIX host.

The source code for the `rcgid` is contained in the SYS:WEB/SAMPLES/RCGID directory in files `rcgid.c`. `rcgid.h` and the `makefile`. You can copy this as well.

4 • Set the appropriate permissions on the executable file.

```
chmod 555 rcgid
```

5 • Start the RCGI daemon, by typing the `rcgid` command using the following syntax:

```
rcgid -p portno [-d usrdir] [-n] [-L] [-l] [-r pat]
[-x:l]
```

The `portno` specifies the port number for the RCGI daemon and it matches the port number specified in the SRM.CFG file. For example:

```
rcgid -p 8004
```

The usrdir specifies the directory where UNIX scripts and files can be found, if you choose not to put them in the default location which is the directory from which rcgid was loaded.

For example, if your scripts are located in /usr/local/cgi, use this command to invoke rcgid:

```
rcgid -d /usr/local/cgi
```

Use the -n switch to suppress the automatic output of a blank line after an HTTP header. If your script produces a type of output other than ASCII or HTML, it must produce an HTTP "Content-Type" header followed by a blank line. By default, the RCGI daemon automatically outputs a header followed by a blank line. If you use the -n switch, your script must take care of generating a blank line after the HTTP headers.

Use the -L switch to restrict connections to local host (loopback) only. This is used for debugging purposes.

Use the -l switch to log the output to a local file instead of using the UNIX syslogd logging feature.

Use the -r pat to restrict connections to hostnames which match the specified pattern (such as *.novell.com, *.tsl.org, and so on).

Use the -x:1 to turn on debug output.

7 • Next, test the rcgid that you have just installed. If you have set up the rcgid alias, try the following from a Web browser:

```
http://webs    238    238erver/rcgid/testscript.pl
```

On the UNIX host enter the testcript.pl as follows:

```
#!/usr/bin/perl
print "Content-type: text/html\n\n";
print "<HTML><HEAD><TITLE>Test
Script</TITLE></Head></HTML>\n";
```

Summary

This chapter described how to create HTML documents that interact with a user. The principal means of doing this is by using HTML forms. When you define HTML forms, you have a choice of using the GET and POST methods for sending form data to the user. The GET method is appropriate for small amounts of data and for generating simple queries. It is also the method used in the ISINDEX tag for sending search keywords. The POST method is a much more general-purpose method that can be used for sending arbitrary amounts of user data to the Web server.

The ACTION attribute of the FORM tag is used to specify the CGI program to execute on the Web server. In a Novell Web Server, you have a choice of using Perl, BASIC, or NetBasic languages to write CGI scripts. The Perl and BASIC scripts are executed by RCGI extensions that accept data on dedicated TCP ports. Starting with Novell Web Server version 3.0, the NetBasic NLM is used to execute the BASIC scripts. The BASIC NLM is not supported. The NetBasic scripts are run using the NetBasic interpreter, which is written as an LCGI extension. You can also implement CGI programs as NLMs.

## CHAPTER 7

Using Perl for Dynamic Content on the Novell Web Server

Perl is a script programming language that originated in the UNIX community. Perl was originally designed for processing system-oriented tasks for the UNIX operating system. In UNIX, most system parameters are stored in text files. Perl excels in processing information in text files and can, therefore, be used for creating and processing HTML content dynamically, based on the user response from a Web client. Highly complex CGI scripts that handle processing of HTML content can be written using Perl.

Today, the most widely used language for writing CGI programs is Perl. One advantage of using Perl is that you can port your CGI scripts between the Novell Web Server and UNIX servers. Using the RCGI interface discussed in Chapter 6, you can even invoke Perl scripts on a UNIX host from a Novell Web Server.

This chapter describes the elements of the Perl language in sufficient depth to enable you to learn the language and to write sophisticated CGI Perl scripts. The latter part of the chapter discusses the sample Perl scripts that ship with the Novell Web Server.

Understanding Perl Basics

If you intend to write CGI scripts that are portable between IntranetWare and UNIX systems, your best choice of language for writing the script is Perl.

This section is written as an overview and a tutorial on using Perl, which is a very popular language for writing CGI scripts. To be an effective IntranetWare Web administrator, you must know the basics of the Perl language because you may have to understand someone else's Perl scripts. Even if you do not intend to write Perl scripts yourself, chances are that you will end up examining Perl scripts written by someone else, or worse still, modifying them yourself!

The CGI scripts that you create for the NetWare server will, of course, be run on the IntranetWare server itself. If you are practicing writing Perl scripts, chances are that you do not have a spare IntranetWare server lying around on which to practice and polish your Perl writing skills. On the other hand, it is highly likely that you have a DOS, Windows 95, or UNIX workstation lying around. If you have a UNIX workstation, you probably have Perl already installed on your system. If you are running DOS or a 32-bit Windows, you can get the Perl interpreter free of charge from the following sources:

- http://info.hip.com (Perl for Window 95)

- http://www.yahoo.com/Computers_and_Internet/Languages/
  Perl (Perl for DOS)

Perhaps Perl is best supported on UNIX systems. You can experiment with Linux, a free version of UNIX that is available on the Internet, or through CD-ROM publishers such as Walnut Creek CDROM at 800-261-6630 or 408-261-6630; and InfoMagic, Inc. at 800-800-6613 or 602-526-9565.

Caldera, Inc., sells a version of Linux called Caldera Desktop Network with NetWare 4 IPX clients, NDS support, and an applications package containing WordPerfect and spreadsheets. You can contact them at

Caldera Inc.
931 W. Center St.
Orem, Utah 84057, USA
801-377-7687
http://www.caldera.com
info@caldera.com

The most widely used version of Perl is Version 4. Perl Version 5 is also available and includes some object-oriented extensions. The version of Perl that ships with Novell Web Server, as of this writing, is Perl Version 5. The discussion in this chapter applies to both Perl Version 4 and 5. However, the object-oriented features of Perl Version 5 are not discussed in this book.

Running Perl Programs

You can run Perl programs using any of the following two methods:

- From the command line

- From a script file

When you run a Perl program from the command line, you place the Perl statements for the program on the command line itself as follows:

```
LOAD PERL -i script      (from the IntranetWare server)
perl script              (from the workstation)
```

Because of limitations on the number of characters you can put in a command line, you can run only simple Perl programs consisting of a few Perl statements from the command line. Also, if you must run the Perl program again using the command line method, you must retype the command line. For short, simple programs, the command line method is quick and convenient, but if you want to reuse the exact program at a future date, you should use the Perl script method of writing the program. The following are examples of running a Perl program from the command line.

You should put the Perl program in a text file, and specify the name of this text file to the Perl interpreter. The text file containing the Perl program is called a *Perl script*. Because Perl scripts are saved in a file, they have a permanence and are not like the transient programs used on the command line.

To find out more about running Perl scripts, you can type the following command:

```
LOAD PERL    -V    (on the IntranetWare server )
perl -v
```

Figures 7.1 and 7.2 show the help screens for the Windows and IntranetWare environment.

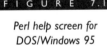

FIGURE 7.1

Perl help screen for DOS/Windows 95

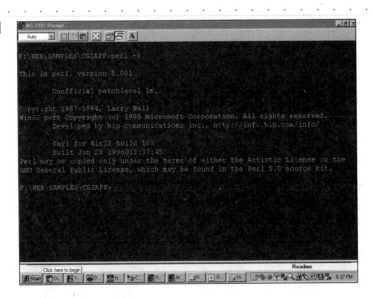

F I G U R E   7.2

Perl help screen for IntranetWare

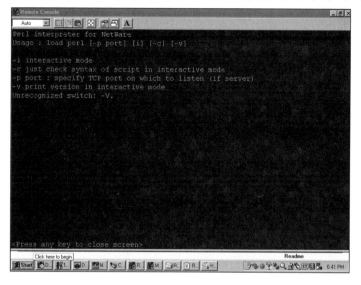

If you load Perl without any arguments, it loads itself as an RCGI extension application and listens on port number 8002. The Perl NLM creates a console screen for itself on the server console with messages similar to the following:

```
PERL: Entered rcgi_main
listening on port 8002
```

Because Perl CGI scripts are sent to the Perl NLM via the RCGI interface, you will see a status message on the Perl NLM console. If you are debugging Perl CGI scripts, you may want to check the Perl NLM console for clues that will help you debug the Perl script.

Understanding the Structure of Perl Programs

Perl programs (or Perl scripts) have a structure that is similar to many other languages. Perl scripts consist of the following program elements:

- ▶ Statements

- ▶ Subroutines

- ▶ Packages

Statements are assignment statements, pattern-matching statements, and control statements (such as if statements, while statements, for statements, and so on). *Subroutines* are methods of encapsulating statements. Invoking the subroutine causes the statements in the subroutine to be executed. The advantage of using subroutines is that commonly used groups of statements can be executed anywhere in your Perl script by invoking the name of the subroutine. *Packages* are used to encapsulate subroutines that provide a set of related actions or functions. Packages are useful for writing Perl *libraries,* which are a collection of subroutines designed for a specific purpose.

Printing from a Perl Script

Consider the following simple one-line program that displays a string of text:

```
print "Hello. I am a simple Perl script\n";
```

This is a print statement that takes a string argument. A *string* is text enclosed in double-quotation marks or single quotation marks. When you run this Perl script, it displays the text of the message. The \n at the end of the string text is the newline character.

The general syntax of the print statement is as follows:

```
print LIST
print (LIST)
print FILEHANDLE LIST
print (FILEHANDLE LIST)
```

The *LIST* is a list of numeric or string values to be printed. The *FILEHANDLE* is a reference to the file on which the output operation is performed. If the *FILEHANDLE* is not specified, the default output file handle is used. The default file handle is a special handle called STDOUT. The STDOUT file handle is a reference to the standard output device, which is usually the console. Thus, in the previous print statement that displays the string, "Hello. I am a simple Perl script\n", the *FILEHANDLE* is STDOUT.

Besides STDOUT, there are other standard file handles such as STDIN and STDERR. The STDIN file handle refers to the standard input device (usually the keyboard). The STDERR file handle refers to the device on which errors are displayed (usually the standard display device, such as the console).

Suppose that you do not want to display the output of the program to the console, but instead want to send the output to a file. You could accomplish this by creating a file handle that references the file. This can be done by using the `open` statement:

```
open(MYFILE, ">xyzzy.out");
```

The ">" preceding the filename opens the file for output only.

Now you can send the output to the `xyzzy.out` file by using the following:

```
print MYFILE "Hello. I am a simple Perl script\n";
```

If no more output is to be sent to the `xyzzy.out` file, you close the file using the `close` statement:

```
close(MYFILE);
```

Thus, the complete Perl script is as follows:

```
open(MYFILE, ">xyzzy.out.");
print MYFILE "Hello. I am a simple Perl script\n";
close(MYFILE);
```

Another way of writing to a file is to change the standard default handle to the file. You can do this using the `select` statement:

```
select (MYFILE);
```

Next, you can send output to the `xyzzy.out` file using the print statement with the default output handle:

```
print "Hello. I am a simple Perl script\n";
```

This statement will write the string to the standard output device, which is now set to the file `xyzzy.out`. Any print statement that does not explicitly reference a file handle will write to the `xyzzy.out` file. If you were to call a Perl subroutine that would normally write to the console by assuming that the default handle is set to STDOUT, you may not get the desired results if the standard output device is set to another file or device. Therefore, you must be careful to reset the standard output device by using a statement such as the following:

```
select (STDOUT);
```

Here is an example of the complete alternative program:

```
open(MYFILE, ">xyzzy.out");
select(MYFILE);
print "Hello. I am a simple Perl script\n";
select(STDOUT);
close(MYFILE);
```

The first `select` statement sets the standard output to the file `xyzzy.out` and the second `select` statement resets the file handle to STDOUT.

There is one minor problem with the previous Perl script. What if these Perl statements were embedded in a larger Perl script? The assumption that the standard output device should be reset to STDOUT will not always be correct, especially if the standard output handle was set by prior Perl statements to a file that was different from STDOUT. To write these Perl statements in a general-purpose fashion so that they do not make any assumption about the prior setting of the default output handle, you can use the `select` statement to return the value of the previous file handle:

```
$prevhandle = select (MYFILE);
```

The `$prevhandle` is a Perl variable (actually, a Perl *scalar* variable) whose value is set to the previous file handle returned by the `select` statement. So, a general-purpose way of writing the previous Perl code would be to save the previous file handle in a Perl variable, and then use this variable to reset the file handle:

```
open(MYFILE, ">xyzzy.out");# Open file for output
$prevhandle = select(MYFILE);    # Select the file
print "Hello. I am a simple Perl script\n"; # Now output
select($prevhandle); # Restore default value of handle
close(MYFILE); # Now close the handle.
```

Now these Perl statements can be embedded in a larger Perl script without any undesirable side effects.

Also notice that the previous code fragment uses the "#" character followed by text. These are called *comments* and are used for making the Perl script more readable, and for documenting the behavior of the Perl script. When the Perl interpreter sees the "#" character it ignores the remainder of the line. If you want to include paragraphs of comments in your Perl script you must begin each line with the "#" character. Perl also ignores any blank lines that it encounters. Blank lines may be used for separating sections of code so that the code is easier to understand.

Redirecting Output

You can explicitly open a file for output, input, or appending by preceding the filename with the "<", ">," or ">>" characters. For example, if you explicitly wanted to open a file for input, you could use the following:

```
open(MYINP, "<test.dat");
```

The use of the "<" before the filename opens the file for input. Actually, leaving out the "<" character has the same effect as opening the file for input. Thus, the following statement is equivalent to the previous statement:

```
open(MYINP, "test.dat");
```

To open a file for output operations, you must precede the filename with the ">" character. You saw this in the examples of the previous section:

```
open(MYFILE, ">xyzzy.out");
```

In the previous open statement, the output file is "rewound" to the beginning. This means that output is written from the beginning of the file. Any prior contents of the file are overwritten. Suppose that you do not want to lose the contents of the output file, but want to append data to the file. An example of this could be in situations when you want to write a Perl script that would log the activity of users logging in to your server. To append to a file, you must precede the filename with ">>" in the open statement:

```
open(WEBLOG, ">>weblogdata");
```

On systems such as UNIX that allow the creation of processes whose output or input can be connected to each other using the "pipe" mechanism, you can use the "|" character as a prefix or suffix to the process name. For example, to read the input of a command who that lists the users that are logged on to the network, you can do the following:

```
open(WHOLIST, "who|");
```

To send data that will be read as input by a process (that is, write to a process), you can use the following:

```
open(LPROUT, "|lpr -Php");
```

The previous command enables data written to the file handle LPROUT to be sent to the process created by executing the following command:

```
lpr -Php
```

This command starts a printer process on a UNIX system.

Flushing Output

The output that is sent to a file handle for printing is normally buffered. This means that when you print a string out as a response to a Web browser, it may not be sent immediately. After the buffer gets full (or nearly full), the buffer contents are sent to the output stream. Buffering of output data gives the appearance of fast output operations at the expense of slightly delayed response in terms of the actual output becoming visible. For many applications (such as printing reports or writing data to a file), the buffering of output data is acceptable and actually desirable because it leads to faster program execution. In the context of a Web browser that is waiting for the output of the Perl CGI script, buffering of output operations will cause the Web browser to appear slow.

For these reasons, many Perl scripts disable the output buffering by setting the value of the special variable $| to a non-zero value:

```
$| = 1;
```

Table 7.1 shows a summary of the some important special variables.

TABLE 7.1	VARIABLE	DESCRIPTION
Summary of Special Variables	$|	When set to non-zero, disables buffering. When set to zero, buffering is enabled.
	$%	Current page number on selected output file handle. Used for report formatting.
	$=	Current page length on selected output file handle. Default value is 60.
	$-	Number of lines left on the page on the selected output file handle. Setting $- to 0 forces a top of form.
	$1..$9	Contains matched subpattern from corresponding set of patterns in parenthesis in the last pattern matched.
	$&	String matched by the last pattern match (excluding patterns matched) in nested blocks that have exited.

(continued)

TABLE 7.1	VARIABLE	DESCRIPTION
Summary of Special Variables (continued)	$`	String preceding whatever was matched by the last pattern match (excluding patterns matched) in nested blocks that have exited.
	$'	String following whatever was matched by the last pattern match excluding patterns matched in nested blocks that have exited.
	$+	Last bracketed match by the last search pattern.
	$_	The default input or the default pattern to be matched.
	$.	Current input line number.
	$/	Current input record separator. Default is newline. Setting to null is same as setting to \n\n. This causes paragraphs separated by an extra blank line to be read.
	$\	Current output record separator. Default is null.
	$,	Current output field separator for the print operator. Default is null.
	$$	Process number of Perl running this script.
	$0	Name of file containing Perl script.
	$[	Index of first element of array. Default is 0.
	$^T	Time of day when Perl script started executing.
	$ARGV	Variable containing the name of the current file when reading from <ARGV>. The ARGV file handle is usually written as <>.

Understanding Perl Scalar Variables and Data

In general, any variable beginning with a "$" character is a scalar variable. The "$" character is followed by a letter, and zero or more combinations of letters, digits and underscores. A scalar variable can hold only a single value at a time. The value could be numeric or a string value. Table 7.1 shows examples of scalar variables that have a special meaning to Perl. Changing these special variables usually has a global effect on all Perl code that is subsequently executed within the Perl script. As part of writing Perl scripts, you may want to define your own scalar variables. The following are examples of distinct Perl scalar variables:

```
$myvar        $color        $user_name
$userName     $Color        $myVar
$sam123_3     $pi_r4_hds    $dovetail
```

A Perl variable consists of the "$" character followed by an arbitrarily long sequence of letters, digits, or the underscore (_) character. Perl variables are case-sensitive. Therefore, the scalar variables $myvar, $myVar, $color, and $Color are all distinct. Scalar variables can be assigned values using an assignment statement consisting of the scalar variable name followed by the "=" assignment operator and an expression that evaluates to a single scalar value (numeric or string data):

```
$variable = scalar_expression;
```

The following are examples of assigning values to scalar variables:

```
$a = 12;        # Assigns $a the value of 10
$b = 1.0e-3;    # Assigns $b the value of 0.001
$c = 0.1eE-2;   # Assigns $c the value of 0.001
$d = "alpha";   # Assigns $d a string value of alpha.
$e = 'alpha';   # Assigns $e a string value of alpha.
                # You will learn the differences between
                # the double and single quotes later in
                # this section.
$d = -314;      # Assigns $d a value of -314. Previous
                # value which is string is replaced by
                # numeric data.
$e = 0377;      # Assigns $e a value of 255 (decimal).
                # Previous value of $e is replaced. Any
                # number followed by 0 is treated as an
                # octal number (base 8).
$f = 0xFF;      # Assigns $f a value of 255 (decimal).
                # Any number followed by 0x is treated as
                # a hexadecimal number (base 16).
$g = -xff;      # Assigns $g a value of -255 (decimal).
           # Notice that the hexadecimal digits A, B,
           # C, D, E, F can be upper or lower case.
```

Perl variables come into existence when they are first used. They must not be defined or declared explicitly. Unless the variable is declared in a subroutine or a Perl package with special qualifiers, the *scope* of Perl variables is global (that is, they can be referenced and modified any where in the Perl program). Later in this chapter you learn how to restrict the scope of Perl variables.

Perl variables that are used without first defining a value have the special value of undef. The undef value translates to a numeric value of 0 in an arithmetic expression, and a string value of "" (null) in a string expression.

Many languages make a distinction between data types (such as integer, floating point, and Boolean). In Perl, all numeric data is internally represented in double-precision format. Perl automatically provides appropriate conversion between numeric data.

Strings can be represented with single quotation marks or double quotation marks. When represented using double quotation marks, any scalar variable embedded in the string will have its value substituted in the string. Consider the following example:

```perl
$pi = 3.14;
$varname = "Mathematical constant PI";
print "$varname has the approximate value of $pi\n";
```

When you run this code fragment, you will see an output similar to the following:

```
Mathematical constant PI has the approximate value of 3.14
```

Notice that the $varname was substituted by its string value of "Mathematical constant PI" and the variable $pi was substituted by its numeric value of 3.14. The \n in the print string represents the new line character and causes a line break between several similar statements.

When you use single quotation marks to represent string data, the Perl interpreter treats it as pure string data and does not attempt to perform any variable substitution. Consider the following code fragment:

```perl
$pi = 3.14;
$varname = "Mathematical constant PI";
print '$varname has the approximate value of $pi\n';
```

When you run this code fragment, you will see an output similar to the following:

```
$varname has the approximate value of $pi
```

Notice that no substitutions were done for the $varname and the $pi variable names. This is because the string to be printed used single quotation marks instead of double quotation marks. Sometimes you may want to override the variable substitution that would normally occur in a double-quoted string. You can do this by preceding the variable name indicator $ by the escape character code (\), which means that the character that follows has a special meaning. You will notice that the use of \n in the previous example signified the code for the newline character. Consider the following code fragment that has the effect of suppressing variable evaluation within the double-quoted string:

```
$pi = 3.14;
$varname = "Mathematical constant PI";
print "\$varname has the approximate value of \$pi\n";
```

When you run this code fragment, you will see the same output as the previous code fragment:

```
$varname has the approximate value of $pi
```

Table 7.2 shows the common escape codes used in Perl.

TABLE 7.2	ESCAPE CODE	DESCRIPTION
Common Escape Codes in Perl	\n	New line
	\r	Carriage return
	\t	Horizontal tab
	\f	Form feed
	\b	Backspace
	\v	Vertical tab
	\a	Bell character (rings bell in old ASCII terminals)
	\e	Escape
	\0ddd	Octal value of *ddd*
	\xhh	Hexadecimal digits of *hh*
	\cX	Any control character (such as CTRL-X in this example)
	\"	The double quotation mark character
	\\	Backslash character
	\l	Lowercase the next letter
	\u	Uppercase the next letter
	\L	Lowercase all following letters until \E
	\U	Uppercase all following letters until \E
	\E	End the effect of \L or \U

Scalar variables can be assigned a *scalar constant* (also called a *scalar literal*) as seen in the previous examples and also *scalar expressions*. Scalar expressions can have numeric or string values. Numeric expressions involve the use of the traditional operators plus (+), minus (-), multiply (*), divide (/), and exponentiation (**). The modulus operator (%) that yields the remainder of an arithmetic division is defined. The following examples illustrate the use of these operators.

```
$u = 3 * 4;          # $u is set to 12
$v = 3 /4;           # $v is set to 0.75
$w = 3 + 4;          # $w is set to 7
$w = $w + 3 ** 4;    # $w is set to 12 + 81 = 93
$x = 3 % 4;          # $x is set to 3
$y = 4 % 3;          # $y is set to 1
$z = 12.5 % 9.7      # Operands are converted to integer
                     # values first. 12.7 becomes 12 and 9.7
                     # becomes 9. The remainder after the
                     # division is 3 so $z is set to 3.
```

The previous statement that sets the value of $w to 93 can also be written using the following shorthand notation:

```
$w += 3 ** 4;
```

The += operator adds to the scalar variable on the left side the value of the expression on the right side. The previous assignment statement is, therefore, equivalent to the following:

```
$w = $w + 3 ** 4;
```

Other shorthand binary assignment operators include the following:

```
-= *=     /=     %=    **=
```

The following assignment statements are equivalent:

```
$var op= expr;
$var = $var op expr;
```

The operator *op* is any of the operators +, -, *, /, %, ** and nearly all other binary operators in Perl.

Other special operators such as auto-increment (++), auto-decrement (--), left shift (<<), right shift (>>), bitwise OR (|), bitwise AND (&), bitwise EXCLUSIVE

OR (^), and bitwise NOT or complement (~), are also defined. The following examples illustrate their uses. The statements listed here all have the same effect (that is, they increment the value of $m by 1).

```
++$m;          # Prefix auto increment
$m++;          # Postfix auto increment
$m += 1;       # Using binary assignment operator
$m = $m + 1;   # Using assignment operator
```

Similarly, the following statements all decrement the value of $m by 1:

```
-$m;           # Prefix auto decrement
$m-;           # Postfix auto decrement
$m -= 1;       # Using binary assignment operator
$m = $m - 1;   # Using assignment operator
```

In the previous examples, the prefix and postfix operators have the same effect. How are they different? When this operator appears on the right side of an assignment operator, it has a different effect:

```
$n = 108;      # $n is set to 108
$p = $n-;      # $p is 108 but $n is 107
$n = 108;      # $n is set to 108
$q = -$n;      # $n is set to 107, and then $q is
               # set to 107.
$n = 108;      # $n is set to 108
$p = $n++;     # $p is 108 but $n is 109
$n = 108;      # $n is set to 108
$q = ++$n;     # $n is set to 109, and then $q is
               # set to 109.
```

The bit-shift operators result in the binary value of the evaluated arithmetic expression being shifted:

```
$a = 1;        # $a set to 1
$a = $a << 2;  # $a set to 4
$a = 9;        # $a set to 9
$a = $a > 2;   # $a set to 2
```

Each left shift has the effect of multiplying the value by 2, and the right shift has the effect of dividing the value by 2.

The bit operators such as bitwise OR (|), bitwise AND (&), bitwise EXCLUSIVE OR (^), and bitwise NOT (~) operate on the individual bits that make up a value. The operators are applied to corresponding bits in each expression. Here are some examples illustrating their uses:

```
$a = 11;       # set $a to 11
$b = 5;        # set $b to 5
$c = $a | $b;  # $c set to 15
$d = $a & $b;  # $d set to 9
$e = $a ^ $b;  # $e set to 6
$f = ~a;       # $f set to 4
```

If you have not come across these operators in other languages, the following explanations of the previous code fragment will help:

Bitwise OR:

```
$a =        1 0 1 1    # Bit pattern for decimal 11
$b =        0 1 0 1    # Bit pattern for decimal 5

$c =        1 1 1 1    # Resulting bit pattern for
                         $a | $b
```

Bitwise AND:

```
$a =        1 0 1 1    # Bit pattern for decimal 11
$b =        0 1 0 1    # Bit pattern for decimal 5

$d =        1 0 0 1    # Resulting bit pattern for
                         $a & $b
```

Bitwise EXCLUSIVE OR:

```
$a =        1 0 1 1    # Bit pattern for decimal 11
$b =        0 1 0 1    # Bit pattern for decimal 5

$e =        0 1 1 0    # Resulting bit pattern for
                         $a ^ $b
```

Bitwise NOT:

```
$a =        1 0 1 1    # Bit pattern for decimal 11
```

```
$f =            0 1 0 0      # Resulting bit pattern for ~$a
```

Perl provides logical comparison operators for numbers: equal (==), not equal (!=), less than (<), greater than (>), less than or equal (<=), greater than or equal (>=), and signed compare (<=>). The signed compare returns a -1, 0, or 1, depending on whether the first operand is less than, equal to, greater than the second operand.

The result of the comparison yields a *false* or *true* value. A *false* value is the number 0, and a *true* value is the number 1.

The operators on string data include concatenation (.), string repetition (x), and comparison operators. Here are some examples of using the concatenation operator:

```
$s = "Life" . " begets ". "life"; # $s is set to
                                   # "Life begets life".
$space = " ";
$t = "Raja". $space . "Yoga";    # $t is set to "Raja Yoga"
$t .= "!";    # $t is set to "Raja Yoga!"
              # Same as $t = $t . "!"
print "He who hates none, who is the friend of all,\n" .
   "who is merciful to all, who has nothing of his\n".
   "own, who is free from egotism, who is even-minded\n".
   "in pain or pleasure, who is forbearing, who is\n".
   "always satisfied, whose life has become\n".
   "controlled, whose will is firm, whose mind and\n".
   "intellect are given unto Me ... such a one is\n".
   "my beloved bhakta. Such a one becomes a yogi.\n\n";
```

The last print statement contains several string literals that are concatenated. It shows how large text paragraphs can be printed using a single print statement.

The string repetition operator specified by the lowercase "x," takes the left operand (string data) and repeats by the number of times specified in the right operator to form a concatenated string:

```
$s = "Hari!";           # Set $s to "Hari!"
$t = $s x 4;            # Set $t to
"Hari!Hari!Hari!Hari!"
```

```
$t = "Har " x (9 > 2);      # Set $t to "Har Har "
$t x= 2;                     # Sets $t to "Har Har Har Har "
                            # Same as $t = $t x 2;
print "=" x 80, "\n";        # Print a line of 80 "=".
```

A common operator used with strings is the chop operator. This is a *unary operator* (that is, it takes a single string value and removes the last character from the string value). Consider the following example:

```
$x = "Success is speedy for the energetic.";
chop($x);       # chops the last character '.'.
chop $x;        # Same as previous statement but
                # without the parenthesis.
```

The first chop operator removes the period (.) from the string and the string becomes "Success is speedy for the energetic". The next chop operator further removes the last character "c," and the value of $x is "Success is speedy for the energeti". The chop operator returns a value that is the character that was removed.

The comparison operators for strings have a different notation than that used for numbers. These operators are equal (eq), not equal (ne), less than (lt), greater than (gt), less than or equal (le), greater than or equal (ge), and signed compare (cmp). The signed compare returns a -1, 0, or 1, depending on whether the first operand is less than, equal to, or greater than the second operand. Here are some examples:

```
$s = "like";
$t = "this";
$at = $s eq "like";  # $at is set to 1
$af = $s eq "Like";  # $af  is set to 0
$bt = $s ne "Like";  # $bt is set to 1
$bf = $s ne "like";  # $bf is set to 0
$ct = $s le $t;      # $ct is set to 1
$cf = "this" le $s;  # $ct is set to 0
$ct = "like" le $s;  # $ct is set to 1
$dt = $s lt $t;      # $dt is set to 1
$df = "like" lt $s;  # $df is set to 0
$et = $t ge $s;      # $et is set to 1
$ef = $s ge "this";  # $ef is set to 0
```

```
$ft = $s ge "like"; # $ft is set to 1
$ft = $t gt $s;     # $ft is set to 1
$ff = "like" gt $s; # $ff is set to 0
$gf = "9" lt "27";  # $gf is set to 0.
$gt = "312" gt "1000"; # $gt is set to 1.
$cmp = "9" cmp "27"; # $cmp set to 1.
```

Why does Perl use a different set of comparison operators used for numeric and string data? Consider the values 9 and 27. In an arithmetic comparison 9 is less than 27, but when compared as strings "9" and "27", the string "9" is greater than "27". This is because the string "9" comes before "27" using the ASCII encodings of the string.

You can create complex logical expressions by combining them using logical AND (&&), logical OR (||), and logical NOT (!). The following are a few examples:

```
$logical1 = $reading >= 1 && $reading <= 100;
$logical2 = $x < 100 || $y;
$logical3 = !($x > 0 && x < 256);
```

Converting Between Strings and Numbers

If Perl expects a string or numeric data of a certain type such as integers, it automatically performs the conversion. For example, the left operand of the repetition operator (x) is expected to be a string and the right operand is an integer. Consider the following statement:

```
$rept = 67 x 3.9;   # $rept is set to "676767".
```

Perl encounters the number 67 as the left operand. Because it is expecting a string value, the number 67 is converted to the string "67". Next, Perl expects to see an integer value for the right operand. Instead, it encounters the non-integer value of 3.9. Perl converts this to an integer by truncating the value of 3.9 to the integer 3. Repeating "67" three times results in the string "676767".

Consider the following example:

```
$ns1 = "11";
$ns2 = "33";
$sum = $ns1 + $ns2; # $sum is set to 44.
```

The variables $ns1 and $ns2 contain string values. When they are added together in the last statement, Perl is expecting numeric operands for the plus (+) operator. Perl, therefore, converts the string values to numeric values and performs the addition. The result is a numeric 44.

When strings are converted to numbers, leading white space and trailing non-digits are ignored. Consider the following example:

```
$ns1 = " 11But this is not a proper number";
$ns2 = "alpha"; # No digits!
$sum = $ns2 - $ns1;  # $sum is set to -11.
```

In the previous example, when Perl encounters the variables $ns1 and $ns2 that contain string data in an arithmetic expression, it converts them to numeric values. The $ns1 variable has a converted value of 11 (all leading white space and non-digit data is ignored). The $ns2 variable has a converted value of 0 because all non-digit data is ignored and the resulting string "" is converted to 0.

Consider the following concatenation example to see what is printed on the console when string data and numbers are concatenated:

```
print  "Catch". (56 - 17*2); # Prints Catch22
```

The concatenate operator is expecting a string value after the concatenate operator (.). Instead, it sees a numeric expression. After the numeric expression is evaluated (value 22), it is converted into a string ("22"), and concatenated to the left operand. The resulting string "Catch22" is then printed out.

All conversions are performed *silently* without generating any errors-however unexpected the actual conversion is.

Reading Input from STDIN

You have seen several examples of printing data, but how do you read data from the keyboard or a file? To read data from the keyboard, you can use the standard file handle STDIN. Recall from the earlier discussion that STDIN is the standard input file handle (usually the keyboard). Consider the following code fragment that reads a line of input from the console and throws away the newline character that terminates the user response:

```
print "Please enter your user name:";
$username = <STDIN>;
```

```
chop ($username);
```

When the <STDIN> is assigned to a scalar variable, a line of input is returned as a string value in the scalar variable. The Perl script will wait until the user enters a response. The response usually has the newline character appended to the end. To remove this newline character, you can use the chop operator.

You can combine the last two statements in the previous example into a single statement as follows:

```
chop ($username = <STDIN>);
```

Note that STDIN contains text lines separated by the newline character, which is treated as a record separator. If you had a file handle to a file containing binary data, the read operator <> would read the entire file. Consider the following example:

```
open (BINARY, "<binfile.dat");
print <BINARY>;      # This will print the entire binary
                     # file on standard output.
$data = <BINARY>;    # $data will contain the entire
                     # binary file data!
```

Defining Perl Arrays

Perl defines two types of arrays: arrays indexed by a range of integer values, and arrays indexed by arbitrary scalar values. This section discusses arrays indexed by a range of integer values. Arrays indexed by arbitrary scalar values are called *associative arrays* (or a *hash*) and are discussed in a subsequent section.

An array variable consists of the character @ followed by a letter, and zero or more combinations of letters, digits, and underscores. The following are all examples of distinct array variables:

```
@list       @names      @Names
@List       @exprs      @Exprs
@LongList   @longlist   @It_Erators
```

The array variable can be assigned an *array literal*, which is a list of scalar values enclosed in parentheses. The following are all examples of array literals:

```
(1, 2, 3, 5, 7, 12) # Array of numeric values. First
```

```
element 1, 2nd element 2,                          # 3rd element 3, 4th
element 5, 5th element 7, 6th
element 12
("Phylos", "Thibetian", -10000, 1800)  # Array of strings and
numbers: 4      elements
("expr" , $el-)               # Array of string and arithmetic
expressions: 2         elements
()               # Array of 0 elements: empty array.
```

Arrays can be built using the list constructor operator (..). For example, the following are equivalent representations of an array consisting of elements 1 to 9:

```
(1..9)
(1, 2, 3, 4, 5, 6, 7, 8, 9)
```

The elements of the list are generated by adding 1 successively to the left operand, until the right operand value is reached or exceeded. If the right operand value is exceeded, the element is not part of the array. Here are some additional examples that show assignment to arrays:

```
@a = (1.1 .. 4.1); # @a is set to (1.1, 2.1, 3.1, 4.1)
@b = (11..13, "C", 4..6); # @b is set to (11, 12, 13, "C",
                          # 4, 5, 6)
@c = (10 .. 9); # @c is set to () an empty array
@d = (1.1 .. 4.0); # @d is set to (1.1, 2.1, 3.1). The
                   # element 4.1 would exceed 4.0 and
                   # is not included.
```

You can assign array variables to array variables. In this case, the contents of the array variables are copied to another array.

```
@Anzimee = (1, -1); # 2 element array
@Phyris = @Anzimee; # @Phyris now is (1, -1)
```

An array variable can occur inside another list, in which case the array elements are merged in position with the list in which it occurs:

```
@lc = ("yellow", "pink", "white",
  "green", "violet-gold");
@rays = ("blue", @lc, "violet");
```

This assigns to @rays the value of ("blue", "yellow", "pink", "white", "green", "violet-gold", "violet").

If the array literal consists of scalar variables, you can use it in the left side of an assignment operator:

```
($x, $y, $z) = ( -1, 2, "cd"); # $x = -1, $y = 2, $z = "cd"
($u, @leftover) = (1, 2, 4, 5) # $u = 1,
                                        # @leftover = (2, 4, 5)
($x, $y) = ($y, $x)  # Swap $x and $y!
($throw, @x) = @x;   # Remove first element of @x
($first) = @x;       # Get first element of @x
@x = (@x, $add); # Add $add as last element of array @x
($x, $y) = (4, 5, 8, 9);# $x = 4, $y = 5. Values 8, 9 are
                    # discarded.
($m, $n, $p, $q) = (3, 6); # $m = 3, $n = 6. $p and $q are
                        # undefined.
```

If an array is assigned to a scalar variable or used in a scalar context, the array returns a number that is assigned is the *length* of the array. The length of the array is the number of elements in the array.

```
$size = (1, 3, 5, 1, 6);   # $size is set to 5
```

You can explicitly force a scalar context by using the scalar function. For example the following code will cause the loop index $x to be set to each of the index values for the array @images.

```
@images = ("image1.gif", "image2.gif", "image3.gif");
for ($x = 0; $x < scalar(@images); $x++)
{
  # Do something
}
```

You can access individual elements of an array by using a subscript notation. By default, the elements of the array are indexed starting from 0. Because the individual elements of the array are scalars, you must precede the array name with a "$" character when referencing an element of an array:

```
@types = ("bmp", "pcx", "tiff");
$first = $types[0]; # $first set to "bmp"
```

You can assign a value to an array element. Doing so changes the original array:

```
@evals = (3.0, 3.7, 3.9, 4.0);
$evals[0] = 3.9; # @evals = (3.9, 3.7, 3.9, 4.0)
$evals[2] += 0.1; # @evals = (3.9, 3.7, 4.0, 4.0)
($evals[0], $evals[3]) = ($evals[3], $evals[0]);
                        # Swaps first and last elements
```

Referencing an element of an array that is not in range returns the undef value. Assigning to an element of an array with an index that is beyond the end of the current array automatically extends the array so that new intermediate values are set to undef.

```
@list = (3, 7, 4);
$x = $list[3]; # $x is undef
$list[3] = 8; # @list is now (3, 7, 4, 8)
$list[6] = 9; # @list is now (3, 7, 4, 8, undef, undef, 9)
```

You can create a slice of an array by using the list constructor operator (..) or enumerating the index values:

```
@scores = (9.2, 9.4, 8.8, 10.0);
@x = @scores[0 .. 2]; # @x is (9.2, 9.4, 8.8)
@y = @scores[3,2,1,0]; # @y is (10.0, 8.8, 9.4, 9.2)
@scores[1,2] = @scores[3,3] # @scores =
                            # (9.2, 10.0, 10.0, 10.0)
@y[0,1] = @y[0,1]; # Swap first and second elements of @y
```

Perl defines special operators for removing elements and adding elements to the ends of the arrays. One set of operators are push and pop, and the other are shift and unshift. The push operator appends a value to the array, and the pop operator removes the last value. You can use the push and pop operation to make the array behave like a stack (see Figure 7.3). The following shows an example of using the push/pop operator;

```
@list = (1, 1, 2, 3);
push(@list, 5);      # @list set to (1, 1, 2, 3, 5)
                     # Same as @list = (@list, 5);
$top = pop(@list);   # $top set to 5. @list is (1, 1, 2, 3)
$top = pop(@list);   # $top set to 3. @list is (1, 1, 2)
```

```
$top = pop(@list);    # $top set to 2. @list is (1, 1)
$top = pop(@list);    # $top set to 1. @list is (1)
$top = pop(@list);    # $top set to 1. @list is ()
$top = pop(@list);    # $top set to undef. @list is ()
```

From the last statement, you can see that using pop() on empty array returns an undef value.

FIGURE 7.3

The Perl push/pop operator makes the array behave like the stack data structure

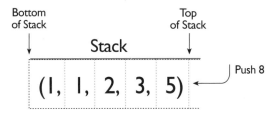
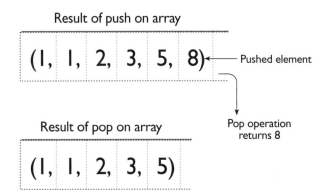

You can push a list of values (an entire array) on an array rather than push single scalar values:

```
@list = (1, 1);
push(@list, 2, 3, 5);    # @list set to (1, 1, 2, 3, 5)
push(@list, @list);      # @list set to (1, 1, 2, 3, 5,
                         #               1, 1, 2, 3, 5)
```

The push and pop operators performed operations on the right end of the array list. If you must add or remove elements from the beginning of the array, you can use the shift/unshift operators. The unshift operator adds elements to the beginning of the array. Existing elements of the array are shifted one element to the right and the array increases in size. You can add a single element or an array list using the unshift operator. The shift operator performs a left shift and removes the first element of the array. The following illustrates the use of the shift/unshift operators:

```perl
@list = (1, 2, 3, 5);
unshift(@list, 1);    # @list set to (1, 1, 2, 3, 5)
                      # Same as @list = (5, @list);
$t = shift(@list);    # $t set to 1. @list is (1, 2, 3, 5)
$t = shift(@list);    # $t set to 1. @list is (2, 3, 5)
$t = shift(@list);    # $t set to 2. @list is (3, 5)
$t = shift(@list);    # $t set to 3. @list is (5)
$t = shift(@list);    # $t set to 5. @list is ()
$t = shift(@list);    # $t set to undef. @list is ()
```

From the last statement, you can see that using shift() on empty array returns an undef value.

If you want to reverse the elements or sort the elements of an array, you can use the reverse or sort operators. The reversal and sorting is done on a copy of the array, and the original array is not altered. If you must change the original array into the sorted or reversed version, you must assign the result of the array and sort operations to the array variable.

```perl
@list = (5, 2, 7, 9);
@slist = sort(@list);        # @slist set to (2, 5, 7, 9)
@rlist = reverse(@list);     # @rlist set to (9, 7, 2, 5)
@elist = reverse(sort(@list)); # @elist set to (9, 7, 5, 2)
@list = reverse(@list);      # @list = (9, 7, 2, 5)
```

The sort operator takes the elements of the array to be ASCII strings. So, sorting for numbers may not be what you may expect.

```perl
@list = (1, 2, 5, 11, 15, 30);
@slist = sort(@list);        # @slist set to (1, 11, 15, 2,
                             #                30, 5)
@scolors = sort("red", "blue", "green");
                             # @scolors set to ("blue",
                             #    "green", "red")
```

Earlier you saw the use of the chop operator in removing the last character of the string value. You can also use the chop operator on arrays. All elements of the array will have their last character removed. Here is an example that removes the newline character from each of the array elements:

```
@lines = ("Associative\n", "arrays\n", "begin with\n",
        "a % symbol\n");
chop (@lines); # @lines becomes ("Associative", "arrays",
               # "begin with", "a % symbol")
```

In the previous section you saw the use of the <STDIN> to return the next line of input when it is assigned to a scalar variable or used in a scalar context. The <STDIN> can also be assigned to an array variable or used in an array context. In an array context, <STDIN> returns all the remaining lines up to the end of the file. For terminal input, the end-of-file is signified by CTRL-D or CTRL-Z. The elements of the array are assigned string values for each line of input. These are usually terminated by the newline character. To remove the newlines for all the lines you could use the chop operator:

```
@lines = <STDIN>;      # Reads all lines in an array context
chop(@lines);          # Removes newlines.
```

Using Perl Control Statements

The examples of Perl code given in the earlier sections of this chapter are deliberately simple and do not show conditional execution of code. Perl enables you to execute statements depending upon the evaluation of a Perl expression. This section will discuss the major types of Perl control statements:

- block statement

- if/unless statement

- while/until loop statement

- for statement

- foreach statement

The `block` statement is a grouping of several Perl statements into a single block enclosed by a pair of braces { }. Perl executes each of the statements in the block in sequence. The `block` statement can be used in any place Perl expects a single statement. `block` statements are primarily useful when used with other control statements to execute a group of statements when a Perl expression evaluates to a true value. The following shows an example of a `block` statement:

```
{
   $x = 1;
   @list = (5, 2, 7, 9, $x);
   @slist = sort(@list);
   $y = pop(@slist);
   $z = shift(@list);
   print "sum = ", $y+$z, "\n";

}
```

Suppose that you wanted to execute a statement or a group of statements depending on the evaluation of a Perl expression. You can do this using the `if` statement that has the following syntax:

```
if (PerlExpression)
{
   PerlStatement;
}

if (PerlExpression)
{
   PerlStatement;
}
else
{
   PerlStatement;
}
```

The *PerlExpression* is any Perl expression and the *PerlStatement* is any Perl statement. The braces around *PerlStatement* are required syntax. If the *PerlExpression* evaluates to true, the first *PerlStatement* is executed; if it evaluates to false the second *PerlStatement* is executed. Here are examples of the use of `if` statements:

```perl
if ($count > 10)
{
  $x = 1;
}
if ($count > 20)
{
  $x = 3;
  @list = (5, 2, 7, 9, $x);
  @slist = sort(@list);
  $y = pop(@slist);
  $z = shift(@list);
  print "sum = ", $x+$y+$z, "\n";

}
else
{
  $x++;
}
```

Perl uses the following rules to determine if an expression evaluates to *true*. The Perl expression is evaluated to a string. If the expression is already a string, no conversion is needed. If it is a number, it is converted to a string. If the string is "0" or the empty string, "", then the expression is false; if it is anything else, the expression is true. The following are example of expressions that evaluate to true or false:

```perl
1        #Convert to "1" first. Evaluates to true.
0        #Convert to "0" first. Evaluates to false.
81       #Convert to "81" first. Evaluate to true.
-3       #Convert to "-3" first. Evaluate to true.
"0"      #Evaluate to false.
"ks"     #Evaluate to true.
"00"     #Not "0" or "". Evaluate to true! Tricky!
"0.0"    #Not "0" or "". Evaluate to true! Tricky!
""       #Evaluate to false
```

```
undef    #Evaluate to false
```

If you only need to execute the statement in the `else` part, there are several ways of writing such a statement:

```
if (expr)
{
}
else
{
    statement;
}

if (!expr)
{
    statement;
}

unless (expr)
{
    statement;
}
```

In the previous three statements, *expr* is assumed to be the same Perl expression. The first statement form with an empty pair of braces is seldom used. The second form is more traditional and is found in many programming languages. The Perl *statement* is executed when the *expr* is false. The last is the Perl `unless` statement. It means the following: The *statement* is executed unless *expr* is true—that is, if the expression is false, the *statement* is executed; and if the expression is true, the *statement* is not executed.

If you must execute one of many code blocks depending on the evaluation of an expression, you can use the following form of the `if` statement:

```
if (expr1)
{
    statement1;
}
elsif (expr2)
```

```
{
    statement2;
}
elsif (expr3)
{
    statement3;
}
else
{
    statement4;
}
```

Each of the expressions, *expr1*, *expr2*, and *expr3*, are evaluated in turn. When any of them evaluate to true, the corresponding statement is executed. Notice the use of the `elsif` reserved word to cascade a number of `if` statements together. The last `else` part is optional. If present, it will be executed only if all other expressions evaluate to false.

If you want to execute a group of statements repeatedly, you can use the `while` or `until` statement:

```
while (expr)
{
    statement1;
    :
    statementN;
}
until (expr)
{
    statement1;
    :
    statementN;
}
```

In the `while`-statement, the group of statements is executed as long as the *expr* evaluates to true. The loop is exited when the *expr* evaluates to false. The `until` statement is the opposite of the `while` statement. In the `until`-statement, the group of statements is executed as long as the *expr* evaluates to false. The loop is exited when the *expr* evaluates to true.

You could use a `while`-statement to read the console input and write to a file. The loop is terminated when an empty line is encountered or the end-of-file is generated:

```
open(OUTFILE, ">data.out");
while (chop($line = <STDIN>))
{
   print OUTFILE, $line, "\n";
}
close(OUTFILE);
```

Another example of the use of the `while` statement that reads standard input is as follows:

```
while (<STDIN>)
{
   chop;
   print;
}
```

When the input operator (<>) is used to read a scalar value, and no explicit scalar variable is assigned, then the value is automatically assigned to the special variable $_. The $_ variable is the default for many operators such as `chop` and `print`. The previous `while` statement is therefore equivalent to the following:

```
while ($_ = <STDIN>)
{
   chop $_;
   print $_;
}
```

If you must read data from the files specified on the command line, you can replace the <STDIN> operator with the *diamond operator* <> as shown in the next example:

```
while (<>)
{
   chop;
   print;
}
```

When the diamond operator reaches the end of the file, it opens the next file specified in the command line and commences reading each line. The diamond operator actually gets the filenames to read from the special array @ARGV. This array is set by the Perl interpreter on startup with the arguments that are specified in the command line. If you change the elements of @ARGV with your own filenames, the diamond operator will read from your specified files instead of the command line files:

```
@ARGV = ("book1.dat", "book2.dat", "book3.dat");
while (<>) # Reads fron book1.data, book2.dat, book3.dat
{
   # Process data in $_
   print;
}
```

Another form of loop statement is the for statement, which has the following syntax:

```
for (intExpr; evalExpr; incrExpr)
{
   statement1;
   :
   statementN;
}
```

This for statement is actually equivalent to the following while statement:

```
intExpr;
while (evalExpr)
{
   statement1;
   :
   statementN;
   incrExpr;
}
```

The meaning of the for-statement is as follows. First the *initExpr* is evaluated. Next, the *evalExpr* is tested to see if it evaluates to true or false. A false evaluation terminates the loop, and a true evaluation executes the statements in the loop. Typically, the *incrExpr* is such that it causes the *evalExpr* to evaluate to a different value the next time around. The *initExpr*, *evalExpr*, and *incrExpr* are all optional. Here are some examples of the use of the for statement:

```
for ($x = 1, @s = (); $x < 10; $x++)
{
  push (@s, $x*3 . " ");
  print @s, "\n";
}
```

Notice that you can use a series of expressions in the *initExpr* and *incrExpr*. In the previous example, $x is set to 1, and @s set to an empty array initially. When the for statement is executed, it produces the following output:

```
3
3 6
3 6 9
3 6 9 12
3 6 9 12 15
3 6 9 12 15 18
3 6 9 12 15 18 21
3 6 9 12 15 18 21 24
3 6 9 12 15 18 21 24 27
```

The following for statement sets up an infinite loop that will not terminate unless a statement in the for-loop terminates the loop, or an external means is used to terminate the loop:

```
for(;;)
{
  statement;
}
```

If you want to execute the statements in a for loop for each value of an array literal or an array, you can use a special form of statement called the foreach statement:

```
foreach $scalar (@arrayname)
{
  statement1;
  :
  statementN;

}
```

The scalar loop variable $scalar (or any other variable name) is set to each element of the array starting with the first element and proceeding to the last element. For each value of the scalar variable, the group of statements is executed. When the loop terminates, the original value of the scalar variables is restored. Here is an example of a `foreach` statement:

```
$x = 100;
print "\$x = $x\n\n";
foreach $x (10, 20, 30, 40)
{
   print $x . " ";
}
print "\n\n\$x = $x\n";
```

This `foreach` statement produces the following output:

```
$x = 100
10 20 30 40
$x = 100
```

Notice that the original value of $x is restored when the loop terminates.

You can control the execution of the loop from inside the loop by executing any of the following special statements:

▶   `last` statement

▶   `next` statement

▶   `redo` statement

The use of the `last` statement terminates the loop. Typically, you use this statement after testing a condition within the loop:

```
while (expr1)
{
   statement1;
   if (expr2)
   {
         last;
```

```
    }
    statement2;
          :
    statementN;
  }
```

In the previous statement, when *expr2* evaluates to true, the `while` loop is terminated. If you have nested loops of `for` or `while` statements and you want to terminate a specific loop, you can use the general form of the `last` statement as follows:

```
last;
last label;
```

The *label* is a reference to a label that can be attached to any loop statement. Here is an example:

```
FIRST: foreach $x (@list1)
{
   SECOND: foreach $y (@list2)
   {

         if ($y < 0)
         {
               last SECOND;
         }
         elsif ($x*$y == 20)
         {
               last FIRST;
         }
         print "product = ", $x*$y, "\n";
   }


}
```

The previous statements print the product of elements of two arrays. When the product is a special value of 20, the outer loop is terminated. This also terminates the inner loop. When the value of `$y` is negative, the inner loop is terminated and the outer loop continues with the next value of its scalar loop variable.

Within a loop, you can skip to the next iteration and omit the execution of the remaining statements in the loop by executing the `next` statement. The `next` statement has the following syntax:

```
next;
next label;
```

The *label* is reference to a label that can be attached to any loop statement.

If you must jump to the top of the loop and redo the loop without evaluating the control expression in the loop, you can use the `redo` statement. The `redo` statement has the following syntax:

```
redo;
redo label;
```

Again, the *label* is reference to a label that can be attached to any loop statement.

Perl has some special types of conditional execution statements that can be used to shorten the amount of typing that you have to do. These are listed next along with their more traditional equivalent forms. You can figure out what these short form statements do by examining their equivalent long forms:

The following is a short `if` statement:

```
expr2 if expr1;
```

The previous is equivalent to the following `if` statement:

```
if (expr1)
{
  expr2;
}
```

The following is a short `unless` statement:

```
expr2 unless expr1;
```

The previous is equivalent to the following `unless`-statement:

```
unless (expr1)
{
  expr2;
}
```

The following is a short `while`-statement:

```
expr2 while expr1;
```

The previous is equivalent to the following `while` statement:

```
while (expr1)
{
  expr2;
}
```

The following is a short `until` statement:

```
expr2 until expr1;
```

The previous is equivalent to the following `until` statement:

```
until (expr1)
{
  expr2;
}
```

Using Perl Associative Arrays

An associative array variable begins with a "%" character, followed by a letter, and zero or more combinations of letters, digits, and underscores. The index to the array can be an arbitrary scalar value called a *key*. Consider the following definition of an associative array:

```
%streets = ("linda", "312 Grant St.", "mary", "300 People
Rd.",
                "anita", "50 Sirius Rd.");
```

The associative array is constructed by enumerating the `key`, `value` pair in a list. The previous statement creates three elements of the associative array `%streets`:

```
Key      Value
"linda"  "312 Grant St"
"mary"   "300 People Rd."
"anita"  "50 Sirius Rd."
```

Each of the elements (values) of the array can be referenced using the following notation:

```
$streets{"linda"}
```

```
$streets{"mary"}
$streets{"anita"}
```

Notice that because the value of an element is a scalar, you must precede it with a "$" character. Also notice the use of the {} for specifying the index that distinguishes it from an index for a normal Perl array.

You can create new elements of the array by assigning values to the array, as shown in the following example:

```
$streets{"melinda"} = "700 Geary St.";
$streets{"katy"} = "130 First St.";
$streets{"betty"} = "22 Lawerence Exp.";
```

The previous statements create three new elements of the array.

If you assign an associative array, you get the key, value pairs of the array. For example consider the following:

```
%ax = ("a", 12, "b", 33, "e", 56);
@x = %ax; # @x set to ("a", 12, "b", 33, "e", 56)
```

You can use the keys() operator to get a list of keys of an associative array, and the values() operator to gets a list of the values.

```
%ax = ("user1", 90, "user2", 50, "user3", 33);
@names1 = keys(%ax);        # @names1 = ("user1", "user2",
"user3")
@names2 = keys %ax;         # Same as @names1.
@scores = values(%ax);      # @scores = (90, 50, 33)
$nelemnts = keys %ax;       # $nelements set to 3. Scalar
context
                            # returns number of elements
```

Here is an example that prints each key, value pair in a key sorted order:

```
foreach $k sort(keys %ax)
{
   print "%ax[$k] = $ax{$k}\n";
}
```

Instead of using the keys operator to iterate over each key of an associative array, you can use the more efficient each operator that returns the key, value pair as an array of two elements. The following prints the name and street address of the %streets array defined previously:

```
while (($name, $street) = each(%streets))
{
   print "$name\t\t$street\n");
}
```

To delete a specific element of an associative array, use the delete operator and specify the value of the array being removed.

For example, the following deletes the score for user2 from the associative array %scores:

```
%scores = ("user1", 99, "user2", 45, "user3", 63);
delete $scores{"user2"};
```

Matching Perl Strings

Perl provides a powerful method to match string data against a template. The template for the data to be matched is called a *regular expression*. The regular expression is included as a string of characters and metacharacters between two forward slashes. A *metacharacter* is a character that has a special meaning.

```
/regular_expression/[g][i][o]
m/regular_expression/[g][i][o]
```

The option "g" is a *global-match option* (that is, it remembers where the last match took place and restarts after the last match if the regular expression is used again). The option "i" is for case-insensitive match; the option "o" is an instruction to the Perl compiler to compile the expression once. You can use the "o" option in situations when you do not expect the value of the *regular_expression* to change. If you want to use a different delimiter than "/" for the regular expressions, you can prefix the regular expression with the character "m" followed by the delimiter character. This is useful if you expect the regular expression to contain the character "/".

The match operator consists of the following characters: =~. Consider the following example:

```
$line = "The computer wizards of Silicon Valley";
if ($line =~ /wizard/)
```

```
{
  print "Match found\n";
}
else
{
  print "Match not found\n";
}
```

The expression $line =~ /wizard/ tests the scalar variable $line to see if there is an occurrence of the characters in the regular expression (wizard, in this case). If the regular expression occurs by itself without the =~ match operator the string being matched is assumed to be in the scalar variable $_. Thus the following two match expressions are equivalent:

```
$_ =~ /wizard/
```

```
/wizard/
```

Here is an example of Perl code that reads standard input and prints only the lines that contain the pattern /wizard/:

```
while (<STDIN>)
{
  print if /wizard/;
}
```

The previous while statement is equivalent to the following:

```
while ($_ = <STDIN>)
{
  if ($_ =~ /wizard/)
  {
        print $_;
  }
}
```

In addition to the =~ match operator, Perl also supports the !~ operator (called the *not match operator*). The !~ operator returns a true value when there is no pattern match and a false value otherwise.

If you want the regular expression to match the beginning of the string, precede the regular expression with the "^" character. If you want the match to occur at the end of the string, place the "$" character at the end of the regular expression. In the absence of these special characters, the match could take place at any part of the string. Here are some examples that illustrate this:

```
/^wizard/     #wizard must occur at the beginning of the
string
/wizard$/     #wizard must occur at the end of the string
/wizard/      #wizard can match any part of the string
```

The regular expression can contain any characters. However, if a metacharacter such as a period (.), asterisk (*), question mark(?), and other characters are encountered, they are treated specially. Table 7.3 shows a list of some common metacharacters in Perl.

TABLE 7.3	METACHARACTERS	DESCRIPTION
Special Characters Used in Perl	.	Any character except a newline
	*	Zero or more of the previous character
	?	One of more occurrences of the previous character
	\d	Any digit 0-9
	\w	Any word character: a-z, A-Z, 0-9, _
	\s	Any space character: \r, \t, \n, \f, space character
	\D	Any character that is not a digit (opposite of \d)
	\W	Any character that is not a word character. (opposite of \w)
	\S	Any character that is not a space character. (opposite of \s)
	{m,n}	*m* to *n* occurrences of the preceding character.
	{m,}	*m* or more occurrences of the preceding character.
	{m}	Exactly *m* occurrences of the preceding character.

The following are examples of regular expressions. The comments show some example string values of $_ that are matched.

```
/a.b/   #Matches acb axb, agb. No match for ab, ba
```

```
/a*b/     #Matches b, ab, aab, aaab. No match for ba, ca
/a?b/     #Matches ab, aab, aaab. No match for b, ba, ca
/\d?/     #Matches any digits: 12, 244, 133 or the null string.
/\w+/     #Matches any string of word characters
/\s*/     #Matches any spaces including the empty string
/\S+/     #Matches any non-space characters
/a{1,5}/  #Matches a, aa, aaa, aaaa, aaaaa
/a{4}/    #Matches only aaaa
/j{3,}/   #Matches 3 or more j characters: jjj, jjjj, ...
```

The codes \w, \W, \d, \D, \s, and \S represent a character belonging to a character class. You can build general classes by including them within square brackets:

```
[aeiou]         #Any lowercase vowel
[aeiouAEIOU]    #Any lower or uppercase vowel
[13579]         #Any odd digit
[0-4]           #Any digit from 0, 1, 2, 3, 4
[0-9\-]         #Any digit or the minus (-) character
[a-zA-Z0-9_]    #Any letter, digit, underscore - same as \w
```

To represent a *negated character class* (that is, a class of characters that does not include the ones specified), use the "^" character immediately following the left bracket ([). Here are some examples:

```
[^aeiouAEIOU]  #Not a vowel
[^a-zA-Z0-9_]  #Not a word character. Same as \W.
[^1369]        #Any character except the digits 1, 3, 6, 9
```

Here are a few examples of regular expressions that use the character class:

```
/[13579]+/       #Any number consisting of odd digits
/.[aeiouAEIOU]/  #Any character followed by a vowel
/.[aeiou]/i      #Same as previous. Use of "i" following
                  the #last / indicates a case
                  insensitive match.
```

If a string character matches a metacharacter and you want to refer to the matched character value, use parentheses around the metacharacter and \1, \2, and so on, to reference the first and second characters that were matched. Consider the following regular expression:

```
/key(.)value(.)\1\2/
```

The following is an example of a string that matches this regular expression:

```
key!value:!:
```

The character "!" matches the first metacharacter (.), and the character ":" matches the second metacharacter(.). The \1 and \2 are references to the first and second matched patterns, which are the characters "!" and ":", respectively. This means that the string data must terminate with a "!:", in this case.

If you want to reference subpatterns in the matched string, you can enclose them in parentheses. The patterns that are enclosed in parentheses are set to $1, $2, .. $9 after a successful match. For example, suppose that you wanted to refer to the two hexadecimal numbers that follow the "%" character, such as that used in URL encoding of special characters. You can use the following:

```
$input = "Hex encoding %2C";
$input =~ /%([\dA-Fa-f][\dA-Fa-f])/;
print $1, "\n"; # This will print 2C
```

If you wanted to separate each of the hexadecimal digits and assign them to $1 and $2, you could use the following:

```
$input = "Hex encoding %2C";
$input =~ /%([\dA-Fa-f])([\dA-Fa-f])/;
print $2,$1, "\n"; # This will print C2
```

Using the hex, oct and sprintf Functions

The hex function can be used to convert a hexadecimal string to its equivalent decimal value. The hex function has the following syntax:

```
hex (expr)
hex expr
```

The *expr* is a string of hexadecimal digits. If *expr* is omitted, it is assumed to be $_. The following are examples of the use of the hex function:

```
$numb = hex("FF");   # $numb is 255.
```

```
$_ = "2A";
$numb = hex;   # argument is "2A". $numb is 42.
$input = "Hex encoding %2C";
$input =~ /%([\dA-Fa-f][\dA-Fa-f])/;  # $1 set to "2C".
$charCode = hex $1;  # $charCode is 44.
```

The last three statements in the previous example show how a hexadecimal string was extracted from a string and converted to its equivalent decimal value. In Perl CGI scripts, this operation is useful in converting a URL-encoded value consisting of "%" followed by hexadecimal character code to the equivalent character code.

If you want to perform the reverse operation of converting a decimal number to a hexadecimal string, you can use the sprintf function:

```
$numb = 255;
$hexstr = sprintf ("%lx", $numb);
print $hexstr, "\n";        # Prints ff.
```

The "%lx" is a field specifier for converting the $numb value to its string format. The "x" is for hexadecimal value and the "l" (letter "ell") qualifier says to consider the number as a "long" value. If a capital "X" were used instead of the lowercase "x," the hexadecimal letters are capitalized. The field specifier has the following general syntax:

```
%m.nx
```

The *m.n* is an optional size of the resultant string. The *x* is one of the format specifiers listed in Table 7.4.

TABLE 7.4	SPECIFIER	DESCRIPTION
Format Specifers for sprintf/printf	c	Character
	d	Decimal number
	e	Exponent format floating-point number
	f	Fixed format floating-point number
	g	Compact format floating-point number
	o	Octal number

(continued)

	SPECIFIER	DESCRIPTION
T A B L E 7.4	s	String
Format Specifers for *sprintf/printf* *(continued)*	u	Unsigned decimal number
	x	Hexadecimal number
	ld	Long decimal number
	lo	Long octal number
	lu	Long unsigned decimal number
	lx	Long hexadecimal number

The oct function can be used to convert an octal number string to its equivalent decimal value. The oct function has the following syntax:

```
oct (expr)
oct expr
```

The *expr* is a string of octal digits. If *expr* is omitted, it is assumed to be $_. If the *expr* starts with a 0x, the oct function treats the expression as a hexadecimal string and converts it to a decimal value. The following are examples of the use of the oct function:

```
$numb = oct("77");    # $numb is 63.
$_ = "026";
$numb = oct;   # argument is "026". $numb is 22.
print oct("0xFF"), "\n"; # prints 255.
```

If you want to perform the reverse operation of converting a decimal number to an octal string, you can use the sprintf function:

```
$numb = 63;
$octstr = sprintf ("%lo", $numb);
print $octstr, "\n";        # Prints 77.
```

Using the Translate Function

The translate function has the following syntax:

```
tr/searchlist/replacelist/[c][d][s]
y/searchlist/replacelist/[c][d][s]
```

The use of y is synonymous to the use of tr—it is just a different notation.

The translate function translates all occurrences of characters in the searchlist to equivalent characters in the replacelist.

For example to translate all occurrences of the "+" character to a " " character in a URL-encoded string, you can use the following:

```
$input = $ENV{'QUERY_STRING'};
$input =~ tr/+/ /; # Translates + to spaces.
```

If a string is not specified in the translate function by the =~ or !~ operators, the translate function operates on the $_ string.

```
$_ = "This is a default string";
tr/a-z/A-Z/; # Translates lowercase to uppercase.
print;   # Prints $_ whose value is
         # "THIS IS A DFAULT STRING"
```

If the "d" option is specified, all characters in the searchlist not specified in the replacelist are deleted. If the replacelist is shorter than searchlist, the last character in replacelist is replicated to match the number of characters in searchlist. If the "d" option is specified, the replacelist is not expanded. If the replacelist is null, a copy of the searchlist is used except when the "d" option is specified; the number of characters replaced is returned.

For example, the following translates all digits from a string and replaces each digit with a blank character:

```
$str = "123first456second789";
$str =~ tr/0-9/ /;   # replacelist is replicated
print $str;          # Prints "   first   second   "
```

The following counts the number of digits in the string:

```
$_ = "123first456second789";
$count =  tr/0-9//;
print $count, "\n"; # $count is 9
```

The following deletes all digits from the string:

```
$str = "123first456second789";
$str =~ tr/0-9//d;   # replacelist is not replicated
print $str;          # Prints "firstsecond"
```

The "c" option at the end takes the complement of the searchlist specified and uses this as the actual search list. This means that the characters in the searchlist are remove from the range of characters in the list \001 to \377, and the resulting list is used as the searchlist. For example, to change all non-digits to spaces, use the following:

```
$str = "123first456second789";
$str =~ tr/0-9/ /c;
print $str; # Prints "123    456    789"
```

The "s" option causes multiple identical consecutive characters of the replacelist in the result string to be replaced with a single occurrence of that character. For example, to squeeze the multiple spaces in the previous example to a single space, use the following:

```
$str = "123first456second789";
$str =~ tr/0-9/ /cs;
print $str; # Prints "123 456 789"
```

To delete all non-digits from a string use the following:

```
$str = "123first456second789";
$str =~ tr/0-9//cd;
print $str; # Prints "123456789"
```

Using the Substitute Function

The substitute function has the following syntax:

```
s/searchpattern/replacetext/[g][e][i][o]
```

The substitute function searches a string for occurrences of the searchpattern and, if found, it replaces the matched pattern with the replacetext. The replacetext is treated as a double-quoted string (that is, variable substitutions will occur in the replacetext). The number of substitutions made are returned. If no substitutions are made a zero is returned. The "g" (global) option causes all matched patterns to be replaced. Without this option, only the first pattern match is replaced. If the searchpattern is empty, the previous search pattern that was found is assumed.

If the "i" option is specified, a case-insensitive pattern match is performed. If the "e" option is used the replacetext is to be evaluated as an expression. Without this option, the replacetext is treated as a double-quoted string. Additional occurrences will cause the resultant string to be re-evaluated as an expression.

If a string is not explicitly specified the substitute operation is performed on the $_ string. If single quotation marks are used, no variable substitutions are performed in the replacetext, except when the "e" option is specified. The use of the "e" option always forces evaluation of the replacetext as an expression.

If the searchpattern contains a $ that looks like a variable, the variable value will be evaluated at run time and substituted in the searchpattern. If you want this evaluation to occur only once, you can use the "o" option.

Here are some examples of the substitute function:

```
$str = "Patterns that contain other patterns contain
other\n";
$_ = $str;
s/Patterns/Expressions/;    # Matches first Patterns
print;# Prints "Expressions that contain other patterns
                         # contain other\n".
s/contain/have/g; # Replaces contain globally
print;# Prints "Expressions that have other patterns
                         # have other\n".
$_ = $str;
s/patterns/expressions/gi; # Replaces globally,
                         # case-insensitive match.
print;# Prints "expressions that have other expressions
    # have other\n".
$_ = $str;
s/other/sprintf("%d", hex("2A"))/g;
print;           # Prints "Patterns that contain sprintf("%d",
hex("2A"))
# patterns contain sprintf("%d", hex("2A"))\n"
$_ = $str;
s/other/sprintf("%d", hex("2A"))/ge;
print;           # Prints "Patterns that contain 42 patterns
contain 42\n";
```

Using the pack and unpack Functions

The pack function has the following syntax:

```
pack (template, list)
```

The values in the *list* are packed in a binary data structure described by *template*. The binary data structure is returned as a string value. This function can be used to convert decimal values to their character representations, or to create complex data structures of the type needed for making a system call to the underlying operating system. For example, the TCP/IP sockets programming interface expects data structures in a particular format. If you want to use the sockets programming interface from Perl, you must create the binary data structure in the expected format.

The *template* is a sequence of characters that describe the fields of the binary data structure. Table 7.5 describes the different data types that can be used to form the binary data structure. Each letter can be followed by a number that specifies the number of times the previous data type is repeated. For example, "CCCC" is the same as "C4". The different field specifiers of the binary data structure may be separated by white space for readability purposes. (White spaces are ignored in determining the format of the data structure.)

Here are some examples of using the pack function:

```
$str = pack("c3", 68, 65, 66); # $str = "DAB"
$hstr = "44";
$char = pack("C", hex($hstr)); # $char = "D"
$str = pack("cxcxc",68, 65, 66); # $str = "D\0B\0A";
```

When you format integers (long integer and short integer values), the order in which the integer bytes are packed depends upon whether the underlying processor uses little-endian or big-endian method for storage. Intel processors used by IntranetWare are *little-endian machines*, which means that the least-significant bytes are stored in lower address memory. Motorola processors and IBM mainframe machines are *big-endian machines*, where most-significant bytes are stored in lower address memory. The following illustrates how integer data is packed on Intel processors:

```
$data = pack("s2", 1, 5); #data = "\1\0\5\0"
$data = pack("i2", 1, 5); #data = "\1\0\0\0\5\0\0\0"
```

TABLE 7.5	DATA TYPE	DESCRIPTION
Template Characters for the pack *Function*	a	ASCII string. Padded with nulls.
	A	ASCII string. Padded with spaces.
	b	Bit string. Low-to-high order.
	B	Bit string. High-to-low order.
	c	Signed character value.
	C	Unsigned character value.
	d	A double-precision floating-point in native format.
	f	A single-precision floating-point in native format.
	h	Hexadecimal string. Least-significant hexadecimal digit first.
	H	Hexadecimal string. Most-significant hexadecimal digit first.
	i	A signed integer value.
	I	An unsigned integer value.
	l	A signed long value.
	L	An unsigned long value.
	n	A short integer in network byte order.
	N	A long integer in network byte order.
	p	A pointer to a string.
	u	A uuencoded string.
	x	A null byte.
	X	Back up a byte.
	@	Null fill to absolute position.

Consider the following example that converts the hexadecimal codes in a URL-encoded string to the equivalent character code:

```
$value =~ s/%([\da-fA-F][\da-fA-F])/pack("C", hex($1))/eg;
```

The use of the pack function converts the hexadecimal string matched after the "%" character to its equivalent character value. The "e" option in the substitute operator causes the pack function to be evaluated to form the replacement string.

The "a" and "A" data types pack the first element of the *list* as a string of the length specified in the repeat count, and pad it with nulls for the "a" data type and spaces for the "A" data type:

```perl
$str = pack ("a4", "ks"); # $str = "ks\0\0";
$str = pack ("A4", "ks"); # $str = "ks   ";
```

The repeat count 6 applies only to the first element in the *list*. So, the following has the same effect as the previous:

```perl
$str = pack ("a4", "ks", "is", "a", "x"); #$str="ks\0\0";
$str = pack ("A4", "ks", "is", "a", "x" );#$str="ks   ";
```

If you want to process the remaining elements in the *list,* you can use multiple specifiers instead of the repeat count:

```perl
$str = pack ("aaaa", "ks", "is", "a", "x"); #$str="kiax";
$str = pack ("a" x 4, "ks", "is", "a", "x"); #$str="kiax";
```

The unpack function is the reverse of the pack function:

```perl
unpack (template, expr)
```

It takes the string in *expr* and unpacks it into an array of values described by the *template*. The *template* data types are the same as that used for pack (see Table 7.5). Here are some examples:

```perl
@ua = unpack("C4", "abcd"); # @ua = (97, 98, 99, 100)
@ua = unpack("a4", "abcd");# @ua = ('abcd')
@ua = unpack("a"x4, "abcd");# @ua = ('a', 'b', 'c', 'd')
@ua = unpack("i2", pack("i2", 1629, 6744));
# @ua = (1629, 6744)
```

Using the split and join Functions

The split function splits a string into an array of strings based on a specified pattern. The following is the syntax of the split function:

```perl
split(/pattern/, expr)
split(/pattern/, expr, limit)
split(/pattern/)
split
```

The *pattern* is used for matching the delimiter used to separate the string *expr*. If *expr* is not specified, the string in $_ is split. The *limit* is used to specify an upper limit on the number of fields into which to separate the string. It is an upper limit on the size of the array returned. If *limit* is not specified, any trailing null value fields are removed.

```
$input="pname=Karanjit+Siyan&addr1=33+Kashi+St.&addr2=Vaikunt
h";
@valuepairs = split(/&/, $input);
# @valuepairs contains the following elements
# "pname=Karanjit+Siyan"
# "addr1=33+Kashi+St."
# "addr2=Vaikunth"
```

As you can see from the previous example, a URL-encoded string can be split along the "&" characters. If you further wanted to split each of the name=value pairs along the "=" character, you can do so by setting up a foreach loop and splitting each element of the array, as shown next:

```
foreach $vp (@valuepairs)
{
        ($name, $value) = split(/=/, $vp);
        $data{$name} = $value;
}
```

The split function separates each element of the array into a $name and $value pair. An associative array %data is then built using the $name as the index. The $value may still contain "+" characters and hexadecimal codes (such as %HH). These are converted by using the translate, substitute, and pack functions that were discussed in earlier sections. The complete foreach loop to perform these translations then becomes the following:

```
foreach $vp (@valuepairs)
{
        ($name, $value) = split(/=/, $vp);
        $value =~ tr/+/ /; # Translate "+" to " "
        # Following replaces %HH with equivalent character
codes.
        $value =~ s/%([\da-fA-F][\da-fA-F])/pack("C",
```

```
hex($1))/eg;
        $data{$name} = $value;
}
```

A *pattern* that matches a null string will split the *expr* string into separate characters. For example the pattern / */ matches zero or more occurrences of the blank character. A zero occurrence of any character is the null string. Also, the null pattern // will separate the string to individual characters. Consider the following example:

```
$str = 'Vaik unth';
@chars = split(/ */, $str);
# @chars = ('V', 'a', 'i', 'k', 'u', 'n', 't', 'h');
# Notice that space was removed because it is a
# delimiter.
$, = " "; # Set the field separator in print to " ".
$\ = "\n"; # Set output record separator to "\n" so
         # print outputs a new line automatically.
print @chars; # Outputs:V a i k u n t h
@chars = split(//, $str);
# @chars = ('V', 'a', 'i', 'k', ' ', 'u', 'n', 't', 'h');
# Notice that space was not removed.
print @chars; # Outputs:V a i k   u n t h
```

Consider the following example that shows the use of *limit*:

```
$str = "kss:1511 Grant St.:Berk.:CA:USA:N
America:Earth:Sol";
($name, $addr1, $otherinfo) = split(/:/, $str, 3);
print "name=$name\naddr1=$addr1\noherinfo=$otherinfo\n";
# This will output the following:
# name=kss
# addr1=1511 Grant St.
# otherinfo=Berk.:CA:USA:N America:Earth:Sol
```

When assigning to an explicit list, instead of an array, and when *limit* is not specified, the *limit* is assumed to be one more than the number of elements in the list. So, in the previous example, if *limit* of 3 was not specified, $otherinfo would be set to "Berk." only and the remainder of the information "thrown" away:

```
$str = "kss:1511 Grant St.:Berk.:CA:USA:N
America:Earth:Sol";
($name, $addr1, $otherinfo) = split(/:/, $str);
print "name=$name\naddr1=$addr1\noherinfo=$otherinfo\n";
# This will output the following:
# name=kss
# addr1=1511 Grant St.
# otherinfo=Berk.
```

The join function is the reverse of the split function, and is used to join a list of elements using the specified expression:

```
join(expr, list)
```

The separate string elements in *list* are joined together into a single string using the value of *expr*. Consider the following examples:

```
$str = join(":", "kss", "1511 Grant St.", "Berk.", "CA");
print $str, "\n";
# This would print the following:
#   kss:1511 Grant St.:Berk.:CA
```

To force each character in a string to be separated by a ":" character, you can use the following:

```
$str = "Perl";
$cstr = join(":", split(//, $str));
print $cstr, "\n"; # Outputs P:e:r:l
```

Here is an example of how you can form a complete path name for an image document from within a CGI script:

```
$imagePath = join("/", $ENV{'DOCUMENT_ROOT'},
                "IMAGES/BIRTHDAY.GIF");
```

If the CGI environment variable DOCUMENT_ROOT is set to SYS:WEB, the $imagePath is set to the following:

```
SYS:WEB/IMAGES/BIRTHDAY.GIF
```

Using the `stat` Function

The `stat` function can be used to return statistics on a file. It can be used for determining the size of a file and other information on the file:

```
stat (filehandle)
stat (expr)
```

The `stat` function returns a 13-element array. Some of the parameters are specific to UNIX and BSD-UNIX derived systems, and may not have a meaning for NetWare. The elements that are returned are described in Table 7.6.

ELEMENT #	VALUE INSIDE ELEMENT
1	Device number
2	Inode number
3	Mode of file
4	Number of links
5	User ID (UID)
6	Group ID (GID)
7	Raw device
8	Size of file in bytes
9	Last accessed time stamp on file
10	Last modified time stamp on file
11	Creation time stamp on file
12	Block size
13	Number of blocks

T A B L E 7.6

Satistics Returned by `stat` *Function*

To see the statistics returned by the stat function on your Novell Web Server, execute the following CGI script (file `stat.pl`) from your Web browser:

```
#!/usr/local/bin/perl
# Previous comment used in case you port script  to Unix.
# File stat.pl
print "Content-Type: text/html\n\n";
$path = "sys:web/docs/index.htm";
@statarray = stat ("sys:web/docs/index.htm");
```

```
@desc = (
  "Device number",
  "Inode number",
  "Mode of file",
  "Number of links",
  "User ID (UID)",
  "Group ID (GID)",
  "Raw device",
  "Size of file in bytes",
  "Last accessed time stamp on file",
  "Last modified time stamp on file",
  "Creation time stamp on file",
  "Block size",
  "Number of blocks"
);
$nelements = @statarray;
print "<html><head><title>Stat
function</title></head><body>";
print "<h1>File name $path</h1>\n";
print "<h2>Number of elements returned by stat =",
$nelements, "</h2>";
print "<h2>Stat array follows</h2>";
print "<pre><i><b>\n";
for ($x = 0; $x < $nelements; $x++)
{
  print "statarray[$x] = $statarray[$x]\t#$desc[$x]\n";
}
print "</b></i></pre></body></html>";
```

Place the previous Perl script in a file `stat.pl`, copy it to the Perl scripts directory (default SYS:WEB/SCRIPTS/PERL), and access the following URL from your Web browser:

```
http://webserver/perl/stat.pl
```

Figure 7.4 shows the result of executing the Perl script using the Novell Netscape Navigator. You can examine this output and consult Table 7.6 to see how the elements returned by the stat function are defined on the Novell Web Server.

Some of the elements of the array have a null value because they are not defined for the Novell Web Server.

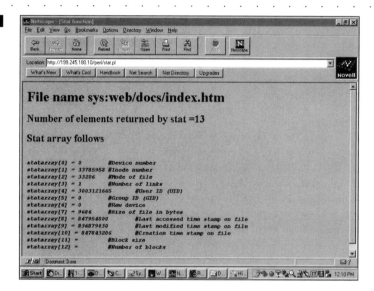

Array returned by stat *function on a Novell Web Server*

Implementing Perl Subroutines

Perl allows you to call modules of code repeatedly and pass arguments to the code module. These modules of code are called *subroutines*. The general syntax of a subroutine is as follows:

```
sub subname
{
  #Perl statements placed here


}
```

You must replace the subroutine name, *subname*, with a valid variable name. Perl (version 4) does not make any provisions for specifying the type and number of parameters as part of the subroutine definition. You could pass to the previous subroutine any number of parameters using the following syntax:

```
&subname(p1, p2, ..., pn);
```

The parameters *p1*, *p2*, ..., *pn* are elements of a list. The Perl parameter initializes the special array @_ with the parameter list. This array is accessible from within the subroutine. Thus, you can access the first, second and third parameters as @_[0], @_[1], and @_[2], respectively.

If there are no parameters to pass, you can call the subroutine using any of the following syntax:

```
&subname();
&subname;
```

The second form is slightly more efficient than the first and is typically used in most Perl code for calling a subroutine without arguments. The following is an example of a subroutine that is used to return a Yes or No answer from a user:

```
$choice = &getyesno("Enter your choice:(y|n)?");
if ($choice eq "y")
{
    // Perform processing for Yes response
}
sub getyesno
{
    local($inp);
    for(;;)
    {
        print @_;
        $inp = <STDIN>;
        chop($inp);
        $inp =~ tr/A-Z/a-z/; # lower case input
        if ($inp eq "y" || $inp eq "n" || $inp eq "q")
        {
            last;
        }
        else
        {
         print "Invalid input. Try again.\n\n";
        }
    }
    $inp;
```

```
} # end getyesno
```

Notice that the array of parameters (a string in this case) is printed out using the @_ array. Also the local variable $inp is defined using the local operator. The scope of the local variable is the subroutine getyesno and any subroutines called by getyesno. The value returned by a subroutine is the value of the last statement executed in the subroutine. In the subroutine getyesno, this is the value $inp on the last statement. You also can use the return operator to return a value from a subroutine. The use of the return operator is slightly slower than using the value of the last expression evaluated. Thus, the last line in the subroutine getyesno could have been the following:

```
return $inp;
```

Another technique that is sometimes used is to extract the parameter values from the @_ parameter array and initialize these to local variables in a subroutine. The following shows how this can be done:

```
sub hostinfo
{
   #Expect 3 parameters for hostname, IP address,
   #and port number.
   local($hostname, $ipaddress, $port) = @_;
   print "Host name = $hostname\n" .
         "IP address = $ipaddress\n" .
         "Port number = $port\n";
}
```

The examples of the Perl subroutines discussed so far passed the subroutine parameters by value. This means that the parameter value that was passed to the subroutine was assigned to a local variable within the subroutine. Changes made to the local variable did not affect the original value that was passed. Sometimes it is necessary to effect change in the original value that was passed to the subroutine from within the subroutine itself. You can accomplish this in Perl by using a parameter-passing method called *pass by name*.

Perl allows you to refer to all values of a particular name by prefixing the name with an asterisk (*). Thus, the asterisk in *xyz refers to all characters (such as $, %, @) that can prefix a variable name. That is, *xyz refers to $xyz, %xyz and @xyz. In Perl this is called *type glob*. When *name is evaluated as a right-side value, it produces a scalar value that represents all objects of that name, including file handle, subroutines, and format names. When *name is used as a left-side value by assignment within a local() operation in a subroutine, it represents a name that is aliased to whatever value was assigned to it. This aliasing mechanism implements passing the value by name. Consider the following Perl program:

```
@xyz = (1, 2, 3, 4, -5, 5, 6, -1);
$\ = "\n"; # End or record is a new line in print()
$, = " ";   # Field space is a blank in print()
print "Before \@xyz = ", @xyz;
&test(*xyz);
print"After \@xyz = ", @xyz;
sub test
{
      local(*abc) = @_;
      foreach $x (@abc)
      {
        $x += 100;
      }

}
```

The subroutine test is passed the type glob *xyz. Within the subroutine the following statement is used to set abc as an alias to whatever was passed to it (that is, @xyz):

```
      local(*abc) = @_;
```

Each value within the passed array is incremented by 100. The output that you will see because of the various print statements is the following:

```
Before @xyz = 1 2 3 4 -5 5 6 -1
After @xyz = 101 102 103 104 95 105 106 99
```

Manipulating Databases

The associative array with its key, value pair can be used as simple databases for accessing stored information. However, associative arrays normally have an existence only when the Perl script is running. When the Perl script terminates, the values in the associative array are lost. Perl provides a method to store Perl associative arrays in files. When a value is stored in the associative array, it is also stored in a file. Other Perl scripts can read this file and access it as if it were an associative array. These special files are called *DBM files*, and the associative arrays are called *DBM arrays*. To define the associative array %FAM and associate it with a file "family", you can use the following:

```
dbmopen(%FAM, "family", $mode);
```

The $mode value is *permission bits* for the file that is created. The permission bits are UNIX-specific and are octal numbers that are in the "owner-group-world" format. On non-UNIX systems, you can set this to the octal number 0777 to provide access to any user for this file. Note that the access control lists, and trustee rights of the operating system under which you are creating this file, will apply. You can perform operations on the %FAM array as if it were an associative array. The difference is that the key, value pairs for the array will be stored in the family file.

When you are finished processing the DBM array, you close it using dbmclose():

```
dbmclose(%FAM);
```

Here is an example that uses the DBM array:

```
dbmopen(%F, "test", 0);
$F{"debi"} = 23;
$F{"karen"} = 33;
$F{"belinda"} = 27;
dbmclose %F;
```

The return value from the dmopen() is true if the open operation is successful. However, this operation will normally create the associated file if one does not exist. If you just want to check if the operation will succeed and not create the files, you can use undef for the mode parameter:

```
dbmopen(%SCORES, "tally", undef) || die "Cannot open tally
file";
```

If the dbmopen() is successful, it will return a true value and there is no need to evaluate the die operator because the overall value is true. If the dbmopen() is not successful, it will return a false value and you must evaluate the operator after the logical OR ("||") to determine the overall value. This will cause the die operator to terminate the program with the indicated message.

Novell Web Server Perl Script Examples

The previous sections have covered sufficient features of Perl so that you can begin to write your own CGI Perl scripts. The Novell Web Server distribution software ships with some sample examples of CGI Perl scripts in the SYS:WEB/SCRIPTS/PERL directory. These sample Perl scripts are

- `echo.pl`

- `cardfile.pl`

- `guestboo.pl`

Since these Perl scripts are already installed on your Novell Web Server you can experiment with these Perl scripts to learn how to write your own Perl scripts. The remainder of this chapter explains how these sample Perl scripts work.

The `cgi-lib.pl` Library

The Novell Web Server ships with a CGI Perl script library that can be used to simplify the writing of Perl scripts. The `cgi-lib.pl` library defines the following Perl subroutines that you can call from your CGI script:

- `MethGet`: This returns a true if this `cgi` call was using the GET request, and false otherwise. It is useful to combine both the form and the script in one place. GET retrieves the form, and POST gets the result.

- `ReadParse`: Reads in GET or POST data, converts it to URL-decoded data, and puts one key=value in each member of the list @in and creates key, value pairs in %in, using \0 to separate multiple selections. If a *variable-glob* parameter (such as *cgi_input) is passed to `ReadParse`, information is stored there, rather than in $in, @in, and %in.

- `PrintHeader`: This prints the "Content-Type" HTTP response header that tells the Web client to expect an HTML document.

▸ PrintVariables: This takes the variables in an associative array as a parameter and returns a string consisting of the values of the variables nicely formatted as an HTML string.

▸ PrintVariablesShort: This takes the variables in an associative array as a parameter and returns a string consisting of the values of the variables formatted as an HTML string. The format uses one line per pair (unless value is multiline).

The sample cardfile.pl CGI script makes use of this CGI library. The source code for this library is shown in Listing 7.1.

LISTING 7.1

cardfile.pl *Script*

```
#!/usr/local/bin/perl - -*- C -*-
# Perl Routines to Manipulate CGI input
# S.E.Brenner@bioc.cam.ac.uk
# $Header:
F:/WEB/SOFTWARE/DISK1/PUBLIC/PERL/VCS/CGILIB.PV_   1.0   10
Nov 1995 17:59:34   LCHEONG   $
#
# Copyright 1994 Steven E. Brenner
# Unpublished work.
# Permission granted to use and modify this library so long
# as the copyright above is maintained, modifications are
# documented, and credit is given for any use of the
library.
#
# Thanks are due to many people for reporting bugs
# and suggestions especially Meng Weng Wong, Maki Watanabe,
# Bo Frese Rasmussen,
# Andrew Dalke, Mark-Jason Dominus and Dave Dittrich.
# see http://www.seas.upenn.edu/~mengwong/forms/   or
```

```
#       http://www.bio.cam.ac.uk/web/                    for more
#                                                      information
# Minimalist http form and script
(http://www.bio.cam.ac.uk/web/minimal.cgi):
# if (&MethGet) {
#    print &PrintHeader,
#       '<form method=POST><input type="submit">Data:'.
#                    '<input name="myfield">';
# } else {
#    &ReadParse(*input);
#    print &PrintHeader, &PrintVariables(%input);
# }
# MethGet
# Return true if this cgi call was using the GET request,
# false otherwise
# Now that cgi scripts can be put in the normal file space,
# it is useful
# to combine both the form and the script in one place with
# GET used to
# retrieve the form, and POST used to get the result.
sub MethGet {
   return ($ENV{'REQUEST_METHOD'} eq "GET");
}
# ReadParse
# Reads in GET or POST data, converts it to unescaped text,
# and puts
# one key=value in each member of the list "@in"
# Also creates key/value pairs in %in, using '\0' to
# separate multiple selections
# If a variable-glob parameter (e.g., *cgi_input)
# is passed to ReadParse,
# information is stored there, rather than in $in, @in, and
%in.
sub ReadParse {
    local (*in) = @_ if @_;
```

```perl
  local ($i, $loc, $key, $val);
  # Read in text
  if ($ENV{'REQUEST_METHOD'} eq "GET") {
    $in = $ENV{'QUERY_STRING'};
  } elsif ($ENV{'REQUEST_METHOD'} eq "POST") {
    read(STDIN,$in,$ENV{'CONTENT_LENGTH'});
  }
  @in = split(/&/,$in);
  foreach $i (0 .. $#in) {
    # Convert plus's to spaces
    $in[$i] =~ s/\+/ /g;
    # Split into key and value.
    ($key, $val) = split(/=/,$in[$i],2); # splits on the
first =.
    # Convert %XX from hex numbers to alphanumeric
    $key =~ s/%(..)/pack("c",hex($1))/ge;
    $val =~ s/%(..)/pack("c",hex($1))/ge;
    # Associate key and value
    $in{$key} .= "\0" if (defined($in{$key})); # \0 is the
multiple separator
    $in{$key} .= $val;
  }
  return 1; # just for fun
}
# PrintHeader
# Returns the magic line which tells WWW that we're
# an HTML document
sub PrintHeader {
  return "Content-type: text/html\n\n";
}
# PrintVariables
# Nicely formats variables in an associative array passed
# as a parameter
# And returns the HTML string.
sub PrintVariables {
```

```
    local (%in) = @_;
    local ($old, $out, $output);
    $old = $*;   $* =1;
    $output .=   "<DL COMPACT>";
    foreach $key (sort keys(%in)) {
      foreach (split("\0", $in{$key})) {
        ($out = $_) =~ s/\n/<BR>/g;
        $output .=   "<DT><B>$key</B><DD><I>$out</I><BR>";
      }
    }
    $output .=   "</DL>";
    $* = $old;
    return $output;
}
# PrintVariablesShort
# Nicely formats variables in an associative array passed
# as a parameter
# Using one line per pair (unless value is multiline)
# And returns the HTML string.
sub PrintVariablesShort {
    local (%in) = @_;
    local ($old, $out, $output);
    $old = $*;   $* =1;
    foreach $key (sort keys(%in)) {
      foreach (split("\0", $in{$key})) {
        ($out = $_) =~ s/\n/<BR>/g;
        $output .= "<B>$key</B> is <I>$out</I><BR>";
      }
    }
    $* = $old;
    return $output;
}
1; #return true
```

The echo.pl **Script**

You can use the echo.pl CGI script for testing and debugging your HTML code. Suppose that you have created an HTML form and you want to see how the values are being received by the Web server and the CGI scripts. You can use echo.pl to view these values. In order to test the echo.pl script, you must define a sample HTML form and specify the echo.pl script in the ACTION attribute of the FORM tag. Here is an example of such an HTML document:

```
<html>
<head>
<title>POST form with echo.pl</title>
</head>
<body>
<form method="POST"
action="http://199.245.180.10/perl/echo.pl">
<h3>Please supply this information about yourself</h3>
<hr>
<input type="text" size=45 name="pname">Name<br>
<input type="text" size=45 name="street1">Street1<br>
<input type="text" size=45 name="street2">Street2<br>
<input type="text" size=45 name="city">City<br>
<input type="text" size=45 name="statepr">State/Province<br>
<input type="text" size=30 name="postalcode">Postal Code<br>
<input size=30 name="email">E-mail<br>
<br>
<input type="reset" value="Clear Form">
<input type="submit" value="Send Form">
</form>
</body>
</html>
```

Figure 7.5 shows the results returned by the echo.pl script upon entering sample data in this form.

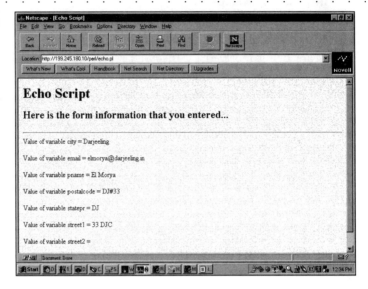

The echo.pl script is as follows:

```perl
require("cgi-lib.pl");
print &PrintHeader;
#print http header
&ReadParse;
#print html header
print "<html>";
print "<BODY TEXT=\"#000000\" LINK=\"#FF0000\">";
print "<BODY BACKGROUND=/images/blue_pap.gif>";
print "<html><head><title>Echo Script</title></head>\n";
print "<body><h1>Echo Script</h1>\n";
print "<H2>Here is the form information that you
entered...</H2><p>\n";
print "<hr>";
foreach $key (sort keys(%in)) {
   print "Value of variable ", $key, " = ", $in{$key}, "<p>\n";
}
#print tail of html
print "<hr>";
print "</body></html>\n";
```

The echo.pl script is interesting from the point of view of the use of the cgi-lib.pl. The cgi-lib.pl is a library of Perl subroutines you can use to carry out common CGI script tasks.

The first statement

```
require("cgi-lib.pl");
```

is a Perl statement that makes the contents of the Perl library cgi-lib.pl available to you.

The next statement

```
print &PrintHeader;
```

has a call to the subroutine PrintHeader. Calling this subroutine causes the standard HTTP header to be printed to the output stream. This header contains the "Content-Type" definition of text/html.

The next statement

```
&ReadParse;
```

reads the form data from the standard input, performs URL decoding of the form data, and places the form data in the associative array %in with the form field names used as the keys.

The next several print statements are the HTML code for providing the appropriate appearance for the data that is output by the foreach statement:

```
foreach $key (sort keys(%in)) {
  print "Value of variable ", $key, " = ", $in{$key},
"<p>\n";
}
```

The loop variable $key is set to each element of an array consisting of the sorted key values in %in. Within the loop the name of the key and its value is printed out.

The cardfile.pl Script

The cardfile.pl script can be used to generate a birthday card, an anniversary card, or a thank-you card. Figure 7.6 shows the form that is displayed when you access the following URL:

```
http://webserver/perl/cardfile.pl
```

After making your selection of the type of greeting, entering your name, and entering the recipient's name, you can select the Create Card button to generate the form. Figure 7.7 shows a sample birthday card that was generated.

The CGI script `cardfile.pl` is shown in Listing 7.2.

F I G U R E   7.6

Display created by `cardfile.pl` *script*

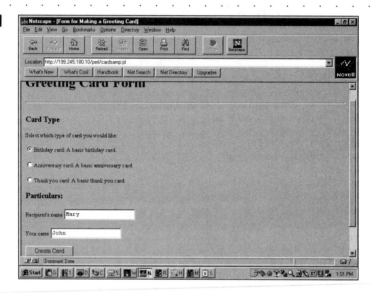

F I G U R E   7.7

Sample birthday card

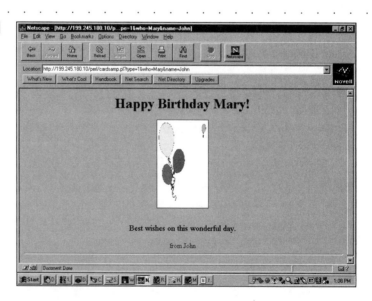

LISTING 7.2

cardfile.pl *Script*

```perl
require("cgi-lib.pl");
print &PrintHeader;
&ReadParse;
if ($ENV{"ARGC"} eq "0") {
print "<HTML><HEAD><TITLE>Form for Making a Greeting
Card</TITLE></HEAD>\n";
  print "<BODY>\n";
  print "<H1>Greeting Card Form</H1>\n";
  print "<HR>\n";
  print "<FORM ACTION=\"/perl/cardsamp.pl\">\n";
  print "<H3>Card Type</H3>\n";
  print "<font size=-1>\n";
  print "Select which type of card you would like:<P>\n";
  print "<INPUT TYPE=\"radio\" NAME=\"type\" VALUE=\"1\"
CHECKED>Birthday card:\n";
  print "A basic birthday card.<P>\n";
  print "<INPUT TYPE=\"radio\" NAME=\"type\"
VALUE=\"2\">Anniversary card:\n";
  print "A basic anniversary card.<P>\n";
  print "<INPUT TYPE=\"radio\" NAME=\"type\"
VALUE=\"3\">Thank you card:\n";
  print "A basic thank you card.<P>\n";
  print "<H3>Particulars:</H3>\n";
  print "Recipient's name <INPUT TYPE=\"text\" NAME=\"who\"
MAXLENGTH=\"32\" value=\"Mary\"><P>\n";
  print "Your name <INPUT TYPE=\"text\" NAME=\"name\"
MAXLENGTH=\"32\" value=\"John\"><P>\n";
  print "<INPUT type=\"submit\" VALUE=\"Create Card\">\n";
  print "</font>\n";
  print "</FORM>\n";
  print "<hr>\n";
  print "Copyright &#169; 1995 Novell, Inc.  All Rights
Reserved.\n";
  print "</body></html>\n";
```

```
        }
        else {
          if ($in{"type"} == 1) {
                  print "<CENTER><H1>";
                  print "Happy Birthday ",$in{"who"},"!";
                  print "</H1>";
                  print "<IMG SRC=\"/images/art.gif\" width=120
        height=200 border=1>";
                  print "<font size=+1>";
                  print "<P>Best wishes on this wonderful day.<BR>";
                  print "</font>";
                  print "<P>from " , $in{"name"},"<br>";
                  print "</CENTER>";
                  print "<hr>";
          }
          elsif ($in{"type"} == 2) {
                  print "<IMG SRC=\"/images/vase.gif\" align=\"right\"
        hspace=20>";
                  print "<CENTER><H1>";
                  print "Happy Anniversary ", $in{"who"}, "!";
                  print "</H1>";
                  print "<font size=+1>";
                  print "<P>You mean so much to me.<BR>";
                  print "</font>";
                  print "<P>Love, ", $in{"name"}, "<br>";
                  print "</CENTER>";
                  print "<P><P><hr>";
          }
          else  {
                  print "<center>";
                  print "<H1>Thank you ", $in{"who"}, "!";
                  print "</H1>";
                  print "<IMG SRC=\"/images/pen.gif\" width=200
        height=200>";
                  print "<P>your good friend, ", $in{"name"}, "<br>";
                  print "</center>";
```

```
  }
}
```

The first three statements are similar to that described earlier for the `echo.pl` file. These statements make the `cgi-lib.pl` library accessible, print the HTTP header, and parse the user input:

```
require("cgi-lib.pl");
print &PrintHeader;
&ReadParse;
```

The next statement is an `if` statement that checks to see if data was supplied:

```
if ($ENV{"ARGC"} eq "0") {
  # Statements for generating form
}
else
{
  # Statements for processing form data
}
```

Recall from Chapter 6 that ARGC contains a count of the arguments submitted to the Perl script. If the ARGC environment variable is set to 0, the HTML code for a soliciting user input is generated. If ARGC is a non-zero value, it means form data was supplied to the Perl script, and this data must be processed to generate the appropriate greeting.

As you examine the statements in the then part of the `if` statement, you will notice that it consists of a series of print statements to send HTML code to the Web client. Contained in the HTML code is the FORM tag sent by the following statement:

```
print "<FORM ACTION=\"/perl/cardsamp.pl\">\n";
```

Because the METHOD attribute is not specified, it defaults to the GET method.

In the `else` part of the `if` statement, you see the code to handle the data that was entered in the form by the user. You see an if statement that checks the value of the form field "`type`" to see the type of card that was selected:

```
if ($in{"type"} == 1) {
  # Statements to generate a birthday card.
}
elsif ($in{"type"} == 2) {
```

```
# Statements to generate an anniversary card.
}
else {
 # Statements to generate a Thank You card
}
```

The statements to generate the cards contain HTML tags that were discussed in the previous chapters. An image is included in the greeting card by using the <IMG> tag.

The guestboo.pl Script

Before understanding what the guest book Perl script does, let's examine how it works. Use your Web browser to access the following URL address on your Novell Web Server:

```
http://webserver/perldocs/guestboo.htm
```

Figure 7.8 shows how this URL address looks in the Novell Netscape Navigator. When you click on the "sign" hyperlink, you will see the form in Figure 7.9 described in the addguest.htm file. Enter sample data in the form and select the Submit Query button. The guestboo.pl script will be executed and you will see a report on the information you submitted (see Figure 7.10).

▶ · ◀

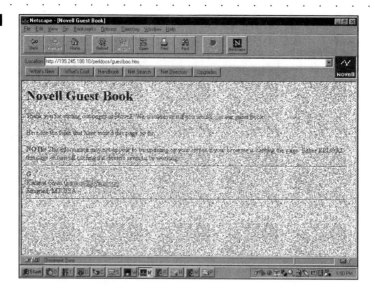

FIGURE 7.9

Add Guest form

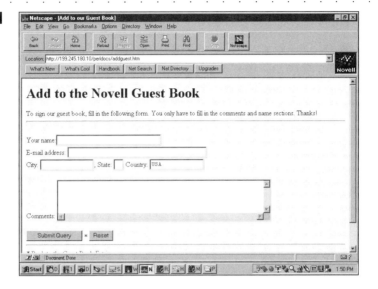

FIGURE 7.10

Report on guest book
information submission

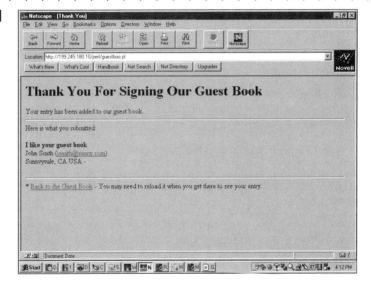

The HTML code in `addguest.htm` is shown next so you can see how the Perl script `guestboo.pl` is specified in the FORM tag:

```
<html><head><title>Add to our Guest Book</title></head>
<BODY TEXT="#000000" LINK="#FF0000">
<BODY BACKGROUND=/images/blue_pap.gif>
<h1>Add to the Novell Guest Book</h1>
To sign our guest book, fill in the following form.
You only have to fill in the comments and name sections.
Thanks!<hr>
<form method=POST action="/perl/guestboo.pl">
Your name:<input type=text name=realname size=30><br>
E-mail address: <input type=text name=username size=40><br>
City: <input type=text name=city size=15>, State: <input
type=text name=state
maxlength=2 size=2> Country: <input type=text value=USA
name=country size=15><p>
Comments:
<textarea name=comments COLS=60 ROWS=4></textarea><p>
<input type=submit> * <input type=reset><hr>
* <a
href="./guestboo.htm">Back to the Guest Book Entries</a><br>
Based on the script and Guest Book Created by: <a
href="mailto:mattw@alpha.pr1.k12.co.us">Matt Wright</a>.
</form></body></html>
```

Notice the FORM tag definition:

```
<form method=POST action="/perl/guestboo.pl">
```

The method of form data submission is POST and the CGI script `/perl/guestboo.pl` is to be executed to handle the form data.

Also notice how the anchor tag

```
<a href="mailto:mattw@alpha.pr1.k12.co.us">Matt Wright</a>
```

can be used to send mail to the address `mattw@alpha.pr1.k12.co.us` once the corresponding hyperlink is selected.

The CGI Perl script `guestboo.pl` is shown in Listing 7.3.

LISTING 7.3

guestboo.pl Script

```perl
#! /usr/local/bin/perl
# ------------------
# Guestbook for the WWW, by Matt Wright
(mattw@pr1.k12.co.us).
# This package is Copyright 1995 by Matt Wright.
# Parts of code taken from:
# Form-mail.pl, by Reuven M. Lerner (reuven@the-
tech.mit.edu).
# This package is Copyright 1994 by The Tech.
# Guestbook is free software; you can redistribute it and/or
modify it
# under the terms of the GNU General Public License as
published by the
# Free Software Foundation; either version 2, or (at your
option) any
# later version.
# Guestbook is distributed in the hope that it will be
useful, but
# WITHOUT ANY WARRANTY; without even the implied warranty of
# MERCHANTABILITY or FITNESS FOR A PARTICULAR PURPOSE.  See
the GNU
# General Public License for more details.
# You should have received a copy of the GNU General Public
License
# along with Guestbook; see the file COPYING.  If not, write
to the Free
# Software Foundation, 675 Mass Ave, Cambridge, MA 02139,
USA.
# ------------------
# Guestbook for the World Wide Web
# Created by Matt Wright          Version 2.1
# Created on: 4/21      Last Modified: 6/1/95
# History can be found in the README file.
#  ***************Set Following Variables Before
```

```
Use!!!*************
# Set this to your server address
$server = "http://".$ENV{"SERVER_NAME"}."/";
# Set this to point to URL style guestbook html file
location.
$guestbookurl = "perldocs/guestboo.htm";
# Set this to point to the actual location of the html
files.
$guestbookreal = "sys:/web/docs/perldocs/guestboo.htm";
$guestlog = "sys:/web/docs/perldocs/guestlog.htm";
# This points to the relative location of this perl script
(this depends
# on what you specify in srm.cfg
$cgiurl = "/perl/guestboo.pl";
#  ***************Set Above Variables Before
Use!!!*************
# Set Your Options:
$mail = 0;                  # 1 = Yes; 0 = No
$uselog = 1;                # 1 = Yes; 0 = No
$linkmail = 1;              # 1 = Yes; 0 = No
$separator = 1;             # 1 = <hr>; 0 = <p>
$redirection = 0;          # 1 = Yes; 0 = No
###############
# If you answered 1 to $mail you will need to fill out these
variables below:
$mailprog = '/usr/lib/sendmail';
$recipient = 'mattw@alpha.pr1.k12.co.us';
# Get the Date for Entry
#$date = `date +"%A, %B %d, %Y at %T (%Z)"`;
#        chop($date);
#$shortdate = `date +"%D %T %Z"`;
#        chop($shortdate);
# Get the input
read(STDIN, $buffer, $ENV{'CONTENT_LENGTH'});
# Split the name-value pairs
@pairs = split(/&/, $buffer);
```

```perl
foreach $pair (@pairs)
{
    ($name, $value) = split(/=/, $pair);
    # Un-Webify plus signs and %-encoding
    $value =~ tr/+/ /;
    $value =~ s/%([a-fA-F0-9][a-fA-F0-9])/pack("C",
hex($1))/eg;
    # Stop people from using subshells to execute commands
    # Not a big deal when using sendmail, but very
important
    # when using UCB mail (aka mailx).
    # $value =~ s/~!/ ~!/g;
    # Uncomment for debugging purposes
    # print "Setting $name to $value<P>";
    $FORM{$name} = $value;
}
# Print the Blank Response Subroutines
&no_comments unless $FORM{'comments'};
&no_name unless $FORM{'realname'};
# Begin the Editing of the Guestbook File
open (FILE,"$guestbookreal");
@LINES=<FILE>;
close(FILE);
$SIZE=@LINES;
# Open Link File to Output
open (GUEST,">$guestbookreal");
for ($i=0;$i<=$SIZE;$i++)
{
    $_=$LINES[$i];
    if (/<META begin>/)
    {
        print GUEST "<META begin>\n";
        print GUEST "<b>$FORM{'comments'}</b><br>\n";
        print GUEST "$FORM{'realname'}";
        if ( $FORM{'username'} )
        {
```

```
            if ($linkmail eq '1')
            {
                    print GUEST " (<a
href=\"mailto:$FORM{'username'}\">$FORM{'username'})</a>";
            }
            else
            {
                    print GUEST " ($FORM{'username'})";
            }
        }
        print GUEST "<br>\n";
        if ( $FORM{'city'} )
        {
            print GUEST "$FORM{'city'},";
        }
        if ( $FORM{'state'} )
        {
            print GUEST " $FORM{'state'}";
        }
        if ( $FORM{'country'} )
        {
            print GUEST " $FORM{'country'}";
        }
        if ($separator eq '1')
        {
            print GUEST " - $date<hr>\n\n";
        }
        else
        {
            print GUEST " - $date<p>\n\n";
        }
    }
    else
    {
        print GUEST $_;
    }
```

```
} #end for
close (GUEST);
# Log The Entry
if ($uselog eq '1')
{
    open (LOG, ">>$guestlog");
    print LOG "$ENV{'REMOTE_HOST'} -
[$FORM{'username'}]<br>\n";
    close (LOG);
}
###############
# Sub Routines
sub no_comments
{
  print "Content-type: text/html\n\n";
  print "<html><head><title>No Comments</title></head>\n";
  print "<body><h1>No Comment?</h1>\n";
  print "You didn't complete the Comments section.
Therefore, your entry was not added to the guest book.
Please enter your comments below.<p>\n";
  print "<form method=POST action=\"$server$cgiurl\">\n";
  print "Your name:<input type=text name=\"realname\"
size=30 value=\"$FORM{'realname'}\"><br>\n";
  print "E-mail address: <input type=text name=\"username\"
value=\"$FORM{'username'}\" size=40><br>\n";
  print "City: <input type=text name=\"city\"
value=\"$FORM{'city'}\" size=15>, State: <input type=text
name=\"state\" value=\"$FORM{'state'}\" size=2> Country:
<input type=text value=USA name=\"country\"
value=\"$FORM{'country'}\" size=15><p>\n";
  print "Comments:<br>\n";
  print "<textarea name=\"comments\" COLS=60
ROWS=4></textarea><p>\n";
  print "<input type=submit> * <input
type=reset></form><hr>\n";
  print "Return to the <a href=$server$guestbook>Guest
Book</a>.\n";
```

```
   print "</body></html>\n";
# Log The Error
   if ($uselog eq '1') {
   open (LOG, ">>$guestlog");
   print LOG "$ENV{'REMOTE_HOST'} - [$shortdate] <b>ERR</b> -
No Comments<br>\n";
   close (LOG);
   }
   exit;
}
sub no_name
{
   print "Content-type: text/html\n\n";
   print "<html><head><title>No Name</title></head>\n";
   print "<body><h1>What's your name?</h1>\n";
   print "You didn't enter your name. Therefore, your name
wasn't added to the guest book.  Please enter your name
below.<p>\n";
   print "<form method=POST action=\"$server$cgiurl\">\n";
   print "Your name:<input type=text name=\"realname\"
size=30><br>\n";
   print "E-mail address: <input type=text name=\"username\"
value=\"$FORM{'username'}\" size=40><br>\n";
   print "City: <input type=text name=\"city\"
value=\"$FORM{'city'}\" size=15>, State: <input type=text
name=\"state\" value=\"$FORM{'state'}\" size=2> Country:
<input type=text value=USA name=\"country\"
value=\"$FORM{'country'}\" size=15><p>\n";
   print "Comments have been retained.<p>\n";
   print "<input type=hidden name=\"comments\"
value=\"$FORM{'comments'}\">\n";
   print "<input type=submit> * <input type=reset><hr>\n";
   print "Return to the <a href=$server$guestbook>Guest
Book</a>.\n";
   print "</body></html>\n";
   # Log The Error
   if ($uselog eq '1') {
```

```
    open (LOG, ">>$guestlog");
    print LOG "$ENV{'REMOTE_HOST'} - [$shortdate] <b>ERR</b>
- No  Name<br>\n";
    close (LOG);
  }
  exit;
}
##########
# Options
# Mail Option
if ($mail eq '1')
{
  open (MAIL, "|$mailprog $recipient") || die "Can't open
$mailprog!\n";
  print MAIL "Reply-to: $FORM{'username'}
($FORM{'realname'}\n";
  print MAIL "From: $FORM{'username'} ($FORM{'realname'}\n";
  print MAIL "Subject: Entry to Guest Book\n\n";
  print MAIL "You have a new entry in your guest
book:\n\n";
  print MAIL "-------------\n";
  print MAIL "$FORM{'comments'}\n";
  print MAIL "$FORM{'realname'}";
  if ( $FORM{'username'} ){
      print MAIL " ($FORM{'username'})";
  }
  print MAIL "\n";
  if ( $FORM{'city'} ){
      print MAIL "$FORM{'city'},";
  }
  if ( $FORM{'state'} ){
      print MAIL " $FORM{'state'}";
  }
  if ( $FORM{'country'} ){
      print MAIL " $FORM{'country'}";
  }
```

```
   print MAIL " - $date\n";
   print MAIL "-------------\n";
   close (MAIL);
}
# Print Out Initial Output Location Heading
if ($redirection eq '1') {
   print "Location: $server$guestbookurl\n\n";
}
else
{
   &redirection;
}
# Redirection Option
sub redirection
{
# Print Beginning of HTML
print "Content-Type: text/html\n\n";
print "<html><head><title>Thank You</title></head>\n";
print "<body><h1>Thank You For Signing Our Guest
Book</h1>\n";
# Print Response
print "Your entry has been added to our guest book.<hr>\n";
print "Here is what you submitted:<p>\n";
print "<b>$FORM{'comments'}</b><br>\n";
print "$FORM{'realname'}";
   if ( $FORM{'username'} ){
      if ($linkmail eq '1') {
         print " (<a
href=\"mailto:$FORM{'username'}\">$FORM{'username'}</a>)";
      }
      else { print " ($FORM{'username'})" }
   }
print "<br>\n";
   if ( $FORM{'city'} ){
     print "$FORM{'city'},";
   }
```

```
    if ( $FORM{'state'} ){
      print " $FORM{'state'}";
    }
    if ( $FORM{'country'} ){
      print " $FORM{'country'}";
    }
print " - $date<p>\n";
# Print End of HTML
print "<hr>\n";
print "* <a href=$server$guestbookurl>Back to the Guest
Book</a> - You may need to reload it when you get there to
see your entry.\n";
print "</body></html>\n";
exit;
}
```

The first several statements in the Perl script set global variables that control the behavior of the Perl script. These statements define $server (which contains the URL address of the Web server), $guestbookurl (which is the location of the guest book HTML document), $guestbookreal (which is the physical path to the guest book HTML document), $guestlog (which is the physical path to the guest log HTML document), and $cgiurl (which is the relative location of the Perl script).

Next, a number of variables are set that control options such as the sending of mail, whether user information is logged, the type of separator to be used, whether redirection is to be used to send user results, and so on.

The next several lines read the form data from standard input, and, after decoding the URL data, place the form data in the associative array %FORM:

```
# Get the input
read(STDIN, $buffer, $ENV{'CONTENT_LENGTH'});
# Split the name-value pairs
@pairs = split(/&/, $buffer);
foreach $pair (@pairs)
{
    ($name, $value) = split(/=/, $pair);
    # Un-Webify plus signs and %-encoding
```

```
$value =~ tr/+/ /;
$value =~ s/%([a-fA-F0-9][a-fA-F0-9])/pack("C",
hex($1))/eg;
    # Stop people from using subshells to execute commands
    # Not a big deal when using sendmail, but very
important
    # when using UCB mail (aka mailx).
    # $value =~ s/~!/ ~!/g;
    # Uncomment for debugging purposes
    # print "Setting $name to $value<P>";
    $FORM{$name} = $value;
}
```

The previous code has been explained in earlier sections in this chapter. As shown earlier, the cgi-lib.pl could also be used to return the form data in the associative array %in. The Perl statements that have been commented out pertain to running the Perl script on UNIX hosts and for debugging the Perl script.

The next two statements check to see if critical data has been supplied in the form fields:

```
# Print the Blank Response Subroutines
&no_comments unless $FORM{'comments'};
&no_name unless $FORM{'realname'};
```

If the comments and realname form fields are not filled out, the no_comments and no_name subroutines are called. These subroutines generate HTML documents that inform the user that he or she should enter the information in these fields and log the error in the error log HTML document. This error log can then be viewed by the Web client. The subroutines are defined in the guestboo.pl file later on.

The next several statements add HTML code to the guest book HTML file so that the next time this file is viewed by the Web client, the user information just submitted will be shown:

```
# Begin the Editing of the Guestbook File
open (FILE,"$guestbookreal");
@LINES=<FILE>;
close(FILE);
```

```perl
$SIZE=@LINES;
# Open Link File to Output
open (GUEST,">$guestbookreal");
for ($i=0;$i<=$SIZE;$i++)
{
    $_=$LINES[$i];
    if (/<META begin>/)
    {
        print GUEST "<META begin>\n";
        print GUEST "<b>$FORM{'comments'}</b><br>\n";
        print GUEST "$FORM{'realname'}";
        if ( $FORM{'username'} )
        {
            if ($linkmail eq '1')
            {
                print GUEST " (<a
href=\"mailto:$FORM{'username'}\">$FORM{'username'})</a>";
            }
            else
            {
                print GUEST " ($FORM{'username'})";
            }
        }
        print GUEST "<br>\n";
        if ( $FORM{'city'} )
        {
            print GUEST "$FORM{'city'},";
        }
        if ( $FORM{'state'} )
        {
            print GUEST " $FORM{'state'}";
        }
        if ( $FORM{'country'} )
        {
            print GUEST " $FORM{'country'}";
        }
```

```
         if ($separator eq '1')
         {
              print GUEST " - $date<hr>\n\n";
         }
         else
         {
              print GUEST " - $date<p>\n\n";
         }
     }
     else
     {
         print GUEST $_;
     }
} #end for
close (GUEST);
```

In the previous code, note that because the file is modified, it is first read using the FILE handle and the results stored in an array @LINES. After reading the file, the FILE handle is closed, and the guest book HTML file is opened for writing using the file handle GUEST. The pattern /<META begin>/ is used as a marker so that user supplied information is added after this tag.

Next, the user entry is logged in the LOG file:

```
# Log The Entry
if ($uselog eq '1')
{
    open (LOG, ">>$guestlog");
    print LOG "$ENV{'REMOTE_HOST'} -
[$FORM{'username'}]<br>\n";
    close (LOG);
}
```

The subroutines no_comments and no_name definition follow next. These are not executed unless called using &no_comments and &no_name.

Next, the mail and redirection options are processed. The $mail option is set to 0 for Novell Web Server because an Internet SMTP mail agent is not yet available from Novell:

```perl
##########
# Options
# Mail Option
if ($mail eq '1')
{
   open (MAIL, "|$mailprog $recipient") || die "Can't open
$mailprog!\n";
   print MAIL "Reply-to: $FORM{'username'}
($FORM{'realname'}\n";
   print MAIL "From: $FORM{'username'} ($FORM{'realname'}\n";
   print MAIL "Subject: Entry to Guest Book\n\n";
   print MAIL "You have a new entry in your guest
book:\n\n";
   print MAIL "-------------\n";
   print MAIL "$FORM{'comments'}\n";
   print MAIL "$FORM{'realname'}";
   if ( $FORM{'username'} ){
        print MAIL " ($FORM{'username'})";
   }
   print MAIL "\n";
   if ( $FORM{'city'} ){
        print MAIL "$FORM{'city'},";
   }
   if ( $FORM{'state'} ){
        print MAIL " $FORM{'state'}";
   }
   if ( $FORM{'country'} ){
        print MAIL " $FORM{'country'}";
   }
   print MAIL " - $date\n";
   print MAIL "-------------\n";
   close (MAIL);
}
# Print Out Initial Output Location Heading
if ($redirection eq '1') {
   print "Location: $server$guestbookurl\n\n";
```

```
}
else
{
  &redirection;
}
```

In the previous code, it is instructive to study how the MAIL file handle is connected to the mail process for output. Note that the SMTP header is sent to the MAIL file handle, and it ends in a blank line, which is then followed by the body of the message.

If the redirection option is enabled, the "Location" HTTP header is used to fetch a request from the specified URL address. If the redirection option is not enabled, then the subroutine redirection is used to supply the information. The subroutine redirection is at the very end of the listing.

Summary

This chapter describes the Perl language in a tutorial fashion. The Perl language elements are discussed in sufficient detail to enable you not only to learn the language, but also to write sophisticated CGI programs in Perl.

The reason Perl has become the language of choice in writing CGI programs is because it has powerful pattern search and text-processing capabilities. Therefore, it can be used to create dynamic comment very easily. One advantage of using Perl is that you can port your CGI scripts between the Novell Web Server and UNIX servers. The latter part of this chapter provided an in-depth discussion of the Perl scripts that are shipped with the Novell Web Server.

## CHAPTER 8

Using BASIC and NetBasic for Dynamic Content on the Novell Web Server

BASIC (which is an acronym for Beginner's All-purpose Instruction Code) is a script programming language that was developed in the 1970s to teach the basics of how to write a computer program. Many people have taken BASIC language classes as part of a computer training curriculum in high school or another educational institution. If you have been using BASIC and feel comfortable with the language, then you may find it easier to write CGI programs in BASIC. Perl is still considered the language of choice for writing professional CGI scripts, and a wealth of sample Perl scripts are available on the Internet.

If you want to access NetWare-specific services, a derivative of BASIC called NetBasic can be used to access NetWare services through the CGI interface. One disadvantage of BASIC and NetBasic is that the CGI scripts written using these languages have limited portability. For example, NetBasic has not been ported to the UNIX platform. There are versions of BASIC available on some UNIX platforms, but it is not the language of choice for systems or applications programming in UNIX.

This chapter describes the elements of the BASIC and NetBasic languages in sufficient depth to enable you to learn the language and to write sophisticated BASIC CGI scripts.

Understanding BASIC

The BASIC language should not be confused with NetBasic. The BASIC.NLM is an implementation of Dartmouth BASIC using an RCGI interface with the following differences:

▸ CONT is meaningless.

▸ PEEK and POKE are invalid statements and cause an error.

▸ SHELL has no effect.

▸ A new string function, form$, facilitates parsing data transmitted using the POST method.

NetBasic is a version of BASIC developed by HiTec Software and licensed to Novell. NetBasic is considerably richer and more powerful than BASIC and is, therefore, a preferred language compared to BASIC. Some of Novell-supplied CGI scripts are written in BASIC, and, therefore, this section briefly exposes you to BASIC. However, the remainder of this chapter concentrates on NetBasic. Starting with Novell Web Server version 3.0, the NetBasic NLM will be used to interpret BASIC scripts. The BASIC.NLM will not be supported. However, there are several interesting examples of CGI scripts written in BASIC and the following section should still prove useful, as it contains examples of writing CGI scripts.

Configuring BASIC on the Novell Web Server

By default, all BASIC programs are stored in the SYS:WEB\SCRIPTS directory. The SYS:WEB\CONFIG\SRM.CFG file contains the following `RemoteScriptAlias` command that determines where BASIC CGI scripts can be placed.

```
RemoteScriptAlias /scripts/ localhost:8001/scripts
```

BASIC scripts are processed by the BASIC.NLM, which must be loaded on the Novell Web Server prior to executing any BASIC CGI scripts. The BASIC.NLM is an example of an RCGI extension application. When BASIC.NLM loads, it listens on TCP port 8001 waiting for execution of BASIC script execution requests through RCGI commands sent through TCP port number 8001 (see Figure 8.1). The previous `RemoteScriptAlias` directive specified that the BASIC scripts should have path alias of `/scripts` and that the BASIC script is executed at the localhost on port number 8001. The `localhost` is a reference to the local Novell Web Server on which the BASIC.NLM is loaded.

Figure 8.2 shows the BASIC.NLM screen when it is loaded on a Novell Web Server. You can examine this screen for status information and troubleshooting tips when debugging your BASIC CGI scripts. As BASIC CGI scripts are sent to the BASIC NLM via the RCGI, a status message appears on the BASIC NLM console. If you are debugging BASIC CGI scripts, you may want to check the BASIC NLM console for clues that will help you debug the BASIC script.

▶ · ◀

FIGURE 8.1

Execution of BASIC CGI scripts by BASIC.NLM

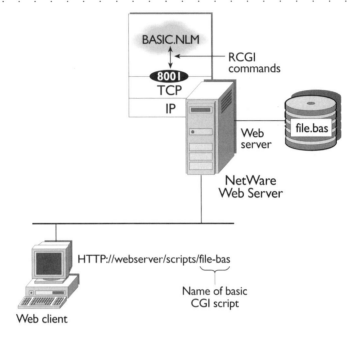

▶ · ◀

FIGURE 8.2

BASIC Server NLM screen

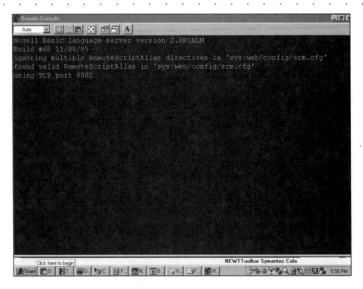

You can specify that the BASIC script be executed on a remote NetWare server instead of a local Novell Web Server by using an alias similar to the following:

```
RemoteScriptAlias /rembasic/ remotehost:8001/scripts
```

You must replace *remotehost* with the hostname or IP address of a remote NetWare Server on which the BASIC.NLM is loaded (see Figure 8.3). Also, the execution of the remote BASIC CGI scripts is specified by a URL address that uses `/rembasic` as the relative path name. For example, to execute a CGI program called `file.bas`, you would specify the following:

```
http://webserver/rembasic/file.bas
```

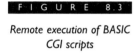

FIGURE 8.3

Remote execution of BASIC CGI scripts

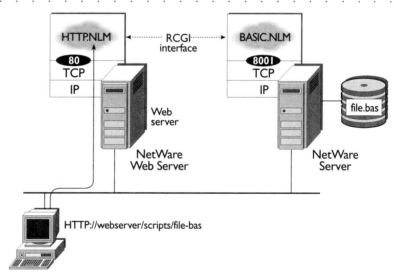

If an error occurs while a BASIC script is running and no error trapping has been set up, the script terminates and the RCGI connection is also terminated.

The Novell Web Server distribution software comes with examples of several BASIC CGI scripts. These include the following:

▶ TESTCGI.BAS CGI-Script to print the value of CGI environment variables

▶ DATE.BAS CGI-Script to print Date/Time Return server date and time

> ▸ CARDSAMP.BAS-CGI script create a Greeting Card using a form

> ▸ SUBS.BAS CGI-Script to take a submarine sandwich using a form

> ▸ 411.BAS CGI-Script to look up employee names in a text database

The following sections discuss the first two examples (TESTCGI.BAS and DATE.BAS) and the last example (411.BAS). The remaining examples are left as an exercise for the reader.

The TESTGI.BAS CGI Script Example

The BASIC that most people are familiar with uses the following language syntax:

linenumber   STATEMENT

The linenumber is any number greater than 1. The line numbers are used to order the statements. Novell's implementation of BASIC for CGI scripts uses the same *linenumber–statement* syntax. Listing 8.1 shows an example of the TESTCGI.BAS BASIC program that ships with the Novell Web Server.

LISTING 8.1

TESTCGI.BAS Program

```
10 rem
20 print "Content-type: text/html"
25 print ""
30 print "<HTML><HEAD><TITLE>RCGI Low-Level Interface
Report</TITLE></HEAD>"
35 print "<BODY>"
40 print "<H1>RCGI Low-Level Interface Report</H1>"
50 print
60 print "<B>argc</B> is <I>", argc$, "</I><BR>"
65 print "<B>argv</B> is <I>", argv$, "</I><BR>"
70 print
100 print "<B>server_software</B> = <I>", server_software$,
"</I><BR>"
```

```
110 print "<B>server_name</B> = <I>",, server_name$,
"</I><BR>"
120 print "<B>gateway_interface</B> = <I>",
gateway_interface$, "</I><BR>"
130 print "<B>server_protocol</B> = <I>", server_protocol$,
"</I><BR>"
140 print "<B>server_port</B> = <I>",, server_port$,
"</I><BR>"
150 print "<B>request_method</B> = <I>", request_method$,
"</I><BR>"
160 print "<B>http_accept</B> = <I>",, http_accept$,
"</I><BR>"
170 print "<B>path_info</B> = <I>",, path_info$, "</I><BR>"
180 print "<B>path_translated</B> = <I>", path_translated$,
"</I><BR>"
190 print "<B>script_name</B> = <I>",, script_name$,
"</I><BR>"
200 print "<B>query_string</B> = <I>",, query_string$,
"</I><BR>"
210 print "<B>remote_host</B> = <I>",, remote_host$,
"</I><BR>"
220 print "<B>remote_addr</B> = <I>",, remote_addr$,
"</I><BR>"
230 print "<B>remote_user</B> = <I>",, remote_user$,
"</I><BR>"
240 print "<B>content_type</B> = <I>", content_type$,
"</I><BR>"
250 print "<B>content_length</B> = <I>", content_length$,
"</I><BR>"
260 if (val(content_length$) <= 0) then 290
270 linput line$
280 print "<B>data</B> = <I>", line$, "</I><BR>"
290 print "</BODY>"
300 rem Standard trailer.  Note variable used to insert
script name in hyperlink below.
```

```
310 rem Hyperlink points to a BASIC script that displays raw
HTML rather than translated HTML.
320 print "<hr>"
330 print "<a href="; chr$(34); "/scripts/convert.bas?";
mid$(script_name$,2); chr$(34);" ><it>";
340 print "See how this script is written.</it></a>"
350 print "<p>"
360 print "Copyright &#169; 1995 Novell, Inc.  All Rights
Reserved."
370 print "</body></HTML>"
400 end
```

This BASIC CGI script prints the CGI environment variables. Figure 8.4 shows the results of executing this CGI script. The following is an analysis of this BASIC program.

The first line contains a REM statement. REM statements are used to add comments to a program. BASIC statements contain one statement per line. The end of the line marks the termination of the statement. You can put multiple statements on a line only if you separate the statements with the ":" character. The print statement as shown in the following lines, sends the output to the standard output channel:

```
20 print "Content-type: text/html"
25 print ""
```

In the case of BASIC CGI programs sending the output to the standard output channel is the same as sending it to the Web server. The previous statements output a MIME content type of text/html and a blank line to mark the end of the HTTP response header.

The following print statements print the HTML tags for displaying the CGI environment variables that follow:

```
30 print "<HTML><HEAD><TITLE>RCGI Low-Level Interface
Report</TITLE></HEAD>"
35 print "<BODY>"
40 print "<H1>RCGI Low-Level Interface Report</H1>"
50 print
```

FIGURE 8.4

Output of the
TESTCGI.BAS script

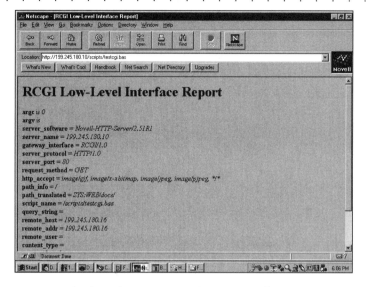

The last statement, which is the print on a line by itself, prints a new line. The next several statements print the values of the environment variables:

```
60 print "<B>argc</B> is <I>", argc$, "</I><BR>"
65 print "<B>argv</B> is <I>", argv$, "</I><BR>"
70 print
100 print "<B>server_software</B> = <I>", server_software$,
"</I><BR>"
110 print "<B>server_name</B> = <I>",, server_name$,
"</I><BR>"
120 print "<B>gateway_interface</B> = <I>",
gateway_interface$, "</I><BR>"
130 print "<B>server_protocol</B> = <I>", server_protocol$,
"</I><BR>"
140 print "<B>server_port</B> = <I>",, server_port$,
"</I><BR>"
150 print "<B>request_method</B> = <I>", request_method$,
"</I><BR>"
160 print "<B>http_accept</B> = <I>",, http_accept$,
"</I><BR>"
```

```
170 print "<B>path_info</B> = <I>",, path_info$, "</I><BR>"
180 print "<B>path_translated</B> = <I>", path_translated$,
    "</I><BR>"
190 print "<B>script_name</B> = <I>",, script_name$,
    "</I><BR>"
200 print "<B>query_string</B> = <I>",, query_string$,
    "</I><BR>"
210 print "<B>remote_host</B> = <I>",, remote_host$,
    "</I><BR>"
220 print "<B>remote_addr</B> = <I>",, remote_addr$,
    "</I><BR>"
230 print "<B>remote_user</B> = <I>",, remote_user$,
    "</I><BR>"
240 print "<B>content_type</B> = <I>", content_type$,
    "</I><BR>"
250 print "<B>content_length</B> = <I>", content_length$,
    "</I><BR>"
```

Notice that the CGI environment variables consist of the environment variable name (see Chapter 6) followed by the "$" character. The next statement checks the value of the content_length$ variable. Variables that end with a "$" character are string values. Variables that do not have the "$" character are numeric values. The use of the val() function converts a string value to a numeric value.

```
260 if (val(content_length$) <= 0) then 290
```

The previous is also an example of an if statement in BASIC. If the content_length$ is zero or negative, execution branches to statement 290. This means that the input to the BASIC script was specified using the GET method. If content_length$ is greater than zero, input must be read from the standard input (that is, input was specified using the POST method). Chapter 6 discusses the GET and POST methods. The following statements read the standard input and display the value of the input:

```
270 linput line$
280 print "<B>data</B> = <I>", line$, "</I><BR>"
```

The linput statement is used to read the value of the input data and assign it to the string variable line$.

The remaining statements provide the end HTML tags for completing the HTML document, and build an anchor tag that can be used by the `convert.bas` script to display the HTML document as uninterpreted (raw) HTML, rather than translated HTML.

```
290 print "</BODY>"
300 rem Standard trailer.  Note variable used to insert
script name in hyperlink below.
310 rem Hyperlink points to a BASIC script that displays raw
HTML rather than translated HTML.
320 print "<hr>"
330 print "<a href="; chr$(34); "/scripts/convert.bas?";
mid$(script_name$,2); chr$(34);" ><it>";
340 print "See how this script is written.</it></a>"
350 print "<p>"
360 print "Copyright &#169; 1995 Novell, Inc.  All Rights
Reserved."
370 print "</body></HTML>"
400 end
```

As you examine the following print statements, you can see that BASIC allows you to print a string of data items when they are separated by the semicolon (;) character. Also, the BASIC function `chr$()` converts an ASCII code to its equivalent string value.

```
330 print "<a href="; chr$(34); "/scripts/convert.bas?";
mid$(script_name$,2); chr$(34);" ><it>";
340 print "See how this script is written.</it></a>"
```

The `mid$(str$, start)` function returns a substring of the string value `str$` starting from *start*. This function is used to strip the leading "/" from the script name. The `chr$(34)` function is used to generate the double-quote character. The previous statements, therefore, output the following anchor tag:

```
<a href="/scripts/convert.bas?scripts/date.bas"><it>See how
this script is written.</it></a>
```

The remaining statements print the copyright notice and the end HTML tags for the generated document.

```
350 print "<p>"
360 print "Copyright &#169; 1995 Novell, Inc.  All Rights
Reserved."
370 print "</body></HTML>"
400 end
```

Notice that the copyright symbol is displayed by inserting the HTML code &#169, and that the last statement is the end statement that terminates execution of the BASIC script.

The DATE.BAS CGI Script for Server Date and Time

The DATE.BAS CGI script shows how to call the BASIC date and time functions in order to return server date and time. Figure 8.5 shows the results of executing the DATE.BAS script. The following is the DATE.BAS script.

```
10 rem BASIC Script to print today's date.
15 rem Copyright (c) 1995 Novell, Inc.  All Rights Reserved.
20 print "Content-type: text/html" : print
30 print "<HTML><head><title>BASIC Date Demo</title></head>"
40 print "<body>"
50 print "Today is "; date$; "."
100 rem Standard trailer.  Note variable used to insert
script name in hyperlink below.
110 rem Hyperlink points to a BASIC script that displays raw
HTML rather than translated HTML.
120 print "<hr>"
130 print "<a href="; chr$(34); "/scripts/convert.bas?";
mid$(script_name$,2); chr$(34);" ><it>";
140 print "See how this script is written.</it></a>"
150 print "<p>"
160 print "Copyright &#169; 1995 Novell, Inc.  All Rights
Reserved."
170 print "</body></HTML>"
200 end
```

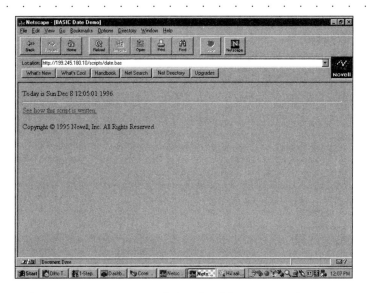

The first two lines are comments, and the third line prints the HTTP response header:

```
20 print "Content-type: text/html" : print
```

Notice that the previous statement is an example of placing two statements on a single line. The `print` command without any argument causes a blank line to be inserted. This blank line signifies the end of the HTTP response header.

The fourth and fifth lines print the beginning tags for the HTML document contents:

```
30 print "<HTML><head><title>BASIC Date Demo</title></head>"
40 print "<body>"
```

The sixth line uses the built-in `date$` function to return the date and time stamp of the Novell Web Server:

```
50 print "Today is "; date$; "."
```

The remaining `print` statements generate an anchor tag to display the uninterpreted BASIC code for the DATE.BAS script, the end tags, and the copyright information for the HTML document.

The 411.BAS Script for Employee Database Lookup

The 411.BAS script performs a lookup in the employee database file given an employee name. Figure 8.6 shows the results of executing the 411.BAS script. The employee database file is kept in the file `scripts/employee.all`, the contents of which are as follows:

```
don juan              (800) 555-1234
shirley doe           (800) 555-1555
john smith            (800) 555-5532
john adams            (800) 555-1776
mary adams            (800) 555-1777
```

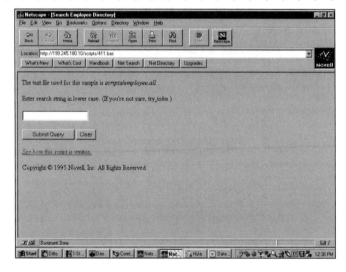

Execution of the 411.BAS script

If you enter the name **john** and press the Submit Query button, you will see the results of the lookup operation displayed in Figure 8.7. The query was submitted using the GET method.

```
http://servername/scripts/411.bas?who=john
```

There were two records returned (see Figure 8.7) because there were two records that both had the name John.

Next, you will learn how the 411.BAS is implemented. The following is a listing of the 411.BAS script:

FIGURE 8.7

*Results of lookup operation
of the employee database*

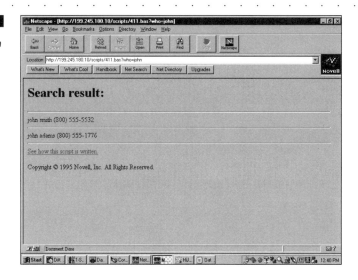

```
1   rem Copyright (c) 1995 Novell, Inc.  All Rights Reserved.
10    rem
15    file$ = "scripts/employee.all"
20    if argc$ <> "0"  then 1000
30    print `Content-Type: text/html` : print
50    print `<HTML><HEAD><title>Search Employee
Directory</title></HEAD>`
55    print "<BODY>"
60    print `<form action="/scripts/411.bas">`
65    print "The text file used for this sample is"
66    print "<I>", file$, "</I>.<P>"
70    print `Enter search string in lower case.  (If you're
not sure, try <i>john</i>.)<p>`
75    print `<input type="text" name="who"
maxlength="32"><p>`
80    print `<input type="submit">`
90    print `<input type="reset" value="Clear">`
100   print `</form>`
110   goto 5000
```

```
1000 ' if arguments, process the form
1001 open file$ for input as 1
1005 on error goto 4090
1020 sstring$ = form$(query_string$, "who")
1025 hits = 0
1030 print `Content-Type: text/html` : print
1035 print "<h1>Search result:</h1><hr>"
1040 while not eof(1)
1050    linput #1, line$
1060    if instr(sstring$, line$) < 1 then goto 1080
1065    print line$
1066    print "<hr>"
1070    hits = hits + 1
1080 wend
1090 close 1
1100 if hits = 0 then print "Sorry, nothing matches your
request.<hr>"
1200 goto 5000
4090 print `Content-Type: text/html` : print
4095 print `error opening employee.all file`
5000 rem Standard trailer.  Note variable used to insert
script name in hyperlink below.
5110 rem Hyperlink points to a BASIC script that displays
raw HTML rather than translated HTML.
5130 print "<a href="; chr$(34); "/scripts/convert.bas?";
mid$(script_name$,2); chr$(34);" ><it>";
5140 print "See how this script is written.</it></a>"
5150 print "<p>"
5160 print "Copyright &#169; 1995 Novell, Inc.  All Rights
Reserved."
5170 print "</body></HTML>"
5200 end
```

The first few lines define the file$ string variable in which is stored the name of the database file:

```
1 rem Copyright (c) 1995 Novell, Inc.   All Rights Reserved.
10   rem
15   file$ = "scripts/employee.all"
```

The next statement checks to see if there were any arguments passed to the BASIC script:

```
20   if argc$ <> "0"   then 1000
```

The previous statement is interesting because if the number of arguments (argc$) is zero, it means that the BASIC script was invoked for displaying the data entry form, and, when the number of arguments is non-zero, the user's data entry is sent to the BASIC script for processing. Therefore, the statements from 1000 on deal with processing data entry and the statements immediately following the if statement are for displaying the data entry form.

Let's first examine the statements for displaying the data entry form:

```
30   print `Content-Type: text/html` : print
50   print `<HTML><HEAD><title>Search Employee
Directory</title></HEAD>`
55   print "<BODY>"
60   print `<form action="/scripts/411.bas">`
65   print "The text file used for this sample is"
66   print "<I>", file$, "</I>.<P>"
70   print `Enter search string in lower case.  (If you're
not sure, try <i>john</i>.)<p>`
75   print `<input type="text" name="who"
maxlength="32"><p>`
80   print `<input type="submit">`
90   print `<input type="reset" value="Clear">`
100  print `</form>`
110  goto 5000
```

The previous statements do the following:

1 • Generate the HTTP response header (line 30)

2 • Generate the HTML tags for the start of the document (lines 50, 55)

3 • Generate the FORM tag for displaying the form fields (lines 60 to 100)

At the end of displaying the HTML form, the execution branches to statement 5000, which generates the standard trailer.

As mentioned previously, the statements starting from line 1000 process the user's data entry. Let's examine these statements:

```
1000 ' if arguments, process the form
1001 open file$ for input as 1
1005 on error goto 4090
1020 sstring$ = form$(query_string$, "who")
1025 hits = 0
1030 print `Content-Type: text/html` : print
1035 print "<h1>Search result:</h1><hr>"
1040 while not eof(1)
1050    linput #1, line$
1060    if instr(sstring$, line$) < 1 then goto 1080
1065    print line$
1066    print "<hr>"
1070    hits = hits + 1
1080 wend
1090 close 1
1100 if hits = 0 then print "Sorry, nothing matches your
request.<hr>"
1200 goto 5000
4090 print `Content-Type: text/html` : print
4095 print `error opening employee.all file`
```

Notice that the statement 1000 shows the use of the single quote character as yet another form of inserting comments in BASIC programs.

Line 1001 shows how you can open a file on a particular channel (in this case, channel number 1):

```
1001 open file$ for input as 1
```

If you were opening the file for writing, you would replace input with output. Line 1005 sets up the error handler using the on error statement:

```
1005 on error goto 4090
```

If any errors are encountered, the script branches to line number 4090 that defines the action to be taken on errors.

The next statement uses the Novell extended BASIC function `form$` to return the value that was specified in the query string:

```
1020 sstring$ = form$(query_string$, "who")
```

The query string is stored in the variable `query_string$`, which is passed as the first argument to `form$`. Recall from the TESTCGI.BAS example that `query_string$` is the name of one of the CGI environment variables. The second argument to `form$` is the name of the form field variable (defined on line 75). The result is the search string to be used for searching the database and is stored in the string variable `sstring$`.

The next three lines initialize the "hits" counter variable, generate the HTTP response header, and generate the heading for the search results:

```
1025 hits = 0
1030 print `Content-Type: text/html` : print
1035 print "<h1>Search result:</h1><hr>"
```

Next follows the loop statement that reads each record of the input employee database file and searches the input record to see if there is a match for the search string that is stored in the `sstring$` variable:

```
1040 while not eof(1)
1050    linput #1, line$
1060    if instr(sstring$, line$) < 1 then goto 1080
1065    print line$
1066    print "<hr>"
1070    hits = hits + 1
1080 wend
```

Notice the syntax of the while statement:

```
while logicalexpression
       statements
wend
```

The *logicalexpression* in this example is `not eof(1)`. The `not` is the logical operator that negates the Boolean expression that follows. The `eof(1)` checks to see if the input channel 1 is at the end of the file. The previous while-statement will, therefore, terminate only when the end-of-file is encountered in reading the employee database file.

Within the while statement, the record is read using the following:

```
1050    linput #1, line$
```

Next, a check is made to see if the search string is found in the input record:

```
1060    if instr(sstring$, line$) < 1 then goto 1080
```

The instr() function returns the number of times the first string argument value is found in the second string argument value. In the previous if-statement, if the search string sstring$ is not found in the input record, execution branches to statement 1080, which is the end of the current loop execution.

If the search string sstring$ is found in the input record, the following statements are executed:

```
1065    print line$
1066    print "<hr>"
1070    hits = hits + 1
```

These statements print the record and the HTML tag for a horizontal line after the record is displayed. The "hits" counter is also incremented.

Lines 4090 to 4095 define the error handling for the BASIC script by displaying an HTML error message.

```
4090 print `Content-Type: text/html` : print
4095 print `error opening employee.all file`
```

Lines 5000 and greater define the standard trailer for the BASIC script, which generates the anchor tag to view the BASIC script and prints the copyright information:

```
5000 rem Standard trailer.  Note variable used to insert
script name in hyperlink below.
5110 rem Hyperlink points to a BASIC script that displays
raw HTML rather than translated HTML.
5130 print "<a href="; chr$(34); "/scripts/convert.bas?";
mid$(script_name$,2); chr$(34);" ><it>";
```

```
5140 print "See how this script is written.</it></a>"
5150 print "<p>"
5160 print "Copyright &#169; 1995 Novell, Inc.  All Rights
Reserved."
5170 print "</body></HTML>"
5200 end
```

Developing with NetBasic

While you can use the standard BASIC NLM, and write BASIC CGI scripts, NetBasic is vastly superior to standard BASIC as a general-purpose programming language used to write CGI scripts. The remainder of this chapter discusses the writing of NetBasic programs.

NetBasic was developed by HiTec Software, who can be contacted as follows:

High Technology Software Corporation
3370 N. Hayden Rd., Suite 123-175
Scottsdale, AZ 85251-6695
Telephone: 602 970-1025
Fax: 602 670-6323
WEB: www.hitecsoft.com
FTP: ftp.hitecsoft.com

Novell has licensed NetBasic for IntranetWare and every copy of the IntranetWare server ships with NetBasic engine in the form of NETBASIC.NLM. The CGI2NMX.NLM in the directory SYS:WEB/LCGI/NETBASIC provides a CGI wrapper interface on the NETBASIC.NLM. In order to run the CGI interface NLM, you must ensure that the following line is configured in the server resource map file SYS:WEB/CONFIG/SRM.CFG:

```
LoadableModule /netbasic/ sys:web/lcgi/netbasic/cgi2nmx.nlm
```

The LoadableModule directive shows that NetBasic runs as an NLM and it processes CGI scripts using the LCGI interface. In the previous example, NetBasic scripts are invoked by specifying the relative path name of /netbasic, as in the following example:

```
http://webserver/netbasic/myscript.bas
```

Tools for Writing NetBasic CGI Scripts

Just as with Perl and BASIC, you can use any text editor to create NetBasic scripts. However, HiTec Software Corporation sells a separate tool called Visual NetBasic that simplifies the creation of NetBasic scripts. You do not need Visual NetBasic to write NetBasic programs. However, if you intend to do serious development of CGI programs and other network scripts using NetBasic it is highly recommended that you purchase the Visual NetBasic GUI tool.

HiTec also sells the WebPro software bundle that includes a Visual NetBasic rapid-development GUI tool to produce NetBasic programs, the NetBasic engine that runs on the server, and their own Web server.

Figure 8.8 shows the Visual NetBasic tool that contains a built-in editor and help documentation on NetBasic Application Programming Interface (API) functions.

F I G U R E   8.8

Visual NetBasic tool

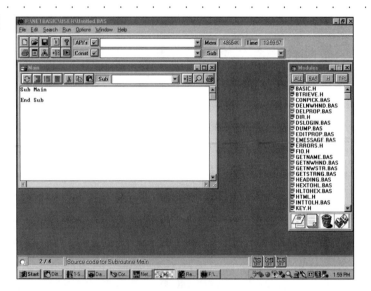

Running NetBasic Programs

You can run NetBasic programs using any of the following methods:

▸ From the server system console

▸ From the NetBasic shell on the system console

▸ Through the CGI

You must first load the NETBASIC.NLM. If you are running a NetBasic CGI script through the CGI, the NETBASIC.NLM and the CGI wrapper NLM (CGI2NMX.NLM) are automatically loaded. If you want to run the NetBasic programs directly, you must load the NETBASIC.NLM from the system console by using the following command:

LOAD NETBASIC

When NETBASIC.NLM loads, it adds the RUN command to the server console. You can use the RUN command to execute any NetBasic script from the console by using the syntax

RUN *NetBasicScriptFilename*

where *NetBasicScriptFilename* is the name of the NetBasic script file. You do not have to specify the default extension of .BAS. A number of sample NetBasic scripts are stored in the SYS:NETBASIC\UTIL directory when NetBasic is installed. If the full path name of the *NetBasicScriptFilename* is not specified, the NetBasic script is assumed to be in the SYS:NETBASIC\UTIL directory. Figure 8.9 shows the results of running the following command from the NetWare Server console:

RUN *VOLINFO*

FIGURE 8.9

Running VOLINFO.BAS on the server console

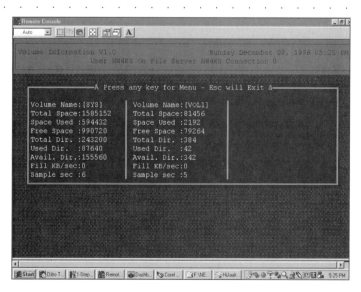

The *VOLINFO* refers to the NetBasic script VOLINFO.BAS that is in the SYS:NETBASIC\UTIL directory. The program that produced the volume information screen is shown in Listing 8.2. You can study this program to get an appreciation of the power of NetBasic, but a complete explanation of this program is not presented here. First, you must learn the elements of the NetBasic language which are presented in the sections that follow.

L I S T I N G 8.2

VOLINFO.BAS Program

```
'(c) Copyright 1993-1996 HITECSOFT CORP. All rights
reserved.
#include "sys.H"
#include "win.H"
#include "key.H"
#include "net.H"
Sub BuildMainMenu
Local("Menu")
Menu = WIN:Menu:Define(20,30)
WIN:Title(" Main Menu ")
WIN:Menu:Item:Add("Change Server    ")
WIN:Menu:Item:Add("Change Check Interval ")
WIN:Menu:Item:Add("Start Monitoring")
WIN:Menu:Item:Add("Exit            ")
Return(Menu)
End Sub
Sub BuildMainWindow
Local("Window")
MainTitle = "Volume Information V1.0"
RPC:Call("","HEADING.BAS",MainTitle)
Window = WIN:Define(6,4,17,77)
WIN:Title(" Press any key for Menu - Esc will Exit ")
WIN:Show
```

```
Return(Window)
End Sub
Sub ChangeDelay
WIN:Define(16,25,18,55)
WIN:Show()
WIN:At(1,1); WIN:Say("Enter Delay Value : ")
WIN:Get(DelayTime)
WIN:Get:Read()
WIN:Close()
End Sub
Sub ChecKDelay
Local("i")
i = 0
Do While (i < Param(1))
    If (KEY:Ready)
        Return
    EndIf
    SYS:Delay(1000)
    i = i + 1
EndDo
End Sub
Sub DoChangeServer
Local("SelectionObject","serverName","con","ConnInfoObject")
SelectionObject = RPC:Call("","SERVPICK.BAS")
If (SelectionObject.Error != 0)
    WIN:Popup("No Server was found!")
    Return
EndIf
If (DATA:Integer(SelectionObject.Key) != KEY_ENTER)
    WIN:Popup("No Server was selected!")
    Return
EndIf
ServerName = SelectionObject.item
```

```
Con = DATA:Integer(SelectionObject.Number)
ConnInfoObject = NET:Connection:Get()
ConnInfoObject.ID = Con
ConnInfoObject = NET:Connection:Set(ConnInfoObject)
If (ConnInfoObject.Error != 0)
   WIN:Popup("Error changing Server!")
   Return
EndIf
RPC:Call("","HEADING.BAS",MainTitle)
End Sub
Sub Main
'Initialize vars.
Choice = 3
DelayTime = 5
VolNumber = 3
VolumeRate = 1
VolumeRateUsage = 0
SaveVolUsed(1) = 0
SaveVolUsed(2) = 0
SaveVolUsed(3) = 0
SampTime(1) = DATE:Utf()
SampTime(2) = DATE:Utf()
SampTime(3) = DATE:Utf()
SampDiff(1) = DelayTime
SampDiff(2) = DelayTime
SampDiff(3) = DelayTime
WIN:Cursor:Hide
MainWindow = BuildMainWindow
MainMenu = BuildMainMenu
Do While (True)
   UpdateWindow(MainWindow,VolNumber)
   CheckDelay(DelayTime)
   If (KEY:Ready)
```

```
          KEY:Read
          If (KEY:Last = KEY_ESC)
              If (YesNo("Exit Volinfo ?"))
                  WIN:Close(MainMenu)
                  WIN:Close(MainWindow)
                  WIN:Heading:Off
                  WIN:Clear
                  WIN:Cursor:Show
                  Quit
              EndIf
          Else
              choice = ProcessMainMenu(choice)
          EndIf
      EndIf
EndDo
End Sub
Sub ProcessMainMenu
Local("choice")
WIN:Select(MainMenu)
choice = WIN:Menu:Start(Param(1))
If (KEY:Last() = KEY_RETURN)
    If (choice = 1)
        DoChangeServer
        WIN:Select(MainWindow)
        WIN:Clear
        WIN:Select(MainMenu)
    EndIf
    If (choice = 2)
        ChangeDelay
    EndIf
    If (choice = 3)
    EndIf
    If (choice = 4)
```

```
          If (YesNo("Exit Volinfo ?"))
              WIN:Close(MainMenu)
              WIN:Close(MainWindow)
              WIN:Heading:Off
              WIN:Clear
              WIN:Cursor:Show
              Quit
          EndIf
      EndIf
  EndIf
  WIN:Hide(MainMenu)
  Return(choice)
  End Sub
  Sub UpdateVolumeInfo
  Local("Vol0","VolumeNumber","Total","Used","DeletedUsed","Fre
  e","UsedDir","Col","Row","VolUsed")
  Local("Blank")
  VolumeNumber = Param(2)
  Vol0 = NET:Volume:Info(VolumeNumber)
  If (Vol0.Error != 0)
      Return
  EndIf
  Total = DATA:Integer(Vol0.Blocks.Total) *
  (DATA:Integer(Vol0.Blocks.Size) / 1024)
  DeletedUsed = DATA:Integer(Vol0.Blocks.Purgable) *
  (DATA:Integer(Vol0.Blocks.Size) / 1024)
  Used = ((DATA:Integer(Vol0.Blocks.Total) -
  DATA:Integer(Vol0.Blocks.Free)) *
  (DATA:Integer(Vol0.Blocks.Size)) / 1024) - DeletedUsed
  Free = DATA:Integer(Vol0.Blocks.Free) *
  (DATA:Integer(Vol0.Blocks.Size) / 1024) + DeletedUsed
  UsedDir = DATA:Integer(Vol0.DIR.Total) -
  DATA:Integer(Vol0.Dir.Free)
  SampTime(VolumeNumber) = DATE:Utf()
```

```
If (SaveVolUsed(VolumeNumber) != 0)
   SampDiff(VolumeNumber) = SampTime(VolumeNumber) -
SaveSampTime(VolumeNumber)
   If (SampDiff(VolumeNumber) > 0)
      VolumeRateUsage = DATA:Integer((Used -
SaveVolUsed(VolumeNumber)) / SampDiff(VolumeNumber))
   Else
      VolumeRateUsage = DATA:Integer(Used -
SaveVolUsed(VolumeNumber))
   EndIf
EndIf
SaveVolUsed(VolumeNumber) = Used
SaveSampTime(VolumeNumber) = SampTime(VolumeNumber)
'Calc. the position for information
Col = 25 * (VolumeNumber - 1)
If (Col = 0); Col = 1; EndIf
Row = Param(1)
'Print("Statistics for volume
",NET:Server:Name(0),"/",Vol0.Name);Newline
Blank = STR:Repeat(" ",10) + " "
WIN:At(Row,Col); WIN:Say("Volume Name:",Blank)
WIN:At(Row,Col); WIN:Say("Volume
Name:[",STR:Sub(Vol0.Name,1,8),"]")
WIN:At(Row + 1,Col); WIN:Say("Total Space:",Blank)
WIN:At(Row + 1,Col); WIN:Say("Total Space:",Total)
WIN:At(Row + 2,Col); WIN:Say("Space Used :",Blank)
WIN:At(Row + 2,Col); WIN:Say("Space Used :",Used)
WIN:At(Row + 3,Col); WIN:Say("Free Space :",Blank)
WIN:At(Row + 3,Col); WIN:Say("Free Space :",Free)
WIN:At(Row + 4,Col); WIN:Say("Total Dir. :",Blank)
WIN:At(Row + 4,Col); WIN:Say("Total Dir. :",Vol0.Dir.Total)
WIN:At(Row + 5,Col); WIN:Say("Used Dir.  :",Blank)
WIN:At(Row + 5,Col); WIN:Say("Used Dir.  :",UsedDir)
WIN:At(Row + 6,Col); WIN:Say("Avail. Dir.:",Blank)
```

```
WIN:At(Row + 6,Col); WIN:Say("Avail. Dir.:",Vol0.Dir.Free)
WIN:At(Row + 7,Col); WIN:Say("Fill KB/sec:",Blank)
WIN:At(Row + 7,Col); WIN:Say("Fill KB/sec:",VolumeRateUsage)
WIN:At(Row + 8,Col); WIN:Say("Sample sec :",Blank)
WIN:At(Row + 8,Col); WIN:Say("Sample sec
:",SampDiff(VolumeNumber))
End Sub
Sub UpdateWindow
Local("j","oldWindow")
OldWindow = WIN:Select
WIN:Select(Param(1))
WIN:Color(WIN_FG_YELLOW + WIN_FG_LIGHT + WIN_BG_BLUE)
WIN:At(1,1); WIN:Say("Checking ...")
WIN:Color(WIN_FG_WHITE + WIN_FG_LIGHT + WIN_BG_BLUE)
j = 1
Do While (j <= Param(2))
    UpdateVolumeInfo(2,j)
    j = j + 1
EndDo
WIN:At(1,1); WIN:Say(STR:Repeat(" ",22))
WIN:Select(OldWindow)
End Sub
Sub YesNo
Return(RPC:Call(NULL,"YESNO.BAS",Param(1)))
End Sub
```

Another way you can run NetBasic programs is by typing the extended command SHELL after loading NetBasic. When you type the SHELL command at the server console, you will see a prompt similar to the following:

```
Copyright messages for NetBasic
<servername>
SYS:\AUTOEXEC.BAS
<servername>
SYS:\>
```

The prompt is set to the server name in <> and the name of the current directory:

```
<servername>
SYS:\>
```

The file AUTOEXEC.BAS is located in the SYS:NETBASIC\USER directory and contains the skeleton of a NetBasic program that you can execute to set up the NetBasic shell environment. The contents of the AUTOEXEC.BAS skeleton program are as follows:

```
Sub Main
' this is your Autoexec
' shell will search the current dir first then the path for
this file
' if it is found, shell will run it
Return
```

You can run any NetBasic script from the shell by typing its name. For example, you can run the CD.BAS script to change your current directory to SYS:NETBASIC\UTIL, by typing either of the following from the shell prompt:

```
CD SYS:NETBASIC\UTIL
CD \NETBASIC\UTIL
```

Next, you can see the NetBasic utilities that are available in this directory by typing the following command:

```
DIR /W
```

Actually, the DIR command runs the DIR.BAS script and it is similar to the DOS command. Figure 8.10 shows the output of the DIR.BAS program.

You can examine the current settings of the NetBasic shell by using the SET command. Figure 8.11 shows an example result of executing the SET command. Notice that this command displays the PATH, PROMPT, and TEMP environment variable settings. You can alter these values by making changes to the AUTOEXEC.BAS file.

FIGURE 8.10

Output of DIR.BAS program

FIGURE 8.11

Output of SET command

The Structure of NetBasic Programs

NetBasic programs (also called *NetBasic scripts*) have a structure that is similar to many other languages. NetBasic scripts consist of the following program elements:

- Statements

- Subroutines

- Classes

Statements are assignment statements and control statements (such as if statement, while statement, for statement, and so on). *Subroutines* are methods of encapsulating statements so that they can be called repeatedly from anywhere within a NetBasic program. Invoking the subroutine causes the statements in the subroutine to be executed. The advantage of using subroutines is that commonly used groups of statements can be executed anywhere in your NetBasic script by invoking the name of the subroutine.

All NetBasic scripts must have a subroutine named main. Here is an example of a simple NetBasic script:

```
sub main
print ("Hello users of NetBasic!")
' Other NetBasic statements
end sub
```

Variable names, subroutine names, and keywords in NetBasic are not case-sensitive. You can use any combination of uppercase or lowercase characters. Comments are added by preceding them with a single quotation mark or by using the rem keyword. The following program is equivalent to the previous program:

```
Sub Main
   PRINT ("Hello users of NetBasic!")
   rem Other NetBasic statements
End Sub
```

NetBasic statements occur one per line. You can place multiple NetBasic statements on a single line provided you separate them with a semicolon (;).

Subroutines can return values, in which case they are called *functions*. Many built-in subroutines in NetBasic are grouped in classes. A *class* is a collection of subroutines/functions and can be organized in a hierarchical fashion. For example the following functions all belong to the NET class:

```
net:stat:bytes:received
net:stat:bytes:transmitted
net:stat:bytes:written
net:stat:disk:bytes:read
net:stat:disk:reads
net:stat:disk:write
net:server:date:get
net:server:date:set
net:server:description
```

Within the NET class are several subclasses such as STAT and SERVER. These subclasses can further be subclassed as shown in Figure 8.12.

FIGURE 8.12

Example class hierarchy in NetBasic

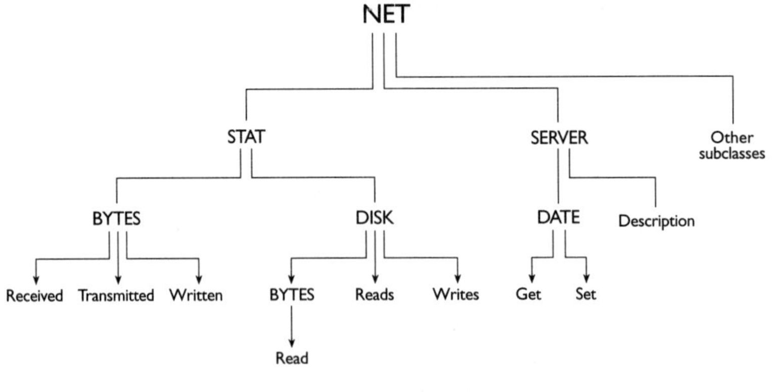

Table 8.1 shows some of the top-level class libraries within NetBasic. The DOC class is an HTML library; the MATH and STR classes are data manipulation libraries; the NDS and NET class are networking libraries; the BTX and ORA classes are database libraries; and the WIN class is a Text-based C-Worthy library function. All the other libraries are system libraries.

T A B L E 8.1	CLASS NAME	DESCRIPTION
NetBasic Class Libraries	BTX	Btrieve database access functions
	COM	Functions for the server serial port
	DATE	System and date functions
	DIR	Directory and server volume manipulation functions
	DOC	HTML tag-generation functions
	FIO	File Input/Output functions
	INI	INI file reading/writing functions
	KEY	Keyboard input functions
	LPT	Server attached printer functions
	MATH	Mathematical functions
	NDS	Novell Directory Services functions
	NET	Novell network functions
	NMX	Network Loadable Module extensions (such as calling C library functions and loading libraries)
	OBJECT	Functions for accessing attributes of objects and creating objects
	ORA	Oracle database access functions
	PARAM	Functions to access parameter information
	PORT	Input and output functions for I/O ports
	RPC	Functions to run external NetBasic programs
	STR	String-manipulation functions
	SYS	Miscellaneous system calls
	WIN	Server based C-Worthy menu functions

NetBasic Objects

Many NetBasic built-in functions (also called NetBasic *commands*) return *object* values. These object values are *instances* of a description of an abstract object or an object template. An object template describes data elements that are members of the object template. The following example helps explain NetBasic objects.

Suppose that you wanted to change the NetBasic shell environment by defining your own AUTOEXEC.BAS file in the SYS:NETBASIC\USERS directory. You can do this by defining the following subroutine in the AUTOEXEC.BAS file:

```
sub main
    ' Set the PATH
    PATH = "NW4KS\SYS:NETBASIC\KSS\;"
    envObj = Env:get("PATH");
    envObj.data = envObj.data + PATH
    Env:set(envObj)
end sub
```

The call to the NetBasic `Env:get()` function returns an environment object. This object has a data component, that can be referenced by using the following:

`objectname.data`

Objects in NetBasic encapsulate data elements. The data elements for objects have well-defined names. Any data element of a NetBasic object can be referenced by using the following syntax:

`objectname.componentname`

In the previous example, the Environment object is named `envObj`, so its component named data is referenced using `envObj.data`. Components of an object are also called *attributes* of that object.

The following statement appends the PATH string to the `envObj.data`:

`envObj.data = envObj.data + PATH`

String values can be concatenated using the "+" operator. Components within an object are separated from the object name by using periods (.), as in the last statement.

The last statement calls the `set` function defined in the class `Env` and passes it the modified `envObj`:

`Env:set(envObj)`

Subclasses and functions/subroutines within a class are separated by the colon (:) character, as in the last statement.

The Environment object is returned by call to the `Env:get()`function. In object-oriented programming, function calls that return an instance of an object are called *factory methods*. Therefore, `Env:get()` is a factory method. In the previous example only the Data attribute of the Environment object was used. The Environment object has two other data attributes: Name and Error. Table 8.2 describes the data attributes of the Environment object.

TABLE 8.2	DATA ATTRIBUTE	DESCRIPTION
NetBasic Environment Object Data Attributes	`Data`	This is a read-write string, and is the value for the environment variable.
	`Error`	This is a read-only integer, and indicates any error encountered during an operation on the object. When no error is encountered, the Error attribute will be zero.
	`Name`	This is a read-write string, and indicates the name for the environment variable.

In addition to the Environment object, NetBasic defines a number of other objects, which are described in Table 8.3. For a complete description of the NetBasic objects and APIs, you can access the online documentation installed on your Novell Web Server at the following URL.

`http://webserver/online/wpguide/index.htm`

TABLE 8.3	OBJECT NAME	DESCRIPTION
NetBasic Objects	Bindery	Provides information for bindery network resources. On a NetWare 4 server, you can set the bindery context on the server using the `SET BINDERY CONTEXT` command so that network resources in the bindery context appear as NetWare 3-emulated bindery objects.

(continued)

T A B L E 8.3	OBJECT NAME	DESCRIPTION
NetBasic Objects (continued)	Connection	Connection objects are used to select a default file server. Prior to logging in, the client must attach to a file server using the `NET:Server:Attach` command. A client can attach to a maximum of 32 file servers. The `NET:Connection:Get` and `NET:Connection:Set` commands are used to select one of the currently attached file servers as the default. Network commands for which the target file server is not specified are presumed to be for the default file server.
	Date	Date objects are used to retrieve the date and time information given the total number of seconds since January 1, 1970. The `DATE:UTF` command is used to determine the total number of seconds between any date and January 1, 1970. For example, the command `Seconds=DATE:UTF("05-10-1997")` is used to store the total number of seconds between January 1, 1970, and May 5, 1997, into the variable `"Seconds"`. The total number of seconds can be supplied to `DATE:Object` command for creating a date object.
	Directory	Directory objects are used to parse the directory information for a path name. Directory objects have some of the attributes of a File object and all of the attributes of a Path object.
	Environment	Environment objects are used to access and change environment variables of NetBasic. The *environment* is a section of memory that is shared among all NetBasic applications. The `ENV:Get` and `ENV:Set` commands are used to read, change, or create environment variables. An environment variable has a name and a data value.
	File	File objects are used to access files.
	Internet	Internet objects are used to locate a process within an Internet-based system. A workstation can run multiple processes, and a network can have many workstations. Multiple networks may be connected to form an Internet-based system.

	OBJECT NAME	DESCRIPTION
T A B L E 8.3 *NetBasic Objects* *(continued)*	Link	Link objects are used by client applications to communicate with server applications. The server application informs clients of its presence by using the advertising protocols that add the server's information to the bindery. Alternatively, the Novell Link Services Protocol (NLSP) can be used to maintain information on services that are available on the network. Link objects currently support both Sequenced Packet Exchange (SPX) and Internet-based Packet Exchange (IPX) protocols.
	Modules	Modules objects are used to return information about loaded NLMs.
	Path	Path objects are used to change the current path.
	Queue	Queue job objects are used to access the jobs in a queue. A *queue* is a central storage mechanism that keeps track of service requests for different clients. The service requests are referred to as *jobs* in the queue.
	Server date	Server date objects are used to retrieve and change the date and time of the default file server.
	Server description	Server description objects are used to retrieve information about the company that distributed the NetWare Operating System (NOS) that is currently running on the default file server.
	System date	System date objects are used to retrieve the system date and time.
	System information	System information objects are used to retrieve information about the system currently running the NetBasic application.
	Volume information	Volume information objects are used to retrieve information about the volumes that are available for the default file server.

Operators and Data Types Within NetBasic

The previous section mentioned the use of the "+" operator to concatenate string values in NetBasic. You can use a number of NetBasic operators, which are listed in Table 8.4 together with a brief description of their meanings and the data types on which the operators work.

TABLE 8.4	OPERATOR	MEANING	TYPES
NetBasic Operators	+	Add/Concatenate	Integer, real, and string
	-	Subtract	Integer, real
	*	Multiply	Integer, real
	/	Divide	Integer, real
	&	Logical AND	Logical
	|	Logical OR	Logical
	=	Equal to	Integer, real, string, and logical
	!=	Not equal	Integer, real, string, and logical
	<	Less than	Integer, real, string, and logical
	>	Greater than	Integer, real, string, and logical
	<=	Less than or equal	Integer, real, string, and logical
	>=	Greater than or equal	Integer, real, string, and logical

The data types used in NetBasic are the following:

- *String*. Strings are enclosed in double quotation marks (for example, "Saint Germain", "Lord Krishna", "El Morya Khan", and so on).

- *Real*. These are numbers that have a fractional part (for example, 3.1415926536, 1.414, and 2.71828).

- *Integer*. These are whole numbers without a decimal point: (for example, 1, 3, 355, and 113).

- *Logical*. These are the Boolean values of true and false.

The comparison operators (=, != , <, <=, >, >=) compare operators of the same type only. Thus, it is illegal to compare an integer or real data type with a string data type in NetBasic.

Operators in an expression are evaluated from left to right. The operators have a precedence that determines which operators are evaluated first. You can use parenthesis in expressions to alter the order of evaluation. The normal precedence of the operators are the following:

1 •   * / &

2 •   + - |

3 •   = != < <= > >=

Variable and Array Declarations in NetBasic

In NetBasic, variables are automatically declared when they are first used. Variables can be up to 32 characters long and are case-insensitive. They consist of an alphabetic character, optionally followed by any combination of alphabetic characters, digits, and underscores (_). The following are all examples of variable names:

```
Ata7     ata7   aTA7
x_abc    X_abc  X_ABC
```

Each of these rows represent the same variable because variable names are not case-sensitive in NetBasic. Variable names are global and can be accessed from anywhere within the source file, unless they are declared local. The scope of a local variable is within the subroutine/function in which it is defined.

Consider the following example of a NetBasic program (file `bcastmsg.bas`) that defines global and local variables:

```
sub main
    MAX_CONNECTIONS = 250
    sendMessages

end sub
sub sendMessages
    local ("connection")
    connection = 1
```

```
        do while (connection <= MAX_CONNECTIONS)

                conObj = Net:Connection:info(connection)
                if (conObj.error = 0)
                        Net:Broadcast:send("Darshan @ 7:00 PM",
    connection)
                endif
                connection = connection + 1
        enddo
    end sub
```

The main subroutine defines the global variable MAX_CONNECTIONS. The scope of this global variable is over the entire source file, including the subroutine sendMessages. The subroutine sendMessages does not have any parameters, so it can be called by either of the following:

```
sendMessages()
sendMessages
```

That is, if subroutines do not have any parameters, the placement of the parentheses () is optional.

Within the subroutine sendMessages, the variable connection is defined as local by using the following statement:

```
local ("connection")
```

The scope of the connection variable is within the subroutine sendMessages, in which it is defined. The general syntax of defining local variables is the following:

```
local ("var1", "var2", ..., "varN")
```

The "..." represent occurrences of one or more variables. The variable names must be enclosed in double quotes. Within sendMessages, a while loop statement is set up which iterates over connections 1 to MAX_CONNECTIONS. The MAX_CONNECTIONS variable is visible within the sendMessages because it is a global variable. For each connection value, connection, the following statement is called to obtain the connection object:

```
conObj = Net:Connection:info(connection)
```

The call to the `Net:Connection:info()` function returns a connection object. The attributes of a connection object are described in Table 8.5. By testing the error attribute of the connection, you can test to see if it's a valid connection:

```
if (conObj.error = 0)
   Net:Broadcast:send("Darshan @ 7:00 PM", connection)
endif
```

TABLE 8.5	DATA ATTRIBUTE	DESCRIPTION
NetBasic Connection Object Attributes	ID	This contains a read/write number that identifies the file server. Each server has a unique connection ID, and clients can attach to a maximum of 32 file servers. The connection ID identifies the target server that will receive all client requests.
	Number	This contains a read-only integer that identifies the client. The number is assigned by the server. When a client attaches to a server, a number is assigned to the client by that server. This connection number uniquely identifies the client among all the connections of the server. When a client is connected to more than one server, each server assigns to the client its own connection number, which may or may not be the same as the connection numbers assigned to that client by other servers.
	Server.Name	This contains the name of the file server.
	Server.ID	This contains the connection ID of the server.
	Error	This contains a code that indicates if an error has been encountered. The Error attribute is read-only integer and indicates any error encountered during an operation on the object. When no error is encountered, the Error attribute will be zero.

If the connection is valid, a broadcast message is sent to that connection by using `Net:Broadcast:send()` command.

Array variables are a special form of variables that can store multiple values (which can be accessed by an *index*). The index can be an integer value, a real value, or string value. The array variable is defined when an index to it is first assigned. For example, consider the following statement:

```
retreats(1) = "Lake Louise"
```

The array `retreats` is now defined. It has a single element that can be indexed by 1. You can define additional elements as follows:

```
retreats(2) = "Half Dome"
retreats(3) = "Darjeeling"
```

With the definition of the previous two statements, the retreats array has three elements defined at indexes 1, 2, and 3. You could even define indexes that are real or string values for the same array, if your application needs it:

```
retreats("shiva") = "Mount Kailash"
retreats(8.5) = "Sri Lanka"
```

With the definition of the previous two statements, the `retreats` array has five elements defined at indexes 1, 2, 3, "shiva", and 8.5.

Array variables cannot be declared local. Once they are declared, their scope is the entire program. In other words, array variables are automatically global variables.

User-Defined Subroutines and Functions

The subroutine `sendMessages` in the previous section is an example of a user-defined subroutine. If you must return a value from the subroutine, use the return statement:

```
return [value]
```

The square brackets around *value* indicate that the *value* is optional. When the *value* is not specified in a return statement, a null value is returned. NetBasic provides a `func` keyword that can be used instead of the `sub` keyword when a value is to be returned. However, NetBasic does not make any internal distinction between them. That is, you could still define subroutines that use the `return` statement to return values. Language purists may prefer to define a function when there is a need to return a value, and a subroutine when there is a need to perform a specified action. The following subroutine and function are, therefore, equivalent:

```
sub pi
    local("pi")
    pi = 355/113
```

```
      return pi
end sub
func pi
      local("pi")
      pi = 355/113
      return pi
end func
```

You can pass parameters to subroutines. In order to obtain the value of the parameter passed to a subroutine or function, you can use the `param()` function:

```
paramValue = param(paramNumber, defaultValue)
```

The `param()` function returns the value of the parameter number, *paramNumber*. The first parameter is 1, the second 2, and so on. The *defaultValue* is optional and specifies a default value to use for the parameter when the parameter is not passed by the calling program.

In order to find out the actual number of parameters that were passed, use the `Param:Count` function:

```
paramCount = Param:count
```

Here is an example of how you could use these two functions:

```
sub main
      ptest(1, 4)
      ' The following QUIT statement is not really
      ' required as execution terminates when there
      ' are no more statements to execute in the main
      ' subroutine. You could use this as part of an
      ' if-statement to prematurely terminate execution
      ' of a NetBasic script.
      quit
end Sub
sub ptest
      local("pi")
      pcount = Param:count
      if (pcount != 2)
```

```
        print ("Incorrect number of arguments")
     return
   endif
   p1 = param(1)
   p2 = param(2)
   print("First parameter = ", p1); newline
   print("Second parameter = ", p2)
end sub
```

Notice that `Param:count` returns the count of the number of parameters, and a test is made to see if exactly two parameters were passed:

```
pcount = Param:count
if (pcount != 2)

        print ("Incorrect number of arguments")
     return
   endif
```

The parameter values were assigned to p1, and p2 and then printed:

```
p1 = param(1)
p2 = param(2)
print("First parameter = ", p1); newline
print("Second parameter = ", p2)
```

Actually, there was no need in the previous code to assign the parameters to p1 and p2, because the previous code could also be written as the following:

```
print("First parameter = ", param(1)); newline
print("Second parameter = ", param(2))
```

Notice the use of the newline function to insert a single new line into the standard output stream.

Importing Declarations

The commands that begin with the "#" character are called *preprocessor directives*. NetBasic defines two such preprocessor directives:

```
#include
#define
```

The #include and #define directives must be in lowercase, which is an exception to the rule that NetBasic is case-insensitive.

When a NetBasic application is run, a component within NetBasic processes the "#" commands, and creates a temporary file that is then executed by NetBasic. This component is called the *preprocessor*. The temporary file is created in the directory specified by the NetBasic environment variable TEMP. If TEMP is not defined, the temporary file is created in SYS:SYSTEM\NMX.

In NetBasic, you can import source code from another file into the current file, using the #include preprocessor directive:

```
#include "filename"
```

The contents of the *filename* that is specified is inserted in the current document when NetBasic encounters the #include directive. The filenames, by convention, have an .H extension, although you can use other extension names. You must specify the double quotation marks around the filename.

The system #include files are, by default, placed in the \NETBASIC\INCLUDE directory, and typically contain constant definitions. As an example, the WIN.H file used for Windows C-Worthy menu interface is as follows:

```
#ifndef _WIN_
#define _WIN_     "(c) Copyright 1993-1996 HITECSOFT CORP.
All rights reserved."
#include "key.H"
#define   WIN_FG_BLACK     0
#define   WIN_FG_BLUE      1
#define   WIN_FG_GREEN     2
#define   WIN_FG_RED       4
#define   WIN_FG_CYAN      3
#define   WIN_FG_MAGENTA   5
#define   WIN_FG_YELLOW    6
```

```
#define   WIN_FG_WHITE      7
#define   WIN_FG_LIGHT      8
#define   WIN_BG_BLACK      0
#define   WIN_BG_BLUE       16
#define   WIN_BG_GREEN      32
#define   WIN_BG_CYAN       48
#define   WIN_BG_RED        64
#define   WIN_BG_MAGENTA    80
#define   WIN_BG_YELLOW     96
#define   WIN_BG_WHITE      112
#define   WIN_BG_BLINK      128
#endif
```

This file defines the color constants used by the C-Worthy programming interface. Notice that the color constants are defined using the #define command:

```
#define name    value
```

Whenever the preprocessor encounters the symbol *name*, it is replaced by *value*.

Here is an example of a simple Windows program that displays a text message within a window. The comments within the program explain the behavior of the program.

```
#include "WIN.H"
sub main
    ' Clears the window
    Win:clear
    ' Define the window: Upper left corner (1,1).
    ' Lower right corner (10, 80).
    ' First number in coordianate is row and second
    ' number is column
    wnd = Win:define(1, 1, 10, 80)
    ' Make the window visible and make it the
    ' default window
    Win:show
```

```
' Set color attribute for informatin to be
' displayed in default window.
Win:color(WIN_FG_YELLOW + WIN_BG_MAGENTA)
' Position cursor at (5,5)
Win:at(5, 5)
' Display message at current cursor setting
Win:say("Welcome to NetBasic windows programming")
' Hide the cursor
Win:Cursor:hide
' Wait for a key press.
Key:read

end sub
```

Control Statements

NetBasic defines only two control statements:

- ▸ if statement

- ▸ do while statement

The control statements that you are familiar with in other languages can be simulated by the previous two control statements.

The if statement has two forms, whose syntax is as follows:

```
if LogicalExpression

   ThenStatements
endif


if LogicalExpression

   ThenStatements
else
```

```
    ElseStatements
endif
```

If *LogicalExpression* evaluates to true, the *ThenStatements* are executed. If it evaluates to false, the *ElseStatements* (if present) are executed. After the evaluation of *ThenStatements* or *ElseStatements*, control branches to the end of the `if` statement.

You have already seen an example of an `if` statement in the subroutine `ptest` discussed in the earlier section, "User-Defined Subroutines and Functions":

```
if (pcount != 2)

    print ("Incorrect number of arguments")
    return
endif
```

The parentheses around (`pcount != 2`) are not necessary. You can write the previous `if` statement as follows:

```
if pcount != 2

    print ("Incorrect number of arguments")
    return
endif
```

You may put parentheses, if you are accustomed to the syntax of languages that require parentheses around the conditional expression *LogicalExpression* (such as C/C++, Perl, Java, and so on).

The second type of control statement is the `do while`:

```
do while LogicalExpression
        Statements
        [loop | exit]
enddo
```

The *Statements* are executed as long as the *LogicalExpression* evaluates to true. At the end of the executing statements in the `do while` loop, control is transferred to the top of the loop, where *LogicalExpression* is evaluated again. As long as

LogicalExpression continues to evaluate to true, the *Statements* are executed. However, if *LogicalExpression* evaluates to False, or the statement `exit` is executed within the `do while` loop, control is transferred to the next statement after the do while statement (that is, the `do while` loop is exited). If the `loop` statement is encountered, within the `do while` loop, control is immediately transferred to the top of the loop where *LogicalExpression* is evaluated again. When the loop statement executes, any statements between the `loop` statement and the `enddo` are not executed.

You have already seen an example of a `do while` statement in the earlier section, "Variable and Array Declarations in NetBasic":

```
do while (connection <= MAX_CONNECTIONS)


    conObj = Net:Connection:info(connection)
    if (conObj.error = 0)
        Net:Broadcast:send("Darshan @ 7:00 PM",
connection)
    endif
    connection = connection + 1
enddo
```

The parentheses around (connection <= MAX_CONNECTIONS) is not necessary. You can write the previous `do while` statement as the following:

```
do while (connection <= MAX_CONNECTIONS)


    conObj = Net:Connection:info(connection)
    if (conObj.error = 0)
        Net:Broadcast:send("Darshan @ 7:00 PM",
connection)
    endif
    connection = connection + 1
enddo
```

You may put parentheses, if you are accustomed to the syntax of languages that require parentheses around the conditional expression *LogicalExpression* (such as C/C++, Perl, Java, and so on).

Printing from a NetBasic Script

The `print` command is used to write information on the standard output device. It is therefore one of the most widely used commands in a CGI NetBasic script (which requires that you write HTTP response headers and HTML content to the standard output device). The syntax of the `print` command is as follows:

```
print(data1, data2, ..., dataN)
```

The *data1*, *data2*, ..., *dataN* are any of the basic data types (such as integer, real, string, logical, and so on). Multiple parameters in the `print` command are separated by commas (,). As the `print` command executes, the current cursor position is updated to the next location where `print` would normally display the next character. If you want to introduce a new line for formatting purposes between two print statements, you can use the `newline` command:

```
print("My Name:", name); newline; print ("Address:", addr1)
```

The default output for `print` and `newline` commands is the standard output device. If you want to change the default output, you can use the `FIO:Output:select` command, whose syntax is as follows:

```
FIO:Output:select(handle)
```

The *handle* is an integer value that represents an output channel. Handles can also be defined for input channels. An input or output handle is usually associated with a file, and the handle is typically created by opening the file. To open a file, you use the `FIO:Open` command which returns the handle to the file. The syntax of the `FIO:Open` command is described next:

```
handle = FIO:Open(filename, mode)
```

The *filename* is a string that represents the path of the file to be opened. The second parameter, *mode*, is also a string that indicates whether the file was opened for input or output operations. The mode values are described in the FIO.H file:

```
#ifndef _FIO_
#define _FIO_     "(c) Copyright 1993-1996 HITECSOFT CORP.
All rights reserved."
#define FIO_READ_ONLY              "r"
```

```
#define FIO_UPDATE                  "r+"
#define FIO_CREATE_WRITE            "w"
#define FIO_CREATE_UPDATE           "w+"
#define FIO_CREATE_APPEND_WRITE     "a"
#define FIO_CREATE_APPEND_UPDATE    "a+"
#define FIO_BINARY                  "b"
#define FIO_TEXT                    "t"
#endif
```

You can include the FIO.H file in your program by using the following:

```
#include "FIO.H"
```

After including the FIO.H file, you can use any of the symbols (such as FIO_READ_ONLY, FIO_UPDATE, and so on) that are defined in the FIO.H file:

```
fin = open("myfile.dat", FIO_READ_ONLY)
fin = open("outfile.dat", FIO_CREATE_WRITE)
fup = open("upfile.dat", FIO_CREATE_UPDATE)
```

If you find it easier to remember the string values for the *mode* parameter, you can use these values directly. For example, the previous open statements could have been written as the following:

```
fin = open("myfile.dat", "r")
fin = open("outfile.dat", "w")
fup = open("upfile.dat", "w+")
```

In both the WIN.H and FIO.H files, you may have noticed the #ifndef preprocessor statement. The statements between #ifndef and #endif are only processed if the _FIO_ symbol is undefined. If this is the first time you are including this file, the _FIO_ symbol is undefined and the #define statements will be processed. The advantage of this technique is that, if the FIO.H was included a second time, there would be no redefinitions of the #define symbols, because the _FIO_ symbol would already have been defined.

Once a file is opened, you can perform any of the operations shown in Table 8.6 on the file.

TABLE 8.6 *File Operations*	OPERATION	DESCRIPTION
	`FIO:Input:select()`	Returns the current handle for the input device.
	`FIO:Output:select (newhandle)`	Selects the standard output device. The function returns the old file handle, so that you can use it to reset the file handle at a later time.
	`FIO:position(handle)`	Returns the current position in the file specified by its handle number.
	`FIO:Seek:bottom (handle [, bytes])`	Sets the current position for the specified file *handle*, by the amount of *bytes* from the bottom of the file. Byte offset for this function is measured from the bottom of the file. The *bytes* parameter is optional. When not specified, the current position is set to the end of the file. The return value is logical true if the current position was changed, and a false if it was not changed.
	`FIO:Seek:top(handle [, bytes])`	Sets the current position for the specified file *handle*, by the amount of *bytes* from the top of the file. Byte offset for this function is measured from the top of the file. The *bytes* parameter is optional. When not specified, the current position is set to the top of the file. The return value is logical true if the current position was changed, and a false if it was not changed.
	`FIO:Seek:byte(handle [, bytes])`	Sets the current position for the specified file handle, by the amount of bytes from 86 386the current position. If bytes is positive, the current position is moved forward. If it is negative, the current position is moved backward. The bytes parameter is optional. When not specified, the current position is set to the top of the file. The return value is logical true if the current position was changed, and a false if it was not changed.

OPERATION	DESCRIPTION
FIO:Read:byte(handle [, bytes])	Reads the specified number of *bytes* from the specified file *handle*. The return is a string value of the number of bytes that were actually read. The *bytes* parameter is optional. When not specified, one byte is read.
FIO:Read:integer ([handle])	Reads one integer from the specified file *handle*. The return is the integer value that was actually read. If *handle* is not specified, data is read from the standard input device.
FIO:Read:real([handle])	Reads one real number from the specified file *handle*. The return is the real value that was actually read. If *handle* is not specified, data is read from the standard input device.
FIO:Read:string ([handle])	Reads one string value from the specified file *handle*. The return is the string value that was actually read. If *handle* is not specified, data is read from the standard input device.
FIO:Write([handle], data1,[, dataN])	Writes one or more specified data values to the specified file *handle*. The return is a logical value true or false, indicating the success of the operation. If *handle* is not specified, data is written to the standard output stream.
FIO:Write:byte(handle, sbuffer, [, bytes])	Writes the specified number of *bytes* in the string buffer, *sbuffer*, to the specified file *handle*. The return is a logical value true or false, indicating the success of the operation. The *bytes* parameter is optional. When not specified, the entire string buffer is written.
FIO:Write:integer ([handle])	Reads one integer from the specified file *handle*. The return is the integer value that was actually read. If *handle* is not specified, data is read from the standard input device.
FIO:eof(handle)	Determines if the current position is at the end of the file.
FIO:close(handle)	Closes the specified file *handle*.

String Manipulation in NetBasic

As part of writing CGI scripts, you must work with text data that is represented as string variables. NetBasic provides a number of string operations in the STR class that you can use for string manipulation.

For example, suppose you want to see if a string occurs in another string. You can use the `STR:search` function to search for a string:

```
position = STR:search(substring, string)
```

The *substring* is searched for in *string*, and the position where it occurs is returned. If the value returned is 0, the string *substring* does not occur in *string*.

```
str1 = "Welcome to NetBasic programming"
ipos = STR:search("come", str1)
' ipos is set to 4
print ("ipos = ", ipos); newline
```

The first character in a string has a position value of 1, and the last character has a position value that is equal to the length of the string. To obtain the length of a string, you can use the following which returns the length of the specified *string*:

```
length = STR:length(string)
```

If you want to extract a portion of a string, you can use the `STR:sub()` function:

```
substring = STR:sub(string, start [, length])
```

The *substring* starting from position *start* and *length* bytes long in *string* is returned. If *length* is not specified, or its value is larger than the string that can be returned, the returned string begins from *start* and ends with the last character in *string*. Consider the following example, which extracts a *substring* value from another *string*:

```
str1 = "Welcome to NetBasic programming"
pattern = "come"
startpos = STR:search("come", str1)
len = STR:length(pattern)
' Substring is rest of string after "come"
substr = STR:sub(str1, startpos + len)
```

You can use the following functions to convert the characters to lowercase:

lowerstring = STR:lower(*string*)

The characters in *string* are converted to lowercase and returned. If you must convert the string to uppercase, you can use the following function:

upperstring = STR:upper(*string*)

The characters in *string* are converted to uppercase and returned. Here is an example:

```
someStr = "If you can keep your head while all about you
are losing theirs..."
upstr = Str:upper(someStr)
' upstr set to "IF YOU CAN KEEP YOUR HEAD WHILE ALL ABOUT
YOU ARE LOSING THEIRS..."
lowstr = Str:lower(someStr)
'lowstr set to "if you can keep your head while all about
you are losing theirs..."
if (lowstr != Str:lower(upstr))
print "Something strange happened!"); newline
endif
```

You can add blank characters to a string to the left or right. The STR:Pad:left() function adds characters to the left, and the STR:Pad:right() function adds characters to the right. Both functions take the string to be padded as the first parameter, and the string length to which the string should be padded as the second parameter:

paddedStr = STR:Left:pad(*string, finalStrLength*)
paddedStr = STR:Right:pad(*string, finalStrLength*)

If you have excessive numbers of blanks to the left or right of a string, you can remove these blanks by using the STR:Trim:left() or STR:Trim:right() function. If you want to trim the blanks on both the left and right of the string, you can use STR:Trim:all() function. These functions take the string to be trimmed as an argument and return the trimmed string.

```
trimmedStr = STR:Trim:left(string)
trimmedStr = STR:Trim:right(string)
trimmedStr = STR:Trim:all(string)
```

Consider a string value that you want to place as a title in a page. The title string value should be 80 columns wide.

```
str = "    My new book          "
tstr = STR:Trim:all(str)
padamount = 40 + Str:length(tstr)/2
title = Str:Pad:left(tstr, padamount)
title = Str:Pad:right(title, 80)
print (title); newline
```

You can create a string with a repeated pattern using the STR:Repeat() function, which takes the string to be repeated as its first parameter, and the number of times it is to be repeated as the second parameter. The repeated string is returned:

```
repeatedStr = STR:repeat(string, times)
```

As an example, the following statement creates a string of 80 "=" characters and prints them to the standard output:

```
print(Str:repeat("=", 80))
```

Data-Manipulation Functions

If you must perform bit arithmetic (such as bitwise OR and bitwise AND), conversion between characters and their ASCII equivalents, or hexadecimal conversions, you can use the DATA class. The functions in the DATA class are described in Table 8.7. These functions are equivalents of many of the Perl functions discussed in Chapter 7, so examples of using the DATA class functions are not provided here.

TABLE 8.7	FUNCTION NAME	DESCRIPTION
DATA Class Functions	DATA:And	Performs bitwise AND operations between two integer values. Usage: `ivalue = DATA:And( ivalue1, ivalue2)`
	DATA:Or	Performs bitwise OR operations between two integer values. Usage: `ivalue = DATA:Or( ivalue1, ivalue2)`
	DATA:Ascii	Determines the ASCII code equivalent of the first character of a string. Usage: `ivalue = DATA:Ascii(string)`
	DATA:char	Converts an integer value to its character equivalent. Usage: `schar = DATA:char( ivalue)`
	DATA:Hex:integer	Determines the decimal value of a hexadecimal number. Usage: `ivalue = DATA:Hex:integer(hex)`
	DATA:integer	Converts any data type to an integer value. Usage: `ivalue = DATA:integer(anydata)`
	DATA:real	Converts any data type to a string value. Usage: `strvalue = DATA:string(anydata)`
	DATA:string	Converts any data type to an integer value. Usage: `rvalue = DATA:real(anydata)`
	DATA:Shift:left	Left shifts the bits in the integer value of the first argument by the number of bits specified as the second argument. Usage: `ivalue = DATA:Shift:left( ivalue, nbits)`
	DATA:Shift:right	Right shifts the bits in the integer value of the first argument by the number of bits specified as the second argument. Usage: `ivalue = DATA:Shift:left( ivalue, nbits)`
	DATA:translate	Converts non-printable characters in a string into spaces. Usage: `strvalue = DATA:translate(strvalue)`
	DATA:type	Returns the type of a variable, *strvarname*. The variable is specified as a quoted string. The value that is returned is "S" for string; "R" for real; "I" for integer; "O" for object; "L" for logical; "U" for unknown. An unknown value is returned if no value is assigned to the variable. Usage: `strtype = DATA:type(strvarname)`

Date Functions in NetBasic

The `DATE:object()` function can be used to return a date object given the number of seconds since January 1, 1970 — the beginning of the Universal Time Format (UTF):

dateobject = `DATE:object(`*seconds*`)`

The `DATE:UTF()` function is used to return the number of seconds since January 1, 1970:

seconds = `DATE:UTF([`*strdate*`] [,` *strtime*`])`

The *strdate* is a date string in the *mm-dd-yy* format, and *strtime* is a time string in *hh:mm:ss* format. If *strdate* is not specified, the current date is assumed. If *strtime* is not specified the current time is assumed.

Table 8.8 describes the attributes of the Date object.

T A B L E 8.8	ATTRIBUTE NAME	DESCRIPTION
NetBasic DATE Object's Attributes	Year	Read-only two-digit string year number (for example, 98, 99).
	UTF.year.century	Read-only two-digit string representing the year number including century (for example, 1998, 1999).
	UTF.year.day	Read-only three-digit string representing the day of the year (for example, 001, 200, 366).
	UTF.year.week	Read-only number representing the week of the year (for example, 01, 52).
	UTF.year.leap	Read-only logical value that is true if the year is a leap year, and false otherwise.
	Month	Read-only two-digit string representing the month of the year (for example, 01, 12).
	UTF.month.name	Read-only string representing the month of the year (for example, January).
	UTF.month.days	Read-only two-digit string representing number of days in the month (for example, 28, 29, 30, 31).
	Day	Read-only two-digit string representing the day of the month (for example, 01, 31).
	UTF.day.name	Read-only string representing the weekday (for example, Monday).

	ATTRIBUTE NAME	DESCRIPTION
T A B L E 8.8 *NetBasic DATE Object's* *Attributes* *(continued)*	Date	Read-only string representing the date in *mm-dd-yyyy* format (for example, 07-07-1999).
	Time	Read-only string representing the time in *hh:mm:ss* (for example, 12:55:33).
	UTF.time.hour	Read-only two-digit string representing number of hours in the day (for example, 01, 12, 23).
	UTF.time.AmPmHour	Read-only two-digit string representing number of hours in a 12-hour cycle of the day (for example, 01, 12).
	UTF.time.AmPm	Read-only string containing AM or PM.
	UTF.time.minute	Read-only two-digit string representing number of minutes in the hour (for example, 01, 30, 59).
	UTF.time.second	Read-only two-digit string representing number of seconds in a minute (for example, 01, 30, 59).
	Error	Read-only integer indicating an error. A non-zero error value indicates an error during an operation on the object.

Consider the following example that prints the date information for the current date and time. You can study this program to see examples of how to use many of the date functions.

```
sub main
    secs = Date:UTF()
    dobj = Date:object(secs)
    if dobj.error != 0
        print ("Error in date object"); newline
    endif
    print(Str:Repeat("=", 80)); newline
    print("Todays date is ", dobj.date); newline
    print("Time is ", dobj.time); newline
    print(Str:Repeat("=", 80)); newline
    if dobj.UTF.year.leap
        print("This year is a leap year")
```

```
else
      print("This year is not a leap year")
endif
newline
print("Week of year is ", dobj.utf.year.week); newline
print("Day of year is ", dobj.utf.year.day); newline
print("Number of days in ", dobj.utf.month.name, " is
", dobj.utf.month.days); newline
end sub
```

Writing CGI Scripts in NetBasic

The NetBasic CGI scripts that you write should be placed in the SYS:NETBASIC\WEB directory. This directory contains a number of sample CGI scripts, all written in NetBasic. NetBasic provides the DOC class and contains functions/subroutines to generate HTML code. The DOC class was designed to hide the complexities of HTML from the CGI programmer. However, you must have some knowledge of HTML to use the DOC class effectively. In some cases, the DOC function/subroutine calls are more verbose than using the print statement to emit HTML code, and sometimes the opposite is the case. If you plan on using only NetBasic to write CGI programs, then it is probably worthwhile to learn to write CGI scripts using the DOC class functions/subroutines. However, the DOC class APIs are not portable to Perl and BASIC. If you also intend to use these or other languages, you should learn to generate direct HTML code. Chapter 5 provides a comprehensive coverage of the essential and some advanced HTML features that can help you become proficient in HTML.

One of the unusual aspects of writing CGI scripts in NetBasic is that you do not need to generate the HTTP response headers, such as:

```
Content-Type: text/html
```

This is because the CGI wrapper NLM, CGI2NMX.NLM, generates the HTTP response headers. If you generate your own HTTP response headers, they will unexpectedly appear as part of the dynamic HTML page that you are generating.

Therefore, you do *not* have to provide the following statements in NetBasic to generate the standard HTTP response header:

```
print ("Content-Type: text/html")
newline; newline
```

NetBasic CGI Script Showing the Use of DOC APIs

This section provides an introduction to using the DOC APIs. For a more complete description of the DOC APIs, refer to the online documentation that comes with the Novell Web Server.

In the following example, you want to write a NetBasic CGI script that displays information on the Novell Web Server volumes. Since you do not have to generate the standard HTTP response header, you can start generating the virtual HTML document. One of the first things you must do is generate the HTML header and body.

You can use the following to generate the HTML header:

```
Doc:Heading("Volume Information")
```

The previous statement produces the following HTML code:

```
<HTML>
<HEAD>
<TITLE>
Volume Information
</TITLE>
</HEAD>
```

If you are familiar with HTML (see Chapter 5), you could have written the previous using the following NetBasic print statement:

```
print("<html><head><title>Volume
Information</title></head>")

Next, you must generate the BODY tag. You can do this by
using the following DOC API:

Doc:Body(DOC_WHITE,DOC_BLACK,"",IMG("nbibg.gif"))
```

The previous statement produces the following HTML code:

```
<BODY BGCOLOR="#FFFFFF" TEXT="#000000"
BACKGROUND="/lcgi/netbasic/nbibg.gif">
```

As before, you could also have used a `print` statement to directly write the previous BODY tag to the standard output.

Next, let's say that you need to generate a <H1> heading. You can do this by using the following:

```
Doc:Tag:begin("H1")
Doc:print("Volume information")
Doc:Tag:end("H1")
```

The previous statements produce the following HTML code:

```
<H1>Volume Information</H1>
```

To display the volume information, you can use the following API to get the volume object:

```
volobject = NET:Volume:info(volumenumber)
```

The *volumenumber* is a number starting with a value of 1 and `volobject` is the Volume information object. Table 8.9 shows the attributes of the Volume information object.

TABLE 8.9	ATTRIBUTE NAME	DESCRIPTION
NetBasic Volume Information Object Attribute	Name	The Name attribute is a read-only string, and contains the name of the volume, up to 16 characters long.
	Blocks.total	The Blocks.Total attribute is a read-only integer, and contains the total number of blocks on the volume.
	Blocks.Free	The Blocks.Free attribute is a read-only integer, and contains the number of unused blocks on the volume.
	Blocks.Purgable	The Blocks.Purgable attribute is a read-only integer, and contains the number of blocks occupied by deleted files on the volume that have not been permanently removed.

ATTRIBUTE NAME	DESCRIPTION
Blocks.Size	The Blocks.Size attribute is a read-only integer, and contains the size of each block in bytes.
Dir.Total	The Dir.Total attribute is a read-only integer, and contains the total number of directories allocated for the volume during installation.
Dir.Free	The Dir.Free attribute is a read-only integer, and contains the number of unused allocated directories that remain on the volume.
Hashing	The Hashing attribute is a read-only Boolean, and contains "TRUE" when hashing is enabled and "FALSE" otherwise.
Removable	The Removable attribute is a read-only Boolean, and contains "TRUE" when the volume is removable and "FALSE" otherwise.
Mounted	The Mounted attribute is a read-only Boolean, and contains "TRUE" when the volume is mounted and "FALSE" otherwise.
Error	The Error attribute is a read-only integer, and indicates any error encountered during an operation on the object. When no error is encountered, the Error attribute will be zero.

You could, therefore, write the following NetBasic code to display volume information:

```
volno = 1
do while true
   volobj = Net:Volume:info(volno)
   if (volobj.error != 0)
        exit
endif

   printvolinfo()

   volno = volno + 1
enddo
```

The previous code sets up a loop for each value of volume number starting from 1. The volume object is constructed using the factory method `Net:Volume:info(volno)`. The error attribute for this volume object is checked. If it is non-zero, the volume object is not valid and this indicates that all possible volume objects for the server have been evaluated. The `printvolinfo()` prints information on the volume:

```
sub printvolinfo
    Doc:hr(2,100)
    Doc:paragraph()
    Doc:print("Volume name: ", volobj.name)
    Doc:break()
    Doc:print("Total blocks: ", volobj.blocks.total)
    Doc:break()
    Doc:print("Free blocks: ", volobj.blocks.free)
    Doc:break()
    Doc:print("Purgeable blocks: ", volobj.blocks.purgable)
    Doc:break()
    Doc:print("Blocks size: ", volobj.blocks.size)
    Doc:break()
    Doc:print("Total directories: ", volobj.dir.total)
    Doc:break()
    Doc:print("Free directories: ", volobj.dir.free)
    Doc:break()
    Doc:print("Hashing: ", volobj.hashing)
    Doc:break()
    Doc:print("Removable: ", volobj.removable)
    Doc:break()
    Doc:print("Mounted: ", volobj.mounted)
    Doc:break()
end sub
```

The previous code draws a horizontal line of a certain width, and then prints the attributes listed in Table 8.9 for the Volume object using `Doc:print()`. `Doc:break()` causes the attributes to be displayed one per line.

At the end of the HTML document, you should generate the end tags for BODY and HTML. You can do this by using the following:

```
Doc:Tag:end("BODY")
Doc:Tag:end("HTML")
```

If you put all the code discussed so far together, you have the following complete listing (file volinfo.bas):

```
' Add all include files and define statements here
#include "html.h"
sub main
    Doc:Heading("Volume Information")
    Doc:Body(DOC_WHITE,DOC_BLACK,"",IMG("nbibg.gif"))
    Doc:Tag:begin("H1")
    Doc:print("Volume information")
    Doc:Tag:end("H1")
    volno = 1
    do while true
        volobj = Net:Volume:info(volno)
        if (volobj.error != 0)
            exit
        endif

        printvolinfo()

        volno = volno + 1
    enddo
    Doc:Tag:end("BODY")
    Doc:Tag:end("HTML")
end sub
' Print volume information ing global object volobj
sub printvolinfo
    Doc:hr(2,100)
    Doc:paragraph()
    Doc:print("Volume name: ", volobj.name)
```

```
        Doc:break()
        Doc:print("Total blocks: ", volobj.blocks.total)
        Doc:break()
        Doc:print("Free blocks: ", volobj.blocks.free)
        Doc:break()
        Doc:print("Purgeable blocks: ", volobj.blocks.purgable)
        Doc:break()
        Doc:print("Blocks size: ", volobj.blocks.size)
        Doc:break()
        Doc:print("Total directories: ", volobj.dir.total)
        Doc:break()
        Doc:print("Free directories: ", volobj.dir.free)
        Doc:break()
        Doc:print("Hashing: ", volobj.hashing)
        Doc:break()
        Doc:print("Removable: ", volobj.removable)
        Doc:break()
        Doc:print("Mounted: ", volobj.mounted)
        Doc:break()
    end sub
```

Figure 8.13 shows the results of running this volinfo.bas CGI script from the Novell Netscape Navigator.

NetBasic CGI Script for Obtaining Statistics on the Server

This section shows you how to write a CGI script for displaying information about the server, the NLMs running on the server, the display screens for the NLMs, and server statistics. The script is written without the DOC APIs for generating the HTML tags. However, the DOC:Var() API is used to obtain the CGI form variable values.

Figures 8.14 and 8.15 show the display produced when the CGI script (websrvr.bas) is run. The screens give you an idea of the type of information displayed for the server.

Figure 8.16 shows the NLM screen for the HTTP console. This display is produced by selecting the HTTP console from the pull-down list and selecting the View NLM Screen button. The code to generate the Screen display is adapted from sample code from HiTec Software.

volinfo.bas *NetBasic script output*

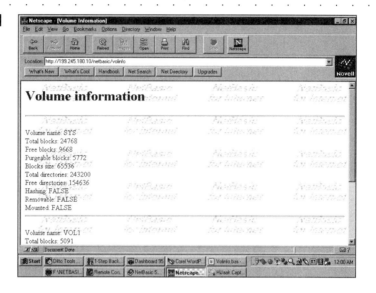

websrvr.bas *display screen 1*

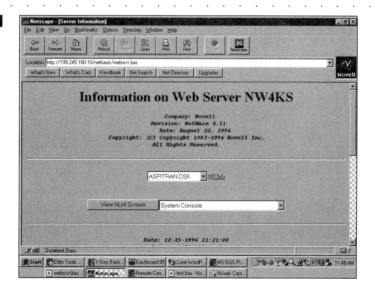

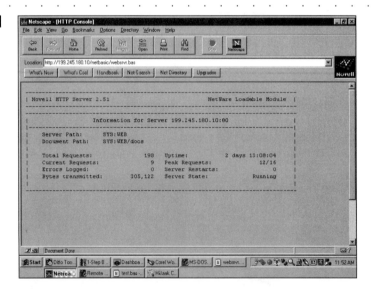

Listing 8.3 shows the websrvr.bas NetBasic CGI script. The analysis of the program is presented after the listing.

LISTING 8.3

websrvr.bas *Script*

```
#include "html.h"
sub main

    screen = Doc:var("screen", "undefined")
    if screen = "undefined"
        ' Display forms and other statistics
        print("<html><head><title>Server
Information</title></head><body>")
        print("<center><h1>Information on Web Server ",
NET:Server:name, "</h1>")
        srvObj = Net:Server:Description
        print("<b><i><pre>"); newline
        print("  Company: ", srvObj.company)  ; newline
        print(" Revision: ", srvObj.revision) ; newline
        print("     Date: ", srvObj.date)     ; newline
        print("Copyright: ", srvObj.Copyright); newline
        print("</pre></i></b><hr>"); newline
        ' Display a list of NLMs
        print("<form>")
        print("<select name=nlms>")
        nextNLM = Net:Module:Name:first
        do while nextNLM != ""
            print("<option>", nextNLM)
            nextNLM = Net:Module:Name:next()
        enddo

        print("</select>NLMs</form><br>")
        ' Enable users to select an NLM screen
        print("<form method=POST action=websrvr.bas>")
        i = Screen:first()
        if ( i != 0 )
```

```
            print("<select name=screen>")
            do while (i != 0)
                print("<option>", Screen:name(i))
                i = Screen:next(i)
            enddo

            print('<input type=submit value="View NLM
Screen">')
            print("</select>")


        endif

        print("</form></center><hr>")
        ' Server statistics
        print("<b><i><center><pre>")
        dateObj = Net:Server:Date:get
        print("Date: ", dateObj.date, " ", dateObj.time);
newline
        print("Server utilization: ",
Net:Stat:Server:utilization); newline
        print("Server transactions: ",
Net:Stat:transactions); newline
        print("Server requests: ",
Net:Stat:Server:requests); newline
        print("Server record locks: ",
Net:Stat:Record:locks); newline
        print("Bytes received: ", Net:Stat:Bytes:received);
newline
        print("Bytes transmitted: ",
Net:Stat:Bytes:transmitted); newline
        print("Bytes written: ",
Net:Stat:Disk:Bytes:written); newline
        print("Bytes read: ", Net:Stat:Disk:Bytes:read);
newline
```

```
        print("Packets received: ",
Net:Stat:Packets:received); newline
        print("Packets transmitted: ",
Net:Stat:Packets:transmitted); newline
        print("Packets routed: ", Net:Stat:Packets:routed);
newline
        print("Directory searches: ",
Net:Stat:Directory:searches); newline
        print("Files read: ", Net:Stat:Disk:reads); newline
        print("Files written: ", Net:Stat:Disk:writes);
newline
        print("Dirty sectors in FAT table: ",
Net:Stat:Fat:Sectors:dirty); newline
        print("Number of FAT sectors written: ",
Net:Stat:Fat:Sectors:written); newline
        print("File creates: ", Net:Stat:File:creates);
newline
        print("File deletes: ", Net:Stat:File:deletes);
newline
        print("File opens: ", Net:Stat:File:opens); newline
        print("File reads: ", Net:Stat:File:reads); newline
        print("File writes: ", Net:Stat:File:writes);
newline
        print("File renames: ", Net:Stat:File:renames);
newline
        print("File bytes read: ",
Net:Stat:File:Bytes:read); newline
        print("File bytes written: ",
Net:Stat:File:Bytes:written); newline
        print("</pre></center></i></b>")
        print("</body></html>")
    else
        ' Process form action for displaying NLM
        ' screen content.
```

```
            sc = Str:Trim:all(screen)
            print("<html><head><title>", sc,
    "</title></head><body>")
                ' Get screen number and place it in sn
                sn = findScreen(sc)
                if (sn = -1)
                    print("<h2>Error in reading screen</h2>")
                    return
                endif
                ' i is line number
                i = 0
                buffer = Data:translate(Screen:text(sn))
                print("<pre>"); newline
                do while i < 25
                    print(Str:Sub(buffer, (i*80)+1, 80))
                    print("<br>")
                    i = i + 1
                enddo
                print("</pre>")
            endif
        end sub
        ' Find screen number, given the screen name passed
        ' as a parameter.
        sub findScreen
            local ("i")
            i = Screen:first()
            do while i != 0
                if Screen:name(i) = param(1)
                    return(i)
                endif
                i = Screen:next(i)
            enddo
            return (-1)
        end sub
```

The logic in the program is contained in one giant if statement.

```
screen = Doc:var("screen", "undefined")
if screen = "undefined"
' Display forms and other statistics
            :
            :
else
' Process form action for displaying NLM
' screen content.
            :
            :
endif
```

The screen variable is defined if the user makes the View NLM Screen selection. If the screen variable is defined, it means that the user has made the selection from an already displayed form. In this case, the else part of the if statement is executed. If the screen variable is not defined, the form must be displayed. In this case, the then part of the if statement is executed.

The then part of the if statement contains the logic to display the following:

▸ The header and body HTML tags:

```
print("<html><head><title>Server
Information</title></head><body>")
print("<center><h1>Information on Web Server ",
NET:Server:name, "</h1>")
```

Notice the use of the <center> HTML tag in the last print statement. Every item displayed between this tag and its corresponding end tag </center>, are placed in the center of the display page.

▸ The Web server information:

```
srvObj = Net:Server:Description
print("<b><i><pre>"); newline
print("   Company: ", srvObj.company)   ; newline
```

```
print(" Revision: ", srvObj.revision) ; newline
print("     Date: ", srvObj.date)      ; newline
print("Copyright: ", srvObj.Copyright); newline
print("</pre></i></b><hr>"); newline
```

First, the srvObj is created by calling the factory method
Net:Server:Description. Next, the attributes of the server object
are printed inside the <pre> ... </pre> HTML tags. The HTML tags
... and <i> ... </i> are used to bold and italicize the display.

▸ The list of NLMs:

```
' Display a list of NLMs
print("<form>")
print("<select name=nlms>")
nextNLM = Net:Module:Name:first
do while nextNLM != ""
        print("<option>", nextNLM)
        nextNLM = Net:Module:Name:next()
enddo

print("</select>NLMs</form><br>")
```

The list of NLMs is displayed as a pull-down list using the <select>
tag defined inside a form. The do while statement is used to
generate a list of NLMs using the <option> tag. Notice that this form
does not have an action attribute defined. You could define an action
attribute, so that when the user selects an option, you can display
additional information on the selected NLM.

▸ A list of NLM screens on the Novell Web Server:

```
' Enable users to select an NLM screen
print("<form method=POST action=websrvr.bas>")
i = Screen:first()
```

```
if ( i != 0 )
  print("<select name=screen>")
  do while (i != 0)
        print("<option>", Screen:name(i))
        i = Screen:next(i)
  enddo

        print('<input type=submit value="View NLM
Screen">')
        print("</select>")

  endif


  print("</form></center><hr>")
```

The logic is similar to that for the form that displayed a list of NLMs. A major difference between this and the previous form is that the action attribute is defined for the form tag. When the user selects one of the NLM screens, and presses the View NLM Screen button, the current websrvr.bas is executed again, but this time the screen variable is defined. This causes the else-part of the if statement to be executed. The Screen:first() and Screen:name() APIs are used to get the number of the screen. The Screen:name(*screen_number*) API is used to get the name of the screen to be displayed in the select field.

▶ Next, a number of statements display server statistics.

```
' Server statistics
print("<b><i><center><pre>")
dateObj = Net:Server:Date:get
print("Date: ", dateObj.date, " ", dateObj.time);
newline
print("Server utilization: ",
Net:Stat:Server:utilization); newline
```

```
print("Server transactions: ", Net:Stat:transactions);
newline
print("Server requests: ", Net:Stat:Server:requests);
newline
print("Server record locks: ", Net:Stat:Record:locks);
newline
print("Bytes received: ", Net:Stat:Bytes:received);
newline
print("Bytes transmitted: ",
Net:Stat:Bytes:transmitted); newline
print("Bytes written: ", Net:Stat:Disk:Bytes:written);
newline
print("Bytes read: ", Net:Stat:Disk:Bytes:read);
newline
print("Packets received: ",
Net:Stat:Packets:received); newline
print("Packets transmitted: ",
Net:Stat:Packets:transmitted); newline
print("Packets routed: ", Net:Stat:Packets:routed);
newline
print("Directory searches: ",
Net:Stat:Directory:searches); newline
print("Files read: ", Net:Stat:Disk:reads); newline
print("Files written: ", Net:Stat:Disk:writes);
newline
print("Dirty sectors in FAT table: ",
Net:Stat:Fat:Sectors:dirty); newline
print("Number of FAT sectors written: ",
Net:Stat:Fat:Sectors:written); newline
print("File creates: ", Net:Stat:File:creates);
newline
print("File deletes: ", Net:Stat:File:deletes);
newline
print("File opens: ", Net:Stat:File:opens); newline
print("File reads: ", Net:Stat:File:reads); newline
```

```
print("File writes: ", Net:Stat:File:writes); newline
print("File renames: ", Net:Stat:File:renames);
newline
print("File bytes read: ", Net:Stat:File:Bytes:read);
newline
print("File bytes written: ",
Net:Stat:File:Bytes:written); newline
print("</pre></center></i></b>")
print("</body></html>")
```

The code for displaying the server statistics is straightforward. It contains a series of `print` statements that display a text string label and the value returned by a NET class API call for returning server statistics.

The `else` part of the outermost `if` statement contains the logic to process the user's selection of the screen to display. It consists of the following parts:

1 • Get the screen text that was selected. `Str:Trim:all()` is used to trim leading and trailing blanks.

```
sc = Str:Trim:all(screen)
```

2 • Generate the head, title, and body HTML tags:

```
print("<html><head><title>", sc,
"</title></head><body>")
```

3 • Convert the screen title text to its equivalent screen number:

```
' Get screen number and place it in sn
sn = findScreen(sc)
if (sn = -1)
  print("<h2>Error in reading screen</h2>")
  return
endif
```

4 • Place a translated version of the screen display in a buffer and generate the <pre> tag:

```
' i is line number
i = 0
buffer = Data:translate(Screen:text(sn))
print("<pre>"); newline
```

5 • Extract each line of display from the string buffer and print it out. At the end, generate the </pre> end tag.

```
do while i < 25
  print(Str:Sub(buffer, (i*80)+1, 80))
  print("<br>")
  i = i + 1
enddo
print("</pre>")
```

The display string buffer is a one-dimensional array that contains the lines of display all concatenated together. The Str:sub() is used to extract 80 characters at a time from the display string buffer.

Table 8.10 shows the attributes for the NetBasic Server object.

TABLE 8.10	ATTRIBUTE	DESCRIPTION
NetBasic Server Object Attributes	Company	The Company attribute is a read-only string, and contains the name of the company that distributed the NetWare Operating System running on the default file server. It is up to 80 characters long.
	Revision	The Revision attribute is a read-only string, and contains the version and revision for the NetWare Operating System running on the default file server. It is up to 80 characters long.
	Date	The Date attribute is a read-only string, and contains the revision date for the NetWare Operating System running on the default file server in *mm-dd-yyyy* format.
	Copyright	The Copyright attribute is a read-only string, and contains the copyright notice for the NetWare Operating System running on the default file server. It is up to 80 characters long.
	Error	The Error attribute is a read-only integer, and indicates any error encountered during an operation on the object. When no error is encountered, the Error attribute is zero.

NetBasic CGI Script for Accessing the Btrieve Database

This section shows you how to write a CGI script for accessing a Btrieve database file. Btrieve is a popular database record manager for personal computers and is used in many accounting packages. In fact, it can be used to build a scalable SQL server. For more information on Btrieve, contact Pervasive Software (formerly Btrieve Technologies) at 1-800-BTRIEVE.

For this example, a simple database will be built that will allow users to add and look up records. You can extend this database to allow update and delete operations. When the CGI script is initially run, it creates an empty Btrieve data file in the server root directory. You can modify the CGI script to create the data file in a more appropriate location. The Btrieve NLM ships with IntranetWare and is loaded when the request is made to access the Btrieve data file.

As in the previous section, this script is written without the DOC APIs for generating the HTML tags. However, the DOC:Var() API is used to obtain the CGI form variable values.

Figure 8.17 shows the display produced when the CGI script (webtriev.bas) is run. You can select either the Lookup or Add radio button. If you are selecting the Lookup button, it is only necessary to enter the value for the Name field. For the Add button, you should also enter the values for other fields. The Btrieve data file is indexed by the Name field value, and it allows you to have entries for duplicate names.

FIGURE 8.17

webtriev.bas *display screen*

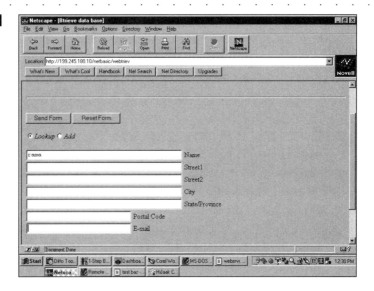

Figure 8.18 shows the results of a lookup for the name "rama." Notice that multiple record matches are displayed, because multiple users with this name were entered. These records were added using the Add option and entering the information on the screen shown in Figure 8.17.

FIGURE 8.18

Results of a lookup of a Btrieve database file

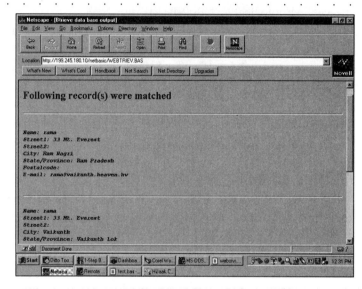

Listing 8.4 shows the `webtriev.bas` NetBasic CGI script. The analysis of the program is presented after the listing.

LISTING 8.4

`webtriev.bas` *Script*

```
#include "basic.h"
#include "btrieve.h"
#include "html.h"
sub main
    local("error")
    error = false
    pname = Doc:var("pname", "undefined")
    if pname = "undefined"
        ' Display HTML form
```

```
        print("<HTML><HEAD><TITLE>Btrieve data
base</TITLE></HEAD>")
        newline

        print("<FORM METHOD=POST ACTION=WEBTRIEV.BAS>");
newline
        print("<H2>Database entry form</H2>"); newline
        print("<HR>"); newline
        print('<input type=submit value="Send Form"> ')
        print('<input type=reset value="Reset Form">')
        newline; newline
        print("<input type=radio name=optype
value=lookup><i>Lookup</i>")
        print("<input type=radio name=optype
value=add><i>Add</i>")
        newline; newline
        print("<input type=text size=45 name=pname>
Name<br>")
        print("<input type=text size=45 name=street1>
Street1<br>")
        print("<input type=text size=45 name=street2>
Street2<br>")
        print("<input type=text size=45 name=city>
City<br>")
        print("<input type=text size=45 name=statepr>
State/Province<br>")
        print("<input type=text size=30 name=postalcode>
Postal Code<br>")
        print("<input size=30 name=email> E-mail<br><br>")

        print("</FORM>"); newline
        print("</BODY></HTML>"); newline

    else
```

```
          ' Process input
          print("<HTML><HEAD><TITLE>Btrieve data base
output</TITLE></HEAD>")
          newline
          print("<BODY>"); newline

          if (!NMX:Lib:Load("BTX"))
              print("Error: Could not locate BTX NLM")
              error = true
          endif
          optype = Doc:var("optype", "undefined")
          if optype = "undefined"
              print("Error: You must select either Lookup,
Add or Update")
              error = true
          endif
          dataFile = "SYS:\TXT.BTV"
          f1size = 45
          f2size = 45
          f3size = 45
          f4size = 45
          f5size = 45
          f6size = 30
          f7size = 30
          recLength = f1size + f2size + f3size + f4size +
f5size + f6size + f7size
          ' Extract the form varables
          street1 = Doc:var("street1", " ")
          street2 = Doc:var("street2", " ")
          city = Doc:var("city", " ")
          statepr = Doc:var("statepr", " ")
          postalcode = Doc:var("postalcode", " ")
          email = Doc:var("email")
          ' If no errors perform database operations
```

```
        if !error
            if !fileExists(dataFile)

                fSpec = makeFileSpec(recLength, 1024, 1)
                fSpec = fSpec + makeKeySpec(1, 45,
BTX_DUP)

                dbCreate(dataFile, fSpec)
            endif
            handle = dbOpen(dataFile)
            if optype = "lookup"
                lookupRec
            endif
            if optype = "add"
                addRec
            endif
            dbClose(handle)
        endif
        print("</BODY></HTML>"); newline
    endif
end sub
' Build the file spec part of the Btrieve file
sub makeFileSpec
    local("fSpec", "recLen", "pageSize", "indexes")
    local("reserved4", "fileFlags", "reserved2", "preAlloc")
    recLen = lowHigh(Param(1))
    pageSize = lowHigh(Param(2,1024))
    indexes = lowHigh(Param(3, 1))
    reserved4 = Str:repeat(Data:char(0),4)
    fileFlags = lowHigh(Param(4,0))
    reserved2 = Str:repeat(Data:char(0),2)
    preAlloc = lowHigh(Param(5,0))
    fSpec = recLen + pageSize + indexes + reserved4 +
```

```
            fileFlags
                fSpec = fSpec + reserved2 + preAlloc
                return (fSpec)
        end sub
        ' Build the key spec part of the Btrieve file
        sub makeKeySpec
                local("keyPos", "keyLen", "keyFlag", "keySpec")
                local("notUsed", "reserved3", "xKeyType", "mKey", "ACS")
                keyPos = lowHigh(Param(1))
                keyLen = lowHigh(Param(2))
                keyFlags = lowHigh(Param(3))
                notUsed = Str:repeat(Data:char(0),4)
                xKeyType = Param(4, Data:char(0))
                reserved3 = Str:repeat(Data:char(0),3)
                mKey = Param(5, Data:char(0))
                ACS = Param(6, Data:char(0))
                keySpec = keyPos + keyLen + keyFlags + notUsed +
        xKeyType
                keySpec = keySpec + reserved3 + mKey + ACS
                return (keySpec)
        end sub
        ' Check for errors in the previous statement
        sub checkError
            if (Param(1) != 0)
                newLine; Print(" Error Number=", Param(1), " On Line
        Number=", Param(2))
                newLine
                Btx:call(Param(3), BTX_CLOSE, "", 0, "", 0)

            endif
        end sub
        ' Convert integer values to a binary string
        sub lowHigh
            local("HI","LO")
```

```
    ' Change the integer byte order and return result as a
binary string.
    LO = Data:char(Math:mod(Param(1), 256))
    HI = Data:char(Param(1) / 256)
    return (LO + HI)
end sub
' Print info on searched/inserted records
sub printinfo
    print("<hr>")
    print("<p><b><i><pre>"); newline
    print("Name: ", pname); newline
    print("Street1: ", street1); newline
    print("Street2: ", street2); newline
    print("City: ", city); newline
    print("State/Province: ", statepr); newline
    print("Postalcode: ", postalcode); newline
    print("E-mail: ", email); newline
    print("</pre></i></b>"); newline
end sub
' Build a record from the fields
sub buildRecord
    local("record")
    record = ""
    record = record + Str:Pad:right(pname, f1size)
    record = record + Str:Pad:right(street1, f2size)
    record = record + Str:Pad:right(street2, f3size)
    record = record + Str:Pad:right(city, f4size)
    record = record + Str:Pad:right(statepr, f5size)
    record = record + Str:Pad:right(postalcode, f6size)
    record = record + Str:Pad:right(email, f7size)
    return (record)
end sub
' Get/extract the fields from the record buffer
sub getRecFields
```

```
        local("rec", "start")

        rec = param(1)
        start = 1
        if recLength != Str:length(rec)
            print ("Problem in getRecFields. Record length = ",
    Str:length(rec))
        endif
        pname = Str:sub(rec, start, f1size)
        start = start + f1size
        street1 = Str:sub(rec, start, f2size)
        start = start + f2size
        street2 = Str:sub(rec, start, f3size)
        start = start + f3size

        city = Str:sub(rec, start, f4size)
        start = start + f4size

        statepr = Str:sub(rec, start, f5size)
        start = start + f5size
        postalcode = Str:sub(rec, start, f6size)
        start = start + f6size
        email = Str:sub(rec, start, f7size)
    end sub
    ' Check if the specified file exists
    sub fileExists
        local ("btfile", "fobj")
        btfile = Param(1)
        fobj = Dir:file:first(btfile)
        if (fobj.error = 0)
            return (True)
        else
            return (False)
        endif
```

```
end sub
' Look up and display records in HTML format
sub lookupRec
    local ("rec", "found", "key")
    key = Str:Pad:Right(pname, flsize)
    rec = buildRecord
    found = 0
    handle = dbGetEqual(handle, rec, rec, 0)
    if dbStatus = 0

        rec = Btx:data:buffer(handle)
        getRecFields(rec)
        do while ((dbStatus = 0) & (key = pname))
            found = found + 1
            if found = 1
                print("<h2>Following record(s) were
matched</h2>")
            endif
            printinfo
            handle = dbGetNext(handle, rec, rec, 0)
            rec = Btx:data:buffer(handle)
            getRecFields(rec)

        enddo
    endif
    if found = 0
        print("<h3>No record was found for ", key, "</h3>")
    else
        print("<hr><h2><i>", found, " record(s) were
found<i></h2>")
    endif
end sub
' Add a record to the database file
sub addRec
```

```
        local ("rec")
        rec = buildRecord
        handle = dbInsert(handle, rec, rec)
        if dbStatus = 0
            printinfo
            print("<hr><h3>Added the previous record</h3>");
newline
        endif
    end sub
    '-------Btrieve Functions-----
    ' Create a Btrieve data file
    sub dbCreate
        local ("btfile", "fSpec", "handle")
        btfile = param(1)
        fSpec = param(2)
        handle = Btx:call("", BTX_CREATE, fSpec,
Str:length(fSpec), btfile, 0)
        checkError(Sys:Error:number, Debug:number - 1, handle)
        dbStatus = Sys:Error:number
        return (handle)

    end sub
    ' Open a Btrieve data file
    sub dbOpen
        local("filename", "mode")
        filename = Param(1)
        mode = Param(2, 0)
        buffer = Str:repeat(" ", 80)
        handle = Btx:call("", BTX_OPEN, buffer,
Str:length(buffer), filename, mode)
        checkError(Sys:Error:number, Debug:number - 1, handle)
        dbStatus = Sys:Error:number
        return (handle)
    end sub
```

```
' Insert a record
sub dbInsert
    local("buffer", "keybuf", "keyno")
    handle = param(1)
    buffer = param(2)
    keybuf = param(3)
    keyno = param(4, 0)
    handle = BTX:Call(handle, BTX_INSERT, buffer,
Str:length(buffer), keybuf, keyno)
    checkError(Sys:Error:number, Debug:number - 1, handle)
    dbStatus = Sys:Error:number
    return (handle)
end sub
' Get first record
sub dbGetFirst
    local("buffer", "keybuf", "keyno")
    handle = param(1)
    buffer = param(2)
    keybuf = param(3)
    keyno = param(4, 0)
    handle = BTX:Call(handle, BTX_GET_FIRST, buffer,
Str:length(buffer), keybuf, keyno)
    dbStatus = Sys:Error:number
    return (handle)
end sub
' Get specified record
sub dbGetEqual
    local("buffer", "keybuf", "keyno")
    handle = param(1)
    buffer = param(2)
    keybuf = param(3)
    keyno = param(4, 0)
    handle = BTX:Call(handle, BTX_GET_EQUAL, buffer,
Str:length(buffer), keybuf, keyno)
```

```
        dbStatus = Sys:Error:number
        return (handle)


    end sub
    ' Get the next record
    sub dbGetNext
        local("buffer", "keybuf", "keyno")
        handle = param(1)
        buffer = param(2)
        keybuf = param(3)
        keyno = param(4, 0)
        handle = BTX:Call(handle, BTX_GET_NEXT, buffer,
Str:length(buffer), keybuf, keyno)
        dbStatus = Sys:Error:number
        return (handle)


    end sub
    ' Close a Btrieve data file
    sub dbClose
        handle = Param(1)
        buffer = Str:repeat(" ", 80)
        handle = BTX:Call(handle, BTX_CLOSE, buffer,
Str:length(buffer), buffer, 0)
        return (handle)
    end sub
```

The logic in the program is contained in the outermost if-statement.

```
        pname = Doc:var("pname", "undefined")
        if pname = "undefined"
            ' Display HTML form
                :
                :
        else
```

```
' Process input
        :
        :
  endif
```

The pname variable is defined if the user defines this form field and submits the form. If the pname variable is defined, it means that the user has submitted the form for processing. In this case, the else part of the if statement is executed. If the pname variable is not defined, the form must be displayed. In this case, the then part of the if statement is executed.

The then part of the if statement contains the logic to display the form. The logic is quite straightforward and consists of print statements to generate the form HTML tags. Form HTML tags are explained in previous sections and also in Chapter 5. The form HTML tag specifies the current NetBasic script in its ACTION attribute:

```
print("<FORM METHOD=POST ACTION=WEBTRIEV.BAS>"); newline
```

When the webtriev.bas is executed again, the pname field should have been defined, and this results in the execution of the else part of the outermost if statement.

The else part of the outermost if statement consists of the following code elements:

▶ The code to generate HTML begin tags for the results to be displayed:

```
print("<HTML><HEAD><TITLE>Btrieve data base
output</TITLE></HEAD>")
newline
print("<BODY>"); newline
```

▶ The code to load the Btrieve library if it is not already loaded:

```
if (!NMX:Lib:Load("BTX"))
  print("Error: Could not locate BTX NLM")
  error = true
endif
```

▶ The code to check if the operation type (Lookup, Add) has been defined:

```
optype = Doc:var("optype", "undefined")
if optype = "undefined"
  print("Error: You must select either Lookup, Add or
Update")
  error = true
endif
```

▶ The code to check which operation has been selected, and print an error if no operation was selected:

```
optype = Doc:var("optype", "undefined")
if optype = "undefined"
  print("Error: You must select either Lookup, Add or
Update")
  error = true
endif
```

▶ The code to define the name of the data file to be used for the database, and the definition of the sizes of the fields in the record, and the record length:

```
dataFile = "SYS:\TXT.BTV"
f1size = 45
f2size = 45
f3size = 45
f4size = 45
f5size = 45
f6size = 30
f7size = 30
recLength = f1size + f2size + f3size + f4size +
f5size + f6size + f7size
```

▶ The code to extract the form field variable values.

```
' Extract the form varables
street1 = Doc:var("street1", " ")
street2 = Doc:var("street2", " ")
city = Doc:var("city", " ")
statepr = Doc:var("statepr", " ")
postalcode = Doc:var("postalcode", " ")
email = Doc:var("email")
```

If you want any of the field values to be mandatory, you should add code to check their values and set the error variable appropriately.

▶ If there are no errors, execute the subroutine LookupRec for the lookup operation, and the subroutine AddRec for the add operation:

```
if !error
  if !fileExists(dataFile)

fSpec = makeFileSpec(recLength, 1024, 1)
fSpec = fSpec + makeKeySpec(1, 45, BTX_DUP)
dbCreate(dataFile, fSpec)
  endif
  handle = dbOpen(dataFile)
  if optype = "lookup"
lookupRec
  endif
  if optype = "add"
addRec
  endif
  dbClose(handle)
endif
print("</BODY></HTML>"); newline
```

Before performing any database operations, a check is made to see if the data file exists. If it does not, it is created by calling the subroutine dbCreate(). Once the existence of the data file is verified, it is opened by calling dbOpen(). The dbCreate() and dbOpen() subroutines are defined later in the code. At the end of performing the database operations the end HTML tags are generated. The file existence test is done by a custom fileExists() function that was written for this purpose:

```
sub fileExists
   local ("btfile", "fobj")
   btfile = Param(1)
   fobj = Dir:file:first(btfile)
   if (fobj.error = 0)
        return (True)
   else
        return (False)
   endif
end sub
```

The fileExists() function uses Dir:File:first() to determine the existence of the file.

The dbCreate() subroutine is used for creating a database file:

```
sub dbCreate
    local ("btfile", "fSpec", "handle")
    btfile = param(1)
    fSpec = param(2)
    handle = Btx:call("", BTX_CREATE, fSpec,
Str:length(fSpec), btfile, 0)
    checkError(Sys:Error:number, Debug:number - 1, handle)
    dbStatus = Sys:Error:number
    return (handle)

end sub
```

As you study this subroutine, you can see that it expects the following parameters:

▸ Name of data file

▸ File specification for the Btrieve data file

All Btrieve calls are made through Btx:Call(). This subroutine expects a fixed number of arguments. Depending on the call, the parameters it expects and returns are different. With the exception of an additional first parameter called handle (set to "" in the call to create a Btrieve file), the remaining parameters have the same description defined in the Btrieve manuals. The Btx:Call() subroutine returns a handle value that is returned by the dbCreate() call. The dbCreate() subroutine is defined to simplify the use of Btrieve functions. If you so desire, you do not have to use the dbCreate() encapsulation of the Btx:Call() function. You can instead call Btx:call() directly.

The call to checkError() is useful as it prints the cause of failure of the previous statement and the line number:

```
sub checkError
    if (Param(1) != 0)
        newLine; Print(" Error Number=", Param(1), " On Line
Number=", Param(2))
        newLine
        Btx:call(Param(3), BTX_CLOSE, "", 0, "", 0)

    endif
end sub
```

The current line number is Debug:number - 1. The Debug:number contains the line number of the statement in which it occurs, which is the call to checkError(). The problem is in the previous line, Debug:number - 1. The system error is reported in Sys:Error:number. All the database encapsulation functions such as dbCreate(), dbOpen(), and so on, set the value of the global variable dbStatus to Sys:Error:number.

The Btrieve file specification includes a data structure that consists of the data file record description followed by one or more key specifications (see Figure 8.19). The *key specification* is a data structure that describes each *key value*, and there is one key specification data structure for each key defined for the Btrieve data file.

FIGURE 8.19

Btrieve data file specification used in creating the file

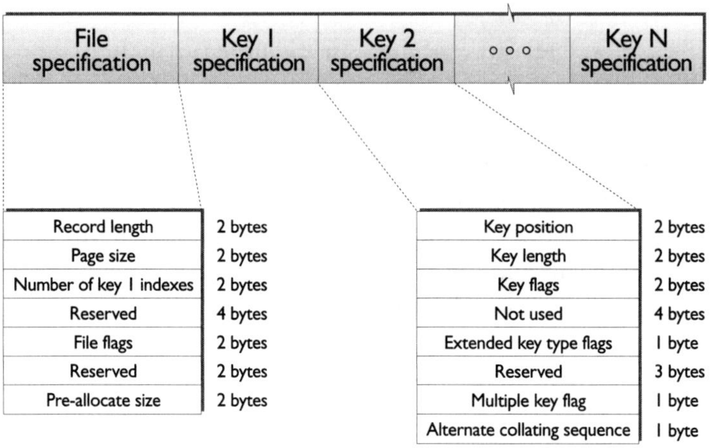

File specification	Key 1 specification	Key 2 specification	o o o	Key N specification

Record length	2 bytes		Key position	2 bytes
Page size	2 bytes		Key length	2 bytes
Number of key 1 indexes	2 bytes		Key flags	2 bytes
Reserved	4 bytes		Not used	4 bytes
File flags	2 bytes		Extended key type flags	1 byte
Reserved	2 bytes		Reserved	3 bytes
Pre-allocate size	2 bytes		Multiple key flag	1 byte
			Alternate collating sequence	1 byte

The file specification is built by calling makeFileSpec() and appending to this data structure the key specifications created by calling makeKeySpec(). The makeFileSpec() subroutine builds the first part of the data structure described in Figure 8.19:

```
sub makeFileSpec
    local("fSpec", "recLen", "pageSize", "indexes")
    local("reserved4", "fileFlags", "reserved2", "preAlloc")
    recLen = lowHigh(Param(1))
    pageSize = lowHigh(Param(2,1024))
    indexes = lowHigh(Param(3, 1))
    reserved4 = Str:repeat(Data:char(0),4)
    fileFlags = lowHigh(Param(4,0))
    reserved2 = Str:repeat(Data:char(0),2)
    preAlloc = lowHigh(Param(5,0))
    fSpec = recLen + pageSize + indexes + reserved4 +
fileFlags
    fSpec = fSpec + reserved2 + preAlloc
    return (fSpec)
end sub
```

In the previous subroutine, 16-bit integer values are converted to a binary string value by calling lowHigh():

```
sub lowHigh
    local("HI","LO")
    ' Change the integer byte order and return result as a
binary string.
    LO = Data:char(Math:mod(Param(1), 256))
    HI = Data:char(Param(1) / 256)
    return (LO + HI)
end sub
```

The Math:mod() function is used to compute the lower-byte value, and division by 256 yields the high-byte value.

The makeKeySpec() subroutine builds the latter part of the file specification structure described in Figure 8.19:

```
sub makeKeySpec
    local("keyPos", "keyLen", "keyFlag", "keySpec")
    local("notUsed", "reserved3", "xKeyType", "mKey", "ACS")
    keyPos = lowHigh(Param(1))
    keyLen = lowHigh(Param(2))
    keyFlags = lowHigh(Param(3))
    notUsed = Str:repeat(Data:char(0),4)
    xKeyType = Param(4, Data:char(0))
    reserved3 = Str:repeat(Data:char(0),3)
    mKey = Param(5, Data:char(0))
    ACS = Param(6, Data:char(0))
    keySpec = keyPos + keyLen + keyFlags + notUsed +
xKeyType
    keySpec = keySpec + reserved3 + mKey + ACS
    return (keySpec)
end sub
```

The lookupRec() subroutine is used to look up records in the database file, given the field name pname, which is used as the key:

```
sub lookupRec
    local ("rec", "found", "key")
    key = Str:Pad:Right(pname, flsize)
    rec = buildRecord
    found = 0
    handle = dbGetEqual(handle, rec, rec, 0)
    if dbStatus = 0

        rec = Btx:data:buffer(handle)
        getRecFields(rec)
        do while ((dbStatus = 0) & (key = pname))
            found = found + 1
            if found = 1
                print("<h2>Following record(s) were
matched</h2>")
            endif
            printinfo
            handle = dbGetNext(handle, rec, rec, 0)
            rec = Btx:data:buffer(handle)
            getRecFields(rec)

        enddo
    endif
    if found = 0
        print("<h3>No record was found for ", key, "</h3>")
    else
        print("<hr><h2><i>", found, " record(s) were
found<i></h2>")
    endif
end sub
```

In the previous code for lookupRec(), the key is constructed by padding the pname value specified by the user with blanks. The reason for doing this is that the key was defined as a fixed size of value flsize.

```
key = Str:Pad:Right(pname, flsize)
```

Next, the call to buildRecord() is used to build a record buffer of the size of the record length:

```
rec = buildRecord
```

Next, the call to dbGetEqual() searches the data file for a record that matches the key value:

```
found = 0
handle = dbGetEqual(handle, rec, rec, 0)
if dbStatus = 0
        :
        :
```

The dbGetEqual() subroutine is called with the handle that was returned from the call to dbOpen(). A dbStatus value of zero indicates that a key match was found. When a key match is found, the record is extracted from the handle value using the following:

```
rec = Btx:data:buffer(handle)
```

The Btx:data:buffer() function is used to extract the record value from the handle and Btx:data:key() is used to extract the key value. In this situation, only the record value is needed. The getRecFields() subroutine is then used to extract the field values from the record string and put them in the global variables pname, street1, street2, city, and so on:

```
getRecFields(rec)
```

The Btrieve data file that was created was set up to support duplicate keys. The dbGetEqual() subroutine finds the first record in the set of records that have duplicate key values. For this reason, a do while loop is set up to look up all records that have the same key value:

```
do while ((dbStatus = 0) & (key = pname))
  found = found + 1
  if found = 1
        print("<h2>Following record(s) were matched</h2>")
  endif
```

```
printinfo
handle = dbGetNext(handle, rec, rec, 0)
rec = Btx:data:buffer(handle)
getRecFields(rec)
```

```
enddo
```

Within the do while loop, the count for the number of key matches is kept, and dbGetNext() is called to get the next record. As before, getRecFields() is called after a new record is fetched to extract its field values. The loop terminates when dbStatus is non-zero, or there are no more duplicate keys. Within the loop, printinfo() is called to generate HTML code to display the matching record. The number of matching records is reported before lookupRec() exits:

```
if found = 0
  print("<h3>No record was found for ", key, "</h3>")
else
  print("<hr><h2><i>", found, " record(s) were
found<i></h2>")
endif
```

The code for printinfo() is straightforward, as it consists of merely print statements to generate the HTML tags and the values of the fields:

```
sub printinfo
    print("<hr>")
    print("<p><b><i><pre>"); newline
    print("Name: ", pname); newline
    print("Street1: ", street1); newline
    print("Street2: ", street2); newline
    print("City: ", city); newline
    print("State/Province: ", statepr); newline
    print("Postalcode: ", postalcode); newline
    print("E-mail: ", email); newline
    print("</pre></i></b>"); newline
  end sub
```

The addRec() function inserts a new record containing the user-supplied information:

```
sub addRec
    local ("rec")
    rec = buildRecord
    handle = dbInsert(handle, rec, rec)
    if dbStatus = 0
        printinfo
        print("<hr><h3>Added the previous record</h3>");
newline
    endif
end sub
```

The addRec() subroutine uses dbInsert() to add the record that was built using the buildRecord() function. If the addition of the record is successful, an HTML message is generated announcing the success. You can study the listing to see how the getRecFields(), buildRecord(), and the other Btrieve functions such as dbOpen(), dbGetEqual(), dbGetNext(), dbInsert(), and dbClose() are written. You can use these Btrieve functions as a template for writing encapsulating subroutines for other Btrieve operations that you may need in your CGI script.

While the CGI program is quite extensive and long because of the many NetBasic support functions that were written, it still lacks a few features that you may want to add. You can extend this CGI script program to perform the following:

▶ Add operations to perform user update and delete. For update and delete, you may require users to enter a password, which is also stored in the data file. You will have to extend the record definition to support a password field. You may want to consider encryption for storing password information.

▶ The name of the user was used as the key, and, since many users could have the same name, duplicate keys had to be supported. A better system would be to define unique user account numbers. This will allow users to uniquely specify using an account number, which record to update or delete.

▸ Add a validation feature so that, if certain critical fields are empty, the record is rejected, and an error message is reported to the user.

Summary

This chapter discussed the BASIC and NetBasic languages. Sample code for BASIC CGI scripts was analyzed to provide an understanding of how to write BASIC programs. The NetBasic language was presented in a tutorial fashion. The NetBasic language elements have been discussed in sufficient detail to enable you to not only learn the language, but also to write sophisticated CGI programs in NetBasic.

NetBasic (with its network extension modules) is particularly useful if you want to access NetWare-specific services. You can access these services through the CGI interface, as seen in the example CGI scripts that were analyzed at the end of the chapter. One disadvantage of BASIC and NetBasic is that the CGI scripts written using these languages have limited portability.

Using Java for Dynamic Content on the Novell Web Server

The Java language was developed by Sun Microsystems and has been licensed by several vendors, including Novell. Java has a number of characteristics that make it suitable for use with Internet applications. Java is not limited to being used exclusively on the Internet. Java's cross-platform portability makes it a good choice for many intranet corporate networks.

On a Novell intranet, Java applications can be run at the user workstation by the Web client, as well as on the IntranetWare server. The IntranetWare server includes built-in support for Java. If your version of IntranetWare does not come with Novell's Java Software Development Kit (SDK), you can download it from the URL `http://www.novell.com/java`. Novell's Java Development Kit is a port of the generic SDK from Sun Microsystems onto the NetWare 4 operating system.

Java is a powerful applications-development language, and usually requires a complete book to cover it effectively. In this short chapter, the basics of the Java language are presented. A number of books are available (including a couple by this author) that you can consult for further details.

Understanding the Java Language

The history of the Java language goes back to April 1991, when a group of Sun Microsystem employees began working on a project code-named "Green." The goal of this project was to develop a system of consumer electronics logic for such devices as ovens, toasters, televisions, videocassette recorders, lights, telephones, pagers, set-top boxes, personal digital assistants, and so on.

The developers quickly discovered a lack of standards in consumer electronics as to what type of processor is actually used. In order to simplify development of the devices, they needed a platform-independent environment. James Gosling at Sun Microsystems initially attempted to extend the C++ language but this approach was abandoned because it was considered to be too much effort and not the best approach from a technical standpoint.

A new language for the Green project was created. This language was initially called "Oak." The name "Oak" was inspired by the oak tree James Gosling saw outside his window. Later on, the name "Oak" had to be discarded because it was being used by an older language. After many hours of brainstorming, inspiration struck one day after the team members visited a local coffee shop. Therefore, contrary to popular opinion, Java is not an acronym such as "Just Another Vague Acronym." The Green team was incorporated into a Sun Microsystems spin-off called FirstPerson, Inc.

In 1993, First Person, Inc. made a bid for the Time-Warner television trial, where many homes were to have experimental video-on-demand hardware for testing. They lost the deal to Silicon Graphics, Inc. In 1994, another deal with the company 3DO fell through, and the prospects of new marketing partners looked bleak. While all this was happening to the original Green team, the Web was gaining larger acceptance, particularly with the development of powerful GUI Web clients that provided the user with considerable flexibility and navigational power.

On May 23, 1995, the Java Environment was announced by Sun Microsystems at SunWorld '95. This was the start of tremendous excitement about creating tools to develop applications in the language. In April 1996, Novell licensed Java for use with the NetWare Operating System.

Popular browsers such as the Netscape Navigator and Internet Explorer incorporate Java-based technology. These browsers can run Java programs that are downloaded from remote Web servers. Java programs for the Web are called *Java applets*. The description of Java applets is embedded in the HTML pages as URL addresses. Since the URL addresses can refer to any computer on the network, the HTTP protocol and the HTML language can be used to distribute code for execution on the intranet or the Internet.

Sun describes its Java language as a simple, distributed, interpreted, secure, architecture-neutral, portable, high-performance, multithreaded, and dynamic language. That is a great many adjectives, and some may even classify them as buzzwords.

Some of these buzzwords have also been used to describe other languages. What makes Java unique is that it is the first language that can be used for writing general-purpose programs, as well as programs designed specifically for use on the Internet and intranets. When used for Internet/intranet applications, the Java programs are typically used in conjunction with the Web clients such as Web browsers. Java programs that are designed to be run from within a Web browser are called *applets*. General-purpose Java programs that can be run standalone (outside of a Web browser) are called *Java applications*.

Java Is Simple

Java was designed with the intent of keeping the language simple, but, at the same time, powerful enough to perform network computing tasks for the Web. This simplicity and power are also helpful in developing applications for intranets.

To meet the goal of simplicity, the designers of the language kept the number of language constructs as small as possible without compromising power. Keeping the language simple makes it easier for people to learn the language, and keeps the compilers small and easier to implement.

The designers also based the language on the C/C++ syntax. Many of the large number of competent C/C++ programmers find the language easy to learn and to migrate to. If you studied Chapter 7 on writing CGI scripts in Perl, you have already picked up the basic syntax of C/C++ and Java.

Some of the features of C/C++ were deliberately removed to keep the Java language simple and secure. As an example, the Java language does not support `goto` statements. Instead, it provides exceptional handling, labeled `break` and `continue`, and `finally` statements. The C/C++ language header files have been removed. There is no #`include` preprocessor directive. Instead, the Java `import` statement is used to selectively import a Java class or all classes in the specified package.

To support the development of large software in a modular fashion, the concept of a package is used. A *package* is a collection of Java code grouped together because of similarity of function. This is similar to the concept of packages in Perl that was briefly discussed in Chapter 7.

Another difference between Java and C/C++ is the removal of support for data structures such as `struct` and `union`. A similar concept can be implemented by the `class` construct in Java. Also, operator overloading and multiple-inheritance capabilities of C++ have been eliminated to keep the Java language simple (although Java does support single inheritance). The multiple-inheritance feature of many object-oriented languages is implemented through the interface feature.

One of the biggest changes in Java from C/C++ is the removal of the direct use of pointers. While pointers in C/C++ are a powerful mechanism, correctly using pointers requires discipline. Without this discipline, it is difficult to ensure that the code that uses them is free of bugs. Real-life experience from maintaining C/C++ code suggests that the use of pointers in C/C++ creates error-prone programs where the bugs can be very subtle. Java automatically handles referencing and dereferencing of language objects. This frees you from the problems of dangling reference pointers, invalid pointer references, memory leaks, and so on. Objects are created dynamically and garbage collection is performed automatically in the background by the Java environment.

Incorrect use of memory allocation is another common source of error in C/C++ programs. By having the Java environment perform this automatically, memory type errors are reduced. The automatic management of memory is particularly valuable in developing Java applications to run on the IntranetWare server. This is because, compared to running NLMs, Java applications are not likely to cause memory leaks or bugs resulting from incorrect pointer usage.

Even though the Java language has been simplified in comparison with C/C++, it comes with a rich set of predefined classes to perform I/O, network, and graphic operations. This makes the Java language easy and powerful enough to develop network-enabled intranet applications. In addition, the Software Development Kit for Java available from Novell provides a number of Java classes that can be used to access Novell network services.

Java Is Object-Oriented

Java is an *object-oriented language*, which means that all programs and data always exist in the context of objects. An *object* is a collection of data and programs that operate on it. The programs that are written specifically for data that resides in the object are called *object methods*. One of the parameters to the object method is the object itself (referred to in the Java language by `this`). As the name "method" suggests, the *object methods* are the mechanism used to operate on the data held in the object. The data and the methods describe the state of the object.

The notion of an object in Java is implemented by the `class` construct. The use of classes is so fundamental to the Java language that it is not possible to write a Java program that does something meaningful without using the `class` construct.

Code reuse is supported in Java by using object inheritance. A class can be derived from another class, which is called *inheritance* or *subclassing*. The Java language comes with useful predefined class hierarchies. At the very top is the special class `Object`. This is the root class from which all other classes are subclasses. By default, a newly created class always inherits from the root class `Object`, even though you may not explicitly define a class from which you inherit. The predefined Java class hierarchies and the additional class definitions from Novell provide the richness of the Java environment for the IntranetWare server platform.

The biggest learning curve in Java is not the language syntax or language semantics, both of which are relatively straightforward and easy to learn. The biggest challenge is in becoming familiar with the predefined class hierarchies, as well as the methods and their purposes. You could, of course, start from scratch and reinvent a new set of class hierarchies to replace the existing rebuilt hierarchies, but you would be much less productive.

Using inheritance, you can always use the concept of code reuse and subclass existing class hierarchies. Because all Java objects are subclassed from `Object`, all Java objects can use the predefined methods for the `Object` class. Where the desired classes hierarchies are not adequate or available, you can always create your own.

Java Is a Robust Language

Robustness in a language means the support for eliminating error-prone constructs both at compile and run time. Java is a strongly typed language, which means that there are well-defined rules on how objects are to be used. For example, you cannot assign a floating-point number to an integer value without loss in precision. The compiler will catch this and other similar errors at compile time. You can explicitly force certain types of objects into others by an explicit type conversion (casting) or writing conversion programs, but this is an explicit action that must be performed by the programmer. This will not be done automatically by the Java language.

The Java memory model performs automatic garbage collection, thus eliminating another important class of runtime errors. Pointers are not directly supported, and this eliminates pointer-related runtime errors (such as inadvertent data overwrites and memory corruption). The Java interpreter also performs such runtime checks as ensuring that array and string accesses are within the bounds of the array size.

Java supports explicit exception handling in the language, which provides the programmer with an additional tool to write robust programs. In addition to the predefined exceptional conditions that indicate potential problems, the programmer can define his or her own exceptions.

Java Is an Interpreted Language

The Java compiler does not produce the machine-language instructions that make up the executable Java program. Instead, the Java compiler produces an intermediate code called *byte-code*. The Java byte-code is read by a Java interpreter that executes it by using an internal model of an abstract machine. The Java interpreter, and the implementation of this abstract machine, are called the *Java Virtual Machine* (JVM). On the IntranetWare server, the JVM runs as an NLM, and Java byte-code is interpreted by this JVM NLM.

The Java byte-code is an architecturally neutral representation of the program. Because the Java program is executed by interpreting the Java byte-code, the Java language is interpretive. In an interpretive environment, the standard "link" phase of patching together the object modules to form a binary executable set of machine instructions vanishes. The linking phase is replaced by the loading of the new class into the Java environment. Interpretive environments such as Java support rapid prototyping and program development.

Just in time (JIT) compilers are also available for those applications that cannot afford the overhead of an interpretive execution of Java code. These JIT compilers translate the byte-code into the machine-language instructions of the computer on which the program is run. This leads to significant improvements in performance. Of course, the output of the JIT compilers is no longer architecturally neutral. However, many Java vendors provide JIT compilers that are specific to the platform on which they run.

Java Is High-Performance

Java is high-performance compared to other scripting languages (such as the varieties of BASIC and Visual BASIC languages, shell scripts, and Perl). It is, however, about 20 times slower than the C language. For many interactive applications, the speed of Java is adequate.

If you want to make the speed of Java comparable with C, you must use JIT compilers. Examples of JIT are available from several vendors (such as Sun, Borland, Symantec, and so on). Web browsers are licensing JIT compilers to provide accelerators for improved performance of applets.

Java byte-code was designed to provide a quick translation from the byte-code format to the machine instructions for processors. So, the performance of byte-code converted to machine instructions is comparable to C/C++ programs.

Java Is Architecture-Neutral

A compiled Java program produces byte-code that is interpreted in the JVM. The byte-code is independent of any specific processor type and machine architecture. This enables the Java code to run on any machine that supports the JVM and Java interpreter.

The architecture neutrality of Java is important for intranets. It enables program code to be written just once in Java. The same program code can then run across a variety of different client or server platforms. Figure 9.1 shows the same Java applet code downloaded into different client platforms.

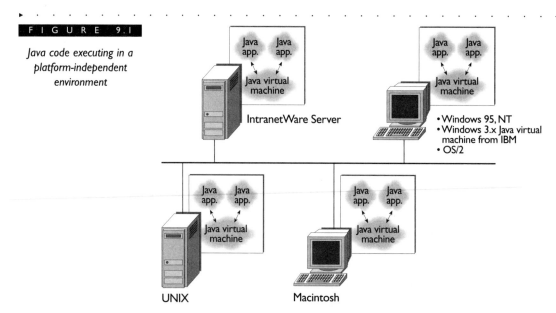

Java code executing in a platform-independent environment

Currently, many organizations spend a great deal of effort and money trying to cover every possible platform they need to support. With different versions of UNIX, Windows NT, Windows 95, OS/2, and Macintosh computers, it is a challenge to write software that can run on all these platforms. Java goes a long way to help with this challenge.

Java Is Portable

Because Java code is architecture-neutral, it can be run on any platform. The code must be written once, and the byte-code can be distributed to different platforms and run unchanged. A constant source of portability problems in other languages is the difference in implementations of the size of basic language data types (such as integers, characters and floating-point numbers). For example, is a basic integer type 16 bits long or is it 32 bits long? In Java, all basic types have the same size, regardless of the platform on which they run. For example, an integer type in Java is always a signed 32-bit value, whether it runs on an IntranetWare server, UNIX machine, or an OS/2 machine. This avoids errors (such as overflow or underflow errors) that typically arise because an incorrect assumption was made about the size of the basic types.

Because Java applets are GUI-based and can be multithreaded, Java programs can only run on those environments that have these features. For example, it would be difficult to have Java applets run on MS-DOS machines that do not support a GUI interface or multitasking.

Java Is a Distributed Language

Java was designed to support applications that run on a network. This network could be the Internet or it could be corporate intranets. Java provides network capabilities by using a predefined language package called java.net. This package contains many classes to simplify network communications between applications running on different computers on a network. Using Java, you can access remote or local files with equal ease. In addition, a virtual circuit network connection is supported by the language, which can be used when building distributed client/server software for intranets.

The Network Computer (NC) uses Java's distributed applications architecture to download applications on demand from a network server.

Java Is a Secure Language

Because Java code is expected to run in a networked environment that can have untrusted host computers, the language was designed with security as a major goal. Java code residing at a Web server can be downloaded and run within the JVM provided by the Web browser, or directly on the IntranetWare server. What is there to prevent viruses and other malicious programs from masquerading as legitimate code and causing damage to the client computer or other computers on the network? A technique many virus programs use to cause damage is to get machine resources by the clever manipulation of address variables such as pointers. This is one of the reasons the Java designers decided not to support pointers in the language. This also eliminates a major security risk.

Memory allocation and layout of classes are done transparently by the Java environment. Because the programmer does not have access to the memory layout, the programmer cannot know the actual memory layout that is used. This makes it difficult for virus programs to access the internal data structures of the Java program.

Before a Java program is interpreted, the Java runtime system performs a *byte-code verification*. Byte-code verification is a formal process in which mathematical algorithms are used to ensure that the program is not violating system integrity. Additionally, programs that are loaded from across the Internet are loaded in a separate namespace than local classes. This prevents a malicious Java applet from replacing standard Java classes.

Java anticipates and protects against traditional techniques used to cause the program to misbehave. It cannot, however, guarantee or claim a 100 percent foolproof environment. There are a number of malicious and wily hackers who will see in Java a new challenge to overcome. As these cases come up, Sun Microsystems and other vendors must plug the security holes and stay one step ahead of these hackers.

While security is important in an Internet environment, it is less so than in the intranet environment. The primary reason for this is that intranets have less exposure to malicious users than the Internet. Since Java is designed to provide a safe execution environment on the Internet, it can certainly meet the needs of most intranets.

Java Is Multithreaded

Java is one of the few languages (Ada is another) that provides support for multitasking in the form of multithreading within the language itself. This means that you can write Java programs where multiple threads are executing "simultaneously." A *thread* is an independent line of execution through a program. Threads can be used to implement parallelism in the program. Each thread performs a specialized function. With several threads running, several parallel activities are taking place. On a single-processor machine, the threads will each have to have their turn executing on the CPU, and so it only appears as if the threads are executing simultaneously. In reality, each thread runs for a duration of time before it is preempted and another thread gets a chance to run. On a multiprocessor machine, threads could be simultaneously executing on different processors. Thus, on an IntranetWare server that is using Symmetrical Multiprocessing (SMP), the threads will execute faster.

To prevent threads from tripping over each other when critical operations are being performed, you can specify *critical regions* by using the `synchronized` keyword.

Most programs that use some form of multitasking or multithreading make low-level calls for system services to the operating system on which they run. Because of differences in system service calls, these programs are not portable to different operating system types. With Java, however, you could write a multithreaded program that could run without alteration on different machines and operating system types.

Java Is Dynamic

Java is a dynamic language in the sense that it loads the classes it needs as they are needed. You can determine at run time to which class an object belongs by checking the run-type information associated with the class. The runtime class definitions makes it easy to perform dynamic linking of classes.

Reviewing the Java Language

As was done with the Perl and NetBasic languages in previous chapters, this section is a short review of the Java language elements. The purpose of this section is not make you an expert Java programmer, but rather to provide a sufficient working knowledge of the Java language elements.

Writing a Simple Java Program

Let's write a simple Java program that will print the following statement at the console:

```
The Light of God never fails!
May you pass every test!
```

You can create Java programs using a text editor, and compile and execute them by using any of the following tools:

- The JDK (Java Developer's Kit) from Sun Microsystems (command line tools)

- Java workshop from Sun Microsystems (visual tools)

- Novell's SDK for Java for IntranetWare

- Visual Cafe from Symantec

- Latte from Borland

- Visual J++ from Microsoft

The program that produces the text described previously is listed next:

```
public class dispmsg
{
    public static void main(String args[])
    {
        System.out.println("The Light of God never
fails!");
        System.out.println("May you pass every test!");
    }
}
```

You must save the Java program in a text file. The name of the file must end with the ".java" extension. With the current release of the Java language, you must save the program with the same name as the class name (in this example, dispmsg.java). If you are developing on the NetWare server, this implies that you are able to create long filenames. Under IntranetWare, you can add the LONG name space (implemented by the LONG.NAM file) to the server volume to add support for creating long filenames.

The *class name* is the name that follows class in the previous program and describes the program fragment that is placed in the braces {}, as shown here:

```
class classname
{
  ...
}
```

The name of the file, in the previous example, must be `dispmsg.java` to match the class name of `dispmsg`. Class names in Java are case-sensitive. Therefore, the following are considered to be three distinct classes.

```
class DispMsg
{
  ...
}
class dispMsg
{
  ...
}
class dispmsg
{
  ...
}
```

Also, notice that because java filenames end with a four-letter "java" extension, you cannot use a MS-DOS editor for creating these filenames. MS-DOS filename extensions are limited to three characters. Under UNIX, filenames are case-sensitive. However, under Windows NT and Windows 95, filenames are not case-sensitive, even though the case is preserved when creating filenames. This means that if you try to create a filename such as `dispmsg.java` in a directory that already has a filename `DispMsg.java`, you will not be able to create a separate filename. In practical terms, this means that in the Windows NT and Windows 95 workstation environments, you must use class names that will *not* lead to conflicts in unique filenames if the Java program is kept in the same directory.

Class structure

Notice that the program code for the dispmsg program is embedded in the following syntax:

```
class classname
{
```

```
    Rest of program code
}
```

In Java, a class is used to define a piece of program code. It begins with the reserved word class followed by the name of the class (*classname*) and then by the brace characters {}. The program code is placed in the brace characters {} that follow the class statement. In Java, the brace characters {} and the program code inside it are called a program *block*. The word class has a special meaning in the Java language and cannot be used for programmer defined data variables and functions. Other reserved words in the dispmsg Java example are public, static, and void.

All Java programs containing program code must have at least one class. Within this class is the actual data and program code that operates on the data. The class mechanism is used in Java to describe the notion of an *object*.

Simple Java objects

An object is a collection of data and programs that operate upon that data. Figure 9.2 shows a conceptual representation of an object. In this figure, the data is shown in the central core of the object. Surrounding the data, in this figure, are programs that operate on the data. Programs defined within an object that operate on the data in the object are called *methods*. In other object-oriented languages such as Small Talk (a language developed Xerox Palo Alto Research), the methods are also called *messages*, and, therefore, some of the Java documentation refers to the programs that operate on data within an object as "messages."

Representing a Java object

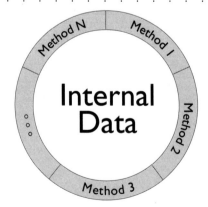

Causing the program in the object to be run is called *invoking a method, calling a method,* or *sending a message* to the object. Conceptually, the idea is that when a method is invoked for the object, or when a message is sent to the object, the program code alters the state of the object that is represented by data in the object (see Figure 9.3).

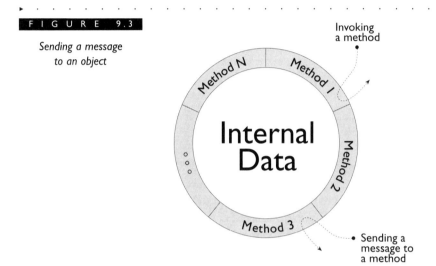

Sending a message to an object

It is not always necessary for a method to modify the data in an object. The method could simply return the current values of the data in the object, or perform some other logic. A method in a Java class corresponds to the functions, procedures, or subroutines in other programming languages such as C/C++, Pascal, NetBasic, Perl, and so on. One major difference is that a method in Java language is always defined within a class or within the syntax of a class, whereas a function, procedure or subroutine in many other languages does not have this association with the object. A Java method has access to all data defined in the class. Other methods outside the class do not automatically have access to the data in the class, unless explicitly granted such access by using reserved words (such as public) preceding the method definition.

Coming back to the dispmsg program, you may notice that the dispmsg program is a trivialized form of a Java object. There is no data in the HelloWord class, and it contains only one method called main.

Definition of the `main` program method

When a Java application is run, control is transferred to the method called `main`. Recall from Chapter 8 that this is similar to NetBasic, which also requires the program `main`. Actually, this convention was originally borrowed from the C language.

Normally, you can assign any name to the methods in a class. However, the name `main` is special because it is the name reserved for the method to which initial program control is transferred when a Java program is run. The `main` method is defined as follows:

```
public static void main(String args[])
{
   Rest of program code for main
}
```

In order to communicate data with a method, you pass *arguments* to the method. Arguments are also called *parameters*. Arguments or parameters are place holders that describe the actual data passed to the method. Arguments follow the method name and are enclosed in parentheses.

Immediately following the method name and arguments is a block of code enclosed in braces {}. In the example of the `main` method, there is only a single argument definition inside the parentheses:

```
String args[]
```

The `String` refers to a built-in class defined in the Java language that is used to contain string data. The Java language defines several useful built-in classes for types of data and functions that are used frequently in many Java programs. In this case, the `String` built-in class is particularly useful for describing string data. *String data* is a sequence of characters and is typically used to describe text data such as messages. String data is represented as a sequence of characters enclosed in quotation marks. You can see an example of string data in the class `dispmsg`:

```
"The Light of God never fails!"
"May you pass every test"
```

The use of `args` immediately following `String` defines the name of the place holder for the type of data to be passed to the method. The brackets [] following the `args` defines the argument `args` to be a reference to an array. Therefore, the argument `args` that is to be passed is an array of `String` objects. For example the first element of args could be the string "The" and the second element could be "coming". Figure 9.4 shows an example of an array of strings that could be passed to the main method.

There is nothing special about the name args used in the main method. You can replace it with another valid variable name, such as shown in the following example:

```
public static void main(String vstr[])
{
   Rest of program code for main
}
```

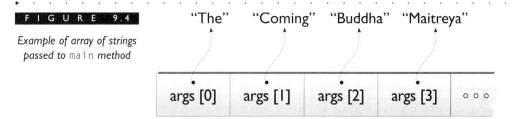

FIGURE 9.4

Example of array of strings
passed to main method

"The"   "Coming"   "Buddha"   "Maitreya"

args [0]   args [1]   args [2]   args [3]   o o o

If your code in the body of the main program must reference the argument passed to main, you must ensure that you use the new name vstr instead of the name args. However, you will find that, as a convention, most Java code uses the name args as the argument for the main program.

Who supplies the array of strings that is passed to the main method? The Java runtime environment passes the string data specified on the command line when the dispmsg Java program is invoked as an array of strings. For example, consider the following invocation of the Java program:

```
> java dispmsg The coming Buddha Maitreya.
```

In this case, the main method is passed the following array of strings:

```
"The", "coming", "Buddha", "Maitreya."
```

In the simple example of the dispmsg program discussed earlier, the body of the main method (that is, code included in the braces {}), contains no further reference to args. However, you must still specify the args parameter as an array of strings, even though your program may not actually use the string.

The `main` method is preceded with a number of modifiers such as `public`, `static`, and `void`. As mentioned previously, these modifiers are reserved words in the Java language and cannot be used as variable names.

The `public` modifier before a method name makes the method "callable" to Java code outside the class. In the `dispmsg` example, there is no other Java code outside the class `dispmsg`, but the caller in this case is the Java runtime environment. The Java runtime environment contains the Java Virtual Machine that processes the Java byte-code, and the Java runtime library code needed for running a Java program. The use of the reserved word `public` before a method name makes the method publicly available (or callable) to any "user" or "client" of the class. In this case, the "user" or "client" is not a human; but actually any other program code that is defined outside the class.

The class defines the object. However, it does not create the actual object. A created object occupies space in computer memory. The class only defines a template for the object. In order to create the actual object, you use the class name to create the object. The following is an example of creating an object from the class `dispmsg`:

```
dispmsg dspobj;
```

The previous statement creates the object `dspobj` from the class (or template) definition `dispmsg`. This process of creating an object from a class definition is called creating an *instance* of the object, or *instantiating* a class. Once you have created a real object, you can invoke the public methods (that is, methods such as `main` that have a `public` modifier) by using a notation such as the following:

```
dspobj.main("The", "coming", "Buddha", "Maitreya.");
```

The preceding example shows how a method in a class is invoked. The general syntax of invoking a methods is as follows:

```
objectname.methodname(arguments);
```

The *objectname* refers to the name of the object (such as `dspobj`). The *methodname* refers to the name of the method (such as `main`) and *arguments* refers to the list of arguments passed to the method.

In general, you must create an instance of the object before invoking its method. The method is then associated with data inside the object. Creating an object from a description of the object is called *instantiating the object*. The class definition of an object is also the description of the object.

There are times when you would like to call a method such as `main` without first creating an instance of the class `dispmsg`. You can do this by using the `static` modifier in defining the method. In the example of the `main` method defined in class `dispmsg`, the `static` modifier is used to indicate that the main method can be invoked without defining an instance of the class such as `dispmsg`. For example if you invoke the following,

```
java dispmsg The coming Buddha Maitreya.
```

the Java runtime environment is able to invoke main in dispmsg by using the equivalent of the following syntax:

```
dispmsg.main("The", "coming", "Buddha", "Maitreya.");
```

Notice that `dispmsg` is the name of the class and not the name of an instantiated object. It is possible to call `main()` in this manner because a method defined with reserved word `static` is associated with all instances of the object of a class, and can be invoked using the following syntax:

```
classname.methodname(arguments);
```

The *classname* refers to the name of the class, *methodname* refers to the name of the method, and *arguments* refers to the list of arguments passed to the method.

The final modifier that is used with the definition for `main` is `void`. In Java, all methods are expected to return a value. However, there are many situations when a method executes some logic, but does not need to return anything. In this case, you must use the modifier `void` before the method name, thereby indicating that no value is expected to be returned by the method.

Printing output

So far, you have learned all aspects of the `dispmsg` class except the single code statement in the following `main` method:

```
System.out.println("The Light of God never fails!");
```

This statement invokes the `println` method defined in the built-in `System` class. The `println` method prints the string to the standard output device, which is usually the computer monitor. After printing the string, the `println` method outputs the newline character, which causes the cursor to be positioned on the next line on the computer screen.

Notice that to use the `println` method, there was no instance of the `System` class defined in the class `dispmsg`. This is because all methods in the `System` class are static and can be invoked by specifying the class name alone.

Compiling and Running a Simple Java Program

In this section, you will learn how to compile and run the simple Java program that you have created on the IntranetWare server. You must have Novell's SDK installed at the IntranetWare server. If your IntranetWare software does not come with the Java Virtual Machine NLM (JAVA.NLM) already installed, you can download it from the Internet site `http://www.novell.com/java`, and follow the instructions to install the SDK. The file that you download is a self-extracting file. Copy the file to the IntranetWare server and run the executable. This will produce a README.TXT file and another executable file. Consult the README.TXT file that accompanies the distribution software for a guideline on how to install the Novell SDK.

The Novell SDK installs on a server volume, and the documentation installs in the \JAVA\DOC directory. The \JAVA\DOC directory contains and `index.html` file that you should open with a Web browser for details on hardware/software requirements, installing, configuring, compiling, and running Java programs.

The current Novell SDK requires 32 MB of server RAM for text applications, and 64 MB of server RAM for running Java GUI applications. Consult the documentation in the \JAVA\DOC directory for other hardware requirements.

After following the instructions to install the Novell SDK, you should restart the server. If you examine the AUTOEXEC.NCF file on the IntranetWare server, you will find that statements similar to the following are added to the file:

```
SEARCH ADD SYS:\JAVA\BIN
SEARCH ADD SYS:\JAVA\NWGFX
```

The SEARCH console command adds the indicated directory to the search path for executing programs from the server console. You can type the SEARCH console command without any arguments to see if the Java directories have been added to the search path.

To enable the IntranetWare server for Java, you should load the JAVA.NLM contained in the `SYS:\JAVA\BIN` directory. The JAVA.NLM implements the Java Virtual Machine (JVM):

```
LOAD JAVA
```

After loading the Java Virtual Machine, a number of additional commands such as JAVAC, JAVA, JAVAH, ENVSET, and so on, that deal with Java program development become available to you from the server console.

If you have not already created your Java program, you can do so, but be sure to name the file with a ".java" extension. You should compile the Java program into byte-code by using the JAVAC program from the IntranetWare server console:

```
JAVAC pathname
```

For example, if the file that you have named is DISPMSG.JAVA in the directory SYS:PUBS\NWEB, then you should use the following command:

```
JAVAC  SYS:PUBS\NWEB\DISPMSG.JAVA
```

To see the complete command line syntax for using the JAVAC compiler, just type JAVAC by itself on the server console:

```
JAVAC
```

After the program compiles successfully, a ".class" file is produced that contains the Java byte-code. You can run the Java byte-code by using the following JAVA command:

```
JAVA classname
```

The *classname* is the name of the Java class that contains the main program. In the case of the example program discussed in the previous section, this class name is dispmsg. However, before you can run the Java program, you must ensure that the Java environment variable CLASSPATH is set to the directory that contains the Java program. To see the current settings for the CLASSPATH environment variable, type the following at the server console:

```
envset
```

The CLASSPATH contains the Java library class files and directories separated by a semicolon (;). Usually, the "." directory is added to the end of CLASSPATH. The "." directory represents the current directory, which is typically set to SYS:\. If your ".class" file is in the SYS:\ directory, you will be able to run the Java program by copying the ".class" file to the SYS:\ directory. For a number of reasons (including system security), this is not desirable. So, you will have to modify the CLASSPATH environment variable by using the following command:

```
envset ExistingValue;YourDirectory
```

The *ExistingValue* is the current setting of the CLASSPATH environment variable. The *YourDirectory* is the name of the directory that contains the Java program that you just compiled.

You are now ready to run the Java program that you compiled. The following is an example of the syntax needed to run the Java program:

```
JAVA   SYS:PUBS\NWEB\DISPMSG.CLASS
```

Java Language Elements

Now that you know how to write a simple Java program, you are ready to explore Java language elements such as variables, operators, control statements, classes, and so on. In this section, you will learn about Java variables, how they are defined and how they can be used in Java statements and expressions. This section also discusses Java classes.

Understanding Built-in Data Types and Operators

A variable's name is described by an identifier. *Identifiers* are names for language entities such as variables, classes, and so on. An identifier in Java can be a sequence of unicode characters of *any* length. There are some limitations on the characters you can use to create the identifier. A Java identifier must begin with a "letter," followed by any combination of letters and digits. A "letter" is a set that consists of the lowercase letters "a" through "z," the uppercase letters "A" through "Z," the underscore (_) character, and dollar ($) character. If the unicode characters defining the scripts of other languages is used, then, the "letter" acquires a broader meaning and can include glyphs from scripts such as Russian, Devanagari, Gurumukhi, Korean, Chinese, Farsi, Japanese, and so on.

To declare a variable, you use the following syntax:

```
datatype var;
datatype var1, var2. ..., varN;
```

The *var*, *var1*, *var2*, and *varN* are variable names and *datatype* is one of the built-in data types, such as the following within the Java language:

▸ byte—8-bit signed integer

▸ short—16-bit signed integer

▸ int—32-bit signed integer

▸ long—64-bit signed integer

▸ char—Unicode character

▸ float—Single-precision floating point

▸ double—Double-precision floating point

▸ boolean—Boolean data type (true or false values)

The *datatype* can also be a Java class, in which case the variable names become object variable names. Here are some examples of Java variable definitions:

```
int       soulsense;
char      honorCode;
long      epochYear;
byte      small_score;
short     height;
boolean found = false;
float     napieranE;
double pi = 3.1415926536;
```

Notice that the variables found and pi are not only defined, but are also set to some initial values. It is quite common in Java to define a variable and also set an initial value for the variable.

Although you can use almost any arbitrary combination of letters for variable names, you cannot use certain combinations of letters as variable names. These special combinations of letters are reserved, and are therefore called *reserved words* or *keywords*. For example, the words int, float, class that you encountered earlier are used in the Java language to define the data types of integer, floating point, and the class construct, respectively. These reserved words cannot be used for programmer-defined names such as names for variables and objects. Table 9.1 defines a list of reserved words in the Java language.

The `null`, `false`, and `true` words appear to be language keywords, but actually they are literal values. The word `null` is used as a value for an object variable that has not been instantiated (or defined). The words `false` and `true` are values for a Boolean data variable. Because these literals are similar to constants such as 278, 1.44, 'k' and so on, they are not included in Table 9.1. Even though these literal words are not formally defined as language reserved words, you cannot use them as programmer-defined names.

T A B L E 9.1				
Reserved Words in Java	abstract	double	int	super
	boolean	else	interface	switch
	break	extends	long	synchronized
	byte	final	native	this
	case	finally	new	throw
	catch	float	package	throws
	char	for	private	transient
	class	goto	protected	try
	const	if	public	void
	continue	implements	return	volatile
	default	import	short	while
	do	instanceof	static	

Java supports a rich set of predefined operators. Most of these operators are taken from the C/C++ language. Table 9.2 shows a list of the Java operators in the order of their highest precedence. That is, operators listed earlier in the table are evaluated before operators listed later in the table.

T A B L E 9.2	LEVEL	OPERATOR TYPE	OPERATOR
Java Operators and Their Precedence	1	Parentheses	()
	2	Postfix operators	[] . (params) expr++ expr--
	3	Prefix unary operators	+expr -expr ~expr !expr ++expr--expr

LEVEL	OPERATOR TYPE	OPERATOR
4	Creation or cast	new (type)expr
5	Multiplicative	* / %
6	Additive	+ -
7	Shift	<< >> >>>
8	Relational	< > >= <= instanceof
9	Equality	== !=
10	Bitwise AND	&
11	Bitwise XOR (EXCLUSIVE OR)	^
12	Bitwise OR	|
13	Logical AND	&&
14	Logical OR	||
15	Conditional	?:
16	Assignment	= += -= *= /= %= >>= <<= <<<= &= ^= |=

T A B L E   9 . 2

Java Operators and Their Precedence (continued)

The following is a Java code fragment that shows the use of some of these operators:

```
// This is a comment
/* Another type of comment */
int     x = 33;
int y, z;
z = y = x;
// The previous sets y to x, and then z to y.
// That is z, y, x have the value of 1.
z++;            // z is incremented and becomes 2.
++x;            // x is incremented and becomes 2
y = x++;
// y is set to 2 (value of x), and then x is incremented
// and becomes 3
z = x + y;
// z is set to 5
y = ++z;
```

```
// z is incremented and becomes 6, then
// y is set to this value and also becomes 6
boolean odd;
odd = (z % 2 == 1) ? true : false;
// This is the "?:" operator.
// z (set to 5) is divided by 2, and the remainder
// of 1 is obtained. This is the definition of % (modulus).
// 1 is then compared with 1 using the equality operator
(==).
// Because the values are equal, the first expression after
"?"
// is evaluated, and "odd" is set to this value. In this
case
// "odd" is set to true. If the expression before "?"
// evaluates to a false value, the expression after ":" is
// evaluated and "odd" is set to its value.
y += 3;
// This is the same as y = y + 3. Since y was 6, it is
// now set to 9.
x -= 3;
// This is the same as x = x - 3. Since x was 3, it is
// now set to 0.
y = 5 << 1;
// This is the left shift operator
// Bit value of 5 is shifted left by 1. Shifting a positive
// number left by 1 is equivalent to multiplying it by 2.
So
// value of y is set to 10.
y = y > 1;
// This is the right shift operator
// Bit value of 5 is shifted right by 1. Shifting a
positive
// number right by 1 is equivalent to dividing it by 2 and
// ignoring the remainder. So value of y is set to 5.
// You could also write the previous statement as the
following:
//        y >= 1;
```

Understanding Java Control Statements

In addition to the assignment statement used in the previous example, Java supports a number of other statement types, such as the following:

- ► block statement

- ► if statement

- ► switch statement

- ► while statement

- ► for statement

- ► do while statement

- ► break statement

- ► continue statement

Block statement

A *block statement* is a grouping of statements within { } brackets. When you examine the main()method from the previous section, note the following general syntax:

```
public static void main(String args[])
{
    // statements
}
```

The block statement (grouping of statements) is shown in bold. The statements can be definitions of Java basic types, assignment, control flow, or even another block statement. A block statement can occur wherever a statement can occur in a Java program. A block statement is also called a *compound statement*.

Variables defined in a block statement have a scope that is confined to the end of the block statement. Unless the reserved word static is used in the definition of a variable, the variable is transient and exists only while the block is being executed. Consider the following code fragment:

```
int     a = 33;
int     b = 44;
{
  int    a;
  a = -99;
  System.out.println("a is set to " + a);
  // The "+" operator for strings is a concatenate operator
  // The value of "a" is set to -99 and not 33.
  // The variable "a" refers to the innermost "a".
  System.out.println("b is set to " + b);
  // The "+" operator for strings is a concatenate operator
  // The value of "b" is set to 44. The variable "b"
      // refers to the outermost "b".

}
System.out.println("a is set to " + a);
// The value of "a" is set to 33 and not -99
// The variable "a" refers to the outermost "a".
System.out.println("b is set to " + b);
// The value of "b" is set to 44. The variable "b"
// refers to the outermost "b".
```

The comments in the previous listing illustrate the meaning of the scope of the variables defined in a block statement.

The if statement

The if statement is used to perform a conditional flow of execution. In the if statement, a Boolean expression is evaluated. If the result of the Boolean expression is true, the "then" group of statements is executed; if the result is false, the "else" of statements is executed. The following illustrates the general syntax of the if statement:

```
if  (BooleanExpression)
    then-statement
[else
    else-statement]
```

The *BooleanExpression* is any Boolean expression. The *then-statement* is any legal Java statement, including the block statement, and is executed if *BooleanExpression* evaluates to `true`. Similarly, the *else-statement* is any legal Java statement including the block statement, and is executed if *BooleanExpression* evaluates to `false`. The brackets [ ] around the `else` part are metacharacters that indicate that the `else` part is optional. These metacharacters are not part of the syntax of the if statement.

The following are examples of if statements. The comments in the code explain the behavior of the `if` statement:

```
// if statement with a single then statement
int x = 108;
int y;
if (x > 0)
    y = -x;    // Because x > 0, y is set to -108
int    z;
if (y < 0)
    z = y + 5; // Because y < 0, z is set to -103
else
    z = y - 5; // Not executed
if (x + y + z > 0)
{
    // The then-statement is a block statement.
    // Because x + y + z is negative, this is not
    // executed.
    x -= 3;
    y -= 3;
    z -= 3;
}
else
{
    // The else-statement is a block statement.
    // Because x + y + z is negative, this is executed.
    x += 3;    // x is 111
    y += 3;    // y is -105
    z += 3;    // z is -100
}
```

Suppose that if the Boolean expression in the if statement evaluates to false, you must execute another if statement. You can code this type of if statement by using the else if statement. Here is an example:

```
if (x == 1)
{
    x -= 3;
}
else if (x == 2)
{
    x += 5;
} // end if
```

In the previous example, you want to execute different statements when the value of x is 1 or 2. In general, there are situations when you want to execute a multiway decision. The following is the general syntax of coding this multiway decision by using an if statement:

```
if (BooleanExpression1 )
    statement1
else if (BooleanExpression2 )
    statement2
else it (BooleanExpression3 )
    statement3

    ...

else if (BooleanExpressionN )
    statementN
[else
    statement-last]
```

The expressions *BooleanExpression1*, *BooleanExpression2*, and so on, are evaluated in the order in which they occur in the if statement. If any of the Boolean expressions evaluates to true, the corresponding statement is executed. Then execution transfers to the end of the if statement and the remaining Boolean expressions and statements are not evaluated. The *statementN* can be any statement including the block statement. The optional else part at the end of the multiway if, is executed only if all other Boolean expressions evaluate to false. Therefore, the else part is used to handle the default code in *statement-last*, if no other conditions (Boolean expressions) are satisfied. If there is no default code, you can omit the last `else` part.

The `switch` statement

A `switch` statement is a special multiway decision statement. The `switch` statement evaluates an expression and executes a group of statements that are labeled by the expression value. The following is the general form of a `switch` statement:

```
switch (expression)
{
  case const1:
        {statement;}
  case const2:
        {statement;}

        . . .
  case constN:
        {statement;}
  [default:
        {statement;}]
}
```

After *expression* is evaluated, it is checked to see if it matches any of the constant values *constN* on the `case` label. If the expression matches the constant `case` value, the group of *statements* listed under it as {*statement;*} are executed. The {} around statement are meant as metacharacters indicating zero or more occurrences of a Java statement, and not meant as the characters for a block statement.

At the end of the execution of the last statement in the `case` statement group, execution continues on to the statements for the next `case` label, *unless* a `break` statement is encountered. When a `break` statement is encountered, execution of further statements in the `switch` statement is terminated, and the control is passed to the end of the `switch` statement. The `break` statement is used to exit to the end of the `switch` statement. Execution will *fall through* to the next `case` label, unless you have a `break` statement.

The `default` label and statements are optional. It is used to catch the situation where the expression value does not match any of the `case` labels. If there is no default action to perform, you do not have to enter any statements for the `default` label.

The case labels and default label can occur in any order, but the case labels must all have different values. Here is an example of a switch statement:

```
int     x = 20;
int     y = -10;
int     z = 30;
// Statements initializing x, y, and z.
switch (x+y) // x + y is 10
{
    case 10: // Matched
           y++;     // y is incremented to -9
    case 20: // Execution drops to this
            // because there is no break in previous
            // case label.
        z *= 2; // z is multiplied by 2, and set to 60
        break; // break statement causes execution to
            // go to end of switch statement

    case 30: // Not executed.
        z += y; // Not executed.
        break;   // Not executed.
        default:  // Not executed.
        y = x + z; // Not executed.
        break;   // Not executed.
} // end switch
```

The while statement

The while statement is used for creating a loop. Most programs must perform some form of repeated action, and the while statement provides a solution for performing this repeated action. The general syntax of the while statement is as follows:

```
while (BooleanExpression)
    statement
```

The *BooleanExpression* is evaluated at the beginning of each loop execution. If this expression evaluates to a true, the *statement* is executed. This *statement* is any Java statement, including the block statement. At the end of the *statement* execution, control is transferred to the top of the loop where *BooleanExpression* is evaluated again. If the *BooleanExpression* evaluates to `true`, the *statement* is executed again. As long as the *BooleanExpression* evaluates to `true`, the *statement* is executed, and this implements a loop. The loop terminates only when *BooleanExpression* evaluates to a `false`. When the loop terminates, control is transferred to the end of the while loop. The following is an example of a `while` statement:

```
int    x = 0;
while (x++ <= 33)
{
    double y, z;
    // The Math Java package is defined in
    // java.lang.
    y = Math.sqrt((double)x);// x is converted to double
first.
    z = Math.atan((double)x);// x is converted to double
first.
    System.out.print("x = "+x);
    System.out.print("sqrt("+x+") = "+y);
    System.out.print("atan("+x+") = "+z);
} // end while
```

This `while` statement will execute until the expression x++ < 33 becomes `false`. This will happen when the value of x before the postfix increment is 34. Within the while loop the value of x will range from 1 to 33. The loop will successively take the square root of x and its arc-tangent value and display the results. Note that, before performing the mathematical operation, the value of x is converted to a double floating-point value. This is because the Math functions expect to be passed a double value. Unlike Perl, Java enforces strict type checking. Between numeric types you can convert one data type to another by using the following syntax:

`(newDataType) expression`

Here *newDataType* is the new data type to convert the *expression* value to.

The `for` statement

The `for` statement also implements a loop. However, unlike the while statement, the `for` statement contains specific constructs for a loop variable initialization, loop test condition, and loop variable change. The general syntax of the `for` statement is as follows:

```
for (InitStmt BooleanExpr; IncrExpr)
    statement
```

Before the start of the loop, the *InitStmt* is executed. This initial statement could be any statement. It is typically an assignment statement that initializes the value of a loop variable that is used to control the execution of the loop. Here are some examples of these assignment statements.

The *InitStmt* is evaluated just once, when the `for` loop is executed. After the *InitStmt* is evaluated, the *BooleanExpr* is evaluated. If the evaluation yields a `true` value, the *statement* is executed. If it yields a `false` value, the `for` loop is terminated and execution proceeds with the next statement after the `for` loop. The *statement* can be any statement, including a block statement. At the end of *statement* execution, the *IncrExpr* is evaluated. The *IncrExpr* is used typically to change the value of the loop variable that was set up in the *InitStmt*. After the *IncrExpr* has been evaluated, the control is transferred to the top of the loop, and *BooleanExpr* is evaluated again. It is important to realize that *InitStmt* is outside the loop, just before the loop begins.

The `for` loop is actually equivalent to the following `while` statement:

```
{
    InitStmt
    while (BooleanExpr)
    {
        statement
        IncrExpr;
    }
}
```

The following is an example of a `for` statement:

```
long decreeStrength = 0;
// This is an example of initializing an array
int PeopleArray[] = { 20, 21, 30, 25,
                      26, 24, 34, 12,
                      40, 50, 60, 33};
// for loop executes 12 times
for (int hours = 0; hours < 12; hours++)
```

```
{
        int N;
        // Example of accessing an array element value.
        N = PeopleArray[hours];
        decreeStrength += N*N;
}
```

The do while statement

The do while statement is yet another type of loop statement. In the while and for statements, the Boolean test is performed at the top of the loop. In the do while statement, the Boolean test is performed at the *end* of the loop. The general syntax of the do while statement is as follows:

```
do
    statement
while  (BooleanExpr);
```

The *statement* can be any Java statement, including the block statement. The *BooleanExpr* is the test condition for the loop. The *statement* is executed first. Next, the Boolean expression, *BooleanExpr*, is evaluated. If this evaluates to true, control is transferred to the top of the loop. If *BooleanExpr* evaluates to false, the loop is terminated and control is transferred to the end of the loop.

The following example shows the use of a do while statement:

```
int      x = 0;
int      xmax = 100
System.out.println("Table of exponent values\n")
do
{
        double y;
        y = Math.exp((double)x);
        System.out.println("texp("+x+") =\t"+y);
} while (x++ < xmax);
```

The do while statement is used less frequently than the while and for loop statements. It is primarily useful in situations where the statement in the loop must be executed at least once, regardless of the Boolean test condition.

The break **statement**

You have already seen how the break statement can be used to exit out of a switch statement. The break statement can be used to exit any block, not just a switch statement. A break statement is typically used in a for, while, or do while loop to exit the innermost loop. Thus, if you have nested loops, a break statement in any loop will only exit the innermost loop in which the break statement occurs.

The following is the general syntax of the break statement:

```
break [label];
```

The label is optional. Without the label, the innermost enclosing block is exited. You can use the label to break out of several nested loops.

The continue **statement**

The continue statement is used inside a loop to skip the remaining statements in the loop, and go to the top of the loop. At the top of the loop, the Boolean expressions (if any) are evaluated and the remainder of the loop execution continues. The continue statement is used to skip the current iteration of the loop, and go on to the next iteration. If a continue statement is executed in a while statement, the Boolean expression at the top of the loop is evaluated next. If a continue statement is executed in a do while statement, the Boolean expression at the bottom of the loop is evaluated next. If a continue statement is executed inside a for loop, the control is transferred to the increment expression (*incrExpr*).

The syntax of the continue statement is the reserved word continue on a line by itself with an optional label:

```
continue [label];
```

When the label is used, the loop will continue to the loop that has the label.

Understanding Classes

In the example of the dispmsg program to display a text message, the Java main() method was embedded inside a class. In Java, you cannot define a method without placing it in the class construct. So, what is a Java class?

A Java *class* is used to describe a Java object. *Objects* are collections of data elements, and methods that operate on the data elements. The Java class has the following syntax:

```
class classname
{
  // class variable definitions
  // class methods
}
```

Class variable definitions can occur anywhere inside the class, but must be outside the methods. Variables defined within the methods are distinct from class variables and are called *local variables*.

Class methods can occur anywhere inside the class. Class methods cannot be nested. That is, class methods cannot have embedded in them the definition of another class method.

Consider the following example of a class definition:

```
class Retreat
{
   int    nAscendedMasters;
   int    nCandidates;
   int    rooms;
   String missionStmt;
   boolean missionSet;
   void setMission(String stmt)
   {
      inti, j; // Local variables

      missionStmt = stmt;
      missionSet = true;


   }
}
```

The previous definition of the class `Retreat` contains five variable definitions: `nAscendedMasters`, `nCandidates`, `rooms`, `missionStmt`, and `missionSet`. These variables are called *class instance variables*. The scope of these class instance variables is from the point of definition to the end of that class. If you compare how the class instance variables are declared and defined with how the local variables are defined in a method, you will see no difference in their syntax. The difference between class instance variables and local variables is the location in which they are placed. Class instance variables are in the class definition, but outside the class methods. Local variables are defined inside the method.

The class instance variable `missionStmt` defines the string object. In Java, string variables are usually represented using the predefined Java class called `String`. The `String` class has a number of predefined methods associated with it that can be used for manipulating the string object and its value.

To declare an object of the class `Retreat`, you can use the following:

```
Retreat darjeeling;
Retreat caveOfLight;
```

These statements define two instances of the `Retreat` class (the objects `darjeeling` and `caveOfLight`). The class instance variables defined for these objects are associated with an instance of an object. The class instance variables are referenced by using the following syntax:

```
instanceobject.variablename
```

The *instanceobject* is the name of the class object (such as `darjeeling` or `caveOfLight`). The *variablename* is the name of the class instance variable defined inside the class. The following are examples of referencing class instance variables:

```
darjeeling.nCandidates
caveOfLight.nCandidates
darjeeling.missionStmt
caveOfLight.missionStmt
```

The class instance variables `darjeeling.nCandidates` and `caveOfLight.nCandidates` have values that are specific to each object instance. The class instance variables occupy different memory and can have different values. For example, `darjeeling.nCandidates` can be set to a value of 33000, and `caveOfLight.nCandidates` can be set to a value of 12000.

Class-wide variables

Class instance variables for separate objects, and have a separate existence. On the other hand, a *class variable* or a *class-wide variable* is common for all class instances. These class variables are preceded with the reserved word static:

```
static type variable = [initialize_value];
```

Suppose that you want to keep track of the total number of times all of the "retreats" defined by the Retreat class have been visited. You cannot effectively use instance variables to keep track of these values, because instance variables are defined for a particular class instance only, and you need global counters for all class instances.

Consider an extension to the class Retreat:

```
class Retreat
{
   // class instance variables
   int    nAscendedMasters;
   int    nCandidates;
   int    rooms;
   String missionStmt;
   boolean missionSet;
   // Class variable
   static long visitors = 0;
   void setMission(String stmt)
   {
       inti, j; // Local variables

       missionStmt = stmt;
       missionSet = true;
   }
}
```

The variable visitors is a class variable because it is preceded by the reserved word static. Its value is initially set to 0, and this variable is used to track the number of visitors. Because the static variable is common to all instances of the class (that is, all class instances refer to the same memory location when accessing the class variable), the following syntax is used to refer to class variables:

classname.variablename

Therefore, to reference the class variable `visitors`, you must use the following syntax:

`Retreat.visitors`

Because the data area storage for class variables is the same for all class instances, changing a class variable will change it for all class instances.

Class constants

Java allows you to define symbolic constants or named constants that are called *class constants*. These can be referred to by an identifier using the following syntax:

`final` *type variable* `=` *initialize_value*`;`

The class constant definition is similar to a class variable definition with the exception of the reserved word `final` preceding the definition. The reserved word `final` indicates that the value assigned by *initialize_value* is the final value (constant value), and it cannot be changed. Any attempt to change the value of the class constant will generate a syntax error when the program is compiled. Thus, `PI` could be defined as follows:

`final double PI = 3.1415926536;`

Following is an example of the use of class constants:

```
class ConstExample
{
   final long MAX_VISITORS = 10000000000;
   public void initiation()
   {
        // The following defines an array of integers
        // of size MAX_VISITORS. The array index
        // always starts from 0. In this example, the
        // maximum index is MAX_VISITORS-1. The new
        // operator is used to allocate space for the
        // array.
        int[] evals = new int[MAX_VISITORS];
        // The following loop initializes the
        // array evals to a zero value.
```

```
       for (int x = 0; x < MAX_VISITORS; x++)
       {
             evals[x] = 0;
       } // end for
  } // end initiation
} // end ConstExample
```

Implementing class methods

Most of the logic for classes is contained in the class methods. Class variables are also important to define because they describe the data structures used in the class methods, but the behavior of the class is contained in the class methods. When you implement classes, you will spend most of the time defining the methods and implementing their logic.

The following is the general syntax of a class method:

```
qualifiers return_type methodname( type1 param1, type2
param2, ... )
{
  ...
}
```

The *qualifiers* are reserved words such as `public`, `static`, and so on. The *qualifiers* are optional, and control how the method is used or accessed by other Java program code. The *qualifiers* value of `public`, `private`, or `protected` control access to the method or class variables:

- ▸ If the method/variable is declared with a `public` keyword, it can be accessed by any Java program within the same file or another file.

- ▸ If the method/variable is declared with a `private` keyword, it can be accessed only by other methods in the same class.

- ▸ If the method/variable is declared with a `protected` keyword it can be accessed only by any subclasses that derive from this class, and all classes in the same package as the declaring class. The last includes the declaring class itself.

CHAPTER 9

NOVELL'S GUIDE TO CREATING INTRANETWARE INTRANETS

▸ If the method/variable is declared with both `private` and `protected` keywords it can be accessed only by other methods in the same class, and any subclasses that derive from this class.

▸ If the method/variable does not have `private`, `protected`, or `public` keyword, it is said to have a default access method. In the default access method, the method/variable can be accessed only by other methods in the same class, and any classes or subclasses in the same package.

The *return_type* is the data type of the value returned by the method. The *return_type* can be a Java basic type (such as `int`, `char`, `float`, and so on), or it can be a class name, or the reserved word `void`. If the reserved word `void` is used, it indicates that no value is returned by the method.

If the method must return an array of values (such as an array of integers), it can be written in either of the following forms:

```
int[] methodname(parameters)
{
    ...
}
```

or

```
int methodname(parameters)[]
{
    ...
}
```

The first method is more intuitive and easier to understand. For these reasons, it is the preferred form.

If a *return_type* is not `void`, you must have at least one `return` statement of the following type:

```
return expression;
```

The data type of the `return` expression must match the *return_type* of the method. If the *return_type* is `void`, you do not have to use a `return` statement. The method will exit when its last statement is executed. If you need to terminate a `void` type method before its last statement, you can use the `return` statement without the expression:

```
return;
```

The parameters are optional and are used to pass data to the method. If there are no parameters for the method, you write the method with an empty list of parentheses ():

```
void methodname()
{
  ...
}
```

The parameter list is a set of variable declarations separated by commas. Writing these parameters is similar to writing class variables or local variables, except that you must use commas to separate them, instead of semicolons. The parameters act as place-holders for the actual parameter value that is passed to the method. The parameters to the method are also called *arguments*. The parameters are also treated as local variables inside the body of the method. Parameters are passed by value. In Java, objects are internally represented by reference (pointer) values. So, when an object is passed, its reference or address is passed by value. This allows object references to be used to access the object whose name was passed inside the class method.

The body of the method can contain any valid statement and expressions such as variable and object definitions, assignment statements, and conditional statements such as `for`, `while`, `do while`, `if`, `switch`, and so on.

The *methodname* is the name of the method and is any valid Java identifier. An *identifier* in Java can be a sequence of unicode characters of *any* length. There are some limitations on the characters you can use to create the identifier. Methods within a class can call each other by using the method name, followed by a list of argument values that match the number and type of parameters for the method being called. Java code that is outside the class, in another method, must use an object name or class name reference for calling the method, as shown here:

```
reference.methodname(parameters);
```

The *reference* is the object name or class name (for static methods). The *methodname* is the name of the method that is being called, and *parameters* is a list of argument values with which the method is being called.

Class constructors and use of this

Class constructors are special methods for classes whose primary purpose is to build an instance of the class. As part of the instantiation of a class, class instance variables and class variables may have to be initialized. The operator `new` is used to allocate space for the object being built. In Java, objects that have been allocated space are not explicitly freed. The Java run time automatically reclaims space for objects that are no longer in use. This process of reclaiming memory space is called *garbage collection*, and it is automatic in Java.

The following shows the general syntax of a class constructor method:

```
qualifiers classname (parameters)
{
}
```

The name of the constructor is the same as the class name. The *parameters* are similar to that used for other methods and are optional. The *qualifiers* can control access to the constructor and are usually reserved words such as `public` or `private`. The use of `private` prohibits the call of the constructor, and hence the instantiation of the class, from outside the class.

An important difference that you may note between constructors and other class methods is the absence of the return type. You may think that because constructors do not have a return type, you can use a return type of `void`. However, this is not allowed by the language.

Java constructor methods are always invoked with the use of the new operator:

```
new  classname(parameters);
```

The *parameters* must match (in number and type) one of the constructors defined for the class. You can overload Java constructor methods. This means that you can define several constructor methods for a class that differ in the parameter number and type. In fact, it is typical to define several constructors for a method. Consider Listing 9.1, which shows a class that defines two constructors.

L I S T I N G   9.1

Class Defining Two Constructors

```
class Retreat
```

```
{
  // class instance variables
  int    nAscendedMasters;
  int    nCandidates;
  int    rooms;
  String missionStmt;
  boolean missionSet;
  // Class variable
  static long visitors = 0;
  void setMission(String stmt)
  {
     missionStmt = stmt;
     missionSet = true;
  }
  // The following is a constructor method
  public Retreat(int ascendedMasters,
        int candidates, int rms, String mstmt)
  {
     // The left hand side of the following assignment
     // statements are class instance variables.
     // The right hand side are the parameter values
     // that were passed to the constructor method.
     nAscendedMasters = ascendedMasters;
     nCandidates = candidates;
     rooms = rms;
     // Note that the call is made to a method
     // in the same class. Such methods are called
     // helper methods.
     setMission(mstmt);

  }
  // Another constructor
  public Retreat(int ascendedMasters,
        int candidates)
  {
        // This calls the previous constructor
```

```
                // with default values for the last
                // two arguments.
                Retreat(ascendedMasters, candidates,
                        1000, "Do Good");


        }


}
// The following is an example of a class in the same
// package that uses the previous class definition.
class Initiate
{
    public static void main(String[] args)
    {
        Retreat az;  // At this point az is set
        // to null because it has
        // not been built as yet.
        // At this point az is set to the object
        // constructed by calling the constructor
        // for Retreat
        az = new Retreat(1000, 10000, 50000,
                    "Care for children");
        // The following instantiates the object dj and
        // assigns it the value constructed by calling the
        // Retreat constructor.
        Retreat dj = new Retreat(2000, 20000, 10000,
                    "Will of God");
        // The following creates a new object brandnew
        // by calling the second Retreat constructor.
        Retreat brandnew = new Retreat(100, 300);


    }
}
```

Java uses a special reserved word called this to refer to the instance of the object. Recall that object methods are invoked using the following syntax:

objectname.methodname(parameters)

The reference to the object itself is passed as an implicit parameter along with the other parameters to the object. This enables the method to refer to the object for which the method was invoked by this. In fact, the class definition of Retreat in Listing 9.1 is the same as the following where the use of this is made explicit. These places where this is used explicitly and was left out in the original definition of Retreat are highlighted in bold.

```java
class Retreat
{
  // class instance variables
  int   nAscendedMasters;
  int   nCandidates;
  int   rooms;
  String missionStmt;
  boolean missionSet;
  // Class variable
  static long visitors = 0;
  void setMission(String stmt)
  {
    // References to class instance variables
    // are with respect to the object this.
    this.missionStmt = stmt;
    this.missionSet = true;
  }
  // The following is a constructor method
  public Retreat(int ascendedMasters,
      int candidates, int rms, String mstmt)
  {
    // The left hand side of the following assignment
    // statements are class instance variables.
    // The right hand side are the parameter values
    // that were passed to the constructor method.
    // References to class instance variables
    // are with respect to the object this.
    this.nAscendedMasters = ascendedMasters;
```

```
            this.nCandidates = candidates;
            this.rooms = rms;
            // Note that the call is made to a method
            // in the same class. Such methods are called
            // helper methods.
            // References to class instance variables
            // are with respect to the object this.
            this.setMission(mstmt);

    }
    // Another constructor
    public Retreat(int ascendedMasters,
    int candidates)
    {
        // This calls the previous constructor
        // with default values for the last
        // two arguments.
        // When this is used as a method name, it
        // is a reference to the class name
        // constructor.
        this(ascendedMasters, candidates,
             1000, "Do Good");

    }


    }
```

Note that when `this` is used as a method name, it is a reference to the class name constructor. Use of `this` is also useful when you want to keep the parameter names for initializing class instance variables the same as the class instance variable names. For example, you could have written the constructor for the Retreat class as follows:

```
public Retreat(int nAscendedMasters,
    int nCandidates, int rooms, String missionStmt)
    {
    // The left hand side of the following assignment
    // statements are class instance variables.
```

```
// The right hand side are the parameter values
// that were passed to the constructor method.
   this.nAscendedMasters = nAscendedMasters;
this.nCandidates = nCandidates;
        this.rooms = rooms;
// Note that the call is made to a method
// in the same class. Such methods are called
// helper methods.
setMission(missionStmt);


}
```

Notice that the parameter names are the same as the class instance variable names. In this case, without the use of this, you would not be able to distinguish between the class instance and parameter names.

Understanding Java Inheritance

Like many object-oriented languages, Java provides the concept of inheritance. *Inheritance* enables you to extend the definition of an existing class by adding code that provides new enhancements and features, without modifying the original definition. This capability leads to reusable code. Consider the following example of a class that implements a circle geometrical object, which will be extended later:

```
class Circle
{
  // The class instance variables are being declared
  // protected. This means that these variables can
  // be used by subclasses of the Circle class.
  protected int xcoord; // X-coordinate of center of circle.
  protected int ycoord; // Y-coordinate of center of circle.
  protected int radius; // Radius of circle.
  // Constructor
  public Circle(int xcoord, int ycoord, int radius)
  {
      this.xcoord = xcoord;
      this.ycoord = ycoord;
```

```
        this.radius = radius;
  }
  draw()
  {
        // Implements the draw method that causes
        // the circle to be drawn.
  }
}
```

When the draw method is called for the circle object, it causes the circle to be drawn. Here is an example of how this class could be used:

```
Circle cobj = new Circle(100, 100, 50);
// Previous statement defines an instance of class Circle
// named cobj. Notice how the constructor is called to
create
// the circle and initialize the cobj to its value.
cobj.draw();
// The previous causes the circle to be drawn.
```

Now suppose that you want to create the concept of a geometrical disk that you can paint with different colors. You can reuse the code for Circle by extending it as shown in Listing 9.2. Read the comments carefully to understand what happens when you extend a class.

LISTING 9.2

Geometric Circle

```
// The Java import statement imports the definition of
// the Color class that is found in the java.awt package.
// If you used the following:
//      import java.awt.*;
// all class definitions in package java.awt become
// known to this program.
import java.awt.Color;
// The Disk class extends the Circle class
// The Disk class is called the parent or superclass.
// The Circle class is called the child class or subclass.
```

```
class Disk extends Circle
{
    // All the non-private class variables and methods
    // of Class are implicitly placed here. This is
    // called inheriting the class variables and methods.
    // This means that you could access the class variables
    // xcoord, ycoord, radius and methods draw(), Circle()
    // in the class Circle as if they were declared here.
    // But you don't have to repeat these definitions
because
    // you are extending the Circle class.
    // The following class instance variable holds the
color
    // of the object. Because it is defined as private, it
    // cannot be referenced directly from outside the
class.
    private Color diskColor;
    // Constructor method. Pay attention to see how we
    // call the parent class constructor.
    public Disk(int xcoord, int ycoord, int radius, Color
dc)
    {
      // Use of the super reserved word refers to the
      // parent class. Here we are calling the constructor
      // for the parent class, Circle. Why?
      // Because, the Disk class "contains" the definition
      // of the Circle class. This came about because we
        // extended the Disk class from the Color class.
This
      // is also called "deriving" from the Color class.
      // When the parent class constructor is called, the
      // circle definition is built.   We need the circle
      // object to be built because the Disk is a Circle
      // with the additional attribute of a color.
      super(xcoord, ycoord, radius);
```

```
    // This sets the disk color, diskColor, defined
    // in the Disk class.
    setColor(dc);
}
// This allows the disk color to be set by
// calling the method. Note that diskColor is
// defined as private. So this is the only way of
// setting the color after the disk has already
// been built.
public void setColor(Color diskColor)
{
    this.diskColor = diskColor;

}
// This fetches the current disk color. Because
// diskColor is defined as private, this is the only
// way of getting the current disk color.
public Color getColor()
{
    return diskColor;

}
// This method paints the disk. Implementation
// details are not shown.
paint()
{
    draw();
    // Now paint the circle with the disk color
    //    :

}
}
```

In Java, all objects are ultimately inherited from Object. The Object class is the root class of all Java objects. In Listing 9.2, the Circle class is inherited from the Object class, even though this inheritance was not explicitly specified.

Therefore, the following class definition which explicitly extends the `Object` class is equivalent to the previous definition of the `Circle` class:

```
class Circle extends Object
{
    // The class instance variables are being declared
    // protected. This means that these variables can
    // be used by subclasses of the Circle class.
    protected int xcoord; // X-coordinate of center of circle.
    protected int ycoord; // Y-coordinate of center of circle.
    protected int radius; // Radius of circle.
    // Constructor
    public Circle(int xcoord, int ycoord, int radius)
    {
        this.xcoord = xcoord;
        this.ycoord = ycoord;
        this.radius = radius;
    }
    draw()
    {
        // Implements the draw method that causes
        // the circle to be drawn.
    }
}
```

Java Applets for the Web Client

The `dispmsg` program presented in earlier sections of this chapter is an example of a Java application. A Java applet is a Java application that runs in the context of a Web browser. Many Java applets are already available from many Internet sites. You can use these applets in your Web pages without knowing how the applets are written. What you do need to know, however, is how to specify the path name to the applets in your Web page. You can also learn to write your own applets to perform specific tasks.

Java applets are typically run from inside a Web browser, as opposed to running as standalone programs. Many Java development environments provide the Applet Viewer program that you can use to run Java applets for debugging and testing purposes. Both the Web browser and the Applet Viewer are GUI programs. In order to display or paint data within the display of these programs, the applet must use Java classes specifically designed for displaying information in a GUI environment.

The size of Java applet code is generally a few kilobytes, and can be downloaded relatively quickly through the Internet/intranet to run inside a Web browser (see Figure 9.5). The location of the applet code is embedded in an HTML file or document. Recall from discussions in previous chapters that HTML documents contain instructions that the Web browsers interpret in order to render the HTML document graphically inside the display of the Web browser.

The applets can enhance the rendering of HTML documents in the Web browser by

- Providing animation

- Accepting interactive input from the user

- Displaying sound (audio clips) with animating images

- Providing graphical elements such as scrolling bars, text area, buttons, and so on

Applets can take advantage of built-in features of the Web browser. For example, applets can use the Web browser's decoder programs for image files such as GIF and JPEG files. By using the Web browser's methods to decode the images, the applet code is insulated against changes in the graphic image format.

The Novell SDK that you can install on the IntranetWare server comes with a number of Java applet samples. By default these applets are placed in the SYS:JAVA\DEMOS directory. Java applets require a GUI environment. In order to run these applets directly from the IntranetWare server console, you must enable the server console for running GUI applications. You can study these Java applets to understand how Java applets can be written.

▶ • ◀

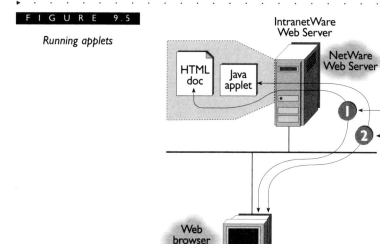

FIGURE 9.5

Running applets

Enabling the IntraNetWare Server to Run GUI Applications

Before enabling the IntranetWare server to run Java applets and GUI programs that use Java's Alternate Windowing Toolkit (AWT) APIs, you must have the JAVA.NLM loaded, and long-name file support enabled (that is, by using the LONG.NAM name space module). Additionally you must have a supported VGA card/monitor and a mouse. To see the list of supported VGA cards, consult the Novell SDK documentation.

Currently, the GUI interface is based on X-Windows. The Novell implementation of the AWT uses a port of XFree86, which behaves much like XFree86 on other platforms. The XFree86 is available at `http://www.xfree86.org`. The memory requirements for running GUI Java applications is 64 MB.

You can run the SuperProbe utility (RSP.NCF) to automatically detect and configure most video/monitor hardware configuration combinations. If the SuperProbe utility fails to correctly autodetect your monitor and/or video card, or if you want more resolutions than SuperProbe assigned your video card, you can edit the configuration file by hand. If you run SuperProbe more than once, the `xf86conf` file (which contains the configuration information) will reset to its default state, thus removing any changes you made to your configuration.

The RSP.NCF file is, by default, placed in the SYS:JAVA\BIN directory and is run from the console. For your information, it runs the following NLM with the specified parameters:

```
load sys:\java\nwgfx\superpro -wr -pa -x11configpath
sys:\java\nwgfx\ -x11loadpath sys:\java\nwgfx\ -x11fvwm
fvwm2
```

Running RSP.NCF will produce two files:

▸ SYS:\JAVA\NWGFX\xf86conf-This is the configuration file for the graphical user interface.

▸ SYS:\JAVA\NWGFX\startx.ncf-This is the NCF file for starting the graphical user interface.

Samples of these files are shown in Listing 9.3. These are useful for debugging your video/monitor configuration and for understanding which NLMs and files are needed for running X-Windows on the server.

LISTING 9.3

xf86conf *Code and*
startx *Code*

```
XF86CONF file:
# xf86conf (x configuration) file generated by helius video
probe.
#
# Copyright (c) 1994 by The XFree86 Project, Inc.
#
# Permission is hereby granted, free of charge, to any
person obtaining a
# copy of this software and associated documentation files
(the "Software"),
# to deal in the Software without restriction, including
without limitation
# the rights to use, copy, modify, merge, publish,
distribute, sublicense,
# and/or sell copies of the Software, and to permit persons
```

to whom the
Software is furnished to do so, subject to the following
conditions:
#
The above copyright notice and this permission notice
shall be included in
all copies or substantial portions of the Software.
#
THE SOFTWARE IS PROVIDED "AS IS", WITHOUT WARRANTY OF ANY
KIND, EXPRESS OR
IMPLIED, INCLUDING BUT NOT LIMITED TO THE WARRANTIES OF
MERCHANTABILITY,
FITNESS FOR A PARTICULAR PURPOSE AND NONINFRINGEMENT. IN
NO EVENT SHALL
THE XFREE86 PROJECT BE LIABLE FOR ANY CLAIM, DAMAGES OR
OTHER LIABILITY,
WHETHER IN AN ACTION OF CONTRACT, TORT OR OTHERWISE,
ARISING FROM, OUT OF
OR IN CONNECTION WITH THE SOFTWARE OR THE USE OR OTHER
DEALINGS IN THE
SOFTWARE.
#
Except as contained in this notice, the name of the
XFree86 Project shall
not be used in advertising or otherwise to promote the
sale, use or other
dealings in this Software without prior written
authorization from the
XFree86 Project.
#
#
****
****
Refer to the XF86Config(4/5) man page for details about the
format of
this file.
#

```
****************************************************************
*********
#
****************************************************************
*********
# Files section.  This allows default font and rgb paths to
be set
#
****************************************************************
*********
Section "Files"
# The location of the RGB database.  Note, this is the name
of the
# file minus the extension (like ".txt" or ".db").  There is
normally
# no need to change the default.
#
#    <template path for video probe nlm >
     RgbPath     "sys:/java/nwgfx/rgb"
# Multiple FontPath entries are allowed (which are
concatenated together),
# as well as specifying multiple comma-separated entries in
one FontPath
# command (or a combination of both methods)
#
# If you don't have a floating point coprocessor and emacs,
Mosaic or other
# programs take long to start up, try moving the Type1 and
Speedo directory
# to the end of this list (or comment them out).
#
#    <template paths for video probe nlm >
     FontPath     "sys:/java/nwgfx/fonts/misc/"
     FontPath     "sys:/java/nwgfx/fonts/75dpi/"
EndSection
#
****************************************************************
```

```
********
# Server flags section.
#
****************************************************************
********


Section "ServerFlags"
# Uncomment this to cause a core dump at the spot where a
signal is
# received.  This may leave the console in an unusable
state, but may
# provide a better stack trace in the core dump to aid in
debugging
#      NoTrapSignals
# Uncomment this to disable the <Crtl><Alt><BS> server abort
sequence
# This allows clients to receive this key event.
#      DontZap
# Uncomment this to disable the <Crtl><Alt><KP_+>/<KP_->
mode switching
# sequences.  This allows clients to receive these key
events.
#      DontZoom
EndSection
#
****************************************************************
********
# Input devices
#
****************************************************************
********
#
****************************************************************
********
# Keyboard section
#
****************************************************************
```

```
********
Section "Keyboard"
    Protocol    "Standard"
# when using XQUEUE, comment out the above line, and
uncomment the
# following line
#    Protocol    "Xqueue"
    AutoRepeat    500 5
# Let the server do the NumLock processing.  This should
only be required
# when using pre-R6 clients
#    ServerNumLock
# Specifiy which keyboard LEDs can be user-controlled (eg,
with xset(1))
#    Xleds    1 2 3
# To set the LeftAlt to Meta, RightAlt key to ModeShift,
# RightCtl key to Compose, and ScrollLock key to ModeLock:
#    LeftAlt      Meta
#    RightAlt     ModeShift
#    RightCtl     Compose
#    ScrollLock   ModeLock
EndSection
#
****************************************************************
********
# Pointer section
#
****************************************************************
********
Section "Pointer"
# Pointer section configured by helius video probe.
    Protocol "PS/2"
    Device   "PS/2"
#    Protocol    "PS/2"
#    Device      "PS/2"
#    Protocol     "Microsoft"
```

```
#     Device        "COM1"
# When using XQUEUE, comment out the above two lines, and
uncomment
# the following line.
#     Protocol      "Xqueue"
# Baudrate and SampleRate are only for some Logitech mice
#     BaudRate      9600
#     SampleRate    150
# Emulate3Buttons is an option for 2-button Microsoft mice
# Emulate3Timeout is the timeout in milliseconds (default is
50ms)
     Emulate3Buttons
     Emulate3Timeout    50
# ChordMiddle is an option for some 3-button Logitech mice
#     ChordMiddle
EndSection
#
******************************************************************
*********
# Monitor section
#
******************************************************************
*********
# Any number of monitor sections may be present
Section "Monitor"
     Identifier   "Generic Multisync"
     VendorName   "Generic"
     ModelName    "Multisync"
# HorizSync is in kHz unless units are specified.
# HorizSync may be a comma separated list of discrete
values, or a
# comma separated list of ranges of values.
# NOTE: THE VALUES HERE ARE EXAMPLES ONLY.  REFER TO YOUR
MONITOR'S
# USER MANUAL FOR THE CORRECT NUMBERS.
#     HorizSync    30 - 38,46-50
```

```
    HorizSync    30-64              # multisync
#    HorizSync    31.5, 35.2    # multiple fixed sync
frequencies
#    HorizSync    15-25, 30-50  # multiple ranges of sync
frequencies

# VertRefresh is in Hz unless units are specified.
# VertRefresh may be a comma separated list of discrete
values, or a
# comma separated list of ranges of values.
# NOTE: THE VALUES HERE ARE EXAMPLES ONLY.  REFER TO YOUR
MONITOR'S
# USER MANUAL FOR THE CORRECT NUMBERS.
    VertRefresh 50-90
# Modes can be specified in two formats.  A compact one-line
format, or
# a multi-line format.
# These two are equivalent
#    ModeLine "1024x768i" 45 1024 1048 1208 1264 768 776
784 817 Interlace
#    Mode "1024x768i"
#        DotClock    45
#        HTimings    1024 1048 1208 1264
#        VTimings    768 776 784 817
#        Flags        "Interlace"
#    EndMode

# This is a set of standard mode timings. Modes that are
out of monitor spec
# are automatically deleted by the server (provided the
HorizSync and
# VertRefresh lines are correct), so there's no immediate
need to
# delete mode timings (unless particular mode timings don't
work on your
# monitor). With these modes, the best standard mode that
your monitor
```

```
# and video card can support for a given resolution is
automatically
# used.
# 640x400 @ 70 Hz, 31.5 kHz hsync
Modeline "640x400"      25.175 640   664   760   800    400   409
411   450
# 640x480 @ 60 Hz, 31.5 kHz hsync
Modeline "640x480"      25.175 640   664   760   800    480   491
493   525
# 800x600 @ 56 Hz, 35.15 kHz hsync
ModeLine "800x600"       36     800   824   896 1024    600
601   603   625
# 1024x768 @ 87 Hz interlaced, 35.5 kHz hsync
Modeline "1024x768"     44.9   1024 1048 1208 1264    768   776
784   817 Interlace
# 640x480 @ 72 Hz, 36.5 kHz hsync
Modeline "640x480"      31.5   640   680   720   864    480   488
491   521
# 800x600 @ 60 Hz, 37.8 kHz hsync
Modeline "800x600"       40     800   840   968 1056    600
601   605   628 +hsync +vsync
# 800x600 @ 72 Hz, 48.0 kHz hsync
Modeline "800x600"       50     800   856   976 1040    600
637   643   666 +hsync +vsync
# 1024x768 @ 60 Hz, 48.4 kHz hsync
Modeline "1024x768"      65     1024 1032 1176 1344    768   771
777   806 -hsync -vsync
# 1024x768 @ 70 Hz, 56.5 kHz hsync
Modeline "1024x768"      75     1024 1048 1184 1328    768   771
777   806 -hsync -vsync
# 1280x1024 @ 87 Hz interlaced, 51 kHz hsync
Modeline "1280x1024"     80     1280 1296 1512 1568    1024 1025
1037 1165 Interlace
# 1024x768 @ 76 Hz, 62.5 kHz hsync
Modeline "1024x768"      85     1024 1032 1152 1360    768   784
787   823
# 1280x1024 @ 61 Hz, 64.2 kHz hsync
```

```
Modeline "1280x1024"   110     1280 1328 1512 1712   1024 1025
1028 1054
# 1280x1024 @ 74 Hz, 78.85 kHz hsync
Modeline "1280x1024"   135     1280 1312 1456 1712   1024 1027
1030 1064
# 1280x1024 @ 76 Hz, 81.13 kHz hsync
Modeline "1280x1024"   135     1280 1312 1416 1664   1024 1027
1030 1064
# Low-res Doublescan modes
# If your chipset does not support doublescan, you get a
'squashed'
# resolution like 320x400.
# 320x200 @ 70 Hz, 31.5 kHz hsync, 8:5 aspect ratio
Modeline "320x200"     12.588 320   336   384   400   200   204
205   225 Doublescan
# 320x240 @ 60 Hz, 31.5 kHz hsync, 4:3 aspect ratio
Modeline "320x240"     12.588 320   336   384   400   240   245
246   262 Doublescan
# 320x240 @ 72 Hz, 36.5 kHz hsync
Modeline "320x240"     15.750 320   336   384   400   240   244
246   262 Doublescan
# 400x300 @ 56 Hz, 35.2 kHz hsync, 4:3 aspect ratio
ModeLine "400x300"     18      400   416   448   512   300
301   602   312 Doublescan
# 400x300 @ 60 Hz, 37.8 kHz hsync
Modeline "400x300"     20      400   416   480   528   300
301   303   314 Doublescan
# 400x300 @ 72 Hz, 48.0 kHz hsync
Modeline "400x300"     25      400   424   488   520   300
319   322   333 Doublescan
# 4802x300 @ 56 Hz, 35.2 kHz hsync, 8:5 aspect ratio
ModeLine "480x300"     21.656 480   496   536   616   300   301
302   312 Doublescan
# 480x300 @ 60 Hz, 37.8 kHz hsync
Modeline "480x300"     23.890 480   496   576   632   300   301
303   314 Doublescan
# 480x300 @ 63 Hz, 39.6 kHz hsync
```

```
Modeline "480x300"          25         480   496   576   632      300
301    303    314 Doublescan
# 480x300 @ 72 Hz, 48.0 kHz hsync
Modeline "480x300"          29.952 480  504   584   624      300   319
322    333 Doublescan
EndSection
#
****************************************************************
*********
# Graphics device section
#
****************************************************************
*********
# Any number of graphics device sections may be present
# Sample Device for accelerated server:
# Section "Device"
#      Identifier     "Actix GE32+ 2MB"
#      VendorName      "Actix"
#      BoardName      "GE32+"
#      Ramdac     "ATT20C490"
#      Dacspeed     110
#      Option     "dac_8_bit"
#      Clocks      25.0  28.0  40.0   0.0  50.0  77.0  36.0
45.0
#      Clocks     130.0 120.0  80.0  31.0 110.0  65.0  75.0
94.0
# EndSection
# Sample Device for Cirrus Logic chip:
#Section "Device"
#      Identifier  "Generic Cirrus Logic"
#      VendorName  "Generic"
#      BoardName   "Cirrus Logic"
#      VideoRam    1024
#      Insert Clocks lines here if appropriate
#EndSection
# Device configured by helius video probe:
```

```
Section "Device"
    Identifier     "ATI 88800GX vgawonder mach64"
    VideoRam     1024
EndSection
# Standard VGA Device:  /* default for vga16 */
Section "Device"
    Identifier     "Generic VGA"
    VendorName     "Unknown"
    BoardName      "Unknown"
    Chipset      "generic"
#     VideoRam     256
    Clocks     25.2 28.3
EndSection
#
****************************************************************
*********
# Screen sections
#
****************************************************************
*********
# The Colour SVGA server
#Section "Screen" helius video probe:
Section "Screen"
    Driver     "svga"
    Device     "ATI 88800GX vgawonder mach64"
    #Driver          "svga"
    # Use Device "Generic VGA" for Standard VGA 320x200x256
    #Device          "Generic VGA"
    #Device          "Generic Cirrus Logic"
    Monitor     "Generic Multisync"
    Subsection "Display"
        Depth          8
        # Omit the Modes line for the "Generic VGA" device
        Modes          "640x480"
        #Modes          "640x480" "800x600" "1024x768"
        #Modes          "640x480" "800x600" "1024x768"
```

```
"1280x1024"
        ViewPort     0 0
        # Use Virtual 320 200 for Generic VGA
        # Virtual      1152 900
    EndSubsection
    Subsection "Display"
        Depth        16
        Modes        "640x480" "800x600" "1024x768"
        ViewPort     0 0
        # Virtual     800 600
    EndSubsection
    Subsection "Display"
        Depth        32
        Modes        "640x400" "800x600"
        ViewPort     0 0
        # Virtual     640 400
    EndSubsection
EndSection
#Section "vga16" helius video probe:
# The 16-color VGA server
Section "Screen"
    Driver       "vga16"
    Device       "Generic VGA"
    Monitor      "Generic Multisync"
    Subsection "Display"
        Modes        "640x480" "800x600"
        ViewPort     0 0
        Virtual      800 600
    EndSubsection
EndSection
# The Mono server
Section "Screen"
    Driver       "vga2"
    Device       "Generic VGA"
    Monitor      "Generic Multisync"
    Subsection "Display"
```

```
          Modes          "640x480" "800x600"
          ViewPort       0 0
          Virtual        800 600
      EndSubsection
EndSection
# The accelerated servers (S3, Mach32, Mach8, 8514, P9000,
AGX, W32, Mach64)
#Section "Screen"
#     Driver       "accel"
#     Device       "Generic Cirrus Logic"
#     Monitor      "Generic Multisync"
#     Subsection "Display"
#         Depth         8
#         Modes         "640x480" "800x600" "1024x768"
"1280x1024"
#         ViewPort      0 0
#         # Virtual     1152 900
#     EndSubsection
#     Subsection "Display"
#         Depth         16
#         Modes         "640x480" "800x600" "1024x768"
#         ViewPort      0 0
#         Virtual       800 600
#     EndSubsection
#     Subsection "Display"
#         Depth         32
#         Modes         "640x400" "800x600"
#         ViewPort      0 0
#         Virtual       640 400
#     EndSubsection
#EndSection
# End helius video probe:
STARTX.NCF file:
load AIO
load AIOPS2
load sys:/java/nwgfx/xlib 127.0.0.1:0
```

```
load sys:/java/nwgfx/xfsvga -ac -xf86config
sys:/java/nwgfx/xf86conf -s 32767
load sys:/java/nwgfx/fvwm2 -f sys:/java/nwgfx/fvwm2/fvwm2rc
```

Note that if your server uses a Microsoft serial mouse instead of a PS/2 mouse, comment the values for the PS/2 mouse protocol and device in the `xf86conf` file:

```
# Protocol "PS/2"
# Device "PS/2"
```

As you examine the sample `xf86conf` file shown in Listing 9.3, you will see the configuration for the mouse drivers under the "Pointer section." You will notice that the default is set for a PS/2 mouse.

Next, enable the Microsoft mouse protocol and mouse device on the COM port by uncommenting the following lines:

```
Protocol "Microsoft"
Device "COM1"
```

Next, edit STARTX.NCF to use a serial mouse by loading the AICOMX mouse driver. For a serial mouse, add these lines to the beginning of STARTX.NCF:

```
load aio
load aiocomx
```

Delete the following line for the PS/2 mouse driver:

```
load aiops2
```

Next, use the following procedure to start the GUI interface.

1 • On the IntranetWare server console, type

```
startx
```

2 • To enable higher default resolution, edit SYS:\JAVA\NWGFX\xf86conf. Uncomment the line in the screen section for video modes up to 1024 x 768, and comment the line for the video mode of 640 x 480. The section with the uncommented line should look like this after editing:

```
#
**********************************************************
# Screen sections
```

```
    #
************************************************************
    # The Colour SVGA server
    #Section "Screen" helius video probe:
    Section "Screen"
        Driver      "svga"
        Device      "Cirrus Logic GD542x"
        #Driver      "svga"
        # Use Device "Generic VGA" for Standard VGA
320x200x256
        #Device      "Generic VGA"
        #Device      "Generic Cirrus Logic"
        Monitor     "Generic Multisync"
        Subsection "Display"
            Depth       8
            # Omit the Modes line for the "Generic VGA" device
            Modes       "1024x768" "640x480" "800x600"
            #Modes       "640x480"
```

Press one the following key combinations to cycle through screen resolutions.

```
<ctrl><alt><+>      To choose the next resolution in
xf86conf.
<ctrl><alt><->      To choose the previous resolution in
xf86conf.
```

If you have not enabled higher default resolutions for the AWT, cycling screen resolutions will have no effect.

3 • To stop the X-Windows interface, toggle to the NetWare console, and restart your server. A less drastic method of stopping the GUI interface is expected to become available in the future.

Tackling Security Concerns for Applets

Because applets are executed from within another program (such as a Web browser), they are not full-featured applications. Applets rely on the Web browser to perform a number of functions (such as the decoding of images). In addition, because of security concerns about downloading executable programs such as applets from an untrusted host, applets have limited file and network access.

As shown in Figure 9.5, applet code is downloaded from a host on the Internet/intranet, and the precompiled byte-code is executed within the Web browser running at the user's workstation. The byte-code interpreter is hardware-platform and operating-system specific, but the byte-code itself is platform independent. To further increase the security of the Java byte-code, a verification process is performed on the downloaded byte-code before it can be run. As part of the verification, all methods and variables referenced in the program are checked to see that they do not violate any Java language conventions. For example, methods and variables in Java are referenced by names. The verification process ensures that this is indeed so, and that the program is not accessing memory areas that may contain other applications or operating system code.

Applets have limited access to the local file system of the workstation on which they run. Generally, applets are not permitted to save files locally, or read files on the local disk. If applets were permitted to do this without any restrictions, a virus applet could alter your files, or even read sensitive information from files on your local disk, and distribute those files to unknown parties on the Internet/intranet. Applets cannot dynamically interact with libraries written for other languages. For example, they cannot load C/C++ libraries in memory and dynamically link to them. Java has the ability to statically link class methods with other language libraries, by declaring the method to be native. Because the code in other language libraries cannot be verified properly, native methods cannot be used in writing applets.

The Web browser may also place limitations on how an applet is run. The Web browser is regarded by the user as a trusted application, as it has access to the local file system. Applets that run in the browser are downloaded from untrusted hosts on the network, and are untrusted applications. In fact, the Web user may not make an explicit choice to run the applet. All that the user may have done is access a Web page, and the HTML document for the Web page (which contains a reference to an applet) will cause the applet to be automatically downloaded to the user's computer. Applets are also restricted to making network connections to the host from which they are downloaded. They cannot establish new connections to other computers on the network. Were an applet able to do so, it could send information to other computers on the network, and perform tasks such as impersonating a user by sending an e-mail on behalf of the user.

Using HTML to Access Java Applets

The following is an example HTML document that references a Java applet:

```
<HTML>
<HEAD>
<TITLE>A simple HelloWorld Applet</TITLE>
</HEAD>
<BODY>
<P>My first applet says:
<BR>
<APPLET CODE="appletURL" WIDTH=300, HEIGHT=300>
Cannot run the Java applet because your web browser is
not Java enabled. Upgrade to the Novell NetScape Navigator.
</APPLET>
</BODY>
</HTML>
```

By now, you should already be familiar with the HTML tags used in the previous HTML code listing. You will notice that there is a new <APPLET> . . . </APPLET> tag for specifying Java applets. The APPLET tag has the following general syntax:

```
<APPLET attributes>
</APPLET>
```

Any text placed between the <APPLET> and </APPLET> tags is ignored by a Java enabled browser. If the Web browser is not Java-enabled, it will ignore the <APPLET> and </APPLET> tags, which it does not understand. Instead, it will display the text between the <APPLET> and </APPLET> tags. This text, as in the previous example, can be used to inform the user that the Java applet cannot be run from the browser.

The *attributes* in the applet tag can contain a number of attribute specifications. In this example, only three attributes (CODE, WIDTH, and HEIGHT) are defined.

A number of other attributes can also be specified. These are discussed in later examples in this chapter.

The CODE="*URL*" attribute specifies the URL location of the applet code. This URL location specifies the file that contains the applet class. Note that this file contains the byte-code for the applet and must be specified using the ".class" extension. If the class file is in a different directory than the HTML file, you can use the CODEBASE="*directory*" attribute to specify the different directory.

The WIDTH and HEIGHT specify (in pixels) the width and height of the bounding rectangle that contains the applet. It is used to specify how big a box to draw for the applet. You should specify appropriate sizes for the applet, taking into account how big a graphics object is painted by the applet.

You can use the ALIGN attribute of the APPLET tag to align the applet with respect to the remainder of the Web page. The following is the syntax of the ALIGN attribute:

```
<APPLET CODE="location" WIDTH=d HEIGHT=d ALIGN=alignvalue>
```

The *alignvalue* can have the values listed in Table 9.4. When the LEFT or RIGHT value is used for alignment, the text will flow as indicated until a <BR CLEAR=*clearvalue*> tag is encountered. Recall that the <BR> tag causes a line break. The CLEAR attribute can be specified to control the behavior of the line break. The *clearvalue* can be LEFT, RIGHT or ALL. A *clearvalue* of LEFT will start the text at the next clear left margin; a *clearvalue* of RIGHT will start the text at the next clear right margin; a *clearvalue* of ALL will start the text on the next line whose left and right margins are both clear.

The align values of TOP, TEXTTOP, MIDDLE, ABSMIDDLE, ABSBOTTOM, BASELINE, and BOTTOM are meant to be used for small applets that would be embedded in a single text line.

You can also use the HSPACE and VSPACE attributes of the APPLET tag to control the amount of space between the applet and the surrounding text. An example of this is as follows:

```
<APPLET CODE="URL" WIDTH=500 HEIGHT=150 HSPACE=90 VSPACE=50>
</APPLET>
```

The values of HSPACE and VSPACE are measured in pixels. A value of 90 for HSPACE will set the space above and below the applet to 90 pixels. A value of 50 for VSPACE will set the space to the left and right of the applet to 50.

· · · · ·

You can also use the <ALT=*alternate*> tag to specify an alternate image of text for Web browsers that are not Java-enabled. The *alternate* is replaced by the URL of the text or image.

TABLE 9.4	VALUE	DESCRIPTION
ALIGN Attribute Values	LEFT	The applet is placed at the left margin of the Web page, and all HTML text that follows the applet tag flows into the space that is to the right of the applet.
	RIGHT	The applet is placed at the right margin of the Web page, and all HTML text that follows the applet tag flows into the space that is to the left of the applet.
	TOP	Sets the applet with the topmost item in the line. The item could be text, applet, or image.
	TEXTTOP	Sets the top of the applet with the top of the highest text in the line.
	MIDDLE	Sets the middle of the applet with the middle of the line.
	ABSMIDDLE	Sets the middle of the applet with the middle of the largest item in the line.
	ABSBOTTOM	Sets the bottom of the applet with the lowest item in the line.
	BASELINE	Sets the bottom of the applet to the baseline.
	BOTTOM	Same as BASELINE.

Passing Parameters to Applets

When you write Java applications, you can pass parameters to the applet. These parameters are usually designed to control the behavior of the program. The parameter values to an applet are passed through the following special PARAM tag:

```
<PARAM NAME=name VALUE=value>
```

The *name* is the name of the parameter, and *value* is its value. For example, if you wanted to specify a color or size for a graphic element in your applet, you could define the following parameters:

```
<PARAM NAME=COLOR VALUE="Magenta">
<PARAM NAME=SIZE VALUE="36">
```

If you were animating an applet and wanted to control its speed, you could define the following value:

```
<PARAM NAME=speed VALUE="5">
```

Here the value of the speed parameter has a meaning that is internal to the applet program. If you are writing your own applets, you can pick any name. If you are using another programmer's applet, you must pass specify the parameter name values that the applet expects.

The parameters to the applet must be specified between the APPLET tag:

```
<APPLET CODE="URL" WIDTH=500 HEIGHT=400 ALIGN=LEFT>
<PARAM NAME=COLOR VALUE="Magenta">
<PARAM NAME=SIZE VALUE="18">
</APPLET>
```

Writing Java Applets

The Java GUI classes are contained in the java.awt package. The AWT classes are an Alternative Windowing Toolkit library of classes that provide the graphic elements (also called *widgets*) for writing GUI-enabled applications. In order to write sophisticated applets, you must familiarize yourself with the classes in the AWT library.

Understanding the Structure of a Java Applet

The applet is a subclass of the class Panel in java.awt package (that is, the class java.awt.Panel). To facilitate the creation of applets, a collection of methods and constructors have been created in the Applet class in the java.applet package. Figure 9.6 shows the hierarchy diagram for the Applet class.

In order to write an applet, you must first extend the java.applet.Applet class:

```
public class MyApplet extends java.applet.Applet
{
  // Your definitions go here.
}
```

Because your applet extends the Applet class, all the public methods described in the Applet class are inherited and available for your use in MyApplet. Some of the Applet class methods are empty (that is, they do not have any code). These are the init(), start(), stop(), and destroy() methods. To use these methods, you must override them and define your own code.

If you supply your own method in your class that has the same name and parameter types as one of the inherited methods, you "override" the inherited method. This means that whenever the method name is called for your extended class, the inherited method from the superclass is not used. Instead, the method that you supply will be called. Within the method that you supply, you are free to call any of the superclass methods, including the method that was overridden.

Most of the functionality of applets is already contained in the Applet class. In order for you to perform functions specific to your class, you must extend the Applet class (as shown previously) and override the init(), start(), stop(), destroy(), and paint() methods. You do not have to override the destroy() method, if your applet does not have any resources that require special handling when the applet terminates. You must, however, at least provide code for the init(), start(), and stop() methods. The init(), start(), stop(), destroy(), and paint() methods are invoked by the Web browser or a Web client application that controls the execution of the applet. The following shows the methods that you must supply in your `Applet` class:

```
public class MyApplet extends java.applet.Applet
{
   // Your definitions go here.
   public void init()
   {
        // Your initialization code
        // goes here.
   } // end init
   public void start()
   {
        // Your start up code
        // goes here.
   } // end start
   public void stop()
   {
        // Your stop code
        // goes here.
   } // end stop
   public void destroy()
   {
        // Your cleanup code
        // goes here.
   } // end destroy
   public void paint(Graphics g)
   {
        // Your paint code
        // goes here.
   } // end paint
}
```

The `init()` method is called when the applet is first loaded. Its primary function is to initialize the applet. This may involve creating instances of classes, setting up initial values of applet data structures, setting parameters, loading images and fonts, and so on. You override the `init()` method in your applet class and add the necessary code.

After an applet has been initialized by the Web browser calling the `init()` method, the Web browser invokes the `start()` method. The `start()` method may be called several times to restart a suspended applet, which may have been suspended by a call to the `stop()` method. Applet suspension can occur if the Web user leaves the Web page on which the applet is displayed by following a link. The applet will be restarted using the `start()` method when the user returns to the Web page. A major difference between `init()` and `start()` is that the `init()` method is called only once during an applet's lifetime, whereas the `start()` method may be called several times. Typically, the `start()` method contains code to display messages, send messages (method invocation) to other objects, create threads to perform parallel execution of applet code, and so on.

If the Web user leaves the Web page on which the applet is displayed, the Web browser suspends the applet by calling the `stop()` method. If the `stop()` method is not called, the applet will consume CPU resources, even though it is not displayed. This is not desirable. So, you must provide a `stop()` method for applet suspension. A suspended applet is restarted by the Web browser by sending the `start()` message to the applet. To implement `stop()`, you must define it to override the `stop()` method in the `Applet` class.

Normally, when an applet terminates the resources used by the objects are reclaimed. However, if you have started additional threads, or have opened files on the Web server, you must release these resources explicitly. This is where the `destroy()` method comes in handy. You use the `destroy()` method for general cleanup of the applet resources. The `destroy()` method that you define overrides the empty `destroy()` method in the `Applet` class. It is not needed in most applets.

The `paint()` method is called whenever there is a need for the browser to redraw the applet. This will occur at least once, after the applet has been initialized, and any time when the browser window is moved, resized, or uncovered after being covered over by another application. If you do not override the `paint()` method, your applet will not do much of anything as far as its display area of the applet is concerned. The argument to the `paint()`method is an instance of the Graphics class. This object defines the graphic context for modifying the display area of the applet. The `Graphics` class is instantiated by the browser and this instance of the object passed to the `paint()` method, and so you do not have to create the object argument. The `Graphics` class is defined in the `java.awt` package, and defines (among other things) methods for drawing lines, ellipses, circles, lines, squares, and other geometrical shapes.

Writing the HelloWorld Applet

Now that you know the structure of applets, you are ready to write a simple Java applet. You will learn to write an applet version of the program `dispmsg` to display messages. The following is the applet version of such a program:

```
import java.awt.Graphics;
class MyApplet extends java.applet.Applet
{
    // init: Override method in Applet
    public void init()
    {
        resize(600, 400);
    }  // end init
    // paint: Override method in Component
    public void paint(Graphics g)
    {
        g.drawString("May you pass every Test!", 5, 10);
    }  // end paint
}
```

Use the `import` statement to import the `Graphics` class:

```
import java.awt.Graphics;
```

This `import` statement is necessary because the `Graphics` class is needed in the `paint()` method. If you are performing several graphics-related tasks and using a number of classes from the `java.awt` package, you could replace the `import` statement by the following to include all the graphics-related classes in the `java.awt` package.

```
import java.awt.*;
```

The previous statement imports all the classes defined in the `java.awt` package.

The `init()` method is used to override the `init()` method in the `Applet` class. This method contains just one line to invoke the `resize()` method. The resize() method is defined in the Applet class. The applet size is resized to the specified dimensions of 600 pixels of width, and 400 pixels of height.

The start(), stop(), and destroy() methods are not defined in the MyApplet class. Therefore, these methods are inherited from Applet class. These Applet class methods do not contain any code and therefore do not provide any functionality. These methods are not needed, because there is nothing to start, stop, or destroy in the applet. The paint() method is called whenever the browser window that displays the applet is moved, resized, or uncovered.

The paint() method contains just one call to the drawString() method of the graphics object that was passed as a parameter to the paint() method. The drawString() method draws the string that is passed at the coordinates <5, 10>. The coordinates are measured in pixels. The origin is the top-left corner. The value of 5 is along the X-axis which, and the value of 10 is along the Y-axis. The Y-axis extends from the top-left corner to the bottom-left corner, and the X-axis extends from the top-left corner to the top-right corner.

To run this applet from a Web browser, you must first define an HTML document that specifies the applet byte-code location. The following is an example of the HTML code that can be used to run this applet.

```
<HTML>
<HEAD>
<TITLE>My Applet</TITLE>
</HEAD>
<BODY>
<H1>My first applet displays</H1>
<HR>
<APPLET CODE="MyApplet.class" WIDTH=300, HEIGHT=300>
If you see this text, you are not running a Java enabled
browser.
</APPLET>
</BODY>
</HTML>
```

Details of the <APPLET> tag were discussed in the earlier section, "Using HTML to Access Java Applets."

As you become familiar with Java, you can use the structure of the Java applet outlined in this section to create more complex applications. Java includes classes for providing multithreading. This means that you can have multiple and separate lines of code execution within the same program. For example, one thread could be used for displaying graphics while other threads are used for executing the applet logic.

Summary

The Java language has become a strategic language for Novell in developing cross-platform applications. The Java language is not limited to being used exclusively on the Internet; it is a good choice for many intranet corporate networks. The Novell SDK shows that Java applications can be run on the IntranetWare platform. This chapter discussed the basics of writing Java programs and many of the key language elements.

As of this writing, Java classes for accessing IntranetWare services are not completely developed. As the Java classes for IntranetWare services become available, future editions of this book will contain material to help you use the IntranetWare-specific Java classes.

Other tools such as Jamba and Java Beans are being developed that allow rapid development of Java programs. Some of these tools enable you to use predefined Java components to create applications.

## CHAPTER 10

Server Side Processing by the Novell Web Server

Previous chapters discussed how to use and write CGI programs to deliver dynamic Web content. The CGI programs run on the Novell Web Server and can deliver server data and HTML documents to Web clients. In certain situations, you may want to provide dynamic Web content with changes to only some of the elements within the HTML document. Rather than write CGI programs to deliver dynamic data to a Web client, you can embed instructions for the server to deliver dynamic data to the Web client without writing CGI programs. These encoded instructions that are processed by the Web server are called *Server Side Includes* (SSIs). This chapter discusses how SSIs can be used to generate dynamic HTML documents.

You also learn two other techniques to generate dynamic data to Web clients: Client Pull and Server Push. These techniques enable you to specify the repeated refreshing of HTML data and the sending of graphic images in succession to produce animation.

Using Server Side Includes (SSIs)

SSIs are directives that are placed in the HTML documents. These directives instruct the Web server to execute external programs and embed their output in the HTML document. You can also specify SSI directives to embed such information as time stamp, server name, size of files, any of the CGI environment variables, and special SSI Environment variables.

The Novell Web Server can be configured to parse HTML documents looking for SSI directives. When the Novell Web Server sees an SSI directive it interprets it and performs the specified action. The SSI directives have the following format:

```
<!--#directive parameter="value"-->
```

Here is an example of an HTML document with the local date and time stamp indicating when the document was accessed:

```
<html>
<head><title>Example of SSI directive</title></head>
<body>
<h1> The AM Network</h1>
<hr>
```

```
Today's date is <!--#echo var="DATE_LOCAL"-->
<hr>
<p>On this day the following special events took
place:<br><br>
Other HTML data
</body>
</html>
```

Figure 10.1 shows how this HTML document (file `ssidate.ssi`) appears in the Novell Netscape browser.

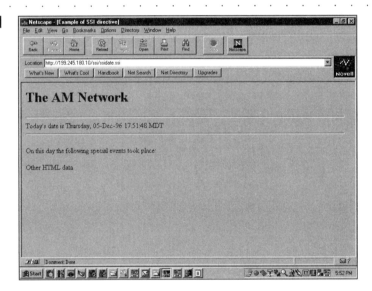

Showing time stamp using the SSI directive

The SSI directive in this example is

```
<!--#echo var="DATE_LOCAL"-->
```

The #echo directive tells the Web server to embed today's date and time in the HTML document. Each time the previous HTML document is accessed, the current local Web server time stamp is displayed.

It is very important that no spaces are inserted between any of the prefix characters "<!--". The following are common mistakes of incorrect syntax in specifying SSI directives:

```
<!-- #echo var="DATE_LOCAL"-->
<! --#echo var="DATE_LOCAL"-->
<--#echo var="DATE_LOCAL"-->
<!--#echo var="DATE_LOCAL">
```

The first two examples have spaces in the string prefix "<!--". The third example is missing the mandatory exclamation mark. The last example is missing the "--" before the ending ">" character. If the SSI directive has incorrect syntax, it is not processed by the Web server and appears as part of HTML data that is rendered by the Web browser, or an error message is generated (see Figure 10.2).

F I G U R E   10.2

Problem of incorrect syntax of SSI directive

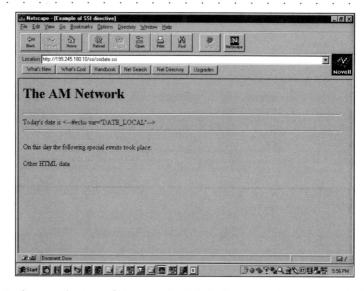

Table 10.1 shows a listing of the standard SSI directives. You can embed these SSI directives anywhere in your HTML document.

T A B L E   10.1

Standard SSI Directives

DIRECTIVE	MEANING
#config errmsg="*value*"	This is used to specify the format of the error message, where *value* can be set to any string value.
#config sizefmt="*value*"	This is used to specify the format of the size of the file in bytes (*value* is bytes) or kilobytes (*value* is abbrev).

TABLE 10.1	DIRECTIVE	MEANING
Standard SSI Directives (continued)	#config timefmt="value"	This is used to specify the format of the time stamps. Several format types can be specified to accommodate differences in how date and time information are displayed.
	#echo var="value"	The value of any of the special SSI variables of CGI variables can be embedded in the HTML document.
	#exec cmd="value"	You can use this to specify an external command that can be executed by the Web server. The output of the external command is inserted in the HTML document.
	#exec cgi="value"	You can use this to specify a CGI program that can be executed by the Web server. The output of the CGI program is inserted in the HTML document.
	#flastmod file	You can use this to insert the last modification date and time for the specified file.
	#fsize file	You can use this to insert the size of the file. The format of the size is controlled by the config sizefmt SSI directive.
	#include file	You can use this to insert the specified text file into the document.
	#include virtual	You can use this to insert the text file whose virtual path is specified into the document.

In addition to the standard SSI directives, the Novell Web Server supports the extended SSI directives shown in Table 10.2. One problem with using the extended SSI directives for a Novell Web Server is that these are not supported on UNIX platforms, and if you have a mix of Novell Web Server and UNIX Web servers, these extended SSI directives are not portable.

TABLE 10.2	DIRECTIVE	MEANING
Extended SSI Directives for the Novell Web Server	`#append file="filename" line="lines"`	You can use this command to append information to a text file whenever a user requests a specific HTML document or submits an HTML form.
	`#count file="filename"`	You can use this command to display the number of times the current file has been accessed.
	`#if "operand1" operator "operand2" operation`	You can use the `#if` command to instruct the server to perform an operation based on the outcome of a logical comparison.
	`#goto "labelname"`	You can use the `#goto` command to jump to the `#label` SSI directive. Any SSI commands or HTML text between the `#goto` command and the `#label` command are skipped.
	`#label "labelname"`	This is the target of the `#goto` SSI directive.
	`#break`	You can use this command to stop the processing of an HTML document. Any HTML code following the `#break` command is not displayed.
	`#calc variablename = "expr"`	You can use this command to calculate arithmetic expressions.

▶ · ◀

Configuring SSIs for Novell Web Servers

Figure 10.3 shows how the SSI directives are processed at the Novell Web Server. When the Web client retrieves an HTML document, the Novell Web Server checks to see of the file has been configured to be processed for SSIs. If the HTML document is configured to be processed for SSIs, the Web server interprets the SSI directives in the HTML document, and embeds the output of executing the SSI directive in the HTML document. The actual text of the SSI directive "<!--#*directive parameter*-->" is removed by the Web server. The output of the SSI directive is substituted in its place.

▶ · ◀

FIGURE   10.3

*Processing of Server Side
Includes*

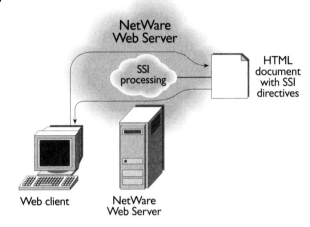

If the HTML document has not been configured to be processed for SSIs, the HTML document is not parsed for SSIs. Instead, it is simply delivered to the Web client as discussed in previous chapters. Any SSI directives in these HTML files will appear as text. To specify which HTML documents are to be parsed for SSI directives, you must name the HTML documents with an ".SSI" extension, and place the document in the Web server directory that has been enabled for Includes processing. By default, the directory SYS:WEB\DOC\SSI is enabled for Includes processing, and you can place the SSI documents in this directory. You can use the Web Manager (see Chapter 4), to enable another Web server directory for Includes processing.

To enable Server Side Includes for a specific directory, follow these steps:

1 • Start the Web Manager program (from \PUBLIC\WEBMGR.EXE).

2 • Select File from the main menu.

3 • Click the Select Server option.

4 • Select the virtual Web server and select OK.

5 • Select the Directories tab.

6 • Select the directory in which you want to enable SSIs from the Existing directories list.

· · · · ·

7 • Select the "Enable includes" check box.

8 • Select Change.

9 • Select OK.

10 • Select Save and Restart, and specify the Web server password.

By enabling the Includes processing for a directory, the "Options Includes" is added for that directory in the SYS:WEB\CONFIG\ACCESS.CFG file. For example, the default SYS:WEB\DOCS\SSI directory that is enabled for SSI processing has the following directives that control access to it in the ACCESS.CFG file:

```
<Directory docs/ssi>
Options Indexes Includes
IndexOptions FancyIndexing IconsAreLinks ScanHTMLTitles
AllowOverride All
<Limit GET>
order allow,deny
allow from all
</Limit>
</Directory>
```

Notice that the Includes options is enabled for the `<Directory docs/ssi>`. If you use the Web Manager program to enable SSI processing for any other directory, you will see the "Options Includes" added for that directory in the ACCESS.CFG file.

Configuring SSIs for UNIX servers

The reason this topic is discussed in a book on the Novell Web Server is that your intranet may contain a mix of UNIX Web servers and Novell Web Servers. UNIX Web servers have a rich heritage of applications that are designed to be run on UNIX Web servers via the CGI interface. CGI programs on the UNIX Web server can be invoked from a Novell Web Server via the RCGI interface (see

Chapter 6). It is, therefore, useful to know how to enable SSI processing on UNIX Web servers. The following instructions are for the UNIX servers based on the Apache and NCSA Web Server.

To specify which HTML documents are to be parsed for SSI directives, you must configure the server resource map file `srm.conf`. You must use the `AddType` directive to specify the MIME type of the SSI document and its extension:

```
AddType MIME_Type Extension
```

For example, to specify that all files with the `.shtml` extension should be processed for SSI directives, add the following to the `srm.conf` file:

```
AddType text/x-server-parsed-html .shtml
```

The MIME content type `text/x-server-parsed-html` specifies a major MIME type of `text` and a subtype of `x-server-parsed-html`. The Web server uses this MIME type description to identify the documents that must be parsed for SSIs.

If you add the following statement to the `srm.conf` file, all HTML files that have an `.html` extension will be processed for SSI directives:

```
AddType text/x-server-parsed-html .html
```

The previous statement will result in the Web server processing even files that do not have SSI directives. This is quite inefficient and will have an impact on server performance. Therefore this type of all-inclusive statement for processing HTML files should be avoided.

Because users can execute external commands by using SSI directives, such commands represent a security hazard that can be exploited by malicious hackers. The Web server offers a method for controlling the type of SSI directives that it will process. You can specify this type of control by specifying the following for using the `access.conf` file:

```
Options option1 option2 ... optionN
```

The options can have values such as `Includes`, `NoIncludes`, `ExecCGI`, and `NoExecCGI`. For example, to enable both Includes and ExecCGI processing (by using the SSI directive `#exec cgi`), you would use the following statement:

```
Option Includes ExecCGI
```

If you wanted to process includes but not the exec SSI directives, you could use the following in the `access.conf` file:

```
Option IncludesNoExec
```

Using SSI Environment Variables

In the following example of an SSI directive, the SSI environment variable DATE_LOCAL tells the Web server to insert the current date and time in the HTML document:

```
<!--#echo var="DATE_LOCAL"-->
```

In addition to DATE_LOCAL, the Novell Web Server understands a number of useful SSI Environment variables. Table 10.3 shows a list of the SSI Environment variables:

TABLE 10.3	VARIABLE	DESCRIPTION
SSI Environment Variables	DATE_GMT	Current date and time at the Web server expressed in terms of Greenwich Mean Time (GMT).
	DATE_LOCAL	Current date and time for the local time zone at the Web server.
	DOCUMENT_NAME	Current document name.
	DOCUMENT_URI	Virtual path to the current document.
	LAST_MODIFIED	Date and time stamp showing when the current document was last modified.
	QUERY_STRING_UNESCAPED	Un-decoded query string. Metacharacters for the command shell are escaped with an Escape.

You are not restricted to using SSI Environment variables. You also can use any of the CGI environment variables shown in Table 6.3 of Chapter 6.

The following is an example of an HTML file (file `ssienv.ssi`) that uses SSI Environment variables:

```
<html>
<head>
<title> SSI Environment variables example</title>
</head>
<body>
<hr>
<h1> Entering the server <!-- #echo var = "SERVER_NAME"--
></h1>
<pre>
<h2>SSI Environment variables</h2>
SSI environment variable DATE_LOCAL set to <!--#echo
var="DATE_LOCAL"-->
SSI environment variable DATE_GMT set to <!--#echo
var="DATE_GMT"-->
SSI environment variable DOCUMENT_NAME set to <!--#echo var="
DOCUMENT_NAME"-->
SSI environment variable DOCUMENT_URI set to <!--#echo
var="DOCUMENT_URI"-->
SSI environment variable LAST_MODIFIED set to <!--#echo
var="LAST_MODIFIED"-->
SSI environment variable QUERY_STRING_UNESCAPED set to <!--
#echo var="QUERY_STRING_UNESCAPED"-->
<h2>CGI Environment variables</h2>
CGI environment variable HTTP_ACCEPT set to <!--#echo
var="HTTP_ACCEPT"-->
CGI environment variable HTTP_CONNECTION set to <!--#echo
var="HTTP_CONNECTION"-->
CGI environment variable HTTP_USER_AGENT set to <!--#echo
var="HTTP_USER_AGENT"-->
CGI environment variable PATH_INFO set to <!--#echo
var="PATH_INFO"-->
CGI environment variable PATH_TRANSLATED set to <!--#echo
var="PATH_TRANSLATED"-->
CGI environment variable QUERY_STRING set to <!--#echo
```

```
var="QUERY_STRING"-->
CGI environment variable REMOTE_HOST set to <!--#echo
var="REMOTE_HOST"-->
CGI environment variable SERVER_NAME set to <!--#echo
var="SERVER_NAME"-->
CGI environment variable SERVER_PORT set to <!--#echo
var="SERVER_PORT"-->
CGI environment variable SERVER_SOFTWARE set to <!--#echo
var="SERVER_SOFTWARE"-->
</pre>
<hr>
</body>
</html>
```

Figure 10.4 shows the processed values of the SSI and CGI Environment variables in the previous HTML file using the Novell Netscape Navigator.

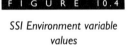

FIGURE 10.4

SSI Environment variable values

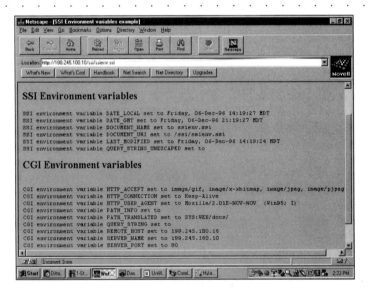

Using Standard SSI Directives

The examples of SSI directives in the previous section all used the #echo directive:

```
<!--#echo var="variable name"-->
```

This section discusses the use of other SSI directives listed in Table 10.1

Using the #config, #fsize and #flastmod Directives

You can use the #config SSI directive to control how date and time, file-size information, and error messages are displayed. The three forms of the #config SSI directives are as follows:

```
<!--#config errmsg="message string"-->
<!--#config sizefmt="abbrev | bytes"-->
<!--#config timefmt="format string"-->
```

You can use the #config errmsg directive to set the error message string that will be displayed when an error is encountered in processing an SSI directive. For example, you could set the error message as follows:

```
<!--#config errmsg="Error[SSI]: Please inform
tsladmin@tsl.org"-->
```

Figure 10.5 shows the error message without the #config SSI directive, and Figure 10.6 shows the error message that is displayed when the previous SSI directive is used. Clearly, the second error message is more useful.

F I G U R E   10.5

Error message without the
SSI directive

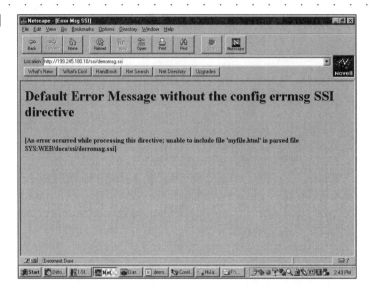

F I G U R E   10.6

Error message with the SSI
directive

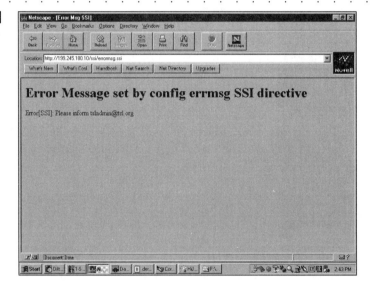

You can use the #config sizefmt directive to set the format of the size of a file. When you set the value of this directive to abbrev, the file size is displayed in kilobytes (KB). For display purposes the size of the file is rounded to the nearest kilobyte. When you set the value to bytes, the file size is displayed in bytes. Consider the following HTML (file fsize.ssi) example:

```
<html>
<head>
<title>File size example </title>
</head>
<body>
<h1> File sizes</h1>
<!--#config sizefmt="abbrev"-->
<b>
<p><h2>Size of file fsize.ssi in kilo bytes is <i><!--#fsize
file=fsize.ssi--></i>
<!--#config sizefmt="bytes"-->
<p><h2>Size of file fsize.ssi in bytes is <i><!--#fsize
file=fsize.ssi--></i>
</b>
</body>
</html>
```

Figure 10.7 shows the file sizes displayed by the previous HTML code using the Novell Netscape browser.

Suppose that you also wanted to display the time a file was last modified. You can use the #flastmod SSI directive to display this time. The many different formats for displaying time include the following:

10/16/99	1:55:00 PM
October 16, 99	13:55:00
Oct 16, 1999	1:55 PM
16/10/99	1:55 p.m.

File size display HTML

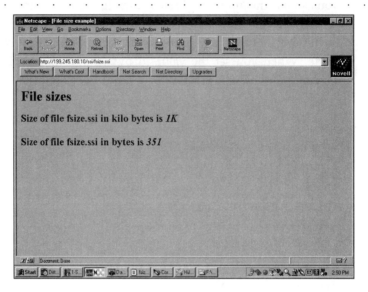

The previous examples represent the same time, even though the format of displaying the time is different. You can use the #config timefmt directive to set the format for the time the file was last modified:

```
<!--#config timefmt="string format"-->
```

The *string format* is used to indicate how the time value is to be formatted. For example, the value of this *string format* in

```
<!--#config timefmt="%b %d, %Y %T"-->
```

will display the following sample time format value:

```
Oct 16, 1998 15:23:33
```

Table 10.4 shows the time format specifiers that can be used in the time format string. The format specifiers are preceded with the percent sign (%) and a letter that follows it.

TABLE 10.4	SPECIFIER	DESCRIPTION
Time Format Specifiers	%a	Day of week abbreviation (for example, Sun, Mon, Tue, and so on).
	%A	Day of week, full format (for example, Sunday, Monday, Tuesday, and so on).

TABLE 10.4	SPECIFIER	DESCRIPTION
Time Format Specifiers (continued)	%b	Month name abbreviation (for example, Jan, Feb, Mar, and so on).
	%B	Full month name (for example, January, February, March, and so on).
	%d	Day of month number. Leading zeros stripped (for example, 1, 2, 3, . . . , 31).
	%D	Date value as *mm/dd/yy* format (%m/%d/%y). Leading zeros stripped (for example, 1, 2, 3, . . . , 31).
	%e	Day of month number formatted as two digits. Single-digit values have leading zeros (for example, 01, 02, 03, . . . , 31).
	%H	Hour in military time, or 24-hour clock format (for example, 1, 2, 3, . . . , 12, 13, . . . , 24).
	%I	12-hour clock format (for example, 1, 2, 3, . . . , 12).
	%j	Day of year (for example, 1, 2, 3, . . . , 366). January 1 is day 1.
	%m	Month number (for example, 1, 2, 3, . . . , 12).
	%M	Minutes formatted as two digits. Single-digit values have leading zeros. (for example, 01, 02, 03, . . . , 59).
	%p	AM or PM format (for example, a.m. or p.m.).
	%r	Time stamp using in following format: "%I:%M:%S AM|PM" (for example, 01:45:33 AM).
	%S	Seconds formatted as two digits. Single-digit values have leading zeros (for example, 01, 02, 03, ..., 59).
	%T	24-hour time formatted as "%H:%M:%S" (for example, 23:15:43).
	%U or %W	Week of year (for example, 1, 2, 3, . . . , 52).
	%w	Day of the week number (for example, 1, 2, 3, . . . , 7). Monday is day 1.
	%y	Year of century (for example, 00, 01, . . . , 99).
	%Y	Year in full format (for example, 1997, 1998, . . . , 2033, and so on).
	%Z	Time zone value (for example, PST, PDT, MST, MDT, CST, CDT, EST, EDT, and so on).

Consider the following HTML example (file `timefmt.ssi`) that displays the time stamp in different file formats:

```
<html>
<head>
<title>Time format example </title>
</head>
<body>
<h1> Time formats</h1>
<b>
<!--#config timefmt="%D %r"-->
<p> File timefmt.ssi last modified on <!--#flastmod file=
timefmt.ssi-->
<!--#config timefmt="%B %d, %Y %T (%A)"-->
<p> File timefmt.ssi last modified on <!--#flastmod
file=timefmt.ssi-->
<!--#config timefmt="%b %d, %Y %T [%a (day %w)]"-->
<p> File timefmt.ssi last modified on <!--#flastmod
file=timefmt.ssi-->
<!--#config timefmt="%d/%m/%y %I:%M:%S %p %Z [year day %j,
week of year %W]"-->
<p> File timefmt.ssi last modified on <!--#flastmod
file=timefmt.ssi-->
</b>
</body>
</html>
```

Figure 10.8 shows the times displayed by the previous HTML code using the Novell Netscape browser.

Using the #include Directive

The #include SSI directive can be used to insert the contents of another file at the point specified by this directive. This can be useful in situations where you have some generic HTML code that you want to include in an HTML file. An example of this is HTML code listing trademarks and copyright notices. Other examples are a thank you note to visitors of your guest book, or the address tag information announcing the author of the page or contact persons for additional information.

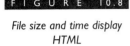

F I G U R E   10.8

File size and time display HTML

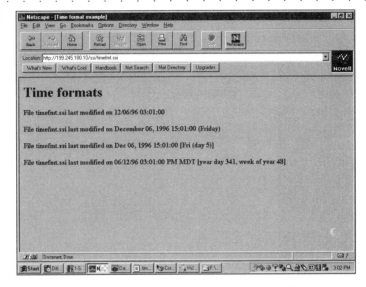

The following shows an example of an HTML document (file `moreinfo.ssi`) announcing further contact information. Notice that this file uses the LAST_MODIFIED SSI Environment variable to inform the user when this contact information was last updated:

```
<address>
<hr>
<pre>
For further information contact the following:
  Web administration questions: tsladmin@tsl.org
  Other questions: tslinfo@tsl.org
              406-222-8300
  This contact information was last modified on <!--#echo
var="LAST_MODIFIED"-->
</pre>
<hr>
</address>
```

You can now include this template contact information HTML code in other HTML documents as follows:

```
<html>
<head>
<title>Include example </title>
</head>
<body>
<h1> Some title</h1>
<b>
<p> Other information...
<br>
<!--#include file="moreinfo.ssi"-->
</b>
</body>
</html>
```

The inclusion of the `moreinfo.ssi` file will cause the contact information in that file to be displayed. In addition, the date and time when this file was last updated will be displayed. This provides the Web user with an idea of how up-to-date is the information in that file.

You can also use a *virtual path* to the filename by specifying the virtual parameter:

```
<!--#include virtual = "path"-->
```

The virtual path is relative to the Web server root. For the Novell Web Server, this defaults to the SYS:WEB directory. Therefore, the virtual path is the path relative to the directory SYS:WEB directory.

You may notice that in the previous example, the LAST_MODIFIED SSI environment variable was used instead of the #flastmod SSI directive. The difference between the LAST_MODIFIED SSI Environment variable and the #flastmod SSI directive shown in the earlier examples is that the LAST_MODIFIED can only display the last modification time stamp of the current HTML document, whereas the #flastmod SSI directive can be used to display the last modification time stamp of any file accessible on the Web server.

Using the #exec Directive

You can execute external commands and have the Web server place their output in the HTML document. The Novell Web Server does not support the #exec SSI directive. However, you can execute the CGI scripts on a UNIX server by using the RCGI interface. The examples of the #exec SSI directive, therefore, apply to UNIX servers. Recall the discussion in Chapter 6 that described how to configure the RCGI interface and run the RCGI daemon on the UNIX server.

To execute an external program, use the following syntax:

```
<!--#exec cmd="external command"-->
```

If the external program produces plain text and not HTML code, you should include the previous directive in the <pre> . . . </pre> HTML tags. Otherwise, the output will be formatted as HTML code. Without HTML tags, the output may not be quite what you expect. Here is an example of how the previous directive can be used on a UNIX system:

```
<html>
<head>
<title> Exec SSI directive </title>
</head>
<body>
<h1> The who commands </h1>
<h2> Who am I?</h2>
<b>
<pre>
I am
  <!--#exec cmd="whoami"-->
</pre>
</b>
<h2> Who is on the system </h2>
<b>
<pre>
The following users are on the system:
<!--#exec cmd="w"-->
</pre>
```

```
</b>
</body>
</html>
```

In the previous example, the UNIX commands `whoami` and `w` are used. The `whoami` gives information on the user who is currently logged on, and the `w` command gives information on all users who are logged on. The output of these commands is enclosed in the <pre> ... </pre> tags to preserve their output format.

Implementing a CGI counter script

In addition to executing external commands, you can include other CGI programs. CGI programs are executed by using the following syntax:

```
<!--#exec cmd="URL of CGI"-->
```

For example, you can execute a CGI program that keeps track of the number of times an HTML page was accessed and display this information as a counter:

```
<html>
<head>
<title>Exec CGI </title>
</head>
<body>
You are the <!--#exec cgi="/perl/counter.pl"--> visitor to
this page!
</body>
</html>
```

The `/perl/counter.pl` CGI program outputs a number for the number of times the page was visited. This number is substituted by the Web server at the point where it encounters the #exec SSI directive in the HTML document. To implement a counter, you must keep track of the number of visits to the page. One way of doing this is to keep the counter in a file that is updated each time the counter CGI program is executed. The counter CGI program will be executed by the #exec SSI directive each time this page is accessed.

Because your home page could be accessed simultaneously by a number of Web clients, you should implement a locking mechanism on the counter data to prevent *race* conditions. A race condition is an operating system term describing a situation when simultaneous attempts to update or read a shared data structure, leading to inconsistent values in the shared data structure. In Perl the flock system call can be used to implement a file lock on the counter data. The flock system call takes the file handle as the first argument and a mode parameter in the second argument. When the mode parameter has a value of 2, the file is locked. When flock is called with a mode parameter value of 8, the file is unlocked. Here is an example of locking and unlocking a file:

```
flock(COUNTER, 2);    # Lock the file COUNTER
flock(COUNTER, 8); # Unlock the file COUNTER
```

Listing 10.1 shows an example of a counter program.

LISTING 10.1

Counter Program

```perl
#!/usr/local/bin/perl
# Previous is for Unix portability
# File counter.pl
$| = 1; # Flush output immediately. Do not buffer.
# Define constants for locking and unlocking of counter
# data file.
$LOCK = 2;
$UNLOCK = 8;
$contact = "tsladmin@tsl.org";
$dataFile = "count.txt"; # Substitute your own
                         # counter data file here.
if (-e $dataFile)
{
    # Verify if file can be read and written
    if (!( -r $dataFile && -w $dataFile))
    {
        &reportError(500, "Counter status",
            "Counter file cannot be read or written");
    }
```

```
    #
    # Open counter file, read it and then close it.
    #
    $visitors = &readCounter;
    #
    # Open the counter file for writing.
    #
    $visitors++;
    &writeCounter;
}
else
{
    # File does not exist.
    # First visitor!
    $visitors = 1;
    if (open(COUNTER, ">" . $dataFile))
    {
        close COUNTER;    # File is now created!
        &writeCounter;
    }
    else
    {
        # Problem creating file
        &reportError(500, "Counter Error",
                    "Problem creating counter data
file");
    }
}
flock (COUNTER, $UNLOCK);
close COUNTER;
print $visitors;  # Print counter value to standard output.
sub readCounter
{
    local ($count);
```

```perl
    open(COUNTER, "<" . $dataFile);
    flock(COUNTER, $LOCK);
    $count = <COUNTER>;
    flock(COUNTER, $UNLOCK);
    close COUNTER;
    return $count;
}
sub writeCounter
{
    open(COUNTER, ">" . $dataFile);
    flock(COUNTER, $LOCK);
    print COUNTER $visitors;
    flock(COUNTER, $UNLOCK);
    close COUNTER;
}
sub reportError
{
     local ($errorcode, $head, $msg) = @_ ;
    print <<EndError;
Content-Type: text/html
Status: $errcode
<head>
<title>$headr</title>
</head>
<body>
<hr>
<h1>$head</h1>
<b>$msg</b>
</hr>
<b><i>Contact $contact</i></b>
</body>
</html>
EndError
```

```
        exit(1);
}
```

The logic for Listing 10.1 is now explained:

```
$| = 1; # Flush output immediately. Do not buffer.
# Define constants for locking and unlocking of counter
# data file.
$LOCK = 2;
$UNLOCK = 8;
$contact = "tsladmin@tsl.org";
$dataFile = "count.txt";
```

The previous code disables output buffering and defines the locking constants $LOCK and $UNLOCK. These constants are primarily defined for improving code readability. The contact person and data filename are also defined. You can substitute a different path name for the counter file. If a full path is not specified, the counter program attempts to create the counter data file in the directory where the CGI counter program is located.

Next, the program checks for the existence of the counter data file by using the following if statement structure:

```
if (-e $dataFile)
{
    # Verify if file can be read and written
    # Other statements in the then part


}
else
{
    # File does not exist.
    # First visitor!
    # Other statements in the else part
}
```

The test -e $dataFile will evaluate to true if the file exists, in which case the then part of the if-statement is executed. If the counter data file does not exist, the else part of the if-statement is executed.

The then part contains the following code, which is executed if the counter data file exists:

```
if (!( -r $dataFile && -w $dataFile))
{
    &reportError(500, "Counter status",
        "Counter file cannot be read or written");
}
#
# Open counter file, read it and then close it.
#
$visitors = &readCounter;
#
# Open the counter file for writing.
#
$visitors++;
&writeCounter;
```

In the previous code, a check is made to ensure that the data file can be read and written. Even though the counter data file may exist, the CGI program may not have sufficient permissions to read or write to this file. The test is done using the following if statement:

```
if (!( -r $dataFile && -w $dataFile))
{
&reportError(500, "Counter status",
"Counter file cannot be read or written");
}
```

If the CGI program does not have sufficient privileges to read or write to the counter data file, the reportError subroutine defined at the end of the program is called. The reportError subroutine displays the message to the Web client and terminates the execution of the CGI script.

After the file is determined to be readable and writeable, the counter data file is read using the following statement:

```
$visitors = &readCounter;
```

The subroutine `readCounter` is defined toward the end of Listing 10.1. It reads the counter data file and returns its value, which is stored in the `$visitors` variable. This variable is then incremented:

```
$visitors++;
```

Next, the `writeCounter` subroutine is called:

```
&writeCounter;
```

The `writeCounter` subroutine updates the counter data value with the incremented counter value.

The `else` part of the `if` statement is executed when the counter data file does not exist. Presumably this is the first time you have set up counter for the home page. First you set the counter value to 1:

```
$visitors = 1;
```

Next, you create the file. This can be done with a call to open the nonexistent file:

```
if (open(COUNTER, ">" . $dataFile))
{
        :
}
```

If the call us successful, the data file is created. The data file is then closed:

```
close COUNTER;    # File is now created!
```

The data file is closed in anticipation of the next statement, which calls the `writeCounter` subroutine to write the counter value of 1 to the counter data file.

```
&writeCounter;
```

The `writeCounter` subroutine opens the data file and after writing the counter value, it closes the file. Because it opens the data file, you must ensure that the data file is not opened when `writeCounter` is called.

Finally, the following `else` part of the `if`-statement is executed if the call to open and create the data file is not successful:

```
&reportError(500, "Counter Error",
             "Problem creating counter data file");
```

The call to `reportError` generates an error report for the Web client and terminates execution of the CGI script.

At the end of the CGI script, the counter value is printed to the standard output:

```
print $visitors;
```

This value is then substituted by the Web server in place of the `#exec cgi` directive.

The subroutines `readCounter` and `writeCounter` are explained next. The subroutine `readCounter` opens the file, reads it and returns the counter value. As you examine the logic in this subroutine, notice that a local variable `$count` is defined. The file is opened and locked. After reading the counter value, it is unlocked and closed, at which point the counter file becomes available to other programs. When the file is locked, other Web clients attempting to access the file will have to wait until it becomes unlocked.

The subroutine `writeCounter` opens the counter data file, writes the value in `$visitors` (global scalar variable) to the counter data file. The file is opened and locked until the write operation is complete. When the file is locked, other Web clients attempting to access the file will have to wait until it becomes unlocked. After the write operation, the file is unlocked, at which point it becomes available to other Web clients.

Because of the widespread use of search engines such as Yahoo, Lycos, and so on, on the Internet, and the registration of home pages on these search engines, the actual counter value may not reflect human users who have accessed these pages. These search engines access the registered pages periodically in order to update their database. Each time these "software robots" access a page that has the `"<--#exec cgi="counter.pl"-->` directive, the counter CGI program will be executed, and this will cause the count to increase by 1. Therefore, the counter values that you see on the Internet are often somewhat inflated and do not represent the actual number of human visitors.

Passing data to a CGI program from the `#exec cgi` SSI directive

You cannot use the query method to pass data to a CGI program from the `#exec cgi` directive. Therefore, the following `#exec cgi` directive causes the Web server to return an error:

```
<!--#exec cgi=juliandf.pl?1/1/97+7/7/99-->
```

In the previous statement, an attempt is being made to pass two date values (1/1/97 and 7/7/99) to the CGI program juliandf.pl. Instead of using the query method to pass the date values, you can specify the date values as arguments to the CGI program:

```
<!--#exec cgi=juliandf.pl 1/1/97 7/7/99-->
```

Within the CGI program juliandf.pl, you can access the date values through the @ARGV array. $ARGV[0] will be set to the first argument of 1/1/97 and $ARGV[1] will be set to the second argument of 7/7/99.

In this example, the CGI program juliandf.pl takes two date values and returns the number of days between these date values. Listing 10.2 shows a sample implementation of such a program in Perl.

juliandf.pl *Program*

```perl
#!/usr/local/bin/perl
# Previous is for Unix portability
# File juliandf.pl
$| = 1; # Flush output immediately. Do not buffer.
if ($#ARGV < 0 || $#ARGV > 1)
{
        print "[Too few or too may arguments]";
        exit(1);
}
$contact = "tsladmin@tsl.org";
$century = 1900;
($month1, $day1, $year1) = &extractDate($ARGV[0]);
$julianDate1 = &julianDate($month1, $day1, $year1);
if ($#ARGV == 1)
{
        ($month2, $day2, $year2) = &extractDate($ARGV[1]);
        $julianDate2 = &julianDate($month2, $day2, $year2);
}
else
```

```perl
{
        $julianDate2 = 0;
}
$daysDiff = $julianDate2 - $julianDate1;
print $daysDiff;
sub extractDate
{
     local ($date) = @_;
     local($month, $day, $year);
     print $date, "\n";

     if ($date =~ m|^(\d+)/(\d+)/(\d+)$|)
     {
          ($month, $day, $year) = ($1, $2, $3);
     }
     else
     {
          print "<<Error in date $date>";
          exit(1);
     }
     if ($year < 100)
     {
          $year += $century;
     }
     ($month, $day, $year);
}
# julianDate: Expect month, day, year format.
# Year should include century
#    $jd = &julianDate(10, 30, 1998);
# Author: Karanjit S. Siyan
#
sub julianDate
{
```

```
        local ($M, $D, $Y) = @_;
        local ($IM, $J);
         $IM = 12 * ($Y + 4800) + $M - 3;
         $J = (2 * ($IM - (int($IM / 12))*12)
             + 7 + 365 * $IM)/12;
         $J = int ($J);
         $J = $J + $D + int($IM / 48) - 32083;
         $J = int ($J);
         if ($J > 2299171)
         {
             $J = $J + int($IM / 4800) - int($IM / 1200) +
    38;
             $J = int ($J);
         }
         return $J;
    }
```

In the previous program code, the dates passed as arguments are converted to Julian date values by calling the julianDate subroutine. The difference between these two Julian date values is then printed using the print statement:

```
$daysDiff = $julianDate2 - $julianDate1;
print $daysDiff;
```

The Julian date is the number of days since 4713 B.C. and is used in astronomy calculations. The Julian date subroutine is accurate for all dates after 4713 B.C. and is useful for computing number of days between any two dates. You can use the ReverseJulianDate subroutine date to convert a Julian date value back to a normal date. For example, if you wanted to find out the date 450 days after a specific date, you would convert the specific date to a Julian date value, add 450 to this value, and use the Reverse Julian date to convert the numeric value back to a date that is 450 days after the specific date. The Perl code for the Reverse Julian date (file rjulian.pl) is as follows:

```
# reverseJulianDate: Returns month, day, year format.
# Year includes century.
#    ($month, $day, $year)= &reverseJulianDate(2450424);
```

```perl
#
# Author: Karanjit S. Siyan
#
sub reverseJulianDate
{
        local ($jd) = @_;
        local ($cjd, $I, $A, $B, $C, $D, $E, $G, $d, $day,
$month, $year);
        $cjd = $jd + 0.5;
        # Note int function returns the integer part
        $I =   int ($cjd);
        $F = $cjd - $I;
        if ($I > 2299160)
        {
            $A = int (($I - 1867216.25)/36524.25);
        }
        else
        {
            $A = $I;
        }
        $B = $I + 1 + $A - int($A/4.0);
        $C = $B + 1524;
        $D = int (($C - 122.1)/365.25);
        $E = int (365.25 * $D);
        $G = int (($C - $E)/30.6001);
        $d = ($C - $E) + $F - int (30.6001 * $G);
        $day = int ($d);
        $month = int (($G <= 13) ? $G - 1 : $G - 13);
        $year = ($month > 2) ? $D - 4716 : $D - 4715;
        ($month, $day, $year);
}
```

The logic behind the Julian date and Reverse Julian date subroutines takes into account several historical correction factors, such as the days from October 5 to October 14, 1582, inclusive, that were abolished by Pope Gregory to get the civil calendar to coincide with the tropical calendar. The explanation of this logic is beyond the scope of this book.

Using Extended SSI Directives

Table 10.2 listed the additional SSI directives available on the Novell Web Server. These *extended SSI* (ESSI) directives are explained next.

Using the #count Directive

The #count SSI directive can be used to display the number of times the current file has been accessed. You could try to use the `counter.pl` script to implement page counts, but the problem is that Novell Web Server does not support the #exec SSI directive.

The syntax of the #count SSI directive is as follows:

```
<!-#count file="filename"->
```

The *filename* identifies what file the server will use to track the number of document hits. The filename can be any valid filename on the server. The counter value is stored as a text string, and the Novell Web Server takes care of all file locking operations to ensure consistency of data.

The following example shows the `counter.ssi` file that ships with the Novell Web Server (in the SYS:WEB\DOCS\SSI directory). This example shows how to use the #count SSI directive to display the number of hits:

```
<HTML>
<head>
<title>SSI Page Counter Demo</title>
</head>
<BODY background="/images/blue_pap.gif" text="#000000">
This page has been loaded <!--#count file="counter.cnt"-->
times.<br>
(Hit the Reload button to see the number change!)
<p>
<hr>
```

```
<! Standard trailer.  Note use of ESSI variable substitution
to insert document name in hyperlink below. >
<! Hyperlink points to a BASIC script that displays raw HTML
rather than translated HTML. >
<a href="/scripts/convert.bas?docs<!--#echo
var="DOCUMENT_URI"-->">
See how this page is written.</a>
<P><a href="/scripts/convert.bas?docs/ssi/counter.cnt">
See what's in the counter file.</a>
<p>
Copyright &#169; 1995 Novell, Inc.  All Rights Reserved.
</body>
</HTML>
```

The counter value is displayed and updated using the following directive:

```
<!--#count file="counter.cnt"-->
```

This `counter.cnt` file is stored in the same directory as the `counter.ssi` file. Figure 10.9 shows the `counter.ssi` file in Netscape Navigator. You can see how the page hit count information is displayed.

FIGURE 10.9

The counter.ssi file in Netscape Naviagtor

The `counter.ssi` file contains anchor tags that invoke the BASIC CGI script `/scripts/convert.bas` to which the name of the file whose contents are to be displayed is passed as a parameter using the GET method. These anchor tags are as follows:

```
<a href="/scripts/convert.bas?docs<!--#echo
var="DOCUMENT_URI"-->"> See how this page is written.</a>
<a href="/scripts/convert.bas?docs/ssi/counter.cnt">
See what's in the counter file.</a>
```

The first anchor tag passes the argument `docs/ssi/counter.ssi` to the `convert.bas` CGI script, and the second anchor tag passes the argument `docs/ssi/counter.cnt` to the convert.bas CGI script. The first argument is actually evaluated by using the `DOCUMENT_URI` SSI environment variable as follows:

```
docs<!--#echo var="DOCUMENT_URI"-->
```

The `convert.bas` CGI script ships with the Novell Web Server and is in the SYS:WEB/SCRIPTS directory. The code for this script is as follows:

```
1 rem Quick program to sanitize HTML files so that browsers
won't eat the HTML
2 rem Copyright (c) 1995 Novell, Inc.  All Rights Reserved.
10 if argc$ = "0" then goto 5000
20 if argc$ = "" then goto 5000
30 file$ = argv$
90 on error goto 4000
100 print "Content-type: text/html" : print
103 print "<title>Contents of "; file$;"</title>"
105 print "<H1>Contents of "; file$;"</H1>"
106 print "<tt><pre>"
140 file$ = lcase$(file$)
142 if file$ = "scripts/411.bas"       then 190
144 if file$ = "scripts/cardsamp.bas"  then 190
146 if file$ = "scripts/convert.bas"   then 190
148 if file$ = "scripts/date.bas"      then 190
150 if file$ = "scripts/subs.bas"      then 190
```

```
152 if file$ = "scripts/survey.bas"     then 190
154 if file$ = "scripts/testcgi.bas"    then 190
156 if file$ = "docs/ssi/counter.ssi"   then 190
158 if file$ = "docs/ssi/counter.cnt"   then 190
160 if file$ = "docs/ssi/date.ssi"      then 190
162 if file$ = "docs/ssi/filestat.ssi" then 190
164 if file$ = "docs/ssi/form.ssi"      then 190
166 if file$ = "docs/ssi/include.ssi"   then 190
168 if file$ = "docs/ssi/insert.htm"    then 190
170 if file$ = "docs/ssi/index.ssi"     then 190
172 if file$ = "docs/ssi/submit.ssi"    then 190
174 if file$ = "docs/ssi/users.txt"     then 190
180 print "<H1>Sorry, illegal file</H1>"
182 print "</pre></tt>"
184 goto 5000
190 open file$ for input as 1
200 linput #1, html$
300 for i = 1 to len(html$)
305 ch$ = mid$(html$,i,1)
310 if ch$ = "<" then print "&lt;"; else if ch$ = "&" then
print "&amp;"; else print ch$;
320 next i
330 goto 200
4000 rem Error-handling routine
4005 if err = 30 then goto 4100
4010 print "Error #"; err; " at line #"; erl; " (argc$ = ";
argc$; ", argv$ = "; argv$; ")"
4100 print "</pre></tt>"
4200 close 1
5000 end
```

The purpose of the previous BASIC script is to display the file contents that may contain HTML codes without causing these HTML codes to be interpreted by the Web browser. The contents of the filename passed as an argument to the CGI script are displayed within the <pre> . . . </pre> HTML tags so that formatting within the file is preserved. Because HTML tags beginning with a "<" and "&" are interpreted by the Web browser, these are searched for and replaced by their HTML codes of "&lt" and "&amp". Only the files listed from lines 142 to 174 are converted. If you want to add your own filename or generalize the CGI script for displaying any file, you must modify the lines 142 to 174.

Using the #append Directive

The #append SSI directive can be used to append information to a text file whenever a user requests a specific HTML document or submits an HTML form. The #append directive uses the following syntax:

```
<!--#append file="filename" line="lines"-->
```

The *filename* specifies the text file to which the data is appended, and the *lines* is an encoding of the information that is added to the text file. You can encode form field names in the *lines* value as follows:

```
&&fieldname&&
```

The following example of a registration form helps explain how to use the #append directive. Figure 10.10 shows the sample registration form (file form.ssi) that ships with the Novell Web Server distribution software. When you enter information on yourself and press the Submit button, the submit.ssi file specified in the ACTION attribute of the FORM tag is executed. This SSI directive displays the screen in Figure 10.11, showing that you have been registered.

In Figure 10.11, you can see that the information was encoded and passed to submit.ssi as the following:

```
submit.ssi?name=Madhoosodan+&street=33+Vaikunth+Lok&city=Vaik
unth&state=HI&zip=999999
```

Chapter 6 discussed this encoding method.

You can select the hyperlink "See what's in *users.txt*" to see how this information is stored in the text file. Figure 10.12 shows the screen that appears when you select this hyperlink. You can see that the text database consists of registration information on users who have been registered so far.

FIGURE 10.10

Display of form.ssi

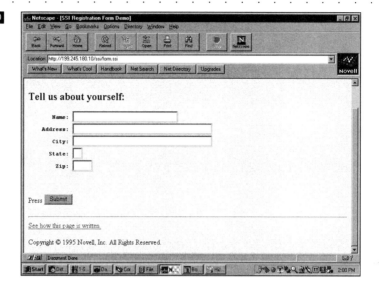

FIGURE 10.11

Feedback on registration information

▶ · ◀

F I G U R E   10.12

Selecting the hyperlink "See what's in users.txt"

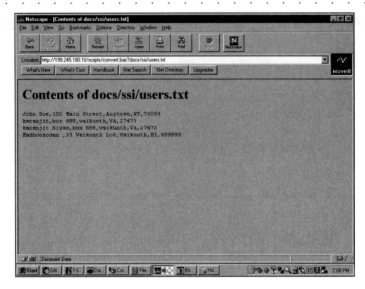

Now that you know what the registration form `form.ssi` does, let's examine how it works. The code for `form.ssi` is as follows:

```
<HTML>
<head>
<title>SSI Registration Form Demo</title>
</head>
<BODY background="/images/blue_pap.gif" text="#000000">
<h1>SSI Registration Form Demo</h1>
<form method=GET action="submit.ssi">
<br>
<h2>Tell us about yourself:</h2>
<TT><strong>
<PRE>
       Name: <INPUT TYPE="text" NAME="name" SIZE="30"
MAXLENGTH="60">
    Address: <INPUT TYPE="text" NAME="street" SIZE="40"
MAXLENGTH="60">
       City: <INPUT TYPE="text" NAME="city" SIZE="40"
MAXLENGTH="60">
```

```
        State: <INPUT TYPE="text" NAME="state" SIZE="2"
MAXLENGTH="2">
          Zip: <INPUT TYPE="text" NAME="zip" SIZE="5"
MAXLENGTH="8">
</PRE>
</strong></tt>
<br>
Press <input type="submit" value="Submit">
</form>
<hr>
<! Standard trailer.  Note use of ESSI variable substitution
to insert document name in hyperlink below. >
<! Hyperlink points to a BASIC script that displays raw HTML
rather than translated HTML. >
<a href="/scripts/convert.bas?docs<!--#echo
var="DOCUMENT_URI"-->">
<it>See how this page is written.</it></a>
<p>
Copyright &#169; 1995 Novell, Inc.  All Rights Reserved.
</body>
</HTML>
```

The previous HTML code is standard HTML code for displaying forms. The details of the form HTML codes are discussed in Chapter 4. What is different about the previous HTML code is that the ACTION attribute in the FORM tag specifies an SSI file:

```
<form method=GET action="submit.ssi">
```

The code for the submit.ssi file is as follows:

```
<HTML>
<head>
<title>You're Registered!</title>
</head>
<BODY background="/images/blue_pap.gif" text="#000000">
<h1>You're Registered!</h1>
```

```
<! The next line appends the registration data to the file
users.txt >
<!--#append file="users.txt"
line="&&name&&,&&street&&,&&city&&,&&state&&,&&zip&&" -->
You have been registered as:<br>
<PRE>
        Name: <!--#echo var='name'-->
     Address: <!--#echo var='street'-->
        City: <!--#echo var='city'-->
       State: <!--#echo var='state'-->
         Zip: <!--#echo var='zip'-->
</PRE>
<center>
<h2>Thank you for registering.</h2>
</center>
<hr>
<! Standard trailer.  Note use of ESSI variable substitution
to insert document name in hyperlink below. >
<! Hyperlink points to a BASIC script that displays raw HTML
rather than translated HTML. >
<a href="/scripts/convert.bas?docs<!--#echo
var="DOCUMENT_URI"-->">
See how this page is written.</a><P>
<a href="/scripts/convert.bas?docs/ssi/users.txt">
See what's in <i>users.txt<i>.</a>
<p>
Copyright &#169; 1995 Novell, Inc.  All Rights Reserved.
</body>
</HTML>
```

The submit.ssi file contains HTML codes to display a feedback form thanking the user for registration. The information on the user's submission is stored in the users.txt file using the #append ESSI directive.

```
<!--#append file="users.txt"
line="&&name&&,&&street&&,&&city&&,&&state&&,&&zip&&" -->
```

Notice that the `line` parameter contains the encoding of the form field values using the notation "&&fieldname&&" to represent the field value. The information that is stored is also displayed to the user using the following HTML code:

```
<PRE>
        Name: <!--#echo var='name'-->
     Address: <!--#echo var='street'-->
        City: <!--#echo var='city'-->
       State: <!--#echo var='state'-->
         Zip: <!--#echo var='zip'-->
</PRE>
```

The field name values are displayed using the #echo var SSI directive. The variables that are specified are the field names. This example illustrates that you are not restricted to displaying the values of CGI and SSI Environment variables. You can also display the field name values that are passed as parameters to the SSI document. The Novell Web Server takes care of automatically decoding the field name values passed as an encoded string.

Using the #if Directive

The #if SSI directive can be used to instruct the Novell Web Server to perform an operation based on the outcome of a logical comparison. The syntax of the #if SSI directive is as follows:

```
<!--#if "operand1" operator "operand2" operation-->
```

The *operand1* and *operand2* are any string or number values that are compared by using the specified *operator*. The *operator* can have the following values:

- ▶ == equal to

- ▶ != not equal to

- ▶ < less than

- ▶ > greater than

- ▶ >= greater than or equal to

- ▶ <= less than of equal to

- ▶ contains The text string in *operand2* is contained (found) in the *operand1* string

The *operation* is the action the Novell Web Server should perform when the comparison of *operand1* and *operand2* is true. Examples of possible operations are the following:

- ▶ goto — Instructs the server to jump to a specific label command

- ▶ print — Instructs the server to print specific text

- ▶ error — Instructs the server to print the current errmsg string

- ▶ break — Instructs the server to truncate the HTML document

- ▶ errorbreak — Instructs the server to print the current errmsg string and then truncate the HTML document

- ▶ printbreak — Instructs the server to print specific text and then truncate the HTML document

As an example, the following #if SSI directive instructs the server to jump to a specific line if the request came from a Mosaic browser. If the request did not come from a Mosaic browser, the server will jump to a different location in the HTML file.

```
<!--#if "&&HTTP_USER_AGENT&&" contains "Mosaic" goto mosaic-->
<p>You are not using Mosaic.
<! Do any special processing for non Mosaic web browsers>
<!--#goto "non-mosaic"-->
<!--#label "mosaic"-->
<p>You are using Mosaic
<! Do any special processing for Mosaic web browsers>
<!--#label "non-mosaic"-->
```

Using the #goto Directive

You can use the #goto ESSI directive to instruct the Novell Web Server to jump to the point in the HTML document identified by a specific #label command. Any HTML text between the #goto command and the #label command is not displayed.

The syntax of the #goto ESSI directive is as follows:

```
<!--#goto "label"-->
```

If the *label* does not contain any spaces, the double quotation marks can be omitted.

In the following example, when the Novell Web Server encounters the #goto ESSI directive in an HTML document, it jumps to the "skipped" label without sending the line in between the #goto and #label commands to the Web client.

```
<!--#goto "skipped"-->
<p>This line is never sent to the web client and hence will
not be displayed.
<!--#label "skipped"-->
<p>This line will be sent to the web browser and displayed.
```

Using the #label Directive

You can use the #label command to mark the spot in the HTML document to which the Novell Web Server jumps when it encounters a #goto ESSI directive that identifies that label as the target.

The label command uses the following syntax:

```
<!--#label "labelname"-->
```

The *labelname* is a string of 254 characters or less. As an example, consider the following:

```
<!--#goto "nextlabel"-->
<p>This line will not be sent by the web server to the web
client and therefore will not be displayed.
<!--#label "nextlabel"-->
<p>This line will be sent by the web server to the web
client and therefore will be displayed.
```

When the Novell Web Server encounters the #goto ESSI directive, it skips the processing of any HTML text until it encounters the #label ESSI directive. This means that the HTML text between the #goto directive and the #label directive will not be sent to the Web client and, therefore, will not be displayed.

Using the #break Directive

You can use the #break ESSI directive to truncate an HTML document so that any HTML text after the #break ESSI directive will not be displayed. The #break ESSI directive has the following syntax:

```
<!--#break -->
```

Consider the following example:

```
<p>This line will be sent by the server to the web client
<!--#break -->
<p>This line will not be sent by the server to the web
client because the document has been truncated and
transmission to the client is terminated.
```

In this example, the HTML text after the #break ESSI directive will not be sent by the Novell Web Server to the Web client. The #break ESSI directive essentially marks an abrupt end of the HTML file.

You will typically want to execute a #break directive based on the result of executing the #if ESSI directive. Here is an example:

```
<!--#if "&&REMOTEHOST&&" != "135.23.66.78" goto "OK"-->
<p> You are not welcome at this host.
<!--#break-->
<!--#label "OK"-->
<p> Hello ....
<! The statements after label OK will be displayed if
requester is not 135.23.66.78>
```

In the previous example, if the Web client has an IP address of 135.23.66.78 you display a message saying that the user is not welcome here, and you do not display any HTML text.

Using the #calc Directive

You can use the #calc ESSI directive to perform mathematical calculations. The #calc ESSI directive has the following syntax:

```
<!--#calc variable = "expression"-->
```

The *variable* is a variable name that you define, and *expression* is an arithmetic expression using operators such as + (add), * (multiply), - (subtract), and / (divide). The operands in the arithmetic expressions can be numbers or other variable names. You can use parentheses to set priorities for the operations. Consider the following example that converts degrees Fahrenheit to degrees Celsius:

```
<!--#calc degF="23"-->
<!--#calc degC="(degF - 32)*5/9"-->
<p>Outside temperature of <!--#echo var="degF"--> Fahrenheit
is same as <!--#echo var="degC"--> Celsius
```

The previous example will print the following

```
Outside temperature of 23 Fahrenheit is same as -5 Celsius
```

Client Pull Versus Server Push

Chapter 9 described how to use Java for Web applications and animation. In addition to Java, you can use techniques such as Client Pull and Server Push to provide image animation. The basis of most animation techniques is to display images in succession so that the human eye averages out the differences in the images to produce the effect of continuous motion.

In Client Pull, the Web client opens a new HTTP connection every time it must access a document (see Figure 10.13). In Server Push, the server maintains an open connection until the necessary data is received by the client (see Figure 10.14).

F I G U R E   10.13

Client Pull

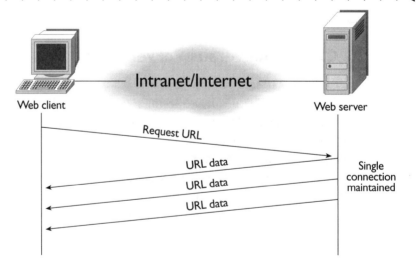

F I G U R E   10.14

Server Push

Client Pull

In Client Pull, a special HTML directive called the META tag is used to refresh the HTML document. The META directive tells the client to retrieve (refresh) the document after a certain period of time:

```
<META HTTP-EQUIV="Refresh" CONTENT="seconds">
```

If you want the META tag to specify a different document, you can specify a URL address as shown here:

```
<META HTTP-EQUIV="Refresh" CONTENT="seconds; URL=urladdr">
```

This META directive can be placed in the HTML document header or as the HTTP response header generated by a CGI program. The META tag tells the Web client to retrieve the document periodically. The META directive simulates the HTTP response header, "Refresh:". The difference is that the HTTP response header, "Refresh:" is nonrepeating. It is processed just once. You can simulate a repeating response header by ensuring that each time the document is accessed it contains the "Refresh:" HTTP header.

The following is an example of a CGI script that repeatedly specifies the HTTP response header, "Refresh:", to cause the document to reload every three seconds:

```
#/usr/local/bin/perl
# Previous statement is for portability to Unix platforms
$timePeriod = 3;
print "Content-Type: text/html\n$Refresh: $timePeriod\n\n";
print <<END;
Other HTML tags go here.
Dynamic behavior such as executing programs
or loading image files can be provided here.
END
exit(0);
```

Server Push

The Server Push is implemented by the server sending the following MIME type to the Web client:

```
Content-Type: multipart/x-mixed-replace;
boundary=delimstring
```

The multipart content MIME type specifies that there are several different content types to follow. The *delimstring* is the string that specifies the boundary between the different content types. For example, if the server wanted to send several GIF files in succession, this could be done by the server sending (or *pushing*) the following content type:

```
Content-Type: multipart/x-mixed-replace; boundary="xxyyzz"
--xxyyzz
Content-Type: image/gif
Content-Length: sizeofimage
GIF Image 1
--xxyyzz
Content-Type: image/gif
Content-Length: sizeofimage
GIF Image 2
--xxyyzz
Content-Type: image/gif
Content-Length: sizeofimage
GIF Image 3
--xxyyzz--
```

The first content type announces to the Web client that multiple data types are to follow. In this case, the data types are GIF images. The boundary string is specified as "xxyyzz". Each data element has its own content type:

```
Content-Type: image/gif
Content-Length: sizeofimage
```

This MIME type of image/gif describes the date element to follow (a GIF image). Note that the boundary string --xxyyzz is used between the data elements; and the boundary string --xxyyzz-- is used to indicate the last "Content-Type." Because the Web sever is "pushing" a graphic image, the "Content-Length" HTTP response header is specified. Its value is the size of the image in bytes.

The following is an example of a Perl script that generates such a stream of "Content-Types":

```perl
#/usr/local/bin/perl
# Previous statement is for portability to Unix platforms
$| = 1; # Disable buffering
$delaySecs = 1;    # Amount of delay between each image push
@images = ("graphic1.gif",
      "graphic2.gif",
      "graphic3.gif",
      "graphic4.gif",
      "graphic5.gif",
      "graphic6.gif");
print "Content-Type:multipart/x-mixed-
replace;boundary=zz\n\n";
for ($x = 0; $x < scalar(@images); $x++)
{
      # Push the graphic file
      print "--zz\n";
      $imageSize = (stat($images[$x]))[7];    # Get size of
image
      print "Content-Type: image/gif\nContent-Length:
$imageSize\n\n";

      if (open(GRAPHIC, "<" .  $images[$x]))
      {
             $N = 10;
             $blockSize = $imageSize/$N;
             for ($b = 0; $b <= $imageSize; $b +=
$blockSize)
             {
                  # Read a block of data and print it
                  # to the standard output.
                    read(GRAPHIC, $blockData, $blockSize);
                    print $blockData;
             }
             close IMAGE;
```

```
                }
                else
                {

                    &reportError(500, "Image file open error",
                        "Problem attempting to open image file");
                }
                sleep ($delaySecs);

        }
        print "--zz--\n";
        exit(0);
        sub reportError
        {
                local ($errorcode, $head, $msg) = @_;
                print <<EndError;
        Content-Type: text/html
        Status: $errcode
        <head>
        <title>$head</title>
        </head>
        <body>
        <hr>
        <h1>$head</h1>
        <b>$msg</b>
        </hr>
        <b><i>Contact $contact</i></b>
        </body>
        </html>
        EndError
                exit(1);
        }
```

The images to be pushed to the Web client by the server are stored in the @images file. The amount of delay between each image pushed to the server is set in $delaySecs. The previous code generates the appropriate HTTP response headers and the boundary string values separating the multipart elements. The size of the graphic image is sent in the "Content-Length" HTTP response header. The for loop is used to transmit the image file in 10 blocks. Each block, except possibly the last block, is one-tenth the size of the image file.

Summary

This chapter discussed how to create dynamic HTML data without using extensive CGI programming. The CGI programs run on the Novell Web Server and can deliver server data and HTML documents to Web clients. In certain situations, you may want to provide dynamic Web content with changes to only some of the elements within the HTML document. Rather than write CGI programs to deliver dynamic data to a Web client, you can embed instructions for the server to deliver dynamic data to the Web client without writing CGI programs. These encoded instructions that are processed by the Web server are called Server Side Includes (SSIs).

Different SSI directives and SSI Environment variables were discussed in detail in this chapter. You also learned two other techniques to generate dynamic data to Web clients: Client Pull and Server Push. Both of these techniques can be used to provide animation and have been explained. The Server Push is more efficient than Client Pull because it maintains only a single connection with the Web server, whereas the Client Pull requires a separate connection for each download of image data.

## CHAPTER II

Integrating the Novell Web Server with NDS

The Novell Web Server comes with an NLM extension that permits Web client users to browse and view the Novell Directory Services (NDS). Because your Novell Web Server could be connected to the Internet, there are a number of security options that you can set to control access to NDS.

In addition to using the NLM extension for browsing NDS, you can write your own CGI scripts to access NDS. The NetBasic language discussed in Chapter 8 contains a number of APIs that can be used to access NDS. You could use this language to write your own CGI scripts to access NDS services.

This chapter discusses how to use and configure the NLM extension for NDS services and how to write NetBasic CGI scripts to access NDS.

Using the Browser Extension NLM

When you install the Novell Web Server, the NDSOBJ NLM is installed in the SYS:WEB/DOCS/CGI/NDSOBJ directory. This NLM is an extension NLM. An *extension NLM* is used to extend the services provided by the Web server in a fundamental way. The NDSOBJ extension NLM enables clients to browse the NDS, a tree of which can be viewed by using Web browsers such as the Netscape Navigator. The NLM extension dynamically generates the HTML pages that contain the NDS tree information. NDS objects in the trees are represented by an icon and the object name (see Figure 11.1).

In order to browse the NDS tree from a Web browser, you must first enable users to run the NDS browser extension.

Enabling the NDS Browser

When you install the Novell Web Server version 3.0 or higher, the NDS browser is enabled by default. In earlier versions of the Novell Web Server, the NDS browser was disabled by default. If the Web browser is the primary interface for the users in the intranet, you should ensure that the NDS browser is enabled so that users can search for resources in the NDS tree. Another reason you may want to enable the NDS browser is if you want external Internet users to read information stored in your NDS trees.

FIGURE 11.1

Viewing the NDS tree from a Web browser

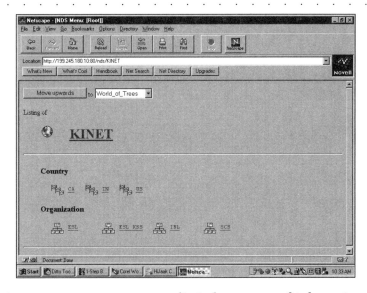

FIGURE 11.1

Viewing the NDS tree from a Web browser

For security reasons, you may want to limit the amount of information that is visible via the NDS browser. By default, the implicit NDS group [Public] is given the Browse NDS object right to the root of the NDS tree. Because NetWare rights are inherited unless blocked by the Inherited Rights Filter (IRF), the Browse object right flows down the entire NDS tree, and users in [Public] can browse the NDS tree. All users, including external Internet users, are automatically in the [Public] group (whether they are authenticated or not), and, therefore, can browse the NDS tree. If you want to prevent users from automatically being able to view a security-sensitive branch in the NDS tree, you must remove the Browse object right from the IRF for the root container of the tree branch.

If you want users to do more than browse the NDS tree—for example, if you want users to see the Phone number and Fax number properties of users—you must assign Read rights to the Phone number and Fax number property of the users. By assigning this right to the [Public] group, all external Internet users have access to this information.

During the Novell Web Server installation, the NDS browser file (NDSOBJ.NLM) is copied to the SYS:WEB/DOCS/CGI/NDSOBJ directory. You must ensure that the following line exists in the server resource map file, SYS:WEB\CONFIG\SRM.CFG:

```
LoadableModule /nds/ sys:web/docs/cgi/ndsobj/ndsobj.nlm
```

When this line is added and the Web server restarted, the Web server receives an HTTP request with the relative path containing /nds/. The Web server maps this to the path for the NDS browser file, sys:web/docs/cgi/ndsobj/ ndsobj.nlm, which is then executed.

If the previous line is not added to the SRM.CFG file, use the following steps to add the line through the Web Manager utility:

1 • Start the Web Manager program. (The program is located in SYS:PUBLIC, which should be in your search path.) Select Start, then select Run, and then type **webmgr**. Select OK.

2 • From the Web Manager program, select File, and then Select Server (see Figure 11.2).

Web Manager selections

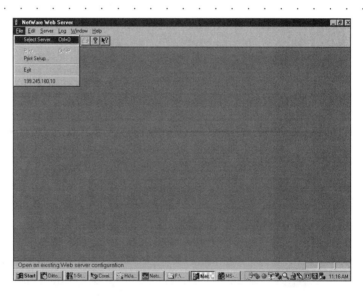

3 • From the "Select Server Root Directory on Web Server" dialog box, select the virtual Web server. Select OK. The Novell Web Server configuration dialog box appears (see Figure 11.3).

Novell Web Server configuration dialog box

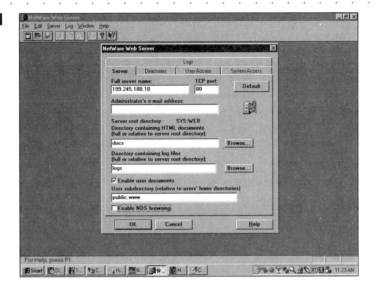

4 • Select the Enable NDS browsing check box, and enable it.

5 • Select OK.

6 • When the Restart Required dialog box appears, select Save and Restart.

7 • You are prompted for the Web server password (that you set when you installed the Web server) to confirm the server reload. Enter the Web server password and select OK.

8 • Exit the WEBMGR.

After completing these steps, you may want to examine the SRM.CFG file to see if the `LoadableModule/nds/...` line has been added. If you move the NDSOBJ.NLM extension file, you must manually edit the mapping of the `LoadableModule` directive in the SRM.CFG file.

Using the NDS Browser

Once the Novell Web Server is enabled for Web browsing you can access the NDS trees, using the following URLs:

```
http://webserver/nds/
http://webserver/nds/ndsobjectname
```

The *webserver* is the DNS hostname or IP address of the Web server. The *ndsobjectname* is the name of the NDS object for the extension to display. Selection of the URLs mentioned previously causes the NDSOBJ.NLM to run. The NDSOBJ.NLM displays a dynamically created page containing NDS tree information. If the first URL format is used, all the trees are available for the user to browse (see Figure 11.4). You can select the NDS tree name that you want to browse.

▶ . . . . ◀

F I G U R E   I I . 4

NDS trees to browse

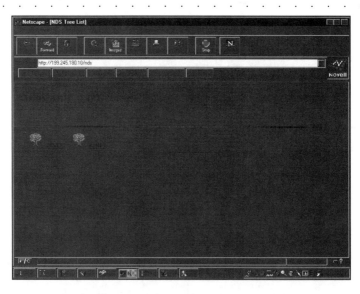

If you want to view a specific NDS object directly, you can use the second URL format. The *ndsobjectname* is the Federated Name, starting with the Tree name. For example, if you want to view the container OU=CORP.O=ESL in the NDS tree KINET, you would use the following URL address:

```
http://webserver/nds/kinet/esl/corp
```

Figure 11.5 shows the results of using the second format of the URL address.

FIGURE 11.5

Directly viewing an NDS object

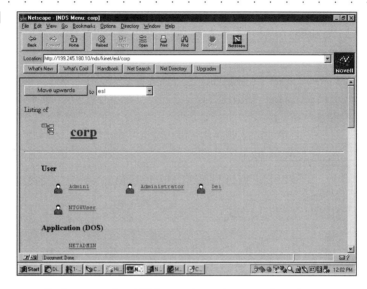

You can generally browse the NDS tree by selecting the object icons on the HTML pages. A "Move upwards" button for moving to one of the selected target destinations is displayed (see Figure 11.5) that enables you to move quickly around the NDS tree.

The Web browser displays icons for the standard NDS objects and a few other objects (such as Btrieve servers, communications servers, IPX/IP gateway server, and so on). You can browse any publicly available information in the NDS tree (that is, any object for which the group [public] has the appropriate rights). By default, [public] only has only the Browse rights to the tree. If you want to view properties of an object, [public] must have the Read property right for the property of the object. You can assign property rights to group [public] by using the standard NetWare Administrator tool.

Enabling the NWADMN3X or NWADMN95 Snap-in Module

The Novell Web Server ships with the NWADMN3X and NWADMN95 snap-in modules that allow the NDS schema to be modified so that additional "Home Page" and "Photo" attributes can be added to and associated for user objects.

If you have a Windows 3.*x* workstation and you are running NWADMN3X.EXE, the snap-in module is the DLL file, WEBSNP3X.DLL. This file is initially copied to the SYS:\PUBLIC directory of the server during Web Server install. To enable the use of this module on Windows 3.*x* systems, you must modify the NWADMN3X.INI file as follows:

1 • Start a text editor to open the \WINDOWS\NWADMN3X.INI file on your workstation.

2 • Add the following line below the [Snapin Object DLLs WIN3X] heading:

```
WEBSNP3X.DLL=WEBSNP3X.DLL
```

3 • Save the file.

If you have a Windows 95 system and you are running NWADMN95.EXE, the snap-in module is initially copied to the SYS:\PUBLIC\WIN95 directory of the server during Web Server install. To enable the snap-in module on a Windows 95 system, follow these steps:

1 • Run the NWADMN95.EXE tool.

2 • Verify that a user object already has the "Home Page and Photo Attributes" button by examining the detail properties screen for the user.

3 • If these buttons exist, then you are finished. If the buttons do not exist, exit the NWADMN95 tool and continue with the following steps.

4 • Run the Registry Editor in the \WINDOWS directory on your workstation. This is the file REGEDIT.EXE (normally in the C:\WINDOWS directory). Figure 11.6 shows the Windows 95 Registry Editor screen.

F I G U R E   11.6

Registry Editor screen

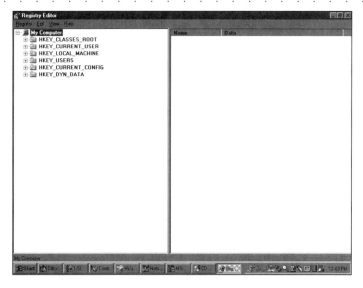

5 • From the Registry menu, select Import Registry File.:

6 • When the Import Registry File dialog box appears, use the browse button to select the SYS:PUBLIC\WIN95\WEBREGED.REG file, and select Open.

7 • If the file is successfully loaded, you will see a message announcing this fact. Close the Registry Editor.

8 • Start the NWADMN95.EXE utility again. When you restart this utility, you will see a message informing you that the NDS Tree does not have the schema extensions to support WEB attributes. Select OK to add the WEB attributes. The "Home Page and Photo Attributes" button is automatically added to all user objects.

The importing of the file WEBREGED.REG in Step 6 adds the WEBSNP95.DLL value under the following key:

```
HKEY_CURRENT_USER\Software\NetWare\Parameters\NetWare
Administrator\Snapin Object DLLs WIN95
```

Figure 11.7 shows the changes that have been made under this key.

FIGURE 11.7

Web Snap DLL changes in
Windows 95 Registry

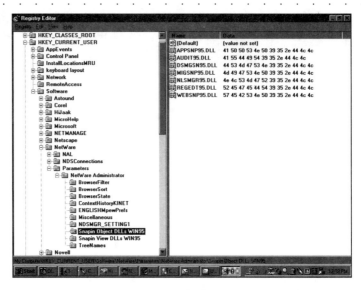

Once you have added the "Home Page and Photo Attributes" button to the user objects, you can add information in these attributes. For adding photographs, use photographs that have been saved in the GIF or JPEG format. For example, to associate a home page or photo with a user object, follow these steps:

1 • Start the NetWare Administrator tool.

2 • Double-click the user for whom you want to configure the home page.

3 • Select the "Home Page and Photo Attributes" button (see Figure 11.8).

4 • To assign a home page to the user, click the Select HTML File button. When the Windows File Open selection box appears, browse the file system and select the HTML file for the user's home page.

5 • To assign a photo, click the Select Photo button. When the Windows File Open selection box appears, browse the file system and select the GIF file for the user's photograph..

6 • Select OK to save your changes.

F I G U R E   1 1 . 8

"Home Page and Photo Attributes" button for the user property

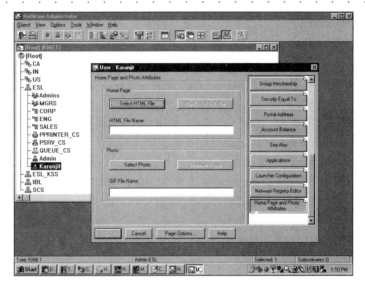

To remove the home page or photograph for the user, follow these steps:

1 • Start the NetWare Administrator tool.

2 • Double-click the user for whom you want to configure the home page.

3 • Select the "Home Page and Photo Attributes" button.

4 • To remove the home page association for the user, click the Remove HTML File button.

5 • To remove the photo association for the user, click the Remove Photo button.

6 • Select OK to save your changes.

Controlling Access to LCGI NLMs

Because LCGI programs such as NETBASIC.NLM and NDSOBJ.NLM can provide unrestricted access to the server, the Novell Web Server provides a special method to restrict access to LCGI programs. To restrict access to LCGI programs, you can create an access.www file in the directory where the LCGI program resides. When a user requests an LCGI server extension in this directory, the Web server prompts the user for a user ID and password.

Once a user is authenticated to use the LCGI extension, full access is available by way of the LCGI program. By default, access to NetBasic LCGI extension is not restricted. This means that full access is available to all NetBasic scripts. Currently, you cannot selectively place access control on different NetBasic scripts. Similarly, once a user is authenticated to use the NDS Object Browser, browsing to all available NDS trees and public object information is permitted.

When NDS browsing is enabled from the WEBMGR, access is not restricted. To restrict access you must create the access.www file. Listing 11.1 shows a well-documented sample access.www file in the WEB\SAMPLES\CONFIG directory.

LISTING II.I

access.www Script

```
# access.www
#
# Please DO NOT use TAB charaters when editing this file.
#
# This file provides local configuration of the web server's
access control
# system.  You can implement the access restriction of a
document directory
# by simply having this local access control file in that
directory.
# The default name for these local control files is
'access.www'
# and it can be set by the 'AccessFileName' in the resource
```

```
configuration
# file: 'srm.cfg'.
#
# Please refer to the User Acess Control section of the
readme.txt file
# for additional relevent information.
#
# This example demonstrates the use of an NDS group and a
list of NDS users
# for the authentication list.
#
# In the global access control files, access.cfg, one should
not specify
# NDS groups and NDS users at the same time, but you can do
that in this file.
# Although The access.www can support both NDS groups and
NDS users at
# the same time, this combination must be handled with care.
The context
# specified in both AuthUserMethod and AuthGroupMethod lines
should be
# identical to minimize confusion.
#
# Syntax:
#
#   AuthType Basic <== Keyword, don't change
#
#   AuthName name
#     name can be any descriptive name that the Browser will
display.
#     One can take advantage of this line to show the context
specified
#     in AuthUserMethod/AuthGroupMethod so those user who
belongs to the
```

```
#    specified context would know that they don't have to type
the
#    fully-qualified user name.
#
#  AuthUserMethod NDS .ou1.ou2...o
#    This signifies that NDS users will be specified in the
access list.
#    The NDS fully-qualified parameter must be a container
object.
#    NOTE THE LEADING PERIOD.  IT IS REQUIRED.
#    For users in the access list (Require User list) that
belongs to
#    this specified container context, they do not have to key
in the
#    fully-qualified name when prompted for user name and
password.
#
#  AuthGroupMethod NDS .ou1.ou2...o
#    This signifies that NDS groups will be specified in the
access list.
#    The NDS fully-qualified parameter must be a container
object.
#    NOTE THE LEADING PERIOD.  IT IS REQUIRED.
#    For users in the specified group (Require Group) that
belongs to
#    this specified container context, they do not have to key
in the
#    fully-qualified name when prompted for user name and
password.
#
#  require user user1 user2 ...
#    Specifies that one or more NDS users in the access list.
#    user* is the name of the user.  If the user NDS context
is already
```

```
#      defined in the AuthUserMethod line, then only the
relative name needs
#      to be specified.  It the user belongs to another NDS
context, then
#      the fully-qualified NDS name mut be specified (with the
leading dot).
#
#   require group gname1 gname2 ...
#      Specifies that one or more NDS groups in the access list.
#      gname* is the name of the group.  The group name should
be a
#      fully-qualified NDS name (with the leading dot).
#
AuthType Basic
AuthName DOCS\ENGR(default context: .eng.icd.novell)
AuthUserMethod NDS .eng.icd.novell
AuthGroupMethod NDS .eng.icd.novell
<Limit GET>
require user mel .sally.mgnt.icd.novell
require group .group1.icd.novell
require group .techies.eng.icd.novell
</Limit>
```

Currently, the Novell Web Server supports three mutually exclusive methods for restricting global directory access using NDS authentication:

1 • Restrict access to all valid users

2 • Restrict access using individual user names

3 • Restrict access using user groups

You can choose only one of the previous methods. These methods are described in more detail in Chapter 4.

Writing CGI Scripts for Accessing NDS

NetBasic comes with a number of NDS-specific APIs that you can use to write CGI scripts to interface with the NDS database. The following sections present you with several examples of writing these scripts. The explanations of how these scripts work will help you understand how to use the NDS APIs.

The default location for NetBasic CGI scripts is SYS:NETBASIC\WEB, so you should copy these CGI scripts to this directory. You can find these CGI scripts on the CD-ROM that accompanies this book. To run the CGI scripts, open the following URL from the Novell Netscape Navigator:

```
http://webserver/netbasic/scriptname
```

The *webserver* is the DNS name or IP address of your Web server, and *scriptname* is the filename of the NetBasic script. The .BAS script extension is optional when specifying the *scriptname*.

Adding User Objects to the NDS Tree

IntranetWare comes with a powerful tool called the NetWare Administrator that you can use to perform generalized functions such as creating, deleting, renaming, or moving user objects. However, you can write your own CGI scripts to perform these functions. The advantages of CGI scripts is that it can be run from the universal Web browser interface, and you can customize the CGI scripts to perform specialized functions.

Figure 11.9 shows the form that is displayed when you run the CGI script NDSUSER.BAS. The form has been filled with sample data. At the very least, you must enter the User Name and Last Name fields, which are required to create the user object. You must also specify the correct context value where you want to create the user. The other fields are optional and represent attributes of the user object.

Figure 11.10 shows the results of submitting the form data to the CGI script. You must press the Send Form button to send the form data. The data that was entered is displayed and the user object is created. You can run the NetWare Administrator tool to verify that the user object has been created. Figure 11.11 shows the attributes of the created user object using the NetWare Administrator tool.

FIGURE 11.9

User object creation form

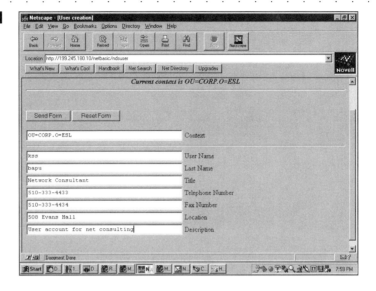

FIGURE 11.10

Results of user object
creation

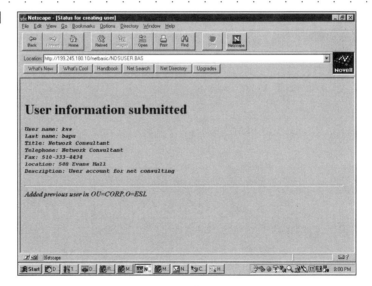

▶ ▶ ▶ . . . . ◀

*User attributes of the
created user account*

Listing 11.2 shows the NDSUSER.BAS program.

NDSUSER.BAS Program

```
' NDSUSER.BAS: This demonstrates the creation of the user
account
' Author: Karanjit S. G. S. Siyan
'
#include "html.h"
sub main
    udf = "undefined"
    uname = Doc:var("uname", udf)
    if uname = udf
        ' Display forms and other statistics
        print("<html><head><title>User
creation</title></head><body>")
        print("<center><h1>Information on user to
create</h1>")
```

```
        print("<b><i>Current context is ",
NDS:Context:Path, "</i></b></center>")
        print("<HR>"); newline
        print("<FORM METHOD=POST ACTION=NDSUSER.BAS>");
newline
        print('<input type=submit value="Send Form"> ')
        print('<input type=reset value="Reset Form">')
        newline; newline

        print("<input type=text size=45 name=context
value=", NDS:Context:Path,"> Context<hr>")
        print("<input type=text size=45 name=uname> User
Name<br>")
        print("<input type=text size=45 name=lname> Last
Name<br>")
        print("<input type=text size=45 name=title>
Title<br>")
        print("<input type=text size=45 name=telephone>
Telephone Number<br>")
        print("<input type=text size=45 name=fax> Fax
Number<br>")
        print("<input type=text size=45 name=location>
Location<br>")
        print("<input type=text size=45 name=description>
Description<br>")
        print("</FORM>"); newline
    else
        ' Process input
        print("<HTML><HEAD><TITLE>Status for creating
user</TITLE></HEAD>")
        newline
        print("<BODY>"); newline
        ' Extract the last name -- mandatory
        lname = Doc:var("lname", udf)
```

```
            if lname = udf
                print("<h1>Error</h1>")
                print("<b>You must define the last name as per
    X.500 specification</b></body></html>")
                return
            endif
            ' Extract the rest of form fields
            title = Doc:var("title", udf)
            telephone = Doc:var("telephone", udf)
            fax = Doc:var("fax", udf)
            location = Doc:var("location", udf)
            description = Doc:var("description", udf)
            print("<h1>User information submitted</h1>")
            print("<pre><b><i>"); newline
            print("User name: ", uname); newline
            print("Last name: ", lname); newline
            ' Display the form fields only if they have been
    defined
            if title != udf
                print("Title: ", title); newline
            endif
            if telephone != udf
                print("Telephone: ", title); newline
            endif
            if fax != udf
                print("Fax: ", fax); newline
            endif
            if location != udf
                print("location: ", location); newline
            endif
            if description != udf
                print("Description: ", description); newline
            endif
            print("</i></b></pre><hr>")
```

```
      ' Set context
      context = Doc:var("context")
      context = NDS:Context:Path
      oldContext = NDS:Context:Path:change(context)
      ' Delete old account if it exists and
      ' Add the new account
      ok = NDS:Delete(uname)
      ok = NDS:Add:user(uname, lname)
      ' Add attributes to the user account
      if title != udf
          ok = NDS:Attribute:Value:add(uname, "Title",
title)
      endif
      if telephone != udf
          ok = NDS:Attribute:Value:add(uname, "Telephone
Number", telephone)
      endif
      if fax != udf
          ok = NDS:Attribute:Value:add(uname, "Facsimile
Telephone Number", fax)
      endif
      if location != udf
          ok = NDS:Attribute:Value:add(uname, "L",
location)
      endif
      if description != udf
          ok = NDS:Attribute:Value:add(uname,
"Description", description)
      endif
      print("<b><i>Added previous user in ", context,
"</i></b>")
    endif
    print("</body></html>")
end sub
```

The main logic in the program is contained in the following enclosing if statement:

```
udf = "undefined"
uname = Doc:var("uname", udf)
if uname = udf
     ' Display forms and other statistics
else
     ' Process input
endif
```

The then part of the if statement is executed when no user data has been entered. At this point, the field uname is not defined. In the then part, the NetBasic print statements generate the HTML form that you saw in Figure 11.9.

The else part of the enclosing if statement is executed when at least some user data is entered. At this point, (at the very least) uname is defined. The else part processes the user input data. The user data is echoed back in a generated HTML document (see Figure 11.10). The user object is created and the attributes, if specified, are added to the user object.

In the then part, the following actions are performed:

I • The HTML header tags are displayed:

```
print("<html><head><title>User
creation</title></head><body>")
print("<center><h1>Information on user to
create</h1>")
```

2 • The current context is displayed:

```
print("<b><i>Current context is ",
NDS:Context:Path, "</i></b></center>")
print("<HR>"); newline
```

The NDS:Context:Path API displays the current context.

3 • The HTML form is generated by print statements:

```
print("<FORM METHOD=POST
ACTION=NDSUSER.BAS>"); newline
```

```
        print('<input type=submit value="Send Form">
')
        print('<input type=reset value="Reset
Form">')
        newline; newline

        print("<input type=text size=45 name=context
value=", NDS:Context:Path,"> Context<hr>")
        print("<input type=text size=45 name=uname>
User Name<br>")
        print("<input type=text size=45 name=lname>
Last Name<br>")
        print("<input type=text size=45 name=title>
Title<br>")
        print("<input type=text size=45
name=telephone> Telephone Number<br>")
        print("<input type=text size=45 name=fax> Fax
Number<br>")
        print("<input type=text size=45
name=location> Location<br>")
        print("<input type=text size=45
name=description> Description<br>")
        print("</FORM>"); newline
```

The FORM action attribute is the NetBasic script itself (that is, the action is performed by the else part of the outermost if statement). The method that is used for submitting the data is POST.

4 • The HTML end tags are generated by the following statement at the end of the outermost statement:

```
        print("</body></html>")
```

In the else part, the following actions are performed. Note that the else part is executed when the form data is submitted for processing.

1 • The HTML header tags are displayed for the output results:

```
            print("<HTML><HEAD><TITLE>Status for creating
user</TITLE></HEAD>")
            newline
            print("<BODY>"); newline
```

2 • The last name (`lname`) is extracted and, if it has not been defined, an error message is generated:

```
            lname = Doc:var("lname", udf)
            if lname = udf
                print("<h1>Error</h1>")
                print("<b>You must define the last name
as per X.500 specification</b></body></html>")
                return
            endif
```

As before, `Doc:var()` is used to fetch the value of the form variable, `lname`. If `lname` is not defined, the variable `udf` is assigned to it. The `udf` variable was set to "undefined" at the beginning of the program.

3 • The remaining form field variables are extracted. `Doc:var()` is used to extract the form field variables.

```
            title = Doc:var("title", udf)
            telephone = Doc:var("telephone", udf)
            fax = Doc:var("fax", udf)
            location = Doc:var("location", udf)
            description = Doc:var("description", udf)
```

4 • The form field values are echoed back as part of the results HTML document:

```
            print("<h1>User information submitted</h1>")
            print("<pre><b><i>"); newline
            print("User name: ", uname); newline
            print("Last name: ", lname); newline
            ' Display the form fields only if they have
been defined
```

```
if title != udf
    print("Title: ", title); newline
endif
if telephone != udf
    print("Telephone: ", title); newline
endif
if fax != udf
    print("Fax: ", fax); newline
endif
if location != udf
    print("location: ", location); newline
endif
if description != udf
    print("Description: ", description);
newline
endif
print("</i></b></pre><hr>")
```

5 • The context in which the user is to be created is set:

```
context = Doc:var("context")
context = NDS:Context:Path
oldContext = NDS:Context:Path:change(context)
```

6 • The user object is created. First, it is deleted, if it exists. You may want to change this logic if you do not want the previous user object to be deleted:

```
ok = NDS:Delete(uname)
ok = NDS:Add:user(uname, lname)
```

`NDS:Delete()` can be used to delete any NDS object. It accepts the name of the object to be deleted as an argument.

`NDS:Add:user()` is used to create the user object. It accepts the user name (login name or common name) as the first argument, and the user's last name as the second argument. There are many other APIs under the `NDS:Add` hierarchy for each of the NDS objects that can be created.

7 • The other attributes specified by the remaining form fields are added. Note that first a check is done to see if these attributes are defined before adding them. This is done to prevent null values of these attributes from being defined.

```
if title != udf
    ok = NDS:Attribute:Value:add(uname,
"Title", title)
endif
if telephone != udf
    ok = NDS:Attribute:Value:add(uname,
"Telephone Number", telephone)
endif
if fax != udf
    ok = NDS:Attribute:Value:add(uname,
"Facsimile Telephone Number", fax)
endif
if location != udf
    ok = NDS:Attribute:Value:add(uname, "L",
location)
endif
if description != udf
    ok = NDS:Attribute:Value:add(uname,
"Description", description)
endif
```

The NDS:Attribute:Value:add() API is used to add attributes to the NDS object. The first argument is the object name to which attributes are to be added. The second argument is the attribute name. You can use the NetBasic documentation or Novell documentation to see the attribute names of user objects. The next section discusses a CGI script for displaying attribute names and attribute information which you can use to discover the attribute names for NDS objects. The third argument is the value to which the attribute should be set.

8 • The message is displayed that announces the user object has been added in the specified context:

```
        print("<b><i>Added previous user in ",
context, "</i></b>")
```

9 • The HTML end tags are generated by the following statement at the end of the outermost statement:

```
        print("</body></html>")
```

Viewing Attributes for NDS Objects

In the previous section, the NDSUSER.BAS script used attribute names for user objects to define attribute values. This section discusses how to write a CGI script to discover attribute values and attribute information.

The CGI script NDSATTR.BAS can be used to display the attributes of an object in the current context. Figure 11.12 shows the form that is displayed when NDSATTR.BAS is run via the CGI interface. You can enter the object whose attributes you want to view, and select the Send Form button to display the objects attributes. Figure 11.13 shows the attributes of the user object "kss" that was created using the CGI script NDSUSER.BAS discussed in the previous section. As you examine Figure 11.13, note the user object attributes CN (common name), Description, Facsimile Telephone Number, L (Location), and so on.

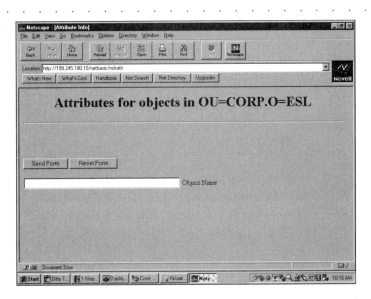

F I G U R E   11.12

Form display for
NDSATTR.BAS CGI script

▶ • ◀

FIGURE 11.13

Attributes displayed by
NDSATTR.BAS CGI script

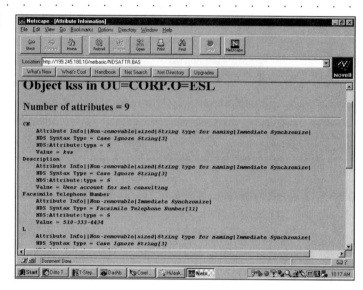

Now let's understand how the NDSATTR.BAS CGI script works. Listing 11.3 shows the NDSATTR.BAS program.

LISTING 11.3

NDSATTR.BAS Program

```
' NDSATTR.BAS: This demonstrates how to display NDS object
attribute info
' Author: Karanjit S. G. S. Siyan
'
#include "html.h"
sub main

    oname = Doc:var("oname", "undefined")
    if oname = "undefined"
        ' Display forms
        print("<html><head><title>Attribute
Info</title></head><body>")
```

```
        print("<center><h1>Attributes for objects in ",
NDS:Context:path, "</h1></center>")
        print("<HR>"); newline
        print("<FORM METHOD=POST ACTION=NDSATTR.BAS>");
newline
        print('<input type=submit value="Send Form"> ')
        print('<input type=reset value="Reset Form">')
        newline; newline

        print("<input type=text size=45 name=oname> Object
Name<br>")

        print("</FORM>"); newline
    else
        ' Process input
        print("<HTML><HEAD><TITLE>Attribute
Information</TITLE></HEAD>")
        newline
        print("<BODY>"); newline
        print("<h1>Object ", oname, " in ",
NDS:Context:path, "</h1>")
        print("<pre><b>"); newline
        count = NDS:Attribute:locate(oname)

        print("<h2>Number of attributes = ", count,
"</h2><hr>"); newline
        next = NDS:Attribute:first
        do while next != ""
            print(next); newline
            NDSAttrType = NDS:Attribute:True:type
            attrInfo = NDS:Attribute:info
            dispAttr(attrInfo); newline
```

```
                        print("    NDS Syntax Type = <i>",
        NDSyntaxType(NDSAttrType), "[", NDSAttrType, "]</i>");
        newline
                        attrValue = NDS:Attribute:value
                        attrType = NDS:Attribute:type
                        print("    NDS:Attribute:type = <i>", attrType,
        "</i>"); newline
                        if (NDSAttrType != 9) & (NDSAttrType != 21)
                            print("    Value = <i>", attrValue,
        "</i>"); newline
                            if NDSAttrType = 24
                                dateObj = Date:object(attrValue)
                                print("            <i>",
        dateObj.date, " ", dateObj.time); newline
                            endif
                        else
                            ' NDS attribute syntax
                            '        9 (octet string)
                            '        21 (stream)
                            count = str:length(attrValue)
                            i = 1
                            print("    Translated Value = <i>")
                            do while i <= count
                                print(Data:translate(str:sub(attrValue,
        i, 1)))

                                i = i + 1
                            enddo
                            print("</i>"); newline
                        endif
                        next = NDS:Attribute:next
                    enddo
                    print("</b></pre>")
                endif
                print("</body></html>")
```

```
end sub
sub dispAttr
    local("attrstr", "count", "i", "code")
    attrstr = param(1)
    count = str:length(attrstr)
    i = 1
    print("    Attribute Info<i>")
    do while i <= count
        code = Str:sub(attrstr, i, 1)
        str = dispCode(code)
        print("|", str)
        i = i + 1
    enddo
    print("</i>")
end sub
sub dispCode
    local ("code")
    code = param(1)
    if code = "H"
        return ("Hidden")
    endif
    if code = "I"
        return ("Immediate Synchronize")
    endif
    if code = "N"
        return ("Non-removable")
    endif
    if code = "P"
        return ("Public")
    endif
    if code = "R"
        return ("Read-only")
    endif
    if code = "S"
```

```
                    return ("Server readable-only")
            endif
            if code = "T"
                    return ("String type for naming")
            endif
            if code = "V"
                    return ("Single valued")
            endif
            if code = "W"
                    return ("Write managed")
            endif
            if code = "Y"
                    return ("Value not synchronized between replicas")
            endif
            if code = "Z"
                    return ("sized")
            endif
            return ("")
        end sub
        sub NDSyntaxType
            local("ndstype")
            ndstype = param(1)
            if ndstype = 0
                    return("Unknown")
            endif
            if ndstype = 1
                    return("Distinguished Name")
            endif
            if ndstype = 2
                    return("Case Exact String")
            endif
            if ndstype = 3
                    return("Case Ignore String")
            endif
```

```
if ndstype = 4
    return("Printable String")
endif
if ndstype = 5
    return("Numeric String")
endif
if ndstype = 6
    return("Case Ignore List")
endif
if ndstype = 7
    return("Boolean")
endif
if ndstype = 8
    return("Integer")
endif
if ndstype = 9
    return("Octet String")
endif
if ndstype = 10
    return("Telephone Number")
endif
if ndstype = 11
    return("Facsimile Telephone Number")
endif
if ndstype = 12
    return("Netaddress")
endif
if ndstype = 13
    return("Octet List")
endif
if ndstype = 14
    return("Email Address")
endif
if ndstype = 15
```

```
                    return("Path")
            endif
            if ndstype = 16
                    return("Replica Pointer")
            endif
            if ndstype = 17
                    return("Object ACL")
            endif
            if ndstype = 18
                    return("Postal Address")
            endif
            if ndstype = 19
                    return("Timestamp")
            endif
            if ndstype = 20
                    return("Class Name")
            endif
            if ndstype = 21
                    return("Stream")
            endif
            if ndstype = 22
                    return("Counter")
            endif
            if ndstype = 23
                    return("Back Link")
            endif
            if ndstype = 24
                    return("Time")
            endif
            if ndstype = 25
                    return("Typed Name")
            endif
            if ndstype = 26
                    return("Hold")
```

```
    endif
    if ndstype = 27
        return("Interval")
    endif
    if ndstype = 28
        return("Syntax Count")
    endif
    return("?Unknown")
end sub
```

The main logic in the program is contained in the following enclosing if statement:

```
oname = Doc:var("oname", "undefined")
if oname = "undefined"
        ' Display forms
else
        ' Process input
endif
```

The then part of the if statement is executed when no user data has been entered. At this point the field oname is not defined. In the then part the NetBasic print statements generate the HTML form that you saw in Figure 11.12.

The else part of the enclosing if statement is executed when at least some user data is entered. At this point, oname is defined. The else part processes the user input data, and the attributes of the specified NDS object are displayed (see Figure 11.10).

In the then part, the following actions are performed:

I • The HTML header and formatting tags are sent to the standard output:

```
        print("<html><head><title>Attribute
Info</title></head><body>")
        print("<center><h1>Attributes for objects in
", NDS:Context:path, "</h1></center>")
        print("<HR>"); newline
```

The current NDS context is displayed in the header text using the
`NDS:Context:path()` API.

2 • The form requesting user input is displayed:

```
        print("<FORM METHOD=POST
ACTION=NDSATTR.BAS>"); newline
        print('<input type=submit value="Send Form">
')

        print('<input type=reset value="Reset Form">')
        newline; newline

        print("<input type=text size=45 name=oname>
Object Name<br>")

        print("</FORM>"); newline
```

The form data is sent using the POST method, and the CGI program to
process the form data (the ACTION attribute) is NDSATTR.BAS. The
form data is processed by the `else` part of the outermost `if` statement.

3 • The end HTML tags are generated after the outermost `if` statement:

```
        print("</body></html>")
```

In the `else` part of the outermost `if` statement, the user data is processed as
follows:

1 • The HTML header and formatting tags for the output HTML page are
printed:

```
        print("<HTML><HEAD><TITLE>Attribute
Information</TITLE></HEAD>")
        newline
        print("<BODY>"); newline
        print("<h1>Object ", oname, " in ",
NDS:Context:path, "</h1>")
```

The object name that was selected and the current NDS context are displayed in the header text using the form field variable `oname` and the `NDS:Context:path()` API.

2 • The pre-format HTML tag is printed so that the output will not be formatted by the Web browser:

```
print("<pre><b>"); newline
```

3 • The `NDS:Attribute:locate()` API is used to obtain the count of the number of attributes that are set for the NDS object. This API takes the name of the NDS object as an argument and sets an internal pointer so that the `NDS:Attribute:first()` and `NDS:Attribute:next()` APIs can be used to traverse through the attributes in sequence.

```
count = NDS:Attribute:locate(oname)

print("<h2>Number of attributes = ", count,
"</h2><hr>"); newline
next = NDS:Attribute:first
```

The number of attributes returned by the call to `NDS:Attribute:locate()` are displayed in the header text.

4 • A `do while` loop is set up to loop through the attributes for the NDS object. At the end of the `do while` loop, the `NDS:Attribute:next()` API is called to get the next attribute. When the next attribute obtained is a null string, the loop is terminated.

```
do while next != ""
    ' Logic to display attribute info and other
data
        '
    next = NDS:Attribute:next
enddo
```

The logic in the `do while` statement is explained in the steps that follow:

1 • The attribute name (next) is displayed. The NDS attribute syntax code is obtained by calling NDS:Attribute:True:type(). This returns a code value that is decoded and displayed later on.

```
print(next); newline
NDSAttrType = NDS:Attribute:True:type
attrInfo = NDS:Attribute:info
dispAttr(attrInfo); newline
```

The NDS attribute information is obtained by calling NDSLAttribute:Info. This returns a string of characters indicating constraints on the attribute received by NDS:Attribute:first() or NDS:Atribute:next(). The constraint codes are H for Hidden, I for Immediate Synchronization of the attribute, N for non-removable, and so on. The dispAttr() subroutine is written to decode these string codes and return a string description of these codes. You can examine the dispAttr() and dispCode() subroutines to see how these codes are decoded.

2 • The NDS syntax codes, and NDS attribute type values are displayed.

```
        print("    NDS Syntax Type = <i>",
NDSyntaxType(NDSAttrType), "[", NDSAttrType, "]</i>");
newline
        attrValue = NDS:Attribute:value
        attrType = NDS:Attribute:type
        print("    NDS:Attribute:type = <i>",
attrType, "</i>"); newline
```

The NDS syntax code was obtained by an earlier call to NDS:Attribute:True:Type. The subroutine NDSyntaxType() is written to translate the NDS syntax code to a string description. You can examine the NDSyntaxType() subroutine to see how this translation is done. This subroutine also contains documentation on the syntax codes.

The NDS:Attribute:type() is used to determine if the attribute value is represented as a String (S), Real (R), Integer or handle (I), Object (O), Logical (L) or Unknown (U) in the NetBasic language.

3 • The attribute value is displayed. However, first a check is performed to see if the value is a nondisplayable string:

```
        if (NDSAttrType != 9) & (NDSAttrType !=
21)
            print("    Value = <i>", attrValue,
"</i>"); newline
            if NDSAttrType = 24
                dateObj =
Date:object(attrValue)
                print("             <i>",
dateObj.date, " ", dateObj.time); newline
            endif
        else
            ' NDS attribute syntax
            '      9 (octet string)
            '      21 (stream)
            count = str:length(attrValue)
            i = 1
            print("   Translated Value = <i>")
            do while i <= count

print(Data:translate(str:sub(attrValue, i, 1)))
                i = i + 1
            enddo
            print("</i>"); newline
        endif
```

The NDS syntax code of 9 or 21 implies that the attribute is an arbitrary Octet String (9) or Stream type (21). These types contain binary data that the Web browser is unable to process.

The else part of the if statement contains the logic to sequence through each binary byte and translate nondisplayable characters to blank by calling the Data:translate() API. The Data:translate() API converts non-displayable characters in the string argument passed to it to blanks.

The `then` part of the `if` statement contains the logic to display ordinary string or integer data. If the attribute is a time value (NDS syntax code of 24), the time value is decoded and displayed. The time attribute value is first converted to a NetBasic Date object by calling `Date:object()`. The Date object accepts the number of seconds since January 1, 1970-the Universal Time Format (UTF). Once the attribute time value is converted to a Date object, its fields are used to display the date and time value.

4 • The end HTML tags are generated after the outermost `if` statement:

```
print("</body></html>")
```

The `dispAttr()`, `dispCode()`, and `NDSyntaxType()` subroutines contain logic to translate various NDS codes to an equivalent string format. The understanding of these subroutines is left as an exercise for the reader.

Viewing NDS Objects in a Container

You can write CGI scripts to browse an NDS container and list the subordinate objects in that container. The NDS_TOP.BAS CGI script shown in Listing 11.4 performs this function. Figure 11.14 shows the form that is displayed when the NDS_TOP.BAS CGI script is executed. The Context field contains, by default, the current context value. You can change it to any legal context value. The root context is specified by using [Root]. Figure 11.15 shows the immediate objects that are to be found in the specified context.

FIGURE 11.14

Form displayed by running the NDS_TOP.BAS CGI script

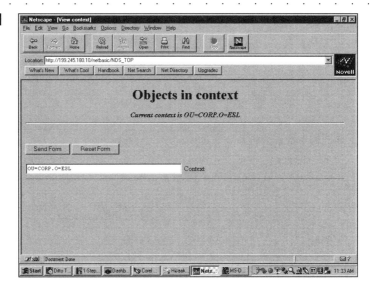

FIGURE 11.15

Display of subordinate objects for the specified context

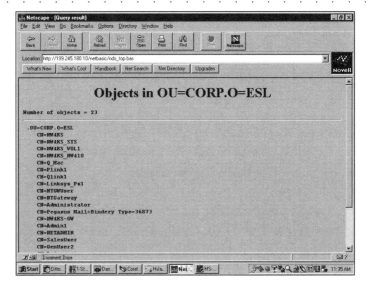

NDS_TOP.BAS Program

```
' NDS_TOP.BAS: This demonstrates how to display subordinate
NDS objects
' Author: Karanjit S. G. S. Siyan
'
#include "html.h"
sub main
    context = Doc:var("context", "undefined")
    if context = "undefined"
        print("<html><head><title>View
context</title></head><body>")
        print("<center><h1>Objects in context</h1>")
        print("<b><i>Current context is ",
NDS:Context:Path, "</i></b></center>")
        print("<hr>"); newline
        print("<FORM METHOD=POST ACTION=nds_top.bas>");
newline
        print('<input type=submit value="Send Form"> ')
        print('<input type=reset value="Reset Form">')
        newline; newline
        print("<input type=text size=45 name=context
value=", NDS:Context:Path,"> Context<hr>")
        print("</FORM>"); newline
        print("</body></html>")
    else
        print("<html><head><title>Query
result</title></head><body>")
        print("<center><h1>Objects in ", context,
"</h1></center>")
        ' Form a complete name for context
        firstChar = Str:sub(context, 1, 1)
        if (firstChar != "[") & (firstChar != ".")
```

```
        context = "." + context
    endif
    offset = 0
    print("<b><pre>"); newline
    enum(context)
    print("</b></pre></body></html>")
    endif
end sub
' Enumerate objects in specified context
sub enum
    local("top", "count")
    top = param(1)
    count = NDS:locate(top)
    next = NDS:first
    print("<b>Number of objects = ", count, "</b><hr>")
    print(str:repeat(" ", offset), top); newline
    offset = offset + 4
    do while (count > 0)
        print(str:repeat(" ", offset), next); newline
        next = NDS:next
        count = count - 1
    enddo

end sub
```

The main logic in the program is contained in the following enclosing `if` statement:

```
context = Doc:var("context", "undefined")
if context = "undefined"
    ' Display forms
else
    ' Process input
endif
```

The `then` part of the `if` statement is executed when no user data has been entered. At this point the form field `context` is not defined. In the `then` part, the NetBasic `print` statements generate the HTML form shown in Figure 11.14.

The `else` part of the enclosing `if` statement is executed when at least some user data is entered. At this point, `context` is defined. The `else` part processes the user input data, and displays the objects in the specified context (see Figure 11.15).

In the `then` part, the following actions are performed:

1 • The HTML header and formatting tags are sent to the standard output:

```
        print("<html><head><title>View
context</title></head><body>")
        print("<center><h1>Objects in context</h1>")
        print("<b><i>Current context is ",
NDS:Context:Path, "</i></b></center>")
        print("<hr>"); newline
```

The current context obtained by calling `NDS:Context:path()` is displayed after the HTML header text.

2 • The form HTML tags and the form field definitions are generated:

```
        print("<FORM METHOD=POST
ACTION=nds_top.bas>"); newline
        print('<input type=submit value="Send Form">
')
        print('<input type=reset value="Reset
Form">')
        newline; newline
        print("<input type=text size=45 name=context
value=", NDS:Context:Path,"> Context<hr>")
        print("</FORM>"); newline
```

The form data is sent using the POST method, and processed by the script NDS_TOP.BAS. This is the same script that is being analyzed here. The else part of the outermost if statement in this script is used to process the data.

3 • The end HTML tags are generated:

```
print("</body></html>")
```

The else part of the outermost if statement performs the following processing of the user input:

I • The HTML header and formatting tags for the results HTML document are sent to the standard output:

```
print("<html><head><title>Query
result</title></head><body>")
print("<center><h1>Objects in ", context,
"</h1></center>")
```

2 • A complete name (also called the *distinguished name*) is formed for the specified context. This name must have a dot (.) in front of it and include all the containers leading to the root. If the context is the root, no dots are specified. Instead, it is represented by the special name [Root].

```
firstChar = Str:sub(context, 1, 1)
if (firstChar != "[") & (firstChar != ".")
    context = "." + context
endif
```

3 • The pre-format HTML tags are generated and the enum() subroutine called with the specified context:

```
offset = 0
print("<b><pre>"); newline
enum(context)
```

The enum() subroutine prints the subordinate objects in the specified context.

4 • The end HTML tags are generated.

```
print("</b></pre></body></html>")
```

Most of the logic for enumerating the subordinates in the context is contained in the enum() subroutine. The enum() subroutine performs the following actions:

I • The local variables are defined. The context parameter is extracted by a call to param() and the NDS:locate() is called to obtain a count of the number of subordinate objects and set an internal pointer so that the NDS:first() and NDS:next() can be used to obtain the first and successive subordinates.

```
local("top", "count")
top = param(1)
count = NDS:locate(top)
next = NDS:first
```

2 • The number of subordinate objects and the top level container are displayed:

```
print("<b>Number of objects = ", count,
"</b><hr>")
print(str:repeat(" ", offset), top); newline
offset = offset + 4
```

The variable offset is a global variable that is used to offset the display string by the specified amount.

3 • The do while statement loops through the successive subordinate objects by calling NDS:next() and prints each of the subordinate objects.

```
do while (count > 0)
    print(str:repeat(" ", offset), next); newline
    next = NDS:next
    count = count - 1
enddo
```

Viewing Last Modified Information for NDS Objects

The NDSDATE.BAS CGI script in Listing 11.5 shows how you can display the last modified date and time stamp information for NDS objects. Figure 11.16 shows the form that is displayed when the NDSDATE.BAS is run. It is, in fact, the same form that was generated by the NDS_TOP.BAS CGI script discussed in the previous section. Figure 11.17 shows the results of submitting the form data. The results are similar to that displayed by NDS_TOP.BAS, with the major distinction that the date and time the subordinate NDS object was last modified is displayed.

Form displayed by running the NDSDATE.BAS CGI script

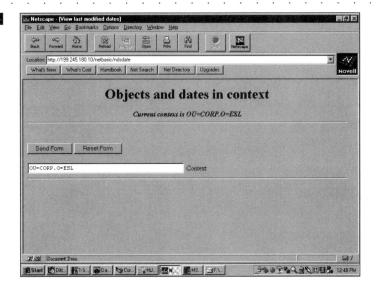

▶ · ◀

F I G U R E   11.17

Display of subordinate objects with the last modified date and time information

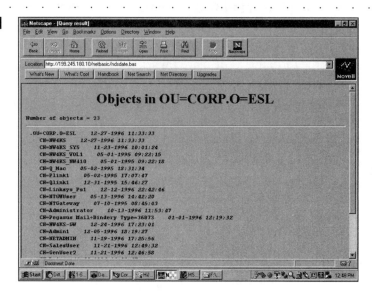

Objects in OU=CORP.O=ESL

LISTING   11.5

NDSDATE.BAS Program

```
' NDSDATE.BAS: This demonstrates how to display the last
modified date
' of NDS objects.
' Author: Karanjit S. G. S. Siyan
'
#include "html.h"
sub main
    context = Doc:var("context", "undefined")
    if context = "undefined"
        print("<html><head><title>View last modified
dates</title></head><body>")
        print("<center><h1>Objects and dates in
context</h1>")
```

```
        print("<b><i>Current context is ",
NDS:Context:Path, "</i></b></center>")
        print("<hr>"); newline
        print("<FORM METHOD=POST ACTION=ndsdate.bas>");
newline
        print('<input type=submit value="Send Form"> ')
        print('<input type=reset value="Reset Form">')
        newline; newline
        print("<input type=text size=45 name=context
value=", NDS:Context:Path,"> Context<hr>")
        print("</FORM>"); newline
        print("</body></html>")
    else
        print("<html><head><title>Query
result</title></head><body>")
        print("<center><h1>Objects in ", context,
"</h1></center>")
        ' Form a complete name for context
        firstChar = Str:sub(context, 1, 1)
        if (firstChar != "[") & (firstChar != ".")
            context = "." + context
        endif
        offset = 0
        print("<b><pre>"); newline
        enum(context)
        print("</b></pre></body></html>")
    endif
end sub
' Enumerate objects in specified context
sub enum
    local("top", "count")
    top = param(1)
    count = NDS:locate(top)
    next = NDS:first
```

```
        dateObj = Date:object(NDS:Date:modified)
        print("<b>Number of objects = ", count, "</b><hr>")
        print(str:repeat(" ", offset), top, "    <i>",
   dateObj.date, " ", dateObj.time, "</i>"); newline
        offset = offset + 4
        do while (count > 0)
             print(str:repeat(" ", offset), next, "    <i>",
   dateObj.date, " ", dateObj.time, "</i>"); newline
             next = NDS:next
             dateObj = Date:object(NDS:Date:modified)
             count = count - 1
        enddo


     end sub
```

The NDSDATE.BAS program is similar to the NDS_TOP.BAS program discussed in the previous section. The major difference is how the `enum()` subroutine is written. The `enum()` subroutine is discussed next. For a discussion of the `main` subroutine, refer to the discussion in the previous section.

Most of the logic for enumerating the subordinates and the last date and time modified information is contained in the `enum()` subroutine. The `enum()` subroutine performs the following actions:

1 • The local variables are defined. The context parameter is extracted by a call to `param()`. `NDS:locate()` is called to obtain a count of the number of subordinate objects and set an internal pointer so that the `NDS:first()` and `NDS:next()` can be used to obtain the first and successive subordinates:

```
        local("top", "count")
        top = param(1)
        count = NDS:locate(top)
        next = NDS:first
```

2 • The number of subordinate objects and the top-level container are displayed:

```
    dateObj = Date:object(NDS:Date:modified)
    print("<b>Number of objects = ", count,
"</b><hr>")
    print(str:repeat(" ", offset), top, "   <i>",
dateObj.date, " ", dateObj.time, "</i>"); newline
    offset = offset + 4
```

NDS:Date:modified() is used to obtain the last modified time of the NDS object that was obtained by a prior call to NDS:locate(), NDS:first(), or NDS:next(). The time is in UTF format and is used as an argument to Data:object() to build a NetBasic Date object. The date and time fields of the Date object are used to display the date and time information.

The variable offset is a global variable that is used to offset the display string by the specified amount.

3 • The do while statement loops through the successive subordinate objects by calling NDS:next() and prints each of the subordinate objects, as well as the last modified date and time information:

```
    do while (count > 0)
        print(str:repeat(" ", offset), next, "
<i>", dateObj.date, " ", dateObj.time, "</i>");
newline
        next = NDS:next
        dateObj = Date:object(NDS:Date:modified)
        count = count - 1
    enddo
```

Note that the Date object is built prior to using its date and time fields that contain the last modified date and time information.

Viewing NDS Partition Information

The NDSPART.BAS program shown in Listing 11.6 illustrates some of the NDS APIs that can be used to display partition information. Figure 11.18 shows the form that is displayed when NDSPART.BAS is executed. You must enter the name of a server that contains partitions. Figure 11.19 shows the partitions that exist on the specified server. Because the server contains a single partition (the master partition), the information that is displayed is very brief.

FIGURE   11.18

Form displayed by running the NDSPART.BAS CGI script

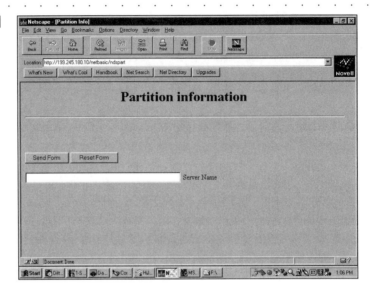

FIGURE   11.19

Display of partition information for the specified server

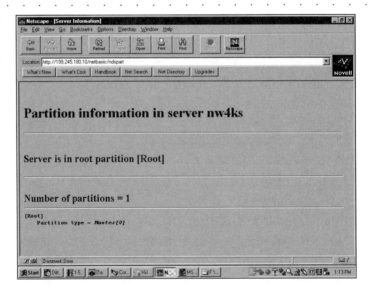

NDSPART.BAS Program

```
' NDSPART.BAS: This demonstrates how to display partition
information
' Author: Karanjit S. G. S. Siyan
'

#include "html.h"
sub main

    sname = Doc:var("sname", "undefined")
    if sname = "undefined"
        ' Display forms
        print("<html><head><title>Partition
Info</title></head><body>")
        print("<center><h1>Partition
information</h1></center>")
        print("<HR>"); newline
        print("<FORM METHOD=POST ACTION=ndspart>"); newline
        print('<input type=submit value="Send Form"> ')
        print('<input type=reset value="Reset Form">')
        newline; newline

        print("<input type=text size=45 name=sname> Server
Name<br>")

        print("</FORM>"); newline
    else
        ' Process input
        print("<HTML><HEAD><TITLE>Server
Information</TITLE></HEAD>")
        newline
        print("<BODY>"); newline
        print("<h1>Partition information in server ",
```

```
sname, "</h1><hr>")
        rootName = NDS:Partition:Root:get(sname)
        print("<h2>Server is in root partition ", rootName,
"</h2><hr>")

        print("<pre><b>"); newline
        count = NDS:Partition:locate(sname)

        print("<h2>Number of partitions = ", count,
"</h2><hr>")
        next = NDS:Partition:first
        do while next != ""
            print(next); newline
            partType = NDS:Partition:type
            print("    Partition type = <i>",
partDescr(partType), "[", partType, "]"); newline
            next = NDS:Partition:next
        enddo
        print("</b></pre>")
    endif
    print("</body></html>")
end sub
' Translates partition code to string description
sub partDescr
    local("pcode")
    pcode = param(1)
    if pcode = 0
        return ("Master")
    endif
    if pcode = 1
        return ("Replica")
    endif
    if pcode = 3
        return ("Subordinate")
```

```
      endif
      return (pcode)
end sub
```

The main logic in the program is contained in the following enclosing `if` statement:

```
sname = Doc:var("sname", "undefined")
if sname = "undefined"
    ' Display forms
else
    ' Process input
endif
```

The `then` part of the `if` statement is executed when no user data has been entered. At this point, the form field `sname` is not defined. In the `then` part, the NetBasic `print` statements generate the HTML form shown in Figure 11.18.

The `else` part of the enclosing `if` statement is executed when at least some user data is entered. At this point, `sname` is defined. The `else` part processes the user input data, and displays the partition information for the specified server (see Figure 11.19).

In the `then` part, the following actions are performed:

1 • The HTML header and formatting tags are sent to the standard output:

```
        print("<html><head><title>Partition
Info</title></head><body>")
        print("<center><h1>Partition
information</h1></center>")
        print("<HR>"); newline
```

2 • The form HTML tags and the form field definitions are generated:

```
        print("<FORM METHOD=POST ACTION=ndspart>");
newline
        print('<input type=submit value="Send Form">
')
        print('<input type=reset value="Reset
Form">')
```

```
newline; newline

print("<input type=text size=45 name=sname>
Server Name<br>")

print("</FORM>"); newline
```

The form data is sent using the POST method, and processed by the script NDSPART. This is the same script that is being analyzed here. The else part of the outermost if statement in this script is used to process the data.

3 • The end HTML tags are generated at the end of the if statement:

```
print("</body></html>")
```

The else part of the outermost if statement performs the following processing of the user input:

1 • The HTML header and formatting tags for the results HTML document are sent to the standard output:

```
print("<HTML><HEAD><TITLE>Server
Information</TITLE></HEAD>")
newline
print("<BODY>"); newline
print("<h1>Partition information in server ",
sname, "</h1><hr>")
```

2 • The name of the partition in which the specified server object is located is printed:

```
rootName = NDS:Partition:Root:get(sname)
print("<h2>Server is in root partition ",
rootName, "</h2><hr>")
```

The NDS:Partition:Root:get() accepts the name of an NDS object as an argument, and returns the partition root node for the object.

3 • The pre-format HTML tags are generated and NDS:Partition:locate() is called with the specified server as an argument. NDS:Partition:locate() returns a count of the number of partitions on the specified server object and sets an internal pointer to the partitions so that calls to NDS:Partition:first() and NDS:Partition:next() return the partition name of the first and successive partitions.

```
print("<pre><b>"); newline
count = NDS:Partition:locate(sname)

print("<h2>Number of partitions = ", count,
"</h2><hr>")
next = NDS:Partition:first
```

4 • The do while loop is used to traverse the partition list and print information on each partition replica that is found:

```
do while next != ""
    print(next); newline
    partType = NDS:Partition:type
    print("    Partition type = <i>",
partDescr(partType), "[", partType, "]"); newline
    next = NDS:Partition:next
enddo
```

NDS:Partition:next() is used to sequence through the partition list. NDS:Partition:type() is used to get an integer code for the partition type. For each partition, the subroutine partDescr() is called with the partition code as an argument. This subroutine returns a descriptive text for the partition code.

5 • The end HTML tags are generated.

```
print("</b></pre>")
print("</body></html>")
```

The partDescr() subroutine contains logic to translate the partition code to a descriptive text. The understanding of this routine is left as an exercise for the reader.

Summary

The Novell Web Server comes with the NDSOBJ.NLM extension that permits Web client users to browse and view the Novell Directory Services. This chapter discussed how to configure the Novell Web Server so that Web browsers can be used to browse the NDS tree. You learned about the security issues concerning the practice of giving external users access to the NDS tree. You also learned how to restrict security for external users by defining the access.www file.

The latter part of the chapter discussed several detailed examples of writing NetBasic CGI scripts to access information in the NDS tree. You also learned how to write CGI scripts to add NDS objects to the NDS tree.

## CHAPTER 12

Installing and Configuring NetWare/IP and DNS for Intranets

If you want to use TCP/IP as your primary protocol on the intranet, you should install and configure NetWare/IP. Even if you do not plan to use TCP/IP as your primary protocol, and you decide to use IPX with the NetWare IPX/IP gateway to communicate with the Novell Web Server, you should still investigate NetWare/IP because NetWare/IP comes with a Domain Name System (DNS) server.

The DNS server implements the DNS protocol that is used for name resolution on the Internet. By running DNS on your IntranetWare server, you can use DNS hostnames instead of IP addresses.

Overview of NetWare/IP

NetWare/IP has the following components:

▸ *NetWare/IP server.* This consists of a series of NLMs that run on the IntranetWare server. These NLMs enable NetWare applications that previously used IPX to use TCP/IP as their transport protocol.

▸ *NetWare/IP client.* This allows a network workstation configured with a NIC to use TCP/IP protocols instead of (or in addition to) the IPX protocol. The NetWare client must be configured to use ODI drivers.

▸ *Domain Name System server.* A NetWare server can be set up as a Domain Name System (DNS) server. The DNS server provides a distributed name lookup service that resolves symbolic names of hosts to their IP addresses. NetWare/IP clients use the DNS to look up the name of their nearest Domain SAP Servers (DSS).

▸ *Domain SAP/RIP Servers (DSS).* These are used as repositories of SAP/RIP information on the network. Service Advertising Protocol (SAP) is used in NetWare networks by NetWare services to advertise themselves to the rest of the network. Routing Information Protocol (RIP) is used to exchange IPX routing information. By using DSS, it is possible to partition networks into domains called *NetWare/IP domains* so that NetWare/IP clients and servers know of services in their NetWare/IP domain only.

Understanding NetWare/IP Domains

NetWare/IP domains should not be confused with DNS domains that are used in IP networks as a general-purpose name lookup service for hostnames. While DNS can be used by a mix of NetWare workstations, NetWare servers, and UNIX-based machines, DSS is used only in NetWare networks. DSS and DNS servers can coexist on a network without any conflict.

Figure 12.1 shows an IP network for three separate departments of the hypothetical organization CaveLight, Inc. These department networks may be in different locations and are connected using IP routers.

Example of a network using NetWare/IP domains

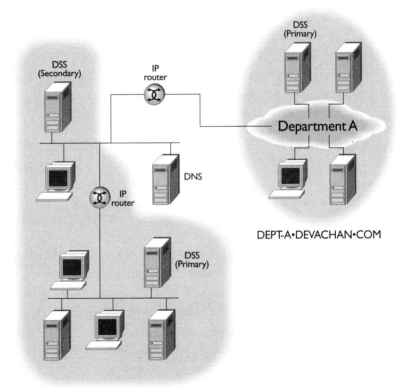

DEPT-A•DEVACHAN•COM

DEPT-BC•DEVACHAN•COM

You can have one logical NetWare/IP domain encompassing the entire network, or you can break the network into several logical domains.

The NetWare/IP domain must have at least one DSS, called the *primary* DSS server. As mentioned previously, the DSS server acts as a repository for all SAP/RIP information. The DSS server broadcasts SAP/RIP information at periodic intervals to workstations and servers within the NetWare/IP domain. By performing this action, it emulates the requirements for SAP/RIP broadcasts for an IPX network. NetWare/IP nodes learn of services on a NetWare network from the DSS. NetWare/IP servers communicate with the DSS periodically to obtain and update SAP/RIP updates. When a NetWare/IP client uses commands such as NLIST SERVER or DISPLAY SERVERS (console command) that require SAP information, the NetWare/IP server responds with information obtained from a DSS server.

It is not necessary for a DSS server to also be a NetWare/IP server. These services can be implemented on separate servers. On a small network, the DSS server and NetWare/IP server can be implemented on the same server.

The primary DSS server supports all NetWare/IP nodes (clients and servers) in its NetWare/IP domain. The NetWare/IP nodes use DNS to find the name of the nearest DSS for obtaining SAP/RIP information.

You may decide to divide the IP network into several logical NetWare/IP domains. Reasons for doing this could be to

- Limit the amount of SAP/RIP information that must be maintained by DSS servers for a domain

- Reduce the processing overhead on a DSS server

You can also increase efficiency by spreading the processing load across multiple DSS servers deployed throughout the network.

Figure 12.1 shows a network divided into two NetWare/IP domains. One NetWare/IP domain encompasses the Department A network and the other NetWare/IP domain encompasses Department B and Department C networks. The NetWare/IP domains are shown with the following names:

DEPT-A.DEVACHAN.COM   (Department A network)
DEPT-BC.DEVACHAN.COM   (Department B, C network)

The choice of names for the NetWare/IP domain such as DEPT-A or DEPT-BC is arbitrary. You should use a convention that meets the needs of your organization. Novell documentation suggests names such as NWIP.DEVACHAN.COM and NWIP2.DEVACHEN.COM as names for the NetWare/IP domain.

The NetWare/IP domain DEPT-A.DEVACHAN.COM has a single primary DSS. The NetWare/IP domain DEPT-BC.DEVACHAN.COM has a primary DSS and a secondary DSS. The secondary DSS is located in the Department C network. This makes it possible for department C network to obtain SAP/RIP information by contacting a local DSS server rather than go across a router (and potentially slow and expensive WAN links) to obtain SAP/RIP information from the primary DSS server for domain DEPT-BC.DEVACHAN.COM.

Figure 12.1 includes a DNS server that is shown outside the NetWare/IP domains. This is to emphasize the point that NetWare/IP domains are used for NetWare-based networks and DNS servers can be use by NetWare and non-NetWare nodes (UNIX, VMS, MVS, and so on).

NetWare/IP Workstation Components

Figure 12.2 shows the NetWare workstation architecture that uses IPX only and Figure 12.3 shows the workstation architecture that uses TCP/IP to access NetWare services.

FIGURE 12.2

NetWare IPX client

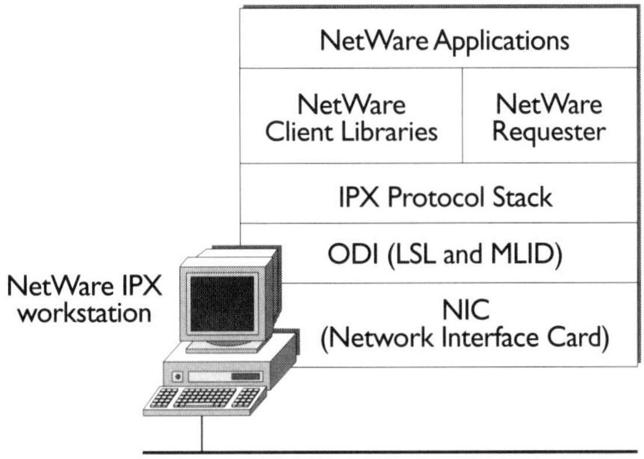

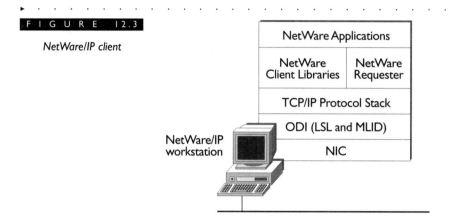

FIGURE 12.3

NetWare/IP client

In Figure 12.2, the bottom layer consists of the NIC hardware that represents Layers 2 and 1 of the OSI model. The ODI interface is implemented by the Link Support Layer, which communicates with the Multiple Link Interface Driver (MLID) for the NIC. The MLID communicates with the network hardware and with the Link Support Layer. The Link Support Layer provides a universal interface to the network adapter that allows a single protocol stack to establish communications with multiple NICs or multiple protocol stacks to communicate with a single NIC.

The SPX/IPX protocols provide the end-to-end transport protocols used by NetWare workstations. The NetWare libraries can be used by applications to access the transport protocols directly. The NetWare shell and the DOS Requester are special-purpose applications that provide file and print redirection.

Compare Figure 12.2 with Figure 12.3. Note that the IPX/SPX protocols in Figure 12.2 have been replaced with the TCP/IP protocol stack in Figure 12.3. The TCP/IP protocol stack implements the transport layer (OSI layer 4). The TCP/IP protocol stack also contains an implementation of the User Datagram Protocol (UDP). UDP is simpler transport protocol than TCP, and is more efficient for both the broadcasts and the requests/replies that are the nature of IP traffic.

The Domain Name System

NetWare/IP contains the file NAMED.NLM that implements the DNS, which is a distributed name-to-IP address database used on many TCP/IP based networks (including the Internet). When a workstation issues a TCP/IP command such as

```
ftp   ftp.novell.com
```

the name of the host `ftp.novell.com` must be resolved to the IP address of the host. The IP address is then used by the TCP/IP protocols to interact with the host. Generally, users find the symbolic hostname easier to remember than the IP address (32-bit number) of the host. The function of DNS is to translate the symbolic hostname to an IP address number that can be used by the protocol software. The term *host* refers to any machine that implements a TCP/IP stack. The resolution of the hostname to its equivalent IP address is performed by DNS protocols. These protocols and mechanisms are described in RFCs 1034, 1035, 1101, and 1183.

The IP Address is a 4-byte (32-bit) number assigned to every interface used by the IP protocol. If a NetWare server has two network interfaces to which IP is bound, a different IP address must be assigned to each of the boards. Most workstations have a single NIC and, if IP is used over this interface, a unique IP address must be assigned for the network interface.

The 32-bit IP address is usually written in a special format called the *dotted decimal notation*. In this notation, each of the four bytes that make up the IP address is expressed as a decimal number. The largest number contained in a byte is 255 and the smallest 0. Therefore, each of the bytes in the dotted decimal notation is a number between 0 and 255, inclusive.

The following is an example of an IP address in a dotted decimal notation:

```
144.19.74.200
```

The decimal number 144 corresponds to the most-significant byte (leftmost byte) of the 32-bit IP address and the number 200 corresponds to the least-significant byte (rightmost byte) of the IP address. The dotted decimal number notation is much simpler to read than the 32-bit number translated as one decimal number. For example, the IP address could also be represented as the single decimal number: 2417183432.

DNS is implemented as a distributed database for looking up name-to-IP address correspondence. Another way of performing the name lookup is to keep the name-to-IP address information in a static file. On UNIX systems, this static file is the `/etc/hosts` file. On NetWare servers, this static file is kept in the SYS:ETC/HOSTS file.

The following is a sample host file format:

```
# Local network host addresses
#
#ident "@(#)hosts    1.1 - 88/05/17"
#
127.0.0.1                 local localhost
144.19.74.1      sparc1 sp1
144.19.74.2      sparc2 sp2
144.19.74.3      sparc3 sp3
144.19.74.4      sparc4 sp4
144.19.74.5      sparc5 sp5
144.19.74.6      sparc6 sp6
144.19.74.7      sparc7 sp7
144.19.75.1      sparc8 sp8
144.19.75.2      sparc9 sp9
144.19.75.3      sparc10 sp10
144.19.75.4      sparc11 sp11
144.19.75.5      sparc12 sp12
144.19.75.6      sparc13 sp13
144.19.75.7      sparc14 sp14
144.19.74.101    cdos
144.19.74.102    server1 s386 nw
144.19.74.103    spws sparcsrv sps ss
144.19.74.201    sparcc1 spc1
144.19.74.202    sparcc2 spc2
```

The IP address 127.0.0.1 is a special address called the *loopback address*. Packets sent to this address never reach the network cable. It can be used for diagnostic purposes to verify that the internal code path through the TCP/IP protocols is working. It can also be used by client applications to communicate with software programs running on the same machine.

Each <IP Address, Host name> pair is expressed on a single line using the style shown in the hosts file. The multiple hostnames for the host are alias names. The protocol software, if configured to perform name resolution using this static host file, will look up the information for resolving a name. Consider the following command:

```
telnet sp7
```

The protocol software uses the following entry in the hosts file to resolve the name sp14:

```
144.19.74.7        sparc7 sp7
```

The name sp7 is an alias for the hostname `sparc7`. The corresponding IP address is 144.19.74.7. The protocol software resolves the name `sp7` to 144.19.74.7. The previous command then becomes:

```
telnet 144.19.74.7
```

There are a number of problems with the static host file approach. As the number of hosts on a network become large. It becomes increasingly difficult to keep this file up to date. Also, many organizations have more than one network administrator. It is difficult for these administrators to coordinate with each other every time host files must be changed. Even keeping this information in a large central static file becomes quickly unmanageable as the number of entries in this file becomes large.

DNS was developed to overcome the problems of name resolution on a large IP network. It provides a distributed database of names and IP addresses. The names could be hostnames or names of mail exchanger hosts. It also has provisions for keeping text descriptions of hostnames and for providing name resolution for other protocol families besides TCP/IP (such as Chaos net, XNS, and so on). It is, however, used predominantly for resolving hostnames for the TCP/IP protocols.

Part of the scheme used in DNS refers to the use of hierarchical names. In the *hierarchical name scheme* used in DNS, names are organized into a hierarchical tree. At the top of the tree is the root domain named by the period symbol (.). Because all names have this common root, the period is omitted when specifying the hierarchical name in most TCP/IP applications. Below the root domain are top-level domains (see Figure 12.4). These reflect how names are organized. Examples of top-level domains are shown in Table 12.1.

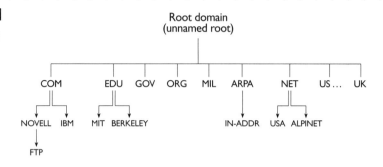

F I G U R E   12.4

Hierarchical names in DNS

T A B L E 12.1	TOP-LEVEL DOMAIN	DESCRIPTION
Examples of Top-Level Domains	COM	Commercial organization
	EDU	Educational institution. Universities, schools, and so on
	MIL	Military
	GOV	U.S. government
	NET	Network provider
	ORG	Organization
	ARPA	ARPANET (now historical, but still used for inverse address mapping)
	US	Country U.S.
	CA	Country Canada
	UK	Country United Kingdom
	DE	Country Germany
	SE	Country Sweden
	FR	Country France
	IN	Country India
	CN	Country China
	JA	Country Japan

The two-letter designations are assigned to country as per the CCITT standards. (The CCITT is an organization based in Geneva that develops standards for worldwide communications.) These are the same country designations used for specifying country objects in Novell Directory Services. Below the top-level domains are middle-level domains. There can be a number of middle level names. Each name is separated by the period (which can never occur as part of the name of a domain). The length of a complete domain name such as

```
madhav.tsl.org
```

cannot exceed 255 characters. In the name `madhav.tsl.org`, the name of the host is

```
madhav
```

This name is in the domain:

```
tsl.org
```

If another host in the same domain had the name sparky, its fully qualified name (FQN) would be

```
sparky.tsl.org
```

Many of the middle-level names refer to names of organizations. An organization is free to define subdomains within the organization. If it does this, it should provide appropriate name services to resolve names in these subdomains. For example, consider the organization DEVACHAN that has been given the domain name:

```
DEVACHAN.COM
```

If this organization has separate networks for its Corporate, Marketing, and Research arms, it could define three separate subdomains named CORP, MKTG, RESCH, and provide a DNS server or a number of DNS servers to resolve names on its networks. The domains in this case would be

```
CORP.DEVAHAN.COM
MKTG.DEVACHAN.COM
RESCH.DEVACHAN.COM
```

Although a DNS server is not required for each domain, it is common to have one or more for each domain being served. In Figure 12.4, there would be several DNS servers for the root domain. These would know about names of the top-level domains such as COM, EDU, MIL, ORG, NET, and so on. Several DNS servers may be used for a domain to perform load balancing, avoid unnecessary network traffic, and for reliability in case the primary DNS server was not available. The COM domain would have one or more DNS servers that know the names of all commercial organizations in the COM domain. Within the COM domain, a subdomain such as IBM.COM will have its own DNS servers for that domain. Hosts within a domain will query the local DNS server for the domain to resolve names. For example, the host WORLD.STD.COM would query the DNS server for the domain STD.COM to find out the IP address of the host FTP.NOVELL.COM or the IP address of ATHENA.SCS.ORG. Once this query is resolved, the results are usually cached locally for a configurable period of time.

The DNS servers for a domain must resolve names of hosts in their domains. They do not need to know about hosts in subdomains if DNS servers are defined for subdomains. Secondary DNS servers in a domain must know the IP address of the primary server in the domain it can contact for resolving a name query. A DNS server must also know the IP address of the parent DNS server.

Relationship Between DNS Domains and NetWare/IP Domains

A NetWare/IP *domain* is defined as a collection of NetWare/IP servers and clients that will receive SAP/RIP information provided by one or more DSS servers in that domain. A NetWare network can be partitioned into multiple NetWare/IP domains. A NetWare/IP domain must exist in the context of a DNS domain. A NetWare/IP domain is created by creating a DNS subdomain with the following properties:

1 • The DNS subdomain must be a subdomain of an existing DNS domain.

2 • The DNS subdomain cannot have subdomains.

After creating the NetWare/IP domain, you must configure NetWare/IP nodes that will belong to this domain with the NetWare/IP domain name.

Consider the organization LIGHTHOUSE that has a registered domain LIGHTHOUSE.ORG. This organization has two existing DNS subdomains for two separate networks for the Engineering and Marketing department as follows:

```
ENG.LIGHTHOUSE.ORG
MKTG.LIGHTHOUSE.ORG
```

It is decided to have a NetWare/IP domain covering the entire Engineering network and two NetWare/IP domains for the Marketing network. To create these NetWare/IP domains, you must first create DNS subdomains. For the DNS domain ENG.LIGHTHOUSE.ORG you can create a NetWare/IP domain as follows:

```
NWIP.ENG.LIGHTHOUSE.ORG
```

For the Marketing network, you must create two NetWare/IP domains. Therefore, you must first create two DNS subdomains of MKTG.LIGHTHOUSE.ORG. You can do this by performing the following:

```
NWIP1.MKTG.LIGHTHOUSE.ORG
NWIP2.MKTG.LIGHTHOUSE.ORG
```

After creating these DNS subdomains, you must configure the NetWare/IP nodes and DSS servers that will be in the NetWare/IP domain with the names of these subdomains.

The DSS Server

In order to provide SAP/RIP information to a NetWare/IP network, you must have at least one DSS server in a NetWare/IP domain. The DSS server holds a database of SAP/RIP information for a NetWare/IP domain. The information in the DSS server may be replicated on multiple DSS servers to improve performance across WAN links and for increased reliability. This section discusses how the DSS server updates its information and how this information is disseminated to other NetWare/IP nodes. This section also discusses the issue of DSS database replication for improved reliability.

Updating DSS Servers

In an IPX-based NetWare server, NetWare services (such as File, Print, and Database services) advertise their existence by using the SAP protocol. These services send SAP broadcast packets every 60 seconds (the actual value is configurable, but 60 seconds is the default). The broadcast packets are sent out over every network interface to which IPX is bound.

In NetWare/IP networks, NetWare services also advertise themselves using SAP. These SAP packets are sent directly to the DSS servers using UDP/IP packets.

When a NetWare server boots, it sends a SAP broadcast advertising its existence. If the server is configured as a NetWare/IP server, it also sends a SAP packet directly to the nearest DSS server using the UDP/IP protocol. The NetWare/IP server sends this information to the DSS server every 5 minutes (the value is configurable). If the DSS server does not receive the SAP refresh information, it times-out the information.

Disseminating DSS Information

In an IPX-based network, NetWare servers listen for SAP packets and cache this information. They then create a temporary bindery entry that lists the services seen by the server. NetWare IPX clients and applications locate these services by looking up the bindery information stored on the server.

NetWare/IP servers also keep a list of available services in the NetWare bindery. They do this by periodically requesting a download of this information from the DSS server. The download occurs at a configurable time interval (the default value is 5 minutes).

Replicating the DSS Database

To increase the reliability and availability of the DSS information, you can have several secondary DSS servers in a NetWare/IP domain. If the primary DSS server is unavailable or too busy to respond to requests by NetWare/IP servers, the secondary server can be used to provide the desired information.

To provide consistency of the DSS information, the DSS database is replicated to all the DSS servers in the NetWare/IP domain. In a large network consisting of slow WAN links, performance can be improved by avoiding the sending of requests for DSS information across the WAN links. This can be achieved by installing a local DSS server on each network so that NetWare/IP nodes can query the local DSS server instead of querying a remote DSS server separated by the slow WAN link. The primary DSS server holds the master copy of the DSS server and the secondary DSS servers hold a Read/Write replica.

SAP/RIP information can be received by DSS servers at different times. This can result in the DSS servers not having the same information. To keep the DSS servers synchronized, the secondary DSS servers contact the primary DSS server at periodic intervals to synchronize their information. If the DSS databases are out of synchronization, the synchronization process will commence. If, at any time, connectivity between primary and secondary DSS servers is lost, the secondary DSS server periodically attempts to establish a connection and initiate synchronization. If the secondary DSS server is activated after being down, it will attempt to synchronize with the primary DSS when it comes up.

To ensure that synchronization is done correctly, each DSS server maintains a database version number for the information stored on it any time. The database version number is changed whenever the database is changed by new information. The database version numbers help the DSS servers determine if the database is out of synchronization. During synchronization, the secondary DSS server uploads to the primary DSS any new records received since the last synchronization. It also downloads any records not in its database. Only changed, deleted, or new records are exchanged, and not the entire database.

Installing and Configuring NetWare/IP

The NetWare/IP is bundled on the CD-ROM that contains the NetWare 4 Operating System. In order to install NetWare/IP, you must mount the CD-ROM that contains the NetWare 4 Operating system at the server. It is also possible to use RCONSOLE to install NetWare/IP, with the CD-ROM installed at the workstation. You must load RSPX.NLM (which autoloads REMOTE.NLM) at the server, and RCONSOLE.EXE at the workstation. After you connect with the server console, the procedure is essentially the same, except that you specify the local CD-ROM drive when prompted for the source of the NetWare/IP distribution.

The complete installation of NetWare/IP consists of the following steps:

1 • Install NetWare/IP.

2 • Configure a DNS server, if one is not available.

3 • Configure a primary DSS server.

4 • Configure NetWare/IP.

If you are interested in just installing DNS services at the IntranetWare server, you must first install NetWare/IP, which contains the DNS files, and then configure DNS. Then you can skip the remaining steps to configure a primary DSS server and the NetWare/IP server. However, if you are interested in installing the complete NetWare/IP and configuring it, you must continue with the configuration of the primary DSS server and the NetWare/IP server.

Installing NetWare/IP

Follow these steps to install NetWare/IP:

1 • Unload any PKERNEL.NLM that might be running, to avoid incompatibility with different PKERNEL NLMs.

   UNLOAD PKERNEL

   At the server console run the INSTALL program.

   LOAD INSTALL

2 • On the IntranetWare server, select Product Options, "Choose an item or product listed above," and Install NetWare/IP.

3 •. When prompted to verify the source path, select the appropriate source and press Enter. You will see the NetWare/IP files being copied to the server.

4 • You will be informed about a README file. Press Esc to continue.

5 • Select No when asked if you want to exit installation. Select Yes if you want to read the README file and start the installation again.

6 • If TCP/IP has not been configured, you will be asked to configure it. See Chapter 3 for information on configuring TCP/IP at the IntranetWare server.

7 • You will see a screen announcing that the NetWare/IP installation is successful and that, if this is your first NetWare/IP server, you should

exit now and use UNICON to configure the DNS server, the primary DSS server, and the NetWare/IP server.

8 • Press Esc to continue.

9 • When asked if you want to configure the NetWare/IP server, answer No, because this is your first NetWare/IP server and you must configure the DNS server, as well as the primary DSS server.

10 • Answer the remaining questions about exiting the NetWare/IP installation so that you can exit the installation.

11 • Exit the INSTALL NLM.

Proceed to the next section on configuring NetWare/IP software.

Configuring DNS

If a DNS server is not available, follow these steps:

1 • You can start UNICON by typing the following command at the server console:

```
LOAD UNICON
```

If asked to log in, specify the server name on which you want to perform NetWare/IP configuration. You must also specify the Admin account name and password.

2 • Figure 12.5 shows the main UNICON screen. You can use the option on this screen to perform most NetWare/IP configuration tasks (see Table 12.2).

▶ · ◀

FIGURE 12.5

Main UNICON screen

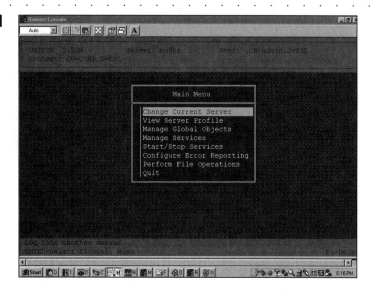

T A B L E 12.2	OPTION	DESCRIPTION
UNICON main screen options	Change Current Server	Used to log in to other NetWare servers for performing NetWare/IP configuration.
	View Server Profile	Used to view global parameters (such as IP address, subnet mask, NetWare information, time zone, and so on) for the IntranetWare server.
	Manage Global Objects	Used to manage global objects (such as users, groups and hosts).
	Manage Services option	Used to configure DNS Server, Hosts information, and NetWare/IP domains.
	Start/Stop Services option	Used to start services that are not running and stop services that are running.
	Configure Error Reporting	Used to set the error reporting level for messages reported to the Product Kernel screen or the AUDIT.LOG file. You can also use this option to specify the maximum size of the AUDIT.LOG file. Setting the error levels can be useful for troubleshooting the NetWare/IP configuration.

OPTION	DESCRIPTION
Performing File Operations	Used to copy files via FTP, edit files, setup the DNS name server database, and create text files from the database.

T A B L E   12.2
UNICON main screen options (continued)

3 • The DNS server must contain <IP Address, Host name> mappings. You can enter these names directly into the DNS database. Each entry in the DNS database is called a *resource record*.

You must first initialize the DNS Master Database. You can do this from the UNICON main menu by selecting Manage Services, DNS, and Initialize DNS Master Database

4 • When prompted for a domain name, enter the Fully Qualified Name (FQN) for the DNS domain. An example would be as follows:

KINETICS.COM

5 • Wait for a few seconds for the "Please Wait" message to disappear. Press Esc.

6 • You will be asked if you want to specify DNS services for subnetworks. Select Yes only if you have subnetworks. The steps that follow assume that you do not have subnetworks.

7 • You will see a status message informing you of the creation of the DNS database. Press Esc to continue.

At this point, you have created the database for the domain name and started the DNS server. The database will initially contain just the hostname record for the NetWare/IP server.

8 • Press Esc a few times to get back to the main UNICON menu.

9 • Now you can add resource records for hostnames and name servers on your network from the UNICON main menu. Select Manage Global Objects, Manage Hosts, and Hosts.

10 • When the "Hosts in the Local Domain" list appears, press the Insert key to add host records, and select an entry to modify its value. Figure 12.6 shows the sample form for adding host records. You must enter only the hostname and the IP address; the other fields are optional. Use the F1 key to get help on the meanings of these fields. Actually, for security reasons, it's best not reveal extra information about the hosts through DNS, and it is preferable not to supply the machine type and operating system information. The reason for this is that "crackers" can exploit machine type and operating system information to learn about the weaknesses of the system.

Add host records for the hosts on your network.

FIGURE 12.6

Host record information

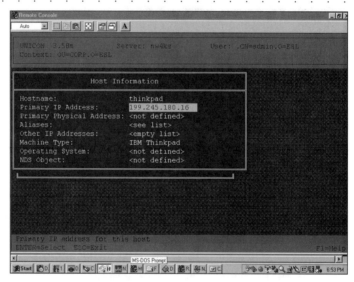

11 • If you plan to use NetWare/IP, you must add a resource record for the DSS servers in the domain you created by following Steps 9 and 10. If you only plan to set up the DNS server, you are finished at this point. You may still want to use Steps 9 and 10 to add additional resource records.

After you have performed the configuration of the DNS system, you may want to add additional information in the DNS database. You can do this by making the following selections from the UNICON main menu:

▸ Manage Services

▸ DNS

▸ Administer DNS

▸ Manage Master Database

▸ Manage Data

When you make the last selection (Manage Data), you will see a list of resource records in the master DNS database on the server. You can modify a resource record by highlighting it and pressing Enter. To add a record, press the Insert and select one of the record types that you can add. To delete a record, highlight it and press the Delete key. You can add the following resource record types to the DNS database:

▸ A—Address record maps names to addresses.

▸ CNAME—Canonical Name specifies an alias for the hostname.

▸ MB—Mail Box identifies a host as a mailbox.

▸ MR—Mail Receive specifies a different domain name to receive mail in place of some previous domain.

▸ MX—Mail Exchanger identifies a host to deliver or forward mail for a domain.

▸ NS—Name Server identifies a name server for a domain.

▸ PTR—Inverse Pointer query records provides mapping of IP addresses to names.

▸ SOA—Start of Authority specifies which server is the best source of information for the data within the domain. Contains many default parameters for caching information.

Configuring the Primary DSS Server

If you plan to configure NetWare/IP, you must have already configured the DNS server as outlined in the previous section. The next step is to configure the primary DSS server, after which you are ready to configure NetWare/IP.

To configure the primary DSS server, the SYS: volume must have 1 MB of free disk space. The amount of system memory needed by the server depends on the number of server nodes in the network. You can use the following formula to determine the memory requirements for a primary DSS server:

Memory in bytes needed on the server =
(Number of servers in the network x 520) + 835,000

If you must set up DSS on a server that belongs to a remote DNS domain, you must add resource records to two master DNS databases:

1 • You must add a name server record to the master DNS database that is servicing your NetWare/IP domain, identifying the DSS server as a name server for the NetWare/IP domain.

2 • You must set up an address record to the master DNS database of the remote domain specifying the IP address and hostname for the server.

To configure the Primary DSS server, run the UNICON NLM and follow these steps to add the DSS subdomain:

1 • Select Manage Services.

2 • Select DNS.

3 • Select Administer DNS.

4 • Select Manage Master Database.

5 • Select Delegate Subzone Authority.

6 • You should see a list of zones and subzones defined in the DNS master database. You must add to it a DNS subdomain for the NetWare/IP domain. To do this, press the Insert key and enter the name of the NetWare/IP domain. If the master domain zone name were KINETICS. COM., you could enter the NetWare/IP domain as follows:

```
NWIP.KINETICS.COM.
```

7 • You should see a list of available hosts that you can enter into the NetWare/IP domain. From the list of available hosts, select the name of the host that is to be the name server for the new NetWare/IP domain. On simple networks the name server is likely to be the same server on which you are running UNICON.

8 • You should see the host you selected added to the name server list for the new NetWare/IP domain.

9 • Repeat Steps 7 and 8 to add optional secondary DSS servers to the NetWare/IP domain.

10 • Repeat Steps 6 to 9 to create other NetWare/IP domains.

11 • After creating a NetWare/IP subdomain (also DNS subdomain), you must inform the DNS server for the parent domain about the new DNS subdomain you have just created. The parent DNS server could be on another node administered by someone else. You will have to request the DNS administrator for the parent domain to add your subdomain to the parent's database.

When a new domain record is added to the parent DNS server, the NetWare DNS server automatically links into the DNS hierarchy by using the information stored in SYS:ETC\DNS\ROOT.DB. This file contains a list of root name servers that are authoritative for the top-level U.S. organizational domains.

Linking to the existing DNS hierarchy
In order for your DNS server to receive queries from outside your domain, you must provide information on your domain name, the names, and the IP addresses of your DNS servers to the parent server. For example, if your new domain is

kinetics.com, and the name server for it is madhav.kinetics.com, you must register this information with the master DNS server that services the com. domain. Typically, most root servers run the Berkeley InterNet Domain (BIND) name system implementation for DNS. This requires the following records to be added to the zone database file for the com. domain:

```
kinetics.com.       IN      NS      madhav.kinetics.com.
madhav.kinetic.com. IN      A       IPaddress
```

The first line is the name server record that identifies the subdomain, kinetics.com, and its name server madhav.kinetics.com. The second line is the address record for the name server madhav.kinetics.com and identifies its IP address. The *Ipaddress* is a place holder for the IP address in the dotted decimal notation.

If the DNS domain above you is administered by someone else, you must register with that administrator and make sure that your records are added to the existing DNS hierarchy.

In order to send queries outside your domain, you do not need to do anything once your DNS server is running. Your NetWare DNS server automatically links into the DNS hierarchy using the information stored in the SYS:ETC\DNS\ROOT.DB file.

Normally, a query for information outside your domain is sent to the root name server for resolution. In order to improve the efficiency of your query for a domain that you manage, you may want to link to another domain so that you can query that domain's name server directly without the overhead of having a root name server resolve your queries. To further improve the efficiency of your query, you may want to send queries by designating one or more name servers as forwarders. The following procedures describe how to use UNICON to view the ROOT.DB file, link directly to another name server, and link indirectly via forwarders. Note that you must link to the existing DNS hierarchy only the first time you create your master DNS database.

To link your domain directly to a DNS server for another domain, follow these steps:

1 • From the UNICON main menu, select Manage Services, DNS, Administer DNS, Link to Existing DNS Hierarchy, and Link Direct. You should see at least the root domain (".") in the list that identifies the fact that your domain name was linked directly to the root.

2 • From the "Root Domains" list, press the Insert key to add the domain to which you want to link, and enter the domain name into the entry box.

3 • To identify the domain's name server, choose the domain name you just added from the "Root Domains" list and press Enter.

4 • To add the name of the server, press the Insert key.

5 • Enter the name of the domain's name server.

6 • To enter the IP address of the name server that you identified in Step 5, highlight the name server and press Enter. Next, press the Insert key and enter the server's IP address.

7 • To return to the UNICON main menu, press Esc a few times.

The utility links your domain as you specified by adding the information you entered in the SYS:ETC/DNS/ROOT.DB file.

You may want to link indirectly via forwarders. *Forwarders* are name servers that have more complete information in their cache than your name server has. If the forwarder is not able to serve the answer to the DNS query from its cache, it will forward the request to other name servers it knows about.

To link indirectly via forwarders, follow these steps:

1 • From the UNICON main menu, select Manage Services, DNS, Administer DNS, Link to Existing DNS Hierarchy, and Link Indirect via Forwarders. You should see a form with three forwarder entries.

2 • Enter the IP addresses of the servers you want to designate as forwarders.

3 • When prompted, select Yes to save your entries.

4 • To return to the UNICON main menu, press Esc a few times.

Creating a replica of the DNS database

For redundancy, reliability, and minimization of network traffic over slower network links, you may want to create one or more replicas of the DNS database on other servers. Follow these steps to do this:

1 • From the UNICON main menu, select Manage Services, DNS, Administer DNS, and Manage Replica Databases. You should see list of replica databases that will initially be empty.

2 • Press the Insert key to create a replica of the DNS database on the server. Fill in the Replica Database Information form as follows:

  ▶ *Domain* specifies the name of the domain for which this replica has a copy.

  ▶ *Nameserver* contains the IP address of the DNS master name server. Three Nameserver fields are provided to enter IP addresses of additional DNS name servers. You should enter at least one name server field.

3 • After filling in the form, press Esc, and answer Yes to confirm the information that you entered.

Configuring NetWare/IP

To configure NetWare/IP, the SYS: volume must have 1 MB of free disk space. The amount of system memory needed by the server depends on the number of server nodes in the network. You can use the following formula to determine the memory requirements for a NetWare/IP server:

Memory in bytes needed on the server =
(Number of servers in the network x 380) + 258,000

Follow these steps to configure the NetWare/IP server:

1 • You should have installed NetWare/IP, and configured DNS and the DSS server.

2 • Load NWIPCFG NLM.

```
LOAD NWIPCFG
```

The main NetWare/IP Configuration screen shown in Figure 12.7 appears.

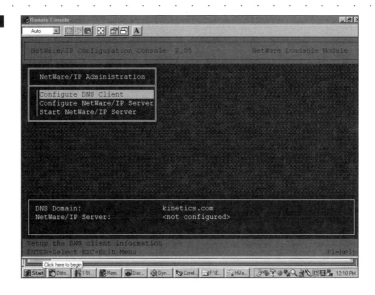

FIGURE 12.7

Main NetWare/IP Configuration screen

3 • If you have not set up the DNS client on the server, you should select Configure DNS Client and enter the DNS domain and its name server's IP address.

4 • Select Configure NetWare/IP Server.

NWIPCFG issues a DHCP request for NetWare/IP information. If a DHCP server responds, you are prompted to confirm the NetWare/IP domain name and primary DSS server name. Chapter 13 discusses setting up a DHCP server.

5 • You should see the NetWare/IP Server Configuration form. Enter the information shown in Table 12.4.

TABLE 12.4	OPTION	DESCRIPTION
Server Configuration Form Options	NetWare/IP Domain	Enter the fully qualified NetWare/IP domain name.
	Preferred DSSs	Enter at least the IP address of the primary DSS server. You can enter an additional four secondary DSS servers for the domain.
	Initial DSS Contact Retries	This is the number of times this NetWare/IP server will retransmit an unacknowledged query to the DSS server on startup. This value can range from 0 to 50, and has a default value of 1.
	Retry Interval	This is the number of seconds this NetWare/IP server will wait before retransmitting an unacknowledged query to the DSS server on startup. This value can range from 5 to 100, and has a default value of 10 seconds.
	Slow Link Customizations	Use this to change the slow link customization parameters.
	Forward IPX Information to DSS servers?	Specifies if this NetWare/IP server should act as a forwarding gateway. A forwarding gateway is used to link IPX to IP networks. The default is No.

6 • Exit to the main menu of the NetWare/IP Configuration screen and select Start NetWare/IP Server.

Configuring DNS Servers on Non-NetWare Platforms

If you are using a non-NetWare platform as a DNS server for a domain, you must consult the documentation for DNS services for that operating system.

On UNIX systems, DNS is implemented by BIND. On BSD-derived UNIX, this is implemented by running the following program:

```
named
```

On SVR4 UNIX, this is implemented by the following program:

```
in.named
```

A DOS-based implementation of BIND is available from FTP Software, Inc. It runs as a Terminate and Stay Resident (TSR) program called NAMED.

BIND uses a file called `/etc/named.boot` that contains a list of other files for holding the zone records for the DNS database. FTP Software's BIND uses the filename NAMED.BOO).

The DNS zone files are text files and have a special format. You can refer to the DNS RFCs referenced earlier in this chapter for information on the syntax of these text records, or consult your operating system's implementation.

If you are using non-NetWare DNS servers for the master domain, you must add a record in its database for the new subdomains that you have created for NetWare/IP. This usually involves using a text editor and adding a record to the zone data file for the DNS server. If you have created a primary DSS named nw4cs.scs.com (IP address 144.19.73.102) and a secondary DSS named ucs.scs.com (IP address 144.19.74.103) for the NetWare/IP domain nwip.scs.com, you should add the following records to the zone data file for non-NetWare DNS:

```
# Domain/Host    Class  RR Type  Data
nwip.scs.com.    IN     NS       nw4cs.scs.com.  # Primary   DSS
nwip.scs.com.    IN     NS       ucs.scs.com.    # Secondary DSS
nw4cs.scs.com.   IN     A        144.19.74.102   # Host record
ucs.scs.com.     IN     A        144.19.74.103   # Host record
```

On most DNS implementations, you will have to restart the DNS service before the changes are registered.

Summary

This chapter discussed the NetWare/IP service, and the basic concepts that you must understand before deploying this service. If you want to use TCP/IP as your primary protocol on the intranet, you should install and configure NetWare/IP. The NetWare/IP software contains the DNS software implemented by the NAMED.NLM. Even if you do not plan using TCP/IP as your primary protocol and you decide to use IPX with the NetWare IPX/IP gateway to communicate with the Novell Web Server, you should still investigate NetWare/IP because NetWare/IP comes with a DNS server.

A detailed procedure on how to install NetWare/IP was presented in this chapter. If you must install DNS services only, you need not configure the DSS server and NetWare/IP server. You need to implement only the first phase of the configuration procedure, which is to install the DNS server.

## CHAPTER 13

Installing and Configuring DHCP for IntranetWare

If you want to use the TCP/IP protocol on the intranet, you must be concerned about setting TCP/IP parameters for each workstation on the network. On large networks, configuring TCP/IP parameters for each workstation on a network can be a difficult and time-consuming task. This is especially true when the TCP/IP parameters such as IP address and subnet masks must be changed. The changes can occur because of a major restructuring of the network, or because the network has a large number of mobile users with portable computers that can be connected to any of the network segments. The network connections to the intranet can be direct physical connections or wireless connections. Because the TCP/IP parameters for computers depend on the network segment they connect to, appropriate values must be set up whenever a computer is connected to a different network segment.

Understanding the consequences of TCP/IP parameter changes requires knowledgeable intranet administrators. For TCP/IP intranets several auto-configuration protocols such as BOOTP (Boot Protocol) and DHCP (Dynamic Host Configuration Protocol) have been developed by the Internet Engineering Task Force (IETF). An IntranetWare server can be configured as a DHCP server, which simplifies the configuration of TCP/IP devices (workstations, servers, routers, and so on) on the intranet. This chapter discusses the DHCP protocol and how it can be configured on an IntranetWare server.

Overview of DHCP

The DHCP protocol is designed for dynamic configuration of essential TCP/IP parameters for hosts (workstations and servers) on a network. The DHCP protocol consists of two components:

- A mechanism for allocating IP addresses and other TCP/IP parameters

- A protocol for negotiating and transmitting host specific information

The TCP/IP node requesting the TCP/IP configuration information is called the *DHCP client*, and the TCP/IP node that supplies this information is called a *DHCP server*. On an IntranetWare network, the DHCP clients are MS-DOS, Windows, OS/2 or UNIX workstations, but the DHCP server can only be a IntranetWare server. The IntranetWare DHCP server can also supply the NetWare/IP parameters needed by a the NetWare/IP server.

Understanding IP Address Management

The DHCP protocol uses three methods for IP address allocation. These methods are the following:

► Manual allocation

► Automatic allocation

► Dynamic allocation

In the *manual allocation* method, the DHCP client's IP address is manually set by the network administrator at the DHCP server, and DHCP is used to convey to the DHCP client the value of the manually allocated IP address.

In the *automatic allocation* method, no manual assignments of an IP address must be made. The DHCP client is assigned an IP address when it first contacts the DHCP server. The IP address assigned using this method is permanently assigned to the DHCP client and is not reused by another DHCP client.

In the *dynamic allocation* method, the DHCP server assigns an IP address to a DHCP client on a temporary basis. The IP address is on loan or "leased" to the DHCP client for a specified duration. On the expiry of this lease, the IP address is revoked, and the DHCP client is required to surrender the IP address. If the DHCP client still needs an IP address to perform its functions, it can request another IP address.

The dynamic allocation method is the only one of the three methods that affords automatic reuse of an IP address. An IP address need not be surrendered by the DHCP client on the expiration of the lease. If the DHCP client no longer needs an IP address (such as when the computer is being gracefully shut down), it can release the IP address to the DHCP server. The DHCP server then can reissue the same IP address to another DHCP client making a request for an IP address.

The dynamic allocation method is particularly useful for DHCP clients that need an IP address for temporary connection to a network. For example, consider a situation where there are 400 users with portable computers on a network and a class C address has been assigned to a network. This enables the network to have 254 nodes on the network (256 − 2 special addresses = 254). Because computers connecting to a network using TCP/IP are required to have unique IP addresses, all 400 computers cannot be simultaneously connected to the network. However, if there are at most only 254 physical connections on the network, it should be possible to use a class C address by reusing IP addresses that are not in use. Using DHCP's dynamic IP address allocation, IP address reuse is possible.

Dynamic IP address allocation is also a good choice for assigning IP addresses to new hosts that are being permanently connected, and where IP addresses are scarce. As old hosts are retired, their IP addresses can be immediately reused. Regardless of which of the three methods of IP address allocation is used, you can still configure IP parameters at a central DHCP server once, instead of repeating the TCP/IP configuration for each computer.

Understanding the DHCP IP Address Acquisition Process

Upon contacting a DHCP server, a DHCP client goes through several internal states, during which it negotiates the use of an IP address, and the duration of the use. The operation of how a DHCP client acquires the IP address can best be explained in terms of a *state transition diagram* or a *finite state machine diagram*. Figure 13.1 shows the state transition diagram that explains the interaction between the DHCP client and DHCP server. This discussion is adapted from the RFCs that describe DHCP operation.

When the DHCP client is first started, it begins in the INIT (initialize) state. At this point the DHCP client does not know its IP parameters, and so it sends a DHCPDISCOVER broadcast. The DHCPDISCOVER is encapsulated in a UDP/IP packet. Recall that UDP (User Datagram Protocol) is implemented by the TCP/IP protocol stack. The destination UDP port number is set to 67 (decimal), the same as that for a BOOTP server. BOOTP is an earlier protocol for allocating IP addresses, but is not as flexible as DHCP. Specifically, the BOOTP server uses a table of IP addresses and network card hardware addresses to assign fixed IP addresses to BOOTP clients.

The DHCP protocol is an extension of the BOOTP protocol. A local IP broadcast address of 255.255.255.255 is used in the DHCPDISCOVER packet. If DHCP servers are not on the local network, the IP router must have DHCP-relay agent support to forward the DHCPDISCOVER request to other subnetworks. DHCP-relay agent support is discussed in RFC 1542.

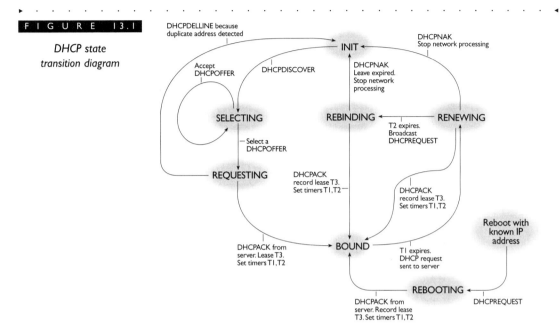

FIGURE 13.1

DHCP state transition diagram

Before sending the DHCPDISCOVER broadcast packet, the DHCP client waits for a random time interval between 1 to 10 seconds. This is to prevent DHCP clients from flooding the network with DHCPDISCOVER requests if they start at the same time. This could occur if the DHCP clients are powered up at the same time (as sometimes happens after a power failure).

After sending the DHCPDISCOVER broadcast, the DHCP client enters the SELECTING state. In this state, the DHCP client receives DHCPOFFER messages from the DHCP servers that have been configured to respond to the DHCP client. The time period over which the DHCP client waits to receive DHCPOFFER messages is implementation-dependent. The DHCP client must select one DHCPOFFER response if it receives multiple DHCPOFFER responses. After selecting a DHCPOFFER message from a server, the DHCP client sends a DHCPREQUEST message to the selected DHCP server. The DHCP server responds with a DHCPACK.

The DHCP client may optionally perform a check on the IP address sent in the DHCPOFFER to verify that the address is not in use. On a broadcast network, the DHCP client can send an ARP (Address Resolution Protocol) request for the suggested IP address to see if there is an ARP response. An ARP response would imply that the suggested IP address is already in use, in which case the DHCPACK from the sever is ignored and a DHCPDECLINE is sent. The DHCP client enters the INIT state and retries to get a valid IP address that is not in use. When the ARP request is broadcast on the local network, the client uses its own hardware address in the sender hardware address field of the ARP packet, but sets a value of 0 in the sender IP address field. A sender IP address of 0 is used, rather than the suggested IP address, so as not to confuse ARP caches on other TCP/IP hosts in case the suggested IP address is already in use.

When the DHCPACK from the DHCP server is accepted, three timer values are set and the DHCP client moves into the BOUND state. These timers are described in the RFCs as the T1, T2, and T3 timers:

▸ The first timer, T1, is the lease renewal timer.

▸ The second timer, T2, is the rebinding timer.

▸ The third timer, T3, is the lease duration.

The DHCPACK always returns the value of T3, the lease duration. The values of timers T1 and T2 may be configured at the DHCP server depending on the implementation. However, if they are not set, default values are used (based on the duration of the lease). The following show the default values used for T1 and T2.

```
T1 = renewal timer
T2 = rebinding timer
T3 = duration of lease
T1 = 0.5 * T3
T2 = 0.875 * T3
```

The actual time at which the timer values expire are computed by adding the timer values to the time at which the DHCPREQUEST that generated the DHCPACK response was sent. If the time at which the DHCP request was sent was T0, then the expiration values are computed as follows:

```
Expiration of T1 = T0 + T1

Expiration of T2 = T0 + T2

Expiration of T3 = T0 + T3
```

RFC 1541 recommends that a "fuzz" factor be added to the timers T1 and T2 to prevent several DHCP clients from expiring their timers at the same time. At the expiration of timer T1, the DHCP client moves from the BOUND state to the RENEWING state. In the RENEWING state, a new lease for the allocated IP address must be negotiated by the DHCP client from the DHCP server that originally allocated the IP address. If the original DHCP server does not renew the release, it sends a DHCPNAK message. The DHCP client moves into the INIT state and tries to obtain a new IP address. If the original DHCP server sends a DHCPACK message, this message contains the new lease duration. The DHCP client then sets its timer values and moves to the BOUND state.

If the timer T2 expires while waiting in the RENEWING state for a DHCPACK or DHCPNAK message from the original DHCP server, then the DHCP client moves from the RENEWING state to the REBINDING state. The original DHCP server may not respond, because it may be down or a network link may be down. Note from the previous equations that T2 > T1, so the DHCP client waits for the original DHCP server for a duration of T2-T1 to renew the release.

At the expiration of a timer T2, a broadcast DHCPREQUEST is sent on the network to contact any DHCP server to extend the lease. The DHCP client is in the REBINDING state. A broadcast DHCPREQUEST is sent because the DHCP client assumes after spending T2-T1 seconds in the RENEWING state that the original DHCP server is not available. The DHCP client tries to contact any DHCP server that is configured to respond to it. If a DHCP server responds with a DHCPACK message, the DHCP client renews its lease (T3), sets the timers T1 and T2 and moves back to the BOUND state. If no DHCP server is able to renew the release after expiration of timer T3, the lease expires and the DHCP client moves to the INIT state. Note that by this time, the DHCP client has tried to renew the lease, first with the original DHCP server, and then with any DHCP server on the network.

When the lease expires (timer T3 expires), the DHCP client must surrender the use of its IP address and halt network processing with that IP address. The DHCP client does not always have to wait for the expiration of the lease (timer T3) to surrender the use of an IP address. It could voluntarily relinquish control of an IP address by canceling its lease. For example, a user with a portable computer may connect to the network to perform a network activity. The DHCP server on the network may set the duration of the lease for one hour. Assume that the user finishes the network tasks in 30 minutes, and now wants to disconnect from the network. When the user gracefully shuts down his or her computer, the DHCP client sends a DHCPRELEASE message to the DHCP server to cancel its lease. The IP address that is surrendered is now available for use by another DHCP client.

If DHCP clients are run on computers that have a disk, the IP address that is allocated can be stored on the disk. When the computer is restarted, it can make a request for the same IP address. This is shown in Figure 13.1 in the state labeled "REBOOTING with known IP address"

Understanding the DHCP Packet Format

The DHCP packet format is shown in Figure 13.2. The DHCP messages use a fixed format for all the fields, except the options field that has a minimum size of 312 octets. If you are familiar with the BOOTP protocol, you will recognize that, with the exception of the flags field and the options field, the message formats for DHCP and BOOTP are identical. In fact, the DHCP server can be programmed to answer BOOTP requests.

▶ · ◀

F I G U R E   13.2

DHCP packet format

◀————————— 32 bits —————————▶

op (1)	htype (1)	hlen (1)	hops (1)
Xid (4)			
sec (2)		flags (2)	
ciaddr (4)			
yiaddr (4)			
siaddr (4)			
giaddr (4)			
chaddr (16)			
sname (64)			
file (128)			
options (312)			

• **Numbers in ( ) represent octets**

· · · · ·

Table 13.1 provides an explanation of the fields used in the DHCP protocol. Only the leftmost bit of the DHCP options field is used (see Figure 13.3). The other bits in the options field must be set to 0.

T A B L E 13.1			
DHCP Fields	FIELD	OCTETS	DESCRIPTION
	op	1	Message op code (message type). A value of 1 means it is a BOOTREQUEST message, and a value of 2 means it is a BOOTREPLY message.
	htype	1	This is the hardware address type. The values are the same as those used for the ARP packet format. For example, a value of 1 is used for 10 Mbps Ethernet.
	hlen	1	This is the hardware address length in octets. Ethernet and Token Ring hardware address length is 6 bytes.
	hops	1	The DHCP client sets this to zero. This is optionally used by relay agents running on routers when they forward DHCP messages.
	xid	4	This is a Transaction ID that is a randomly generated number chosen by the DHCP client when it generates a DHCP message. The DHCP server uses the same Transaction ID in its DHCP messages to the client. The Transaction ID enables the DHCP clients and servers to associate DHCP messages with the corresponding responses.
	secs	2	This is filled by the DHCP client. It is the seconds elapsed since the client started trying to boot.
	flags	2	(Flags) The leftmost bit is used to indicate if this is a broadcast message (bit value of 1). All other bits must remain zero.
	ciaddr	4	This is the DHCP client's IP address. It is filled by the DHCP client in a DHCPREQUEST message to verify the use of previously allocated configuration parameters. If the client does not know its IP address, this field is set to 0.
	yiaddr	4	This is the DHCP client's "your IP address" returned by the DHCP server.

(continued)

TABLE 13.1	FIELD	OCTETS	DESCRIPTION
DHCP fields (continued)	siaddr	4	If the DHCP client wants to contact a specific DHCP server, it inserts the server's IP address in this field. The DHCP server's IP address may have been discovered in prior DHCPOFFER, DHCPACK messages returned by the server. The value returned by the DHCP server may be the address of the next server to contact as part of the boot process. For example, this may be the address of a server that holds the operating system boot image.
	giaddr	4	This is the IP address of the router that runs the relay agent.
	chaddr	16	This is the DHCP client's hardware address. A value of 16 octets is used to allow different network hardware types. Ethernet and Token Ring use only 6 octets.
	sname	64	This is an optional server hostname if known by the DHCP client. It is a null-terminated string.
	file	128	This is the boot filename. It is a null-terminated string. If the DHCP client wants to boot with an image of the operating system downloaded from a network device, it can specify a generic name such as "unix" for booting a UNIX image in a DHCPDISCOVER. The DHCP server can hold more specific information about the exact operating system image needed for that workstation. This image name can be returned a fully qualified directory path name in the DHCPOFFER message from the DHCP server.
	options	312	This is an optional parameters field.

FIGURE 13.3

DHCP Options format

B	0	0	0	0	0	0	0	0	0	0	0	0	0	0	0

Most of the DHCP messages sent by the DHCP server to the DHCP client are *unicast messages* (that is, messages sent to single IP address). This is because the DHCP server learns about the DHCP client's hardware address in messages sent by the DHCP client to the server. The DHCP client may request that the DHCP server respond with a broadcast address by setting the leftmost bit in the options field to 1. The DHCP client will do this if it does not know its IP address yet. The IP protocol module in DHCP client will reject a datagram it receives if the destination IP address in the datagram does not match the IP address of the DHCP client's network interface. If the IP address of the network interface is not known, the datagram will still be rejected. However, the IP protocol module will accept any IP broadcast datagram. Therefore, to ensure that the IP protocol module accepts the DHCP server reply when the IP address is not yet configured, the DHCP client will request that the DHCP server reply using broadcast messages instead of unicast messages.

The options field is variable in length, with the minimum size extended to 312 octets, so that the total minimum size of a DHCP message is 576 octets, which is the minimum IP datagram size a host must be prepared to accept. If a DHCP client needs to use larger size messages it can negotiate this using the "Maximum DHCP message size" option. Because the "sname" and "file" fields are quite large and may not always be used, DHCP options may be further extended into these fields, by specifying the 'Option Overload" option. If present, the usual meanings of the "sname" and "file" are ignored, and these fields are examined for options. Options are expressed using the T-L-V (Type, Length, Value) format. Figure 13.4 shows that in DHCP, the option consists of a 1-octet Type field, followed by a 1-octet Length field. The value of the Length field contains the size of the Value field. The different DHCP messages themselves are expressed using a special Type value of 53. The option values that describe the DHCP messages are shown in Figure 13.5.

F I G U R E   13.4

Generic format for DHCP messages

1 octet	1 octet	N octets
Type (1)	Length (1)	Value (N)

FIGURE 13.5

*Option format values for all
the DHCP messages*

Type 53	Length 1	Value 1	DHCPDISCOVER
Type 53	Length 1	Value 2	DHCPOFFER
Type 53	Length 1	Value 3	DHCPREQUEST
Type 53	Length 1	Value 4	DHCPDECLINE
Type 53	Length 1	Value 5	DHCPACK
Type 53	Length 1	Value 6	DHCPNAK
Type 53	Length 1	Value 7	DHCPRELEASE

DHCP on an IntranetWare Server

Now that you understand how DHCP works, you can better understand the parameter choices involved in installing, configuring and administering DHCP servers.

The DHCP protocol format is a superset of the BOOTP protocol. Because of this, the NetWare DHCP service is backward-compatible with BOOTP clients. A DHCP server responds to a BOOTP request as if it were a DHCP request. All assigned IP addresses for BOOTP clients are treated as permanent lease assignments in DHCP, and the addresses are not reused.

If you have an existing BOOTP server configuration on your server, the configuration information for it is stored in the SYS:ETC/BOOTPTAB file. When you install DHCP, the installation program migrates the contents of the SYS:ETC/BOOTPTAB file to the SYS:ETC/DHCPTAB file, which contains the configuration information for the DHCP server. After the migration of the BOOTP information, you should not make changes to the BOOTPTAB file, because these changes are not copied automatically to the DHCPTAB file.

The following sections describe in detail the procedures for maintaining and administering DHCP servers for the IntranetWare server.

To configure the NetWare DHCP service, follow these steps:

1 • Install the NetWare DHCP service.

2 • Define subnetwork profiles for each subnetwork using DHCP services. If your network does not use subnetting, define a single subnetwork profile.

3 • List IP addresses that are to be assigned statically.

4 • Define a list of nodes that you do not want the DHCP server to reply to.

5 • Load the DHCP Server NetWare Loadable Module.

The NetWare DHCP service is configured and managed by the DHCP Configuration utility (DHCPCFG).

Installing the DHCP Server on an IntranetWare Server

As with most NetWare products from Novell, the NetWare DHCP service is installed using the NetWare Installation Utility (INSTALL.NLM). This section discusses the procedure for installing the DHCP server. You must mount the NetWare OS CD-ROM either at the server or the workstation. If you are using the CD-ROM at the workstation you should log in to the server remotely by using RCONSOLE.EXE. If you are using the CD-ROM at the IntranetWare server, you should mount the CD-ROM at the server using the appropriate drivers.

Follow these steps to install the DHCP server:

1 • Run INSTALL:

```
LOAD INSTALL
```

2 • From the INSTALL main menu, select "Product options," "Choose an item or product listed above," and "Install NetWare DHCP."

3 • When prompted, specify the location of the installation source files, and press Enter.

4 • You will see the DHCP files copied and then you will see the INSTALL menu.

5 • Select Install Product.

6 • From the list of servers, select the server on which you want to install the NetWare DHCP service.

7 • Select Yes to start installing the NetWare DHCP service.

8 • You will see a status of the file copy operation. At the end of the file copy you will see a report that the installation was successful. Press Enter to continue.

9 • Press Esc a few times and answer Yes to exit the installation utility.

Defining Subnetwork Profiles

After installing the DHCP service, you must define a subnetwork profile. A *subnetwork profile* contains configuration information for a specific TCP/IP subnetwork. When you install the DHCP server, the DHCPCFG tool automatically creates an initial subnetwork profile for each of the network cards in the NetWare server. You should edit the initial subnetwork profiles to reflect the actual configuration information you want the DHCP server to return to DHCP clients.

Follow these steps to customize the subnetwork profile created automatically during installation:

1 • Run the DHCPCFG NLM:

```
LOAD DHCPCFG
```

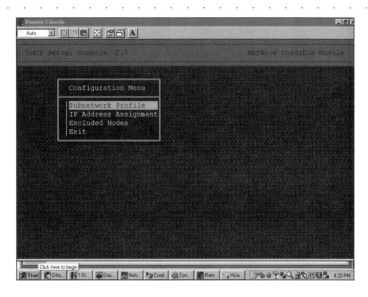

F I G U R E   13.6

DHCP Configuration menu

2 • The DHCP main configuration menu shown in Figure 13.6 appears.

3 • Select Subnetwork Profile

4 • A list of subnetwork profiles appears. The subnetwork profile name is listed under the column Subnetwork Name. If you want to change the name of a subnetwork profile, choose the profile you want to modify from the list of subnetwork profiles, press F3, and enter the new name.

5 • To view/modify the Subnetwork Profile parameters, highlight the profile you want to modify from the list of subnetwork profiles and press Enter (see Figure 13.7).

The information in the Subnetwork Profile form is returned to the DHCP client on that subnetwork when it issues a DHCP request. When a client makes a DHCP request, the DHCP server determines the correct configuration information for that client based on the subnetwork the client is connected to. These fields are explained in Table 13.2.

▶ · ◀

FIGURE 13.7

Subnetwork profile form

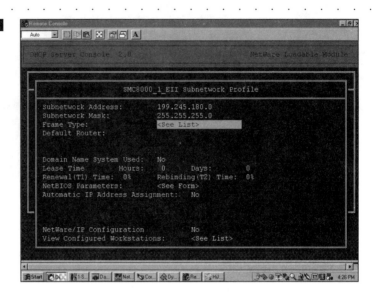

6 • Edit the subnetwork profile configuration as necessary and press Esc.

7 • Select Yes to save your changes.

8 • Press Esc to return to the DHCP main menu.

TABLE 13.2	FIELD	DESCRIPTION
Subnetwork Profile Form Fields	Subnetwork Address	This field defines the IP subnetwork for which you can view/modify the information.
	Subnetwork Mask	The IP subnetwork mask for the subnetwork whose profile you are viewing/modifying.
	Frame Type	The frame type used for this subnetwork. Selecting this field shows a list of frame types. You can add or subtract from this list by pressing the Insert and Delete keys, respectively.
	Default Router	This is used to specify the default router for the subnetwork.

T A B L E 13.2	FIELD	DESCRIPTION
Subnetwork Profile Form Fields (continued)	Domain Name System Used	If this field is set to Yes, you must supply the domain name, and the IP address of at least one DNS server. You can specify IP addresses of from one to three DNS servers, which are tried sequentially. By selecting Yes, you are linking the IP address supplied by the DHCP server with its registered host name in DNS.
	Lease Time (Hours, Days)	This field is used to specify the duration of the lease. This is the T3 timer discussed earlier in this chapter.
	Renewal (T1) Time	This is the renewal timer, T1, discussed earlier in this chapter. It is specified as a fraction of the T3 timer. If you want to use the RFC suggested defaults, supply a value of 50 percent.
	Rebinding (T2) Time	This is the rebinding timer, T2, discussed earlier in this chapter. It is specified as a fraction of the T3 timer. If you want to use the RFC suggested defaults, supply a value of 87 percent or 88 percent.
	NetBIOS Parameters	This form enables you to specify the parameters for running NetBIOS over TCP/IP. You can specify the NetBIOS over TCP/IP Name Server option, which enables you to configure a list of IP addresses for NetBIOS name servers. This option enables DHCP clients that use NetBIOS over TCP/IP to request a list of NetBIOS name servers from the DHCP server. You can specify the NetBIOS over TCP/IP Node Type option. This option enables you to configure a list of NetBIOS node types such as B-node (broadcast nodes), P-node (Point-to-Point nodes), M-node (Mixed nodes), and the H-node. You can specify the NetBIOS over TCP/IP scope option. The *NetBIOS scope* is the population of computers across which a registered NetBIOS name is known. NetBIOS multicast and broadcast datagram operations must reach the entire extent of the NetBIOS scope. DHCP enables you to define the NetBIOS scope. For additional information on NetBIOS over TCP/IP, consult the RFCs 1001 and 1002.

(continued)

TABLE 13.2	FIELD	DESCRIPTION
Subnetwork Profile Form Fields (continued)	Automatic IP Address Assignment	When set to Yes, you will see an additional form to specify a range of IP addresses to assign automatically on a demand basis. When assigning IP addresses automatically, the DHCP server assigns to the DHCP client the next available IP address from a range of IP addresses. The IP address range may include all IP addresses for a network segment or a subset of IP addresses. For automatic IP address assignment, you must define the start and end IP address for the IP range. Addresses that are outside the designated range are available for static assignment by the DHCP server. When set to No, statically assigned IP addresses are used. Static assignments are based on a defined list of hardware address-to-IP address associations.
	NetWare IP Configuration	When set to Yes, you can specify the NetWare/IP configuration parameter that can be obtained via DHCP. Set this to No if you are not using NetWare/IP. You need to specify NetWare/IP configuration information only if NetWare/IP clients on the subnetwork are using DHCP or BOOTP to obtain their TCP/IP and NetWare/IP configurations. If TCP/IP and NetWare/IP are configured to use locally set parameters, you should set this field to No.
	View Configured Workstations	This is used to display a list of assigned IP addresses to DHCP clients. This also displays the physical address of the workstations running DHCP clients, and whether the IP address was assigned automatically.

Creating a Subnetwork Profile

Once installed, the DHCP server automatically creates a subnetwork profile for each of the network cards installed on the DHCP server. For networks that are not directly connected to the DHCP server (connected by an IP router), you must manually create a new subnetwork profile the DHCP clients on that network. You must also configure the connecting IP routers with DHCP or BOOTP forwarding relay agents.

Follow these steps to create a subnetwork profile.

1 • Run the DHCPCFG NLM:

LOAD DHCPCFG

2 • Select Subnetwork Profile

3 • A list of subnetwork profiles appears. Press the Insert key and enter the name of the profile.

4 • Enter the subnet address for the subnetwork profile.

5 • The Subnetwork Profile form appears. The information in the Subnetwork Profile form is returned to the DHCP client on that subnetwork when it issues a DHCP request. When a client makes a DHCP request, the DHCP server determines the correct configuration information for that client based on the subnetwork the client is connected to. These fields are explained in the previous section.

6 • Edit the subnetwork profile configuration as necessary and press Esc.

7 • Select Yes to save your changes.

8 • Press Esc to return to the DHCP main menu.

Setting Up Static IP Address Assignments

A *static IP address assignment* is a manually created entry in the DHCP server database that associates an IP address with a specific network node. This is in contrast to *automatic IP address assignment* where the DHCP server creates an IP address assignment for each DHCP client.

You may want to statically assign addresses in situations when a DHCP or BOOTP client has an established IP address, or in situations when a NetWare server or a UNIX host, has an IP address within the range of IP addresses that you designated for automatic assignment.

To set up a static IP address assignment, you need the following:

▸ The workstation name, which can be a label of up to 48 uppercase or lowercase letters

▸ The static IP address that you want the DHCP server to assign to the DHCP client

▸ The physical (or MAC) address of the DHCP client

The physical address for Ethernet and Token Ring network boards is expressed as six hexadecimal bytes separated by colons (for example, 00:00:C0:00:31:BA). For ARCnet network boards, you specify a hexadecimal byte (for example, 5C). You can obtain the client's MAC address by inspecting the label attached to the NIC, or by entering the following command at that workstation:

```
NLIST USER /A
```

Follow these steps to create a new IP address assignment:

I • Start the DHCPCFG utility:

```
LOAD DHCPCFG
```

2 • Select IP Address Assignment.

3 • When the list of IP Address Assignments appears, press the Insert key.

4 • When prompted, enter the workstation name.

5 • The Workstation IP Address Assignment form shown in Figure 13.8 appears.

6 • Enter the workstation IP address in the Internet Address field.

7 • Enter the workstation's physical address with each hexadecimal byte separated by a colon.

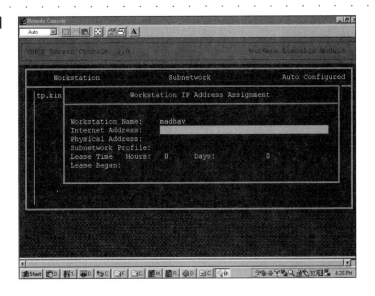

FIGURE 13.8

Workstation IP Address Assignment form

8 • Exit the Workstation IP Address Assignment form by pressing Esc. (For static entries, the Lease Time field will show 0 days, 0 hours and cannot be edited.)

9 • Select Yes to save the new assignment.

10 • Press Esc to return to DHCPCFG main menu.

Defining Excluded Nodes for a DHCP Server

The DHCP server assigns IP addresses to any workstation that sends a DHCP request. If there are nodes on your network that you do not want to receive IP address assignments, you can ensure that they do not have a DHCP client configured to make such a request. Additionally, you can exclude them by adding them to the excluded nodes list. The DHCP server will not send a DHCP reply to any workstation that is listed on the excluded nodes list.

To exclude a node, you specify its physical address. You can also exclude a group of nodes by using the wildcard character in place of the node portion of the MAC address. NetWare DHCP accepts the asterisk (*) as a wildcard character. As an example, you can exclude all nodes using a particular type of network board, by specifying an asterisk (*) for the manufacturer ID portion of the MAC address. Follow these steps to create an excluded nodes list with the DHCPCFG utility:

1 • Start the DHCPCFG utility:

```
LOAD DHCPCFG
```

2 • Select IP Address Assignment.

3 • When the list of Physical Addresses appears, press the Insert key.

4 • When prompted, enter the physical address of the excluded workstation or a wildcard version of the physical address for a group of workstations.

5 • Enter a comment indicating why the workstation is excluded.

6 • Repeat Steps 3 to 5 as needed.

7 • Press Esc to exit from the list of excluded addresses.

8 • Select Yes to save the new assignment.

9 • Press Esc to return to DHCPCFG main menu.

Loading DHCPSRVR

Once you have configured the NetWare DHCP server, you are ready to load the DHCPSRVR NLM that implements it. You use the following command to load the DHCP Server NLM:

```
LOAD DHCPSRVR [-t x] [-a y] [-h]
```

The options have the following meanings:

▶ -t x specifies the time interval that the DHCPSRV checks to see if the DHCPTAB file has changed. The default value is 60 seconds.

▸ -a y specifies the time interval that the DHCPSRV checks to see if the lease time for an address has expired. The default is 10 minutes.

▸ -h displays a help message.

Summary

One of the major configuration and maintenance problems with a TCP/IP network is the amount of effort needed to ensure that each TCP/IP node has the correct TCP/IP parameters On large networks, manually configuring TCP/IP parameters for each workstation can be a difficult and time-consuming task. Mobile users who connect with laptop/notebook computers to different TCP/IP network segments must be configured with TCP/IP parameters (such as IP address and subnet masks) that are consistent with the subnetwork they attach to. Most computer users do not have the knowledge to make these changes manually. The DHCP protocol automatically assigns the correct IP address and other TCP/IP parameters to the connecting node. With DHCP, IP addresses are allocated on a lease of a specific duration. If a TCP/IP node needs the IP address for a duration that is longer than the lease, it must renew the release from the DHCP server. The DHCP protocol is also flexible enough to permit permanent leases.

## CHAPTER 14

Installing and Configuring FTP Services for Intranets

If your intranet uses TCP/IP, or is connected to the Internet (which primarily uses TCP/IP), the file-transfer protocol (FTP) is useful for transferring documents and information in files. Historically, FTP was the primary method for transferring documents between computers on the Internet. Today, many Internet users send files as attachments to e-mail messages, but FTP still remains a convenient method for transferring files between disparate systems.

The IntranetWare server distribution software comes with an FTP server that can be installed and configured on the IntranetWare server. This chapter discusses how FTP can be used, as well as how you can install and configure FTP services on an IntranetWare server.

Overview of Using FTP

Figure 14.1 shows an example of the flexible use of FTP. This figure shows an FTP client accessing multiple FTP servers on a TCP/IP internetwork. The FTP commands to each of the different FTP servers in Figure 14.1 is the same. These commands can be issued manually for command line FTP clients, or automatically by GUI-based FTP clients. After a user learns the FTP commands for command line FTP clients, no additional training is required for accessing FTP server services even though the FTP server may be hosted on a VAX/VMS, UNIX, an IBM mainframe, or a NetWare server platform.

Figure 14.1 shows FTP with two components: the FTP server and the FTP client. The *FTP server* is implemented on a wide variety of third-party platforms such as UNIX, NetWare server, VAX/VMS, MVS, OS/2, Windows NT, and DOS/Windows. The *FTP client* also is implemented by many vendors. The following are a few examples of FTP clients:

▶ LAN Workplace from Novell

▶ UNICON FTP Client on IntranetWare server

▶ PC/TCP from FTP Software

▶ PC/NFS from Sun Microsystems

▶ Chameleon NFS from NETMANAGE

FTP servers and clients in
an intranet/Internet

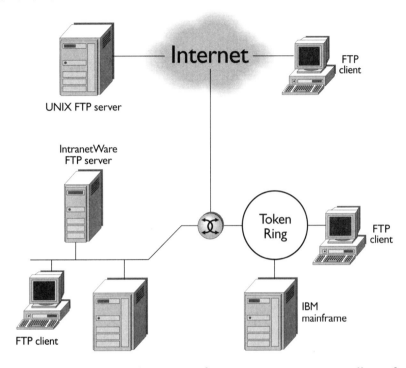

The FTP server can run on a wide variety of operating systems. Regardless of the operating system on which the FTP server runs, the FTP client uses the authentication mechanism of the underlying operating system that runs the FTP server. This means that the user generally needs a user account on the FTP server. The files and directories to which the user has access on the FTP server are restricted by permission settings for the user account. The FTP user uses the same password to log in to the FTP server as the one used to log in to the operating system running on the FTP server. An important exception to requiring a user account on the operating system is a special account called the *anonymous FTP user account*. This account enables any user to access the FTP server and is generally used to provide a limited access to the files on the FTP server.

If the IntranetWare server is set up as an FTP server, IntranetWare users can use their usernames and passwords to log in as FTP users to that server. When the users log in as FTP users to an IntranetWare server, they are given the same file access privileges they have in their IntranetWare user accounts.

Because DOS/Windows 3.x does not have an underlying username and password authentication scheme, most FTP server implementations for the DOS/Windows 3.x environment provide an additional configuration module to define FTP users and passwords.

Using FTP

Figure 14.2 shows an example of a typical FTP session on a NetWare FTP server. Notice that the command to access the NetWare server is the following:

```
ftp servername
```

When you make a connection to the FTP server, the FTP server sends a status message identifying itself and informing you that it is ready. You must type the username and password for that NetWare system.

You can use the ? key or FTP HELP command to obtain additional information on using FTP commands (see Figure 14.3).

F I G U R E   14.2

Start of FTP client session

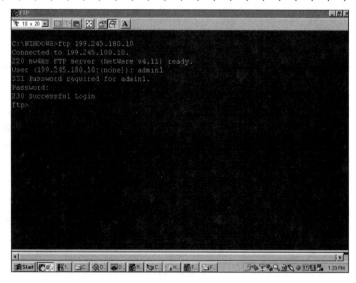

F I G U R E   14.3

Help on FTP commands

To transfer a file to the local FTP client, use the following command:

`get remotefile [localfile]`

If you do not specify the *localfile*, it is assumed that it has the same name as the *remotefile*.

To transfer a file to the FTP server, use the following command:

`put localfile [remotefile]`

If you do not specify the *remotefile*, it is assumed that it has the same name as the *localfile*. You can transfer a file to the FTP server only if the user account under which you are logged in has privileges to create a file in the FTP server's directory. You navigate the FTP server's directory system by using the FTP `cd` (change directory) command. To change the directory of the local system (FTP) client, you can use the `lcd` (local change directory) command.

Figure 14.4 shows the use of the FTP `cd` and the `pwd` commands. Notice that the directory names on the NetWare FTP server are referred to in UNIX style. Therefore, the directory SYS:PUBLIC is referred to as `/sys/public`.

F I G U R E   14.4

Example of using cd *and*
pwd FTP *commands*

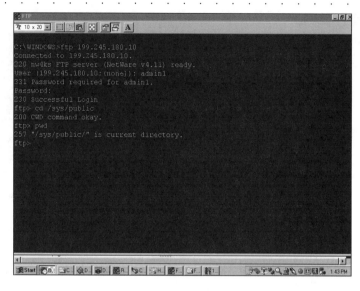

Figure 14.5 demonstrates how to use the FTP `dir` command to see a list of file/directories in the root (`/vol1`) directory of the NetWare FTP server. Notice that the directory listings are displayed in the UNIX style, even though the NetWare file and directory permissions are displayed.

F I G U R E   14.5

Example of using the
dir *FTP command*

Figure 14.6 shows how to use the FTP get and put commands. According to the figure, the following FTP file-transfer commands were issued:

```
get afile
get afile local.afl
put printers.txt   /vol1/printers.txt
```

The first command transfers the file called afile on the NetWare FTP server to the local directory on the FTP client. The name of the local file is the same as the remote file (afile) because the local filename is not specified. Note that FTP also reports the size of the file and the length of time required to transfer the file.

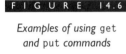

Examples of using get *and* put *commands*

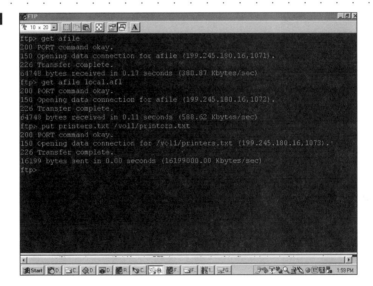

In the second FTP get command, the same remote file (afile) is transferred but given a different local name (local.afl). Notice also that the second file transfer is much quicker than the first. The reason is that NetWare caches the file on initial access. The second access to the file is taken from cache and is, therefore, faster. The last command is a put command to transfer the file printers.txt to the FTP server. Table 14.1 shows a description of some of the FTP commands.

TABLE 14.1	COMMAND	DESCRIPTION
Example FTP Commands	get *remotefile [localfile]*	Transfers *remotefile* from a remote system to a local directory
	put *localfile [remotefile]*	Transfers *localfile* from a local system to a remote host
	mget *file1* ...	Transfers multiple files from a remote system to a local directory
	mput *file1* ...	Transfers multiple files from a local system to a remote host
	dir	Lists directory contents on a remote system
	ldir	Lists directory contents on a local system
	pwd	Prints the full path name of current directory on a remote system
	lpwd	Prints the full path name of current directory on a local system
	cd *dirpath*	Changes the directory to *dirpath* on a remote system
	lcd *dirpath*	Changes the directory to *dirpath* on a local system
	type [ascii | binary]	Sets transfer mode to ASCII or Binary
	struct [stream | record]	Sets transfer structure to Stream or Record

Understanding FTP Transfer Modes

FTP supports two types of transfer modes: ASCII mode and Binary mode. The *ASCII mode* is used for transferring text files and performs automatic end-of-line conversions between different operating systems. If a text file is transferred from a UNIX system to a DOS system, for example, FTP automatically adds an extra carriage return required for DOS text files at the end of each line of text. Similarly, if a text file is transferred from a DOS system to a UNIX system, FTP automatically strips from the end of each line of text the extra DOS carriage return that is not required for UNIX text files.

The *Binary mode* (also called *Image mode*) is used for non-text files such as program files, image files, and binary data. You should not transfer these types of files by using ASCII mode. If you do, any occurrence of end-of-line characters in binary data could cause end-of-line translation, which could modify the binary data.

Figure 14.7 shows how ASCII and Binary commands are used for transferring files. The following commands are used to transfer the files:

```
ascii
get getaddr.c
binary
get getaddr.exe
```

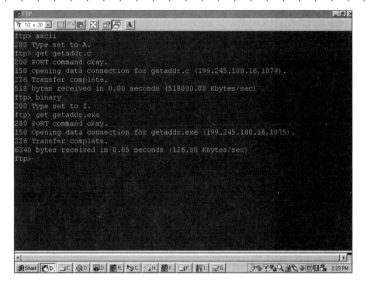

*Transferring text and
binary files in FTP*

Before transferring the C program file (ASCII text) called GETADDR.C, the FTP client is placed in ASCII mode. Before transferring the GETADDR.EXE binary file, the FTP client is placed in binary mode.

You also can use FTP to set the transfer structure. The two file structures from which you can choose are stream and record. The *stream* transfer structure interprets the file as a stream of bytes. This structure is the most commonly available transfer method. The *record* transfer structure interprets the file as a sequence of records. This transfer structure is not commonly used. It was used in the older TOPS-10 operating system environment, which provided support for it.

The previous examples of FTP showed the use of FTP commands to transfer files. Some vendors (such as NETMANAGE's Chameleon NFS and Novell's LAN Workplace/Workgroup products) offer a graphical interface for using FTP.

Understanding Directory Name Conventions

The FTP clients see NetWare path names and directory listings in UNIX-style format. The following are examples of NetWare path names seen and specified in the FTP client:

```
SYS:PUBLIC\CLIENT appears as /sys/public/client
VOL1:APPS\DB\MEMOS appears as /vol1/apps/db/memos
```

The general syntax for converting NetWare-style names is

/volumename/pathname

where *volumename* is the NetWare volume name, and *pathname* is the NetWare directory path name. You must use these names in their lowercase form.

The NetWare FTP server can handle path names of 255 characters or less. The FTP server also supports the UNIX wildcards (* and ?). These characters are useful in the FTP `mget` and `mput` commands that you can use for transferring multiple files with a single command.

The NetWare FTP server supports the use of two periods (..) to refer to the parent directory. The following FTP command, for example, makes the parent directory the current working directory on the NetWare FTP server:

```
CD ..
```

The NetWare FTP server supports the tilde (~) character, which expands to the path name of the NetWare user's home directory.

Examining the NFS Name Space

The NetWare FTP server supports the `quote site` command that enables the FTP client to view the FTP server's directories in the DOS name space or the NFS name space, regardless of the name space on the NetWare volume. When the NetWare FTP server is initially configured for NFS name space, file operations for volumes that do not have NFS name space take place in the DOS name space.

You can use the FTP `quote site` command to specify the name space used for viewing the files. The following is the general syntax for this command:

```
quote site { dos | nfs }
```

To view the name space as a DOS name space, use this command:

```
quote site dos
```

To view the name space as an NFS name space, use this command:

```
quote site nfs
```

Figure 14.8 displays the alternate views of the FTP server's directories in the DOS or NFS name space by using the quote site DOS command. Figures 14.10 and 14.11 demonstrate the use of the quote site DOS and quote site NFS commands. Notice the message that appears when these commands are used. When the quote site DOS command is used, the operations are only for volumes that support the DOS name space (all NetWare volumes support the DOS name space). When the quote site NFS command is used, the operations are only for volumes that support the NFS name space. Also note the differences in directory listings of the two name spaces. The NFS name space directory listing in Figure 14.11 includes the full long names of the files in Figure 14.10.

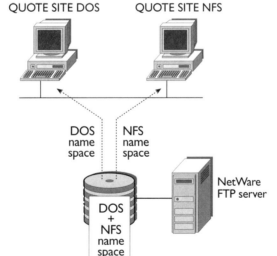

F I G U R E   14.8

The quote site command for alternate views

QUOTE SITE DOS   QUOTE SITE NFS

DOS
name
space

NFS
name
space

NetWare
FTP server

DOS
+
NFS
name
space

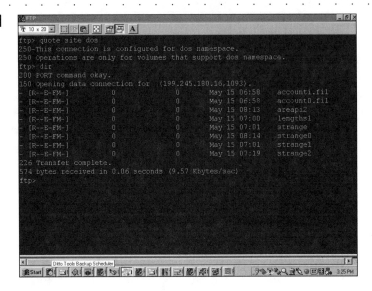

Another difference between the DOS name space and NFS name space is the way symbolic links are handled.

Using Symbolic Links in DOS and NFS Name Spaces

If a symbolic link is retrieved from the FTP server in the NFS name space, the file or directory that is the target of the symbolic link is returned. This behavior is expected for UNIX symbolic links. If a symbolic link is retrieved from the FTP server in the DOS name space, however, the file that is returned is the filename of the target of the symbolic link, not the contents of the target file. The reason is that symbolic links appear in the DOS name space as text files that contain the name of the file or directory being pointed to.

Figure 14.11 shows a symbolic link /sys/data/symexamp/slink to the file /sys/data/symexamp/test.dat. The contents of the file test.dat are the following:

```
John Taggart stepped out of the awning of 1801 Maiden Lane. It
was a typical hot day in Summer...
```

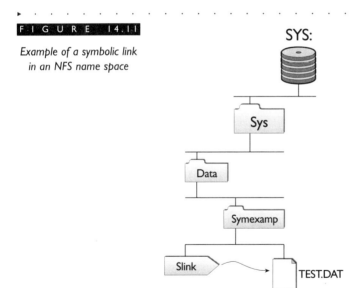

Example of a symbolic link in an NFS name space

SYS:

Sys

Data

Symexamp

Slink

TEST.DAT

Figure 14.12 demonstrates an attempt to read the contents of the symbolic link file /sys/data/symexamp/slink transferred by using the NFS name space. Notice that the displayed contents are the contents of the target file test.dat.

▶ · ◀

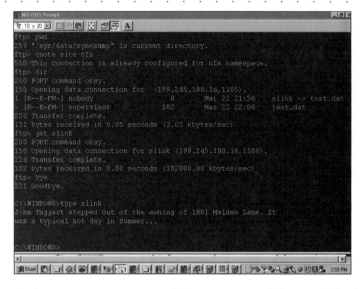

FIGURE 14.12

File transfer of a symbolic link in the NFS name space

Figure 14.13 shows an attempt to read the contents of the symbolic link file /sys/data/symexamp/slink transferred by using the DOS name space. Contrast the results of Figure 14.13 with those of Figure 14.12. Notice that the displayed contents are *not* the contents of the target file test.dat but the name of the target symbolic link test.dat

▶ · ◀

FIGURE 14.13

File transfer of a symbolic link in the DOS name space

Using the `quote stat` Command

Another extension of the NetWare FTP server is the `quote stat` command. You can use the `quote stat` command to inquire about the status of an FTP connection to the NetWare FTP server and the best parameters for retrieving a file. The following is the general syntax of this command:

```
quote stat [ pathname ]
```

The `quote stat` command by itself, with no path name specified, displays information on the status of the connection (see Figure 14.14). If you use the `quote stat` command on a file, the command displays information about the best set of FTP parameters for retrieving the file (see Figure 14.15). This information is displayed in the following format:

```
Type   Format    Structure   Mode   Pathname
```

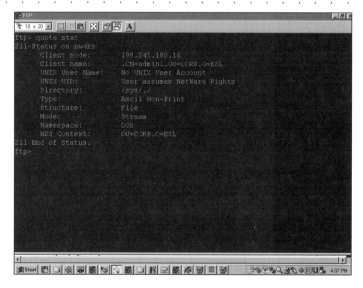

Example of the quote
stat *command*

▸ . . . . ◂

Example of the quote stat
file command used on a file

Table 14.2 contains the meanings of the preceding fields.

Output of the quote
stat *Command*

FIELD	MEANING
Type	Data transfer type—"A" for ASCII, or "I" for Image (binary)
Format	Data transfer format—"N" for nonprint (used for ASCII and IMAGE), or a number specifying local byte size
Client node	Client hostname or IP address
Client name	NetWare username
Unix User Name	UNIX username
Unix UID	UNIX user ID for the UNIX username
Directory	Current working directory
Structure	Transfer structure—"F" for file structure, or "R" for record structure
Mode	Transfer mode—"S" for stream structure, or "R" for record structure
Namespace	Current name space
NDS Context	Current NDS context

Accessing NetWare FTP Servers Without FTP Support

The NetWare FTP server contains a feature that enables NetWare servers without FTP services to be accessed through a NetWare FTP server. In Figure 14.16, the NetWare server NWCS has FTP services, whereas the NetWare server MADHAV does not have FTP services. The FTP client can access the NetWare FTP server and, through this connection, access files on the NetWare server MADHAV.

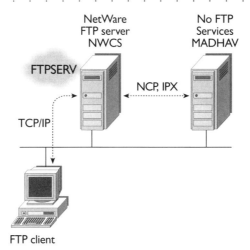

F I G U R E   14.16

Accessing other NetWare servers via the FTP server

You must reference the path names for the NetWare server without FTP services by using the following special syntax:

```
//netware_server_name/volume_name/file_pathname
```

You must reference the file `madhav/sys:public/sata/memo.txt`, for example, by using the following name:

```
//madhav/sys/public/data/memo.txt
```

You must, however, adhere to some restrictions and requirements for accomplishing the connections shown in Figure 14.16. These rules include the following:

- A NetWare account must exist on the NetWare server (without FTP services) with identical username and password to the NetWare FTP server.

2 • Anonymous users cannot access files on NetWare servers without FTP services.

3 • FTP clients can access only DOS name space on NetWare servers without FTP services.

4 • The NetWare server without FTP services must be configured with the following command:

```
SET REPLY TO GET NEAREST SERVER=ON
```

To refer to a file on a NetWare server that does not have FTP services, use the following syntax:

```
//servername/volumename/pathname
```

Installing the IntranetWare FTP Server

The IntranetWare software comes with a CD that contains the FTP server and the UNIX/NetWare print gateways. The following sections will describe the installation of the FTP server and its configuration.

Installing the IntranetWare FTP Server

As with most NetWare products from Novell, the NetWare FTP server is installed using the NetWare Installation utility (INSTALL.NLM). You must mount the NetWare OS CD-ROM either at the server or at the workstation. If you are using the CD-ROM at the workstation, you should log in to the server remotely using RCONSOLE.EXE. If you are using the CD-ROM at the server, you should mount the CD-ROM at the server using the appropriate drivers.

Follow these steps to install the FTP server:

1 • Run INSTALL:

```
LOAD INSTALL
```

2 • From the INSTALL main menu, select "Product options" and "Install a product not listed."

3 • When prompted, specify the location of the installation source files, press F3 and enter **NWUXPS:NWUXPS** if the CD is mounted at the server, or **drive:\NWUXPS** if the CD is mounted at the workstation. Replace *drive* with drive letter for the CD-ROM at the workstation.

4 • You will see the FTP files copied and then the INSTALL menu appears.

5 • Press Esc to continue when you are informed about the existence of the README.TXT file.

6 • Select No if you are asked if you want to stop the installation to read the README.TXT file.

7 • Enter the drive letter of the server boot drive (usually drive C:).

8 • Select Yes to install the online documentation.

9 • If you do not have a document viewer installed, select Yes to install the document viewer.

10 • You will see installation status messages as the remaining files are copied to the IntranetWare server.

11 • The UNICON NLM will load. Log in as administrator.

12 • A menu for configuring DNS and Network Information System (NIS) locally or remotely then appears. You will be presented with the options shown in Table 14.3.

TABLE 14.3	OPTION	DESCRIPTION
DNS and NIS Configuration Options	Local DNS and Local NIS	This configures the local IntranetWare server as the master DNS and master NIS server. The NIS services were originally created by Sun Microsystems to store hostname-to-IP address mapping information, user/group accounts, and so on.

(continued)

TABLE 14.3	OPTION	DESCRIPTION
DNS and NIS Configuration Options (continued)	Remote DNS and Remote NIS	This sets the IntranetWare server as a client to a remote DNS server and NIS server, which have already been installed and configured. Storing of host information and configuration must be done on the remote server. You can use UNICON to view information on the remote servers, but you cannot modify this information.
	Remote DNS and Local NIS	This sets the IntranetWare server as a client to a remote DNS server. The IntranetWare server is set as a master NIS server. This option requires that the host information be managed on the remote DNS server. You can use UNICON to view information on the remote DNS server, but you cannot modify this information.
	No DNS and Remote NIS	This sets the IntranetWare server as a client to the remote NIS server. Also, the IntranetWare server is not using DNS. Instead, it is using the remote NIS. This option requires that the host, user, and group information be managed on the remote NIS server. You can use UNICON to view information on the remote NIS server, but you cannot modify this information.

13 • Make the appropriate selection and fill out the form which will ask you for the NIS/DNS domain names and domain servers. Press Esc to continue.

14 • If you have already installed DNS/NIS service, do not initialize the database, unless you want to delete earlier information on the system.

15 • Follow the instructions to complete the installation and restart the server.

Configuring the IntranetWare FTP Server

After installing the FTP server and restarting the IntranetWare server, you must configure the FTP server. The configuration of the FTP server is done by using the UNICON NLM. You can use UNICON to create a general guest user account called the Anonymous user account. When an FTP client requests access using the Anonymous user account, the user can supply any password. This password is not checked against any user account on the IntranetWare server. As part of configuring the Anonymous user account, you must set specify the login directory for the Anonymous user, which by default is the root of the volume SYS: (/sys). If you have UNIX clients on your network, or if you are connected to the Internet, you should also add the NFS name space to the server volume that the FTP users will be logging on to. You can add the NFS name space by running the following commands just once for each volume to which you are adding NFS name space:

```
LOAD NFS
ADD NAME SPACE NFS TO volumename
```

Another configuration task you should perform is to set the NetWare shareable attribute for the files that you expect the FTP clients to be downloading concurrently.

Follow these steps to configure the FTP server:

1 • Start UNICON from the IntranetWare server console:

```
LOAD UNICON
```

2 • Log in to the server by supplying and Admin username and password.

3 • From the UNICON main menu select Manage Services, FTP Server, and Set Parameters.

4 • Figure 14.17 shows the FTP Server Parameters screen. The fields on the FTP Server Parameters screen have the meanings shown in Table 14.4. If you have a second volume on the IntranetWare server, you should change the Anonymous User's Home Directory to a directory other than the sys:\ directory.

5 • Next, verify that the Anonymous user is mapped correctly. You can do this from the UNICON main menu by selecting Manage Global Objects, Manage Users, and All Entries. The Anonymous user should appear in both the NetWare and UNIX columns. If not, enable the Anonymous user account as specified in Step 4.

FIGURE 14.17
FTP Server Parameters screen

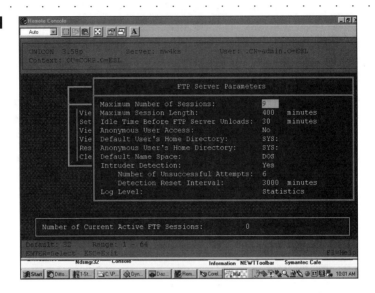

TABLE 14.4	FIELD	DESCRIPTION
FTP Server Parameters Fields	Maximum Number of Sessions	The maximum number of simultaneous sessions that are permissible.
	Maximum Session Length	Maximum number of minutes an FTP session can be active.
	Idle Time before FTP Server Unloads	The number of minutes the FTP server remains resident in memory before unloading, if there are no open FTP sessions.
	Anonymous User Access	When set to Yes, it enables the Anonymous user account; otherwise, it disables it.
	Default User's Home Directory	The home directory for a user who does not have a home directory on the IntranetWare server.
	Anonymous User's Home Directory	The home directory for the Anonymous user account.
	Default Name Space	The default name space used for FTP for non-UNIX clients.
	Intruder Detection	Determines if intruder detection is enabled or disabled. If enabled (set to Yes), the fields Number of Unsuccessful Attempts and Reset Intruder Interval have a meaning.

(continued)

TABLE 14.4	FIELD	DESCRIPTION
FTP Server Parameters Fields (continued)	Number of Unsuccessful Attempts	The number of unsuccessful attempts are allowed before information is logged. The number of attempts is tabulated only within the time period specified by the reset interval.
	Detection Reset Interval	The time interval within which unsuccessful login attempts are tabulated.
	Log Level	This can be set to a value of None (disables logging), Logins (Records login information), Statistics (FTP server statistics including logins are recorded), or File (records descriptions of FTP transactions including logins and statistics).

If you have a second volume on the IntranetWare server, you should change the Anonymous User's Home Directory to a directory other than the `sys:\` directory.

6 • If you have enabled the Anonymous user account, verify that the home directory for the Anonymous user account is owned by the Anonymous user and that file access is set up correctly. You can perform this task from the UNICON main menu by selecting Perform File Operations and View/Set File Permissions. Enter the path for the Anonymous user's home directory and press F9 to view file information. Verify that the NFS permission for the home directory is set as follows:

`[U = rwx] [G = --] [O = --]`

This means that the user owner's permission for the home directory is set to read, write, and execute. No permissions are assigned for the group ID and the rest of the world (others).

Restricting access to FTP server

You may want to deny FTP access to specific users who may not be trustworthy. You can use UNICON to define which users that can access the FTP server by creating an FTP access file. The FTP access file is `sys:etc/restrict.ftp`. This is an editable text file that you can use to define FTP access. The RESTRICT.FTP file uses a specialized syntax that is described in this section. If RESTRICT.FTP is empty or does not exist, no FTP access is permitted to the server.

To view or edit the FTP access file, follow these steps:

1 • Start UNICON:

LOAD UNICON

2 • From the UNICON main menu, select Manage Services, FTP Server, and Restrict FTP Access. The screen shown in Figure 14.18 appears.

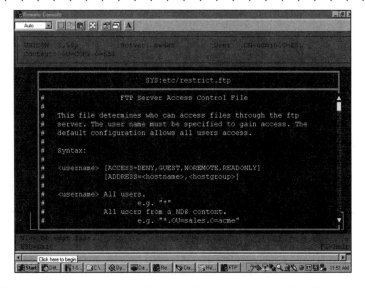

Edit the file using the syntax described in the comments in the file. Listing 14.1 shows a sample RESTRICT.FTP file that allows all users access to the FTP server.

L I S T I N G 14.1

Sample RESTRICT.FTP File

```
#                 FTP Server Access Control File
#
#    This file determines who can access files through the ftp
#    server. The user name must be specified to gain access. The
#    default configuration allows all users access.
```

```
#
#    Syntax:
#
#    <username>  [ACCESS=DENY,GUEST,NOREMOTE,READONLY]
#                [ADDRESS=<hostname>,<hostgroup>]
#
#    <username>  All users.
#                    e.g. "*"
#                All users from a NDS context.
#                    e.g. "*.OU=sales.O=acme"
#                NDS user relative to the default context.
#                    e.g. "bill"
#                Complete Canonicalized NDS name.
#                    e.g. ".CN=Admin.O=acme"
#
#                <username> is required and must be the first
#                field in the line.
#
#    ACCESS=     This option limits user access to the server. This
#                option is case sensitive and is not required.
#
#    DENY        Denies access to the server. This parameter
#                overrides a previously declared global access.
#
#    GUEST       Restricts the user to the home directory on the
#                server running the FTP server.
#
#    NOREMOTE    Restricts the user to the local server.
#                User cannot access any remote servers.
#
#    READONLY    Restricts the user from storing any files on the
#                server.
#
#    ADDRESS=    This option restricts access for users from
#                a specific host or set of hosts (hostgroup).
#                This option is case sensitive and is not required.
```

```
#
#    Examples:
#
#    1. The following example specifies that all users have
#       access to the local server but cannot access remote
#       NetWare servers.
#
#    * ACCESS=NOREMOTE
#
#    2. The following example specifies that all users from the OU
#       called SALES have full access, but must connect from the
#       host <hostname>.
#
#    *.OU=SALES.O=ACME ADDRESS=hostname
#
#    3. The following example specifies the user ADMIN cannot access
#       the FTP server.
#
#    ADMIN.O=ACME ACCESS=DENY
#
#    The following default entry of "*" allows all users access to
#    ftp server.
*
```

Viewing FTP Log Files

The FTP server uses two log files: FTPSERV.LOG (which maintains an activity record for FTP sessions) and INTRUDER.FTP (which maintains a record of failed login attempts). The FTPSERV.LOG file is kept in the SYS:ETC directory, and the INTRUDER.FTP is kept in the SYS:SYSTEM directory for tighter security.

The FTPSERV.LOG file records information on logins and FTP activity. The amount and type of information is controlled by the Log Level parameter in Figure 14.17. Login activity is recorded per user session. The information is recorded when the session ends. The activity record for that session is appended to the FTPSERV.LOG file with a double line separating the entries for each session.

To display this file, from the UNICON main menu/select Manage Services, FTP Server, and View FTP Log File. The following is a sample FTPSERV.LOG file:

```
------------------

Wed Jan  8 10:29:14 1997 FTP Session Starts from 199.245.180.16.
Wed Jan  8 12:09:13 1997 2 files copied from server.
0 files copied to server.
Wed Jan  8 12:09:13 1997 FTP Session Ends from 199.245.180.16.
------------------

------------------

Wed Jan  8 12:09:26 1997 FTP Session Starts from 199.245.180.16.
Wed Jan  8 12:10:04 1997 0 files copied from server.
0 files copied to server.
Wed Jan  8 12:10:04 1997 FTP Session Ends from
199.245.180.16.------------------
```

The Intruder Log File is SYS:SYSTEM\INTRUDER.FTP. It records information about unsuccessful login attempts. You can set the intruder detection parameters on the screen in Figure 14.17.

The information recorded in the INTRUDER.FTP file includes the following:

▸ Time of attempted access

▸ Login name of the user attempting access

▸ Incorrect password

To view the INTRUDER.FTP file, from the UNICON main menu select Manage Services, FTP Server, and View Intruder Log File. The following is a sample INTRUDER.FTP file that shows several attempts to log in with an incorrect password:

```
Intruder Alert. Host thinkpad.kinetics.com at address
199.245.180.16 has exceeded the limit
Time 1-08-97 12:20:27pm  User .CN=admin1.OU=CORP.O=ESL used
password dada .
Time 1-08-97 12:20:13pm  User .CN=admin2.OU=CORP.O=ESL used
password ddd .
```

```
Time 1-08-97 12:17:12pm  User .CN=kss.OU=CORP.O=ESL used
password add .
Time 1-08-97 12:17:00pm  User .CN=admin2.OU=CORP.O=ESL used
password ad .
Time 1-08-97 12:16:43pm  User .CN=kss.OU=CORP.O=ESL used
password ksspwd .
Time 1-08-97 12:16:31pm  User .CN=admin2.OU=CORP.O=ESL used
password admin2pw .
Time 1-08-97 12:10:16pm  User .CN=admin2.OU=CORP.O=ESL used
password admin2pw .
```

Starting FTP Service

The operation of the NetWare FTP server is shown in Figure 14.19. The NetWare FTP server is implemented by two NLMs: INETD.NLM and FTPSERV.NLM. The INETD.NLM is an implementation of the Internet daemon used in UNIX systems. The INETD.NLM listens on well-known ports (such as the FTP port 21), waiting for incoming connection requests. When INETD.NLM receives a TCP connection request on port 21, it knows that this request is an FTP connection request, and it loads the FTPSERV.NLM.

FIGURE 14.19

Operation of INETD.NLM in starting FTP service

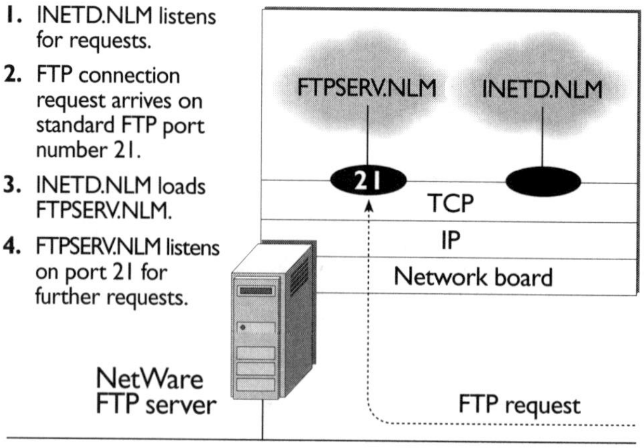

1. INETD.NLM listens for requests.
2. FTP connection request arrives on standard FTP port number 21.
3. INETD.NLM loads FTPSERV.NLM.
4. FTPSERV.NLM listens on port 21 for further requests.

The FTPSERV.NLM remains in NetWare server memory as long as active FTP connections exist. FTPSERV.NLM is automatically unloaded when there are no more active FTP connections and the Idle Time Before FTP Unloads parameter period (see Figure 14.17) has expired.

You can use UNICON to start or stop the FTP server by performing the following steps:

1 • Start UNICON:

```
LOAD UNICON
```

2 • Log in as Admin user.

3 • Select Start/Stop Services.

4 • You should see a list of running services. If FTP Server is not in the list, you can start it by pressing the Insert key and selecting FTP Server. If FTP Server is in the list, and you want to stop the FTP Service, highlight FTP Server in the list and press the Delete key.

Another way to start and stop the FTP server is to load or unload the INETD.NLM. The INETD.NLM can be activated by the LOAD INETD command. The INETD.NLM requires the existence of the preconfigured file SYS:ETC\INETD.CFG. The following are the contents of the INETD.CFG file:

```
# Internet services syntax:
#  <service_name> <socket_type> <proto> <server_pathname>
ftp stream tcp ftpserv
#
# The Tftp service is provided primarily for booting.
# Most sites run this
# only on machines acting as "boot servers."
#
#tftp dgram udp tftpserv sys:tftpboot
```

The INETD.CFG file lists the services that are started by INETD.NLM and whether the protocol is a stream protocol or datagram protocol. It also lists the name of the protocol. The name of the service can be found in the SYS:ETC/SERVICES file which defines the port number for the service. Listing 14.2 shows the contents of the SERVICES file. The FTP and TFTP (Trivial File Transfer Protocol) service information is highlighted in bold.

LISTING 14.2

SERVICES File

```
#
# SYS:ETC\SERVICES
#
# Network service mappings.  Maps service names to transport
# protocol and transport protocol ports.
#
echo        7/udp
echo        7/tcp
discard     9/udp     sink null
discard     9/tcp     sink null
systat      11/tcp
daytime     13/udp
daytime     13/tc
netstat     15/tcp
ftp-data    20/tcp
ftp         21/tcp
telnet      23/tcp
smtp        25/tcp    mail
time        37/tcp    timserver
time        37/udp    timserver
name        42/udp    nameserver
whois       43/tcp    nicname      # usually to sri-nic
domain      53/udp
domain      53/tcp
hostnames   101/tcp   hostname     # usually to sri-nic
```

```
sunrpc       111/udp
sunrpc       111/tcp
#
#
# Host specific functions
#
tftp         69/udp
rje          77/tcp
finger       79/tcp
link         87/tcp     ttylink
supdup       95/tcp
iso-tsap     102/tcp
x400         103/tcp               # ISO Mail
x400-snd     104/tcp
csnet-ns     105/tcp
pop-2        109/tcp               # Post Office
uucp-path    117/tcp
nntp         119/tcp    usenet     # Network News Transfer
ntp          123/tcp               # Network Time Protocol
NeWS         144/tcp    news       # Window System
#
# UNIX specific services
#
# these are NOT officially assigned
#
exec         512/tcp
login        513/tcp
shell        514/tcp    cmd        # no passwords used
printer      515/tcp    spooler    # experimental
courier      530/tcp    rpc        # experimental
biff         512/udp    comsat
who          513/udp    whod
syslog       514/udp
talk         517/udp
route        520/udp    router routed
```

```
new-rwho    550/udp  new-who    # experimental
rmonitor    560/udp  rmonitord  # experimental
monitor     561/udp             # experimental
ingreslock  1524/tcp
snmp        161/udp             # Simple Network Mgmt Protocol
snmp-trap   162/udp  snmptrap   # SNMP trap (event) messages
```

Normally, you should not have to change the INETD.CFG or SERVICES file for FTP services. To stop FTP services on the NetWare FTP server, unload INETD. If an active FTP connection exists, you must unload FTPSERV.NLM first. The following are the general commands for stopping FTP services on a NetWare FTP server:

```
unload FTPSERV
unload INETD
```

Summary

FTP is very useful for transferring documents and information in files across an intranet or the Internet. The IntranetWare server distribution software comes with an FTP server that can be installed and configured on the IntranetWare server. This chapter discussed how to install the FTP server on the IntranetWare server and how to configure FTP services on an IntranetWare server using UNICON. You also learned how to access the FTP server using an FTP client and the different commands and modes that can be used to access the FTP server.

What's on the CD-ROM

The material on the CD-ROM is organized into four subdirectories:

- ▸ CODE

- ▸ JAVASDK

- ▸ PERLW32

- ▸ WINPERL

CODE

The \CODE subdirectory on this CD-ROM contains code listings from examples used throughout this book.

JAVA SDK

This subdirectory contains a self-extracting file for installing the beta version of IntranetWare SDK for Java 1.1. To install the SDK, double-click this filename.

PERL for Win32

This program is located inside a subdirectory labeled \PERLW32. Within that subdirectory is another subdirectory labeled \PERL5. Within the \PERL5 subdirectory is a file named INSTALL.BAT. To install the binary version of Perl for Win32, run INSTALL.BAT from DOS by typing INSTALL at the DOS command line prompt. If you are running Windows, traverse the directories until you see the INSTALL.BAT filename. Double-click the filename.

This script adds Perl-related entries to the Registry and creates the directory \PERL\BIN. If this directory already exists, then the INSTALL program looks there for the file PERL.EXE. If the file exists, it will be run to determine its version number and then renamed to PERL.{VERSION #}.EXE. If the PERLE.EXE file does not exist, the INSTALL program adds \PERL\BIN to your path. A log of the installation session is created in the file \PERL5\INSTALL.LOG.

Copy any of your own scripts or library files into the \PERL\BIN directory. This allows you to run those scripts from any other directory.

For the latest version of Perl for Win32, visit ActiveState's Web site at `http://www.ActiveState.com`.

WINPERL

The WinPerl program is contained in the \WINPERL subdirectory. Within in that subdirectory are two subdirectories called \PERL4003 and \PERL4100. Inside both of these directories are files called WINPERL.EXE. Double-clicking these filenames will start the WINPERL program.

The \PERL4003 subdirectory contains the Debug version (beta.3) of WinPerl for Win32. The \PERL4100 subdirectory contains the Educational version (that is, version 1.0) of WinPerl for Win32.

This program runs in Windows 95. It does not run in Windows 3.x.

Index

database
  employee, 411.BAS script for lookup, 370–377
  manipulation in Perl, 326–327
  version numbers in DSS servers, 669
database server, client access to, 15–16
Date attribute, for NetBasic Server Object, 436
date functions, in NetBasic, 416–418
DATE NetBasic class library, 391
Date object (NetBasic), 394
  function to return, 416
date stamp, SSI directive for, 554–555
DATE.BAS CGI script, 368–369
DATE_GMT SSI environment variable, 552
DATE_LOCAL SSI environment variable, 552, 553
day of week, in SSI time format, 558
daylight savings time (DST), 58
dbCreate() subroutine (NetBasic), 452–453
dbGetEqual() subroutine (NetBasic), 457
dbInsert() routine (NetBasic), 459
DBM files, 327
dbmopen function (Perl), 327
<DD> tag (HTML), 160
DDN (Defense Data Network), 4
DE domain, 664
Debug:number (NetBasic), 453
debug output, from rcgid daemon, 263

decimal value
  converting to hexadecimal string, 310
  converting hexadecimal string to, 309–310
  converting octal number string to, 311
  NetBasic function to convert hexadecimal to, 415
declarations, importing to NetBasic, 403–405
decode.pl file, 233–235
default access method, in Java, 502
default destination path, for copying server boot files, 50
default label, in Java switch statement, 491
Default Name Space parameter, for FTP Server, 730
default page, 11
default router, for subnetwork profile form, 700
default source path, for copying server boot files, 50
Default User's Home Directory parameter, for FTP Server, 730
Defense Advanced Research Projects Agency (DARPA), 2
Defense Data Network (DDN), 4
#define directive (NetBasic), 403, 404
definition list in HTML, 160
definition style, 151
DEFROUTE Bind parameter, for IP protocol, 73, 75
delete operator (Perl), for associative array, 305

DELPHI, 5
destroy() method (Java), 536, 538
Detection Reset Interval parameter, for FTP Server, 731
<DFN> tag (HTML), 151, 154, 156
DHCP client, 686
  IP address acquisition process, 688–692
DHCP client IP address, in DHCP, 693
DHCP message
  generic message, 695
  option format values for, 696
  size of, 695
DHCP packet format, 692–696
DHCP protocol
  fields used in, 693
  on IntranetWare Server, 696–707
  IP address allocation in, 687–688
  overview, 686–696
DHCP-relay agent support, 688
DHCP server, 33, 686
  defining excluded nodes, 705–706
  installing on IntranetWare Server, 697–698
  multiple on WAN, 39
  static IP address assignments in database, 703–705
  Web server as, 38
DHCPACK message, 689–690, 696
DHCPCFG utility
  for excluded nodes list creation, 706

IDG BOOKS WORLDWIDE, INC.
END-USER LICENSE AGREEMENT

Read This. You should carefully read these terms and conditions before opening the software packet(s) included with this book ("Book"). This is a license agreement ("Agreement") between you and IDG Books Worldwide, Inc. ("IDGB"). By opening the accompanying software packet(s), you acknowledge that you have read and accept the following terms and conditions. If you do not agree and do not want to be bound by such terms and conditions, promptly return the Book and the unopened software packet(s) to the place you obtained them for a full refund.

1. **License Grant**. IDGB grants to you (either an individual or entity) a nonexclusive license to use one copy of the enclosed software program(s) (collectively, the "Software") solely for your own personal or business purposes on a single computer (whether a standard computer or a workstation component of a multiuser network). The Software is in use on a computer when it is loaded into temporary memory (i.e., RAM) or installed into permanent memory (e.g., hard disk, CD-ROM, or other storage device). IDGB reserves all rights not expressly granted herein.

2. **Ownership**. IDGB is the owner of all right, title, and interest, including copyright, in and to the compilation of the Software recorded on the disk(s)/CD-ROM. Copyright to the individual programs on the disk(s)/CD-ROM is owned by the author or other authorized copyright owner of each program. Ownership of the Software and all proprietary rights relating thereto remain with IDGB and its licensors.

3. **Restrictions on Use and Transfer.**
    (a) You may only (i) make one copy of the Software for backup or archival purposes, or (ii) transfer the Software to a single hard disk, provided that you keep the original for backup or archival purposes. You may not (i) rent or lease the Software, (ii) copy or reproduce the Software through a LAN or other network system or through any computer subscriber system or bulletin-board system, or (iii) modify, adapt, or create derivative works based on the Software.

    (b) You may not reverse engineer, decompile, or disassemble the Software. You may transfer the Software and user documentation on a permanent basis, provided that the transferee agrees to accept the terms and conditions of this Agreement and you retain no copies. If the Software is an update or has been updated, any transfer must include the most recent update and all prior versions.

4. **Restrictions on Use of Individual Programs.** You must follow the individual requirements and restrictions detailed for each individual program in Appendix D of this Book. These limitations are contained in the individual license agreements recorded on the disk(s)/CD-ROM or printed in this book. These restrictions may include a requirement that after using the program for the period of time specified in its text, the user must pay a registration fee or discontinue use. By opening the Software packet(s), you will be agreeing to abide by the licenses and restrictions for these individual programs. None of the material on this disk(s) or listed in this Book may ever be distributed, in original or modified form, for commercial purposes.

5. Limited Warranty.

(a) IDGB warrants that the Software and disk(s)/CD-ROM are free from defects in materials and workmanship under normal use for a period of sixty (60) days from the date of purchase of this Book. If IDGB receives notification within the warranty period of defects in materials or workmanship, IDGB will replace the defective disk(s)/CD-ROM.

(b) IDGB AND THE AUTHOR OF THE BOOK DISCLAIM ALL OTHER WARRANTIES, EXPRESS OR IMPLIED, INCLUDING WITHOUT LIMITATION IMPLIED WARRANTIES OF MERCHANTABILITY AND FITNESS FOR A PARTICULAR PURPOSE, WITH RESPECT TO THE SOFTWARE, THE PRO-GRAMS, THE SOURCE CODE CONTAINED THEREIN, AND/OR THE TECHNIQUES DESCRIBED IN THIS BOOK. IDGB DOES NOT WARRANT THAT THE FUNCTIONS CONTAINED IN THE SOFTWARE WILL MEET YOUR REQUIREMENTS OR THAT THE OPERATION OF THE SOFTWARE WILL BE ERROR FREE.

(c) This limited warranty gives you specific legal rights, and you may have other rights which vary from jurisdiction to jurisdiction.

6. Remedies.

(a) IDGB's entire liability and your exclusive remedy for defects in materials and workmanship shall be limited to replacement of the Software, which may be returned to IDGB with a copy of your receipt at the following address: Disk Fulfillment Department, Attn: Novell's Guide to Creating IntranetWare Intranets, IDG Books Worldwide, Inc., 7260 Shadeland Station, Ste. 100, Indianapolis, IN 46256, or call 1-800-762-2974. Please allow 3-4 weeks for delivery. This Limited Warranty is void if failure of the Software has resulted from accident, abuse, or misapplication. Any replacement Software will be warranted for the remainder of the original warranty period or thirty (30) days, whichever is longer.

(b) In no event shall IDGB or the author be liable for any damages whatsoever (including without limitation damages for loss of business profits, business interruption, loss of business information, or any other pecuniary loss) arising from the use of or inability to use the Book or the Software, even if IDGB has been advised of the possibility of such damages.

(c) Because some jurisdictions do not allow the exclusion or limitation of liability for consequential or incidental damages, the above limitation or exclusion may not apply to you.

7. U.S. Government Restricted Rights. Use, duplication, or disclosure of the Software by the U.S. Government is subject to restrictions stated in paragraph (c) (1) (ii) of the Rights in Technical Data and Computer Software clause of DFARS 252.227-7013, and in subparagraphs (a) through (d) of the Commercial Computer— Restricted Rights clause at FAR 52.227-19, and in similar clauses in the NASA FAR supplement, when applicable.

8. General. This Agreement constitutes the entire understanding of the parties and revokes and supersedes all prior agreements, oral or written, between them and may not be modified or amended except in a writing signed by both parties hereto which specifically refers to this Agreement. This Agreement shall take precedence over any other documents that may be in conflict herewith. If any one or more provisions contained in this Agreement are held by any court or tribunal to be invalid, illegal, or otherwise unenforceable, each and every other provision shall remain in full force and effect.

License Agreement for PERL for Win32

GNU GENERAL PUBLIC LICENSE
Version 2, June 1991

Preamble

The licenses for most software are designed to take away your freedom to share and change it. By contrast, the GNU General Public License is intended to guarantee your freedom to share and change free software—to make sure the software is free for all its users. This General Public License applies to most of the Free Software Foundation's software and to any other program whose authors commit to using it. (Some other Free Software Foundation software is covered by the GNU Library General Public License instead.) You can apply it to your programs, too.

When we speak of free software, we are referring to freedom, not price. Our General Public Licenses are designed to make sure that you have the freedom to distribute copies of free software (and charge for this service if you wish), that you receive source code or can get it if you want it, that you can change the software or use pieces of it in new free programs; and that you know you can do these things.

To protect your rights, we need to make restrictions that forbid anyone to deny you these rights or to ask you to surrender the rights. These restrictions translate to certain responsibilities for you if you distribute copies of the software, or if you modify it.

For example, if you distribute copies of such a program, whether gratis or for a fee, you must give the recipients all the rights that you have. You must make sure that they, too, receive or can get the source code. And you must show them these terms so they know their rights.

We protect your rights with two steps: (1) copyright the software, and (2) offer you this license which gives you legal permission to copy, distribute and/or modify the software.

Also, for each author's protection and ours, we want to make certain that everyone understands that there is no warranty for this free software. If the software is modified by someone else and passed on, we want its recipients to know that what they have is not the original, so that any problems introduced by others will not reflect on the original authors' reputations.

Finally, any free program is threatened constantly by software patents. We wish to avoid the danger that redistributors of a free program will individually obtain patent licenses, in effect making the program proprietary. To prevent this, we have made it clear that any patent must be licensed for everyone's free use or not licensed at all.

The precise terms and conditions for copying, distribution and modification follow.

GNU GENERAL PUBLIC LICENSE TERMS AND CONDITIONS FOR COPYING, DISTRIBUTION AND MODIFICATION

0. This License applies to any program or other work which contains a notice placed by the copyright holder saying it may be distributed under the terms of this General Public License. The "Program", below, refers to any such program or work, and a "work based on the Program" means either the Program or any derivative work under copyright law: that is to say, a work containing the Program or a portion of it, either verbatim or with modifications and/or translated into another language. (Hereinafter, translation is included without limitation in the term "modification".) Each licensee is addressed as "you".

Activities other than copying, distribution and modification are not covered by this License; they are outside its scope. The act of running the Program is not restricted, and the output from the Program is covered only if its contents constitute a work based on the Program (independent of having been made by running the Program). Whether that is true depends on what the Program does.

1. You may copy and distribute verbatim copies of the Program's source code as you receive it, in any medium, provided that you conspicuously and appropriately publish on each copy an appropriate copyright notice and disclaimer of warranty; keep intact all the notices that refer to this License and to the absence of any warranty; and give any other recipients of the Program a copy of this License along with the Program.

You may charge a fee for the physical act of transferring a copy, and you may at your option offer warranty protection in exchange for a fee.

2. You may modify your copy or copies of the Program or any portion of it, thus forming a work based on the Program, and copy and distribute such modifications or work under the terms of Section 1 above, provided that you also meet all of these conditions:

a) You must cause the modified files to carry prominent notices stating that you changed the files and the date of any change.

b) You must cause any work that you distribute or publish, that in whole or in part contains or is derived from the Program or any part thereof, to be licensed as a whole at no charge to all third parties under the terms of this License.

c) If the modified program normally reads commands interactively when run, you must cause it, when started running for such interactive use in the most ordinary way, to print or display an announcement including an appropriate copyright notice and a notice that there is no warranty (or else, saying that you provide a warranty) and that users may redistribute the program under these conditions, and telling the user how to view a copy of this License. (Exception: if the Program itself is interactive but does not normally print such an announcement, your work based on the Program is not required to print an announcement.)

These requirements apply to the modified work as a whole. If identifiable sections of that work are not derived from the Program, and can be reasonably considered independent and separate works in themselves, then this License, and its terms, do not apply to those sections when you distribute them as separate works. But when you distribute the same sections as part of a whole which is a work based on the Program, the distribution of the whole must be on the terms of this License, whose permissions for other licensees extend to the entire whole, and thus to each and every part regardless of who wrote it.

Thus, it is not the intent of this section to claim rights or contest your rights to work written entirely by you; rather, the intent is to exercise the right to control the distribution of derivative or collective works based on the Program.

In addition, mere aggregation of another work not based on the Program with the Program (or with a work based on the Program) on a volume of a storage or distribution medium does not bring the other work under the scope of this License.

3. You may copy and distribute the Program (or a work based on it, under Section 2) in object code or executable form under the terms of Sections 1 and 2 above provided that you also do one of the following:

a) Accompany it with the complete corresponding machine-readable source code, which must be distributed under the terms of Sections 1 and 2 above on a medium customarily used for software interchange; or,

b) Accompany it with a written offer, valid for at least three years, to give any third party, for a charge no more than your cost of physically performing source distribution, a complete machine-readable copy of the corresponding source code, to be distributed under the terms of Sections 1 and 2 above on a medium customarily used for software interchange; or,

c) Accompany it with the information you received as to the offer to distribute corresponding source code. (This alternative is allowed only for noncommercial distribution and only if you received the program in object code or executable form with such an offer, in accord with Subsection b above.)

The source code for a work means the preferred form of the work for making modifications to it. For an executable work, complete source code means all the source code for all modules it contains, plus any associated interface definition files, plus the scripts used to control compilation and installation of the executable. However, as a special exception, the source code distributed need not include anything that is normally distributed (in either source or binary form) with the major components (compiler, kernel, and so on) of the operating system on which the executable runs, unless that component itself accompanies the executable.

If distribution of executable or object code is made by offering access to copy from a designated place, then offering equivalent access to copy the source code from the same place counts as distribution of the source code, even though third parties are not compelled to copy the source along with the object code.

4. You may not copy, modify, sublicense, or distribute the Program except as expressly provided under this License. Any attempt otherwise to copy, modify, sublicense or distribute the Program is void, and will automatically terminate your rights under this License. However, parties who have received copies, or rights, from you under this License will not have their licenses terminated so long as such parties remain in full compliance.

5. You are not required to accept this License, since you have not signed it. However, nothing else grants you permission to modify or distribute the Program or its derivative works. These actions are prohibited by law if you do not accept this License. Therefore, by modifying or distributing the Program (or any work based on the Program), you indicate your acceptance of this License to do so, and all its terms and conditions for copying, distributing or modifying the Program or works based on it.

6. Each time you redistribute the Program (or any work based on the Program), the recipient automatically receives a license from the original licensor to copy, distribute or modify the Program subject to these terms and conditions. You may not impose any further restrictions on the recipients' exercise of the rights granted herein. You are not responsible for enforcing compliance by third parties to this License.

7. If, as a consequence of a court judgment or allegation of patent infringement or for any other reason (not limited to patent issues), conditions are imposed on you (whether by court order, agreement or otherwise) that contradict the conditions of this License, they do not excuse you from the conditions of this License. If you cannot distribute so as to satisfy simultaneously your obligations under this License and any other pertinent obligations, then as a consequence you may not distribute the Program at all. For example, if a patent license would not permit royalty-free redistribution of the Program by all those who receive copies directly or indirectly through you, then the only way you could satisfy both it and this License would be to refrain entirely from distribution of the Program.

If any portion of this section is held invalid or unenforceable under any particular circumstance, the balance of the section is intended to apply and the section as a whole is intended to apply in other circumstances.

It is not the purpose of this section to induce you to infringe any patents or other property right claims or to contest validity of any such claims; this section has the sole purpose of protecting the integrity of the free software distribution system, which is implemented by public license practices. Many people have made generous contributions to the wide range of software distributed through that system in reliance on consistent application of that system; it is up to the author/donor to decide if he or she is willing to distribute software through any other system and a licensee cannot impose that choice.

This section is intended to make thoroughly clear what is believed to be a consequence of the rest of this License.

8. If the distribution and/or use of the Program is restricted in certain countries either by patents or by copyrighted interfaces, the original copyright holder who places the Program under this License may add an explicit geographical distribution limitation excluding those countries, so that distribution is permitted only in or among countries not thus excluded. In such case, this License incorporates the limitation as if written in the body of this License.

9. The Free Software Foundation may publish revised and/or new versions of the General Public License from time to time. Such new versions will be similar in spirit to the present version, but may differ in detail to address new problems or concerns.

Each version is given a distinguishing version number. If the Program specifies a version number of this License which applies to it and "any later version", you have the option of following the terms and conditions either of that version or of any later version published by the Free Software Foundation. If the Program does not specify a version number of this License, you may choose any version ever published by the Free Software Foundation.

10. If you wish to incorporate parts of the Program into other free programs whose distribution conditions are different, write to the author to ask for permission. For software which is copyrighted by the Free Software Foundation, write to the Free Software Foundation; we sometimes make exceptions for this. Our decision will be guided by the two goals of preserving the free status of all derivatives of our free software and of promoting the sharing and reuse of software generally.

NO WARRANTY

11. BECAUSE THE PROGRAM IS LICENSED FREE OF CHARGE, THERE IS NO WARRANTY FOR THE PROGRAM, TO THE EXTENT PERMITTED BY APPLICABLE LAW. EXCEPT WHEN OTHERWISE STATED IN WRITING THE COPYRIGHT HOLDERS AND/OR OTHER PARTIES PROVIDE THE PROGRAM "AS IS" WITHOUT WARRANTY OF ANY KIND, EITHER EXPRESSED OR IMPLIED, INCLUDING, BUT NOT LIMITED TO, THE IMPLIED WARRANTIES OF MERCHANTABILITY AND FITNESS FOR A PARTICULAR PURPOSE. THE ENTIRE RISK AS TO THE QUALITY AND PERFORMANCE OF THE PROGRAM IS WITH YOU. SHOULD THE PROGRAM PROVE DEFECTIVE, YOU ASSUME THE COST OF ALL NECESSARY SERVICING, REPAIR OR CORRECTION.

12. IN NO EVENT UNLESS REQUIRED BY APPLICABLE LAW OR AGREED TO IN WRITING WILL ANY COPYRIGHT HOLDER, OR ANY OTHER PARTY WHO MAY MODIFY AND/OR REDISTRIBUTE THE PROGRAM AS PERMITTED ABOVE, BE LIABLE TO YOU FOR DAMAGES, INCLUDING ANY GENERAL, SPECIAL, INCIDENTAL OR CONSEQUENTIAL DAMAGES ARISING OUT OF THE USE OR INABILITY TO USE THE PROGRAM (INCLUDING BUT NOT LIMITED TO LOSS OF DATA OR DATA BEING RENDERED INACCURATE OR LOSSES SUSTAINED BY YOU OR THIRD PARTIES OR A FAILURE OF THE PROGRAM TO OPERATE WITH ANY OTHER PROGRAMS), EVEN IF SUCH HOLDER OR OTHER PARTY HAS BEEN ADVISED OF THE POSSIBILITY OF SUCH DAMAGES.

END OF TERMS AND CONDITIONS

Appendix: How to Apply These Terms to Your New Programs

If you develop a new program, and you want it to be of the greatest possible use to the public, the best way to achieve this is to make it free software which everyone can redistribute and change under these terms.

To do so, attach the following notices to the program. It is safest to attach them to the start of each source file to most effectively convey the exclusion of warranty; and each file should have at least the "copyright" line and a pointer to where the full notice is found.

> <one line to give the program's name and a brief idea of what it does.>
> Copyright © 19yy <name of author>
>
> This program is free software; you can redistribute it and/or modify it under the terms of the GNU General Public License as published by the Free Software Foundation; either version 2 of the License, or (at your option) any later version.
>
> This program is distributed in the hope that it will be useful, but WITHOUT ANY WARRANTY; without even the implied warranty of MERCHANTABILITY or FITNESS FOR A PARTICULAR PURPOSE. See the GNU General Public License for more details.
>
> You should have received a copy of the GNU General Public License along with this program; if not, write to the Free Software Foundation, Inc., 675 Mass Ave, Cambridge, MA 02139, USA.

Also add information on how to contact you by electronic and paper mail.

If the program is interactive, make it output a short notice like this when it starts in an interactive mode:

> Gnomovision version 69, Copyright © 19yy name of author
> Gnomovision comes with ABSOLUTELY NO WARRANTY; for details type 'show w'.
> This is free software, and you are welcome to redistribute it under certain conditions; type 'show c' for details.

The hypothetical commands 'show w' and 'show c' should show the appropriate parts of the General Public License. Of course, the commands you use may be called something other than 'show w' and 'show c'; they could even be mouse-clicks or menu items—whatever suits your program.

You should also get your employer (if you work as a programmer) or your school, if any, to sign a "copyright disclaimer" for the program, if necessary. Here is a sample; alter the names:

> Yoyodyne, Inc., hereby disclaims all copyright interest in the program 'Gnomovision' (which makes passes at compilers) written by James Hacker.
>
> <signature of Ty Coon>, 1 April 1989 Ty Coon, President of Vice

This General Public License does not permit incorporating your program into proprietary programs. If your program is a subroutine library, you may consider it more useful to permit linking proprietary applications with the library. If this is what you want to do, use the GNU Library General Public License instead of this License.

The "Artistic License"

<u>Preamble</u>

The intent of this document is to state the conditions under which a Package may be copied, such that the Copyright Holder maintains some semblance of artistic control over the development of the package, while giving the users of the package the right to use and distribute the Package in a more-or-less customary fashion, plus the right to make reasonable modifications.

Definitions:

"Package" refers to the collection of files distributed by the Copyright Holder, and derivatives of that collection of files created through textual modification.

"Standard Version" refers to such a Package if it has not been modified, or has been modified in accordance with the wishes of the Copyright Holder as specified below.

"Copyright Holder" is whoever is named in the copyright or copyrights for the package.

"You" is you, if you're thinking about copying or distributing this Package.

"Reasonable copying fee" is whatever you can justify on the basis of media cost, duplication charges, time of people involved, and so on. (You will not be required to justify it to the Copyright Holder, but only to the computing community at large as a market that must bear the fee.)

"Freely Available" means that no fee is charged for the item itself, though there may be fees involved in handling the item. It also means that recipients of the item may redistribute it under the same conditions they received it.

1. You may make and give away verbatim copies of the source form of the Standard Version of this Package without restriction, provided that you duplicate all of the original copyright notices and associated disclaimers.

2. You may apply bug fixes, portability fixes and other modifications derived from the Public Domain or from the Copyright Holder. A Package modified in such a way shall still be considered the Standard Version.

3. You may otherwise modify your copy of this Package in any way, provided that you insert a prominent notice in each changed file stating how and when you changed that file, and provided that you do at least ONE of the following:

a) place your modifications in the Public Domain or otherwise make them Freely Available, such as by posting said modifications to Usenet or an equivalent medium, or placing the modifications on a major archive site such as uunet.uu.net, or by allowing the Copyright Holder to include your modifications in the Standard Version of the Package.

b) use the modified Package only within your corporation or organization.

c) rename any non-standard executables so the names do not conflict with standard executables, which must also be provided, and provide a separate manual page for each non-standard executable that clearly documents how it differs from the Standard Version.

d) make other distribution arrangements with the Copyright Holder.

4. You may distribute the programs of this Package in object code or executable form, provided that you do at least ONE of the following:

a) distribute a Standard Version of the executables and library files, together with instructions (in the manual page or equivalent) on where to get the Standard Version.

b) accompany the distribution with the machine-readable source of the Package with your modifications.

c) give non-standard executables non-standard names, and clearly document the differences in manual pages (or equivalent), together with instructions on where to get the Standard Version.

d) make other distribution arrangements with the Copyright Holder.

5. You may charge a reasonable copying fee for any distribution of this Package. You may charge any fee you choose for support of this Package. You may not charge a fee for this Package itself. However, you may distribute this Package in aggregate with other (possibly commercial) programs as part of a larger (possibly commercial) software distribution provided that you do not advertise this Package as a product of your own. You may embed this Package's interpreter within an executable of yours (by linking); this shall be construed as a mere form of aggregation, provided that the complete Standard Version of the interpreter is so embedded.

6. The scripts and library files supplied as input to or produced as output from the programs of this Package do not automatically fall under the copyright of this Package, but belong to whomever generated them, and may be sold commercially, and may be aggregated with this Package. If such scripts or library files are aggregated with this Package via the so-called "undump" or "unexec" methods of producing a binary executable image, then distribution of such an image shall neither be construed as a distribution of this Package nor shall it fall under the restrictions of Paragraphs 3 and 4, provided that you do not represent such an executable image as a Standard Version of this Package.

7. C subroutines (or comparably compiled subroutines in other languages) supplied by you and linked into this Package in order to emulate subroutines and variables of the language defined by this Package shall not be considered part of this Package, but are the equivalent of input as in Paragraph 6, provided these subroutines do not change the language in any way that would cause it to fail the regression tests for the language.

8. Aggregation of this Package with a commercial distribution is always permitted provided that the use of this Package is embedded; that is, when no overt attempt is made to make this Package's interfaces visible to the end user of the commercial distribution. Such use shall not be construed as a distribution of this Package.

9. The name of the Copyright Holder may not be used to endorse or promote products derived from this software without specific prior written permission.

10. THIS PACKAGE IS PROVIDED "AS IS" AND WITHOUT ANY EXPRESS OR IMPLIED WARRANTIES, INCLUDING, WITHOUT LIMITATION, THE IMPLIED WARRANTIES OF MERCHANTIBILITY AND FITNESS FOR A PARTICULAR PURPOSE.

WE WROTE THE BOOK ON NETWORKING

Novell Press® and IDG Books Worldwide

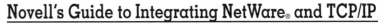

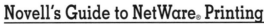

Novell's CNE® Study Guide for Core Technologies

by David James. Clarke, IV

The ideal preparation guide for the two non-NetWare specific exams required for CNE® certification: Service and Support (801) and Networking Technologies (200). This study guide contains real-world case studies, sample test questions and other valuable information. You'll also receive the exclusive Novell NetWire Starter Kit, the ClarkTests v.2 and MICROHOUSE I/O Card Encyclopedia demo.

932 pp plus CD-ROM
$74.99 USA
$104.99 Canada
0-7645-4501-9

Novell's CNA℠ Study Guide for IntranetWare™

by David James Clarke, IV and Kelley J.P. Lindberg

A must for system managers studying for their CNA℠ credential. Organized and easy-to-read, this resource covers all CNA course material including NetWare 2.2 and NetWare 3.1x with real-world scenarios, sample tests and a live on-line NetWare lab. The accompanying Novell Advantage CD contains Novell exclusive software.

700 pp plus CD-ROM
$69.99 USA
$96.99 Canada
0-7645-4513-2

Novell's CNE® Study Guide for IntranetWare™

by David James Clarke, IV

Learn all aspects of Novell's IntranetWare CNE program as well as NDS design and implementation. Covers certification courses 520, 525, 526, 532 and 804. Includes a free Novell Support Connection CD plus hundreds of CNE test questions.

1600 pp plus CD-ROM
$89.99 USA
$124.99 Canada
0-7645-4512-4

Novell's Four Principles of NDS™ Design

by Jeffrey F. Hughes and Blair W. Thomas

Take full advantage of the powerful new features of the NetWare 4 operating system with this clearly illustrated reference guide zeroing in on four essential Novell Directory Services (NDS) design principles: physical infrastructure, organizational structure, optimal partition size and minimum replicas placements, and time synchronization.

343 pp
$39.99 USA
$54.99 Canada
0-7645-4522-1

SMART BOOKS™
from the Novell Experts

CD-ROM Installation Instructions

Insert the *Novell's Guide to Creating IntranetWare Intranets* CD-ROM in your CD-ROM drive (for example, drive D:\). In Windows 95, use My Computer or Explorer to view the root directory of the CD-ROM.

To view a code listing from the book, double-click on the Code folder and then on the file you wish to view. You can use a text editor such as WordPad to view the .PL, .BAS, and .HTM source code. Use a Web browser such as Internet Explorer to view the results produced by the .HTM source files.

To install the programs on the CD-ROM (beta version of IntranetWare SDK for Java 1.1, Perl 95, and WinPerl), open the folder corresponding to the software and double-click on the appropriate executable or batch file. For additional installation instructions, see the appendix named "What's on the CD-ROM"

IDG BOOKS WORLDWIDE REGISTRATION CARD

RETURN THIS REGISTRATION CARD FOR FREE CATALOG

Title of this book: Novell's Guide to Creating IntranetWare™ Intranets

My overall rating of this book: ❑ Very good [1] ❑ Good [2] ❑ Satisfactory [3] ❑ Fair [4] ❑ Poor [5]

How I first heard about this book:

❑ Found in bookstore; name: [6]   ❑ Book review: [7]

❑ Advertisement: [8]   ❑ Catalog: [9]

❑ Word of mouth; heard about book from friend, co-worker, etc.: [10]   ❑ Other: [11]

What I liked most about this book:

_____

_____

What I would change, add, delete, etc., in future editions of this book:

_____

_____

Other comments:

_____

_____

Number of computer books I purchase in a year: ❑ 1 [12]   ❑ 2-5 [13]   ❑ 6-10 [14]   ❑ More than 10 [15]

I would characterize my computer skills as: ❑ Beginner [16] ❑ Intermediate [17] ❑ Advanced [18] ❑ Professional [19]

I use ❑ DOS [20] ❑ Windows [21] ❑ OS/2 [22] ❑ Unix [23] ❑ Macintosh [24] ❑ Other: [25]_____
                                                                                    (please specify)

I would be interested in new books on the following subjects:
(please check all that apply, and use the spaces provided to identify specific software)

❑ Word processing: [26]   ❑ Spreadsheets: [27]

❑ Data bases: [28]   ❑ Desktop publishing: [29]

❑ File Utilities: [30]   ❑ Money management: [31]

❑ Networking: [32]   ❑ Programming languages: [33]

❑ Other: [34]

I use a PC at (please check all that apply): ❑ home [35] ❑ work [36] ❑ school [37] ❑ other: [38] _____

The disks I prefer to use are ❑ 5.25 [39] ❑ 3.5 [40] ❑ other: [41]_____

I have a CD ROM: ❑ yes [42]   ❑ no [43]

I plan to buy or upgrade computer hardware this year: ❑ yes [44]   ❑ no [45]

I plan to buy or upgrade computer software this year: ❑ yes [46]   ❑ no [47]

Name: _____ Business title: [48] _____ Type of Business: [49]

Address (❑ home [50] ❑ work [51]/Company name: _____)

Street/Suite# _____

City [52]/State [53]/Zipcode [54]: _____ Country [55] _____

❑ **I liked this book!** You may quote me by name in future
   IDG Books Worldwide promotional materials.

My daytime phone number is _____

IDG BOOKS

THE WORLD OF
COMPUTER
KNOWLEDGE